Becoming Lunsford Lane

Becoming Lunsford Lane

The Lives of an American Aeneas

CRAIG THOMPSON FRIEND

The University of North Carolina Press
Chapel Hill

This book was published with the assistance of the Z. Smith Reynolds Fund of The University of North Carolina Press.

Set in Minion Pro by Westchester Publishing Services
Manufactured in the United States of America

Library of Congress Cataloging-in-Publication Data
Names: Friend, Craig Thompson, author.
Title: Becoming Lunsford Lane : the lives of an American Aeneas /
    Craig Thompson Friend.
Description: Chapel Hill : The University of North Carolina Press, [2025] |
    Includes bibliographical references and index.
Identifiers: LCCN 2025001937 | ISBN 9781469685342 (cloth ; alk. paper) |
    ISBN 9781469683867 (epub) | ISBN 9781469687766 (pdf)
Subjects: LCSH: Lane, Lunsford, 1803-approximately 1863. | Enslaved persons—
    North Carolina—Raleigh—Biography. | Free Black people—North Carolina—
    Raleigh—Biography. | North Carolina—Social conditions—19th century. |
    BISAC: BIOGRAPHY & AUTOBIOGRAPHY / Cultural, Ethnic & Regional /
    African American & Black | SOCIAL SCIENCE / Ethnic Studies / American /
    African American & Black Studies | LCGFT: Biographies.
Classification: LCC E444.L26 F75 2025 | DDC 306.36209275655092 [B]—
    dc23/eng/20250304
LC record available at https://lccn.loc.gov/2025001937

Cover art: *Lunsford Lane (1803–ca.1863)*. Reprinted from *Lunsford Lane; or Another Helper from North Carolina,* by William George Hawkins (Crosby & Nichols, 1863). Courtesy American Antiquarian Society via Wikimedia Commons.

For product safety concerns under the European Union's General Product Safety Regulation (EU GPSR), please contact gpsr@mare-nostrum.co.uk or write to The University of North Carolina Press and Mare Nostrum Group B.V., Mauritskade 21D, 1091 GC Amsterdam, The Netherlands.

Dedicated to

Roderick Glenn Turner

who, through his quiet compassion,
his persistence in the face of difficulties,
his buoyant sense of humor,
his generosity of forgiveness,
his optimism that things will work out,
his dignity when confronting racism,
his passion for storytelling,
and his genuineness
has embodied, for me, what it means to be
a Black man in the United States.
This book reflects him,
and although he may not realize it,
he made it better,
as he has my life.

Thus, ord'ring all that prudence could provide,
I clothe my shoulders with a lion's hide
And yellow spoils; then, on my bending back,
The welcome load of my dear father take;
While on my better hand Ascanius hung,
And with unequal paces tripp'd along.
Creusa kept behind; by choice we stray
Thro' ev'ry dark and ev'ry devious way.
I, who so bold and dauntless just before,
The Grecian darts and shock of lances bore,
At ev'ry shadow now am seiz'd with fear,
Not for myself, but for the charge I bear.

—Virgil, *The Aeneid*, Book II, 19 B.C.E.

If you are not a reality, whose myth are you?
If you are not a myth, whose reality are you?

—Sun Ra, 1970 CE

Contents

Illustrations

Becoming Lunsford Lane

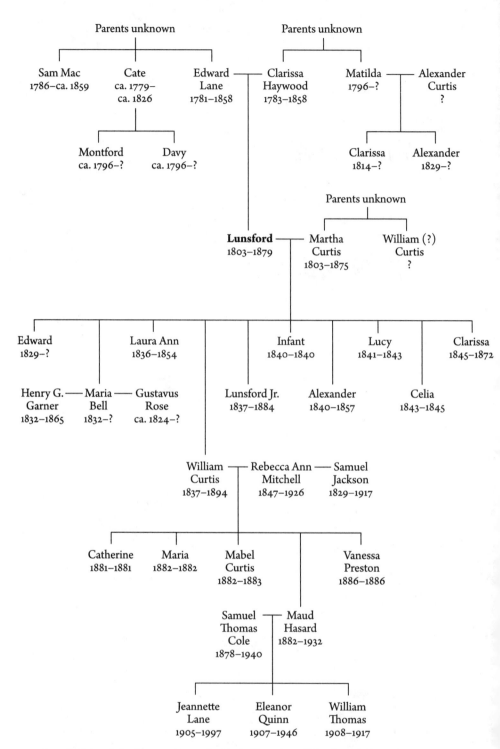

Lunsford Lane's family tree. Drawn by Craig Thompson Friend.

Introduction

The Storyteller

In the evenings, as the sun fell behind oaks and pines, casting long shadows across Raleigh, North Carolina, Clarissa fed dinner to her enslavers and their children before returning to the small kitchen in which she lived with her toddler, Lunsford. When her husband's enslavers permitted, Ned joined his wife to sit in the quiet, enjoying a meal and the intimacy of their young family before the demands on their time began anew. What they did with their family time is not known, but Clarissa and Ned most likely shared stories with their boy, drawing from a collective ancestral wisdom: origin stories, tales of trickster animals, rumors of flying Africans—a canon of folktales that circulated among the enslaved communities of the American South.[1]

Sometimes, the story was about people who flew. "The slaves was out in the field workin'. All of a sudden they got together and started to move round in a ring. Round they went faster and faster. Then one by one they rose up and took wing and flew like a bird," imagined Clarissa. "The overseer heard the noise and he came out and he saw the slaves rise up in the air and fly back to Africa. He ran and he catched the last one by the foot just as he was 'bout to fly off," as her hand grasped the air. On other evenings, Ned conjured a rabbit who scampered through his son's dreams. "Br'er Rabbit kept asking him, and the Tar-Baby, she kept on sayin' nothin', till presently Br'er Rabbit drew back with his fist, he did, and blip he tuck her on the side of the head. His fist stuck, and he couldn't pull loose. The tar held him. But Tar-Baby, she stayed still, and Br'er Fox, he laid low." Imbued with the sorrow of generations of enslavement and told at night when enslavers were out of range of ear and eye, the stories were sweet, lyrical, and rebellious, warning about Br'er Foxes and Br'er Bears, and dreaming of escape, freedom, and better times.[2]

Across Edenton Street, Ned's sister, Cate, told similar tales to her twin sons, but as nursemaid to her enslavers' children, her storytelling belonged to the White children who commanded not only her labor but her culture. A lifetime before Joel Chandler Harris collected the folk memories of Black America to create his fictional Uncle Remus for White readers, Black storytellers like Cate, Ned, and Clarissa negotiated their tradition of subversive storytelling, sharing with White children what they hoped their own children would interpret differently.

Storytelling sits at the heart of identity and memories. When Lunsford was grown in the early 1840s, his own story joined the canon, although it never became as ubiquitous as others did. It inspired many Black Americans but found more appeal among White Americans eager to envision an end to slavery and drawn to the myth of self-making. Born on May 30, 1803, Lunsford was the only child of Clarissa Haywood and Ned Lane. He lived and labored thirty-two years enslaved until 1835, when he arranged for an acquaintance to purchase him using money that Lunsford had earned and saved. A year later, he traveled to New York, where he obtained emancipation papers, returning southward as a free man with a new name—Lunsford Lane. Determined to purchase and emancipate his family, he found employment in the governor's office, bought a house, and turned it into a home by negotiating to have his still-enslaved wife and children join him.[3]

In the summer of 1841, when magistrates tried to enforce a law that required people emancipated outside of North Carolina to leave the state, he fled northward and began sharing his narrative, what quickly became known among abolitionists as "The Story." He first recited it on November 4, 1841, at an antislavery meeting in Hingham, Massachusetts, and although he hesitated to call himself an abolitionist, he became one of the most popular antislavery speakers of the day. For nine months during 1841 and 1842, as he circulated throughout New England, thousands, upon hearing that "Lunsford Lane was coming," crowded to see the man who had made money while in bondage—the rare self-made man in the enslaved Black body. Audiences clamored to hear his parable of Southern oppression, self-determination, and Northern redemption. They came to understand the extent to which he, like millions of enslaved women and men in the Southern United States, yearned "to be rocked in their cradle of Liberty,—oh, how unlike being stretched on the pillory of slavery!"[4]

When Lane arrived in Weymouth, Massachusetts, in late January 1842, Anne Warren Weston, a former leader of the Boston Female Anti-Slavery Society and still among the vanguard of Bostonian abolitionism, described how the church "thronged to suffocation, benches in all the aisles." She hoped that his speech would "provide a good effect for the Cause." Lane did not disappoint, describing what it had meant to be enslaved, how he had arranged his freedom and supported his still-enslaved family, and the efforts to purge him from North Carolina. The Story captured American imaginations. Even in his absence, people told it in church sermons and antislavery speeches, always concluding, as did Lunsford, with the ultimate, often unarticulated, cliffhanger: Would Lane return southward and successfully rescue his family?[5]

In April 1842, he returned to Raleigh and composed the final chapter of The Story. As Lunsford stepped off the train with enough cash in his pocket to purchase his wife and children, the crowd that greeted him was just as electrified as those in New England but far less welcoming. City commissioners detained him, accusing him of antislavery lecturing and dragging him before a kangaroo court in a room overflowing with curious voyeurs acting as an impromptu jury. He told The Story that he had practiced so many times, joking about how he raised money from Northern audiences that "drank" it in "as the fat of the land." Without evidence of abolitionism, the superintendent of police released Lane, but as Lunsford recovered his luggage at the train station, a mob swarmed him, futilely rummaging for abolitionist literature in his trunk. Frustrated, they turned on their guest and "raised me from the ground and carried me on their shoulders. Then I was indeed high and lifted up. Thus I was carried, as in a whirlwind, towards the gallows. Then my heart sunk within me. I thought all was gone."[6]

All was not lost. Weeks later, The Story was resolved as Lunsford and his family paraded into the 1842 annual meeting of the American Anti-Slavery Society in Manhattan. Called to tell The Story again, he arose before some of the greatest speakers of the age: Frederick Douglass, Stephen Symonds Foster, Henry Highland Garnet, Abby Kelley, Wendell Phillips, Charles Lenox Remond, James McCune Smith, Lewis Tappan, and other giants of American abolitionism. "I have for twelve months been going from house to house," Lane began, "and from place of business to place of business, to tell my story, and ask for help, so that my history is known to you and many others." He abandoned the well-worn tale so many had already heard, improvising a concluding chapter of how he escaped the mob and redeemed his family. One observer declared, "It was heart speaking to the heart. The whole audience was melted to tears."[7]

Realizing The Story's potential, a month later, Lane sat down with "a friend" to put it to paper. *The Narrative of Lunsford Lane* demonstrated how Lunsford had learned the power of storytelling: that however truthful the bedrock of his story, there was always room for imagination, leaving out some details, highlighting others, filling in gaps with suspect memories and minor fictions, and tailoring it to what audiences wanted to hear or read. In the narrative that he spun, Lunsford crafted a parable from the American myth of self-making, situating him to claim an empowering and rewarding individualism seldom associated with Black Americans, particularly those enslaved. As historian W. Sherman Savage summarized a century later, the moral of The Story was that "his was a very telling argument against slavery, for here was a law-abiding citizen who had made a contribution to the economic system of North Carolina." Presented as truth, at least some of The Story, some of the most significant parts, was the stuff of fantasy.[8]

And yet, The Story was never Lane's full biography. What happened to the man who found freedom and family? Over the years, the cradle of liberty was not as restful as he imagined. Like so many others who made lives of freedom after years of enslavement, the economic challenges were overwhelming. He lived another thirty-seven years, moving from job to job and dragging his family from place to place: Cambridgeport, Massachusetts; Oberlin, Ohio; Wrentham, Massachusetts; Woonsocket, Rhode Island; Worcester, Massachusetts. Lane bought houses in all but Woonsocket, assuming multiple mortgages on each, never making enough money to make payments, taking financial losses, and eventually belying the myth and exposing himself as a most unsuccessful self-made man. In Worcester, his wife and daughters outperformed him as real estate investors, but who, in the 1860s, had heard of self-making women, much less self-making Black women? Their successes made his failures even more egregious.[9]

Lunsford's celebrity added to his troubles, drawing racial animus in some quarters and resentment of his abolitionism in others. For a decade, he relied on his name recognition to make money, but as his celebrity began to fade, he found himself replaced on the abolitionist lecture circuit by newer faces with fresher stories. He refused to let go of his fame, using his name to sell herbal medicines and to take a position for which he was not particularly prepared: steward of Worcester's Wellington Hospital.

Slowly, Lunsford Lane lost those he loved and had worked so hard to redeem. He and Martha mourned an infant's death in 1840. Two more young children—Lucy and Celia—died in the 1840s. His parents, Edward and Clarissa, and two older children—Laura Ann and Alexander—died over the next decade. Of the children who reached adulthood, his three sons—Edward, William Curtis, and Lunsford Jr.—left home, and only Lunsford Jr. looked back. By the late 1860s, only daughters Maria Bell and Clarissa remained in the house, closer to their mother as her relationship with their father deteriorated. By 1872, Martha and Lunsford were estranged. She moved to Jersey City, New Jersey, where she died three years later. He went to Norwich, Connecticut, then Brooklyn, and finally Manhattan, dying in a tenement house in 1879 alone. When buried, Lunsford Lane had no obituary and no gravestone, the barren burial site evidencing how forgotten he had become, and not only by his children. He disappeared from history. Not even close friends such as Charles Spear, supporters like Anne Warren Weston, or members of the abolitionist fraternity such as Frederick Douglass and Lewis Clarke knew that Lunsford was no longer with them.

———

Becoming Lunsford Lane: The Lives of an American Aeneas is the first book-length biography of Lane since 1863. Although a straightforward trajectory of his life, as well as those of his parents, wife, and children, it is not a simple biography. Lunsford Lane lived many lives populated by many people. He was an enslaved man until 1835, a free Black Southerner between 1835 and 1842, and a Black Northerner from 1842 to 1879. He was a Black man trying to determine what it meant to be an American, often wanting to celebrate himself as a self-made man but uncertain about tearing down the veil of racism that hung between him and opportunity. He was a man who drew many audiences over his lifetime because he was willing to write his life to meet their expectations and not his realities, creating a mythical Lunsford Lane which he could not control as it overwhelmed his life and his own sense of self.[10]

Because of *The Narrative of Lunsford Lane*, which Lunsford dictated in 1842, we think we know him—the young man who, between 1803 and 1842, lived in the South enslaved and then free. We have some idea of the Lunsford Lane of the next twenty years through William G. Hawkins's 1863 *Lunsford Lane*. Like the *Narrative* before it, however, Hawkins's biography embellishes The Story and distorts the realities of Lane's life. In other words, Lunsford Lane and his biographer—and everyone who subsequently wrote about him—were unwilling, consciously or not, to reveal the full person. The older Lunsford Lane, in roughly the last seventeen years of his life, is essentially unknown.

How Lunsford Lane negotiated Blackness in an era increasingly defined by hardening conceptualizations of racial distinctions is a central theme of his biography. Race, of course, had always been part of the American narrative. Since 1640, when John Punch, an African indentured servant in Virginia, had been caught trying to run away and received a different sentence—lifelong enslavement—than two European indentured servants who fled alongside him, Blackness had been criminalized. By the end of the seventeenth century, racial categories had developed in Western thought: French physician François Bernier, for example, cataloged Europeans, Africans, East Asians, and Lapps. Despite hundreds of thousands of those Europeans arriving in the Americas as unfree labor, slave laws of the mid-seventeenth century through the early eighteenth century exposed White colonials' general agreement that Blackness demanded *permanent* enslavement. There was little doubt about Blackness by the nineteenth century, although debate remained as to just how Black someone was if they had a White ancestor.[11]

Whiteness was an altogether different matter. Bernier had cast a large net in defining Europeans, including peoples of North Africa, India, the Middle East, Southeast Asia, and North America. Although thinkers like taxonomist Carl Linnaeus, naturalist Georges-Louis Leclerc the Comte de Buffon, and political philosopher Thomas Jefferson attempted to define Europeans more narrowly, the only consensus that emerged about who was White manifested in legal definitions. Beginning with the 1790 census, the government of the new United States categorized people as "White," "Slave," and "All other free persons." It was a definition of exclusion: White was not enslaved or other.[12]

In the subtitle to Lane's narrative, it was not to enslavement but to "the crime of wearing a colored skin" that he attributed his challenges and troubles. Over a century of laws dictated Blackness in North Carolina, and in 1830–31, the state passed one of the most restrictive Black codes in the nation. In an era of increasingly defined racial lines, laws and the systems of surveillance designed to enforce them dictated Black lives. That reality made The Story more threatening to White Southerners and more inspirational to Black Southerners and antislavery Northerners of both races.

Except it was more imagined than real. Throughout his life, Lunsford was cautious, conservative, and willing to wait for change rather than force it. In The Story, he crafted a more determined version of himself, one that aligned with cultural assumptions about Black men, self-making, and fatherhood. He did not intend it as an act of resistance, although its subversion of racial assumptions and stereotypes questioned not only the White enslavement of Black Americans but challenged many abolitionists' hesitance to free enslaved peoples by any means necessary. Lunsford's biography is one of life writing: his own intentional, and sometimes incidental, shaping of personal and public identities. By so transparently exploring himself as enslaved and then free, as son, husband, and father, as a political and economic citizen, and as a Black American, Lane invited audiences to consider how one human negotiated the powerful forces of nineteenth-century American enslavement and racism to pursue love, family, security, freedom, and self-making.[13]

In addition to his life writing, Lane constructed his public persona through the spoken word. As Massachusetts politician and author Edward Griffin Parker declared in 1857, it was the "Golden Age of American Oratory," blossoming from an earlier era when men of wealth and education drew from classical rhetorical styles to entertain and inspire audiences who, elite like them, appreciated their ideas and perspectives. By the 1830s, the evangelical language of the Second Great Awakening, the public appeals of social reform, and the popular entertainments of theater and professional lecturing transformed oratory. Middling and even lower-class audiences expanded the market for performances that ranged from heart-wrenching to sidesplitting to every emotion betwixt.[14]

The timing could not have been better for abolitionists. They organized lecture circuits and promoted dynamic orators like Frederick Douglass, Charles Lenox Remond, Wendell Phillips, William Lloyd Garrison, and Lunsford Lane. But it did not come as easily to Lunsford as it did for the others. Parker claimed that the great orators were gifted "with the germ of genius," stimulated by "a felicity of situation, and the unfaltering application of a life to accomplish their development." Lane had that germ of genius, but he did not relish lecturing as did Douglass, Lane's early circuit partner. Abolitionist audiences were fickle, quickly losing interest in one individual's cause when another came along. Lunsford watched his popularity and source of money wane with the arrival of new speakers such as George Latimer, Lewis Clarke, and Henry Bibb, all freedom seekers who represented an alternative message about the route to freedom. Always financially pressured and regularly reminded of the precarity of life as children and parents died, Lunsford struggled to find a higher purpose beyond making a buck. He became a good storyteller but never a great orator.[15]

Through his storytelling, Lunsford Lane empowered abolitionists to mythologize him, another biographical theme. Joseph Warren Cross, pastor of the Congregationalist Church of West Boylston and vice president of the Massachusetts Abolition Society, compared Lane to a demigod: "His exploits so far exceed those of Eneas, that could Virgil hear his story, he would be ashamed of his own hero, and confess that Lane's *facts* were much superior to Maro's fictions." In the eighth century BCE, Aeneas, son of Aphrodite, played a minor yet important role in the Homeric poem *The Iliad*, defending Troy against the Greeks during the Trojan War. Seven centuries later, as the Roman Empire arose, Publius Vergilius Maro situated Rome's origins in older antiquity by turning to a hero Julius Caesar and Augustus Caesar claimed as their ancestor, one clearly favored by the gods. Virgil built upon Maro's narrative, making Aeneas the central figure of *The Aeneid*, written between 29 and 19 BCE. As a *pietas*, a man of loyalty, duty, and respect for others, Aeneas led his family from Troy despite losing his wife and having to carry his father. Dido, queen of Carthage, momentarily distracted Aeneas from his destiny until Mercury reminded him of his duty to the mission. In *The History of Rome*, written between 27 and 9 BCE, Titus Livius completed the legend, describing Aeneas's conquest of the peoples living on the lands on which Rome arose, his death, and his apotheosis into immortality as Jupiter Indiges. Aeneas remained a powerful figure in Western literature, appearing as late as the fourteenth century CE in *Sir Gawain and the Green Knight* as the ancient ancestor of the legendary King Arthur.[16]

Cross and other abolitionists embraced the parallels between The Story and Aenean mythology, both of which portrayed men driven by piety, not in its religious meaning but as a sense of duty and devotion to family. Like Aeneas, who saved most of his family from the collapse of Troy and inevitable death, his enemies permitting him and his family to flee out of respect for his righteousness, Lane liberated most of his family from the South's cruel system of enslavement, escaping harm in their last moments in North Carolina because of his piety, reflecting both his own uprightness and the righteousness of his cause. Although Lane did not carry his father out of Raleigh, he acted similarly by ensuring that his mother joined him in freedom. Lane's demigod-like mythology became so powerful that abolitionists reflexively proclaimed his children "young immortals."[17]

Cross envisioned Aeneas in Lunsford. Yet, Aenean lore held that Aeneas and his lineage were progenitors of European ethnicity: that Aeneas's great-grandson, Brutus, was the fabled founder from whom "Britain" derived as a place and a people. Cross envisioned a new embodiment of Aeneas—in a Black body. He was not the first. In the early 1590s, Shakespeare had hinted the same in *Titus Andronicus*, in which the love interest of Tamora, queen of the Goths, is Aaron "the Moor." During a bit of sexual role play, Tamora casts her paramour as Aeneas to her Dido. When two other characters come upon the couple in the woods, the racial epitaphs fly: "swarthy Cimmerian," "spotted, detested, and abominable," "a barbarous Moor." Of course, Moors from North Africa were not Cimmerians from western Asia, and the racial jumbling must have confused audiences. Still, they knew that Cimmerians and Moors were not Anglos. What mattered was that Aaron was darker and different. Shakespeare designated Aaron an Aeneas explicitly through a tryst with Tamora's Dido and implicitly in Aaron's effort to save their mixed-race son from certain death by fleeing Rome.[18]

Over the centuries, actors who portrayed Aaron applied oil to their faces as crude blackface. But the character's claim that he would always be a Moor, that "all the water in the ocean / Can never turn the swan's black legs to white," extended only so far as the stage. By the 1780s, Whitening (read: civilizing) Black and Brown bodies animated British imperialism and, half a century later, White America's manifest destiny. Cross's characterization of Lunsford Lane as the Black American Aeneas, "superior" to Virgil's Aeneas in his heroism and more authentic in his narrative, testified to abolitionism's role in that civilization process. The Blackness of Lunsford's skin would never disappear, but he could acquire the Whiteness of heroism and self-making.[19]

Lane was less sophisticated in reconciling himself with The Story. He mythologized his life through the simple trope of the self-made agent of capitalism, tapping into themes of agency and activism that have been powerful influences on how we understand Black American history. The great sociologist and historian W. E. B. Du Bois argued that, by taking control of their destinies through education, "the Best of this race" would "guide the Mass away from the contamination and death of the Worst." In the nineteenth century, those who exceeded society's racist expectations and their own self-doubts became the "exceptional negro." The problem with such stereotypes is that originally conceived as beneficial to the larger Black community, they inevitably evolved to commend individuals who, having mastered capitalism, celebrity, and proximity to the ideals of the White middle class, somehow received better treatment and acceptance within the larger American culture, including having biographies written of them.[20]

Scholars and politicians, Black and White, have celebrated Lunsford Lane as an "exceptional negro," primarily based on the myth of his entrepreneurial self-making. Legal historian W. Sherman Rogers argued that entrepreneurialism historically provided a "foundation of excellence" for Black Americans and that Lane's story is a "particularly illuminating example of the ingenuity and resourcefulness." In 2015, North Carolina's Governor Pat McCrory issued a proclamation for Black History Month, wholeheartedly appropriating the mythical narrative, recognizing Lane as "believed to be the state's first Black American inventor, who, while enslaved, invented a pipe and special tobacco blend that allowed him to purchase his freedom and move his family." That proclamation does not accurately reflect the historical record, only the legend.[21]

Such is the mythology of Lunsford Lane, much of which emanated from the idea that Lane was a good entrepreneur, the inaccuracy of which is key to this biography. He made only enough money—$1000 [$30,400 in modern purchasing value]—to free himself and took thirteen years to do so. He begged for the $3000 [$91,200] to free his family. He lost money on every landed property he owned over his lifetime. He was a hustler his entire life. The question must be asked: Why have we needed to imagine Lunsford Lane as a successful entrepreneur? For some audiences, The Story personified the ideal of the self-made man: if an enslaved Black man could empower himself economically, self-making certainly was available to anyone who was unrestricted by enslavement and racism. The Story allowed other listeners and readers to elevate some Black individuals, as embodied in the men and a few women who had known enslavement and then performed abolitionism, above the faceless masses who could not achieve standards of exceptionalism, respectability, and excellence. For others, particularly among the enslaving class, The Story allowed some to believe that if Lunsford and other Black Americans could act as entrepreneurs and find freedom, enslavement and racism must not have been *so* oppressive or *so* insurmountable.

We do not have to ascribe agency and activism to Lunsford Lane. He simply *was*. As literary scholar Badia Ahad lamented in 2021, "Rarely do Black people ever reap the glory of simply being." Despite the mythology, Lunsford was no self-made agent of capitalism. It was not so unusual for an enslaved man to make money and aspire to freedom. It was not unique for a free Black Southern man to own a house and raise a family. It was not abnormal for a Black Northern man to do what he could to pursue happiness. His humanity and story deserve recognition because, like Aeneas, he endured. He found ways to survive enslavement, racism, and their attendant violence. Lunsford

Lane just lived. Was that not enough to ask of a nineteenth-century Black American? Is it not enough to ask of anyone?

Beginning on that November day in 1841 when Lunsford Lane first related his story to a public audience, reinforced on a June day in 1842 when he dictated it to "a friend," and embedded in American mythology through the proclamations of abolitionists such as Cross and Hawkins, each iteration of The Story removed us further and further from the real Lunsford Lane. His biography is one of *becoming*: of transforming from a flesh-and-blood real human into a mythological American, losing himself and his family in the process. The identity that Lunsford created, abolitionists applauded, White Southerners disparaged, Black Americans lionized, scholars perpetuated, and which became part of a timeless canon of folktales was always a caricature. It almost killed him in the South, and it made life exceedingly difficult in the North. We have never known Lunsford Lane: he wore the proverbial trickster's mask well. His true story is so much more than The Story, speaking to the joys and tragedies of human relationships, illuminating the rewards and frustrations of trying to live a good life, and celebrating the miracle, for a nineteenth-century Black American, of persisting. Trapped by his own mythology, Lunsford Lane was far more complex, important, and human than The Story ever allowed.

Comments on Style

While relating the life of one man and his family, this biography is also the story of Black and White residents of the United States across the late eighteenth, nineteenth, and twentieth centuries. The reader will, at times, come across lists of names: people who stretched alongside Lunsford Lane on the pillory of enslavement and others who rested with him in the cradle of freedom. Many are remembered only on enslavers' wills and estate inventories or in local and state legal and transactional records. For most, their brief mention in the biography of another is their only footprint in history. I honor them, for although they did not leave traces by which their stories may be fully recounted, often forbidden from doing so, their lives mattered.

Since Lunsford is an uncommon name, governmental officials recorded it with a variety of spellings, including Lanceford, Laneford, Langford, Lansford, Lonsford, Lunceford, and Lundsford. I standardized the name as Lunsford, the spelling he employed in *Narrative of Lunsford Lane.* In the cases of other names and words, I retained original spellings and capitalizations. During his first twenty-three years, Lunsford Lane was simply Lunsford. I refer to him by first name when discussing those years and regularly throughout the rest of the biography. Some readers may bristle at my familiarity, but I have done so specifically for clarity. Employing just his surname, which at one time was Haywood and then became Lane, can be problematic as there are many other Lanes and Haywoods. For similar reasons, I reference his father, Ned, solely by first name until 1801, and his mother, Clarissa, and wife, Martha, by first name until 1842, when they both took their husbands' surnames.[22]

I converted historic monetary values into rough estimates of modern buying power, providing a general sense of historical values rather than a categorical statement of absolute worth. Estimates of modern purchasing power are indicated in brackets following historical monetary figures. For example, "he took a loan for $50 [$1,730]."[23]

I gave extensive thought to the appropriateness of quoting verbatim those primary sources that employed the term "nigger." It is a violent word, one that should not be given the power to insist that we treat it delicately by moderating it with "the n-word" or "n——." Individuals used the term toward Lunsford Lane on several occasions, and recognizing its cruelty and hideousness is crucial to understanding the nation in which he lived and moved. I am grateful to Elizabeth Stordeur Pryor for her intellectually honest and emotionally mature meditations on the topic. Pryor argued that using "scare quotes" or a replacement term "creates a barrier meant to protect the reader or to signal the squeamishness of the writer who would have chosen any other word." She concluded that avoiding the word suggests "that we all know exactly what this word means," a presumption about which "we should not be so sure." Still, for quoting the word, I apologize to anyone who may be offended.[24]

I reflected similarly on the capitalization of "Black," "Indigenous," and "White." Compelling arguments have been made for capitalizing Black and Indigenous to reflect the shared racial identities and communities that peoples created when enslavement and colonialism stole their original geographies and cultures. Scholars and journalists have been more hesitant to capitalize "white," arguing, as the *New York Times* explained, that "white does not represent a shared culture and history in the way Black does." I disagree with that conclusion. White Americans did—and do—share a culture, one that is as historically constructed as Blackness and Indigeneity, drawing from as great a variety of geographies and cultures as those identities, and one that became embedded in legal, economic, political, and social systems that elevated White Americans with authority and privilege over others. Whiteness as a historical construct and force is central to this story. I concur with the American Psychological Association's argument that "to not name 'White' as a race is, in fact, an anti-Black [and, I would add, anti-Indigenous] act which frames Whiteness as both neutral and the standard," and that we must name "White as a race as a way to understand and give voice to how Whiteness functions [and functioned] in our social and political institutions and communities."[25]

PART I

Freedom on the Pillory of Slavery

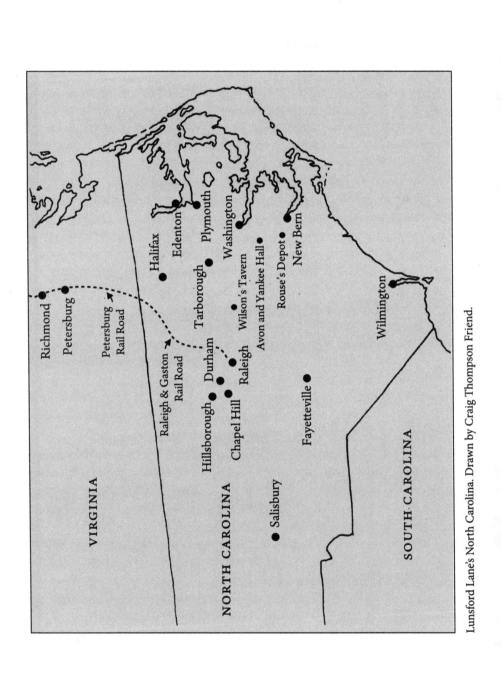

Lunsford Lane's North Carolina. Drawn by Craig Thompson Friend.

Chapter 1

Ned and Clarissa

Lunsford Lane never had the luxury of reconstructing his genealogy. It is not that he lacked curiosity. Only a handful of Black Americans knew their ancestries, treasuring tales passed through their families, but as Frederick Douglass asserted, "Genealogical trees do not flourish among slaves." For most, among them Lunsford, knowing and being with parents was a gift, and as he related when telling The Story, the only ancestors he knew by name were his father, Ned, and mother, Clarissa. Their stories are where he began his story, as shall we.[1]

———

In 1781, Ned opened his eyes and saw his two-year-old sister, Cate, welcoming him into their corner of the world, several hundred acres in North Carolina's eastern Piedmont. Upon hearing of the baby, their enslaver, Joel Lane, christened him Young Ned, distinguishing the infant from an enslaved man who suddenly discovered he was to be Old Ned. Five years later, Young Ned and Cate greeted a younger brother, Sam.

We do not know who fathered the three siblings. Even the identity of their mother is speculative, likely one of two women: Flora or Hasty. Flora was the first human whom Joel Lane purchased and enslaved. In 1761, twenty-three-year-old Joel settled several hundred acres and married seventeen-year-old Martha Hinton, daughter of one of the region's largest landowners. To assist his young wife, he bought fourteen-year-old Flora for £60 [$13,180]. Over the next seven years, the Lanes created a household: Martha birthed Henry, James, and William; and Joel purchased Dick, Jack, Stanter, and Young Sam. Enslaved people planted gardens, tended livestock, cooked and served meals, and as their enslaver accumulated thousands of acres over the 1760s and 1770s, they cleared and cultivated the new grounds.[2]

Flora, Dick, Jack, Stanter, and Young Sam were a family on the Lane farm as well. They came from large farms in the eastern part of the state where enslaved communities formed around the emotional support provided each other as they watched parents, spouses, and children disappear to the slave trade or succumb to the violence of enslavement. In the Piedmont, farms were smaller. Opportunities to create support networks proved challenging, and smaller numbers of enslaved laborers, particularly women, meant that most enslaved men never found long-term loving relationships. Maybe Dick, Jack, Stanter, or Young Sam found love with Flora, or she might have loved a man who lived and labored on a nearby farm. The matron of the enslaved community on Joel Lane's farm (and before 1777, probably the only enslaved woman), Flora was young, thirty-three years old when Ned was born. Of course, Joel Lane may have forced her into a relationship, and she may not have loved her children's father at all. Possibly, Ned, Cate, and Sam did not share the same paternity.[3]

Or Ned's mother might have been Hasty, whom Lane purchased in the early 1780s. If so, then her husband, Ned, might have been his father, making some sense of their enslaver's insistence on distinguishing between "old" and "new." Old Ned was not that old. He lived another thirty years at least, and Hasty twenty years longer than him. After the turn of the nineteenth century, when Young Ned found himself on a different estate, he encouraged his new owner to find and restore his family. His sister Cate and her two sons soon joined Ned, as did Hasty and Old Ned. Still, they might have been more chosen family than blood relations. Their relationship to Young Ned is hypothetical at best. If neither Hasty nor Flora was Ned's mother, she was someone lost to history and, maybe, even to her own children, having died or been sold away before they could appreciate her. If so, then Hasty and Flora and other enslaved women surrogated as aunts to Cate, Young Ned, and Sam.[4]

The puzzle of Young Ned's parentage cannot be solved because enslavers did not permit enslaved people to be narrators. Silencing their voices dehumanized them, denied their ancestries, and weakened their kinship ties. Enslaved people clung to family memories, but slaveowners preferred to supplant remembrances of enslaved parents with affinity and loyalty to lineages of ownership. Whoever she was, Young Ned's mother passed little ancestral knowledge to her children, and Ned remembered more about Joel Lane than he did his mother, seemingly sharing no memories of her with his own son.[5]

In contrast, enslavers actively preserved their genealogies. Churches tracked White family lines through birth, marriage, and death records. Local governments drew on family histories to enforce patrilineal land laws. Joel Lane could trace his ancestry. Family lore held that there might have been a connection to Ralph Lane, who had helped Walter Raleigh establish the Roanoke colony in 1585. More verifiable was that his great-great-great-grandfather, Thomas Lane, had arrived in Jamestown in 1613. Three generations later, Joel was the youngest of six sons. His eldest brother, John, successfully petitioned the colonial assembly for their share of their mother's inheritance. By 1760, the Lane brothers were among the colony's wealthiest siblings. Joel Lane spent the rest of his life determined not to waste his inheritance, investing in the things that retained value: land and enslaved humans.[6]

Joel and Mary Lane's home, Raleigh, NC. Photograph by Craig Thompson Friend.

So, in the 1760s, Joel Lane bought land in the eastern Piedmont and enslaved laborers to work it. As a representative to the colonial General Assembly, he proposed a new county, canvassing to be named a commissioner for the new Wake County and gaining a voice in locating a courthouse, jail, and stocks adjacent to his farm at the intersection of the New Bern-Hillsborough and the Fall Line roads, a crossroads that became known as Wake Court House. Over the 1770s, Lane acquired more land and enslaved more humans, acquiring one or two at a time, although the records are sparse as to who they were and whence they came. By 1790, twenty-seven enslaved people lived on Lane's farm, most of whom were young, positioning Lane to act as a patriarch. Of the five people whom Lane originally purchased—Flora, Dick, Jack, Stanter, and Young Sam, who were at least in their late thirties by the early 1790s—it seems that only Jack remained. Hasty, Old Ned, and others acted as aunts and uncles to an increasingly younger enslaved community, including Young Ned, Cate, and Sam.[7]

By the 1780s, White Americans' ability to trace their ancestries suggested a coherence and continuity in their families that they argued could not be found among Black families. Some years later, the Supreme Court of North Carolina articulated what had always been assumed: marriage among enslaved peoples, "consisting of cohabitation merely, by the permission of their owners, does not constitute the relation of husband and wife." Enslaved people had families, "frail as may be the right, and temporary the enjoyment," but they did so only through "the necessities or caprice of their owners." Slaveowners expanded definitions of "family," couching ownership of other humans in language of kinship and intimacy, insisting that enslaved people on each farm or town lot were members of the household. Like many enslavers, Joel Lane presumed to replace Black parental figures with himself, evidenced by the ease with which he named a child and even renamed an adult.[8]

Enslaver was a powerful status, one backed up by the political, legal, economic, and social structures that buttressed eighteenth-century American slavery, a system designed to extract the labor of Black people and many Indigenous peoples, confine them to limited geographies, control their actions, restrict their opportunities, and make them "less than" the White people around them. To ensure social order, in 1716, North Carolina's colonial government layered expectations onto enslavers that they police the people they enslaved, provide permissions for enslaved peoples to travel, and emancipate only for "honest & Faithfull service." When it came to making decisions about the lives of the enslaved, in some ways, slaveowners were as constrained by the law as were those they owned.[9]

Over the eighteenth century, laws that dictated Black Carolinians' lives became more restrictive. When rebellion flared up among enslaved peoples along South Carolina's Stono River in 1739, terrifying White residents throughout the American colonies, North Carolina's assembly tripled the size and scope of its Black code, empowering White indentured servants as "Christians" with legal status and rights, and granting them personal agency and protections denied "heathen" Black and Indigenous peoples, whether enslaved or not. Policing powers expanded beyond individual enslavers so that sheriffs could track down people fleeing from enslavement and stifle threats of insurrections.[10]

The new laws redefined the criterion for emancipation from "honest & Faithfull service" to "meritorious service," an unarticulated concept borrowed from a 1723 Virginia law. White folk generally agreed that if an enslaved person exposed a potential uprising or thwarted a murder plot, they served meritoriously, and the law expressly encouraged that sort of espionage. But if an enslaved person was simply honest and faithful without causing any problems for their enslaver, was their service equally meritorious? Or did the idea require something more uniquely praiseworthy, such as saving a White child from drowning or thwarting the theft of a White man's property? The assembly abdicated its role in defining meritorious service, leaving county courts to determine worthiness case by case. Still, for those who earned emancipation through meritorious service, freedom was illusory. The law prohibited them from remaining with families and friends, demanding they abandon the colony within six months or risk being seized and publicly auctioned back into enslavement, not for five years as defined by the previous Black code, but for life. Having left North Carolina, emancipated peoples could return for no longer than one month without risking a similar fate.[11]

In 1753, the General Assembly again amended the Black code, allotting to each county three searchers who seasonally invaded the homes of enslaved peoples to look for and confiscate weapons. If patrollers found anything suspicious, they wielded authority to lash offenders thirty times or nail ears to pillories and then cut them off. The law expected enslavers to impart justice as well, reminding them that the colony could do only so much in controlling Black Carolinians and demanding they take more responsibility for the humans whom they enslaved.[12]

By the 1780s, then, Joel Lane and all slaveowners benefited from a system of laws, sheriffs, searchers, and courts that buttressed their own scrutiny and control of Black folk. Lane knew the system well, having served as a Halifax County sheriff in 1761 and 1762, following in the footsteps of his elder cousin, Joseph Lane, who embodied the many levels of surveillance. As enslaver, Joseph monitored the people he forced to labor and live on his farm. In 1751, as sheriff, he arrested an enslaved man for a felony, supervising the trial as justice of the peace, and upon the guilty verdict, ordering the man hanged and possibly acting as the executioner. As a searcher, he participated in a 1758 shooting of an enslaved man attempting to flee. Legally and personally, Joseph Lane committed to enslaving humans. Upon his death, he divided Tom, Cate, King, Annaca, Mingo, Ploughman, Jack, Cleony, Vilet, Daffiny, and Affrica among his siblings and their "Heirs and Assigns for ever."[13]

Forever—the Black codes ensured that enslavement disabled personhood and delivered a lifelong sentence for Black Carolinians who, unless they fled, had a very narrow and ill-defined path to freedom. In contrast to indentured laborers, most of whom were White people but also some free Black folk who chose to contract their labors, enslavement was neither contractual nor limited. Meritorious service—used as an incentive to inspire loyalty and hard work—remained a purposefully vague concept because most White people found it difficult to fathom anything that enslaved people could do that truly warranted rescinding their enslavement.

————

That Joel Lane enslaved Cate, Young Ned, Sam, and two dozen more people mattered, then, for his needs, ambitions, and scrutiny dictated their lives. When Martha Lane died in 1771, his enslaved people raised his children until he remarried—Martha's sister, Mary. Over the next decade, his enslaved people looked after the five children to whom Mary gave birth. When Joel Lane acquired a tavern license in 1772 to serve people visiting the county's civic buildings, his enslaved people prepared the drink and food and quartered and pastured guests' horses. When he joined other White Americans in 1776 in shedding his "oppression" by signing a pledge denouncing taxation without representation, his enslaved people did not make it their revolution despite hearing rhetoric of liberty as they served guests, watching examples of rebellion from passing militias, and picking up rumors of enslaved laborers rebelling to the east. When Lane, as a member of the Wake County Council of Safety, became an entry taker in 1778, tracing ownership rights for lands abandoned by fleeing Loyalists and acquiring almost four thousand acres for himself, his enslaved people went to work turning the new grounds into old fields. When the war raging across the other colonies finally arrived in North Carolina, and Lane received an exemption from military duty, his enslaved people raised and prepared the pork, bacon, beef, and corn that he sold to American troops. When he hosted the Provincial Congress in his tavern in 1781 and 1783, receiving £15,000 [$2,708,000] in reimbursement on each occasion for "house rent, pasturage, &c.," his enslaved people took care of the guests and their horses.[14]

In return for his enslaved people's work and loyalty, Joel Lane remained committed to manumission *only* for the murky reason of meritorious service, which apparently none of his enslaved people ever provided. As a representative in the Provincial Congress in 1777, he voted to remind White Carolinians inspired by other motives—such as the world-shattering concept that "all men are created equal"—that the people they freed would be jailed and sold back into enslavement. Only meritorious service as certified by a county court warranted freedom, and in the 1787 General Assembly, he voted against a bill allowing for personal emancipations by enslavers who, "out of conscience," wished to free humans whom they enslaved.[15]

In early 1792, commissioners paid Joel Lane £1,378 [$251,570] for one thousand acres adjacent to his farm on which to situate a new state capital to be named Raleigh. The General Assembly approved a plan for the town, and lots went on sale. Carpenter Rodham Atkins bid to construct a new State House, listing his friend Joel Lane as security for his character and ability to complete the work. From the people who cleared 250 acres of "old fields" to the workers who molded the bricks to the men who assisted Atkins and his hired carpenters, the State House arose, like Joel Lane, by benefit of enslaved labor. It symbolized a town, state, and culture indebted to slavery. Enslaved people, numbering over 100,780, comprised over one-quarter of the state's population. Twenty-seven of them remained bound to Joel Lane, and he added another five by 1795.[16]

Then, on March 29, 1795, Joel Lane, fifty-six years old, died. He left substantial properties to his three eldest sons. The younger seven children inherited the bulk of the "Estate real and personal": lands, livestock, household goods, and enslaved humans. The enslaved Lane "family" received nothing. Through war and peace, had they all not served faithfully, even meritoriously? Lane proved constant to the end. Twenty-two of the thirty-two enslaved people, including Young Ned's brother, Sam, were dispersed among Lane's children. The other ten, including Young Ned and Cate, were to serve Mary Hinton Lane during her widowhood. She died four days later.[17]

Now orphaned, the younger seven Lane children separated into guardians' homes. Only John was of age and eligible to take his inheritance: sixteen hundred acres, "all my Stock of Cattle and Hoggs," and Affie, Austen, Clansey, and Peter. Each of the other children received furniture and three enslaved humans. As the youngest son, Thomas inherited the house and several thousand acres of land, although he could not take ownership until he came of age.[18]

Despite Joel Lane's significant wealth, he left considerable debt. To settle the estate's arrears, his sons, Henry and James, inventoried the properties and planned a sale. In October 1795, horses, sheep, cows, hogs, and bee hives went on the auction block, as well as the tools of the enslaved laborers: flat irons, iron pots and pans, sheep shears, butter churns, saws, looms, harnesses, cotton and linen wheels, bellows, an anvil, hammers, tongs, grind stones, brushes, spice mortars, coffee pots, hoes, shovels, and harnesses. The farm ceased to be a working one. Young Ned, Cate, and the enslaved laborers originally assigned to Mary Lane, and who remained on the farm, went into trusteeship, hired out to earn some profit toward the estate's debts.[19]

Other enslaved people departed the Lane farm as each Lane child moved into the home of a guardian. The state required guardians to take "the Custody and Tuition of such Child or Children" by posting £2000 [$242,110] bond, a considerable financial investment meant to guarantee that guardians adequately raised orphans and protected their inheritances. In return, while the children were in their care, guardians benefited from unencumbered use of orphans' lands and enslaved laborers. Ten-year-old Sam bid goodbye to

Cate and Ned as seventeen-year-old Martha Lane took him, Phill, and Salley into the home of William Hinton, her maternal uncle. The other Lane orphans scattered among other relatives, and the enslaved community disintegrated—forever. Only the ten assigned to Mary remained behind, joined by Jimboy, Jeffrey, and Cloe, inherited by ten-year-old Thomas. Because Thomas received the Lane farm, the guardianship law required him to leave a "sufficient Number of Slaves to cultivate and Improve the same," even as he moved into his elder brother's house.[20]

Amidst the chaos of Black families and the Black community being ripped apart, in 1796, seventeen-year-old Cate became pregnant. She might have found a lover, possibly one of the enslaved men. By the time Cate's twins arrived, only five men remained—Jimboy, Jeffrey, Will, Old Ned, and Jack. She might have met a man who lived nearby on an adjacent farm, or, since the estate executors lived miles away and surveillance was lax, she might have been raped by any of the men, White or Black, who interacted with the under-supervised enslaved people. Whatever the circumstance, by the end of 1796, Cate was mother to Montford and Davy. Fifteen-year-old Ned became an uncle.

The little bit of freedom that enslaved people experienced on the old Lane farm masked the threat of sale that weighed on Young Ned, Cate, and the others. Henry and James Lane made minimal headway in settling their parents' estate, collecting £108 [$16,770] on the debts owed and selling off "great parts" of the properties. When Henry died unexpectedly in January 1797 without a will of his own, he left behind a household vulnerable to the machinations of his father-in-law, John Hinton, who grabbed custody of Henry's properties, including the profits from the sales of the Lane assets. Family drama ensued. Elizabeth Lane Haywood and her husband, Stephen, charged that her half-brothers had mismanaged the estate. When Elizabeth's eldest full brother, John Lane, took over the executorship, she convinced him to sue Hinton for £5,000 [$776,400], the projected income from the land sales. In December 1800, the case resolved with Hinton paying "all the Assets of the defendant's intestate," far less than what Elizabeth expected: £252 [$30,500].[21]

Henry Lane's death left two of the Lane orphans without a guardian. John Lane took in young Joel, but none of the immediate Lane family assumed guardianship for Thomas, turning instead to a cousin, Martin Lane, an unsuccessful carpenter who recently had lost his Raleigh town properties to delinquent taxes. Unable to cover the requisite guardian bond, Martin relied on two other relatives to guarantee it. By spring 1798, he settled into the old Lane manor to raise Thomas, secure and improve the estate, and supervise Young Ned, Cate, and the other enslaved people awaiting their futures.[22]

The farm returned to order, taking in £1,397 [$220,490] by the end of 1798, much of which came from hiring out enslaved people to nearby farmers and craftsmen. In 1799, carpenter Rodham Atkins rented Jimboy for $50.30 [$1,230] a month, agreeing to provide him "one shirt of ozenabriggs"—a course, unbleached linen imported from Osnabrück in lower Saxony, properly spelled "osnaburg"—and "one pair of breeches of Negro Cotton"—a cheap and course cotton and wool cloth produced in New England manufactories for Southern markets. John Lane and Martin Lane hired out others on similar terms, making good money from the labor even as they avoided obligations to clothe and feed the people whom they enslaved. In late 1798, Young Ned found himself among those hired out, rented by John Haywood to help renovate a house in the new capital town. Ned left behind all that he knew—his sister, his nephews, and the Lane farm—heading for town lot 210, just north of the new State House. He was seventeen years old.[23]

The Haywoods of Edgecombe County were one of the most established and prominent families in North Carolina. When Elizabeth Lane Haywood sued over the profits from the sale of her father's lands, her husband Stephen Haywood was at her side. He was the youngest of four brothers who inherited their family's lineage, wealth, and status. The brothers were men on the move. Between 1797 and 1804, all four relocated to Raleigh, their families eventually occupying four town blocks and forming a clan of Haywoods whose prestige in town and state politics was recognizable well into the nineteenth century. In time, they enslaved hundreds of people on plantations back east, farms north of Raleigh, and their town lots.

The eldest brother, John Haywood, moved to Raleigh in 1797 because state law required the State Treasurer, a position he had held for a decade, to reside in the new capital. In June, he purchased town lot 210, on which sat a fine house facing the State House to the south, and he hired Young Ned to help renovate the residence. Haywood bought a farm beyond Raleigh's northern boundary to support the town house. He soon courted Eliza Eagles Asaph Williams of Mt. Gallant plantation in New Hanover County. In March 1798, they married. He was forty-three, and his young bride, who he called Betsy, was seventeen, the same age as Young Ned.[24]

Eliza knew well the social and political expectations that accompanied marriage among the elite. Her parents, John Pugh Williams and Jane Davis Williams, were among the Cape Fear region's foremost citizens, her father an honored Revolutionary War veteran and six-term veteran of the state House of Commons. He bought and sold on the slave market, and thirty-nine enslaved laborers worked Mt. Gallant by 1790. By the time Eliza Williams became Eliza Haywood, her world was one of large farms, good society, and enslaved humans.[25]

John Haywood, 1755–1827. From Portrait Collection, circa 1720–1997, North Carolina Collection. Courtesy of Wilson Special Collections Library, University of North Carolina at Chapel Hill.

But that world had yet to manifest on lot 210 where the town house was under renovation. The newlyweds lived in Casso's Inn and Stables, which sat just south of the State House, advertised as "A Capital Inn" where politicians and other men gathered for dinners, conversations, and other entertainments. When John Haywood first arrived in Raleigh, he had taken up residence at Casso's Inn. He and Eliza celebrated their wedding there in February 1798, and Eliza moved in with him until, three months later, as her pregnancy began to show, she abandoned Raleigh for her parent's farm. Over the decades, Eliza's mother, Jane Williams, a few months younger than John, resented her daughter's marriage to a man over twice her daughter's age, openly competing with him for Eliza's attentions. When Eliza returned to Mt. Gallant, John confessed that "I should feel greater love and affection for your Mother if she did not so completely rival me in the affections of her Daughter." Jane Williams certainly influenced her daughter, but Eliza's refusal to remain in Raleigh surely reflected concern, maybe even horror, at the thought of raising an infant above a tavern.[26]

Five months later and late in her pregnancy, in October 1798, Eliza Haywood returned to Raleigh and her husband, briefly. Her mother tempted her back to Mt. Gallant, insisting that "we are angry with ourselves ever since that we did not make Mary go with you." Mary, an enslaved midwife, "has acted in that Capacity for 31 little Black folks among our own, and never lost one but Mother and Child all do well." The offer appealed to Eliza who was frail and frightened, but John insisted she stay. Weeks later, she received another invitation from her mother, reminding her that "Mary is full as good—and she is here to Nurse and wait upon you altogether." Of course, nothing stopped Jane Williams from sending Mary to Raleigh, but by November, daughter asked her mother whether it would be respectable to leave John again. "I see not the least impropriety in your coming down and it is quite Natural that you should want to do so," Williams replied and then, to up the ante, she reminded her daughter that "here is as good a Midwife as is generally to be met with, and an Excellent wet Nurse in Nancy." Over John's protests, Eliza left again and, after December, when she gave birth to Eliza Eagles Haywood (called Betsy John by the immediate family), remained at Mt. Gallant. By the time Young Ned arrived at lot 210 in November 1798, then, John Haywood was alone in Raleigh.[27]

Ned found the house, in its state of renovation, a disaster. The town was even messier, a new capital growing into its own with the sorts of residents, mostly men of lesser status than the State Treasurer, who showed up to make a quick profit as carpenters and bricklayers, office seekers, tavernkeepers, and peddlers. John Haywood should have stood out as a man of respectability, but in his unrenovated house with a rented enslaved laborer, he did not display the social status that Jane Williams expected for her daughter. Eliza stayed where life was familiar and comfortable, where she had the support of her parents, two sisters, and a community of enslaved people who served her.

With some urgency, Haywood contracted Rodham Atkins, whose work on the State House established him as Raleigh's "eminent house carpenter," at least in his own advertisements. Atkins had laborers in tow: young White men who indentured as apprentices, enslaved Black men whom he purchased, and other enslaved men whom he hired, such as Jimboy from the Lane estate. John Haywood, too, rented the labor of more enslaved men to assist with the renovation. "I have pulled down the Stair Case and am endeavoring by divers alterations and improvements to make our dwelling House more comfortable," he bragged to his wife in February 1799, claiming as his own the manual labor of Ned and other hired enslaved men.[28]

Atkins's progress on lot 210 went slowly. Newly elected governor William R. Davie warned John Haywood that the carpenter, with so many projects underway, neglected his obligations. For months, Haywood's house on lot 210 sat unreconstructed with walls and stairs demolished, Atkins excusing his neglect on the winter weather. Frustrated by the slow pace, Haywood dismissed the enslaved men whom he had hired, sending them back to their owners by mid-March 1799. "All the Negroes free and gone off except Ned," he wrote to his wife, "some to one House—some to another."[29]

With Ned to help, Haywood turned his attentions to landscaping, reporting to Eliza that "Our Garden is ploughed up a first time, but is neither laid off nor freed from Rubbish; nor has the Weather for many days past been such as to suffer working it." Ned tilled the ground; John claimed the labor. Haywood reveled in "having a Gardner," assuring his wife that because Ned was available, "I am under the necessity of attending to the laying off the Walkes, which have never yet been made:—I must see too to the planting some Grape Vines I have, as well as to the planting our pease &c." Grapes and peas were only the beginning. The residence would become a great house with labyrinthine walks coursing around trees and shrubbery, flowers in open vistas, and exotic plants that inspired conversation. "This you will agree is employment in abundance," he appealed to Eliza, "especially for a man who has no one but Ned, an awkward Boy, to assist him."[30]

John Haywood wrote of gardening and torn-down staircases to coax Eliza back to Raleigh. He had to find a way to compete with his mother-in-law, particularly the enslaved midwife and nursemaid with whom she bribed her daughter. He promised to purchase "a Maid, that would look decent, be handy, trusty, a good Nurse for our Daughter, and one whose Conduct guided by her good sense would be such as would always please you and recommend her." He bought Kizzy, who showed little interest in serving the Haywoods and often disappeared at night to keep company with "a Mr Blair, an Irishman, who it was said had become enamored of her." Haywood had bought Kizzy to use her body to nurse his child. He soon sold her to Blair, who used her body for his sexual pleasure. His search for a nursemaid resumed: "Many Negroes have lately gone through this place for Sale, but I have not been able to find one which I thought would answer the purpose."[31]

John's efforts impressed neither Eliza nor her mother. An as-yet-found nursemaid, uncultivated gardens, and an unrenovated house were not the only deterrents. Eliza expected a better society, something else that John seemed incapable of providing. By early 1799, John Haywood insisted to his wife repeatedly that, as other respectable men such as his brothers relocated to the capital town, "Raleigh is like to be much improved in point of Society all at once."[32]

Ned did not join his employer at Casso's Inn. He remained at the house on lot 210, alongside several of Haywood's enslaved laborers brought to Raleigh from the Edgecombe farm. As winter thawed in early April 1799, work began anew. Husband wrote wife that "taking away the stairs has made one pretty large room. . . . I have put another window in the next largest room, intending your Piano shall stand there." Of course, every time John Haywood wrote "I," he meant Ned, those whom Haywood had relocated from Edgecombe

County, and those working for Atkins. They were the ones putting another window in the piano room as they continued to tear down, build up, plaster, paper, and paint.[33]

Still, Eliza refused to return, promising to bring the baby as soon as Atkins completed renovations to the great house, renovations that would evidence her husband's status, provide the space for the social events that John expected her to host, and prove John's love for her. John Haywood did not wait. In late April 1799, he sent his brother Sherwood to retrieve what was rightfully his. By early May, Eliza and Betsy John arrived in Raleigh. Before the month was out, Eliza's mother followed.[34]

————

During the months of renovation, Young Ned occasionally glanced eastward, just across Wilmington Street, where a young woman named Clarissa worked the gardens behind Sherwood and Eleanor Haywood's house. In contrast to the quiet, underused property on which he lived, lot 225 was a busy household with a lively kitchen where "the house servants lodged and lived, and here the meals were prepared for the people in the mansion," as Clarissa's son later described.[35]

In early 1799, John Haywood had purchased lots 208, 209, 224, and 225 on his brother Sherwood's behalf—a full town block that included a substantial house, the kitchen, and other outbuildings, composing a landscape of enslaved labor that stirred guests and passersby to envy his brother's leisure and status. Sherwood was thirty-seven years old and recently appointed a federal loan officer with a workplace adjacent to John's office in the State House. Sherwood's wife, Eleanor, was twenty-three, the eldest child of Philomen Hawkins III and Lucy Davis of Pleasant Hill farm in Granville County, where she prepared for her destiny as the wife of "a man of respectability," as Lunsford recalled him.[36]

Sherwood and Eleanor brought two young daughters and about twenty enslaved people with them to Raleigh to work the town estate and a farm some miles north of town—known as St. Mary's—that sustained the household. Among the enslaved were Clarissa, Matilda, and their mother. Clarissa had been born in 1783. Like Ned's parents, her mother and father remain obscure. She was biracial, so she counted at least one White male ancestor, possibly an Irish or English indentured servant who mingled among the enslaved women or an enslaver or overseer who raped a female ancestor. She was sixteen years old when she accompanied the Haywoods to Raleigh. That she, her sister, and her mother served the family rather than working the farm suggests a favored status. They crammed alongside other enslaved women into the small outbuilding that served as a kitchen behind Sherwood and Eleanor's house.[37]

Sherwood Haywood,
1762–1829. Privately
owned. Photograph
by Joshua Steadman.
Courtesy of Betsy
Haywood.

Noisy, smoky, and smelly kitchens inhabited by enslaved cooks were a world apart from the rooms where their enslavers ate. Enslaved domestics lived where they worked, immediate to the families who controlled them. At least one stout table, some cast-iron pots, and several straw mattresses lay about such kitchens. When cooks doubled as laundresses, massive copper kettles lined the kitchens' walls alongside the cast-iron pots, ropes swung overhead for hanging clothes, and dressers provided ironing and storage space.[38]

By the 1790s, new ideas about White women's place in the home and who should be seen and unseen in household operations reshaped thoughts about kitchens. In the North, where capitalism and the rhetoric of revolution began to reject enslavement in favor of free labor, cooking moved into main houses as kitchens became centers for White women's domestic culture. Laundering remained a dirty affair, hidden away in basements or outbuildings, still done by servants, some still enslaved. In the South, as capitalism embraced slavery, kitchens moved farther from great houses, situated among storehouses, stables, privies, smithies, smokehouses, and slave quarters as just another site of enslaved labor. An observer remarked as early as 1724 that wealthier Southerners located "the *Kitchen* apart from the *Dwelling* House, because of the Smell of hot Victuals, offensive in hot Weather," but it was not only the odors that stirred White Southerners to distance kitchens farther from their homes. Although enslaved cooks and servers evidenced slaveowners' status, their labor was best left unseen.[39]

Clarissa served as a cook and laundress, and she managed the small garden near the kitchen, always under Sherwood and Eleanor Haywood's watchful eyes from a veranda that stretched around three sides of the house. Eleanor trusted Clarissa, assigning the keys to the pantry to her. As Clarissa pulled weeds and tended her work, she occasionally glanced westward, just across Wilmington Street, to where a young man laid paths in the garden when the weather permitted.[40]

––––––––

In December 1799, John Lane, still settling his parents' estate, advertised a forthcoming auction: Susannah (nicknamed Suckey), Archer, Cate and her sons, and Young Ned. Enslaved people on the old Lane farm became quick capital to pay off lingering debts from Joel and Mary Lane's estate, now four years unresolved. Throughout 1799, Will, Old Ned, Hasty, Old Rose, Jack, and Vilot had disappeared, all presumably sold. Rumor of the impending sale spread widely, exciting interest from Henry Haywood Jr., seventy miles to the east in Edgecombe County. "If those are to be sold," he wrote his brother, John, "I must beg of you to let me no when as I should wish to be at the sale." On January 10, 1800, John Lane ushered in the nineteenth century by selling the last vestiges of his parents' eighteenth-century farmstead. Five of the six enslaved humans sold, John recording the transactions with the Wake County Court:

One Negro girl Sucky to Dugald McKithen	£131 . . 0 . . 0 [$15,860]
Three Negros by the Names of Cate, Davy and Munford to Nath'l Lane	£272 . . 10 . . 0 [$32,940]
One Negro Boy by the [name] of Archer to Jn. Lane	£194 . . 0 . . 0 [$23,480]

Young Ned did not stand on the auction block that day. He did not even bother to show up.[41]

By January 1800, Ned had been working on lot 210 for a little over a year, and despite his being an "awkward boy," the State Treasurer had arranged to own him, offering a price that John Lane accepted a couple months later, selling the last of thirteen enslaved humans. On March 10, Lane penned the sale into the county records: "One Negro by the name of Ned to John Haywood, £200 . . 10 . . 0 [$24,220]."[42]

With that, John Lane had only one task remaining. About twenty months later, he put his parent's house up for rent, displacing Thomas and his guardian, Martin, who moved to a nearby farm. Five years later, when Thomas Lane turned twenty-one years old, he claimed his inheritance—the manor house and surrounding lands. By then, John Lane planned to move to Tennessee, and there was little to keep Thomas or Martin in Raleigh either. Martin sold the farmhouse and mill where he and Thomas lived, and Thomas sold the Lane estate and one of his enslaved people, Cloe. His sister Dorothy's husband, Allen Gilchrist, bought the property and agreed to "bargain sell and convey" Thomas's other inherited properties. When the Gilchrists moved into Dorothy's childhood home, three people formerly enslaved by her father—David, Judy, and Brittain—strangely found themselves returning as well. It must have seemed empty without the rest of their community who had once served Joel Lane and his family.[43]

———

After Sherwood Haywood delivered Eliza to her husband in July 1799, she made clear that she continued to disapprove of Raleigh, staying only long enough to get pregnant again. John became desperate. When Young Ned badgered him about reuniting him with his sister and nephews, Haywood recognized an opportunity. Within nine months, he purchased Cate and her sons from Nathaniel Lane for 555 Spanish milled dollars [$12,860]. Haywood had his gardener in Ned, and he now found a midwife and nursemaid in Cate.[44]

Eliza had made clear, however, that the unrenovated house was the real problem. Upon arriving in Raleigh years earlier, John had also bought lot 190 just down the street. When adjacent lot 191 became available, he grabbed it. If he could develop those properties, his wife might be more inclined to stay. They were convenient to the State House but not contiguous to it. Two blocks away, the business and busyness of government were not so immediate, and a larger estate would give her and their children room to breathe.[45]

John decided to relocate the great house from lot 210, a cheap alternative to building a new house. In January 1800, he hired Jim, an enslaved man from New Bern who "has had a great deal of Experience in that line of business" to "accomplish your house moving." Over the next few months, Haywood contracted carpenters and hired more enslaved laborers to install piers under the house, planning to raise it and move it to the new lots. On May 19, onlookers gathered to watch the undertaking. The scaffolding failed, the house tilted, and one of the piers snapped, sending splintered lumber through the crowd. Ned survived unharmed, but the projectiles struck three other workers, killing Saul, a hired-out enslaved laborer. A "melancholy event," declared a local newspaper. John Haywood seemed most concerned about his liability, insisting that "the accident might have befallen himself or any other person engaged in raising the House." Still, he took responsibility for the enslaved man's death, the price he paid discouraging him from possibly repeating the tragedy. He put lot 210, its house, and outbuildings up for sale. Eliza Haywood remained at Mt. Gallant.[46]

In October, John Haywood began purchasing materials to build a new great house on lots 190 and 191, but the work did not begin in earnest for another seven months. In May 1801, he hired James and Robin, enslaved bricklayers, to complete the foundation. Other hired enslaved laborers and Haywood's own enslaved people worked alongside hired carpenters and house joiners to raise the house. Rumor was that it resembled the ancestral Haywood home at Dunbar: a two-story residence with classical columns and large chimneys buttressing each end. A wide hall extended from the front door to the back doors, with a parlor to the right and a great room for entertainment to the left. Three large bedrooms and a smaller one occupied the second floor. Carpenters carved moldings, mantels, and wainscoting as house joiners installed doors, windows, and staircases. It was to be Raleigh's most opulent residence.[47]

Even before its completion in November, the great house served the social role expected of a Haywood home. John warned his wife that she would "return to a troublesome scene—to a place filled with Members of the Assembly—to a House crowded with disagreeable guests—and to a Husband oppressed and worn down with the multiplicity of cares and business." Eliza Haywood undoubtedly determined never to go back.[48]

Among the outbuildings surrounding the Haywoods' new house was a stable where Young Ned took up residence. His room was eight by eighteen feet, with immediate access to the horse stall and a storage chamber. A cleaning trough ran through all. He became accustomed to the clip-clop of horse hooves, an occasional whinny, and the smell of hay and manure. It was where, in the chaos of the Haywoods' expanding social world, Young Ned transformed into Ned Lane.[49]

Seldom did enslaved people have a choice as to names because White enslavers controlled their public identities, often by christening enslaved babies, inscribing their names onto inventories, and naming them in runaway ads and announcements of estate sales. Occasionally, a first name given by an enslaved parent to their baby stuck, or at least reemerged later if the individual found freedom. Surnames were rarer. When they did appear, they often represented past or present owners. On John Haywood's and Sherwood Haywood's inventories, names resonated with genealogies of enslavement: Austin Ford, Tom Bird, Peter Bird, Joe Branch, P. Hawkins, S. T. Hawkins, Charles Gaston, Henry Bryan, Henry Mitchell, and the Curtises—Phil, Austin, and Ned. Yet, in John Haywood's household, enslaved people who

John and Eliza Haywood's home, Raleigh, NC. Photograph by Craig Thompson Friend.

had been on the Lane estate—Cate, her sons, and Old Ned and Hasty—did not carry the Lane surname. Similarly, in Edgecombe County, where Elizabeth and Stephen Haywood inherited several of her father's enslaved laborers, Moses, Frederick, and Kissey did not use the Lane name.[50]

Around the turn of the nineteenth century, Ned began to be known as Ned Lane. Unlike his sister and others formerly enslaved by the Lanes, he chose his surname, although his selection is curious. Black cultural ways did not include family surnames, so when Black Americans appropriated one, it often made a political statement. They took names different from those of their owners to separate themselves and their families from their enslavers. Ned appropriated the only surname he had known, one of consequence—Lane. It no longer held power over him, but it made clear that he was not a Haywood.[51]

None of the Haywoods seemed to care how Ned Lane fashioned his identity. If he served faithfully, they overlooked a little independence. In fact, John Haywood counted on it. Awkward Ned grew into a reliable man, beginning to travel alone, serving as Haywood's courier across the state, carrying letters with the directive "By Ned" and, as in August 1801 during one of Eliza Haywood's brief visits to Raleigh, traveling alone to Wilmington to pick up drapes and a straw bonnet from her mother.[52]

Again, Eliza remained in Raleigh only briefly, and when she returned to Mt. Gallant a month later because she so missed her family, John conceded that her sister could move permanently with her to Raleigh. Rather than send his brother Sherwood to retrieve Eliza, he sent Ned Lane, giving him horses and sixty dollars [$1,390], "as much Money as I suppose will be Sufficient to carry him & the Horses to Wilmington—to find and stable the Horses whilst they remain there:—and to pay *all expenses* incident to travelling on your return." Beginning with those days renovating the house on lot 210, John Haywood became reliant on Ned Lane so that, as Ned traveled back from Wilmington with Eliza Haywood and the children, he functioned as an instrument of John's patriarchy. Through Ned Lane, John Haywood demanded that his wife return to the family estate. Never again did she stay away so long.[53]

After completion of the new house in late autumn of 1801, Eliza made Raleigh her home. She found it difficult to travel, pregnant for six of the next seven years and physically ill throughout much of that time. As children filled the house, Ned Lane became Uncle Ned, a familiarity that laid bare the household's power dynamics, for even the toddlers commanded his time and attention. Responsibility for the children, though, lay with Ned's sister, Nurse Cate, who proved her own indispensability. Some months after the 1801 birth of the Haywoods' second child, Eliza's mother reassured her daughter that the boy would soon be able to sit up "if Cate takes pains to learn him." Eliza's constant pregnancies and her unfailingly "exhausted state" placed the burden of infant care on Nurse Cate.[54]

Further exhausting Eliza was the relentless hospitality required of her. She complained that when visitors called upon her as Mrs. John Haywood, she had to "shew the Person whoever it is great Respect and attention and this being the case we must thank them instead of blameing them." Twelve days before Christmas in 1803, her husband invited a houseful of General Assemblymen to dinner. The Haywoods owned a long table that seated twenty-six and a side table that accommodated four more. "And that has been the Number every other Day since," Eliza grumbled after four evenings of entertaining state legislators. She was exhausted: "The Children all Night and the People in the Day." When the General Assembly's December term ended, "the Federal Court meets the first of January, and I shall have the same Trouble over again."[55]

Just as John Haywood once took credit for laying gardens and tearing down stairs, Eliza Haywood's letters intimated that she did all the domestic work herself. The demands on energy and time had to be tolling for a sickly and constantly pregnant woman, but Eliza dismissed the work of her enslaved laborers as insufficient and undeserving of recognition. With Ned's purchase in March 1800, followed by the acquisition of Cate in November, John staffed the household to attend her. In September 1801, he added Moses, a thirty-year-old "Cook as well as Field hand," to aid Cate in the kitchen. Two months later, twenty-one-year-old Lewis joined the enslaved community. At the end of December, so too did Old Ned and Hasty, purchased from Rodham Atkins, who had acquired them in the selloff of the Lane estate. Seven enslaved people labored on the town estate, and a dozen more worked on the 595-acre farm along Crabtree Creek, raising vegetables, fruits, and meats for the Haywood family. Eliza was far from alone in her domestic work, but she did not acknowledge the work of her enslaved cooks and servers. "I have no Person to assist me but our own Black People," she complained, but in her persistently exhausted condition, she relied on them to clean, garden, prepare, and serve.[56]

By the spring of 1803, all of John's brothers and their families arrived in the capital town with dozens of enslaved people. In the autumn of 1798, Henry Haywood Jr. brought his wife, Ann Shepard Haywood, to their new Raleigh home on town lot 177, attended by four enslaved people, with another six working a farm north of town. Five enslaved people served in Sherwood and Eleanor Haywood's townhome just across Edenton Street and one block to the west from John and Eliza. Ten others labored on the 116-acre St. Mary's farm. In 1802, Stephen Haywood joined his brothers in the capital town. He had wed Elizabeth Lane in 1796, and they lived at Dunbar, watching the rest of the family migrate to the capital town. When they arrived in Raleigh, they set up house to the northeast of John Haywood's estate, again just across Edenton Street. Like his brothers, Stephen purchased a farm just north of town, but he did not people it with enslaved laborers for another year. Frederick, whom Elizabeth Lane Haywood inherited upon her parent's death, preceded his enslavers to Raleigh, having been sold to Rodham Atkins in 1799 as a carpenter's assistant but not remaining long with Atkins who traded him to Hogg & Adams, brokers who specialized in acquiring and reselling landed and human properties. Frederick disappeared into the slave market—forever.[57]

John Haywood's brothers and their wives aspired to have grand homes to rival the one built by the State Treasurer for Eliza, if not in size, at least in elegance. In 1805, dissatisfied with the one town lot, Henry purchased lots 206, 207, 222, and 223, between Stephen's and Sherwood's properties, already situated with a large house and outbuildings. The Haywood clan carved out a notable family presence in Raleigh, overseeing large households comprised of White dependents and enslaved Black folks on cultivated town estates supported by nearby farms. Every Black body signified their enslavers' aspirations and achievements. As Clarissa labored in the kitchen serving Eleanor and Sherwood Haywood, as Ned delivered John Haywood's letters across the state, and as Cate taught Eliza and John's children to walk, they represented the Haywoods and symbolized the clan's wealth and status.[58]

Chapter 2

Learning Enslavement

Over her lifetime, Clarissa walked across the yard from the detached kitchen to the main house tens of thousands of times, climbing the stairs to the veranda to serve Eleanor and her guests, gathering whisps of family gossip. In early May of 1803, Eleanor and Eliza shared stories of sorrow and joy. Eliza's father had died days earlier, having drunk himself to death at Mt. Gallant. She was already planning the journey to comfort her mother and sisters. She had good news to share as well, displaying a small baby bump. Six months later, she gave birth prematurely to her fourth child, Fabius Julius, putting both mother and child in danger. They survived, and the boy would go on to enjoy a distinguished career as a physician, innovator in the use of chloroform, Confederate surgeon, and cofounder of the North Carolina Medical Society. Eleanor Haywood also had exciting news. She, too, was pregnant although, at two months, the baby bump was less conspicuous. In mid-December, she would give birth to her fourth child, Thomas. Unlike his cousin Fabius, Thomas would not survive his first night.[1]

As Eleanor hosted family and friends, Clarissa awaited nearby. It was particularly challenging in early May 1803. She, too, was pregnant, eight months along. Her back and legs ached. When she retreated to the kitchen, she found little peace as women maneuvered kettles and skillets around the blazing fire, clanging heavy lids loudly against cast-iron pots.[2]

Amid the chaos, on May 30, Clarissa gave birth to a boy. She had known his father, Ned Lane, for four years. If Clarissa and Ned married, neither the law nor the church sanctioned their love. They dedicated themselves to each other privately, but they could not bind themselves exclusively, for they had other families who insisted on their devotion. Eleanor Haywood soon relied on Clarissa not only as a cook and laundress but to raise her daughters, and Ned was Uncle Ned to the future doctor Fabius and his siblings. When Clarissa gave birth that spring morning, she and Ned began their own family, one always in tension with the families who enslaved them.[3]

"My infancy was spent upon the floor, in a rough cradle, or sometimes in my mother's arms." Clarissa's son's earliest memory came from his mother, shared with him later in life, easily read as melancholic and related to him with regret. She could lift him and embrace him, but only "sometimes." Clarissa and other enslaved mothers lamented their babes' futures and their inability to give more attention. Her time was not her own. It belonged to Sherwood and Eleanor. So, too, did the newborn. He joined their inventories as another enslaved human. If his name mattered to his owners, then Sherwood Haywood, like Joel Lane, would have greeted the child with one. The Haywoods appeared rather indifferent to the infant.[4]

Instead, Ned Lane christened his son after a man whom he met years earlier—Lunsford Long of Halifax County. Lunsford had an ancient Anglo meaning as "one who dwells by the crossing on the Lune," supposedly a location in Sussex, England. At the turn of the nineteenth century, it was a rare name in the United States, at least as a first name. Five men, all of them White Carolinians, sported the first name as did approximately eighteen boys, most from the Carolinas as well. Among them was Lunsford Long. Born in the mid-1760s, Long was Joel Lane's cousin. By 1790, he owned a modest farm, worked by two enslaved people whom he inherited, alongside two hundred acres in northeastern North Carolina and five thousand acres on "western waters." In August 1794, he married "the celebrated and much admired Miss Rebecca Jones" of Edgecombe County, and the first of their two daughters arrived eleven months later. He sold the western lands, investing his profits in enslaved humans. Within a decade, he worked fifty-six people on his Halifax County farm.[5]

At some time in the early 1790s, Long met Young Ned on the Lane farm. After Joel Lane's death, Long, as clerk of the Halifax County Court, continued to journey to Raleigh to meet with State Treasurer Haywood. Upon encountering Ned Lane again, Long expressed "a high opinion for the slaveman and his accommodating child, so much so that he became their friend and benefactor," inspiring Ned to name his son after the benevolent White man. This memory, recalled over five decades later, is suspect. After all, if accurate, Ned Lane's son went some time without a name or with a name discarded possibly as late as 1809 in memoriam when Long died, "desiring to retain remembrance of so kind a man."[6]

It was an ill-chosen recognition. As kindly as Long treated Ned Lane, he did not similarly consider the people he enslaved. Upon Long's death, the executor delivered to the daughters only the enslaved humans whom their mother had brought into the marriage as her dower, dividing the rest among Long's other heirs, separating enslaved parents from children and husbands from wives. The daughters expected more, and the North Carolina Supreme Court agreed, concluding that Long spoke "of the negroes *generally*, as stock, without particularizing them by name," and "as stock is to be diminished by deaths, so it must be kept up and supported by its natural increase." Ned Lane's son became Lunsford in honor of a man who equated enslaved humans with beasts of burden.[7]

Ned Lane's home, aka the Haywood stable, Raleigh, NC. Photograph by Craig Thompson Friend.

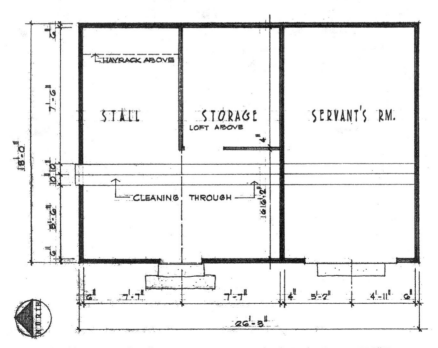

Interior, "Stable, Haywood Hall, 211 New Bern Ave., Raleigh, Wake County, NC." From Survey HABS NC-229 RAL 8, sheet 20, Historic American Buildings Survey. Courtesy of Library of Congress Prints & Photographs Division, Washington, DC.

Cate's home, aka the Haywood kitchen, Raleigh, NC. Photograph by Craig Thompson Friend.

In that moment when Ned Lane met Lunsford Long on the Haywood estate, his son had been with him. The rule that a child followed the enslaved status of his mother usually relegated children to their mothers' spheres. Although a street separated Clarissa's and Lunsford's lives on Sherwood Haywood's town lot from Ned's world at John Haywood's house, on occasion, when Clarissa worked the garden or became overwhelmed with cooking and laundering, Ned Lane's son joined him in his spaces where Lunsford also came to know his Aunt Cate and his cousins, Montford and Davy, living nearby in a twelve-by-eighteen-foot kitchen.[8]

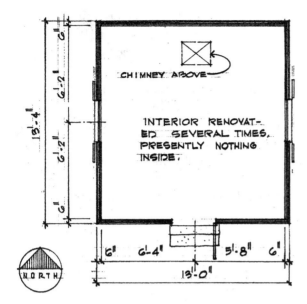

Interior, "Kitchen, Haywood Hall, 211 New Bern Ave., Raleigh, Wake County, NC." From Survey HABS NC-229 RAL 8, sheet 20, Historic American Buildings Survey. Courtesy of Library of Congress Prints & Photographs Division, Washington, DC.

Ned Lane gave his son a first name, but he did not endow his son with the surname that he had appropriated, and Lunsford had no claim to it, having followed his mother into enslavement. Some two decades later, in 1828, Lunsford recorded his full name—Lunsford Haywood—in the baptismal records of the Baptist church. Indifferent to the child's first name, Sherwood Haywood imposed the mark of ownership in due course. Lunsford belonged to the Haywoods, and for his first thirty-two years, he was a Haywood in the genealogy of enslavement.[9]

––––––––

As a child, Lunsford learned specific lessons from Ned and Clarissa about being Black and enslaved: the dangers he faced due to his race and enslavement, the unjust treatment he might face from authorities, the threat of being kidnapped, and the need to appease enslavers to avoid being sold away, "this worst (to us) of all calamities." Lunsford's parents did their best to prepare him for the world, and there was no shortage of examples from which to draw.[10]

The story of Peter Bird was one such tale that Lunsford's parents shared with him. Years earlier, in mid-January 1798, before Ned arrived on lot 210, guests gathered at Casso's Inn and Stables to celebrate John and Eliza Haywood's marriage. Some of John's enslaved domestics worked the party, among them Peter Bird. Having finished serving the guests, Bird returned to lot 210. As he passed the State House, he heard a commotion and saw a trunk tumble from the window of the State Treasurer's office, three men climbing out behind it. Bird called out the robbers, who responded with stones and bricks, forcing him to flee back to Casso's where he interrupted the wedding party. As John Haywood and others followed Bird to the State House, the thieves deserted the chest and ran, authorities capturing only Phillimon, an enslaved man.[11]

North Carolina's Black code trapped Phillimon between the judge's demand that he identify the White men who forced him to steal and the threat those White men posed should he speak their names. He remained silent, even as the judge threatened to hang him. The court kept its word. In May, Phillimon swung from the public gallows on Fayetteville Street, a warning to all enslaved people of what meritorious service unquestionably was not.[12]

Phillimon's silence and sacrifice did not protect the conspirators. Authorities discovered that the trunks contained not cash but papers from the office of Secretary of State James Glasgow, where William Tyrell, Phillimon's enslaver, clerked. Peter Bird, quite by happenstance, exposed a scandal. Glasgow and Tyrell had been stealing western lands granted to North Carolina's Revolutionary War veterans. Tyrell placed his name on other people's surveys and land grants, and Glasgow awarded lands to people who never fought in the war, issuing grants "to himself and others, on forms of warrant without any signature." The General Assembly had both men arrested for fraud. In the end, Glasgow and Tyrell paid fines, but neither hanged from the public gallows.[13]

Late in 1798, as Peter Bird helped renovate the house on lot 210 alongside Young Ned, he petitioned the General Assembly to reward him for his meritorious service, arguing that the legislature already "would have rewarded a White man for such an essential service by a large sum of Cash." Bird wanted to "be set free from his master as a reward he has rendered the state," concluding that "to a man in Slavery, no reward can be so valuable as . . . being emancipated." John Haywood agreed since Bird "has also shown himself obliging and affectionate toward me." The assembly emancipated Bird, praising him as "an encouragement to similar instances of virtue & honesty" and compensating Haywood £200 [$31,560].[14]

Peter was as free as a bird, but he did not fly. Although the assembly did not exempt him from having to leave North Carolina, Bird remained, heading a household of five free Black Raleighites and one enslaved person. Some meritorious service, apparently, came with absolution from the law, not officially but through local constables not enforcing it. If sheriffs and searchers looked the other way, emancipated people could ignore the law. White Raleighites tolerated Peter Bird's presence. After all, he demonstrated unquestionable loyalty to them. Other enslaved peoples, including Ned Lane and Clarissa, witnessed what came from meritorious service, a term with which many were familiar, even if they were unsure of what it entailed. Among enslaved people, when another enslaved person found freedom, everyone spoke of it, even to their children.[15]

Yet, for emancipated people like Peter Bird, freedom also brought insecurity. A sheriff could decide, at any moment, to enforce the law. More immediate was that no longer guarded by the system of laws, slave owners, sheriffs, searchers, and courts, they lacked protection. Bird and other free Black folks had little recourse against attacks on their properties and bodies. As they told stories, Clarissa, Ned, Cate, and other enslaved parents expressed the dread of enslaved parenthood. Tales resonated with uncertainties about their children's futures. Their security and lives, like their names, relied upon the good graces of White people. There was always a sliver of hope that, like Peter Bird, serendipity might make one meritorious enough. There was also the incessant terror of being abducted. Fear of being snatched, Lunsford recalled about his childhood, "was like that of having the heart wrenched from its socket; while the idea of being conveyed to the far South, seemed infinitely worse than the terrors of death." Too many friends and relatives disappeared, their inabilities to protect themselves creatively portrayed as mired in tar, and their sudden disappearances imaginatively described as flying. Lost ancestors, missing friends, stolen children—the enslaved folk of the South wandered among the specters of the past.[16]

Black parents were not alone in telling stories. Accounts of enslaved peoples on the run filled Raleigh's two newspapers, edited by William Boylan and Joseph Gales. From New Jersey, Boylan moved to Raleigh in May 1799 to serve the Federalist Party as editor of the *Raleigh Minerva*. Three months later, the British-born Gales relocated from Philadelphia, and in October, the Jeffersonian Republican Party's *Raleigh Register* was born. The editors' perspectives and politics could not have been more different, but they agreed on the enslavement of Black Carolinians.[17]

Immediately, the two editors were at each other's throats over the state's lucrative printing contracts. The political rancor of the national election of 1800 raised anxieties and heated debates, which exacerbated their animosities. Boylan spent years disparaging Thomas Jefferson's fitness for the presidency, printing editorials and letters that emphasized the president's relationship with his enslaved sister-in-law, Sally Hemings. Mocking the president's 1801 inaugural call to set aside partisanship for nationalism—"We are all Republicans, we are all Federalists"—Boylan sarcastically pontificated how "we are all Black and we are all white, and consequently all Brigands—Huzza for massa Jefferson." Boylan and many others believed that racial mixing, socially and sexually, denigrated White people, a point driven home in a conundrum he posed: "If according to the sage of Monticello, a full blooded Congo negro, is cousin German to an Ourang Outang, what relationships does there exist, between said Ourang Outang and young Tom J____; whose grand mother was a full breed Congo, and whose father & grandfather, were human beings?"[18]

Although Gales did not employ equally racialized language, similar attitudes about race were common among the Jeffersonians. Their leader once pondered whether the "Oranootan" did not prefer "Black woman over those of his own species." Yet, the politicizing of Jefferson's relationship to Hemings tempered their racialized rhetoric. Gales represented a more insidious racism. Like the party that he represented, Gales keenly felt the incongruence between the principles articulated by Jefferson in the Declaration of Independence and their beliefs in the biological inferiority of people of African descent. Upon arriving in Raleigh in September 1799, Gales noted that the town contained "not more than 1,000 inhabitants and at least one third were slaves or free colored persons." If those three hundred and so enslaved peoples became free, Gales could not envision a peaceful and harmonious coexistence. They would have to go, maybe to the African lands of their ancestors, but the logistics were unimaginable, and the possibility of mass emancipation inconceivable. Enslavement was necessary.[19]

Gales was little different from Boylan in agreeing on the sacredness of a racial system that ensured separation between allegedly civilized Americans and their heathenish neighbors. Both newspaper editors normalized that system by advertising enslaved people as parts of estates, publicizing slave auctions, promoting the hiring out of enslaved laborers, and warning of runaways. In the pages of the *Raleigh Minerva* and *Raleigh Register*, Gales and Boylan battled politically, but every runaway advertisement and every notice of the availability of enslaved laborers to be purchased or hired out assured their readers that most White Carolinians united behind Black enslavement.

Lunsford's childhood in the early 1800s coincided with an increase in runaway advertisements that intensified White Raleighites' anxieties about the Black people, seen and unseen, around them. Raleigh constantly seemed full of strangers. The business of government drew thousands into the capital annually, among them, people negotiating a gauntlet of sheriffs, searchers, patrollers, and vigilantes as they wandered northward in search of freedom, scattered eastward or westward in search of family, or just hid, unsure of where to go. In the shadows of North Carolina's State House, Lunsford and other enslaved children came upon frightened and desperate humans, the flying Africans of their bedtime stories who taught them new stories of the horrors of the Deep South.[20]

Most were men between fifteen and thirty years of age, many displaying what Lunsford called the "lash-mangled" evidence of their enslavements.

Charles had "the Marks of a late Whipping on his Back" and a broken arm. Burn scars marred Eady's left hand. One of Bob's ears had been cropped and the other marked "as if it had been nailed to a post." Frank had lost both ears. "J. Hill," the mark of their enslaver, had been branded into Harry's and Fecarrow's cheeks, and Harry had more on his forehead and chest. Advertisements such as that for Frank, who was "very artful and plausible, and will attempt to pass as a free man," made every unfamiliar Black man a potential threat to White readers.[21]

Enslavers theorized where enslaved people planned to go, but no one knew their locations, and that hidden presence portended something horrific. When enslaved Virginians rebelled in 1800, White Southerners became anxious about the runaways in their midst. When enslaved Virginians rebelled again in early 1802, sparking rumors of violence in Halifax and Northampton counties east of Raleigh, White anxieties became panic. In June, patrollers arrested over one hundred enslaved people in Bertie, Martin, and Halifax counties on charges of committing "great havoc," accused of planning to murder all White men, older White women, and uncooperative Black people, reserving younger White women as wives to serve them. In Raleigh, one citizen demanded greater surveillance of Black residents, complaining that there were not "a sufficient number of patrollers so as to patrole the streets every night."[22]

By July 1805, fear defined race relations. Just southeast of Raleigh, patrollers arrested fifteen people suspected of plotting against their enslavers. A court determined the instigator to be Syraz, an elderly man once enslaved by Sherwood Haywood. Clarissa knew him. A court found him and two others guilty, sentencing one to burn alive and the others to hang. Rumor circulated that someone from Raleigh had called on Syraz to acquire some poison "to make his master better to him." Had the person returned to the capital to exact vengeance? Which Raleigh enslaver was under threat? Did anyone dare eat meals prepared by their enslaved cooks? Were Clarissa and Cate cautioned not to let anyone enter their kitchens? Were they suspected? The Haywoods and all Raleigh slaveowners watched their domestics with paranoia, and the people they enslaved responded with a distrust of their own.[23]

Lunsford grew up in this culture of fear, coming to know some of the runaways. "I had conversed with many slaves who had escaped from the rice and cotton farms of Georgia and Alabama," and although their stories "added nothing to my happiness," they made Lunsford aware of his unique circumstance. He was not like the desperate people he met, physically deformed by labor and punishment, emotionally impaired by enslavement's psychological tortures, unsure of where to go and how to survive.[24]

Insurrection, poisoning, murder—rumors of Black violence associated with fleeing enslaved peoples circulated widely as racial tensions intensified. By

1812, when Lunsford was nine years old and as the United States fell into war with England, many enslaved peoples sensed opportunity anew. Over the next few years, Raleigh's newspaper editors listed double, eventually triple, the number of runaway advertisements they had before the war. White Carolinians described enslaved people who tried to escape as an internal danger that paralleled the external threat of the British. One White resident demanded that Governor William Hawkins exempt wealthier White citizens from militia service so they could remain vigilant against the threat of "insurrection or invasion." An uprising never manifested. The runaways never showed themselves. Enslaved laborers never rebelled. Free Black people never challenged White control.[25]

Instead, with enslaved and free Black people discouraged from helping freedom seekers, Raleigh began to resemble the refined society that John Haywood once prophesized to Eliza, built on the backs of Ned Lane, Clarissa Haywood, and the capital's other enslaved—and controlled—peoples. Like Ned's toil in the Haywood gardens, enslaved cooks, carriage drivers, doormen, gardeners, messengers, carpenters, cabinet makers, and brick layers did much, if not most, of the demanding work in planting high society in the capital. Those who did not labor in town did so on farms around Raleigh, raising vegetables, fruits, and livestock for the town's families and markethouse.[26]

Enslavers benefited directly from enslaving other humans, but as local newspapers' promotion of the institution demonstrated, slavery was of concern to all White people whether they enslaved a human or not. As Pennsylvania jurist George M. Stroud explained of North Carolina's Black code in the 1820s, the laws that framed enslaved lives situated Black people "under the like restriction in relation to *every white* person, without discrimination as to character, and with but little consideration as to motives." Control of Black populations—enslaved, free, and runaway—ensured stability and White authority, economically and politically privileging all White people by situating them to pursue their ambitions without regard to the needs or aspirations of Black folk. It bound White Carolinians, indeed all White Americans, across class, gender, and partisan lines.[27]

As the War of 1812 closed, Lunsford turned twelve years old, surrounded by a brood of Haywood children ranging from nineteen years old to just a couple months: eight in Sherwood's house, nine in John's, three in Henry's, and five in Stephen's. Later in life, his memories included playing with the White children and witnessing how, as they grew into the Haywood genealogy of wealth, status, and political influence, they evolved into his enslavers. There were other children enslaved by the Haywoods on the town estates, among them his cousin Clarissa, born in 1814. She was the first child of his mother's sister, Matilda, and Alexander Curtis, enslaved by newspaper editor William Boylan. Other young Curtises arrived over the next fifteen years—Phil, born 1814; Austin, born 1823; Alexander, born 1826 (only Alexander can be verified as Matilda and Alexander's child). Most enslaved children lived on the farms beyond town, among them Lunsford's cousins, Montford and Davy, who, when they turned fifteen years old in 1810, began laboring on the Crabtree Creek farm. In his cousins, Lunsford saw his own future as a farm laborer, but Ned Lane's and Clarissa Haywood's significant statuses on John Haywood's and Sherwood Haywood's estates, respectively, positioned him better than other enslaved children.[28]

Living in the kitchen behind the slaveowners' house ensured a better diet: "We used to have corn bread enough, and some meat." After Clarissa cooked for Sherwood and Eleanor Haywood's family, she put cornmeal balls in the pot liquor—the juices left behind after preparing meats or greens, filled with vitamins and minerals that boiled out—and placed the vat in the yard. Lunsford and other children set upon it with their spoons. From the veranda, Eleanor Haywood ordered the older children to eat slowly to give the younger ones a chance. On occasion, Sherwood Haywood visited the yard with cakes and other confections for the enslaved children.[29]

As Lunsford entered his teens, the Haywoods put him to work cutting wood and gardening alongside Clarissa. Over the years, Ned Lane shared his horticultural knowledge with Lunsford, hoping to position his son to secure stature in Sherwood Haywood's household. Ned and Clarissa's son never became a gardener, but those lessons in the gardens proved invaluable over time.

For Ned Lane, gardening skills made him indispensable to his enslavers. Although John was Eliza's husband, Ned became her companion, albeit an involuntary one who was more a workmate than a friend. They were the same age, a generation younger than John Haywood, sharing similar resentments of the patriarchal cage in which they lived. Struggling physically and emotionally, Eliza made the garden her sanctuary, and it became the epicenter of her relationship with Ned. She acted as the horticulturist, researching and ordering plants and seeds, corresponding with other gardeners throughout the nation, and directing Ned's manual labor as he prepared the soil, planted, hoed, pruned, raked, and weeded. She established a working friendship with William Prince Jr., owner of the Linnaean Botanic Gardens and Nurseries in Flushing, New York, and among the nation's foremost gardening experts. She spent so much time in the garden that her daughter, Betsy John, regarded the space as "holy grounds" after her mother's death.[30]

Every compliment paid Eliza as a great gardener, such as her brother-in-law's praise for her as "the only person that ever raised a Magnolia from the Seed," testified to Ned Lane's green thumb. When Thomas Haywood described his parents' garden in 1827, he unwittingly recounted Ned's skills in implementing Eliza's vision: "Our Box Edging is I think without the slightest partiality (& I have seen a good deal of it) most excellent. We have a Court Yard in front of our house comprising as much as half an acre which we mean to crowd & have indeed already filled with The American Arbor Vitae, . . . your Firs—the Wreath Rose—the Cherokee Rose—& the Chinese or monthly blooming Rose." Who did Thomas think dug the holes, fertilized the soils, planted the foliage, and trimmed the hedges?[31]

Eliza Haywood, after all, could not do the gardening herself. In her perpetually exhausted state, she labored to make it through each day. As early as 1800, her "cough and spitting" became so notable that it drew concern from her husband's business associates. She suffered the cough the rest of her life and grew frustrated with the public's awareness of her condition, feeling it a burden to entertain neighbors and friends who thought obligated to "visit the sick Constantly." In 1804, upon the birth of her fifth child, Eliza "unexpectedly Fainted quite away, neither breath nor pulse." Terrified, her mother wrote, "Great God, I thought She was gone for ever." When finally revived by the physician, Eliza whispered, "for God's Sake help me—so many little children." In early 1806, she hemorrhaged during childbirth, causing her sister to wish that "she may never have an other child for I am very certain she can't undergo it." Over the next six years, John Haywood curtailed his libido, and Eliza Haywood's health gradually improved as she convalesced in the garden. In 1811, John impregnated her again, and the Haywoods had four more children over the next seven years.[32]

Ned Lane's forced companionship to Eliza Haywood competed with his marriage and fatherhood. In the first two decades of the nineteenth century, he often found himself away from Clarissa and Lunsford. When not assisting Eliza, he chaperoned her mother to and from Raleigh. John Haywood provided his mother-in-law with part of a Raleigh town lot where she could live, and he planned to convert a small building into a home for Ned, who could assist her. But "the house which you saw as Ned's new House on my lott," she informed her daughter, "I intend to make or rather finish as Habitable as *He* can make it for a resort for myself." *He* was John Haywood. She seldom wrote his name, the tension between them having subsided little over the decades. By 1816, Ned Lane served Jane Williams as much as he did the Haywoods, spending long stretches at Mt. Gallant attending to her demands. "I made Ned search for Sallad Dishes," she reported about a forthcoming dinner, "but none but some flat with Scallop edges like those you have."[33]

When Jane Williams died in July 1818, Ned Lane returned to the Haywood estate permanently. Eliza's grief over her mother's death worsened her already precarious condition. She miscarried soon thereafter, an event that almost took her life. John restrained himself for another three years. In 1822, the Haywoods welcomed yet another daughter who became their first to die in infancy, less than a year after her birth.[34]

With hesitation, then, in 1824, John Haywood informed Betsy John that her mother was pregnant again, remarking that her siblings "generally will dislike the circumstance." Given their mother's physical weakness, the tragedies of the past few years, and John's age at sixty-nine years, his children's negative reactions were understandable. Their concern was not just for Eliza's physical health. Over twenty-two years and eleven children, Eliza managed with Nurse Cate's help, each baby exacting a toll on both women. Sometime between 1815 and 1824, Cate died, no more than forty-four years old. When Eliza Haywood's child arrived in January 1825, he was sickly, and she eagerly handed him over to Young Esther, who was ill-prepared to raise him.[35]

Throughout Eliza Haywood's poor health, multiple pregnancies, six-year convalescence, and her mother's death, she increasingly depended on Ned Lane. She often sent him to the market in the mornings and set him up with credit accounts at local stores. When the economy collapsed during the Panic of 1819, she expected him to pay from his own pocket and be reimbursed. In March, Eliza paid Ned for "money of his own laid out for me," then again in September for "Eggs Chickens and Sloat," and in November for "articles bought." Eliza was not without resources, of course, but she positioned Ned as a financial go-between with local stores, putting him constantly on call to shop, deliver letters, and drive the family around Raleigh and beyond.[36]

Across Edenton Street, as a teenaged Lunsford Haywood gardened and chopped wood, only occasionally seeing his father, he became aware of "the difference between myself and my master's White children," better understanding why he crossed paths with so many runaways. In Sherwood and Eleanor's home, their children William and Lucy were closest in age to Lunsford. Lucy always viewed Lunsford as her playmate, insisting decades later that she considered him a friend and continued to feel for him as she did when they were children. Lunsford only remembered how the two Haywood siblings suddenly began to order him about, encouraged by their parents to do so, reminding Lunsford that he was not a playmate but a slave.[37]

Like enslaved children, the children of slave owners learned their roles. They watched parents order laborers about. They saw enslaved people punished, separated, and sold. They accompanied their parents to slave auctions. They heard adults fret over runaways and insurrections. They came to recognize the advantages that came with wealth, family reputation, and the color of their skin. The Haywoods carefully cultivated the racial distinctions between free and enslaved, including keeping their laborers illiterate. "I was not permitted to have a book in my hand," Lunsford resented. "To be in the possession of anything written or printed, was regarded as an offence." As there was not yet a law in North Carolina that prohibited enslaved Carolinians from learning to read, if there was offense, it was the Haywoods who took it, wishing to emphasize how White and free differed from Black and enslaved. Later in life, Lunsford noted that Eleanor "took uncommon pains to prevent" him and his mother from learning to read and write. Clarissa could spell only one word: "baker."[38]

In Lunsford's years of self-awakening, he watched the Haywoods sell enslaved peoples, and the dread and fears of childhood tales increasingly rang true. He became fixated on the possibility of being separated from his parents. Distressed over the sales of friends, fearful of being kidnapped or sold away, and realizing "that I was never to consult my own will, but was, while I lived, to be entirely under the control of another," his childhood anxieties became a "state of mind hard for me to bear." Despairingly, he imagined "from day to day, and from night to night, how I might be free." Years of meeting runaways put the thought into Lunsford's head that he, too, could fly.[39]

Lunsford knew more and more people, enslaved by Haywoods, who took flight. Sam, sold from a Haywood estate in April 1816, refused to move to Tennessee with his new enslaver and headed back to Raleigh, "having relations among the Negroes of Mr. Haywood's." The following year, Stephen Haywood sold Sam Freeman as a house servant, but Freeman took a small horse, a good saddle, and a road out of North Carolina. John Haywood had more luck than his brother in keeping the people whom he enslaved, hiring some to do menial labor and others to learn trades, increasing their market values. He lent out Jacob in 1820, and Brutus worked as a house painter in Salisbury. Nancy Woods lived in his house in New Bern with her daughter Nancy and son Virgil, as well as multiple children whom she raised: William, Brutus, Venter, Jane, and George. In early 1825, she asked John Haywood to apprentice Virgil to a tailor or shoemaker. Although better situated to take flight than John Haywood's field hands and enslaved domestics, none of the people whom he hired out, most living far from his watch, ever flew.[40]

Neither did Lunsford. It might have been his devotion to his parents. It might have been because he met runaways who had not succeeded, cowering and despondent in the shadows. It might have been that he could not muster the bravery because flight required a stoic resignation to the worst of fates if caught. No, there had to be a more reasonable path. Lunsford decided to stay in Raleigh which seemed as good a place as any for an enslaved man to pursue freedom.

Raleigh's most prominent free Black man was schoolmaster John Chavis, whose prominence and pedantry contrasted with the clandestineness and brokenness of runaways. Born to free Black Carolinians around 1763, fifteen years later, he enlisted in the Fifth Regiment of Virginia and fought in the Revolutionary War. In the early 1790s, through a scholarship program for "poor and pious youth" known as the Leslie Fund, he attended the College of New Jersey, an institution dominated by New Light Presbyterians. Led by John Witherspoon, the college embraced the Scottish Enlightenment and its natural rights philosophy, teaching that liberty came with obligations assigned to one's station by God. Chavis finished his education at Liberty Hall Academy, a Presbyterian school in Lexington, Virginia. The Lexington Presbytery approved him to ride circuits in southern Virginia and into North Carolina. By 1806, Chavis moved to Raleigh and opened a school in which he taught both White and Black children. Two years later, he segregated the Black students to an evening school "for the accommodation of some of his Employers, to exclude all Children of Colour from his Day School."[41]

Although widely respected throughout Raleigh, John Chavis barely survived on his income from preaching and teaching. In 1815, he took a loan for £50 [$5,550] to purchase 110 acres of Wake County farmland. John Haywood signed as security for the loan, as did Willie P. Mangum, one of Chavis's former students who would go on to serve in the United States House of Representatives from 1823 to 1826 and the United States Senate from 1830 to 1836. As the loan came due, Chavis nervously approached Haywood on occasion to explain why he could not make payments. "Using every means of industry to raise money, yet such is the times, that I cannot neither make up profitable schools, nor collect the money for those I do make up after it is due," he wrote in May 1822. He hoped that Haywood and "my worthy friend Judge Mangum to keep me alive, until I can either raise money by my school or by my crop." When Chavis finally had some cash in October, he visited Haywood's house and then the State House but found the State Treasurer in neither place. Inexplicably, he did not visit the bank to make payment, and then he worried that there might be "disappointment on that acc.t." His hunch was correct. Haywood suggested to Mangum that they just accept their loss and pay it off before more interest accrued.[42]

Chavis's status and connections were rare for a free Black man, modeling a Black manhood for young Lunsford and other aspirants to freedom. Lunsford appreciated how his own presence among the Haywoods situated him to associate with some of the same prominent White families who benefited the schoolmaster, creating a space in which he might develop similar financial and personal networks. The state granted free Black men the vote, which promised a modicum of citizenship if Lunsford could gain freedom. As for education, he faced an immediate obstacle: Sherwood and Eleanor's resistance to educating the enslaved.

As an example of free Black manhood, however, Chavis was problematic. Education, citizenship, and access to Raleigh's White world which profited him, and to which Lunsford aspired, came with a cost. Despite Chavis's status with White former students, whom he affectionately called "sons," he often felt disrespected and questioned their subtle racism. "Is it my colour, or my insignificance or the gross ignorance, which my many letters contain, is the reason why you have never condescended to answer one of them?" he demanded of Mangum early in their epistolary relationship. In chastising Abraham Rencher, a Democratic congressman, Chavis insisted that "if I am Black, I am free born American & a revolutionary soldier & therefore ought not be thrown intirely out of the scale of notice." In a White-dominated society, the subtle silences of his "sons" occasionally left Chavis deeply doubtful that he had overcome any prejudices.[43]

Chavis was a man stuck between the races. He pursued a life few Black men and even fewer Black women could imagine, particularly in the South. It was a life wrought with vulnerability, as most Black Carolinians understood through cautionary tales about the tenuousness of living as a free Black person. Lunsford aspired to that life.

Chapter 3

Toward Rational Liberty

On a Sunday evening in 1820, Lunsford Haywood sat down beside his mother in the Baptist Church. Founded in 1812, the congregation originated with fourteen enslaved Black and nine White Raleighites who met on the second floor of the State House. Within four years, they built their first church on Person Street, facing a town common where they occasionally gathered for outdoor worship, laying claim to it as their "Baptist grove." The congregation was the oldest of Raleigh's interracial churches. Clarissa joined in the late 1810s, insisting, as mothers are inclined to do, that her son join her.[1]

Lunsford seldom could. Beginning in his mid-teens, early on Sundays, he escorted Sherwood and Eleanor Haywood and their children to either the Methodist church or the Presbyterian church, wherever the Episcopalians chose to worship since they had no home of their own. He waited just beyond the narthex doors, listening to sermons and common prayers. After returning the Haywoods to their home, he took the horses to St. Mary's, where they grazed as he tended crops. Their care allowed him to escape momentarily. Sometimes, the family demanded Lunsford drive them about in their carriage to visit friends and show off their wealth. Occasionally, at dusk, he again accompanied the Haywoods to wherever the homeless Episcopalians gathered for vespers. Upon delivering the family home yet again, if time permitted, he wandered to the small church where his mother waited. After hours of songs and more hours of preaching, he walked Clarissa home. She took her bed with the other women in the detached kitchen. He took up his blanket and his place on the dining room floor in the main house, close to the fireplace and the people who called on him at all hours of every day.[2]

Lunsford recalled a Sunday in 1820 when he finished his chores and arrived in time to hear junior pastor Josiah Crudup elaborate on Ephesians 6:5: "Servants be obedient to them that are *your* masters according to the flesh, with fear and trembling," Crudup chastened Black congregants, emphasizing "*your* masters," expecting them to grasp how the commandment applied not to their relationship with the almighty God of the Baptist faith but to their subservience to White people in the here and now. Crudup had a lesson for the White congregants as well, turning to Luke 12:47. "And that servant, which knew his lord's will, and prepared not himself, neither did according to his will," the preacher extolled, "shall be beaten with many stripes."[3]

The sermon might as well have been a stump speech. Crudup was campaigning for the state legislature as a Jacksonian. (Years later, he proclaimed that although Andrew Jackson had faults, even the "sun himself has spots.") Some members of the Baptist congregation, many of the White ones, were among his future voters. He assured them that he supported the enslavement and control of their fellow Black congregants.[4]

Crudup's political opponent was Stephen Haywood, the youngest of the Haywood brothers, "a steadfast and uniform Republican, of incorruptible integrity, devoted to the Republican institutions of his country." Among those institutions was the Raleigh Auxiliary Society, a branch of the American Colonization Society. Crudup and other critics questioned the Society's work, whether it posed a slippery slope to the gradual abolition of slavery. The premise that Black Americans could govern themselves, albeit across the Atlantic in Liberia, challenged proslavery propositions that Black people needed White folk to feed, house, and protect them. How could White Baptists, indeed, how could any White Carolinians trust Haywood to sustain the institution of slavery and guard them against the menace of emancipated and runaway Black people? Vote Crudup![5]

Black congregants, larger in numbers but not in power, listened as the preacher bellowed about God's goodness "in bringing us over to this country from dark and benighted Africa, and permitting us to listen to the sound of the gospel"—as if Christianity and Islam had not been competing for African souls for centuries. As much as Lunsford Haywood despised Crudup's message, he relished good oratory, and the preacher's politically honed eloquence proved inspirational. It won Crudup public office, and it left an impression upon Lunsford of the power of oratory that he never forgot.[6]

———

Rumors spread quickly around Raleigh. In late 1820, the rumors were about the Haywoods. The state assembly opened an investigation into John's activities as State Treasurer, a position in which he collected tax revenues, made payments on behalf of the state, sued individuals who failed to pay for state-appropriated lands, and kept his accounts "fully, fairly, finally and completely settled and balanced." As security against John's handling of the state's money, the law required an annual oath to uphold public interests and a surety bond equal to the balance of all funds in the treasury, as well as expected revenues for the next year, just in case he mishandled the money. Some years, he both swore the oath and made the bond. Most years, he did one or the other. A few years, he did neither.[7]

Beginning in 1813, state senator Willis Alston, a Halifax County planter and leading member of the House of Commons, openly questioned the Haywoods' lifestyle, suggesting they lived far more opulently than John's income allowed. By 1820, many other North Carolinians suspected the same, noting Haywood's lackadaisical attitude toward his annual oath as evidence of his duplicity. Alston heard gossip of shoddy record-keeping, dishonest reporting of cash reserves, and an inappropriate $25,000 [$533,663] loan to the State Bank of North Carolina in 1811.[8]

Then, there was that business back in 1798 about the western land frauds that had led to Phillimon's hanging and Peter Bird's freedom. Rumors were that Treasurer Haywood, in return for a little money under the table, had lent state funds to friends for their private land speculations and credited them for unpaid taxes. In a 1794 letter to former surveyor John Gray Blount, among the largest landowners in the nation, John had inquired about "a mode in which a friend might effect the business of getting rich in the land-Speculation way.... I have no wish to make money in this way myself, but I have brothers as poor as Job, who are a great tax to me." Had Bird, who discovered the thieves on the evening of John and Eliza Haywood's marriage, incidentally initiated a chain of events that would expose his enslaver's complicity in the scheme? If so, John's cleverness in avoiding investigation ended twenty-two years later.[9]

John Haywood became a victim of his genealogy. Over six decades earlier, in 1753, as Treasurer for the Northern Counties of North Carolina, his grandfather John Haywood came under suspicion as he collected rents and fees for John Carteret, the Earl of Granville, a descendent of one of the original Lord Proprietors of Carolina. A Grand Jury indicted Grandfather Haywood, but the Governor's Council interceded, ordering the attorney general to enter "Nolli Prosequi"—"unwilling to pursue"—in the records. Five years later, a Lower House committee investigated Granville's land sales and implicated two surveyors for committing fraud and overcharging fees: Grandfather Haywood's sons, William and Sherwood Haywood (John, Sherwood, Henry, and Stephen's father and uncle, respectively). More importantly, Grandfather Haywood had overcharged for making entries, forced one claimant to pay twice for a deed, and refused testimony for an appeal. The House accepted the committee report but again did nothing to discipline the Haywoods.[10]

Tensions boiled for six years until January 1759 when colonists rioted in Edenton. They crashed into the head land agent's house, taking him hostage until he gave them a bond of a "most unusual Nature." Days later, when news circulated that Treasurer Haywood had died at Dunbar, the mob stormed his home and dug up his body to verify his deadness, leaving his corpse lying on a garden path. When the Edgecombe County sheriff arrested a few rioters, the mob broke open the Halifax jail to release their friends. Governor Arthur Dobbs denounced the "traitorous Conspiracies" and demanded arrests and punishments, but the damage was done. Colonial Carolinians realized that violence offered an effective recourse against a system that protected its own, a lesson they took with them to revolution.[11]

Sixty-one years later, rumors of impropriety hung about State Treasurer John Haywood's neck like a noose. Unlike his grandfather, he could not rely on the protection of an aristocratic colonial elite. He faced a more dangerous jury: the age's emerging democratic impulses that openly distrusted men of money. Willis Alston, the self-styled representative of the great masses, demanded the investigation. Insulted by the "unfriendly and malicious Threats of this Gentleman," John Haywood welcomed the probe to restore "his integrity in the discharge of his official duties." So, he called for an investigation of himself, first by the Comptroller and then by the Committee of Finance. In the end, he expected a report that "will be *to him* more valuable than any boon that the State can bestow, and *to his children* more precious than any bequest he can make them."[12]

John Haywood was not disappointed. Within weeks, the committee concluded its work, declaring him a model state official over his thirty-three-year career: no irregular balances, no accounting mistakes, no shell games as he moved funds among accounts, no misleading statements about the state's cash reserves. He should have known better than to offer a questionable loan to the State Bank in 1811, but since the legislature authorized it, he had acted legally.[13]

John Haywood's acquittal relieved his children, nephews, and nieces, a gift "more precious than any bequest he can make them." But they were privy to private conversations that the General Assembly never heard. As John Haywood's nephew, William Henry Haywood III, wrote years later to Betsy John Haywood, "Strange mysteries hang about the fate of our fathers and families." They were mysteries that soon doomed many.[14]

———

Stephen Haywood, the youngest of the four brothers, always lived in his siblings' shadows. John's civic service as State Treasurer was renowned if suspect. Sherwood served as federal commissioner of loans. Henry was a clerk of the United States Federal Court. Stephen aspired to join them in public service.[15]

Stephen and Elizabeth Lane Haywood were in Raleigh less than three years when, in 1805, Elizabeth died. She was twenty-five years old and the mother of two sons. Stephen did not remarry for four years, an uncommon delay for a widowed father of young children and suggestive of his deep grief. In late summer 1809, he embarked on life again, wedding his sister-in-law Eleanor's sister, Delia Hawkins. Seven years later, citizens elected him to the state's

House of Commons, where he served for two years before winning election to the state Senate in 1819. Then, in 1820, his reelection campaign faltered. It did not help that his brother faced an investigation or that his opponent was Josiah Crudup, the dynamic and popular Baptist preacher. Stephen lost the election, and although it might have satisfied him when Crudup vacated the seat because the state constitution forbade ministers from holding public office if they continued to preach, Stephen still had lost, and it wounded him. He faded from public service.[16]

Four years later, on September 11, 1824, fifty-three-year-old Stephen died, leaving Delia and eight children behind. The public announcement mourned how "the death of this worthy and respectable citizen has made a chasm in the link of affection which has so long united the hearts of four brothers in tenderness and love." Beyond the brothers, so bound were the lives of the Haywood families with those of the people they enslaved that the death of a patriarch held far-reaching implications for every member of the household.[17]

Stephen's death was the moment when the "strange mysteries that hang about the fate of our fathers and families" began to reveal themselves. The debt that Delia inherited as executrix of Stephen's will was substantial enough that, in his will, he directed her to sell the farms. It was also public enough that city commissioners did not expect her to cover the annual property taxes. About one month after Stephen's death, they advertised a public auction of her town lots. She turned to her brothers-in-law, John and Sherwood, who paid her property taxes through 1828, avoiding confiscation and sale of her home.[18]

Like so many other widows, Delia Haywood quickly devised ways to protect what remained of her husband's estate, secure a future for her children, and keep the wolves at bay. She demanded repayment of all debts owed to her late husband, put up for sale the Edgecombe County farm and the farm north of Raleigh, and began renting rooms to members of the General Assembly. She offered ten available rooms, each with a fireplace. In 1829, she enlarged her house to accommodate even more guests, turning her once genteel home into a boarding house.[19]

Delia always had a resource for quick money: the enslaved property. In his will, Stephen Haywood listed those working in the Raleigh townhouse and on the Wake County farm—Gray, Isaac, York, Sandy, Jo, Davy, Anderson, William, Abraham Jr., Willie, Charles, Luke, Frank, Allen, Milly, Sarah, Anny, Eliza, Caroline Jr., Kissey, Ruby Jr., and Darius. He instructed Delia to select ten from those who attended her during her lifetime. The unselected and those on the Edgecombe farm were divided among their children. In January 1828, Delia hired out her ten and sold the rest, among them Mark, who fled his new owner months later and somehow hid in Raleigh for at least a year. Among those she kept was Davy Littlejohn, "a bright mulatto man, about 5 feet 10 inches high, slender made, with the mark of the cut of a knife on one of his cheeks, 2 or 3 inches long." He was a skilled carpenter who had helped to build the Old West dormitory at the state university in Chapel Hill. Davy bid his time. In December, he abandoned Raleigh, taking a horse with him. Delia futilely offered $20 [$628] for his return. She could afford little more.[20]

Delia Hawkins Haywood struggled, but she established a precedent for her sisters-in-law, who soon found themselves having to call in debts, sell lands, rent out rooms, hire out enslaved workers, and, as a last resort, put some enslaved people up for sale. Just down Edenton Street, Lunsford and others watched as Delia sold their friends and family members. What if Sherwood died? As Lunsford recalled, his enslaver "had now the reputation of being wealthy; but should death suddenly call him away, I had nothing to hope from his selfish wife."[21]

———

On March 2, 1825, citizens filled doors and windows along Fayetteville Street, waving as a parade labored toward the State House. The Raleigh militia led, followed by a couple of elegant carriages greeted by a twenty-one-gun "federal salute." Just that morning, its occupants traveled from Halifax, the latest leg of a fourteen-month tour that the Marquis de Lafayette undertook to celebrate the Revolutionary War semicentennial. Governor Hutchins G. Burton privately welcomed the nation's guest before delivering a public address that echoed the dozens of proclamations that the Frenchman heard time and again during his tour. The company then went to John Haywood's house for a light meal.[22]

After refreshments, the group gathered at the State House, where William Polk, one of North Carolina's remaining Revolutionary veterans, addressed a large crowd with praise for Lafayette's "purest love of liberty." Inside the State House stood Antonio Canova's statue of George Washington, commissioned in 1821. Local lore holds that having just dined with the Haywoods, Lafayette viewed the statue with Betsy John Haywood. Upon seeing Washington carved in marble, the Marquis assured his hosts that "the likeness was much better than he expected to see."[23]

Then, they were off to dinner at the Government House, a governor's mansion built in 1816 at the south end of Fayetteville Street, with music followed by toasts: to George Washington, the people, rational liberty, President James Monroe, the "unanimity of parties," Lafayette "who estimated, as but *dust in the balance,* all the blessings of life, when in the opposite scale were placed liberty and freedom," and finally, woman—"her manners give refinement to our social intercourse, and her virtue is the talisman that guards our own."

In honor of the Marquis and William Polk, John Haywood offered a generously worded salute to the Battle of Brandywine in which both had fought when "French and American blood first flowed together." The crowd then migrated to the Eagle Tavern for a ball, a full-length portrait of Washington chaperoning their frivolity. The next morning, the distinguished men of Raleigh gathered for breakfast before bidding their guest goodbye at a farewell reception.[24]

For Lafayette, his journey across the American South was bittersweet. As a member of his entourage regretted, "They who so sin against the liberty of their country—against those great principles for which their honored guest poured on their soil his treasure + his blood, are not worthy to rejoice in his presence." Throughout the trip, Lafayette frequently engaged and enraged audiences, commenting that "I would never have drawn my sword in the cause of America, if I could have conceived that thereby I was founding a land of slavery." Did Lafayette say that to Raleigh's leading citizens, most of whom, like his Revolutionary peer William Polk, were prominent slaveowners? Upon arriving in New Orleans four weeks after departing Raleigh, Lafayette wrote to his daughters, "There is one point to which I decidedly cannot resign myself: that is slavery, and the anti-Black prejudices. I believe that in this respect my travel might have been useful."[25]

Lafayette's condemnations of slavery derived from his commitment to rational liberty. As described decades later by celebrants of Scottish Enlightenment thought, rational liberty was a freedom neither unrestrained nor unregulated. It was "not of that popular despotism which coins the whims of the mob into laws . . . nor of that anarchy in which the misgovernment of the ignorant, the bigoted, the brutal and the vile, sooner or later, invites the inauguration of Octavious and the Empire." Benjamin Franklin, George Washington, Thomas Jefferson, James Madison—the men who led the revolution and shaped the new nation knew well the writings of David Hume, Lord Kames, and Adam Smith, and they warned that mobs and monarchs, obligated to no one, were the enemies of liberty. John Witherspoon, the young nation's foremost advocate of Scottish Enlightenment thought, taught generations of young men, including Raleigh's John Chavis, that liberty came with responsibilities to others.[26]

Then, the French Revolution erupted, elevating the stakes of defining liberty. Fearing the unrestrained mobs, in 1790, English philosophe Edmund Burke framed rational liberty as freedom checked by individual wisdom, judiciousness, and moral obligation to others, and regulated by government. The alternative to rational liberty was anarchical freedom, the self-interested mob celebrating a "servile, licentious, and abandoned insolence, to be our low sport for a few holidays, to make us perfectly fit for, and justly deserving of slavery, through the whole course of our lives." Absolute, unfettered liberty inevitably resulted in tyranny.[27]

Lafayette tried to direct France toward rational liberty, consulting with Thomas Jefferson in 1789 to draft the *Déclaration des droits de l'Homme et du Citoyen*. Situating himself between the mob and the monarchs, Lafayette, commander of the French National Guard, found it increasingly difficult to keep order and his head. He fled France in 1792 as Burke and all of Europe watched in horror while revolution devoured reason and liberty. Austrians arrested him as an agitator, and he remained imprisoned until 1797 when France's aspiring tyrant, Napoleon Bonaparte, having climbed to power atop the destruction of the mobs, negotiated a prisoner release. As a citizen, Lafayette continued to promote rational liberty, but he gradually faded from public service. When Napoleon finally fell in 1814, Albert Gallatin, Secretary of the United States Treasury, congratulated his friend Lafayette: "I think every friend of rational liberty and of humanity must rejoice at the overthrow of the detestable tyranny under which you and a great part of Europe groaned."[28]

A decade later, in early January 1825, as Lafayette undertook his tour of the United States, he dined with both houses of the United States Congress, where they lauded him as the "Apostle of rational Liberty, unawed by the frowns of Tyranny, uninfluenced by the blandishments of Wealth, and unseduced by popular applause." It was a title that he carried proudly on his tour. So, as wealthy Raleighites celebrated the nation's guest, they acclaimed rational liberty as well, oblivious or indifferent to how it conflicted with their own enslavement of others.[29]

Enslaved waiters and cooks worked the dances and dinners, listening to Enlightenment ideals of rational liberty as they served the petty tyrants who controlled their lives. Lunsford Haywood was among them, consuming the rhetoric of rational liberty as he waited upon the Marquis. The following morning, as Lunsford served at breakfast, Lafayette sought him out and tipped him ten silver dollars [$312], one for him and the rest to be shared among his fellow servers.[30]

When recalling the 1820s, the speeches are what Lunsford Haywood remembered most clearly, not just when Lafayette visited but during subsequent visits by other notable guests. In November 1825, another celebration occurred at the Eagle Tavern to welcome Vice President John C. Calhoun and his family. Following dinner and toasts, the South Carolinian spoke briefly on the unsurpassed patriotism of North Carolinians, concluding with a toast to "North Carolina: the first to assert American Independence; she will be among the last of the States to abandon the principles in which that great event and our admirable political institutions originated." Lunsford, again serving a public dinner, relished Calhoun's eloquence. Then, a party followed in honor of

Floride Calhoun, welcomed by Betsy John Haywood since her father chaired the committee in charge of the festivities, and her mother was too exhausted to host.[31]

Over the next few years, Lunsford waited at dinners for Whig senators George E. Badger and Willie P. Mangum, Episcopal bishops John Stark Ravenscraft and Levi Silliman Ives, and Justice William Gaston and Chief Justice Thomas Ruffin of the North Carolina Supreme Court. Each speaker impressed him with the rhetoric of liberty that infused their remarks, captivating their White audiences and their enslaved Black waiters.[32]

Speechmaking belonged to White men, taught in academies and perfected in oratory societies. When enslaved people overheard public speeches, as Lunsford Haywood later remarked, "the two senses of seeing and hearing in the slave are made doubly acute by the very prohibition of knowledge." On Sunday afternoons following public dinners and patriotic celebrations, Lunsford and other servers gathered at a nearby spring to regale each other with memorized speeches, rehearsing for unrealized citizenship, claiming their own Americanness through their own voices, and critiquing White hypocrisy with select words and clever puns, drawing occasional laughter from their audiences. Then, they all fell into a debate about the substance of the speeches.[33]

By the mid-1820s, Lunsford became a regular waiter at public events, oversaw operations in Sherwood Haywood's household, and drove Eleanor and Sherwood about town. Occasionally, he escorted Sherwood to the Edgecombe plantation, where over 150 people labored in cotton and corn fields. Plantation culture differed dramatically from the town estate and even the St. Mary's farm. Haywood left control to an overseer, making occasional visits to arrange shipment of farm productions to the small port of Washington, North Carolina, and on to New York. Gathering crops in autumn, pig slaughtering and bacon curing in winter, harvesting the fisheries in spring—enslaved people lived and labored quite differently than Lunsford's domestic experiences. He noted their leisure time, often dedicated to drinking, gambling, and thieving. Sherwood extended latitude to his overseer, Mr. Warren, in managing the enslaved and, over the years, lost several enslaved laborers to Warren's impatience. On one occasion, Warren set his hunting dogs on an enslaved man who died as they tore him apart.[34]

On other occasions, Lunsford escorted Eleanor farther east to Chocowinity to visit her eldest daughters, Sarah Leigh and Nancy Hawkins, who married into the wealthy and politically connected Blount family. In late spring 1827, Eleanor's unmarried teenager Maria Toole and her recently widowed daughter Delia Haywood Williams joined in the journey. Two enslaved women packed boiled tongue, cheese and biscuits, sweet buns, brandy, and wine into the carriage alongside luggage and gifts for Eleanor's grandchildren. Lunsford drove, Jacob attended, and the two women accompanied as waiting maids. As Lunsford later recalled, Eleanor "was a woman of large ideas" and "thought she filled a large space in the world, and that many eyes in the town were turned upon her, and she did not wish to disappoint them." As the carriage swelled with gifts, supplies, and people, Eleanor instructed Lunsford to drive them around town so they could be seen before turning to the open road.[35]

The journey was routine. About forty miles along the way sat Wilson's Tavern, the only public house that the Haywoods patronized. Not that they particularly liked Jake Wilson, whom they found to be crass and poor company, but the tavern could be reached in one day, and accommodations were adequate. The Haywood women and their maidservants took their rooms. Lunsford and Jacob slept on the kitchen floor.

By three the following afternoon, the travelers reached Washington, where Sarah and Nancy brought their young children to see their grandmother and aunts. Eleanor preferred Washington over Chocowinity. The town was a center of trade, particularly with Northern markets. Tobacco, cotton, corn, and bacon shipped to New York, and luxuries returned to fill Washington's stores. Three days of reunion ensued with good eating and shopping, replacing the gifts for the grandchildren with elegant clothes to be envied in Raleigh.

On the evening before their return journey, Nancy and Sarah invited guests to dinner, among them the Jaquiths—a Northern teacher and his Southern newlywed. Although Lunsford did not give their names, they were most likely Henry W. Jaquith and Lucy Tallman Jaquith, who married earlier in 1827 and were visiting her family in Onslow County before returning to their home in Indiana. As the conversation turned to enslavement, Jaquith criticized North Carolina, which, blessed with soils and a good climate, failed to embrace ideas of thrift, enterprise, and liberty: "If free, requited labor were only added, what a paradise we should behold." Eleanor responded, "Why, Mr. Jaquith, you perfectly astonish me by the extravagance of these remarks, and had you not married a Southern lady, you would be in danger of a coat of tar and feathers."

"Yes, madam," Jaquith retorted, "the best argument I suppose you capable of replying. Had I time, I could produce abundant testimony from Southern statesmen and others, all concurring in the view I have given of the institution. Not many years since, Thomas Marshall stated in the Virginia Legislature, that 'Slavery is ruinous to the whites. It retards improvement, roots out an industrious population, banishes the yeomanry of the country, deprives the spinner, the weaver, the smith, the shoemaker, the carpenter of employment and support.'" After a moment, Eleanor conceded, "I admit that Judge Marshall held many very unsound opinions on the subject, but you will find few Southerners of much ability or reputation agreeing with him." Jaquith disagreed, tracing a genealogy of Southern antislavery thought from Marshall to Charles J. Faulkner, a member of the Virginia House of Delegates, to Charles Fenton Mercer, who cofounded the American Colonization Society and represented Virginia in the United States House of Representatives, to George Washington. The two bantered back and forth, with Jaquith concluding, "You and I have lived to see slavery abolished in Pennsylvania, and the wealth and enterprise of its citizens far surpassing her neighbors, Maryland and Virginia. The day of North Carolina's deliverance must come, and let us pray that it may not come in blood!"[36]

Lunsford stood in the shadows before, quite abruptly, interjecting: "I beg your pardon, mistress, for interrupting your conversation but as we are to leave early in the morning on our journey homeward, I came to ask if you have any special orders about preparations for leaving?" As if seeing Lunsford for the first time—"his fine form, his ease and grace of manner, his intelligence, and correct use of language"—Jaquith declared, "This man is out of his place; Nature has endowed him with rare abilities; and as a freeman, with a Northern education, he might rise to eminence, and become a deliverer of his race." For Lunsford, Jaquith's assessment was revelatory.

The next day, Eleanor awoke in a disagreeable mood. As the carriage began its journey homeward, a local farmer on a dogcart rode up alongside them, a Black man tied by his hands and feet to the back where the dogs typically sat when taken on a hunt. The driver knew Eleanor as a distant cousin, which made it difficult for her to discourage his company when he announced that he had just retrieved Isaac from the Washington jail. When the unwelcomed guest fell behind, she griped, "I wish Galt and his runaway had followed their own way, and not troubled us with the company; many people will think I have been to Washington on the mean errand of slave-catching."

Around noon, the party arrived at a spring and decided to stop for a meal. The Haywood women picnicked in the shade, served by the maidservants, as Galt explained to Eleanor how he purchased Isaac only nine months earlier and the man thrice wandered back to Washington to be with his wife and child: "I have almost made up my mind never to buy a married negro again." Lunsford and Jacob attended to the horses as they watched Isaac work the ropes and eventually free himself. He did not fly but joined Lunsford and Jacob, drawing attention from the picnickers. Galt was irate, demanding that Isaac behave and return to the Galt farm.

"I must be allowed to see my wife, and children sometimes, and the overseer says I shall not," Isaac pleaded. "I only want to go once a month." The enslaved man and his enslaver negotiated there, in front of Lunsford, until Galt conceded that Isaac could have four days with his family in Washington, although he would have to find his own way there and then back to the farm. Exuberantly, Isaac bounded away, a small bundle of meat and bread provided to him by the Haywood daughters. The maidservants packed the carriage, all climbed aboard, leaving Galt behind, and they arrived at Wilson's Tavern as the sun set. The next morning, they were on their way again, pulling up to the Raleigh house in mid-afternoon, Sherwood greeting their return.

The 1820s were full of lessons for Lunsford Haywood. From John Chavis, he learned that education, citizenship, and networking shaped free Black manhood. From Lafayette, Lunsford heard of rational liberty and its responsibility for others' liberty as well. Isaac taught Lunsford how a man took it upon himself to exert his manhood, evidencing how enslavement was negotiable if one were clever or at least insistent enough. Henry Jaquith showed Lunsford that beyond North Carolina, there was a big world with ideas more appealing than the racialized justifications for enslaving other human beings that Lunsford heard time and again at public speeches, from church pulpits, and overhearing White conversations. Lunsford came to realize that, given the opportunity, he could rise.

Chapter 4

Becoming Lunsford Lane

On November 18, 1827, John Haywood died, and Eliza joined her sister-in-law Delia in widowhood. Given the questions raised seven years earlier about John's handling of the state treasury and his obstinance in reporting to the General Assembly thereafter, a joint select committee examined the treasurer's accounts. The news surprised all: $68,906.80 [$2,094,000] was missing from the state's coffers, more than half of the State's annual budget. John had posted no bond for 1826 or 1827, so when the legislature uncovered the discrepancies, the State had no recourse but to sue his estate. "We are brought to ruin," Fabius Haywood fretted to a family friend.[1]

As executor of his father's will, George Washington Haywood called in debts, but the $1,751.59 [$53,240] he collected could not assuage state officials who seized most of John's assets, including the enslaved inventory. John Haywood's mismanagement proved particularly devasting to the hundreds of humans whom he had enslaved. In his will, he bequeathed nineteen enslaved people to Eliza: Ned Lane listed first, followed by Moses, Toney, Sally, Jacob (identified as a shoe-maker), Esther (the cook), Lydia, Young Ester (the nursemaid), Mary, Lucy, Crawford, Hardy, John, Peter, Edmund, Patty, Ben, Jordan, and Doctor. Although legal tradition held that they should have remained part of Eliza's widow's dowry, the State confiscated all of them on the premise that the house comprised her life estate, her one-third of the inheritance. John had intended to shield other enslaved people, such as Nancy Woods and the family in New Bern, who were to be given "time to procure a master or masters and to the person or persons thus selected by them, I desire them to be sold," and Brutus, who was to remain in Salisbury, hired out as a painter. The State's confiscation of John's estate swept all of them into chaos. None were safe as John had wished.[2]

Normally, in auctioning debtors' properties, sheriffs sold non-enslaved property first, followed by the enslaved properties, and finally land. John Haywood's debt was so substantial, however, that Eliza lost slaves, land, and personal effects at the same time. Over three days in February and March 1828, the State auctioned off several of the enslaved humans, profiting nearly $24,600 [$788,500]. Lunsford realized his childhood fears as his father climbed upon the auction block on the first day, but Eliza's friends in state

Eliza Williams Haywood, 1781–1832. From Portrait Collection, circa 1720–1997, North Carolina Collection. Courtesy of Wilson Special Collections Library, University of North Carolina at Chapel Hill.

government permitted her to make the only bids. To save Ned Lane, Jacob, Mary Jenny, Lilila Bellay, Hasty, Moses, Sally, Young Esther and her two children, and Kezzeah and her three children, Eliza paid $1,780 [$57,050], more than half of which went toward the first four purchases. Although well below market value, her expenses still pushed her further into debt. Years later, William Henry Haywood III advised his aunt to sell her bank stock to pay off the "debt due to your negro-purchases."[3]

As enslaved people went to auction, Fabius Haywood attempted to save Lunsford's cousins, the sons of Cate, the woman who "suckled three of us: She is now dead but I bear a regard and feeling to her children, which I do not to other negroes." Davy and Montford, "smart, active and intelligent young men," one a carpenter, the other an overseer, remained on the farm north of Raleigh. They were "good servants," Fabius assured a family friend who lent him the money to rescue them from the auction block.[4]

The rest of the enslaved inventory, those not saved by Eliza or Fabius, became casualties of John Haywood's fiscal mismanagement. Some took advantage of the moment. Burwell and Dick, sold at auction in February 1828, escaped by June. In early August, the new State Treasurer, William S. Robards, unsuccessfully attempted to apprehend Virgil, who allegedly fled to New York. In December, Isaac took flight from the man who purchased him at one of the auctions. A month later, another enslaver advertised for Peter Wolf, acquired at another auction, who had convinced Mark, purchased at the sale of Stephen Haywood's estate years earlier, to join him in flight.[5]

Sales of enslaved and landed properties did little to reduce the debt. Not until late 1831 did the real estate garner $5,163 [$182,040], a mere fraction of the $47,000 [$1,657,000] that officials demanded. The State requested a reassessment of John Haywood's estate. When a jury found $7,160 [$252,450] in assets yet unpaid, State Treasurer Robards griped that the judgment was "not regarded as worth any thing," arguing that the actual amount plus accumulated interest was closer to $17,740 [$625,480]. Eliza Haywood fretted that she would end up homeless, although her brother-in-law assured that the "law of the land *will* protect you, and the Legislature, even if it was disposed, (which it is not) could not turn you out of your House, or strip you."[6]

Although Eliza expressed hatred of hosting over the decades, as early as September 1828, she desperately opened her home to members of the legislature "who may honor her with their patronage." Within a year, she advertised rooms for "Travellers—Gentlemen & their Families—Boarders by the day, week, month, or year—School children for any length of time." Guests received access to a "beautiful and highly cultivated garden" and a "good stable," and since both were Ned Lane's realms, the guests had access to him as well. On the eve of legislative sessions, Eliza served meals to assemblymen, welcoming into her home many of the men who stripped her and her family of their inheritance. She accommodated twenty-five to thirty guests at a time in a "number of detached rooms, besides those in the main building."[7]

With the Wake County farm gone, the yard around the house became the vegetable garden, increasing work for Ned Lane and other enslaved people who previously had relied on farm laborers to sustain the household. Her supplier, James L. Belden's Garden Seed in Wethersfield, Connecticut, received fewer orders for ornate plants and increased requests for Early China beans, large Lima beans, blood red beets, early yellow turnips, York cabbage, red Dutch cabbage, Drumhead cabbage, orange carrot, cauliflower, celery, cress, cucumber, eggplant, golden Sioux corn, ice lettuce, nutmeg melons, green citron melons, silver onions, parsley, parsnip, peas, radish, spinach, and winter squash. Eliza, who complained for years about hosting John's political and business colleagues, became a hostess beyond compare, and her house became one of Raleigh's "favorite boarding houses."[8]

————

By the late 1820s, Ned, Clarissa, and Lunsford remained a family separated. Lunsford continued to join his mother at the Baptist Church when he could. The congregation had grown to over two hundred congregants, too many for the small church, forcing relocation to a larger wooden building on the north end of Moore Square. Over two-thirds of the congregation were enslaved or free Black members, so most services were at night after enslaved workers finished their daily toils. A sexton lit tallow candles to illuminate the interior and rang the bell to announce worship. A committee formed to consult with Black members on their religious experiences, recruiting Joseph, one of Sherwood Haywood's enslaved laborers, as a deacon to officiate communion for Black congregants. Enslaved laborers on the Haywood estates, some recruited by Joseph, joined: Hannah from Sherwood and Eleanor's estate and Jethro and Zilpha from Eliza's estate. They, in return, enlisted family and friends. Twenty more enslaved people from the Haywood rosters accepted baptism, among them Clarissa and nine whom Sherwood allowed to travel from St. Mary's for Sunday services. They sat in segregated spaces, and in the church minutes, they occupied segregated membership lists. Ned Lane never joined, but Lunsford Haywood did, obtaining from Eleanor "a written permit (a thing always required in such a case)" to be baptized on April 27, 1828.[9]

As did many enslaved peoples, Lunsford developed a stormy relationship with Christianity. John Chavis once described Raleigh's Black population as "very indifferent respecting religion." Discouraged from learning to read and expected to trust preachers' interpretations of the Bible, enslaved people often viewed organized religion suspiciously, with Lunsford noting, "Many of us were as highly civilized as some of our masters, and as to piety, in many instances their superiors."[10]

One local Episcopal minister, George Washington Freeman, rector of Christ Church between 1829 and 1840, drew favorable attention from Raleigh's enslaved community until the day when he argued that the Bible taught "that it was the will of heaven from all eternity we should be slaves, and our masters be our owners." Like so many White Christians, Freeman struggled to condemn enslavement, although he cared about the spiritual well-being of his enslaved neighbors. In his own discourses on biblical justifications for enslaving humans and the duties of slaveowners to the people they held in bondage, Freeman openly opposed emancipation because he believed free Black people lived miserably.[11]

Lunsford grew weary of Christian preachers who acted friendly toward Black Carolinians and yet argued to sustain their enslavement. He criticized organized Christianity as a faith of hypocrisy, denying the lessons of individual liberty to enslaved peoples and insisting on submission and obedience: "The first commandment impressed upon our minds was to obey our masters, and the second was like unto it, namely, to do as much work when they or the overseers were not watching us as when they were." Such messages sounded "strangely in the ears of freedom." Enslavement was contrary to both the rational liberty of the young nation and the religious self-determination of the New Testament.[12]

Sometimes, church membership is not about faith, and Lunsford's decision to join the Baptist Church soon after his experience with Lafayette suggests as much. Christian clergy preached a theology of Black submission to White authority, one that he could not reconcile with the "love of principle [that] prevailed over the love of power," as Lafayette put it, when "virtue triumphed over ambition." With missionary zeal, rational liberty could expel the darkness of despotism, and what were enslavers if not petty tyrants eager to exert what power they had over the powerless? But the rational part of rational liberty required those with freedom to wield it morally, with care for others. White enslavers, despite their pronouncements of Christian faith, failed at rational liberty. The Declaration of Independence proclaimed that the Creator authored human freedom, which, in Lunsford's words, White Americans "without God's consent, had stolen away."[13]

Lunsford Haywood did not attend the Baptist church, then, for eternal salvation. It offered more immediate benefits, providing space and time in which to contemplate rational liberty, to indulge "in the exercise of my own conscience—a favor not always granted to slaves." Prohibited from reading and writing on the Haywood estate, he used the church to gain "instruction," learning "by stealth" to read and think about a life of principle, virtue, and duty. The Baptist Church was a place in which Lunsford separated himself from the Haywoods, found his voice, and acquired the skills of literacy that, to him, symbolized freedom.[14]

When a teenager, Lunsford received a basket of peaches from his father and sold them. Later, he peddled some marbles that he won playing with other boys. Years later, Lunsford's remembrance of those transactions testified to the hope they raised "of purchasing at some future time my freedom." Yet, his work as an enslaved laborer interfered with those aspirations. He spent his days running errands for the Haywoods, pasturing horses, and working at St. Mary's. Sherwood invested little in the farm, peopling it with older enslaved laborers and the children of those serving on the town estate. Lunsford performed his share of farm work most weeks, returning to Raleigh well after sundown each time to spend late-night hours cutting wood to sell first thing the next day.[15]

The first hint that Lunsford planned to make money to purchase himself was in 1824 when he began wandering to the markethouse each morning to do the Haywoods' shopping, visiting the stores of Benjamin B. Smith and Joseph & William Peace "to convey the idea to by-standers that he was acting for the aristocracy of the town." It was a charade. He shopped for himself, purchasing items cheaply and storing them in the cellar of Smith's store to resell later. Shopkeepers paid Lunsford for shelving goods and creating displays on the sidewalks. Presaging his success as a waiter at public affairs, he discovered that good service brought tips. Richard Bennehan, an Orange County planter and one of the state's more influential men, occasionally visited Sherwood and Eleanor and paid Lunsford a dollar [$35] each time. When Gavin Hogg, a Raleigh lawyer, began regularly courting Sarah Leigh Haywood Blount, who had returned from Chocowinity after her husband died in 1828, he, too, tipped Lunsford usually a dollar. Gratuities became foundational to Lunsford's moneymaking, and when the legislature convened, he made a bundle. Assemblymen resided in nearby hotels and boarding houses, staying up late at night and often requiring assistance back to their rooms after an evening of heavy drinking. Some mornings, Lunsford skipped shopping to visit boarding house rooms where he polished boots, brushed clothes, and prepared "early morning bitters" to dispel the hangovers. The senators and congressmen paid well.[16]

Then, one day in the mid-1820s, Ned Lane shared a secret with his son: he had an idea for flavoring tobacco. Lunsford imagined a new opportunity. For some time, he had sold smoking tobacco to members of the legislature as he helped them to their boarding house rooms, but he made little profit because he purchased high-quality tobacco and scratched out a few pennies in reselling it. With Ned's idea, Lunsford could purchase poorer quality tobacco at cheap rates, mask the imperfections to "manufacture a good article out of a very indifferent material," and boost his profits. In the night hours, after he attended to the Haywoods' demands and tucked inebriated legislators into their beds, Lunsford and his father flavored smoking tobacco that Lunsford then peddled for fifteen cents [$4.60] per packet. Sales were meager and profits slow to arrive—$1000 [$30,400] over the next decade, roughly $100 [$3,040] a year. As an enslaved man, Lunsford could spend little of the money without drawing attention.[17]

From reselling goods to acting as a private manservant to producing tobacco, Lunsford's enterprises were common. Over his lifetime, however, Lunsford would watch others amplify his entrepreneurial activities as if they—and he—were exceptional. Desperate to show that enslavement could not have been *that* bad if someone such as Lunsford could aspire to and achieve freedom through entrepreneurialism, historians and politicians perpetuated the myth and still do. While the profits from tobacco sales contributed to Lunsford's freedom, he needed other sources of money before he could purchase himself and his family.[18]

Lunsford was neither singular in his economic ingenuity nor particularly good at it. In preindustrial America, people always bartered, learned trades, engaged in multiple jobs, and imagined new products to sell. Those activities persisted into the nineteenth century, even as an industrial and market revolution transformed the American economy. One North Carolinian recalled how, among Black Carolinians living in Raleigh and other large towns, "the apter males became barbers, fiddlers, or Jacks-of-all-trades." Of course, they were almost always free Black men unless, like Lunsford, an enslaved man held enough status to advantage himself. They "eked out with a petty traffic in the rude articles of their own make, such as chairs, splint baskets, horse-collars and door-mats made from shucks and bark, 'dug' troughs, bread-trays, etc." Others hauled wood, mixed hangover remedies, and flavored tobacco. As the editorialist concluded, "In fact, they were largely, perforce, a class of piddlers, and like piddlers everywhere more indispensable than any other element of the community."[19]

Since the mid-1700s, political philosophers tried to define what "piddlers" were, arguing that economies functioned better without government intervention, guided instead by the decisions of individual producers and consumers. Jean-Baptiste Say, the leading economic philosopher of the 1820s and a co-founder of the world's first business school, articulated assumptions about piddlers, seeking to understand how person-to-person trade fit into emerging market-oriented economies. His definition of entrepreneur was a simple and longstanding one: the word meant "between takers," one taking goods and the other taking payment. Central to taking was production, traditionally made possible through the passage of knowledge from master to apprentice or, as in Lunsford's case, from father to son. Takers acquired the knowledge of their craft, the materials needed to produce, and the ability to execute their ideas. Lunsford trained for years under his father as a horticulturalist. If he wanted to be a tobacconist, he had to learn which quality of tobacco he needed and how to flavor it. In the early nineteenth century, it seemed that any person, enslaved or free, with a bit of ingenuity could be branded an entrepreneur.[20]

Economic changes emerging in Western European nations and the United States across the eighteenth and nineteenth centuries demanded a reimagining of piddlers. New industries, transportation, and communication made it possible for takers to evolve from producers of goods to managers of manufacturing. As Say anticipated, new "entrepreneurs d'industrie" became men of production costs, profit margins, and bottom lines. They became the symbols of nineteenth-century capitalism, still takers but hardly piddling. They operated on grand scales with more intention, reinventing themselves from takers into investors and profiteers, consolidating production, distribution, and sales under their management.[21]

Motivation distinguished emerging ideas of entrepreneurs from piddlers. Banks, insurance companies, corporations, and laws arose as part of a financial system that encouraged greater economic risks. Some Americans—male, White, and socially connected—directly benefited from the new institutions. Men of wealth picked and chose when to economically engage, strategizing their futures by calculating investments and risks and pursuing profit for profit's sake, an attitude that piddlers, many of whom struggled to survive, could ill afford.[22]

Most Americans did not embrace the emerging concept of entrepreneurship. "Entrepreneur" could not be found in Noah Webster's 1828 *An American Dictionary of the English Language* or twenty years later in George and Charles Merriam similarly titled dictionary. Well into the nineteenth century, when the term popped up in American usage, it was Say's original definition of the term: the older idea of the piddler, often one who scratched out little, if any, immediate profit. Across the nineteenth century, piddling increasingly became referred to as "hustling," a term previously applied to prostitutes and thieves, indicative of how the emerging entrepreneurial class frowned upon piddlers as disrupting the more structured capitalist economy to which they aspired.[23]

New ideas about entrepreneurialism posed a particular problem in the South. American slaveowners fully embraced it themselves, investing in staple-crop production and enslaved labor, engaging markets, aligning with large-scale factory producers, gaining investment loans from financial institutions, pursuing profits so that they could live in luxury, and reinvesting the rest, often in speculative ventures such as new plantations on western borderlands. Capitalistic success fueled their individual liberties, so they knew well the relationship of economic empowerment to political freedom. By minimizing others' access to investment loans, regulating the quality of agricultural exports, restricting public land use, erecting local markethouses to guide piddlers toward "more appropriate" market participation, and other mechanisms, planters and other monied men monopolized capitalistic opportunities, economically and politically dominating the piddlers around them.[24]

Lunsford Haywood and other enslaved piddlers, then, existed in an entrepreneurial milieu dominated by economic and political elites. Operating on the margins of the exploding capitalist economy, they grew vegetables, caught fish, hunted squirrels and rabbits, kept chickens and pigs, cut and hauled wood, flavored tobacco, and sold their wares at markethouses and to regular customers. Some Black folk, both free and enslaved, trained as painters, plasterers, furniture makers, blacksmiths, hostlers, and waiters, making them valuable contributors to Raleigh's more formal economy, but the benefits of that economy remained beyond their grasp. Some free Black residents like John Chavis enjoyed access to loans but only through the assistance of wealthy White men, and a few enslaved people such as Ned Lane had book credit in local stores granted on the reputations of their enslavers. Most Black piddlers operated in a cash nexus, accumulating income slowly and limiting consumption and investments, particularly among enslaved people saving toward purchasing freedom.[25]

Enslaved piddlers faced an additional obstacle to their economic activities: race. Across the 1700s and early 1800s, Black codes consistently curtailed their economic activities. In 1826, North Carolina's General Assembly passed more expansive restrictions. Only with written permission from their enslaver could an enslaved person sell or buy goods, and only during daylight hours. The law listed items forbidden in trade with enslaved peoples, including tobacco. White folk who traded with an enslaved person without government permission faced a $100 [$3,040] fine. Enslaved piddlers received thirty-nine lashes at the public pillory.[26]

So, as Lunsford Haywood enacted his scheme to make money, he did so as a piddler, violating the laws restricting enslaved enterprise. He sold tobacco, contrary to the law, often at night, another transgression, and without written permission from the Haywoods, yet again against the law. Sherwood and Eleanor tolerated Lunsford's waiting at dinners and dances and his evening and morning catering to state legislators—both of which provided plenty of gossip—but he hid the tobacco production and sales from them. Lunsford knew he was acting illegally, clandestinely storing his stock in the basement of Smith's store and hiding his earnings from the Haywoods. Only one thing protected him from thirty-nine lashes: many of his tobacco customers were legislators who had passed the code forbidding such hustling. They willingly broke their own law as they consumed Lunsford and Ned's product.[27]

Legislators and other White Carolinians gave Lunsford and other enslaved peoples a bit of economic independence because, as the North Carolina Supreme Court later concluded, it purportedly strengthened the genealogy of enslavement: "These slight indulgences are repaid by the attachment of the slave to the master and his family, by exerting his industry and honesty, and a spirit to make and save for the master as well as for himself." Black codes that regulated trade with and among enslaved peoples implicitly recognized "a sort of ownership by slaves of certain articles . . . which shows that there is a universal sense pervading the whole community, of the utility, nay, unavoidable necessity, of leaving to the slave some small perquisites, which may be called his and disposed of by him as his"—a small sliver of humanity in an inhumane system.[28]

So, even as Lunsford's economic ventures put him in conflict with state law, theoretically, his piddling bound him more closely to the Haywoods and their network of wealthy and powerful White Carolinians. When he took money from legislators, they sanctioned his hustling as acceptable, providing the social capital that he needed to make his efforts pay off. Yet, try as he might to conceal his tobacco sales and profits, Lunsford gradually became visible to the Haywoods, to merchants who also sold tobacco, and to White piddlers who, as they too moved from activity to activity, job to job, scraping money together any way they could for sustenance, came to view him as unwanted competition. He hid his activities as much to mask his achievements as to avoid the law.[29]

————————

Among the few men of God whom Lunsford Haywood trusted were Presbyterian ministers. On one occasion, likely at the town's Fourth of July celebration in 1824, Reverend William McPheeters publicly declared, "It is impossible to enslave an intelligent people." Lunsford took the message to heart. McPheeters had arrived in Raleigh in 1810 to serve as principal of the Raleigh Academy. Six years later, he held a service in the State House, and Raleigh's Presbyterian congregation took shape. Twenty-six congregants gathered for worship, including eleven women, one of them Nancy Holmes, a free Black woman.[30]

Although not the first interracial congregation in Raleigh, the organization of the Presbyterian Church marked a sea change in the relationship of Christianity to enslavement in the capital town. The congregation filled with individuals who, if not dedicated to the abolition of enslavement, were at least willing to discuss it openly. By 1819, McPheeters led congregants in organizing the Raleigh Auxiliary Society for Colonizing the Free People of Colour of the United States. When the society met for the first time, most attendees, including Joseph Gales, William Boylan, and William Peace, were Presbyterians. A few, like Sherwood Haywood, John Haywood, and Charles Manly, were Episcopal allies. When William Meade, an agent for the American Colonization Society, visited later that year, he found "the highest talents, authorities, and wealth of the State were present." By 1821, even more wealth and talent joined the society, including a couple of Raleigh's largest slaveowners, Thomas P. Devereux and William Polk; prominent businessmen like William Hill, Jeremiah Battle, and William Peck; as well as the organization's first female subscriber, Susan D. Nye, a teacher from New York recruited for the Raleigh Academy.[31]

Gales, the dedicated Jeffersonian editor of the *Raleigh Minerva*, who, for decades, held the party line that although reprehensible, enslavement was necessary, began lobbying for public support for colonization, printing reports as to how "colonization is no novelty. . . . It is not a dream." For Nye and McPheeters, whose faith shaped their antislavery sentiments, colonization offered a solution to the sin of enslavement. But for most members of the American Colonization Society, colonization provided a solution to "flying slaves," common parlance for freedom seekers. As Robert Goodloe Harper of Maryland put it when he cofounded the society in 1816, colonization in Africa would not only address the enslaved laborer who neglected "work as much as possible, to withdraw himself from it altogether by flight, and sometimes to attempt direct resistance," but would provide asylum for free Black Americans who contributed "greatly to the corruption of the slaves, and to aggravate the evils of their condition, by rendering them idle, discontented, and disobedient." Raleigh's Auxiliary Society languished, however. By 1825, a member expressed surprise upon seeing a society report in the local newspaper, "not having heard of it for years, I supposed it was defunct." Frustratedly, McPheeters directed his attention elsewhere, organizing a school for the deaf and mute. In 1828, he made clear his intentions to step down as pastor, and the congregation invited Thomas P. Hunt to the pulpit.[32]

Lunsford Haywood met Hunt soon after the minister's arrival. A former Virginia planter, Hunt became an ardent advocate of temperance and colonization, freeing the people whom he enslaved and sending most of them to Liberia. His stay in Raleigh was short-lived, only two years, largely because he was so forthright about his abolitionism. He commonly reprimanded church members who mistreated enslaved laborers and regularly preached on the demoralizing influence of enslavement. Two men whom he emancipated served as his waiter and driver. Lunsford remembered how they sat in Hunt's study, reading his books, imagining that he, too, could become a free man and cultivate his mind.[33]

Lunsford Haywood visited Hunt regularly, and he was there one day when William Polk, Raleigh's oldest Revolutionary War veteran and largest enslaver, called. Alexis De Tocqueville's *Democracy in America* sat open on a table, and Polk took the opportunity to interrogate Hunt about it. Claiming not to have read the book, he asked if rumors about Tocqueville's unfavorable opinion of Southern institutions were true. Hunt responded with a prolonged review in which he critiqued enslavement as contrary to "true democracy." Polk responded, "If this be true, and our civilization is to become homogeneous, I can see no escape from a terrible and protracted contest in the future, unless, indeed, the South becomes a distinct confederacy, which might be effected by peaceable means." Hunt retorted, "The severe justice of the Puritan character, to say nothing of the great interests of humanity, both in Europe and America, which would be involved, would not admit of so peaceable a separation as you and I might desire."[34]

As Polk packed to leave, he turned to Lunsford, snidely commenting, "I suppose we are to have another happy free negro in our midst, to make our happy slaves all unhappy. I hope that you will have the good sense to use your liberty as not abusing it." At least among the enslavers, word had spread of Lunsford's nighttime activities and obvious aspiration.[35]

In late 1827, Lunsford began to court Martha Curtis, an enslaved woman working the lands where Lunsford's father had labored as a boy—the old Lane farm, now owned by William Boylan. Unlike his old adversary Joseph Gales, Boylan had little evolved in his thinking about enslavement from his earlier days as a newspaper editor. Selling his interest in the *Minerva* in 1810, Boylan became more politically active: four terms as a Federalist in the General Assembly, a leader in the internal improvements movement, organizer of the Peace Party to oppose the War of 1812, supporter of a state bank, and treasurer of the North Carolina Agricultural Society. He also emerged as a significant planter, purchasing the Lane farm and house from Allen Gilchrist in 1818 and transforming it into a cotton farm, which he called Wakefield.[36]

One of Boylan's many acquaintances was Christopher Curtis, who owned 168 acres north of Raleigh, adjacent to Sherwood Haywood's farm. Curtis enslaved twenty-five people in 1815 but was growing too old to supervise them. His son, Anderson, showed no interest in being a farmer, investing his own money in a store along Fayetteville Street. Anderson advertised for an overseer "who understands the culture of corn and wheat" to manage his father's farm, but when Christopher Curtis passed away late in the year, Anderson decided to sell the land and the laborers. Closing his father's estate proved difficult. Few people responded to his demand that his father's debtors repay their loans. Then, in June 1816, during a fire that consumed over fifty buildings along Fayetteville Street, looters pilfered Anderson's store, stealing a pocketbook that contained the documents related to his father's estate and promissory notes from customers. Anderson warned his clients not to pay on the stolen notes, and then he closed shop, selling the rest of his father's properties, including the enslaved laborers, to cover the now unrecoverable debts.[37]

So, in 1817, enslaved peoples with the surname Curtis began showing up on slave inventories around Raleigh. Sherwood Haywood purchased Jane Curtis and her daughter, Eliza, as well as Austin Curtis, Phil Curtis, and Ned Curtis. William Boylan, hesitating to drain the labor force on his profitable Chatham County farm to work his experimental cotton farm in Raleigh, also bought enslaved Curtises—Alexander, who married Clarissa's sister, Matilda, and Martha, her brother, and their mother.[38]

By all accounts, William Boylan was kind to enslaved domestics and field hands, but he was the same man who once took a cane to Joseph Gales, decrying his opponent as an African baboon. Boylan's eldest son, John, suffered a harsher reputation. By 1823, John was twenty years old and, with his father preoccupied with the Auxiliary Society and other political interests, empowered to run the Boylan properties. "He was a mighty hard man to git along with," recalled one of the Boylans' enslaved humans, Elias Thomas, a lifetime later. William Boylan entrusted management of his properties to John, who did not hesitate to physically abuse or even kill enslaved people whom he could not control. Rumors circulated that John whipped a man to death on the Chatham farm. On another occasion, he gave a Raleigh neighbor permission to shoot an enslaved man who habitually ran away, and soon thereafter, the Black man died in the neighbor's field, shot in the head. So, too, did Martha Curtis's family suffer under John's temper. Facing the overseer's wrath and the whipping post, her brother ran. John shot him in the back, maiming him for life. When Lunsford began to call on Martha around 1827, then, it opened possibilities for her to escape the hell of the Boylan farm.[39]

Martha was not Lunsford's first choice, however. Two years earlier, he had pursued Lucy Williams, enslaved by Thomas Devereux, a reporter for the North Carolina Supreme Court. Devereux enslaved Lucy and six other humans on his town lot. For whatever reasons, Lunsford "failed in my undertakings," so discouraging him that he gave up on marriage. He then met Martha. His description of their courtship was businesslike: "I fell in with her to whom I am now united, Miss MARTHA CURTIS, and the bargain between us was completed." Years later, when Lunsford recollected The Story, Martha often faded to the background, framed by her husband in a most patriarchal manner as someone under his control rather than someone he loved.[40]

Lunsford "next went to William Boylan, and asked him, according to the custom, if I might 'marry his woman.' His reply was, 'Yes, if you will behave yourself.' I told him I would. 'And make her behave herself?' To this I also assented." The exchange was not a courtesy call as practiced commonly among free individuals but obligatory. The state did not recognize Lunsford's and Martha's right to wed as enslaved individuals. It was the enslaver's role to supervise such unions, and Boylan insisted on a catechism of proper married behavior, including manly restraint of women. He situated himself as the arbiter of Lunsford and Martha's marital morality. Even if allowed to live separately from Boylan, Martha remained legally his and a part of his household. By acknowledging Boylan's claim over Martha, Lunsford Haywood conceded her primary relationship as that with her owner. When they married in

May 1828, Lunsford and Martha imagined that what God joined together, no one could sunder, but marriage between an enslaved wife and husband was a secondary relationship, one tolerated by two owners.[41]

For about a year, Martha remained in Boylan's household, provided with "sufficient food and clothing to render her comfortable." Lunsford, increasingly money conscious as he saved toward freedom, did not spend much on his wife "except to procure such small articles of extra comfort as I was prompted from time to time." In February 1829, marked by Lunsford as "nine months and one day" after their marriage, a son was born: Edward, named for his grandfather. Two and a half years later, a daughter, Maria Bell, arrived. Martha and Lunsford's marriage appeared healthy and strong. Years later, as Lunsford dictated The Story, he crowed how his bond with Martha had not been broken, and when freed from the oversight of enslavers in 1842, "now it cannot be, except by a higher power."[42]

Sadly, it was a premature conclusion about the rest of their marriage, for Lunsford seemed to never recognize how Martha was not an incapable dependent. When she saw an opportunity, she took it. After the birth of her second child, she negotiated with William Boylan to sell her and the children to Benjamin B. Smith, the merchant in whose cellar Lunsford stored his tobacco and goods. Smith was also Martha's "class-leader" in religious instruction at the Methodist Church, yet another interracial congregation numbering eighty-five White congregants and 135 Black congregants in 1833. Late that year, Smith purchased Martha, Edward, and Maria Bell for $560 [$20,260].[43]

Benjamin B. Smith wore his faith on his sleeve, teaching at the Methodist Church and managing the North Carolina Bible Society. Like many people, he was a reluctant activist, regularly requiring a nudge to act on his beliefs. He critiqued heavy drinking, particularly that undertaken in the taverns of Grog Alley near his store on Fayetteville Street, but he refused to join the temperance movement until Presbyterian minister Thomas P. Hunt pointed out how inebriated hooligans threatened the security of Smith's store and home. Once prodded, Smith became fully intolerant of alcoholic consumption, pouring his stock of liquors and wines into the street: "The news was circulated, and such running with tin kettles and cups was seldom ever witnessed."[44]

Smith similarly disapproved of enslavement but hesitated to act. As a youth, he had inherited an enslaved woman, Lenda. Even after Smith married Laura Worthington in 1819, Lenda continued to organize and serve the frequent parties for which he and Laura became widely known. By the 1820s, Lenda married and bore a child, Washington. Smith's affection for the enslaved woman who grew up with him extended only so far. When Washington reached fifteen years of age in the mid-1820s, Smith sold him to an enslaver in south Wake County. Although only twenty miles away, Lenda never saw her son again. It was years before she even met someone who could console her that Washington was still alive. Bennet T. Blake, a Methodist minister and enslaver, assured her that her son was worth "five hundred dollars" [$17,700], offering no news about Washington's health or happiness. Lunsford witnessed the conversation, interpreting it as another example of Christianity's hollowness.[45]

Lenda still served the Smiths when Martha and her children arrived in the household. Martha's familiarity with Benjamin quickly proved a problem. He warmly called her "Patsy," a playful nickname that Lunsford did not use and that Laura, Smith's wife of fourteen years, surely disliked. Laura denied Martha "a chance to prove that she was honest in the affairs of the household," directing Lenda not to share the key to the pantry. Although conditions were difficult at the Boylan farm, Martha quickly realized that, despite Benjamin B. Smith's friendship, life in the Smith household was a challenge. Laura was stern, and Benjamin was cheap. As Lunsford sarcastically criticized when recalling the meager meals that Smith served to Martha and the children, "such luxuries were more than he could afford, kind and Christian man as he was considered to be."[46]

Concerned about his family's welfare, Lunsford began supplying clothes and food to Martha and the children. Opportunities to select and wear clothing allowed a bit of expression and self-identity, stamping Lunsford Haywood's imprimatur on his family and distinguishing his family from other enslaved families. He spent so much on clothing and food for his family that his savings dwindled to five dollars [$180], which he lost soon thereafter as he took the horses to graze at St. Mary's.[47]

And the Smiths' presence curtailed Lunsford and Martha's marital intimacy. Having moved out of more cloistered quarters on the Boylan farm into the Smith house, Martha lost the little privacy that she enjoyed. They did not have another child for three years.

Despite Lunsford's baptism, the tobacco, the conversations, the marriage to Martha, and the children, he described his existence as tedium: "So my life went wearily on from day to day, from night to night, and from week to week." He continued to sleep on the parlor floor in Sherwood and Eleanor Haywood's house, about six blocks away from Martha and the children.[48]

On October 5, 1829, the monotony ended. The "man of respectability" Sherwood Haywood died, and his "selfish wife" Eleanor became the third widow Haywood. Lunsford had witnessed the pain of separation and loss inflicted upon those enslaved on Delia's and Eliza's estates, and he anticipated

Eleanor Hawkins
Haywood, 1776–1855.
Privately owned.
Photograph by Joshua
Steadman. Courtesy of
Betsy Haywood.

worse on Eleanor's estate. Sherwood, after all, was not as wealthy as Lunsford assumed or Eleanor feigned. In fact, unlike Delia's and Eliza's surprises at the circumstances left behind by their husbands, Eleanor knew well the financial woes that burdened her family. Sherwood reminded her and everyone else on his deathbed, dying "very much embarrassed with debt."[49]

Sherwood's position as United States Commissioner of Loans had disappeared in 1817 with the creation of the Second Bank of the United States. Although President James Madison appointed him a commissioner for the Raleigh branch, the pay was less than the previous position. To sustain the family's standard of living over the next dozen years, Sherwood accumulated debt, a lot of it. In April 1828, he cosigned on a bond and provided security for his nephew, William Henry Haywood III, to gain a cashier position at the State Bank of North Carolina. In October, Sherwood took a new position as an agent for the Bank of Newbern, offering his real estate and half of his chattel properties as bonds. Then, only a month before his death, he used the remainder of his enslaved property as security against a $6,000 [$196,950] loan from the bank.[50]

The total debt upon his death neared $40,000 [$1,313,000]. Decades later, Eleanor's executors claimed that she did not sell lands or enslaved properties to pay off the debt because a depressed economy portended "ruinous prices." The reality was that she dared not sell because several banks held liens that she could not meet with the profits, putting the rest of the estate in jeopardy. To survive, she began taking loans from the Bank of Newbern to cover estate debts and support her children. She successfully paid off one loan, but recognizing the threat that collectors would eventually confiscate her enslaved and landed properties, she decided to sell some of her enslaved laborers at auction.[51]

Having watched Ned Lane on the auction block four years earlier, Clarissa worried about her and her son's fates. Months later, nearing fifty years of age and undoubtedly tired of serving the Haywoods, she accompanied Eleanor's daughter, Lucy Davis Haywood, to New York. Lucy was to wed John S. Bryan in February, and the trip was a pre-wedding shopping spree. Once in Manhattan, Clarissa made clear her intention to abandon Lucy, as well as Lunsford, Ned Lane, her sister Matilda, the Haywoods, Raleigh, all of it. In the end, Clarissa did not fly. "I often think of the time when you went to New York with me," Lucy reminisced later in life, "how I persuaded you to stay." Lucy narcissistically imagined that Clarissa declined freedom and returned southward for her sake when Clarissa just could not abandon her family.[52]

Clarissa and Lucy returned to a Haywood household in chaos. Eleanor, five of her children, twenty-one enslaved people, and two free Black residents remained on the town estate, and another thirty-eight enslaved humans worked the St. Mary's farm, maintained "only to take care of invalid and aged slaves, and breeding women with several children." When Eleanor calculated profits from the larger Edgecombe farm at the end of 1829, it brought in $1,335 [$43,800] in cotton sales, enough to shave $500 [$16,400] off her bank loan and settle other obligations but not enough to meet family needs.[53]

Desperate for more money, Eleanor hired out thirty-three of her enslaved laborers, including Lunsford. But the profits were thin, so, in February 1830, she decided to sell. She, Delia, and two other widows appointed Eleanor's son, Robert W. Haywood, to disburse their lands in Warren and Granville Counties. In April, Eleanor parted with the first of her enslaved humans, London, who immediately flew. She might have profited $350 [$11,500] from his sale, but when he disappeared, she lost the profit and paid an additional $33.50 [$1,100] for authorities to track him down. She advertised for the return of a stray bay horse within days of London's escape, and the ad strangely attributed to the horse what was certainly her thinking about London: "I suppose that he is trying to get to my plantation in Edgecomb, where he was raised." Neither the horse nor London were seen again. Clarissa and Lunsford became more anxious as Eleanor sold numerous children from parents, two husbands from their wives, and one wife from her husband, the profits from which situated Eleanor to pay off one-sixth of Sherwood's outstanding debt.[54]

In 1831, Eleanor's brother-in-law and last remaining Haywood brother, Henry, and his son, William Henry III, tried to salvage what they could of Sherwood's estate. They paid off the bond that Sherwood had posted years earlier on young Henry's behalf, and arranged for Thomas Devereux, to whom Sherwood most recently had indebted himself, to take the house and other landed properties as collateral until "a Judgement [be] rendered against the said Sherwood Haywood on said bond." Only then, nearly a decade later, did Devereux "reconvey the said property or such part thereof as might remain," selling the properties back to Eleanor Haywood for $1 [$35].[55]

Whether it was London who stole Eleanor's horse or not, only two horses remained for which Lunsford Haywood was responsible. The following year, a thief took both—"one with a star and the other with a blaze face." Eleanor had no money to replace them. As Lunsford's responsibilities at the Haywood house diminished, he became increasingly nervous that Eleanor might sell him, particularly as rumors of her overwhelming debt circulated. His hiring out probably saved him. Hoping to avoid sale and unhappy with working for someone else, Lunsford approached Eleanor about leaving the arrangement and hiring his own time. She agreed, and they settled on $120 [$4,250] per year. It was a risky request. The State Assembly outlawed self-hire in 1794, so both he and Eleanor kept silent about the arrangement.[56]

Free to act on his own time, Lunsford no longer hid his tobacco production. Encouraged, he threw himself into flavoring and marketing tobacco, and he found local stores eager to sell the product on commission. Some of the legislators whom he sobered up in the mornings took the tobacco back to Fayetteville, Salisbury, Chapel Hill, and other hometowns. Nervous about exposing his success to local authorities, who sometimes interfered with the practice of hiring out when they thought the enslaved piddler was too successful, Lunsford continued to live humbly. He made sure to pay Eleanor promptly each year but pretended he could barely meet the payment. It is possible that even Martha did not know of his profits.[57]

Despite its promise, the agreement with Eleanor Haywood posed a dilemma. Lunsford suspected that, had she been more aware of his activities, she would boost the rate for his self-hire or curb it altogether. He knew she did not have good fortune allowing her enslaved laborers to hire themselves out. Hoping to squeeze more money from loaning out enslaved laborers, Eleanor had brought thirty-three-year-old Joe Branch and his family from the Edgecombe farm to Raleigh, where he could hire out as a blacksmith. The Haywoods had valued Branch so much that, in 1828, Sherwood had purchased Branch's wife Tempe and son Needham to keep him happy. When the

Branch family arrived in Raleigh, Tempe was around twenty-nine years old and "quite an intelligent and genteel looking negro," and young Needham, around seven years old, "can read and write." Then, at the end of 1831, all three were gone "without license." Eleanor could ill afford their loss, needing to establish that they were her property before anyone else laid claim. An ad appeared in the *Raleigh Register*:

50 or 100 Dollars Reward,

Will be given for negro Joe and his Wife and Son, who left Raleigh about Christmas. Joe is about 35 years of age, 6 feet high, walks a little *lame*, has a down look, a Blacksmith by trade—complexion not very Black.—His Wife is of middle stature, and I believe her complexion is rather Blacker than her husband's. His son is about 9 or 10 years old. If these Negroes are taken and confined in any Jail within the State, $50 will be given; if out of the State $100.[58]

Years had passed since that trip to Washington, North Carolina, when Eleanor worried that people, upon seeing her with her distant cousin, might think she involved herself in "the mean errand of slave-catching." In the financial desperation that followed Sherwood's death, others' opinions mattered no longer. Anticipating Joe, Tempe, and Needham's flight northward, she offered a reward in the *Norfolk Herald*, *Richmond Enquirer*, and *Baltimore Patriot*. With no luck in recapturing the freedom-seeking family, she enlisted her son, Rufus, to track them down.[59]

Chapter 5

The Insistence of Whiteness

From meritorious service to regulations on Black piddlers, law—legislated and adjudicated—structured Black lives. Entangled state regulations, city ordinances, and racial expectations became a patch of thorns that scratched every Black person who lived in or moved through Raleigh. In 1816, *Haywood v. Craven's Executors* set legal precedents about how enslaved peoples could gain or lose freedom. John Craven had died in 1808, leaving land and thirty enslaved persons to his sister and setting up a trust to arrange for their freedom upon her death. When she died, she had left a will that gifted the enslaved laborers to a friend, the youngest Haywood brother, Stephen, who sued to overturn Craven's wishes. When *Haywood v. Craven's Executors* reached the North Carolina Supreme Court in 1816, the justices agreed that John Craven's use of a trust to ensure his wishes was improper, consequently restricting enslavers' abilities to emancipate through their wills.[1]

Other laws and judicial decisions expanded White authority over Black Carolinians. In early 1828, Elizabeth Jones of Chowan County inherited an enslaved woman named Lydia. Jones was a minor, so her guardian assumed control over Lydia, hiring the woman out to John Mann of Edenton. When Mann tried to whip Lydia, she fled, and as she ran, he shot her, wounding her for life. Lower courts indicted Mann for battery. When the case arrived at the North Carolina Supreme Court in 1830, newly appointed justice Thomas Ruffin wrote the majority decision, concluding that Mann and other White Carolinians could not be indicted for assaulting the people they enslaved. In the opinion of the court, "the power of the master must be absolute, to render the submission of the slave perfect."[2]

Yet, John Mann was not Lydia's legal enslaver. He hired her, and this one fact made *State v. Mann* far more consequential. Ruffin expressed concern that previous judicial decisions and unenforced codes led to a "mildness of treatment and attention to the comforts of the unfortunate class of slaves." He had enough of the laxity of enforcement of Black codes, such as those that Lunsford Haywood manipulated for his own profit. Given the "disparity in numbers between whites and Blacks," Ruffin viewed enslaved people as threats to the stability and security of White life if "the police now existing may be further relaxed." Since the seventeenth century, North Carolina lawmakers worked to define what it meant to be a Black person in both enslavement and freedom, but the Supreme Court's decision in *State v. Mann* revealed without a doubt what it meant to be a White person, opening the way for all White men, indeed, all White people, to exert physical authority over their enslaved neighbors. *State v. Mann* announced the 1830s as a decade of expanding White rights and privileges, often at the expense of lost opportunities for Black folks, whether free or enslaved.[3]

In October 1830, a scuffle erupted in Boston, Massachusetts. Several Black men confronted a White gang who regularly congregated on Belknap Street, near the First Independent Baptist Church of People of Color, known as the African Meeting House, pitching racial slurs and insults at passersby. Southern newspapers, including Raleigh's *North-Carolina Star*, relished the opportunity to spread news of Northern racial discord, blaming the Boston incident on a recently published pamphlet: *Walker's Appeal to the Colored Citizens of the World.*[4]

To hear White Southerners describe it, *Walker's Appeal* was the most dangerous document ever written. Born circa 1796 to a free woman in Wilmington, North Carolina, David Walker moved to Boston by the mid-1820s, speaking openly against enslavement and racist assumptions of Black inferiority. Writing directly to his fellow Black Americans, Walker condemned Thomas Jefferson's "orang outang" theory—that Black inferiority was natural and undisputable. "See this, my brethren!! Do you believe that this assertion is swallowed by millions of the whites?" Walker argued for the "complete overthrow of the system of slavery, in every part of the country," and he denounced the "colonizing trick" promoted by groups like the Raleigh Auxiliary of the American Colonization Society. Walker petitioned White readers to reflect on their own complicity in perpetuating enslavement and enslaved Black people to rise and free themselves should nothing change. By late 1830, copies of *Walker's Appeal* arrived in North Carolina, purportedly circulated, according to one Raleighite, by "misguided & deluded fanatics" intent on "exciting our colored population to scenes at which the heart sickens on the bare recital."[5]

Even White citizens sympathetic to ending enslavement reacted warily to *Walker's Appeal*. "I never read any better adapted to lead the slave to revolution and fiendishness," decried Presbyterian minister Thomas P. Hunt. "Whatever sin there was in slavery, even sinners were not to be expected to have the door opened for the midnight assassin, and unrelating avengers to enter and bathe their hands in the blood of their babes." Rumors quickly spread of Black residents ready to spill blood, inciting some White Raleighites to physically attack their Black neighbors.[6]

The State Assembly responded with the nation's most aggressive Black code, a compilation of sixty-one laws, some dating from 1715, supplemented by thirty new acts passed in 1830 and 1831, including prohibitions on enslaved people living independent of slaveowners, cohabitating with free Black people, and preaching in public. The code placed new restrictions on free Black life, making illegal any gambling with enslaved people or peddling goods without a county license. Neither could they, or anyone, teach enslaved peoples to read or write, leading to the closing of John Chavis's school months later. "If slaves were taught to read," argued one legislator as he waved *Walker's Appeal* in the State House, "they would be more likely to read the inflammatory publications of the day." The code's proponents reasoned that reading and writing excited "dissatisfaction" among enslaved laborers and resulted in "insurrection and rebellion."[7]

The legislature was not done and revisited the pathway to freedom for enslaved peoples. In reaction to *Walker's Appeal*, the legislature stripped county justices of their power to interpret meritorious service. Enslavers wishing to free their enslaved laborers were to petition a Superior Court, giving six weeks of public notice in the *State Gazette* and paying $1,000 [$35,450] as bond to ensure that the newly freed person would "honestly and correctly demean him, her or themselves, while he, she or they shall remain within the State of North Carolina."[8]

Emancipated people could not stay long in North Carolina. Within three months, they had to leave "and never afterwards come within the same." If they did not leave or if they later returned, they could be arrested and sold back into enslavement, the profits from which would be split between wardens of the poor and whoever turned in the unwelcome visitor. If an enslaver emancipated their chattel through a last will and testament, the process became more onerous. Unless the executor of an estate paid double the bond, emancipation could not be initiated until two years after the probate. Freedom no longer demanded meritorious service; it required money. Still, meritorious service remained a consideration, particularly for enslaved people over fifty years old who could be freed without public notice if the enslaver or executor provided a $500 [$17,725] bond and swore that the enslaved person had not paid them to petition for emancipation. Meritorious service remained in the language of the code, defined by what it was not: "Meritorious service must consist in more than mere general performance of duty."[9]

The Black code of 1830–1831 was a proactive effort by White Carolinians to thwart racial terror, but the anxieties persisted. In late August 1831, news arrived of Nat Turner's rebellion in Southampton County, Virginia, during which rebels killed over fifty White Virginians, and dozens of Black Americans died in retaliation. In Raleigh, unfounded rumors circulated that two thousand enslaved people had burned Wilmington, killed hundreds of its White residents, and prepared to advance on the capital, which was "on guard around the clock for several weeks." White Carolinians became particularly vigilant about the Black folks moving among them. North Carolina's assembly passed a law empowering three local justices to call out the militia to track down runaways who were "in any way alarming the citizens of any county."[10]

Proslavery politicians grabbed the moment to denounce all antislavery literature, connecting *Walker's Appeal* and "the first fruits of their diabolical projects" to another new and dangerous publication, *The Liberator*, an abolitionist newspaper "circulated openly among the free Blacks of this city." Under the guise of confiscating literature, constables rounded up about a dozen free Black Raleighites and imprisoned them. A White gang murdered a free Black family in their home. The state militia went on guard around the clock. White men too old to serve in the militia formed a "senior volunteer association," authorizing themselves to help Raleigh's city guard in patrolling its streets. The legislature made it easier to call up the state militia to suppress insurrection and capture "outlawed and runaway negroes." To curb communication among Black Carolinians, the legislature required Black piddlers to purchase an eight-cent [$2.80] license and certify good character with seven justices to peddle outside of their home counties. Still, legislation in reaction to Turner's Rebellion was thin because the legislature had codified so much in the 1830–31 session.[11]

Lunsford Haywood's world turned dramatically upside down. In just two years, all his plans dissipated. As an enslaved man, he could no longer hire his own time or peddle his tobacco as freely as he had, taking his enterprises underground as the presence of the city guard, the state militia, and the senior volunteer association transformed Raleigh into a police state, at least for Black residents. He had the consent of his enslaver and the indifference of White legislators, merchants, and ministers as he pursued his ventures, but now they, too, faced greater scrutiny in dealing with an enslaved man. New emancipation procedures meant he would have to raise an additional $1,000 to post as his bond, for certainly, Eleanor would never cover the expense. He questioned whether the pursuit of freedom was worth the effort because, if emancipated, he would have to abandon North Carolina, Martha, the children, and his parents.

Fire made his decision for him. It was an occasional visitor to Raleigh, most notably in 1816 when it destroyed many stores, taverns, inns, and homes that stood between the State House on Union Square and the Government House some five blocks down Fayetteville Street. In January 1831, the State House roof caught fire, requiring the laying of a new one. As workers soldered zinc nails into place, some hot coals ignited the roof again, and flames devoured the building within hours. "Seldom has the eye witnessed so awful a spectacle as this vast building in one concentrated blaze, streaming from every window and a vast column from the roof," described a local newspaper. Strong winds from the west threatened to spread the fire across the street toward the new Episcopal Church, the State Bank, and—one block beyond—Eliza Haywood's house and Ned Lane's stable quarters. Instead, the State House roof, layered with zinc, pulled the entire structure and the fire inward and downward upon Conova's statue of George Washington. Only his arm, leg, and head survived.[12]

Even before the State Assembly debated how to rebuild, in early January 1832, fire broke out again a few blocks to the south in an outhouse behind Pulliam's Millinery Store, where someone dumped ashes from the store's fireplace. Houses and shops in the surrounding blocks were "small, and built of scantling," many hurriedly rebuilt after the 1816 blaze when, only by exploding buildings to impede the fire's progress, residents had kept it from threatening the State House. Sixteen years later, as fire from the millinery spread along Fayetteville Street and westward along Hargett Street, citizens again tried to slow it by fruitlessly blowing up Turner & Hughes's bookstore and pulling down the city markethouse. Flames overtook some seventy structures, including Benjamin B. Smith's store. He and other merchants "lost nearly the whole of their Stock in Trade."[13]

"Too much praise cannot be bestowed on the coloured population who used every exertion in their power to be serviceable on the occasion," announced *The Raleigh Register*. Lunsford was certainly among them, but probably not for altruistic or civic reasons. In Smith's basement lay all of Lunsford's stock. He lost everything as fire lapped up his dreams of freedom.[14]

When Eliza Haywood died on July 19, 1832, her son Thomas wrote the obituary, celebrating his mother as "an eminent *practical florist and horticulturalist.*" The few enslaved laborers who had survived the auctions following her husband John's death faced uncertain fates. She directed that Jacob, Old Esther, and Mary Jenny be sold to settle debts, insisting that Esther, who had nursed the youngest Haywood children, at least remain among the immediate White family. Then Eliza did what Joel Lane and John Haywood had not. She granted Ned Lane (as well as Moses and Sally) freedom for "meritorious services," leaving the nature of that service undefined and jeopardizing chances that a Superior Court or the General Assembly might approve his emancipation. Even if Ned Lane was to be free, his emancipation came with a condition: "That Ned may continue to live with my three daughters as long as they keep house together upon their providing him with clothes & board & paying him a reasonable compensation, providing he is willing so to do." Eliza left the house to those three daughters—Betsy John, Rebecca Jane, and

Frances Ann—until it could be sold for $6,000 [$212,700]. If it did not sell within six years, she directed the cost be reduced to $5,000 [$177,250], and if not successful, then to be auctioned at any price. Ned Lane could be free, but only by agreeing to raise the Haywood girls, keeping him at their service for possibly another six years until 1838, when Frances turned eighteen years old.[15]

The prospects for Ned's emancipation were meager. During the 1820s, emancipation had become far more charged with racial and political implications. In two of three cases that went before the North Carolina Supreme Court between 1824 and 1832, the justices decided against emancipation and only found in favor in the third case because the enslaver freed the enslaved person specifically for demonstrable "faithful and meritorious service." Following *Haywood v. Craven's Executors* in 1816, the entire system—from Superior Courts to Supreme Court to General Assembly—became stingier and increasingly obsessed with the consequences of individual emancipations.[16]

White enslavers could not afford the visibility of free Black people. "Our slaves," wrote a White Carolinian, "when they look around them and see persons of their *own color* enjoying a *comparative* degree of *freedom*, and assuming privileges beyond their own condition, naturally become dissatisfied with their lot, until the feverish restlessness of this disposition foments itself into insurrection, and . . . breaks down every principle of duty and obedience." As another decried, "Experience has shown that those free Negroes were at the bottom of all riots and rebellions among our slave population." In 1827, the General Assembly reduced the number of potentially trouble-making free Black residents by placing new restrictions on individuals who acquired freedom in North Carolina, like those applied to individuals who found freedom in another state. After twenty days, any newly free Black person faced arrest and a penalty of $500 [$15,250], and if they could not pay, ten years of labor. If they did pay, they could remain another twenty days and then leave or pay another $500. The conditions became codified in the Black code of 1830–1831.[17]

For Ned Lane, Eliza Haywood's failure to properly emancipate him proved fortunate. Although she directed her executors to grant Ned his freedom, after the requisite two-year wait, they never initiated the emancipation process by filing a petition, giving public notice, or posting a bond. In the early 1830s, the climate was not favorable. All petitions to emancipate in 1832 failed to pass the General Assembly. A couple of petitioners were persistent, appealing again in 1833 with some success, but new petitioners were denied. Only one new applicant found freedom in 1833. In 1834 and 1835, another ten petitions went before the legislature, with only one approved. Had Eliza Haywood's executors pursued Ned Lane's freedom, the chances of legal emancipation were slim.[18]

Of course, if Eliza or her executors had petitioned the legislature successfully, Ned Lane might have lingered about Raleigh for years without anyone challenging his presence. Then again, he might have been run out of the state, forced to abandon his family and guardianship of the Haywood girls. He had Eliza's will that promised his emancipation, but he did not pursue it, and he did not push the executors, Fabius and Washington Haywood, to initiate the process. If the Haywoods wished him to remain in service, protecting and raising the young women, they had to ignore their mother's wishes, keeping Ned legally enslaved even as they treated him as a free man. So, Ned Lane remained in the Haywood house, choosing family over freedom as Clarissa had done years earlier.

————

At midnight on March 11, 1834, authorities invaded the New York City home of John Lockley and took him, his wife, and their son to prison. Rufus Haywood identified them as Joe Branch, Tempe Sugg, and Needham, Eleanor Haywood's runaways whom he had been chasing for two years. Under an 1828 revision of New York law, a claimant such as Rufus Haywood could submit a writ of habeas corpus to force fugitive slaves like Joe, Tempe, and Needham into court. The same statute permitted the accused to respond with a writ *de homine replegiando*, a legal measure through which they could demand a jury trial. In response to Southern enslavers' efforts to enforce the Fugitive Slave Act of 1793, many Northern states enacted laws permitting writ *de homine replegiando* to protect Black residents and White Northerners' rights to assist them. Most White Northerners were not necessarily antislavery, but juries were not friendly to enslavers' claims, and they little tolerated Southerners invading their communities and arresting their neighbors. So, Joe Branch submitted a writ *de homine replegiando* to pursue a jury trial.[19]

Coincidentally, another case concerning a fugitive slave and his enslaver, *Jack, a negro man, v. Mary Martin*, wound its way through New York's judicial system. When the case finally reached the state Supreme Court of Judicature in 1834, the justices concurred with the lower courts, striking down *de homine replegiando* as contrary to the federal fugitive slave law of 1793 and refusing Jack his jury trial. Based upon *Jack v. Martin*, the court similarly denied Joe, Tempe, and Needham their right to a jury trial.[20]

In 1835, the New York Court for the Correction of Errors sustained the decision of the Supreme Court of Judicature, concluding that both principle and precedent had established that slavery was a national issue into which the states had no authority to intervene and that an enslaved person, regardless of how long they had escaped enslavement and how much property they had accumulated to establish themselves as a citizen, "was not entitled to trial by jury, or by any other mode different from that prescribed by the laws of congress." Political activists worked for the next six years to encourage the

New York legislature to reinstate the jury trial protection as part of its personal liberties law of 1840, but that was too late for Joe, Tempe, and Needham. Rufus Haywood convinced the judge of their identities, and they returned to Raleigh, where Eleanor Haywood put them up for auction, destroying their family by selling them to separate purchasers for a total of $1,600 [$55,600]. In the end, her vengeance was not worth her effort. She paid her son over $3,100 [$107,750] in salary and expenses.[21]

For Eleanor, worse than the financial loss was that the episode thrust the Haywoods into the national debate over the morality of enslavement, bringing Eleanor the type of attention she resented. Details of the court case circulated widely through *The Emancipator* and *The National Gazette and Literary Register*. Some of Eleanor's Southern friends celebrated her persistence and New York's striking down of *de homine replegiando*, defining enslavement rights so clearly that anyone who "impedes their exercise" was "a violator of the public peace."[22]

In the North, however, the story became a condemnation of the Haywoods as characteristic of the slaveocracy. The American Anti-Slavery Society grabbed onto the story as one of many injustices that gave it purpose. In its first annual report, a few pages after the editors denounced colonization as a vacuous scheme built upon White racism, they related Joe, Tempe, and Needham's arrest, celebrating a revelation that emerged during the trial: "(and we see no reason to doubt it,) that this alleged fugitive is a *first cousin* to Dr. Rufus Haywood, the pursuer," implying that one of the Haywood patriarchs, "a brother of the Hon. Sherwood Haywood," was Joe Branch's father. More likely, Joe Branch's father was Sherwood himself. Eight years later, when Lunsford dictated his story for publication, he used precise language when referencing "my master's white children" and "white boys," as if to differentiate them from other boys and children whom Sherwood fathered. Such a public revelation sullied the Haywood name. No wonder Eleanor vindictively destroyed Joe Branch's family on the auction block.[23]

On the Haywood estates, at the Baptist Church, and in private homes and public functions to which Lunsford escorted Eleanor Haywood and her family, he was privy to conversations about defending enslavement and Northerners' opposition to it. Just as he witnessed Eleanor's debate with Jaquith years earlier, he overheard her complain about Joe, Tempe, and Needham's ingratitude and the New York court case in which they embroiled her family, and he watched as she sold the Branch family, separating them from each other—forever.

Well into 1833, politicians debated whether to rebuild the State House in Raleigh. Why not relocate to a more vibrant economic center such as

Fayetteville along the Cape Fear River? State senator Henry Seawall suggested many reasons why not Fayetteville, including the region's Black population, which was "greater than the white." He did not need to argue too much. Advocates for relocating the State Capitol fought among themselves and failed to mount a successful coalition to force change. So, on the Fourth of July in 1833, a procession marched from the Government House to Union Square, where three thousand people gathered to watch the laying of a cornerstone, followed by orations and a reading of the Declaration of Independence. Governor David L. Swain declared that, with granite quarried about one and one-quarter miles to the southeast, the new building would be "almost imperishable" as "the Capitol of a free State."[24]

Construction of a capitol proved a metaphor for North Carolina's evolving political climate. The Democratic Party had boosted Andrew Jackson to the presidency in 1828 and again in 1832, with overwhelming popular and electoral votes from North Carolina. The Government House saw a succession of Democratic governors between 1828 and 1836, the lone exception being David L. Swain. And if there was to be a new capitol, why not a new government? A group of constitutional reformers, among them William Henry Haywood III, aspired to wrestle the state from the grip of monied interests and address the "anti-republican, unjust, and oppressive" system of representation. In 1832, some tied the new capitol to a constitutional convention, insisting that it could not be rebuilt without "the authority of the people in Convention met for said purpose." In 1835, reformers pushed a bill through the Assembly to call a constitutional convention. It survived the less-democratic Senate by a single vote.[25]

North Carolina's most prominent men arrived in Raleigh in early June 1835, gathering at the Government House to address undemocratic features of the state's 1776 constitution. Over the course of a week, delegates created a more balanced regional representation in the General Assembly and transferred the election of the governor from the General Assembly to the popular vote. Such changes were, in the end, about as democratic as the new constitution would become. White men twenty-one years of age who paid public taxes gained the right to vote for the Governor and members of the House of Commons, but land ownership remained a qualification for voting for Senators.[26]

On the eighth day, a committee resolution came forth to restrict, if not fully revoke, voting rights for free Black Carolinians. Debate was furious. Joseph Daniel of Halifax argued that "cultivating a good understanding with the most respectable portion of our free persons of color" would make them "very serviceable to us in case of any combination for evil purposes among their brethren in bondage." Warren County's Weldon Edwards questioned whether repealing suffrage from free Black men who owned landed property resulted in taxation without representation. Jesse Wilson of Perquimans County worried that "the moment a free mulatto obtains a little property, and is a little favored by being admitted to vote, he will not be satisfied with a black wife. He will connect himself with a white woman." Greene County's Josiah Crudup, the preacher who once angered Lunsford, confessed that "no man could wish more than himself, to see the race of men in question raised from their present degradation," but "some intelligence and moral character were necessary to qualify a man to exercise this privilege." William Gaston of Craven County claimed that John Chavis and other free Black men of the time were "chiefly the sons of White women, and therefore entitled to all the rights of free men." Arguments to preserve free Black suffrage swayed few opponents, and Black Carolinians' voting rights ended by a vote of sixty-six to sixty-one. James W. Bryan of Carteret County articulated the winning argument: "This is a nation of white people—its offices, honors, dignities, and privileges, are alone open to, and to be enjoyed by, white people."[27]

When John Chavis died three years later, he had lost everything—the school, his citizenship, his vote, and his passion for engaging his "sons." Chavis stopped writing letters in 1837, disgusted by the stripping of his citizenship and the outlawing of Black preaching and teaching. That year, he published one of his last sermons, titled "The Atonement," in which Chavis argued for the equality of all humankind in the afterlife. As a theological contemplation, the tract was full of allusions to racial intolerance and bigotry, too much for the Presbytery, which refused to fund publication. In 1778, John Chavis had pledged allegiance to a nation that, by 1837, he realized had no loyalty to him. Although a local newspaper sympathetically reported his death as "passing a long pilgrimage here on earth," family legend holds that, soon after he was accused of breaking the law against teaching Black children to read, several people invaded his home and clubbed Chavis to death, the first violent act in what would become a purge of Raleigh's free Black community.[28]

The constitutional convention and its disfranchisement of Chavis and other Black Carolinians evidenced a conservative backlash arising across the South in reaction to the emergence of Northern abolitionism. At the beginning of the 1830s, William Lloyd Garrison commenced *The Liberator* as an antislavery newspaper, announcing in its first year his intent to form an abolitionist society. In 1833, the American Anti-Slavery Society appeared, citing scripture to declare enslavers "man-stealers" and insisting "that the slaves ought instantly to be set free, and brought under the protection of law." Garrison openly encouraged scattering antislavery tracts, "like rain-drops, over the land." *Walker's Appeal* was only the first, then, of an anticipated library of abolitionist literature that would inspire enslaved Black Southerners to rebel.

In response, proslavery thought, seldom heard anywhere in North Carolina before 1835, found a foothold in the state constitution, transforming enslavement into the ideological foundation for a White Carolinian way of life.[29]

From 1796 until 1831, North Carolina's State House served a state that legitimized enslavement and flourished from enslaved labor. Then it burned, and the decision to disfranchise Black Carolinians in 1835 meant that, when finished, the new building stood not as "the Capitol of a free State," as Governor Swain pronounced, but a monument not only to enslavement but to White supremacy. When Raleighites gathered again for the Fourth of July in 1836, among the procession were stone cutters, masons, and carpenters who worked on the capitol, all hired and all White. Not participating were Black laborers: twenty-nine quarrymen, eight carpenters, eight blacksmiths, and forty-nine hired-out enslaved people who had carried bricks, moved stones, dug foundations, and removed trash. Nine of them came from Betsy John Haywood's house just down the street.[30]

———

For Black Carolinians, the 1830s were a decade of turmoil and terror. Laws and judicial decisions asserted White superiority, forcing thousands of Black folks to adjust their lives to new realities. Proslavery advocates shifted justification for enslaving from a necessary evil to a positive good that benefited enslaved peoples as much as it did their enslavers. There was no room for enterprising Black men in the new racial order. Lunsford acted the loyal and faithful servant, a role that mattered not only in Eleanor Haywood's household but throughout Raleigh. He performed the part even as he pursued his freedom through prohibited economic activities. To avoid arrest and potentially separation from all he loved, he needed to know the script—the laws that dictated Black life—and the spaces in which to perform.[31]

Years later, as Lunsford told The Story, he cited the laws that framed his quest for freedom. He understood the prohibition on hiring his own time from Eleanor: "It is contrary to the laws of the State, for a slave to have command of his own time in this way." He recognized that "the laws forbid emancipation except for 'meritorious services.'" He knew the section of the 1830–31 Black code that codified "if the free person of color so notified, does not leave within the twenty days after receiving the notice, he may be arrested on a warrant from any Justice, and be held to bail for his appearance at the next county court, when he will be subject to the penalties specified above; or in case of his failure to give bonds, he may be sent to jail." Laws dictated Black lives.[32]

So, too, did White perceptions. One day in the late 1820s, Sherwood Haywood sent Lunsford to tailor James Litchford for a new suit. A proper servant and waiter needed to look the part. "I suppose," inquired Litchford, "nothing could induce you to become a free man. You would not take Your freedom if it were offered you. You must be a happy man to be allowed to wear such fine clothes as these, your master has ordered you." Any response that Lunsford offered would unquestionably get back to the Haywoods and not only to them. What message did it send if one of the most visible and comfortable of enslaved Black Raleighites claimed to be miserable? If Lunsford Haywood thought of freedom and escape, who among the enslaved community would not? White anxieties over emancipations and insurrections did not need encouragement. So, Lunsford hesitated before replying. "Oh, of course, no person ever had so kind a master as Mr. H.," he declared. "I often think myself very ungrateful for the favors I receive." He meant none of it. He acted as a trickster, donning the mask of the faithful and loyal servant even as he subverted the rules to his advantage.[33]

Tricksters dominate folk cultures, often as the central figures in folk tales, parodies, and satires. Among Black Americans, African folk traditions of tricksters persisted as well, taking animal, divine, and human shapes. Èṣù, the Yoruba trickster god, limps as he walks because one foot remains affixed in the godly realm even as he traverses the human world. From their use of Br'er Rabbit, Railroad Bill, Brother John, and other tricksters, nineteenth-century Black Americans converted African folk tales into critiques of the greatest inequity found in a "free" nation: enslavement. Lunsford Haywood and other enslaved peoples appropriated the boldness, if not the tactics, of tricksters into their own lives.[34]

For all the credit given tricksters in folklore, few storytellers contemplated the turmoil within the trickster as she or he outmaneuvered their adversaries. Tricksters often appear amoral, doing what they must do to survive. But most humans wrestle with morality. As the tailor took his measurements, Lunsford Haywood's hesitance was one such moment of moral internal dialogue. What exactly did these clothes represent? Were they to symbolize the Haywood family's wealth and status, or were they for his pleasure? Did the Haywoods care at all about his comfort and happiness? In retelling the episode decades later, Lunsford added that when he said that he often felt "very ungrateful" to the Haywoods, he purposefully misled the tailor. He insisted that he had meant that he was unappreciative "to the Lord"—another moment of tricking as he framed his story for a religious audience. As the tailor measured chest and waist, collar and shoulders, inseam and outseam, Lunsford came to the realization that he owed nothing to Sherwood and Eleanor, couching that decision in the language of moral gratitude. Undoubtedly, the tailor told the Haywoods of Lunsford's appreciation.[35]

Lunsford also owed nothing to other White residents of Raleigh. Gabriel's conspiracy in 1800, the Northampton rebellion in 1802, Vesey's conspiracy in

1822, *Walker's Appeal* in 1829, Turner's Rebellion in 1831, and the omnipresent yet seldom seen runaways—time and again, White Carolinians reacted to perceived threats of Black violence by tightening the screws on enslaved and free Black life. For Lunsford Haywood, at least, enforcement was inconsistent, random, and as he phrased it, "winked at." With his stock destroyed in the fire of 1832 and confident that White authorities continued to wink, Lunsford Haywood started anew. He navigated the Black code that prohibited him from hiring out his time, required he get a permit to sell goods, made it nearly impossible for him to sell those same goods in counties beyond Wake, barred him from selling the tobacco that seemed his best option for making money, and made illegal his efforts to learn to read and write. He needed another product to earn greater sales and more money but reduce the possibility of arrest.[36]

The tobacco had been Ned Lane's idea; the pipe was Lunsford's. He saw smokers occasionally burn their lips on pipe stems when tobacco blazed. Imagining the pipe bowl as a whiskey still, he attached a hollowed-out reed to the bowl, allowing excess heat to escape, creating a cooler, more pleasing, and less painful smoke. He sold each pipe for ten cents [$3.50], again targeting his sales to the legislators and throwing in a little tobacco free of charge. The capitol remained under construction, but he met them every morning in front of the Presbyterian Church where the assembly convened, and he sold to them every evening as he escorted them from taverns to their quarters in local inns and boarding houses. Sales of pipes were permitted, but every other step of his piddling—selling tobacco, doing so without written permission from Eleanor, occasionally after sunset—remained against the law. The lawmakers to whom he sold would implicate themselves if he was brought to trial. The rabbit drew the foxes into the briar patch with him, and he made good money off them.[37]

———

For the rest of his life, Lunsford celebrated September 9, 1835, as his day of freedom. It was a Wednesday when he found Eleanor Haywood on the veranda, and together they calculated his value at $1,000 [$34,750]. It had taken at least a decade for him to save enough. He gave the cash to Benjamin B. Smith, anticipating that the widow Haywood would agree to the price. Later that day, Smith paid Eleanor, and when she signed over Lunsford Haywood's enslavement to Smith, Lunsford felt he was free.[38]

Lunsford planned this transaction for some time, and as Eleanor's financial situation worsened, the moment was ripe with opportunity. She had sold the nine-hundred-acre Chatham County farm in April. Lunsford feared enslaved laborers would soon follow. Desperate for money, Eleanor could cheat him out of his profits, a common occurrence among self-hired enslaved peoples. Through Smith, Lunsford offered her quick cash, and she accepted the offer because it was more than she could make from hiring him out, allowing him to self-hire, or putting him to work. Yet, Lunsford was not free. North Carolina law allowed manumission only for "meritorious service," a standard unacknowledged in Lunsford Haywood. Legally, he remained enslaved to Smith.[39]

Lunsford moved into the merchant's household, and he and Martha found an opportunity to celebrate. Nine months later, in the late summer of 1836, they welcomed a daughter, Laura Ann. That they lived in the home of Laura Smith might have been a coincidence, but every child seems to have been named after someone: Edward, for Lunsford's father; Laura Ann, for Laura Smith, perhaps. (If so, then the relationship between Martha and Laura clearly improved over the years.) About ten months after Laura Ann, twin sons—William Curtis and Lunsford Jr.—joined the family, the former seemingly named for Martha's brother, and the latter obviously for his father. The only child whose name perplexes was Maria Bell. There were no Marias perched in the family tree, although, given the naming patterns, it is plausible that Maria was Martha's mother's name. The succession of births after 1835 suggests that Lunsford lived with Martha in the Smith household for at least two years.[40]

But Lunsford did not remain technically enslaved that long. In August 1836, like hundreds of other White Carolinians, Smith fled the sweltering heat and humidity by traveling to Manhattan to meet Northern suppliers and sample new goods for his rebuilt Raleigh store. In the past, Laura Smith had accompanied her husband, but in 1836, she conceded her place to Lunsford. Maybe inspired by his mother's experience in Manhattan, he realized the opportunity at hand. He colluded with Smith to "escape" in New York and gain his freedom, bypassing the process of emancipation in North Carolina—no weeks of advertising on Smith's part, no need to argue for meritorious service, no bond which the stingy Smith would never cover and toward which Lunsford would take unknown years to save. Smith's annual trip to New York was an ideal opportunity.[41]

In the autumn of 1836, New York City was still a city of enslavement. In 1799, the New York state legislature had passed a series of emancipation laws to gradually end enslavement, beginning with children born into enslavement after the enactment of the law. There were thousands who remained without hope of freedom, people born before July 1799. Then, in 1817, the Gradual Emancipation Law revised its predecessor. All enslaved people born before July 1799 would receive freedom on July 4, 1827. Those born between 1817 and 1827, registered as "apprentices" rather than as "slaves," remained unfree for another twenty-one years. The promise was that there would be no enslaved peoples in New York by the late 1840s. When Lunsford and Benjamin stepped into Manhattan in 1836, there were still seventeen enslaved people and countless "apprentices" in the city, the last representatives of a dying institution.[42]

New York's 1817 law included a clause that "if any person, so held as a slave, shall be introduced or brought into this state, . . . he or she shall be and is hereby declared free." So, as Lunsford Haywood walked through Manhattan, he marched into freedom. "And a queer and a joyous feeling it is to one who has been a slave," he later recalled. "I cannot describe it, only it seemed as though I was in heaven. I used to lie awake whole nights thinking of it." A local judge wrote up the emancipation papers, and then Lunsford and Benjamin B. Smith went shopping for supplies for Smith's store. In mid-autumn 1836, two free men—one Black, one White—began their journey homeward to Raleigh.[43]

Not only was Lunsford no longer enslaved, but he was also no longer a Haywood. When he arrived in Raleigh, he was Lunsford Lane, his new name as much a rejection of his enslavement by Sherwood and Eleanor Haywood as his father's appropriation of Lane once had rejected his enslavement by John and Eliza Haywood. The trickster journeyed to North Carolina a new man.[44]

And yet, Smith and Lane returned to Raleigh under the pretense that Smith still enslaved him. The town was more agitated about race relations than ever. One thousand antislavery pamphlets had arrived in Charleston, South Carolina, compliments of the American Anti-Slavery Society. News, and a few of the pamphlets, quickly spread to North Carolina. White Carolinians gathered in Hillsborough to denounce "Northern Fanatics," and in Pittsboro, where they demanded local postmasters "suppress the circulation of papers of an incendiary character." For years, Southern newspaper editors had reported the activities of Northern abolitionists, and the American Anti-Slavery Society's postal campaign magnified their scrutiny. They praised meetings such as one in Worcester, Massachusetts, during the summer of 1835, where the audience hissed at the antislavery lecturer, tore up his notes, and ran him out of town. They condemned the "great anti-slavery meeting" of early autumn 1835, the first of the New York Anti-Slavery Society. And they became suspicious of mail sent to free Black Carolinians, fearing the dissemination of *Walker's Appeal* and other antislavery tracts.[45]

———

Years later, Frederick Douglass exclaimed, "I am now in the eyes of American law considered a thief and a robber, since I have not only stolen a little knowledge of literature but have stolen my own body also." By that same logic, Lunsford Lane might have argued that in the eyes of America, he was now an entrepreneur, having acquired his own body and more than a little knowledge not only about producing tobacco and pipes but also managing sales and marketing by wrapping the tobacco in paper printed with "Edward and Lunsford Lane." It was quite a moment: a commercial product not only independently produced by two Black men, both enslaved as far as the public knew, but marketed with new names. Lunsford shed the Haywood surname publicly, and Edward discarded the familiar Ned employed by his enslavers. Still, to avoid drawing attention to himself, Lane sold his goods as an enslaved man with his enslaver's permission. No one need know he was a free man yet.[46]

Orders for tobacco and pipes addressed to "Edw'd & Lunsford Lane" began to arrive at the Raleigh post office. "I became known not only in the city, but in many parts of the State, as a tobacconist." Lunsford's claim should be read cautiously. Stores throughout the state widely advertised tobacco products, often with statements such as "10 Boxes smoking Tobacco—prepared in Guilford county; a new article to be tried by those who love the pipe." They advertised "choice tobacco" of good or superior quality, sometimes flavored as "honey dew tobacco." No one advertised Edw'd & Lunsford Lane tobacco or pipes. His reputation as a tobacconist circulated by word of mouth in small circles, primarily among legislators.[47]

Still, tobacco sales boomed, particularly as Raleigh filled with politicians recently elected to statewide office. It was the first gubernatorial race under the rules of the constitution of 1835, including direct popular vote without the participation of free Black men. Early in the campaign, Edward B. Dudley of Wilmington appeared as the frontrunner. A Whig with substantial experience in the General Assembly and the United States Congress, Dudley openly despised Andrew Jackson and Martin Van Buren. He promised North Carolinians an extensive internal improvements program to enhance the state's economy and bind it to the rest of the nation. Dudley campaigned against incumbent Richard Dobbs Spaight Jr. by suggesting that the Democrat might reinstate Black voting rights. Democrats responded that Dudley "thinks it to be our duty to give our daughters in marriage to the indian savages!!!" The accusation perverted Dudley's position on the Cherokees of western North Carolina. He simply suggested that White Carolinians settle around them so that "the Indian character, if the breed remained, would become *extinct*." For Democrats, however, only one thing was as repugnant a thought: "Had Gen. Dudley advised us to liberate our negroes for the purpose of intermarrying with them."[48]

Although the election took place in early August 1836, results trickled in and not until well into September did officials declare Dudley the winner by four thousand votes, ending the parade of Democrat governors. "REDEEMED!! REGENERATED!! AND DISINTHRALLED!!" declared a Whig paper. With

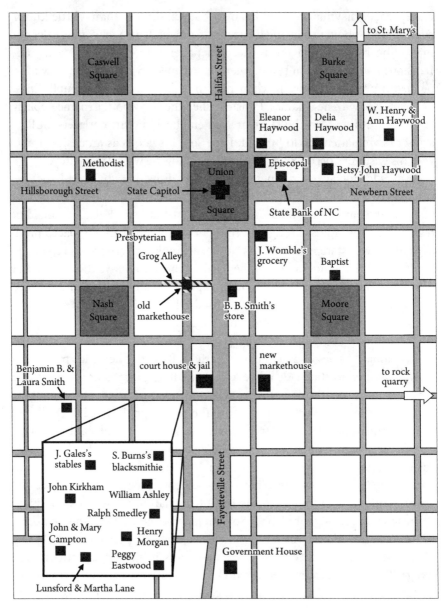

Lunsford Lane's Raleigh, circa 1840. Drawn by Craig Thompson Friend.

the capitol still under construction, senators and congressmen squeezed into the hall of the Government House at the foot of Fayetteville Street, and Chief Justice Thomas Ruffin swore Dudley into office. But declarations of a shift in the state's politics were premature. Democrats retained a narrow majority in both houses of the state assembly, and they appropriated much of Dudley's internal improvements program, hoping to steal his thunder. They could not. He outmaneuvered his opponents and took full credit for legislative successes, boosting his popularity.[49]

For the hundreds of White laborers in Raleigh who voted Democratic in 1836, the Whig victories and Dudley's bluster over *his* internal improvements plans infuriated. Only a year earlier, during the constitutional convention, Democrats secured White voting rights and erased Black voting rights, certain that the move would deliver control of state government. Now, the Whig Dudley was governor. In late June, as Whigs planned the state's Independence Day celebration, hundreds of Democratic mechanics and laborers gathered across town to "confer and co operate with a committee of the citizens of Raleigh, in making arrangements for the two bodies to celebrate the day in conjunction." The Whigs rejected their offer. The ceremonies went as expected: a procession, prayer, a reading of the Declaration of Independence, and an oration. The only mechanics or laborers to participate were those employed in building the capitol.[50]

Dudley was a friend to more than just the Cherokees. His private secretary, Christopher C. Battle, hired Lunsford Lane as his attendant. Battle attended frequent meetings of the Board on Internal Improvements and the Literary Board, but he also responded to summonses of the Governor's Council. Unable to give "attention to the Executive Office, which the Private Secretary had formerly done," Battle employed Lane as a "door-keeper" to wait on the Governor and staff the office, including filing documents, delivering mail, and waiting upon committee meetings. Lunsford's hire was not merely practical. The Governor knew Lunsford from years earlier when Dudley joined the Haywood clan by marrying Elizabeth Haywood, daughter of Henry Haywood Jr. The new Whig governor wanted the optics of a Black man serving a central role in his office. Expecting resistance, he never asked the legislature to approve the hire.[51]

Lunsford's years of networking as a waiter and an attendant to drunk politicians paid off. He had a salaried job: $4 [$131] a month. He also "kept my eyes and ears open as well as I could." The only drawback, and a crucial one at that, was that Lunsford could no longer sustain the fiction that he was enslaved.[52]

Chapter 6

Freedom in a Briar Patch

For over three decades, Ned Lane helped to raise John and Eliza Haywood's children. After Eliza's death in 1832, for the first time in his life, he served the Haywoods of his own choice. He lived with Betsy John, Rebecca, and Francis, but they were no longer girls. The youngest, Francis, was fifteen years old. What Ned did not bargain for was that the daughters were not the only Haywood children in the house. Three brothers—seven-year-old Edmund Burke, eighteen-year-old William Davie, and twenty-six-year-old Thomas Burgess—also remained. If they became too much of a burden, Edward Lane had a route to freedom and could initiate it at any time.

Betsy John Haywood was the most exciting woman in Raleigh. She turned down a marriage proposal in the late 1810s, and the family prophetically worried she would never wed, her father insisting that she consider Nathaniel Macon, the great Republican politician thirty-eight years her elder, as a potential suitor. She politely refused. When she visited the nation's capital in the early 1820s, she returned to Raleigh inspired by the city and its social scenes, modeling new fashionable dresses that left "bosoms and necks . . . almost entirely bare." Betsy John was educated, sociable, and tended to laugh too loudly at the most inopportune moments, which is why, as she grew up, her father relied more on his daughter to host guests like Lafayette and Calhoun than he did his perpetually sick wife, Eliza.[1]

In 1837, however, Betsy John faced a difficult situation. She had less than twelve months before the executors auctioned the two-acre estate with its large two-story house, nine outbuildings, and garden "in a high state of cultivation, . . . arranged as to unite the most beautiful flower garden with a large one for the cultivation of Vegetables." She and her siblings wanted to keep the house in the family, devising a plan to grant their interests to Betsy John who then sold the estate to her brother-in-law, Charles Manly. In turn, Manly offered it back to Betsy John at a significantly reduced price, with her brothers making up the difference with Manly. She was ecstatic. "Can I ever cease to remember that through the liberality of my three elder brothers," she rejoiced, "I am enabled to remain in the home of my childhood!"[2]

Still, Betsy John needed money to feed the occupants, send her younger brothers to college, and maintain a house that was slowly becoming a money pit. Fabius recommended his sister open a school, and another brother, Alfred Moore, insisted that "their will not be sufficient Time, for the Notice; unless you Advertise at once." When her sister Rebecca married and moved to Wilmington in early 1834, Betsy John grasped the opportunity. Months later, she and Frances had twenty-seven girls in their classes, and Ned Lane served them all. At least the students went home each evening, giving Uncle Ned some relief.[3]

Four years later, Betsy John decided to transform her academy into a girls' boarding school. Her cousin, William Henry Haywood III, thought, "There is no situation in Raleigh better suited for the school than your house." She would have to do something about her brothers. Burke was still young, and once she finalized his guardianship, Betsy John could manage him, but how could she draw young female boarding students with William and Thomas living in the house? William had returned to Raleigh the previous year with a degree from the University of Pennsylvania School of Medicine but was restless and floundering in purpose. Thomas had struggled a decade longer, dropping out of a Connecticut military academy in 1827. He scoffed at the overly masculine culture of the academy, preferring art to discipline and pretty women to manly culture: "I have not as yet learnt to drink wine smoke cigars—swear—how many Girls hearts I have broken." William Henry Haywood III warned Betsy John that her brothers, "being grown men cannot live with you." Yes, it was best that William and Thomas leave.[4]

Fortuitously for Betsy John, three years earlier, the eldest Haywood sons, John and Washington, had invested in a 320-acre farm in Greene County, Alabama. Washington remained in Raleigh, but John moved to Alabama to manage the cotton farm. When economic depression struck with the Panic of 1837, the cotton market collapsed, and John hesitated to expand the farm, limiting the number of enslaved peoples he migrated there. Only Charlotte, a nursing mother, invalid Abner, pregnant Sarah Ann, and Maria were "at the hoe & poor hands too." By late 1838, the economy seemed to rebound. John solved both his and Betsy John's problems, having Thomas and William escort seventy-three enslaved laborers, many formerly on John and Eliza Haywood's rosters, to the rich cotton fields of the Old Southwest.[5]

By the end of 1839, Betsy John had her boarding school, and her adult brothers and sisters were gone, except for twenty-two-year-old Frances, who, like Betsy John, would never marry, dedicated to the boarding school for the next five decades. With no more Haywood children to raise, Uncle Ned might have felt released from his obligation, but he stayed—an arrangement of convenience. He had room and board and proximity to his wife, son, and grandchildren. In return, he catered to Betsy John, Frances, and dozens of precocious, aspiring Southern belles.

———————

Unlike Lunsford's father, who, despite his unrealized freedom, was in a secure situation at the Haywood house, Martha and the children remained exposed to the whims of enslavement in a potentially unfriendly household, and his mother remained enslaved to Eleanor Haywood, who continued to face financial challenges. As a free man, he could have petitioned for their freedom, but the General Assembly had become miserly with emancipations, letting petitions die in committee even when based on "merit and good behavior." In the late summer of 1838, one of Lunsford's friends, Henry Patterson, who inherited his freedom from his White mother, lobbied the legislature to emancipate his wife, Emeline, fearing what would happen should her enslaver die. Patterson made the case for her "industry, quietness & good order." He gained the support and signatures of eighty-five White Raleighites, including Benjamin B. Smith, William Boylan, and William Henry Haywood III. In early December, Patterson's petition died by two votes.[6]

With Smith's help, maybe Lunsford Lane could free his wife and family without appealing to the legislature. He offered to buy them, reaching an agreement with Smith to purchase them for $1,000 [$32,820]. Lunsford was too eager. Smith increased the price to $3,000 [$98,470], a figure more aligned with rates in the New Orleans slave market. Lunsford pushed back, negotiating and eventually settling on $2,500 [$82,050] to be paid in five annual installments, the first due months later in January 1839. Lunsford sacrificed a bit of his freedom in contracting with Smith, becoming indebted to someone who expected Lane to not only make the payments but provide for the family as well, even though Smith still enslaved them.[7]

Lunsford could not so easily protect his mother. Eleanor Haywood relied on Clarissa as much as ever, renewing her social life after several years of mourning Sherwood's death and desperately trying to salvage the inheritance. Clarissa catered regular afternoon teas, during which Eleanor aspired to regain her social prominence. As Eleanor's children brought their own children to visit, Clarissa again found herself Aunt Clarissa. How many times must she have wondered what life would have been like had she stepped into the pandemonium and freedom of Manhattan years earlier?[8]

When the Panic of 1837 threw the national economy into chaos, Eleanor faced a new round of demands from her creditors, selling a large tract of land in Edgecombe County to stave them off. She then turned to her enslaved inventories, selling as many as twenty-four from St. Mary's. For enslaved laborers, including Clarissa, economic depression brought day after day of dread.

When Eleanor relocated another seven enslaved laborers from St. Mary's to the Raleigh estate, only seven people remained on the farm, making clear that she no longer expected it to sustain the town estate.[9]

The economic troubles of the late 1830s made Lunsford Lane's purchase of a lot and house in 1838 quite remarkable. In early October, he paid $53.50 [$1,750] for part of town lot 53, an oddly narrow parcel of land with only 35 feet fronting Cabarrus Street and 218 feet stretching northward. Real estate purchases were simple: because real estate transactions were between takers, they were localized, with laws varying from state to state. Property laws in North Carolina differed from those in Massachusetts, which contrasted with those in Ohio. Usually, a neighbor or acquaintance sold property to an individual who then became indebted for the sale price. Most did not seek mortgage loans from financial institutions. The mortgage market existed for businesses and individuals with enough real and personal property to provide collateral. Lunsford and other buyers of meager means might apply for a mortgage loan with the help of one or two wealthy White men to cosign. In most cases, purchasers simply registered their mortgages with the county court, acknowledging their debt to the person from whom they bought the property.[10]

Upon signing the deed, Lunsford became an owner but not *the* owner. North Carolina property law retained English common law traditions that distinguished between the equitable ownership of the purchaser and the legal ownership of the seller. The seller of the sliver of lot 53 was Joseph Gales, the retired editor who once battled his editorial nemesis William Boylan in the newspapers and in the streets. Even though Gales retained the legal upper hand, Lane held interest in the property through his right to redeem it, and he could use it as collateral toward other loans. Robert Williams Haywood, one of Lunsford's childhood playmates and the state's adjutant general, witnessed the transaction, attesting to his faith in Lunsford's ability to pay off the terms of payment.[11]

Soon, Lunsford's economic success, evidenced by his property purchase, drew attention. Drury Lacy, the new Presbyterian minister and a member of the Auxiliary Society, spent an afternoon trying to convince him to migrate to Liberia, promising that citizens of Raleigh would pay his expenses. What of Lane's wife and children? Lacy promised that Lunsford would find a new spouse in Liberia, and Martha would eventually find a new man in Raleigh. "If this proposition had been made at a time when I was in a situation to purchase the freedom of my wife and little ones," Lane reflected years later, "with that understanding that they were to accompany me to that paradise of the colored man—so considered, at least, by the Southern people—I would gladly have entertained the proposition, but as it proposed only my own removal, I simply said I would consider it."[12] Lane's family mattered more than a free life.

Weeks after he bought the house, Martha and the children—Edward, Maria Bell, Laura Ann, William, and Lunsford Jr.—moved in with him, with Benjamin B. Smith's blessing. Lunsford and Martha christened their new home with a flourish. Another child arrived nine months later, dying soon after birth.[13]

A free man housing an enslaved family was not unusual in Southern towns. White demands for craftsmen, servants, and other laborers created markets for hiring enslaved peoples, and often, slaveowners found it more convenient and lucrative to allow those whom they enslaved to just live with partners. The Black code of 1830–31, however, forbade "any free negro or free person of colour to intermarry or cohabit and live together as man and wife with any slave." Should constables decide to question Martha and the children living independently of their enslaver, Smith faced a $100 [$3,280] fine for permitting them to do so. In such circumstances, enslavers negotiated ways to guarantee that they continued to oversee and control their enslaved humans. As Lane described, Smith signed a bond that "transferred my family into my own possession," explaining the arrangements for anyone who questioned six enslaved people living separately from their owner, although Smith remained answerable for them. The bond, combined with the clothing that Lunsford had bought his family, distinguished them from enslaved peoples, making his family appear free, at least to the 1840 census taker. Census takers were not patrollers; they just wanted numbers. So, the census taker counted and made assumptions about the seven people crammed into the small house.[14]

If Smith and Lane pretended that little had changed, magistrates would not demand Lunsford leave North Carolina or charge Smith with allowing his enslaved people to live with a free Black man. Ironically, the deception drew attention. In August 1839, a grand jury decided that Lunsford had broken the law. He was an emancipated man who had come to North Carolina and lived freely for four years, well past the twenty-day window allowed by law. At its next session, the Wake County Court of Pleas and Quarter Sessions ordered the sheriff to arrest the "Defendant slaves of Benjamin B. Smith"—Lane and another free Black man, Isaac Hunter—for "going at large as freemen and having their own time." Like Lane, Hunter had gained his freedom in New York and returned to live in North Carolina. Smith did not correct the court's assumption about enslaving the men, offering a $500 lien on his properties as surety that both men would appear at court in February. The situation was more than a charade: the court refused to acknowledge Lane's and Hunter's emancipations, and later that of Waller Freeman, who also gained his emancipation in New York and then returned to Raleigh.[15]

Despite the fire of 1832, Benjamin B. Smith's miserliness in providing for Martha and the children, and the economic malaise brought on by the Panic of 1837, by January 1839, Lunsford made enough money for the first annual payment to purchase his family. In 1840, Martha gave birth to another son, Alex, the seventh child to join the family. Considering the increasing number of children, Smith did not raise his asking price for the family's freedom.[16]

———

Lot 53 sat four blocks south of the construction at the State Capitol and half a block to the west, occupying the southeastern quadrant of a town block. Farther west, by two blocks, sat Benjamin and Laura Smith's home. The Lanes' immediate neighbors were small landowners, many of them free Black folk and a few White residents of meager means. A stable stood nearby where Joseph Gales continued to keep his horses.[17]

Even Whig newspapers described free Black folks as "poor," "malicious," "vengeful," "harassing," "begrudging," and "loitering around the corn field fences of their white neighbors, in broad day light, just for the purpose of hearing something or seeing something to the disadvantage of those white neighbors"—a projection of what White people had done to their Black neighbors, enslaved and free, for over a century through searchers, patrollers, and their own intrusions. Lunsford Lane was not a poor loiterer, dallying about, waiting for White Raleighites to stumble. He was busy making a life and a family, and so were his neighbors.[18]

Next door to the Lanes lived the Camptons—John, Mary, and their son, Richard. Nine years younger than Lunsford, John had been free his entire life, thriving as a successful carpenter and house joiner, one of Raleigh's more economically successful Black men. Although free Black men such as John Chavis and Lunsford Lane relied on White men to secure property purchases, by 1840, several Black men were fiscally sound enough to fill that role, Campton among them. Since at least 1837, he bought and sold town lots, gradually amassing some money and a reputation for assisting others in their dreams to rise, acting as surety for Sam Jones's property purchase and co-signing on Waller Freeman's property deed.[19]

Alongside John Campton's co-signature on the deed was that of Henry I. Patterson. Born three years after Lunsford Lane, Patterson, like Campton, always lived a free man. He was a plasterer and brick mason, occupying lot 61 with his wife, Emeline. Twice, he applied to the State Assembly to emancipate her: the first in 1838 when the assembly voted it down, and the second in late 1840 when his petition died in the Committee on Private Bills. A Democratic congressman introduced a bill directly on the floor to aid Patterson. It failed eighty-two to twenty-nine, and Emeline remained enslaved.[20]

The recipient of Campton and Patterson's goodwill was Waller Freeman, a friend of Lunsford Lane. In 1804, his father, a free Black farmer named Lewis

Freeman from Chatham County, purchased Waller's mother, Maria, from her enslaver. Before the deal was complete, Maria gave birth to Waller, and the infant followed his mother into enslavement even as she walked away from it, forced to leave her baby behind. As Waller grew up, he was sold to enslaver after enslaver, finally ending up among the Haywoods. Eleanor Haywood's daughter and son-in-law, Delia and George E. Badger, purchased Waller in the late 1820s. In their household, he met his future wife, Eliza, an enslaved domestic. In 1832, Waller's father arranged to purchase his son but kept him enslaved so Waller could remain in the state, hiring his son out to Raleigh merchant Ruffin Tucker. Three years later, Freeman petitioned the General Assembly for his freedom, but the appeal died in committee. So, in October 1837, as Lunsford Lane had done two years earlier, Waller accompanied his employer to Manhattan, where Tucker helped him log a deed of manumission with the city register. Like Lunsford, Waller returned to North Carolina knowing well the prohibition against him staying more than twenty days, but if Lane could hide in plain sight, why not he? Waller and Eliza began to create a family. In 1840, he bought a parcel of land for $50 [$1,770] on the eastern edge of Raleigh and built a home, but he lived there alone. Eliza and their children—Julia, Emily, William, Francis, and Henry—remained enslaved on the Badger estate.[21]

Isaac Hunter, too, was an acquaintance of Lunsford, having been arrested together for "going at large as freemen and having their own time." Born enslaved in 1809 onto the inventory of Theophilus Hunter Jr., by his teens, Isaac found himself sold to a Raleigh shoemaker. John Holloway struggled as a boot and shoemaker, often finding himself behind on debts, including in 1823 when the city auctioned off "George, Alexander, and Bill, Boot and Shoe-Makers; Sam, a Blacksmith, and Letitia, a valuable house girl," all confiscated from Holloway to cover back taxes. Isaac's situation was uncertain, and like Lunsford, he decided to find a way to freedom. Holloway permitted him "to do small jobs for himself and by great industry and saving he accumulated from his small gains a sum sufficient to buy himself." Enslaver and enslaved agreed on a purchase price of $800 [$24,450], and the young man set to work making the money, opening a cobbler shop in Chapel Hill. Several years later, when Hunter paid his enslaver half of the asking price, Holloway decided that Hunter was worth more, raising it to $1,200 [$36,675]. For years, Hunter traveled the state, crossing into Virginia and even into Northern states, plying his trade and making money. Around October 1838, Hunter paid Holloway the original asking price plus interest and traveled to New York where, like Lunsford Lane and Waller Freeman before him, Hunter acquired emancipation papers and then returned to Raleigh convinced he could live freely.[22]

One might wonder why, as Isaac Hunter traveled into Northern states, he did not just fly. As with so many free Black men, such as Henry Patterson and Lunsford Lane, he wanted to secure more than his freedom. Isaac aspired to save his wife and children from enslavement as well. On William Boylan's estate, where Martha Lane's brother continued to labor despite his debilitating injury, lived Emily and their three young children—William, Betsy, and Hezekiah. In late 1839, Isaac convinced Boylan to sell Emily and the children for $2,800 [$91,900]. Hunter paid half of the bill and agreed to pay the remainder by February 1842.[23]

Another friend of the Lanes was Allen Jones, seven years Lunsford's senior. As a celebrated blacksmith in the 1820s, having "shod all the stagehorses on the routes," Jones became well-known and successful. In 1828, when Delia Haywood settled her husband's estate, she sold Jones's wife, Tempe, and their three children—Monroe, Bethana, and Charles. A year later, Allen Jones bought them for $600 [$19,700], and by the time the census taker arrived in Raleigh in 1830, he and Tempe had added William and John to the family. Two years later, he bought a house on a parcel of lot 128 and set up a new blacksmith shop. He committed to helping other Black Raleighites, counting five enslaved and four free people in a separate household that he purchased in 1841. They were individuals he tried to protect legally, as in 1832 when he purchased a plot of land on the east side of town, the house and orchard sitting on it, and the occupant—Ephriam Andrews. Jones helped Black land purchasers such as Rachel Campton and Sam Jones by co-signing their deeds as a trustee. He also committed to the uplift of Black children in Raleigh, joining with local Quakers to establish a school just beyond the town limits.[24]

A neighbor of the Lanes, John A. Copeland Sr., five years younger than Lunsford, was, like John Campton, a carpenter and house joiner by trade, engaged in that work since emancipated by his enslaver's will in the late 1810s. He married Delilah Evans in 1831. Never enslaved, Delilah worked as a hired servant alongside two other free women and six enslaved domestics in the house of Thomas and Ann Devereux. In 1839, upon inheriting several farms and over fifteen hundred enslaved people, Thomas abandoned a profitable legal practice to become a full-time planter and enslaver, keeping a house in Raleigh for social and political access. Delilah, nursemaid to the Devereux children, received "allotments of food and clothing" as her pay and often accompanied the family to visit Ann's relatives in New England. Since Delilah was free, the Devereuxes did not worry that she would fly. She could leave at any time, but she was anchored emotionally to her husband and growing family in Raleigh. Her frequent absences and meager compensation burdened

John with sustaining their three young sons, John Anthony Jr., George, and Henry, who, in the same age range as the Lane twins, became friends with William Curtis and Lunsford Jr.[25]

A distinct free Black community thus took shape in Raleigh, anchored by the Camptons, Freemans, Pattersons, Joneses, Hunters, Copelands, and Lanes, but the southern neighborhoods in which they lived were not comprised entirely of free Black households. Peggy Eastwood, a widowed White woman, lived next door to the Lanes. Silas Burns, a White blacksmith from Massachusetts who came to Raleigh to join in building the capitol and a prominent member of the Raleigh Mechanics Association, occupied a nearby blacksmith shop. John H. Kirkham, a tinware worker, purchased a lot adjacent to Lane and John Campton in March 1841. Their lives and property histories relate the economic realities that bound free Black Raleighites and White working-class Raleighites together.[26]

There were others living in the neighborhood as well, runaways hiding and relying on free Black families to help them survive. When Eleanor Haywood sold Colin to a Georgia farmer in 1839, he found his way back to Raleigh, evading discovery for years. He was the vanguard of a stream of Haywood runaways seeking to reconnect with families destroyed by Delia Haywood's desperation, then Eliza's, and finally Eleanor's. They wanted to undo the tragedies of separation, with little hope that they could truly go home again. In his conversations with them, Lunsford Lane was reminded that, unlike the small farm at St. Mary's where he occasionally had labored, the enslaved laborers on the cotton farms of the deep South, including John Steele Haywood's Alabama farm, felt "the rigors of bondage with no cessation,—torn away sometimes from the few friends they love, friends doubly dear because they are few, and transported to a climate where in a few hard years they die—or at best conducted heavily and sadly to their resting place under the sod, upon their old master's plantation." It made Lunsford's "blood run to chill." The runaway notice for Colin downplayed such conditions, wondering "what did Whitey do that could have made them run?"[27]

Rumors of hidden runaways drew White attention to the homes of Raleigh's free Black families, and beginning in 1831, a three-person board— the slave patrol committee—appointed and supervised guards to keep the peace and maintain racial order. Seven years later, Raleigh's commissioners passed a series of city regulations to control free Black residents. To acquire a permit to simply live in the town, free Black people had to prove "honest, industrious and peaceable character." The city watch patrolled the town every night, keeping an eye out "particularly in respect to Fire" but also all "suspicious or disorderly persons." Yet, it was not Black folks' drinking and carousing that the city needed to worry about.[28]

––––––––

Edward Dudley proved an effective governor, and he expected to win reelection in the fall of 1838 and expand the power of the Whigs in the General Assembly in the process. His Democratic opponent, former governor John Branch, embraced the Independent Treasury Bill, a proposal by President Martin Van Buren to remove government funds from state banks and place them in the hands of a federal agency. During another national depression, it was an unpopular plan, even among many Democrats, and it doomed Branch's campaign. The Whigs retained the governorship and added representatives to the assembly. The Capitol remained unfinished, delayed by problems transporting the quarried granite. The General Assembly moved to a new location, abandoning the Presbyterian Church in which they had met since the burning of the State House, renting a "very spacious building" at the corner of Fayetteville and Market Streets owned by Benjamin B. Smith. Although they could not occupy the Capitol, Whigs hoisted a flag over it in celebration not only of their electoral victories but also of the United States Congress's defeat of the Independent Treasury Bill, infuriating Democrats who decried the partisan "desecration of the capitol of the State."[29]

Lunsford Lane continued in the Executive Office. He served committees, guarded closed-door meetings, and practiced reading and writing. He occasionally slipped a pipe and pack of tobacco labeled "Edward and Lunsford Lane" into the pocket of a passerby. His salary was enough to sustain the family, but he needed more income to meet the house payments and save toward his family's freedom. As an enslaved teen, he had first gone to work chopping wood. As a free man, he returned to it, cutting wood every night and delivering it to a woodyard every morning. He purchased two horses and a cart, offering hauling services. For $5.33 [$190], he bought a strip of land adjoining his lot, 2 feet fronting Cabarrus and 218 feet deep, providing access to McDowell Street and room to erect a storage shed for his wood and his wagon. During "busy operations," he hired someone to help.[30]

All seemed to be going well until Jordan Womble won his first local election. As a deacon and clerk for the Baptist church since the mid-1820s, Womble seemed comfortable in the interracial congregation, but when he lost his grocery store in the fire of 1832, his attitude toward Black Raleighites changed. They were unwanted economic competition. Although a Whig, he became increasingly conservative in his racial politics. When requested to superintend a Black parishioners' gathering in the mid-1830s, he refused. In January 1839, he won election as a town commissioner, representing the working-class eastern ward, gaining the title "esquire," and serving as a justice on the Court of Pleas and Quarter Sessions. Ten months later, when the Court directed the sheriff to arrest Lunsford Lane and Isaac Hunter for acting as free men, Womble was one of the three justices who signed the warrant.[31]

1839 was notable not only for Lunsford's arrest but for a new wave of economic anxiety as the nation experienced deeper depression with a second panic. "The Hard Times, the Reduction of Wages, and prices of produce and property & stagnation of business" injured working-class Carolinians. Years earlier, local mechanics and laborers imagined long-term work in constructing the State Capitol at $1.25 to $1.50 [$41 to $49] per day, but as the work stretched over years, many laborers demanded better wages. Commissioners dismissed them from the project, turning to Northern craftsmen and drawing criticism for depriving White working-class Carolinians, "their wives and little ones of bread." As further insult, the State paid the new workers $2 [$66] per day plus their expenses to Raleigh. Northern laborers alone did not threaten Southern White laborers' job security. "What branch of mechanic have we in our country in which we do not find negroes often distinguished for their skill and ingenuity?" demanded North Carolina Democrat Charles Fisher. "In every place we see them equalling the best white mechanics." Many of them, still enslaved, found themselves hired out to work on the Capitol.[32]

As the Capitol neared completion, so did nine years of pent-up anger. "A few proud Aristocrats who would consider themselves contaminated by coming in contract with a mechanic or a laborer, have snatched the reins and knowing the forbearance of this class of men, assume to be dictators for their respective townships and counties," complained one mechanic, warning that working-class laborers "knowing that 'resistance to tyrants is obedience to God,' may rise in their strength and as freemen and American citizens as well as Democrats, assert their rights and bring you down from your assumed importance." Disgruntled laborers gathered in the groggeries to drink, complain, and gamble their frustrations away. In his campaigns for commissioner, Womble positioned himself among them as a champion of their cause, and they reelected him to his commissioner's seat for the next three years.[33]

In seeking the 1840 gubernatorial nomination, Whig John Motley Morehead held a rally in April, speaking for ninety minutes on the failures of Jacksonian Democracy and the virtues of presidential Whig candidate William Henry Harrison. Then, he promoted granting suffrage to free Black people, "exhibiting his character in its true light, of a Patriot, Statesman, and excellent citizen." Many in the working class who did not have sufficient property to vote for the state Senate wondered why propertied Black Carolinians deserved full voting rights before them. In early October, as Whigs poured into Raleigh for their state nominating convention, the prospect of Whig victory and the re-enfranchisement of Black Carolinians became too much to bear for thousands of White Carolinians.[34]

Race became a central theme of the 1840 presidential campaign. Democrats rumored that William Henry Harrison intended to use surplus revenue to emancipate enslaved people and "is in favor of selling white men for debt." The accusations put Harrison on the defensive, forcing him to condemn abolition and declare that neither the states nor the federal government could "do any thing to remove it, without the consent of those who are immediately interested." The Whigs retorted that *The Emancipator*, the newspaper of the American Anti-Slavery Society, admired and extolled Democrat Martin Van Buren, who, in 1821, denounced efforts to strip free Black men of voting rights. Whigs depicted his defense of "beloved free negroes" as "hostility to poor people." North Carolina Whigs insisted that the Democratic gubernatorial nominee, Romulus Saunders, when a member of the House of Representatives, supported the gradual abolition of enslavement. Saunders pushed back, repeatedly claiming that his opponent Morehead was the true abolitionist at heart, warning voters of "Morehead and his colored sympathies," declaring the Whig "dangerous in the extreme to allow free Blacks the privilege of voting for the emancipation of their slave brethren."[35]

With racial lines clearly drawn in the Carolina red clay, Lunsford Lane and Isaac Hunter did not show up at the Court of Pleas and Quarter Sessions in February 1840. Benjamin B. Smith attended, queried by justices about the missing plaintiffs, and again required to give surety of $250 [$88,620] for each of his "slaves" who refused to appear. The justices levied a judgment *nisi* against Lunsford and Isaac: that unless they appeared before the next court in May, Smith would lose "his goods and chattels, lands, and tenements."[36]

Amid the racialized and politicized atmosphere of early summer 1840, Whigs and Democrats gathered in Raleigh to celebrate the opening of the new State Capitol and, more generally, Raleigh's coming of age. It was a three-day affair with a parade, dinner, toasts, public readings of congratulations, the illuminating of Capitol Square and the Government House, two-hour excursions aboard the recently completed Raleigh & Gaston Rail Road, and two nights of dancing in the Senate chamber: "They ate and drank, and danced—What then? They danced, and drank, and ate again!" And they toasted "the City of Oaks, with her Grecian Capitol." The town finally achieved the sociability and respectability that John Haywood had promised Eliza so many years earlier.[37]

Lunsford Lane was among the servers who heard the toasts, watched the dancing, and escorted drunk celebrants back to their hotel rooms. He had been moving the Executive Office into the new Capitol, alongside the first-floor offices of the Secretary, Treasurer, and Comptroller. The Senate and Hall of Representatives inhabited the second floor, with a rotunda separating them. The third floor housed the Supreme Court and a library. Edward Dudley had about six months remaining as governor, and Lunsford was uncertain if his own tenure in state government would end with Dudley's. In early August, when Morehead won the governorship, riding a wave of Whig victories that gave the party the Senate and House as well, he extended an offer to Lunsford to continue in the Executive Office, proving his critics correct about "his colored sympathies." Lane accepted.[38]

As Lunsford had suspected for some time, his advantages in Raleigh had been winked at time and again. With so many working-class White people struggling and angry, a free Black man in service to the Governor felt like a slap to their faces. Jordan Womble certainly thought so, as did another town commissioner and justice of the peace, Willis G. Scott, who had been among those who penalized Benjamin B. Smith for failing to control his "slaves." Two weeks after Morehead's victory, Womble and Scott approached Lane, handing him a note. "Read it," ordered Womble, "or if you cannot read, get some white man to read it to you."[39]

To Lunsford Lane, a free man of Colour

Take notice that whereas complaint has been made to us two Justices of the Peace for the county of Wake and state of North Carolina that you are a free negro from another state who has migrated into this state contrary to the provisions of the act of assembly concerning free negroes and mulattoes now notice is given you that unless you leave and remove out of this state within twenty days that you will be proceeded against for the penalty proscribed by said act of assembly and be otherwise dealt with as the law directs given under our hands and seals this the 5th Sept. 1840.

Unless he left, Lane faced imprisonment and a five-hundred-dollar [$17,700] fine. Staying in Raleigh threatened his freedom and also the long-term prospect of purchasing his family. Even if he remained and paid the fine, only twenty days stood between him and rearrest and repayment. The winking had stopped. Lunsford could no longer hide, quite visibly, in the briar patch.[40]

———

As Lunsford Lane experienced when Womble and Scott handed him his walking papers, the fall of 1840 marked a moment when White Carolinians no longer willingly overlooked Black activities. Womble and Scott were magistrates who acted on the petitions of citizens, and someone was unhappy that Lane existed as a free Black man. That someone also disapproved of Isaac Hunter and Waller Freeman, who, with Lunsford, were the only three men who had traveled to New York to gain emancipation. In September 1840, each received notice that he had twenty days to leave before a fine, imprisonment, and sale back into enslavement.

In the waning months of Dudley's administration, Lane asked his powerful employer to aid him in requesting that the law be suspended. Lane's supervisor, C. C. Battle, composed a letter of support.

> Lunsford Lane, a free man of Color, has been in the employ of the State under me since my entering on my present situation. In the discharge of the duties I had from him, I have found him prompt, obedient, and faithful. At this particular time, his absence to me would be much regretted, as I am now just fixing up my books and other papers in the new office, and I shall not have time to learn another what he can already do so well. With me the period of the Legislature is a very busy one, and I am compelled to have a servant who understands the business I want done, and one I can trust. I would not wish to be an obstacle in the execution of any law, but the enforcing of the one against him, will be doing me a serious inconvenience, and the object of this letter is to ascertain whether I could not procure a suspension of the sentence till after the adjournment of the Legislature, say about 1st January, 1841.

It was a bureaucrat's letter, full of concern for the workings of government rather than Lane's future. Washington Haywood, once Lunsford's childhood playmate and now a Wake County attorney, convinced Womble and Scott to delay initiating the twenty-day countdown until the legislature considered Lane's appeal, a courtesy they extended to Hunter and Freeman as well.[41]

Lane then penned his petition, most likely with Battle's help, asking to "remain a limited time within the State, until he can remove his family." Drawing upon many years of mingling with the White social and economic elite, Lunsford gathered signatures from Eleanor Haywood; physician Fabius Haywood; state adjutant general Robert W. Haywood; Martha's former enslaver, William Boylan; his employer in the governor's office, C. C. Battle; Charles Manly, an assistant clerk in the House of Commons who married into the Haywood clan and was the governor's brother-in-law; state attorney general Hugh McQueen; merchants William and Joseph Peace; Baptist pastor Amos J. Battle; Presbyterian minister William McPheeters; and the editor of the *Baptist Recorder*, Thomas Meredith. Lane found twenty-six signatories. Most were Whigs. Some, such as McPheeters, once populated the Raleigh Auxiliary of the American Colonization Society. All believed that their status aided Lane's cause. Still, privately, Lunsford fretted, "And why must I be banished? Even after I entertained the first idea of being free, I had endeavored so to conduct myself as not to become obnoxious to the white inhabitants, knowing as I did their power, and their hostility to the colored people."[42]

Among working-class Carolinians, regardless of race, their need to make money took them from job to job and enterprise to enterprise, making them competitors for survival. Simple subsistence was hard for all working-class people, but the Black codes further disadvantaged Black piddlers, hustlers, and laborers, and the sudden decisions to enforce the twenty-day rule added to anxieties by threatening not only Hunter's, Freeman's, and Lane's economic activities but the stability of their families. The Court of Pleas and Quarter Sessions, already frustrated by Lane's and Hunter's failures to appear on previous occasions, demanded new bonds. Benjamin Smith had already paid $750 [$26,600] on Lunsford's behalf, so Lane turned to his patron Robert W. Haywood, who had assisted him in purchasing a house and attempted to protect Lunsford by petitioning to permit him to remain in North Carolina. Five hundred dollars [$17,700] later, the court scheduled Lane's case for February 1841, as were Hunter's and Waller's cases.[43]

Desperately, Isaac Hunter rushed to announce his intentions "to apply to the next General Assembly for a modification of the laws relating to free persons of color, so as to permit me to reside in my native State." On December 2, his petition arrived in the House of Commons, where the secretary promptly referred it to the Committee on Propositions and Grievances. Twenty-two of those who signed Lunsford's petition also signed Hunter's appeal, but Isaac found an additional forty-four supporters, including his former enslaver John Holloway and Benjamin B. Smith, who, strangely, had not signed Lane's petition. Within a week, the committee recommended the House pass the petition. Hunter "is regarded by many of the most intelligent and respectable persons of the City," the committee concluded, "and he is well known as being honest, industrious, peaceable, and orderly." Although opponents tried to indefinitely postpone the resolution, the House eventually sent it to the Senate by a fifty-eight to forty-six count.[44]

Even as the Committee on Propositions and Grievances amended and completed consideration of Hunter's petition, on December 7, Lunsford Lane's appeal arrived in the House and went into committee. He also posted notice: "I intend to apply to the next General Assembly of this State for a modification of the laws relating to Free Negroes, so as to allow me to remain in my native State and among my kindred." The words "among my kindred" revealed Lunsford's motivations. He lived with his family. Leaving North Carolina was synonymous with abandoning them. Just as he once peddled tobacco from boarding house to boarding house and on the steps of the State House, he now wandered from legislator to legislator, pleading with them to support his petition, at one point breaking down in tears as he begged them to allow him to stay. Some snidely replied that he had been better off enslaved.[45]

On December 11, Hunter's resolution moved on to the Senate as Lane's petition sat in the House's Committee on Propositions and Grievances. Hunter's appeal went to the committee anew, was amended, and then considered on December 21, passing on its second reading. He could remain in the state, but the amendment limited his time to only twenty additional days. Later that same day, in the House of Commons, Waller Freeman submitted his petition "from many citizens of Raleigh and vicinity in his behalf," and it was read and sent to the Committee on Propositions and Grievances. He, too, placed notice in the newspaper of his intentions, and word that the Senate approved Hunter's petition made his own chances look good. Lane and Freeman had reason for optimism.[46]

Yet, on December 23, the House postponed Lane's petition indefinitely. Even as the Senate and House approved the amendment on Hunter's petition on December 29, it was clear that Lunsford Lane was not viewed the same way as Hunter. Something had gone wrong. The House of Commons received a petition from over 125 citizens complaining about fellow citizens who lobbied the General Assembly "for the relief or emancipation of several Negroes who live in the City of Raleigh or its vicinity." Decrying the increasing numbers of free Black people "already becoming a nuisance to [the] whole southern country," the memorialists demanded nullification of emancipations acquired beyond the state's boundaries.[47]

When Freeman's resolution returned from the committee, the House had approved it on December 26 despite many assemblymen distrusting wording that Freeman remain and "reside in my native State," seemingly indefinitely. On January 9, the House instructed Freeman to withdraw his petition, refusing to consider it further. Lane's petition suffered the same problem. He requested "to remain a limited time within the State, until he can remove his family also." How long was "a limited time"?[48]

On the same day that Freeman lost his fight, D. H. Guyther, a Whig ally of the governor, reframed Lane's resolution to request that Lane "remain and reside in this State for twelve months from and after the first day of January next." The House passed it, sixty-two to thirty-four. Two days later, in the Senate, Lane's resolution failed, nineteen to seventeen, even after a request for reconsideration by another ally of the governor. Lane waited outside the Senate chamber "that I might receive the earliest news of the fate of my petition." He later regretted that: "I should have gone within the senate chamber, but no colored man has that permission. I do not know why, unless for fear he may hear the name of Liberty." But it was not the name of liberty that he heard as the chamber doors swung open. A senator exited who, upon seeing

Lane, delightfully snarked, "Well Lunsford, they have laid you out; the nigger Bill is killed." The Senate instructed Lane to withdraw his petition and papers, dashing his dreams. Like Freeman, Lane's prospects of emancipating his family dissipated. He carried the petition and testimonials with him for decades, relics of a lost battle.[49]

For most of his life, Lunsford Lane enjoyed an advantaged position among Black Raleighites and a privileged reputation among White Raleighites. His decision to seek emancipation in New York redefined him, at least in the eyes of legislators. It made him a citizen of New York, where Black citizens had the right to testify in court and trade with whomever they wished. For Lane—and Hunter and Freeman as well—the petition was an admission that he was no longer a Carolinian. He broke the law that required free Black persons from another state to remain only twenty days. He wanted the law altered for his specific case. To legislators, many of whom knew Lane personally from years of him helping them to beds at night, waking them in the mornings, and selling them hangover concoctions and flavored tobacco, Lane became foreign. In the final resolution that the House considered, someone even inserted the words "aledging himself to be" when noting his free status.[50]

If the General Assembly's considerations of all three petitions were about rights, then all would have received the same verdicts, but when the General Assembly extended the time a free Black person could remain in North Carolina or when it emancipated an enslaved wife or drew any conclusion about Black Carolinians, the decisions were about the condition of a specific person, not collective rights. Lunsford Lane lost favor in Raleigh. The winking had definitely ended.[51]

Since the Whigs controlled both houses of the General Assembly, partisanship naturally played a small role in the support given the petitioners, but the Senate's final decision clearly did not indicate any loyalty to the Whig governor occupying the Executive Office where Lunsford worked. Most Whigs in the South supported Black enslavement as much as their Democrat colleagues, and the rules of enslavement were at play. Enraged over the audacity of three emancipated men testing the limits of the Black code, many members of the House of Commons resolved to revise the rules by which individuals could be emancipated, targeting specifically how "it has become usual for slaves, purchased by persons who agree to hold them for the purposes of emancipation." The White transgressor faced a fine and imprisonment; the free Black person would be jailed and sold back into enslavement. The bill narrowly failed late in December.[52]

Although Isaac Hunter had another twenty days, that was not enough time to raise the money to purchase Emily and the children. He still owed William Boylan $1,400 [$49,650]. With $422 [$14,650] in his pocket, Hunter fled

North Carolina in early January 1841, headed first to Washington, DC, then Philadelphia, and on to New York. In each city, he earned money and solicited contributions toward his family's freedom, eventually raising $3,108 [$108,020]. Upon his return to Raleigh in late February 1842, magistrates arrested Hunter. William Boylan interceded, insisting that Isaac came only to pay his debt. The transaction was made: Hunter bought his family, including two new sons, Isaac Jr. and Matthias. The Hunters fled North Carolina, settling in Brooklyn, where Isaac resumed his shoemaking trade and advertised as a physician. Over the years, he and Emily lost a child but had four more. In May 1852, after a man assaulted twelve-year-old Isaac Jr., Hunter protested that "John Stevenson, a *white* man beat, bruised and mangled my son. Isaac H. Hunter is *colored* in a shameful manner"—his emphasis on skin tones attesting to the weight of the racism that he experienced in the South and carried to the North. Isaac Hunter died in the summer of 1876, heavily in debt, leaving his wife and grown children to deal with the resulting lawsuits.[53]

Waller Freeman and his brother, John Freeman, abandoned Raleigh days after Isaac Hunter, soon after the General Assembly rejected his petition. They journeyed to the nation's capital, where Eliza and the children had been taken by her enslaver, George E. Badger after he accepted President William Henry Harrison's invitation to serve as Secretary of the Navy. Freeman negotiated with Badger to emancipate the family for $1,800 [$62,550], and he began to work towards their freedom.[54]

Lunsford Lane remained in Raleigh longer than the others. On the last day of December, the House's Finance Committee considered whether his pay as an attendant to the governor was reasonable and warranted. Determining that the State had not fully compensated Lane for his work since July, the committee resolved that Lunsford should receive $24 [$830]. Democrats eagerly took advantage of the investigation to debate whether C. C. Battle had the authority to hire an attendant in the first place. Governor Dudley had employed staff with abandon: clerks to sell Cherokee lands, a surveyor, agents to sell subscriptions for a proposed railroad, and Lane. They portrayed Whig spending as excessive. In a critique titled "Views of the Whiggery," they condemned those who "have charged to extravagance the necessary and inevitable expenses of the General Government, and thus raised a false clamor for electioneering purposes." The hiring of clerks, a surveyor, an attendant, and railroad solicitors had "no legislative authority." Democrats in the Senate blocked compensation for Lane. To further emphasize Whig corruption, they noted that Lane was to receive eighty cents [$27.50] a day as doorkeeper for the Governor's Council, but only when it was in session, typically one day a month. Instead, Lane had earned a $4 [$140] monthly salary. He already received more compensation than he deserved.[55]

Only when many of the Democrats took a legislative break did Whig legislators manipulate the rules to pass the resolution, ordering the Public Treasurer to give Lane backpay and formerly ending Lane's employment. He received his money in mid-January and left North Carolina soon thereafter.[56]

When the Wake County Court convened in February 1841, Lane, Hunter, and Freeman had long since fled the state, threatening the bonds that Benjamin B. Smith, Robert W. Haywood, Charles Manly, and A. B. Stith had posted for their court appearances. The sureties requested a delay until the May term, again posting $500 [$17,375] for each man. Still, the Court passed judgment, concluding that neither Lane, Hunter, nor Freeman was free, insisting that, having broken the law and avoided court trial, they were fugitives from the law. The Court then found Smith guilty of "indentured hiring slaves their own time," fining him $2 [$70] and court costs.[57]

It is ironic that, given the runaways whom Lunsford Lane met over the years, his flight from North Carolina was not the type of fugitivity he ever imagined. Lane pushed the law as far as he could in Raleigh, and as he traveled northward, he, too, was a runaway—not as an enslaved man seeking freedom but as a free man evading "the crime of wearing a colored skin."

Chapter 7

The Quest

Lunsford Lane needed help. Years earlier, when he and Benjamin B. Smith had visited New York, Lane met several abolitionists and developed relationships that he strengthened during trips in 1836 and 1839. They might provide guidance, if not money, to his cause. Joining him on the journey was shoemaker John Jones, once enslaved by former governor David L. Swain.[1]

Travel went smoothly to Washington, DC. With letters of introduction in hand, Lane and Jones called upon Joseph Gales, son of the former editor of the *Raleigh Register*, who remembered Lunsford's father from gatherings at John Haywood's house. In 1805, Gales had moved to Washington, where he cofounded the *National Intelligencer* and, in 1813, formed the partnership of Gales and Seaton, which became the official printer to the United States Congress. As Lane remembered it, after a short visit, Gales offered "a few lines to our mutual friend, Gideon Smith, of Baltimore; you may have some trouble in getting through."[2]

The trouble was kidnapping. Lunsford had known since childhood that White men often snatched free Black people to sell in the Deep South's slave markets. By the early 1830s, kidnapping was an epidemic across the Upper South. Kidnappers targeted Black travelers, anticipating that their victims had few local connections to vouch for their identities, seizing them "on suspicion as runaway slaves, thrust into prison, confined sixty days or more, and sometimes sold into bondage for their jail fees" as abolitionists described. As Lane and Jones traveled from Washington to Baltimore, they moved among enslaved peoples, freedom seekers, and free Black travelers from the South and the North. Opportunities for kidnappers abounded.[3]

As in Raleigh, where a city guard, sheriffs, searchers, a voluntary citizens patrol, and individual slaveowners occupied multiple levels of policing over Black residents, Baltimore, too, was an enslavers' city with layers of surveillance. The police and a less official citizens' patrol enforced laws and guarded the city. Within the system, kidnappers posed as enforcers of the status quo. The federal Fugitive Slave Act of 1793 allowed them to hold a suspected runaway slave, appeal to a local magistrate for certification to take the victim into custody, and return the person to their enslaver for a handsome reward. Maryland laws assumed a Black person to be enslaved until confirmed otherwise, and if proven to be free, the law assumed some criminality.[4]

In 1841, Baltimore housed three commercial slave dealers who actively rewarded kidnappers, including the infamous Hope H. Slatter, who openly defended his mission "to buy negroes and send them to the South." Slatter held enslaved people in a prison on Pratt Street, which he advertised as "large, light and airy, and all above ground, with a fine large yard for exercise, with pure delightful water within doors." Others called it "a well-known hell on earth" where humans, as many as forty at a time, crammed into small cells until prices at the New Orleans markets became favorable. When British abolitionist Joseph Sturge, cofounder of the British and Foreign Anti-Slavery Society, toured the United States with American poet and abolitionist John Greenleaf Whittier in 1841, he confronted Slatter about the morality of the business, specifically the separation of families. It was easy to demonize Slatter, but Sturge also questioned, "*Who* is most guilty in this atrocious transaction—the *slave owner*, who sold thee the woman and child at Baltimore *thou*, the transporter of them for ever from their husband and parent—*the purchasers* of the mother and child at New Orleans, where they may be for ever separated from each other—or the *citizen* who, by his vote and influence, creates and upholds enactments which legalize this monstrous system?"[5]

Lunsford Lane and John Jones arrived in Baltimore on a Saturday, lodging at Henry A. Butler's boarding house. A free Black man, Butler catered to Black visitors, making his establishment a regular target for kidnappers. The next morning, Lane and Jones attended worship services at different churches, and afterward, Lane waited at the boarding house for Jones to return for dinner. He did not wait long. Three White men, identifying themselves as constables, entered and arrested Lunsford, escorting him to Pratt Street, where they had imprisoned his traveling companion.[6]

Lunsford carried his papers—his letters of introduction, his manumission, and a permit to travel. When he realized that they had confiscated Jones's papers, he shared only the permit, fearful they would destroy the others. Lunsford insisted that he was a free man, promising to prove Jones's freedom at trial the next morning before Justice of the Peace Joseph Shane. Reluctantly, his captors allowed him to return to the boarding house, where Butler dampened his hopes, relating how Shane seldom decided a case in favor of accused fugitives, despite any abundance of evidence. Lane needed someone with more clout to help and reached in his pocket for another piece of paper: Gales's introduction to Gideon Smith, editor of the *American Turf Register and Sporting Magazine*, a monthly dedicated primarily to horseracing. Smith's connections were extensive, among them Thomas Yates Walsh, an attorney with a reputation in Baltimore's criminal courts as "a master at cross-examination, a keen wit and a magnetic pleader before a jury."[7]

The next morning, Walsh and Lunsford stood before Esquire Shane. The officers claimed they received letters requesting they capture two men who escaped enslavement in North Carolina, but when Walsh demanded they present the letters, they could not. He dove into a masterful lecture on the rampant kidnapping of free Black people in Baltimore and the "unprincipled men" who gobbled them up for the New Orleans slave trade. In the absence of proof of Lane's and Jones's enslavements, Walsh demanded Shane consider the evidence of their freedom. Both men had emancipation papers and letters of introduction from White men whom Shane and Walsh knew in Washington and Raleigh. Walsh offered to have Gideon Smith testify how he knew Benjamin B. Smith and the circumstances behind Lane's emancipation.[8]

Then Walsh turned to his defendants' character: "How had these men come into the city? Not in the night time, crawling away under cover of the forest to escape the sight of men, but in broad daylight, upon one of the public conveyances; they repair to a respectable boarding-house, kept by a colored man, known in this city for his uprightness of character." He queried, "How did they spend their Sabbath? Not secreted from the public, shut up in those secluded hiding-places for runaways, but they arrange their plans, as Christians should, to attend the house of God on the day set apart for his worship." Such were hardly the actions of men in flight. As for the men who stalked their prey in the shadows, Walsh denounced them as "not the authorized officers of the law, but agents of individuals interested in consigning free persons to slavery." The judge conceded Walsh his case, and Lane and Jones escaped Slatter's kidnapping syndicate. A month later, a free Black man from New York, Solomon Northup, was less fortunate, kidnapped and confined in William H. Williams's slave pen in the District of Columbia before being sold southward into twelve years of enslavement.[9]

After an evening at Butler's inn sharing stories of Lane's bravery and Walsh's cunning legal mind, the Carolinians set out the next morning. In Philadelphia, Lane sought out a Mr. Cauthen, recently involved in the rescue of three kidnapped men. Cauthen recommended Lane attend an abolitionist meeting where he would find activists sympathetic to those who "escaped the 'gins and traps' of the soulless slave-trader." At the gathering, Lunsford shared his designs to purchase his family, the collection plate circulated, and, suddenly, he realized what he needed to do. Money could be made just by asking for it.[10]

The events in Baltimore terrified Lane, and after the visit to Philadelphia, he returned to Raleigh to check on his family and gather more documents to secure his travels to New York and Boston. He arrived in early May. Five leading citizens signed a testimonial confirming that "his habits are temperate and industrious, that his conduct has been orderly and proper, and that he has for these qualities been distinguished among his caste." Church clerk

Madison Royster certified Lane's membership in the Baptist Church and his "good moral, Christian character." Lane handed Benjamin B. Smith $1,070 [$39,500] and promised the parcel of lot 53 on which the family lived, signaling that when Lane returned to rescue his family, it would be his last time in North Carolina. Finally, Lunsford bought Laura Ann, his seven-year-old daughter, paying Smith $250 [$9,230] for her and receiving in return a bill of sale. "Know all men by these presents, that for and in consideration of the sum of two hundred and fifty dollars, to me in hand paid, I have this day bargained and sold; and do hereby bargain, sell and deliver unto Lunsford Lane, a free man of color, a certain negro girl by the name of Laura, aged about seven years, and hereby warrant and defend the right and title of the said girl to the said Lunsford and his heirs forever, free from the claims of all persons whatsoever."[11]

Then, Lunsford and Laura Ann slipped out of North Carolina before magistrates could corner him. On May 18, the Wake County Court of Pleas and Quarter Sessions convened. When *State v. Lunsford Lane* came up on the docket, he was not there, although years later, he claimed that he attended. The court entered a judgment *nisi* against him, but it was the last time the case arose in court. Robert Haywood lost the bonds that he had posted on Lane's behalf, as did Benjamin B. Smith. Isaac Hunter and Waller Freeman similarly avoided their cases, and their sureties lost the money posted on each man's behalf. Smith nagged Lunsford about repayment of the lost money for at least the next year.[12]

———

By the end of May, Lunsford and Laura Ann arrived in Manhattan where he sought out Henry D. Turner, a former Raleigh merchant who had moved to New York City and who happily wrote another recommendation for Lane, praising his "uniform good conduct." From Lunsford's three previous visits, he was familiar with Manhattan, and for the next three months, he and Laura Ann found refuge there.[13]

Lane began to meet and maneuver through abolitionist circles. He needed $1,380 [$50,950] as final payment to Smith, and he convinced two New York benefactors to pledge $300 on the condition that he first raise the other $1,080. Luckily, hundreds of abolitionists had descended on the city. Just a year earlier, abolitionism splintered between political abolitionists determined to use American politics to end enslavement and the Garrisonians who envisioned abolition as part of a much larger moral transformation of American society. In May, the two organizations held competing meetings in Manhattan, "the American Anti Slavery Society (the branch which goes for Garrison and the 'rights of women')" convening on May 11, and the newly organized

"American and Foreign Anti Slavery Society, (the branch of the abolitionists opposed to Abby Kelley, Garrison, nonresistance, &c.)" holding its own convention just down the street the following day. One report dismissed both meetings: "The two National Anti-slavery societies had considerable to say—a good deal of it in abuse of each other." Lunsford arrived only weeks after the rival meetings, and the contentious aftermath was his introduction to the abolitionist movement.[14]

Lane connected with the "Old Organization"—the Garrisonian wing—and, at some point, met the grand man himself, William Lloyd Garrison, who easily might have dismissed Lane's efforts to purchase his family. During the 1830s, before Lane's first trip northward to secure his emancipation, abolitionists had debated the morality of buying enslaved peoples' freedom. In 1832, Garrison denounced colonizationists, who raised money to send emancipated peoples to the American colony of Liberia, asserting that "it is wrong, and consequently sinful, to give money, or any other pretended equivalent, for 'the bodies and souls of men,' under any pretence whatever." The American Anti-Slavery Society, which Garrison helped to found the following year, took his lead and asserted in its Declaration of Sentiments that "no compensation should be given to planters emancipating their slaves, because it would be a surrender of the great fundamental principle, that man cannot hold property in man." Another cofounder, Lindley Coates, summarized abolitionists' anxieties about their own complicity in the nation's peculiar institution when he argued that, in purchasing the freedom of enslaved peoples, "I would be increasing the traffic in, and enlarging the market for men, women and children" since the enslaver "need not care whether his market is at the south or at the North . . . seeing how his object is to make money out of them."[15]

If Garrison was true to his principles, he should have refused Lane and, as he did in the past, critiqued audiences who contributed to Lane's cause "without ever dreaming that they were trampling upon moral principle in so doing." Garrison did none of that. Instead, he embraced Lane, for whom the issue was neither ethical nor philosophical but personal, inviting him and Laura Ann to Boston. They arrived in late August.[16]

Lane related his story to Garrison who printed it in the September 17 issue of *The Liberator*, introducing Lane to abolitionists everywhere as "a modest, intelligent man, and very prepossessing in his appearance." The Story came first, followed by documentation that Lane had acquired over a year: the complaint given him by Womble and Scott, the intercessions made by Washington Haywood and C. C. Battle, Lane's petition, letters of support from Henry D. Turner, Weston Gales, and Madison Royster, and finally Laura Ann Lane's bill of sale signed by Benjamin B. Smith. "Mark how coolly the transfer is made on the part of the seller!" raged Garrison. "Yet, remember, it is a father buy-ing his own child in republican, christian America: Horrible!" The article con-cluded with a plea for donations to free Lane's family from "the prison-house of bondage," and it could not wait: "Whatever is to be done for Lunsford must be done quickly."[17]

Readers were skeptical, and money trickled in, with Garrison reporting every step of Lane's meager progress. By October, Lunsford "collected but a very small sum," although he garnered promises of "assistance and co-operation" from Boston clergy. Garrison printed a letter received from Ger-rit Smith of Peterboro, New York, who sent $30 [$1,110] and regretted that it "is when the claims of such a case come before me, that I especially feel the folly and wickedness of my 'non-resistance' to the importunities of my friends for my name and credit." Smith was a rising star of the Liberty Party, the political arm of the abolitionist movement, but he had developed a reputa-tion for being "mild," justly earned as his letter to Garrison revealed. As one critic put it, "The moment he was an abolitionist, he lost *caste* and was put among the off-scourings." In other words, Smith lost social standing as he em-braced antislavery, and the effect emasculated him. Still, his gift to Lane fore-shadowed his future as an abolitionist when he would directly aid enslaved people in purchasing freedom and free people in establishing themselves. If Smith "could have beheld the grateful emotions which were depicted in his countenance," *The Liberator* reported of Lane's receipt of the $30, "he would have realized afresh, what he has felt ten thousand times over, how true is the declaration, that 'it is more blessed to give than to receive.'"[18]

News of Lane's cause spread across the North. In Hingham, Massachusetts, a local newspaper editor chastised his more conservative neighbors who avoided debates over enslavement and abolition, believing Southern slave-owners' rights to property constitutionally sacred. Lane's situation offered the opportunity to test whether such people "who dislike Slavery, but are opposed to the Abolitionists" backed up their sentiments with cash.[19]

The argument was ingenious, casting Lane as a property owner as well, with sharp critiques of White Southerners' disregard for Black Southerners' property privileges. Upon paying for his freedom, Lunsford became a property owner, "seized of himself." He carried "a deed of the property (or in other words, free papers)" because the "*prima facie* evidence (viz. his color)" of en-slavement would always precede any claims to freedom. He would also have to purchase his family as property to fulfill their freedom. Then came the strike: "It is a North Carolina abstraction, that tenacious as they are of the right of property in human beings, that right can only vest in people of light complex-ion." The challenge was made. "Now, Anti-Abolitionists, and all ye who insist that the Southerners ought not to part with their slaves without being paid for them," the editor threw down the gauntlet, "here is a chance for you. . . . Please form a line,—walk up single file,—and lay down your money one at a time. We beg of you not to confuse and overwhelm us by rushing in all at once." Lunsford Lane went to Boston to raise money to save his family, but he quickly became a symbol of redemption-by-purchase, as he phrased it, that forced northerners, White and Black, abolitionist and anti-abolitionist, to wrestle with their convictions about buying freedom.[20]

On November 1, Lane called on Charles J. Spear in Boston. A Universalist and leader in the ending of capital punishment, Spear felt under the weather but begrudgingly welcomed the company. Lane shared his story, causing Spear to ponder, "Oh! How strange! In a land boasting of its free institutions, a man should be unable to have his own wife and children!" But he offered no donation. Two days later, Lane again visited, begging Spear to use his influence to solicit donations. Spear responded with a series of purely academic questions: What was food like in the South? Enslaved labor? Slave auctions and slave traders? The reception of abolitionist literature? He expressed "a deep interest" in Lunsford's situation and hoped Lane would "live to see his wife and children free!" But Spear offered no assistance and, again, no money.[21]

Frustrated and dejected, Lunsford arrived at the quarterly meeting of the Old Colony Anti-Slavery Society in Hingham three days later. The Society advertised for "timid souls to come out; and for folks that have been afraid of other folks' opinion, to show that they have a mind of their own." Warning was given that "If you do go, put both hands to your ears—for horrible things will be said." William Lloyd Garrison addressed the crowd, of course, as did Edmund Quincy, Samuel J. May, and Stephen Symonds Foster, but the draw was a relatively unknown speaker: Frederick Douglass.[22]

Twenty-three-year-old Douglass had arrived in Massachusetts three years earlier under the pseudonym Bailey and accompanied by twenty-five-year-old Anna Murray. They settled in New Bedford, a town heavily populated with formerly enslaved peoples, some emancipated, others self-liberated. Bailey and Murray had a common law marriage, taking on the name Johnson to signify their new start. When the two wed later that year, they again changed the surname to Douglass. For years, the Douglasses made a home in New Bedford, and Frederick attended local abolitionist meetings, learning the craft of antislavery oratory. Later in life, he noted the impact of the first political speeches he heard, one by Oliver Johnson, a confidant of Garrison, and another by Massachusetts Democratic congressman Caleb Cushing.[23]

Like Lane's experiences with Lafayette and Calhoun, early speeches inspired Douglass's passion for oratory. "It was enough for me to listen," he described, "to receive and applaud the great words of others, and only whisper in private." In early August 1841, Douglass uttered his own first great words at a meeting of the Massachusetts Anti-Slavery Society on Nantucket. He told his story of enslavement, prompting Garrison to declare, "I think I never hated slavery so intensely as at that moment." It initiated three months of lecturing in over twenty towns across eastern New England, accompanied by a mentor, John A. Collins, editor of the abolitionist magazine *The Monthly Offering.* By the meeting of the Old Colony Anti-Slavery Society, Douglass had gained a bit of a reputation as "a very eloquent speaker" who "will give us a fair specimen of what the colored man can do in the intellectual way," but he was still far from a household name.[24]

Lunsford Lane was unknown as well, his reputation made solely through Garrison's newspaper. One Highamite wrote that, on the first evening of the meeting, "We had the pleasure of shaking hands with Lunsford Lane, and did not find our fingers soiled enough to speak of, though he clutched them pretty considerable hard." Moving through circles that respected him as a free man, Lane was awkward, and on the second day of the convention, in the morning before the Society officially convened, when he arose to appeal for donations, his speech was brief and unmoving, a simple "statement to the audience, and appeals to them for assistance to enable him to purchase his family from slavery."[25]

Later, when Garrison reported the meeting, he felt obligated to exaggerate Lane's performance, pleading, "How could such a case as Lunsford Lane's be presented to such an audience as was assembled, without exciting in its emotions too deep for utterance?" Anticipating skepticism, he asked, "Why stood he there pleading for a pittance of the hard-earned wealth of New-England's yeomen? Was he incapable of taking care of himself, of earning his own living, that he must come to the barren shores of New-England to solicit charity? Was he an imposter, playing upon the credulity of the people, in order to filch their pockets?" Garrison reassured that "No, there was no mask to be taken off." In comparison to Lane's lackluster presentation, all that needed to be conveyed about the other Black participant's speech was that "our friend Douglas, too, produced a very powerful effect."[26]

Lane's speech, fleeting and ineffective, sparked a conversation that overtook the morning's agenda, delaying a planned debate on the role of political action in abolitionism. John A. Collins expressed reservations about "*ransoming* of slaves by abolitionists." Enslaved people who escaped, like Douglass, "depreciated the value of slaves in the market," while enslaved people who purchased their freedom, like Lane, gave monetary value to enslavement. Since Collins could not do the same for "a poor fugitive with whom he had conversed the day previous,—no more than for the millions still groaning in slavery," he could not justify giving to Lunsford. Samuel J. May, cofounder of the American Anti-Slavery Society, concluded that refusing to help Lane purchase his family was "a matter of principle." After all, the American Anti-Slavery Society long ago denounced compensating enslavers. One attendee, a bit impassioned in the moment, proposed to dissolve the Union rather than pay to free enslaved people. Another participant turned to a friend and whispered, "But I would buy my own wife and children, were they in slavery, why should I not help Lane buy his?"[27]

Then, Frederick Douglass arose. His four brothers and a sister remained enslaved, and although he was not raising funds for their emancipation, he "would be glad to see something done to cheer the heart of one who had been a brother bondman." Yes, insisted Douglass, it was distasteful, maybe even unprincipled, to pay slaveowners as "they ride about in their carriages with the finest of cloth on their backs, with rings on their fingers, and in the enjoyment of every luxury that wealth can buy." But was nothing owed to the enslaved laborers? "Who earns it all? Whose labor pays for it? The poor slaves! Their masters bend not a finger in labor, and then are mean enough in soul to pocket the hard earnings of the poor slave, without giving him anything but just bread enough to support life from day to day, that he may still toil on to enrich them."[28]

Charles Spear, who declined to help Lane days earlier, sat in the audience with his brother, John Murray Spear. John arose to support purchasing enslaved people's freedom. "If my child is seized, and threatened with all the horrors of slavery, what is union to me?" bellowed Spear. "Do I not love my child better than that union?" Pointing to Lane, he continued, "One sits before you, sir, whose wife and six children are now in the clutches of slavery, this is the first anti-slavery meeting he has ever attended." As later reported, several attendees welled up with tears as Spear dramatized Lane's appeal: "'Give me my wife,' he cries, 'what is your Union to me?' . . . But if the question ever should come between Union and Truth, hesitate not for Truth." As his brother spoke, Charles Spear's reticence of the previous week melted.[29]

Despite Douglass's and Spear's opinions, attendees decided not to circulate the collection box, delaying donations until after the Society's evening session to absolve abolitionists from endorsing redemption-by-purchase "or the scheme of purchasing slaves, generally." Cheered by the prospects, Lane became a new man. After the evening session, he spoke again and told his story with a new vigor "in such a manner as to force conviction of its truth, on the minds of all present." Garrison then grabbed the spotlight, demanding with righteous indignation how any system could be tolerated in which a man could only gain possession of his own child "for the sum of $250." The collection box came out, and when combined with some gifts Lane solicited the next morning, he pocketed nearly fifty dollars [$1,850] towards his family's emancipation.[30]

The meeting of the Old Colony Anti-Slavery Society opened Lane's eyes to the task before him. Raising money from those who wanted to abolish enslavement was as challenging as maneuvering the laws created by those who wished to retain it, and the debate over redemption-by-purchase remained a serious obstacle to any success. In eliciting sympathies and soliciting money, his story—The Story—proved a far more effective tool than his mere presence and simple appeal. But Lane's success had come from making The Story about family, not principle. Late in November, John Gill, editor of the *Hingham Patriot*, articulated the argument. Would abolitionists "prefer that these children of Lane should continue in slavery, to take part in a bloody insurrection into which the excitements in the North have a powerful tendency to arouse in the colored population of the South?"[31]

As Lunsford learned to negotiate Northern abolitionism, he could forget, at least momentarily, about the surveillance of Southern enslavers. By the end of November, news of the Old Colony Anti-Slavery Society circulated to Raleigh. As *The Weekly Standard* reported, "Among the orators who flourished on that occasion was Lunsford Lane, well known here, and a runaway slave under the disguised name of Douglas." Local newspapers, mostly Democratic rags, expressed minimal interest in Lane specifically, determined instead to raise the alarm that Northern abolitionists and their Southern Whig allies wanted to fill national offices with candidates sympathetic to the antislavery cause, warning that "where ever the 'whigs' have obtained power, in the States, they have done all the mischief they could on this disturbing question." Notice was made that Lane pleaded for funds to purchase his family: "We are not told how the subject ended, but guess the collections on the occasion lacked a 'bucket' full of being sufficient for the purpose."[32]

Surely, someone told Martha that Lunsford's name was in the newspaper, speculating that he could not raise the money. The family remained in the house on Cabarrus Street, reliant on Benjamin B. Smith. Someone took all the wood out of Lunsford's shed with a promise to pay $100 [$3,690], but the cash never came. Lunsford received letters at the Boston post office in mid-December, and although the authors are impossible to determine, Smith was among the correspondents, assuring Lane of his family's safety, checking on when he would see Lane again, and inquiring whether Lunsford had news from Isaac Hunter about the bail money Smith had paid on his behalf.[33]

So, too, must Edward Lane and Clarissa Haywood have heard about their son's activities. Clarissa continued under the threat of Eleanor's financial troubles. Edward remained in Betsy John Haywood's house, still doing some of the shopping, which required him to wander the stores along Fayetteville Street nearby.

As fall turned to winter, Lunsford continued to solicit donations. After a visit to New Haven, Connecticut, he and Laura Ann took the stagecoach to Boston. A snowstorm slowed their travel, and upon arriving at Springfield, Massachusetts, the stage stopped at an inn. The innkeeper asked the occupants, "Do you stop here, or go on?" Lane decided to stop for the night. It was dark, the snow clouds blocking the moonlight. "Walk in, walk in," the keeper encouraged, taking Laura Ann in his arms to carry her. As the interior light illuminated the scene and Laura Ann's skin complexion, the innkeeper dropped her to the floor, turning to Lane and declaring, "You can't stop *here*." Lunsford pleaded, only to receive, "You shan't stay." Lane begged the landlord if there was a "friend to the colored man in Springfield." "I know of none but Dr. Osgood," came the reply. "He likes 'niggers,' they say."[34]

As the clock approached midnight, Lunsford and Laura Ann arrived at Samuel Osgood's door. The pastor of the First Church of Christ invited them in, but Lunsford politely refused, asking for directions to a friendly public accommodation. Osgood knew of one, instructing Lane to "tell them Dr. Osgood wishes them to take good care of you, and Laura Ann—leave your bill *unpaid*, I will settle it, and come and take breakfast with me in the morning." It was more than Lunsford could accept, and he was grateful that the darkness of the night hid his tears. The next morning, Lane paid his own bill and caught the five o'clock stage. For years, he recalled how Osgood spared him and Laura Ann from sleeping in the snow-covered street.[35]

By January 10, 1842, when Lane spoke at the Chardon Street Chapel in Boston, he had raised $1,900 [$70,160], more than he needed. "Hear him! Cheer him!" the advertisements exclaimed. Several speakers addressed the hall in anticipation of Lane relating "the particulars of his case to the audience." He raised another $126 [$4,650].[36]

Accompanying Lane was Charles Spear, now fully dedicated to Lane's cause. Eight years earlier, Spear began advocating for debt reform in Massachusetts, denouncing the laws because "Numerous evils result:—families are ruined:—credit is impaired:—the moral and physical strength is destroyed." He paralleled imprisonment for debt to enslavement itself, arguing that both institutions made a person more like "brutes than human beings," "allowed every creditor to chain his debtor," and exposed "him daily in the market place as we do a wild beast." Just as John A. Collins served as Frederick Douglass's mentor, Spear became Lane's travel companion and guide. Feeling "the luxury of doing good," he "gave up myself to Mr. Lane." Spear quickly recognized that helping Lane could be profitable. "I was getting myself out also," he crowed upon returning from Boston, having profited $70 [$2,580] and "about $125 for Mr. Lane! This was doing a great business. I enjoyed a great deal." But Spear's conscience was not clear. He rationalized in his diary that, although he hated taking money from audiences for himself, why "should my family suffer in advancing the interests of others?"[37]

When Lane and Spear arrived in Weymouth on Sunday, January 23, they found the doors of Union Church locked. Its minister, Jonas Perkins, notorious for refusing abolitionist lecturing from his pulpit, promised to take up a collection for Lane, and during morning services, the good reverend "told the story & took up $23 [$850] & notice was given of a meeting at the Universalist House in the evening" where Lane would speak. Yet, Perkins scheduled a competing prayer meeting, encouraging his congregation to forego Lane's lecture. That evening, the minister met a largely empty church, most of his congregants flocking to rumors that "Lunsford Lane was coming." So many people crowded into the Universalist House that additional benches had to be brought into the aisles. John Murray Spear, Charles's brother, opened with prayer, and then he and Charles spoke before introducing Lane, who, as Anne Warren Weston recalled, "told his story very well & for the space of an hour answered all the questions speered at him." His audience could picture every moment as if they had experienced it themselves, but of course, they could only imagine because all of them were Northern folk, mostly White but a few Black, vainly trying to empathize with Lane's enslavement and desperation to save his family. For them, The Story was, well, a story, albeit an inspirational one. Lane garnered another $41 [$1,510], and the congregation sang "elegant anthems" before Cyrus M. Burleigh, editor of the antislavery The Unionist and secretary of the American Anti-Slavery Society, delivered a lengthy address.[38]

When Weston wrote her sister of the evening's events, she noted, almost as an afterthought, that "Lunsford had his little girl with him." Laura Ann regularly traveled with her father. She was a student at the Abiel Smith School, an all-Black public school opened in 1834 near Boston's First Independent Baptist Church. Black and White faculty taught over one hundred Black students. The school's all-White administration was often at odds with the city over insufficient supplies and outdated textbooks. For Laura Ann Lane, who never knew she could learn to read or write, congregate with other students, and act like a child, it must have seemed magical.[39]

A week later, Lunsford joined a three-day antislavery meeting in Boston. He again engaged Frederick Douglass and another Black abolitionist, Charles Lenox Remond. Garrison was there, too, but Lane met a new crowd of White abolitionists, including Wendell Phillips, Abner Belcher, Abby Kelley, and James Canning Fuller. Delegates from throughout New England and New York attended, so many that the gathering moved to the State House to accommodate the throng. Debates became contentious, particularly a motion that abolitionists call out clergy who "constitute the main strength of slavery in our land." Remond praised the resolution in a lengthy speech during which he noted that, for the first time, a Black abolitionist occupied the convention speaker's chair. Douglass had convened the session on the previous evening, an inspiring moment of Black empowerment in what traditionally had been seen as a White movement. Later, Douglass spoke as well, telling his own story in "the best speech of the evening," in which he mimicked the "southern style of preaching to slaves."[40]

New Yorker James Canning Fuller reported that Lane was not among the advertised speakers, but "he shone brightly" and the attendees begged him to relate The Story. Lane happily obliged, collecting $131 [$4,840]. John A. Collins again objected "that the principle of buying slaves was wrong under all circumstances," but as he wrote of the day's events in his diary, Charles Spear laughed that Collins "was too late, for we were counting the money as he was talking!"[41]

One can only imagine Lane's experience. He had heard Douglass briefly in Hingham, but here was Remond as well, widely considered among the most eloquent of abolitionist speakers. He was second only to Wendell Phillips, who influenced abolitionism's entire school of speakers with his mannerisms, intonations, and cadences. Lane always loved oratory, but the words of Lafayette and Calhoun paled in comparison to the inspirations of Phillips, Remond, Douglass, and Garrison. In the opinions of some White attendees, Lane shared that spotlight. "Both Frederick and Lunsford Lane are noble specimens of humanity," concluded Fuller, although his admiration did not translate into aiding Lane's cause. Weeks later, Garrison publicly questioned why Fuller had not contributed.[42]

Lane, Douglass, and Remond were three distinct types of abolitionist speakers. Remond critiqued Southern enslavement from a distance, having never experienced it. Born into a well-to-do free family in Salem, Massachusetts, in 1810, Remond became an anti-slavery activist as a teenager. By 1840, he was an agent of the Massachusetts Anti-Slavery Society with a reputation as an articulate and persuasive lecturer. Years later, observers compared his rhetorical fieriness to that of Patrick Henry. Douglass, in contrast, denounced the institution as something that was behind him. Born enslaved in rural Maryland in 1818, Douglass escaped but remained a fugitive from Maryland enslavement laws. By 1841, he made a home with Anna and two children, Rosetta and Lewis Henry.[43]

Lane, the eldest of the three Black abolitionists at the meeting, more cautiously negotiated his critiques of enslavement because the system still enslaved a part of him. He, too, escaped the South but as a legally emancipated man. Despite having responsibility for his daughter Laura Ann, he could not make a home in New England because Martha and the other children remained enslaved. Like Èṣù, the Yoruba trickster god hobbled by one foot anchored in the godly realm as the other foot traveled the world, Lunsford limped from one abolitionist meeting to the next, one foot affixed with his family in enslavement while the other trekked across New England.

After Boston, Lane was on the road again to East Abington on January 28, where he collected $36 [$1,330]. Five days later, he and Spear journeyed to Plymouth where, Spear cryptically noted, "I have never seen a stranger sympathy in all the meetings we have had for Mr. Lane." They counted another $60 [$2,220] for Lunsford's cause. On February 4, they attended the tenth annual gathering of the Massachusetts Anti-Slavery Society in Boston without intending to solicit contributions. Upon hearing of Lane's presence, the delegates voted to have him relate The Story. Spear described how, in pleading the cause of three million enslaved people, Lunsford collected a few more dollars, anticipating that "Mr. Lane will soon be off now for his family. Heaven prosper him."[44]

In early January, Lunsford Lane had the money to emancipate his family, yet he remained in Massachusetts through the month, and February and March. Something about the abolitionist cause kept him in New England. He became curious about abolitionism's political arm, the Liberty Party, whose state convention was in mid-February. When the party gathered in Boston's Faneuil Hall, Lunsford met Henry Highland Garnet, the foremost Black advocate for political action against enslavement. Born in Chesterville, Maryland, in 1815, Garnet spent nine years enslaved before escaping with ten other family members. They survived in New York City, where Garnet attended the African Free School and began a career in abolitionism. Lane again heard a young Black man give a powerful speech against which The Story paled in comparison. The audience demanded Lane speak as well, and he raised another $33 [$1,220].[45]

Over the next few weeks, Lunsford Lane prepared to return to Raleigh, where his family awaited. He arranged Laura Ann's continued schooling and for her care should he not return. In late March, James Canning Fuller, embarrassed by Garrison's public admonition, sent $25 [$920] to The Liberator's offices with a memo that read, "I hope, when he goes South, he will do well, and on his return leave not a hoof behind of his family, and that he and they may be abundantly blessed, settle where they may." That was Lane's plan. He wrote Benjamin B. Smith, asking him to secure permission from Governor

Morehead to return to North Carolina. The governor authorized Smith to send a statement granting twenty days of safety but did not write one himself. That should have given Lane pause.[46]

––––––––

Lunsford stepped into Raleigh on April 23, a cool spring Saturday. He planned a quick visit, much like he had done the previous May when he purchased Laura Ann. He would pay Smith, pack up the family, and be on the way to Boston by Monday morning. As he stepped from the train, Lunsford realized it would not play out as he anticipated.

Three months earlier, Raleigh had held its annual city elections, and Jordan Womble's courting of the White working-class vote paid off again, not only for his reelection but also for the campaigns of other local Democrats, Daniel Murray among them. Murray won a commissioner's seat for the city's middle ward and, having heard rumor of Lunsford's impending arrival, led a patrol to arrest him as he stepped from the train. Murray and Womble arranged with Raleigh's recently elected superintendent of police, Thomas D. Loring, editor of the local Democratic newspaper in which he criticized Lane's New England activities, to hold a "call court." Upon finding City Hall, atop a new market house, locked, they sought the largest available space as the crowd of onlookers grew. It was the spacious meeting room in Benjamin B. Smith's store.[47]

Democrats in Raleigh determined to make a point to the Whigs, to the community, and to Lane. Since the Whigs' state convention just weeks earlier at the State Capitol, Democrats targeted Governor Morehead's campaign for reelection, denouncing his "favoritism to his own 'pets.'" Morehead had hired his sixteen-year-old nephew as his private secretary. He employed carpenters from Guilford County, his home county, to work on the governor's residence, "slighting the Mechanics of Wake." Although gone from Raleigh for nearly a year, Lunsford Lane, too, appeared to be one of Morehead's favorites, retaining the doorman title and salary even in his absence. It was a position that many White Carolinians believed no Black man should hold. Lane's return to Raleigh, then, could not have been more poorly timed.[48]

Smith's meeting room overflowed with spectators as Loring read the charge: delivering abolitionist lectures in violation of an 1836 state resolution that condemned "the measures of the Northern Abolitionists." How did Lunsford plead? Lunsford donned his trickster hat, explaining how he was not an abolitionist lecturer. He offered to recite The Story—the events that forced him to leave Raleigh, his desire to rescue his family, and his "last resort" to "call up on the friends of humanity in other places, to assist me." He had wandered "house to house, from place of business to place of business, and from church to church," relating the same tale that he now shared with them. Had his donors been abolitionists? He never asked. He was just happy to take their money. Had his speeches been anti-slavery? No more than the speech he gave at that moment.[49]

By the conclusion of The Story, William Boylan and Charles Manly had arrived at Smith's store to defend Lane, convincing Loring to release his prisoner. When James Litchford, the tailor who once measured Lane for a new suit of clothes, warned that a mob waited outside, Boylan and Manly arranged a guard to escort Lunsford to the train station, encouraging him to leave his money with Litchford to settle his business. The mob followed, determined to investigate further, searching Lane's trunk and carpetbag for "abolition papers." As they did, the city guard escorted Lane to the jail for his own safety. Benjamin B. Smith awaited him, and they devised a scheme whereby Lunsford would slip out after nightfall and sneak to Boylan's farm, the farm where his father had been born as Young Ned into the inventory of Joel Lane, where his wife Martha had picked cotton, and where her brother continued to struggle from once being shot in the back. Lunsford would wait there, on the lands watered with the sweat and tears and blood of his loved ones, until he could board the train the next morning.[50]

As the eight o'clock hour approached, Lane stepped into the night and into the hands of the mob, nearly one hundred strong. Sidney Bumpas, the new minister at Raleigh's Methodist Episcopal Church, described the throng as "composed principally of the very lowest classes of the people." Raleigh lawyer David W. Stone considered them a "most disagreeable mob." Lane later named a few of the men: merchant Willis Scott, who once had accompanied Jordan Womble in handing Lane his walking papers, journeyman printer William Andrews, who eagerly carried a bucket of tar, and Lunsford's next-door neighbors: tinsmith John Kirkham and blacksmith Silas Burns. Their interest in Lane was not new. Two years earlier, these men and other members of the mob had petitioned the General Assembly, demanding it deny emancipation to Lunsford as well as Isaac Hunter and Waller Freeman.[51]

The mob half carried, half dragged Lane to a wooded hill on the east end of Raleigh, adjacent to the quarry from which the granite came for the recently completed State Capitol. Off in the distance, the town's gallows stood well within view. Here he was, surrounded by the mob, the unrestrained and unregulated people about which Lafayette had warned, threatening his life, his rational liberty, and his pursuit of happiness. Someone demanded Lane "tell us the truth about those abolition lectures you have been giving at the North." One of them entreated, "You were always, Lunsford, when you were here, a clever fellow, and I did not think you would be engaged in such business as giving abolition lectures." Fearing they would hang him, Lunsford mustered the courage that, for decades, he witnessed among freedom seekers hiding in Raleigh's shadows, resigned to the worst of fates for the noblest of causes. Months of debate over redemption-by-purchase paid off as Lane sincerely replied that "abolitionists did not believe in buying slaves, but contended that their masters ought to free them without pay." He turned the question upon his captors: "How then could they suppose me to be in league with the abolitionists?"[52]

Frustrated and furious, the men stripped Lunsford and brought forward the pine tar, determined to mete out their own justice. Tarring as a form of public torture had proved irresistible to rebellious American colonists in the 1760s and 1770s determined to leave their marks on oppressive customs officials and Loyalists. As they tarred their way to independence, the ideal of popular sovereignty gave ideological validation to the brutality of tarring. The practice returned in the 1830s, employed by anti-antislavery mobs against White neighbors sympathetic to abolition. In 1837, mobs attacked an abolitionist in Alton, Illinois, riding him on a rail about town for hours before tarring and feathering him and throwing him into the Mississippi River. They then turned on the printing office where he worked, the business of Elijah Lovejoy, whom they murdered two months later.[53]

So, the mob decided to tar Lunsford Lane to reassert the stain of enslavement through a product that once had sustained North Carolina's reliance on enslaved labor. William Andrews dipped his hands into the bucket—suggesting that the pine tar was not hot—and prepared to smear it across Lunsford's body. Once boiled down, the resin is naturally sticky and need not be heated to adhere. Lane's neighbor, Silas Burns, stopped the journeyman, cautioning, "Don't put any in his face or eyes." Three others joined in, covering their victim's face as the tar poured over him. Someone ripped open a pillow and shook it over his head, replacing his pilfered clothes with a coat of feathers.[54]

Then, the mob was done. "They gave me my clothes," Lane later recalled, "and one of them handed me my watch which he had carefully kept in his hands; they all expressed great interest in my welfare, advised me how to proceed with my business the next day, told me to stay in the place as long as I wished, and with other such words of consolation they bid me good night." They were gone as swiftly as they struck, an anticlimactic conclusion to the most horrifying moment of Lunsford Lane's life.[55]

Lunsford's character saved him. "You were always . . . a clever fellow": the mob begrudgingly respected that part of Lane, for he, like they, hustled to survive. He was one of them, moved among them, sold them tobacco, hauled their wood, sat in the same church, lived next door. Two decades later, Lane drew his own conclusion about the event: "They felt that they had now degraded me to a level beneath them," but it was more than that. Lane sinned against them, not by any action but by what he embodied—the freedom of Black people. They believed they had a right, indeed an obligation, to confront it, emboldened by over a century of Black codes, the strengthening of Whiteness over the 1830s, and state supreme court decisions that demanded White Carolinians police their Black neighbors. As Lane resolved, racial hatred drove the mob: "There were many, who did not own the hair of a slave, who were ready to crush me to the earth."[56]

And yet, despite seeing Lunsford's Blackness, the mob's attack on him was not solely racial. The mechanics in the mob construed Lane as a threat to their own ambitions. "The members of the Raleigh Mechanics Association," one of them had toasted at a Fourth of July banquet the previous summer. "May they ever strive to elevate themselves to the great good and moral standing of the illustrious Benjamin Franklin and Roger Sherman; brother Mechanics of the olden stamp." In a 1793 autobiography, Benjamin Franklin articulated self-made manhood as "industry, economy, and perseverance," personal characteristics that warranted individual freedom. Roger Sherman, a Connecticut merchant, clerk, and surveyor, became so successful at self-making that he achieved renown as the only person to sign the Articles of Association of 1774, the Declaration of Independence, the Articles of Confederation, and the United States Constitution—the four great founding compacts.[57]

By the 1820s, the self-made ideal applied to men of various professions, but always White men. William H. Crawford, running for president in 1824, styled himself as a "self-made man; has risen from obscurity by his own exertions," and because of that effort, he "knows how to appreciate true merit." In defining self-made manhood in 1828, Samuel Phillips Newman, chair of Rhetoric and Oratory at Bowdoin College, claimed that Crawford "saw that all his resources were in himself, and he resolved that the power of these resources be tried." Over the 1820s and 1830s, Americans increasingly applied the label of self-made man to White men such as David Rittenhouse, John Sevier, Nathaniel Bowditch, Davy Crockett, Henry Clay, Daniel Webster, Martin Van Buren, Lewis Cass, and Amos Kendall. According to Clay, self-made men acquired "whatever wealth they possess by patient and diligent labor." The ideal assumed that any man could pursue monetary wealth and others' esteem, the only restrictions being those of the marketplace, which included racial limitations.[58]

Raleigh's mechanics dreamed that they, too, could work, persevere, and climb into self-made manhood. If Franklin and Crockett could rise from humble origins, why not they? The answer stood before them. Free Black carpenters, tinsmiths, joiners, blacksmiths, and tobacco manufacturers competed with White carpenters, tinsmiths, joiners, blacksmiths, and tobacco manufacturers. Lunsford Lane bragged that "In the manufacture of tobacco I met with considerable competition, but none that materially injured me." He stood out from the local Black population, more successful than other tobacconists Black and White, and socially visible within the governor's office. He stole their futures. So, the mob desecrated his prominence. His tarring and feathering, his humiliation, standing naked in a field as they covered him with the product of enslaved hands—that was the expiation for his sin against them. Through their ritual of atonement, they granted Lane the right to live.[59]

Lunsford found his way to his family at Smith's house. Having assumed the worst, Martha and the children received him with tears of relief and joyous laughter. Lunsford's embarrassment can only be imagined. Martha began the arduous task of removing the vandalism. Only intense scrubbing or use of irritating solvents like turpentine removes tar, taking hair and occasionally skin with it. Afterward, for the first time, Lunsford held his infant daughter Lucy, born during his months in New England. Then, a rap at the door disrupted their celebration. A few of the mob came to apologize, promising Lunsford safety through the night. He did not believe them. The governor's office posted a guard outside the house for the family's protection.[60]

The next morning, Lane recovered his money from Litchford and redeemed his family from Benjamin B. Smith. While Martha and the children packed their possessions, he went to say "good-bye" to his parents. Clarissa was despondent. As Lunsford remembered, Eleanor Haywood "could not witness the sorrow that would attend the parting with my mother." Eleanor, whom Lunsford once dismissed as selfish, wrote a pass for Clarissa and "told her to go with me, and said that if I ever became able to pay two hundred dollars for her, I might; otherwise it should be her loss." In curious contrast, Lunsford left no remembrance of his goodbye to his father.[61]

Rumor brought hundreds of Raleighites, including many from the previous evening's activities, to the train station to see the Lanes off. As *The Liberator* reported, "There was not so great a crowd when Lafayette went through Raleigh." Realizing the continued threat, Lunsford sent his family to board the train and walked down the tracks to climb aboard as it passed. The Raleigh & Gaston Rail Road departed at ten o'clock on the morning of April 25. As the Lanes rode northward, they turned their backs on the mob, the racialized violence and trauma, and the enslavement of the South. They also left behind their families—Martha's brother, Lunsford's cousins, the Baptist church, their friends and neighbors, and their patriarch, Edward Lane.[62]

From the shadows, Edward may have watched his family depart. He might have boarded the train with them, but he did not, his manumission never legally ensured. What might Betsy John Haywood or her brothers do should he break the commitment he made to them and the girls in her boarding school? He remained enslaved according to North Carolina law, despite Eliza Haywood's final wishes a decade earlier. He was unwilling to become a fugitive slave for the rest of his life, always looking over his shoulder for an enslaver in pursuit.

Even in the aftermath of the horror of the mob, Lunsford was thinking about The Story. As he left that April morning, he instructed Benjamin B. Smith to write a "certain gentlemen in Boston"—Garrison—and confirm the story of the mob that Lane was about to share across New England. In return, Garrison would reimburse the $1000 that Smith had posted to the Wake County Court as bond for Isaac Hunter. Smith wrote, but the reimbursement never came, despite Smith inquiring again months later.[63]

————————

"We merely wished to let the aristocracy know that they should not have their own way," declared one of the men who released the tar-covered Lunsford Lane. For years, Lane benefited from connections to well-off White men in state government and among Raleigh's merchants, two groups that recently were tightening the screws on the town's working class. Because authorities had winked at Lane's breaking of the law repeatedly, the mob justified their vigilantism because "no proceedings, lawfully, were taken against him." David W. Stone denounced the mob's "lawless acts with the 'tar bucket' and a 'coat of feathers'" and hoped that some of them would eventually appear in the superior court so they could be taught "that this is a land of laws yet." Instead, the assault on Lunsford Lane unleashed "the fury of the mob" on Raleigh, as Sidney Bumpas described. But Bumpas and Stone wrote their thoughts in private diaries and correspondence. Public condemnations never came. To the contrary, locals lightly joked about the episode, as when a reporter claimed to overhear several members of the mob discussing how tarring and feathering, "if applied correctly, is an excellent remedy for the rheumatism—it draws to such perfections."[64]

Inspired, the mob organized as the Raleigh Regulators, printing and posting handbills threatening anyone who challenged them. The Saturday following their attack on Lunsford, they marched about a mile and a half beyond town to destroy the school for free Black children that Allen Jones had organized with local Quakers.[65]

A nasty editorial appeared in late April 1842 in The Rasp, a weekly rag printed by nineteen-year-old Wesley Whitaker Jr., who did not take journalism too seriously, filling the paper with jokes, light poetry, and sarcasm and reveling in others' descriptions of The Rasp as "saucy" and "racy." Whitaker was an active officer in the local mechanics association and a "good Democrat." Although he promised to "speak plain facts," he was a sensationalist, excelling even the Democratic *Weekly Standard* in its condemnation of "the notorious" Lunsford Lane. "Will the Old North State—can she remain mute, while her delightful City of Oaks is made the harbor of fanatics who would see every white infant beheaded and rejoice in seeing abolitionism established?" squalled Whitaker. "Our blood boils at the thought, that one, who is a well known fanatic, and an enemy to our institutions, should be suffered to plant his footsteps on southern soil!" Whitaker reveled in the mob's attack and Lane's humiliating tarring and feathering. "Ostrich-like, he was suffered to wend his way to the hospitable roof of his *sapient* protector." The young editor spoke the mind of many White Raleighites who found the events of late April a reminder that free Black people threatened Raleigh's social order.[66]

In November, the superintendent of police, Loring, petitioned the General Assembly, complaining that his efforts to police enslaved and free Black folks had become ineffective because the state did little to enforce its own laws, neither the one that prohibited free Black people from preaching, nor the one that limited their stays upon returning to North Carolina, nor the one that restrained "unscrupulous fanatics" from engendering rebellion. Like Lane, some of those who returned to North Carolina visited Northern cities "where the doctrines of abolitionism are openly as well as secretly advocated and advanced." Even the twenty-day window granted initially to Lane, Isaac Hunter, and Waller Freeman gave them time to infect their enslaved kin and friends with ideas of rebellion and escape. Loring's response to "the machinations of the reckless spirit of Abolitionism" was to clamp down on his Black neighbors.[67]

Black Raleighites found the attack on Lane, the terrorism of the Raleigh Regulators, and Loring's effort to increase a police presence a frightening precursor. Six months after the mob destroyed Allen Jones's school, he "was forcibly taken from his own house, in the dead of night, by a mob, and so beaten, bruised and mangled, that doubts are entertained of his recovery." Although several White residents condemned the beating in a public meeting, they also blamed the victim, who "rendered himself somewhat obnoxious" by advocating for Black education and subscribing to the *National Intelligencer*, the nation's leading Whig paper.[68]

On March 1, 1843, Jones's family joined a caravan of free Black families headed for New Richmond, Indiana: John and Delilah Copeland, unmarried blacksmith John Lane, John and Mary Campton, and Calvin Terry, whom, a week later, enslaver Joseph B. Hinton advertised as a runaway, suspecting that Allen Jones, "of *lynching* notoriety," had lured the young man away. In New Richmond, the group met Amos Dresser, an abolitionist who, some years earlier in 1835, had been publicly whipped in Nashville, Tennessee, for possessing abolitionist literature. Dresser encouraged them to continue on to

Oberlin, Ohio, where the threat of kidnapping was less menacing than in New Richmond. The travelers turned eastward.[69]

Of Lunsford Lane's neighbors and friends, only Henry Patterson remained in Raleigh, but life became more difficult for him as well. He struggled to make mortgage payments as plastering and bricklaying jobs went to White laborers, and by late 1844, he nearly lost the house before he remortgaged through Weston Gales. Patterson did not become financially secure enough to pay off the property until 1847. Over the 1840s, he and Emeline, still enslaved albeit to Henry, who had purchased her, had a daughter and four sons—Mary, Henry, John, Chany, and William—but their time in Raleigh ended in 1852 when the family packed up, joined by Henry's brother, John, and his family, following the trail blazed to Oberlin for them years earlier.[70]

For decades, the North Carolina General Assembly attempted to weaken the influence of its free Black residents. In 1840, Raleigh's magistrates decided that they needed to confront three emancipated men who lived among them. As a result, the Hunters and Freemans fled by the spring of 1841, and the Lanes followed a year later. The terror of Lunsford Lane's assault, Allen Jones's lynching, and the continued mobbing inspired a wave of free Black emigration. They were not men or women who secured emancipation in New York but people who always lived in North Carolina, many free throughout their lives, who turned their backs on their home and the racial violence that made it home no longer.

For enslaved men and women in Raleigh, the path to freedom traveled by Lane, Hunter, and Freeman disappeared under the pressure of the mob. The small group of men—Benjamin B. Smith, Robert W. Haywood, Charles Manly, and A. B. Stith—who had aided individuals in their quests for freedom were as close to abolitionists as one would find in Raleigh, protecting Lunsford, Isaac, Waller, and their families, accompanying the men to Manhattan to secure their emancipations, and willing to spend their own funds to help the men negotiate the court system. The Raleigh Regulators condemned Smith as the "*sapient* protector" who helped Lunsford. Threatening "the point of the bayonet," the editor of *The Rasp* rallied the mob against Smith and the others and "any man, who professes Southern principles" who might, in the future, "declare himself the friend of the aggressor." The warning was enough to dissuade them from helping other enslaved people pursue freedom in the future.[71]

PART II

Restless in the Cradle of Liberty

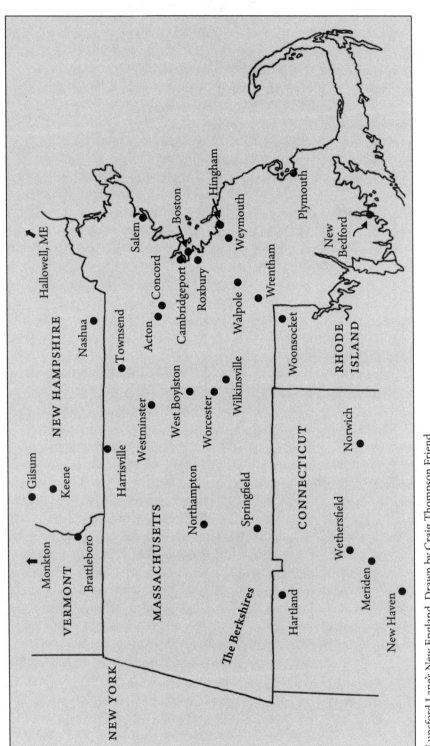

Lunsford Lane's New England. Drawn by Craig Thompson Friend.

Chapter 8

The Search for Identity

"Phizzz-zzz-zzz" roared the steam engine on the Raleigh & Gaston Rail Road as the Lanes rode northward through Wake Forest and Henderson to Ridgeway, where the track turned eastward, crossing the Roanoke River at Gaston. There, the family transferred to the Petersburg Rail Road, taking them into Virginia and their connection to the Petersburg & Richmond Rail Road. Once in the state capital, the Lanes transferred again, taking the Richmond & Fredericksburg Rail Road to northern Virginia, where they dis-embarked, joining other travelers clamoring into carriages to ride nine miles to the Potomac River and the steamboat *Baltimore*. From the decks of the *Baltimore* as it chugged along its sixty-mile, five-hour trip up the Potomac, they caught sight of Mount Vernon slowly falling to ruin on the western bank and a white presidential palace ahead of them as they approached the District of Columbia. They then boarded the Washington & Baltimore Rail Road, transferring again in Baltimore to the Philadelphia, Wilmington & Baltimore line. In the City of Brotherly Love, they changed to the New Jersey Rail Road, finally arriving in Jersey City before finding a boat to voyage across the Hud-son River into Manhattan. The entire journey took over fifty hours.[1]

Lunsford Lane could not afford the fare for his family, and as he had so many times over the past year, he relied on the generosity of strangers. Seymour W. Whiting, treasurer for the Raleigh & Gaston Rail Road Company, paid the family's way to Petersburg. Epenetus P. Guion, a Raleigh hotelkeeper and federal mail carrier along the Great Southern Route, covered them to Washington. Then a Philadelphian, name forgotten, helped them the rest of the way. Each benefactor enabled the Lanes "to pass on unmolested," as Lunsford phrased it, escorting the family at each exchange. Rail cars were inti-mate spaces, and Lunsford expected "to be detained at several places on our way." Every stop, every transfer offered opportunities for a child to be snatched, property stolen, violence inflicted, or the family arrested as suspected fugitive slaves. Among their fellow travelers was John Kirkham, one of the Lanes' for-mer neighbors who had joined the mob in tarring Lunsford. He jumped off at every stop to harass the family and decry Lane as an abolitionist and insur-rectionist. Still, all went as well as the Lanes could expect, although a trunk containing their better clothes disappeared in Washington.[2]

By the 1840s, the concept of "flying slaves" had evolved, replacing Africa as the locus of freedom with the Northern United States and Canada. As Lunsford's mother, wife, and children rode above ground in rail cars, they, too, were flying slaves, travelling through spaces between enslavement and freedom. With the promise of happiness before them, the journey enthralled and empowered them. Clarissa Haywood took on Edward's surname and became Clarissa Lane, Martha transformed from Martha Curtis to Martha Lane, and Lunsford converted his son Alex's name to Alexander. "I want all that belongs to us," he avowed.[3]

Weeks later, as Lunsford stood before an abolitionist audience in Manhattan's Broadway Tabernacle, he related how, upon being told to leave North Carolina two years earlier, "It prostrated my hopes. My money was lost, my bright expectations were lost—my family was lost, and I was lost." Although the money was thin, upon arriving in the North in 1842, Lunsford had recovered his family, his dreams for the future, and himself.[4]

With its steeple climbing 135 feet into the sky, the Broadway Tabernacle towered over Sixth Avenue and West 34th Street, its Gothic Revival sandstone architecture dwarfing the residential neighborhood. Twenty-five hundred people could fill its "audience-room," a circular auditorium with eight tiers of seats and magnificent acoustics. Among abolitionists, the church was sacred ground. Lewis Tappan, cofounder of the American Anti-Slavery Society, helped to found it in 1836. The great evangelist and abolitionist Charles G. Finney served as its original minister. In its hall in 1838, William Lloyd Garrison raged about how "the slaveholders of the South have done us all cruel injustice. . . . And now, we will have our revenge." The following year, during the sixth annual meeting of the American Anti-Slavery Society, Andrew Harris, among the nation's first Black college graduates and a leader in the Black intellectual and antislavery communities, spoke from the platform, fiercely protesting to attendees that "If the blood of the innocent, which has been shed by slavery, could be poured out here, this audience might swim in it—or if they could not swim they would be drowned." In 1840, Tappan and other Tabernacle leaders funded the defense of the *Amistad* rebels, fifty-three Mende captives who, the previous year, successfully took control of the ship transporting them to Cuba and enslavement. When a United States ship seized the *Amistad*, the Mendes found themselves mired in legal cases threatening to permanently enslave them. In March 1841, the United States Supreme Court heard *United States v. Amistad*, upholding a lower court decision favoring the Mendes' return to Sierra Leone. Many of the defendants eventually stood on the stage in Broadway Tabernacle, thanking the congregation before returning to Africa as free people.[5]

In early May 1842, the American Anti-Slavery Society convened in Broadway Tabernacle for its ninth annual gathering, and on the second morning, a little over a month after Lunsford Lane had departed New England to redeem his family, debate erupted over purchasing the freedom of enslaved people. An opponent was in mid-sentence when the church doors groaned open. Heads turned to see "a middle-aged, noble-looking, keen-eyed man, coming in with a child in his arm—accompanied by his wife, who seemed in the prime of life, and a group of bright looking children." Whispers that "it was Lunsford Lane, with his emancipated family" swelled to a collective euphoria as Lunsford, Martha, and six of their seven children—Edward, Maria Bell, William Curtis, Lunsford Jr., Alexander, and Lucy—crossed the hall, the audience huzzahing and applauding as the family climbed the platform. (The Lanes' seventh child, Laura Ann, having arrived in the North earlier with her father, was in school in Boston.) Someone suggested that debate be suspended, but the meeting chairman invited Lunsford to the podium as "the best advocate for the resolution" to redeem enslaved peoples. It all seemed so impromptu as if they had just stepped off the boat into Manhattan, but the Lanes had been in New York for over two weeks before they strode into Broadway Tabernacle. Their timely entrance during a debate over redemption-by-purchase was most certainly choreographed.[6]

Unlike the full, albeit smaller houses to which Lunsford had spoken over previous months, the cavernous Broadway Tabernacle was emptier than not. Disagreements that rent the abolitionist movement into old and new organizations over the past three years had taken their toll. Even within the organizations, members fought over politics, the effectiveness of moral suasion, and redemption-by-purchase. Garrison was among those not in the room to see Lane's return, boycotting the meeting because the Executive Committee refused to schedule a debate on "a repeal of the Union between the North and the South—or in other words, between liberty and slavery." Others followed Garrison's lead so that attendance was "rather lean, the body of the Tabernacle not being half filled, to say nothing of the galleries." Had anyone anticipated Lunsford Lane's arrival in New York City, the opportunity to hear his conclusion to The Story might have drawn thousands and filled the temple.[7]

Lunsford began by introducing his family, declaring, "It is a source of great rejoicing to my heart to present to this meeting, these, in whom my life consists." He explained the previous twelve months—the agreement with Benjamin B. Smith, how the magistrates' warning to leave North Carolina left him feeling lost, how he cried as he begged legislators to consider his petition to remain, how he fled with Laura Ann and placed her in school "to which I never in my life had the honor of carrying a pitcher of water to the scholars," his solicitations across the North, his return to Raleigh, the call court, and the mob. The effect of his emotional appeals to the audience was commanding. Listeners called out: "Where did you live? . . . You have not told us that, yet" and "How did you get away?"[8]

With the Broadway Tabernacle audience engrossed, Lane spun his new climatic chapter of The Story. Insistent on their Southern justice, the mob had carried him toward the town gallows, causing him to fear that "all was gone," but "I then looked anxiously about me, expecting to see the rope and the gallows, for I thought they were going to hang me; but had not dared to do it at the common gallows. While I was looking about, I saw a bucket, and wondered what it was for. Soon a pillow was brought, and then I perceived the bucket was full of tar. They stripped off the remainder of my clothes, and covered me with tar almost from my head to my heels. Then opening the pillow, they covered me liberally with the equipment of an Anti-Slavery lecturer." Lunsford paused dramatically as his audience roared with laughter and cheers. As their ecstasy subsided, he described how the self-satisfied mob let him return to his family, how the Lanes slept little that night, how they boarded a train the next morning for the journey northward, and how, as his family stepped from the railcar into the City of Brotherly Love, "I heard the shackles fall from those who are dearer to me than life."[9]

Then, for his audience's entertainment, Lane theatrically pulled a piece of paper from his pocket, identifying it as the bill of sale for his family and evidencing how purchasing freedom was "like a bill for selling any other property." Lane's friend, Charles Spear, took the stage and read Benjamin B. Smith's description of Martha as a "dark mulatto woman" and the names of the children, each arising or, in the case of the youngest ones, being lifted by their father before the audience. Invited to speak to the crowd on redemption-by-purchase, Lane never mentioned the topic, and yet, he made his point about the righteousness of saving other humans at any cost, inspiring his audience to consider their own emotional—and financial—investments in Black America.[10]

Abolitionists understood and managed the optics of their meetings. Frederick Douglass's mentor, John A. Collins, wrote William Lloyd Garrison earlier in 1842, advocating that Douglass become more visible as a spokesperson for the movement: "Our cause is far advanced, that the public have itching ears to hear a colored man speak, and particularly A SLAVE." Douglass resented being handled and introduced as "'chattel'—a 'thing'—a piece of southern 'property'—the chairman assuring the audience that it could speak." Still, abolitionists did not stop packaging him for public consumption. Following a particularly impactful speech in 1844, *The Liberator* described Douglass as "an insurgent slave, taking hold of the right of speech, and charging on his tyrants the bondage of his race." Except for Lunsford, the Lanes, too, were enslaved, evidenced by the folded receipt in his vest pocket, drawn out and read as audiences gasped in awe. Abolitionists, and White Northerners generally, wanted to hear the voices of enslaved folk, or at least gaze at them.[11]

Over the previous fall and winter, Lunsford had made a name for himself as a unique celebrity: the free Black man striving to save his enslaved family. In Broadway Tabernacle, he transformed into a popular speaker, embodying the lessons learned over years of admiring orators. In Raleigh, he had listened to speeches by men trained in a classical style usually reserved for the White elite. They inspired patriotism and liberty by appealing to the mind. Lane heard, as well, the sermons of White clergy, men also trained in classical oratory whose words, too, were meant for the mind, often to convince audiences of the scriptural righteousness of enslavement. On Sundays, Lunsford had engaged his own debating society around a spring in Raleigh, where he practiced classical oratory with other enslaved speechmakers.[12]

By the 1840s, another form of oratory emerged on American stages and from American pulpits, one more attuned to affecting hearts as well as minds, a more democratic rhetoric that required little formal training. Lane had watched and heard two of the best in this new form—Charles Lenox Remond and Frederick Douglass, both more self-trained than schooled and using rhetorical tactics not only to make audiences think but to stir their emotions.[13]

For years, Remond framed character as a racial issue, denouncing how, in the United States, "the rights, privileges and immunities of its citizens are measured by complexion." He placed manhood at the intersection of race and citizenship, and because Black men could not achieve full citizenship, they could never be complete men: "If the Union had been formed upon the supposition that the colored man was a *man*, a man he would have been considered, whether in New Hampshire or Kentucky." Among abolitionists, models of Black manhood were few, their imaginations stifled by an insistence that enslavement impeded true marriages and fulfilling fatherhoods. Remond offered a model for Black manhood, but he did not represent the rehabilitation of manhood that many abolitionists expected to see from those who escaped enslavement. Throughout the 1820s and 1830s, literature like *Walker's Appeal* informed Northerners' perceptions of enslavement, framing Black manliness as angry and resentful, exhausted by the hypocrisy of "enlightened and Christian" Americans who, if not enslaving Black people, at least supported it for their own security and profit. Abolitionist Hosea Easton insisted that emancipation meant little without enabling manhood: "Merely to cease beating the colored people, and leave them in their gore, and call it emancipation, is nonsense." Only a societal shift in thought about race, one that required the nation "no longer act the part of the thief," would "kindle anew the innate principles of moral, civil and social manhood, in the downtrodden colored American."[14]

Yet, Easton, Remond, and other Black abolitionists of the 1830s were usually men who had not experienced enslavement. Although they had plenty about which to be angry, they could not embody the rage of enslaved Black manhood described by Walker. Men who experienced enslavement did not speak widely on the topic, partially because the abolitionist movement was too embryonic in the early 1830s and then too convulsed in the late 1830s to arrange and manage their performances. William Grimes, who escaped enslavement in 1815 by stowing away on a ship to New York City and authored the first of the American-printed slave narratives, seemingly never lectured. Before he died of consumption in 1830, David Walker spoke of his own life on only a few occasions to Black audiences, encouraging them to acquire educations equal to that gained by White people.[15]

And then came Frederick Douglass, in whom the imagery of anger and resentment found in early representations of Black manhood became personified. Years later, he recalled how, as an enslaved man, he was a "man of war" haunted by "dreams, horrid dreams of freedom through a sea of blood." At an antislavery meeting in Boston in January 1842, Garrison introduced Douglass as epitomizing how "A chattel becomes a man." Three years later, in his *Narrative*, Douglass explained, "You have seen how a man was made a slave; you shall see how a slave was made a man," prefacing his description of how he finally had tolerated enough from his enslaver, "At this moment— from whence came the spirit I don't know—I resolved to fight; and, suiting my action to the resolution, I seized Covey hard by the throat; and, as I did so, I rose. He held onto me, and I to him. My resistance was so entirely unexpected, that Covey seemed taken all aback. He trembled like a leaf. This gave me assurance, and I held him uneasy, causing the blood to run where I touched him with the ends of my fingers."[16]

Douglass was a natural at reaching hearts with his performances of angry and resentful Black manhood, but in 1841 and 1842, he was still cultivating his emotional style of oratory. As one observer described upon hearing Douglass speak, "His eyes would now flash with defiance, and now grow dim with emotions he could not control." Douglass combined emotional pleas with denunciations of "the system" and the sanction that religion gave it. Early, he mastered the expressive performance of oratory and, alongside Remond, transformed the nature of abolitionist oratory in the nineteenth-century United States.[17]

In contrast, Lunsford Lane, having learned the art of emotional rhetoric from Remond and Douglass, remained "modest" and cool in his delivery. He knew that The Story was powerful enough to invite listeners' financial investments. Audiences waited anxiously for the rumor that "Lunsford Lane was coming" and then went out to hear him and cheer him. But convincing audiences of an argumentative point was an entirely different matter. In his speech in Broadway Tabernacle, when "the thrill of joy ran through the assembly," as Charles Spear described, Lane demonstrated that he finally mastered the new oratory.[18]

Lane proved to be unlike other abolitionist speakers. Once enslaved and then free, he understood Douglass's rage against enslavement and Remond's exasperation with racism, but he did not demand abolition or racial justice. That Lane refused to frame his cause as abolitionism did not escape notice. "He never dared say he was an abolitionist in N. C.," remarked one commentator when describing Lane's appearance in Broadway Tabernacle, "but on this platform, I say, if any man ought to be an Anti Slavery Lecturer, Lunsford Lane is the man." He *ought* to have been an abolitionist, but he did not call himself antislavery, and few others appear to have done so either.[19]

Instead, Lane preached the sacredness of family, framing his manly identity through "these, in whom my life consists" and "those in whom my life was hid," inviting audiences to identify with his plight through their own personalities as fathers and mothers, daughters and sons. And they did. Months earlier, abolitionist Increase J. Smith, weighing opposition to redemption-by-purchase against Lane's pursuit to purchase his family, decided that he "could not blame Lunsford for his course . . . in his relation of husband and father." For Northern audiences, Lane's appeal to fatherhood made the abstraction of enslavement tangible. He was a man so thoroughly dedicated to his family and to "all that belongs to us" that he never seriously considered flying from the South, and he willingly risked re-enslavement, tarring and feathering, even death to save his family. The reception to Lane's speech in Broadway Tabernacle was a celebration of the Black family and the victory of Black manhood.[20]

––––––––

Appropriately, many antislavery meetings convened in churches because abolitionism was religion, and abolitionists acted as—and in some cases were—itinerant preachers, traveling and evangelizing from town to town, hoping to proselytize the gospel of antislavery. Charles Spear related his own conversion upon hearing Lunsford Lane speak: "By being associated with him,

I have lost my prejudices; have made myself more free, and advanced the cause of abolition," he rejoiced, concluding, "It has cost me much labour and toil, but I believe that I shall find a warm friend here that will never forsake me."[21]

Philadelphia was where the Lanes first had stepped into the land of liberty, and Manhattan was where they experienced the roar of the crowd celebrating their freedom, but Boston, "where the stern, cruel, hated hand of slavery could never reach us more," was Lunsford's destination. As he fundraised over the previous year, he met hundreds of Massachusetts abolitionists who eagerly donated because they saw him as a cause. Days after Lane's Broadway Tabernacle speech, Spear, still feeling the warm passion of conversion, accompanied the Lanes to Boston where they met with his brother John, far more radical than Charles and determined to use both politics and religion to reform American society. The Lanes moved into the home of Lewis and Anna Dyer Ford, members of the New England Anti-Slavery Society who lived south of Boston in Abington and frequently opened their home in the 1840s and 1850s to some of the most famous of Black abolitionists. Lewis recalled how the Lanes "were a happy family, and I enjoyed their visit hugely," Lewis Ford recollected decades later. Despite other worthies whom the Fords hosted, "I had no visitors that I can today, in November 1889, look back upon with greater pleasure and pride, than that joyful slave family who felt me worthy a visit from them."[22]

The next several weeks were a whirlwind of travel and speechmaking. On May 15, Charles Spear accompanied the Lanes to the home of Nathanial Colver, Baptist minister of Tremont Temple in Boston and ardent abolitionist. Lunsford told The Story, and shortly thereafter, Colver accompanied the Lanes to the American Baptist Anti-Slavery Convention at his church, where Lane again related The Story. The congregation "return our thanks to God for His kind interposition in delivering our brother Lunsford Lane and family from the land and power of American Slavery." The collection plate circulated to aid Lane "in repaying a debt contracted by procuring the emancipation of his mother," and no one complained about redemption-by-purchase. Months later, Lunsford sent Eleanor Haywood the $200 [$7,380] she had requested as Clarissa's value.[23]

On May 22, Lunsford spoke at the annual meeting of the Massachusetts Abolition Society, three of his children joining him on stage. Newspapers across the North reported how "A most thrilling effect was produced upon the audience." Three days later, the entire family stood on the stage at the convention of the New England Anti-Slavery Society at Chardon-Street Chapel in Boston. A day later, the Lanes attended a meeting of temperance advocates at the Massachusetts State House, among whom was John H. W. Hawkins, leader of the Washingtonian Movement, a temperance fellowship of former alcoholics who believed that mutual support, friendship, and shared experiences helped their peers remain sober. Hawkins's twenty-one-year-old son, William, joined his father and gained his first impression of The Story and Lane's family. (Two decades later, William G. Hawkins would discover Lunsford anew and write Lane's first biography.) After the collection plate circulated, Spear concluded, "This finishes the whole story. We have redeemed him and set him upon the world."[24]

Again, Spear might have considered Lunsford's work complete, but Lane was not done. If there was money to make from telling The Story, Lunsford intended to continue sharing it and his family with audiences. In late May, he joined Frederick Douglass at the annual meeting of the New England Anti-Slavery Society. The distinction between the two men could not have been clearer. Lane received an "enthusiastic reception" for his family story, but despite what he had learned about public speaking, he was still a storyteller foremost, and reports of the meeting expressed more interest in his wife and seven children than his message. Douglass gave a rousing address that "makes color not only honorable but fashionable," bringing him praise as a "heroic figure" and foretelling his career.[25]

Audiences had reason to not fully embrace Lane as an orator. They wanted him to declare his loyalty to the cause, but he continued to refuse the label "abolitionist." In late June, he took Martha and the children to a meeting of the Plymouth County Anti-Slavery Society. Mary Weston reported that "he told his story, & as he had to do it in short time it was well told." Well enough, in fact, that attendees lauded Lunsford, declaring that although "the coat of tar and feathers bestowed upon him by the mobocrats of Raleigh, N. C. was not merited on account of his advocacy of the principles of abolition," there should no longer be disbelief "in the minds of slaveholders, that he deserves an anti-slavery dress." Like the suit of tar and feathers forced upon him in Raleigh, the antislavery fashions in which abolitionists clothed him were just as unwelcome.[26]

Even as Northern audiences vacillated on whether Lunsford Lane represented abolitionism or not, back in North Carolina, there was little doubt that he was an abolitionist. News arrived in Raleigh that the American Anti-Slavery Society honored the "scoundrel" in Broadway Tabernacle. Depicting the Society's entire membership as Black abolitionists, young firebrand Wesley Whitaker Jr. portrayed Lane seated beside "the sable president" before an audience of "thousands of the knotty headed tribe." Although Whitaker advertised his paper, The Rasp, for readers "who are fond of fun and a good joke . . . and especially to juveniles," in reporting about Lane, he always remained far more serious in tone even as he fabricated almost everything. Whitaker warned of Lunsford's appearance in New York that "the half is not yet told," claiming to expose the American Anti-Slavery Society's mission to dissolve the Union.

"But this is nothing," he continued; they took steps to arm "abolition missionaries" who would equip every enslaved person with a knife "with which he may cut his master's throat!" Whitaker insisted that his was "no exaggerated account," egging on the Raleigh Regulators to retaliate against Benjamin B. Smith and other Lane defenders in Raleigh: "You know your duty too well."[27]

Among those defenders was Betsy John Haywood and several of her brothers, but they were potentially powerful enemies, and neither Whitaker nor his Raleigh Regulator friends were up to that challenge. The most vulnerable person in Betsy John Haywood's household was Edward Lane, who continued to serve the boarding school students. Sometime in late July or August 1842, Betsy John sent him to market, giving him written consent to be out and about. It should have been enough, but a paper permit would not repel a lead ball. For months, the city guard was on heightened alert against Black rebellion and White mobs, and White resentment of Lunsford Lane was everywhere. Well after sunset, as Edward returned to the Haywood house, a supposed city guardsman shot him in the back. He lay convalescent for months.[28]

Beginning with Lunsford's telling of The Story to William Lloyd Garrison in August 1841, every iteration contributed to an American history that Black writers had begun putting to paper. They pushed back against a national narrative that accepted without critique Thomas Jefferson's depiction of Black Americans that "in memory they are equal to the whites; in reason much inferior, as I think one could scarcely be found capable of tracing and comprehending the investigations of Euclid; and that in imagination they are dull, tasteless, and anomalous."[29]

White scholars, such as George Bancroft, whose education at Harvard College and the University of Göttingen well prepared him for a career as the mid-nineteenth century's preeminent historian, assumed the cultural and intellectual authority of White America. In his ten-volume *History of the United States*, he echoed the Jeffersonian mantra. From Bancroft's perch, the historical heroes of the United States were the Europeans who colonized North America, particularly his native New England, and led a revolution against British oppression. Enslaved peoples benefited from that march toward liberty—"That America should benefit the African, was always the excuse for the slave-trade"—but Africans and their progeny were merely observers to White courage and sacrifice. As formerly enslaved Samuel Ringgold Ward, an abolitionist, newspaper editor, and historian, critiqued in 1855, White America insisted that "our history is that of the chain, the coffle gang, the slave ship, the middle passage, the plantation-hell!"[30]

That Lunsford Lane and hundreds of thousands of other Black Americans could not trace their ancestries beyond their grandparents, if even that, permitted White historians and audiences to dissociate them further from the history of the United States. As Frederick Douglass noted, "You have no ancestry behind you" was the impediment that Black Americans faced in celebrating the past.[31]

In the early nineteenth century, then, Black history foremost became a search for ancestry. In 1834, the National Convention of Colored Peoples crafted a Declaration of Sentiments in which delegates insisted that Black Americans lay claim "to be the offspring of a parentage, that once, for their excellence of attainment in the arts, literature and science, stood before the world unrivalled." That parentage was in Africa which "extended to Greece and Rome those refinements that made them objects of admiration to the cultivators of science." Some of the earliest Black authors, such as James W. C. Pennington, opened their histories by highlighting the greatness of African civilizations—a direct response to White observers who argued that Blackness could never nurture creativity and dismissed Black poets, artists, authors, and orators as "either whites, or so intermixed as to have the benefit of white intellect."[32]

"When I cast my eyes in the bright annals of fame among whites," wrote Black abolitionist, lecturer, and women's rights advocate Maria W. Stewart, "I turn my eyes within, and ask my thoughts, 'Where are the names of our illustrious ones?'" To overcome the historical portrait of Black Americans passively watching White Americans create the United States, thinkers identified Black heroes who demonstrated intelligence, reason, imagination, and a commitment to the nation's purest principles. They considered it critical to connect to the Revolutionary War through the valor of Black ancestors. At the 1840 gathering of the American Anti-Slavery Society, Henry Highland Garnet predicted of Black patriots who fought for independence that "truth will give them a share of the fame that was reaped upon the field of Lexington and Bunker Hill. Truth will affirm that they participated in the immortal honor that adorned the brow of the illustrious Washington." Fifteen years later, William C. Nell published *The Colored Patriots of the American Revolution*, one of the first histories of Black America. "THE colored race have been generally considered by their enemies, and sometimes even by their friends, as deficient in energy and courage," Nell explained. "This little collection of interesting incidents, made by a colored man, will redeem the character of the race from this misconception, and show how much injustice there may often be in a generally admitted idea."[33]

Black historians and abolitionists understood the value of hero worship within a nation just beginning to write its history, and they fashioned Black heroes to buoy a collective, public resistance to the emerging White national narrative. At the National Convention of Colored Citizens in 1843, Garnet demanded that the names of Denmark Vesey and other brave heroes be inscribed alongside great revolutionaries such as "Moses, Hampden, Tell, Bruce and Wallace, Toussaint L'Ouverture, Lafayette and Washington." He considered Vesey, who hanged in July 1822 for allegedly plotting a revolt against enslavement, a "martyr to freedom."[34]

Heroes need not have led armies. Freedom seeker Jermain Wesley Loguen imagined Black men as "Divine instrumentalities for Divine ends" who became "conspicuous in the intellectual and moral firmament." Years later, James McCune Smith, a free New Yorker, doctor, and abolitionist, declared that, when considering American culture and liberty, "we live in the heroic age of our country, and the negro is the hero."[35]

In 1842, Lunsford Lane was among the first of the new heroic age, and according to abolitionist audiences, for all the right reasons: family, manhood, and freedom. The Story became so familiar so quickly that, in his absence, others told it to antislavery meetings and church gatherings, as in January 1842 when the minister of Weymouth's Union Church denied Lunsford access but related The Story in Lane's stead, and at a July 1842 meeting of the Plymouth County Anti-Slavery society when preeminent legal mind Joel Prentiss Bishop, recently arrived from New York's heavily evangelical Burned-Over District to edit *The Social Monitor and Orphan's Advocate*, "employed himself in the afternoon in telling Lunsford's little narrative of getting his wife & children" although Lane had done so hours earlier to the same crowd.[36]

In the summer of 1842, Congregationalist minister Joseph Warren Cross declared Lane an American demigod comparable to Aeneas. Cross knew White Americans would grasp the comparison. Virgil's *The Aeneid* held a special role in binding national ambitions to the glory of the ancient republics. From Benjamin Franklin and John Adams to Benjamin Rush, James Madison, and Alexander Hamilton, the founding generation cited Virgil regularly and instinctively. On his mantelpiece, George Washington displayed bronze statuettes of Aeneas carrying his father from Troy, accompanied by his wife and son. Students in grammar schools and female academies revered Aeneas's exploits. Colleges required applicants to translate passages from *The Aeneid* for entrance examinations. Politicians referenced *The Aeneid* in debates about the moral and spiritual virtues of manifest destiny since Aeneas had been driven westward "by destiny design'd." From the works of James Fenimore Cooper, Ralph Waldo Emerson, and Henry David Thoreau to those of Nathanial Hawthorne, Walt Whitman, and Herman Melville, Aenean lore appeared throughout the literature of the American Renaissance.[37]

As a living member of the American pantheon, at least among the antislav-ery crowd, Lunsford Lane represented much more than moral continuity with ancient piety and virtue. Two years after Cross's proclamation of Lunsford as the American Aeneas, radical abolitionist Stephen Symonds Foster enumer-ated Lane among the inheritors of the American Revolution. Reflecting upon why enslaved Americans did not "assert their freedom, and meet the invaders of their rights in mortal combat," Foster puzzled, "Why is not Madison Wash-ington George Washington? And why are not Charles Remond, and Frederic Douglass, and Lundsford Lane, the Henrys, and Hancocks, and Adamses, of a second American Revolution?" In his ambition to remake the United States through abolitionism, Foster imagined a new founding generation.[38]

What Foster meant by associating Lunsford Lane with one of the Adam-ses is perplexing. Both Samuel and John could be abrasive and polarizing, unpopular with many who saw their brand of revolution as dangerous and embraced by others who viewed them as models of radical passion. Lunsford Lane did not elicit such extreme reactions. Although attuned to other Black abolitionists' critiques of slavery and racism as exposing the vacuousness of American ideals, Lunsford so embraced ideas of progress and opportunity that he could not concur with that appraisal. His audiences were less shocked or angered than those who listened to Remond and Douglass. They were con-soled in their beliefs that American self-making had worked for Lane and it could work for all.

Possibly, Thomas Jefferson offered insight when, in comparing Samuel Adams to his loquacious cousin John, he concluded that "mr. Samuel Adams, altho' not of fluent elocution, was so rigorously logical, so clear in his views, abundant in good sense, and master always of his subject that he com-manded the most profound attention whenever he rose in an assembly by which the froth of declamation was heard with the most sovereign contempt." What Lunsford lacked in eloquence compared to Douglass and Remond, he gained in stature when he arose on a stage, doing so with the gravity of an elder statesman, of someone who knew of what he spoke. He was "a man of character,—one in whom every human passion seems softened and subdued," according to an anonymous letter writer who met Lane in Bedford, Massa-chusetts, in March 1844. "So mild are his manners, that we are at once drawn towards him." Lunsford Lane was not loud, fiery, or insistent, and yet, people listened.[39]

Alongside Remond, Douglass, and other Black abolitionists, Lane was a revolutionary aspiring to transform a slaveholding republic into a new nation. Abolitionists, particularly Black abolitionists, were in revolt, drawing inspi-ration from the earlier revolution against tyranny to point out White Ameri-cans' hypocrisy. They aimed to recreate the United States, to turn the world upside down. Black abolitionists wanted a history of Black America that informed the cause. So, when authors such as William Nell and William Wells Brown wrote histories of Black America in the 1850s and 1860s, they positioned the antislavery movement as a second American Revolution to fulfill the promise that all men are, in fact, created equal. As Nell explained, in fighting another American revolution, "all, of every complexion, sect, sex and condition, can add their mite, and so nourish the tree of liberty, that all may be enabled to pluck fruit from its bending branches; and, in that degree to which colored Americans may labor to hasten the day, they will prove valid their claim to the title, 'Patriots of the Second Revolution.'"[40]

Yet, like Samuel Adams and other older revolutionaries, radical in the context of the 1760s but replaced by a new generation eager to take up the cause by the mid-1770s, Lane would not remain on the frontline of change as a new generation of more radical abolitionists took control of the movement—Henry Bibb, John Brown, Stephen S. and Abby Kelley Foster, Henry Highland Garnet, Thomas Wentworth Higginson, Harriet Jacobs, Sojourner Truth, and Frederick Douglass. As American politics heated and abolitionists thirsted for hypercritical condemnations of Southern patriarchs, other Black abolitionists and their stories rose in popularity and influence, pushing the more conciliatory and modest Lane into the shadows. Heroes and gods endure only as long as a culture or a movement needs them.

———

Despite Lunsford Lane's reluctance to identify as antislavery, abolitionists integrated him into their history as devoted to a cause. In the early 1840s, he became the face of purchasing freedom, both self-purchase and redemption-by-purchase.

The philosophical problem at the center of abolitionists' debate over purchasing freedom was that property ownership was the cornerstone of the American economy and society. "Property must be secured," John Adams declared in 1790, "or liberty cannot exist." Land ownership freed many men—and quite a few women—from dependence upon others, providing the source from which wealth, or at least sustenance, came. Enslaved property provided the labor by which greater comfort and prosperity could be realized. In the early nineteenth century, most White Americans, even some Black Americans, interpreted Garrisonian abolitionists' demands to dismantle chattel property rights as an affront to a basic principle of American identity.[41]

By the 1840s, self-purchase began to chip away at those reservations. When Lunsford Lane and others contracted with enslavers to purchase themselves, their transactions were well within the rules of American property law and practice. Of course, enslavers did not want redeemed people cluttering their towns. To retain the racial dynamics cultivated over a century of law, enslavers in North Carolina and other states established barriers: restricting enslaved peoples' economic activities, limiting enslaved peoples' rights to own property themselves, requiring redeemed people to leave towns and states, and gradually prohibiting enslaved peoples from contracting. Still, such laws were only as effective as their enforcement, and most Southern legislatures recognized slaveowners' rights to do as they wished with their enslaved humans, which created opportunities for many enslaved peoples to negotiate emancipation. Consequently, few abolitionists questioned the morality of self-purchase. It occurred within the bounds of American property law and, alongside manumission-by-will, was the only legal route to freedom available to enslaved people.[42]

In contrast, Lunsford's ambitions to purchase his family had elicited vocal disapproval from some abolitionists. Had he accomplished the entire family's freedom while remaining in Raleigh, they would have viewed it as an extension of his self-purchase. Instead, after Lane purchased himself, he spent years as a free man aspiring to redeem his family, including those months in New England where he drew abolitionists into the ethics of redemption-by-purchase.

Redemption-by-purchase was not a common expression, but it was an important and familiar concept, originating among the colonizationists of the 1820s. Senator Rufus King from New York suggested that federal surplus from public lands sales be used to purchase enslaved peoples, stipulating that emancipated peoples then leave the United States. Building upon King's proposal, Presbyterian minister and colonizationist Loring D. Dewey argued that American enslavement could be eradicated within forty years by purchasing the freedom of sixteen- to thirty-year-old enslaved peoples—those in child-bearing years—at $3,925,000 [$119,950,000] annually, transporting those populations to Liberia and removing "the source of increase" in the United States. Given the grandiosity of the proposal and the contentiousness of national politics around slavery, a federal plan never materialized, and advocates turned to more local efforts, as in 1830 when Thomas Cruse of Baltimore offered to purchase the freedom of all locally enslaved women "in the view of no more slaves being born in our fair city."[43]

Debates amplified after 1831 when Benjamin Lundy, a Quaker and abolitionist, founded the *Genius of Universal Emancipation* monthly in which he contemplated King's earlier proposal, arguing that the government should pay a reasonable sum "upon the express condition that ALL shall CERTAINLY be emancipated in due time." Without such a guarantee, Lundy considered any action, such as the purchase of a single enslaved person, a validation of enslavers' claims that humans could be held as property. William Lloyd

Garrison rebuked Lundy, insisting that even mass emancipation, if achieved through purchase, was an affront: "The way to overthrow slavery is to bring truth to bear in a burning focus upon their consciences; and to show to the people that a slaveholder . . . is a man-stealer, who violates the principles of humanity, religion and justice." It was an inconvenient reality, after all, that by entering the enslaving market, even the most well-intentioned purchasers of freedom incidentally increased demand for enslaved laborers.[44]

Lundy found Garrison and the Society's position untenable. It was easy for Garrison to oppose purchasing freedom philosophically, but if his father and mother were enslaved by "some 'barbarian' in the Turkish or Algerine dominions," would Garrison "consent to their 'ransom'"? Garrison hesitated, "We know not how far we might be *tempted* to purchase the liberty of some dear one, in such a case; but as to the purchase itself, we could never be brought to acknowledge any property or right in the slaveholder, which the payment of money as an apparent equivalent tacitly admits." So, no, Garrison would not ransom his parents from Algerine enslavement![45]

When, in the late summer of 1833, Great Britain ended enslavement in the empire's Caribbean colonies through redemption-by-purchase, Lundy enjoyed a momentary vindication. Garrison, in London when Parliament approved payment of £20 million [$2,851,000,000] to slaveowners, most of whom were absentee landlords, was flummoxed, decrying the decision "as an abandonment of the high ground of justice" and emphasizing how many Britons worried about newly freed people insurrecting against the empire. A year later, Garrison could not ignore that redemption-by-purchase worked on a grand scale. Not a single report of racial violence came from the colonies, and Garrison conceded that "the abolition act is in the full tide of successful experiment."[46]

Pathetically, considering that success, Garrison insisted that although the American Anti-Slavery Society denounced such emancipations, redemption-by-purchase emanated from the "same principles" held by the society. Pro-slavery advocates in the South delighted in watching Garrison and other abolitionists twist into moral and rhetorical knots over redemption-by-purchase. "Let them buy the freedom of the enslaved," mocked the editor of the *Southern Christian Herald*. "Ah! this would be a test of their benevolence, or their philanthropy. Such generosity as this, would speak more powerfully than all their essays and resolutions, their pamphlets and periodicals."[47]

Then, in the summer of 1841, Lunsford Lane had shown up in Massachusetts, wandering from meetings of local antislavery societies and temperance societies to community gatherings organized specifically to hear him tell The Story. Every time he spoke, he ended with an appeal for donations to redeem his family. The Story, with its emphasis on the earnest and industrious Lane working toward his family's freedom, was harmless enough, but when printed for the first time in *The Liberator* in the summer of 1841, Lane shared all the documents that he carried with him from North Carolina, including the bill of sale for his daughter, "a certain negro girl, by the name of Laura, aged about seven years." Eight months later in Broadway Tabernacle, Lane lifted high another bill of sale that read: "I have this day bargained, sold and delivered unto Lunsford Lane, a free man of color, one dark mulatto woman named Patsy, one boy named Edward, one boy also named William, one boy also named Lunsford, one girl named Maria, one boy also named Ellick, and one girl named Lucy, to have and to hold the said negroes free from the claims of all persons whatsoever." Lunsford Lane was exactly what the voices of anti-redemption-by-purchase feared—a slave buyer—leaving no doubt that enslaved people and freedom itself were commodities. Despite Lane's praise as an Aeneas and revolutionary, his was not the historical narrative of Black America that abolitionists and Black historians imagined or wanted.[48]

The reception given Lane's success and his family shocked Garrison, John A. Collins, and even Frederick Douglass, who insisted that humans could not be, or at least should not be, commodified. For nearly a decade, arguing that enslaving was a crime against humanity and God, the American Anti-Slavery Society opposed compensating enslavers, insisting that more immediate emancipations—escaping and even insurrection—were "not wronging the master, but righting the slave, restoring him to himself." Lane disagreed, not with the premise that enslaved peoples should be restored to themselves but rather about whose place it was to decide upon the nature of that restoration. It was not up to Garrison, the Society, or abolitionists but to enslaved peoples to determine the appropriate means by which to acquire their freedom.[49]

Opponents of redemption-by-purchase remained silent until Lane's speech in Broadway Tabernacle drew so much attention. A week later, a letter writer to *The Liberator* demanded, "Can those abolitionists, who advocate the doctrine of immediate emancipation—who contend that the slave has an equitable moral claim to his liberty, and that the master has no claim upon such servant or slave, consistently contribute any thing for the liberation of such servants from bondage? and thus practically acknowledge claims which, in words, they deny?" Hundreds of members of the American Anti-Slavery Society had dropped coins in Lane's collection box. If they were willing to do it for Lane, the writer continued, "may not the reason which might be urged for a departure from an acknowledged principle in one case be urged for such departure in a thousand?" The moral of Lane's story was clear and applied to every enslaved human—redemption-by-purchase was as good a means to freedom as any. Garrison snappily retorted, "It is no part of the policy or design of abolitionism to BUY OUT slavery, either by wholesale or retail—far from it." Yet, Garrison embodied the contradiction suggested by the critic, divorcing his moral principles from his support for the individual. Months earlier, after criticizing "how coolly" Benjamin B. Smith sold Laura Ann to Lunsford Lane, Garrison had pleaded for donations to free Lane's family from "the prison-house of bondage."[50]

After Broadway Tabernacle, Frederick Douglass became more resolute and vocal in opposing redemption-by-purchase. When he first met Lunsford Lane in the fall of 1841, Douglass had supported Lane's solicitations, but by May 1842, he was thoroughly anti-purchase, openly denouncing the practice: "I would rather see fifty dollars paid into the treasury of the anti-slavery society, than fifty thousand dollars spent in buying up slaves. Mr. Garrison was right when he said he did not want to spend time and strength in breaking off a few leaves, or even boughs; he wanted to ascertain how many strokes at the root would make the whole tree fall."[51]

Douglass, William Wells Brown, Henry Bibb, and other Black abolitionists personally familiar with enslavement adamantly rejected redemption-by-purchase until opportunities arose to purchase their own freedom or that of a fellow abolitionist. Garrison also came around, acknowledging in 1847 that he saw "no discrepancy in saying that a certain demand is unjust, and yet being willing to submit to it, in order to save a brother man, if this is clearly made to be the only alternative left to me." The occasion was Douglass's emancipation. A Delaware abolitionist argued that Garrison supported the redemption-by-purchase of his "dear friend" even though he "has never reasoned in this way before, . . . and I presume never would." Garrison retorted that he had no choice since "compensation was the only means that could release him." Garrison and Douglass became targets of ridicule. Men with whom they once agreed about the immorality of redemption-by-purchase turned on them, with one commentator editorializing that "we feel mortified, and full of shame . . . that a man like Douglass should have cheapened himself to $750 [$27,700] before the slaveholders." William Wells Brown followed in dismissing his previous reservations when, in 1854, after five years in Europe, friends offered to purchase his freedom and make it possible for him to return to the United States. Only Bibb rejected the purchase of his freedom, arguing that paying ransom for enslaved people who escaped and lived in the North for years, such as himself and Douglass, was a betrayal of abolitionism. It was best to let slave hunters take freedom seekers back to the South so that they could inspire rebellion from within.[52]

In contrast, over the 1840s, Lane remained true to his cause, consistently pro-purchase, inserting "redemption by purchase" directly into the title of his narrative as advocacy for others, and lifting high the bills of sale and parading his family across stages during his retellings. He associated his ability to purchase his family with his own manly self-making, teaching audiences that redemption-by-purchase was an acceptable way to end individual enslavement.

Consequently, embedded in The Story as it evolved was a thorough acceptance of the chattel principle of enslavement—Lunsford Lane had been property, as had his parents, his wife, and his children. Even Garrison acknowledged the bill of sale as a transfer of property, however disturbing the implication. "I could not legally purchase it," Lane noted of freedom, but he could purchase his family's bodies. In fact, only because they had been property could they be redeemed, a reality that forced abolitionists, Lane's enemies in the South, and even later scholars to wrestle with *how* he could have been a consumer of human property.[53]

Chapter 9

The Reluctant Abolitionist

In mid-June 1842, Lunsford Lane, thirty-nine years old, seven years free, wandered Boston's Cornhill Street. The neighborhood was Boston's printers' row, many of the offices aligned with reform: the evangelical American Tract Society, the Congregationalists' *Boston Recorder*, the Universalists' *Christian Freeman*, the American Sunday School Union's *Gazette of Education and Sunday School Journal*, the Baptists' *Christian Reflector*, the Methodist Episcopal Church's *Causeway Ladies' Repository*, the Massachusetts Temperance Union's *Temperance Journal*, and William Lloyd Garrison's abolitionist *The Liberator*.[1]

Lunsford pulled his coat collar close to his face. The weather was odd in New England for early summer. A cold front pushed westward across the region, drizzling freezing rain over Massachusetts and dusting Vermont and New Hampshire with snow. It was a good day for a man from North Carolina to shelter indoors, warm himself by a fireplace, and spin a tale "solicited by very many friends to give my narrative to the public." As he opened the door to *The Liberator* office, one of those reformers, "a friend," greeted him, assigned to translate his words into a manuscript to "relate the story to the public." Like the "many friends" who encouraged Lane to tell his story, "a friend" was someone Lunsford barely knew.[2]

Lane was not entirely cooperative. His hope to avoid arguing anything, wishing simply to "describe slavery generally, and in the narration of my own case," just did not do for the abolitionists funding the publication of his narrative. "A friend" was to take Lane's dictation, occasionally alter a verb or revise an intent, hoping to make Lane's words more antislavery in tone. "Give us the facts," John A. Collins once told Frederick Douglass. "We will take care of the philosophy."[3]

After a brief nod to his former enslaver and his parents, Lane began in the most natural way, with his birth: "I was not born a plantation slave, nor even a house servant under what is termed a hard and cruel master." As the words drifted from his lips, they joined a cacophony of voices that arose in the 1820s and reached over 130 strong by the 1880s: men and women who recounted formerly enslaved lives to ghostwriters and publishers, generating a canon of slave narratives. The stories' details varied, but the narrators united in the refrain that "I was born a slave." Well, *most* narrators joined in that chorus.

Lane's declaration was so unlike others' claims, the only narrative to employ the negative in describing birth into enslavement, defining who he was by declaring what he had never been. His birth claim was unique, as uncommon as a winter storm in June.[4]

For people who experienced enslavement, birth claims provided natural places to begin their autobiographies. Just as enslavers had dehumanized enslaved peoples by stripping them of narrative power, abolitionists humanized them, empowering them to speak to the most emotional issue of their lives and the most divisive topic of their era—American slavery. Even Frederick Douglass, who by the 1850s, could command audiences' attention without a birth claim, knew its power in making him more relatable, expounding in the first chapter of *My Bondage and My Freedom*: "I am a *slave*,—born a slave, an abject slave, even before I made part of this breathing world, the scourge was platted for my back; the fetters were forged for my limbs."[5]

Not so for Lunsford Lane. Compared to Douglass's and other narrators' statements, Lane rejected the idea that being born enslaved defined him. He refused to be abject, scourged, fettered, marked by either the debilitating work of farm enslavement or the abuse that he associated with difficult enslavers. Lane insisted that his story was unlike that of any other. The unconventional birth claim confirmed it.

Although Lane's ghostwriter mediated the shape of the narrative, Lunsford made it his own, controlling the essence of The Story and exhibiting his mastery of storytelling. *The Narrative of Lunsford Lane* is foremost a classical hero's tale, making easy the comparison to Aeneas, but it also includes elements of trickster tales common to Black American folklore, captivity narratives that had become popular in the late 1830s, and a mythology of the self-made man that was gaining popularity in American culture.

In *The Narrative of Lunsford Lane*, Lane is the classical hero. His adventure begins in the ordinariness of Black Southern life, constrained by enslavement and the law. He receives his call to adventure from his father, who encourages Lane to make money and purchase his freedom. He finds a mentor, albeit a problematic one, in Benjamin B. Smith, who introduces Lane to the mystical otherworld of the free North, where the laws that circumscribe Black life are unfamiliar yet liberating. He returns home to negotiate a series of trials—Smith's indifferent treatment of his family, a series of laws that erode his opportunities to make money, the magistrates' demand that he abandon Raleigh and his family, his appeal to the State Assembly. He travels to the otherworld, where he finds allies among abolitionists who are the keepers of a great treasure: the money with which he would free his family. Once Lane acquires his reward, he faces his final and greatest trial in the mob and the realization of his own mortality. He arises, phoenix-like, from their symbolic erasure of his humanity, now a master of himself prepared to lead his family to freedom. The Story is the classical monomyth and the telltale that Lane knew well the craft of storytelling.[6]

But *The Narrative of Lunsford Lane* is more than the classical hero's journey. It is also a trickster tale. Lunsford puts on masks throughout the narrative, simultaneously playing son and father, enslaved and entrepreneurial, free and oppressed, conciliatory and resistant, manipulated and manipulator, victim and hero. By the 1840s, narrators—and biographers more generally—began to view the individual not as a coherent and unchanging personality but as performative, allowing the subject to manifest as different selves to evidence self-reliance, self-control, and self-improvement. The tension in Lane's *Narrative* is between those performative selves.[7]

As a trickster tale, *The Narrative of Lunsford Lane* reveals how Lunsford had consumed the folk culture of the enslaved South. He recounted how he negotiated the Br'er Foxes—whether the Haywoods who enslaved him or the members of the State Assembly who tried to define him legally. He described escaping the Br'er Bears, who ensnared him with their own version of a tar baby and a bag of feathers. He related a family flying above ground aboard a train out of the South until, as they stepped into Philadelphia, they "passed into another world." The folk tales were not only a way to conceptualize enslaved Black lives but also encouraged Lane's approach to life, critiquing racial dynamics even as he claimed authority over his own narrative. Wittingly or not, Lane positioned himself as the trickster, not just in multiple simultaneous roles but at the crux of multiple simultaneous forces—disorder and order, evil and good, death and life, bondage and freedom.[8]

Lane portrayed racism, not enslavement, as the cause of his troubles and sorrow. Technically, *The Narrative of Lunsford Lane* is not even a slave narrative. Lane's enslaved life comprises a mere quarter of the book. It is, instead, a race narrative, and it mimics the foremost race literature of his age— American captivity narratives. In the first part of the *Narrative*, Lane desires freedom from the Haywoods who enslave him and from the state that confines him through laws and policing. It is a storyline that resembles Revolutionary-era tales like *A Narrative of Colonel Ethan Allen's Captivity*. Then, Lane relates how a threatening crowd took him captive and how he escaped death to be reconciled to his family, like colonial captivity stories such as *Narrative of the Life of Mrs. Mary Jemison*. Not coincidentally, Allen's, Jemison's, and other older captivity narratives enjoyed a literary revival at the turn of the 1840s, just as Lane began to relate The Story, making audiences receptive to his version of a captivity narrative.[9]

Yet, Lunsford's *Narrative* could not be a captivity narrative in the traditional sense. Yes, it tells the story of a man's struggle against the petty tyrants who held him captive, the despotism of the slaveocracy, and the tyranny of the mob, culminating in Lane's justly deserved freedom, but by the 1840s, the captivity narrative as a quest for freedom was a plot line for justifying *White* liberty: Anglo-Saxon liberation in colonial America, and then White independence in the Revolutionary era. In claiming freedom, White Americans racialized liberty as their privilege, a legacy from their English heritage.

Freedom conceptually became inseparable from Whiteness, carried in the "Saxon seed, with its instinct for liberty and law, for arts and for thought," as Ralph Waldo Emerson asserted. From the Greeks to the Romans to the Saxons to the Anglos to White Americans, freedom evolved as a racial inheritance, normalized over centuries in the rhetoric and imagery of breaking the shackles. Not surprisingly and most ironically, Hiram Powers's *The Greek Slave*—a fully nude, White female figure with wrists enchained, carved in 1858—became the most acclaimed visual representation of enslavement in nineteenth-century America.[10]

It was a centuries-old belief among most White Americans, including some abolitionists, that Black dependence was as natural as White independence. Indeed, many White people struggled to imagine how enslaved Black Americans truly desired something that was not innate to their heritage, distinct as they were from the "Saxon seed." When enslaved people sought freedom—through self-purchase, running away, or insurrection—few White Americans thought they did so out of a pure longing for liberty, dismissing Black liberation time and again as incited by White troublemakers, inspired by abolitionist literature, or in mimicry of White revolution. As White Americans racialized freedom, so too did they normalize an expectation of Black inferiority and subordination, embedding it in politics, the law, societal norms, and cultural representations.[11]

As Lane dictated his *Narrative*, he invented a public persona from the cultural notions familiar to him, including White Americans' ideal about the quest for freedom and the racial prejudice that he faced daily. He recognized how, in the land of the free, "wearing a colored skin" while not enslaved was a crime against the monopoly that Whiteness held on freedom. As his new abolitionist friends declared, in breathing the air of White liberty, Black people, too, could inhale freedom, but not evident in the speeches echoing from abolitionist meetings was the fact that to be truly deserving of freedom as White Americans defined it, Black people somehow had to claim Whiteness, either through bloodlines or through qualities considered to be innately White. It was the same philosophy that underlay meritorious service as a rationale for emancipation in Southern states.[12]

So, Lunsford portrayed himself as more acceptable, more aligned with cultural notions of Whiteness, explicitly embracing what nineteenth-century

White Americans assumed to be their unique cultural values: personal virtue, dedication to family, and a work ethic—in other words, self-made manhood. When *The Autobiography of Benjamin Franklin* had appeared in 1793, it introduced a unique mythology to the American canon: the self-made ideal, beginning with the author's unlikely origins, the event that triggered his aspirations to rise, his industry and perseverance, and the rewards of success—public virtue, social respectability, and "philosophical reputation." These ideals permeate The Story as manifested in Lane's speech at the American Anti-Slavery Society. As he stood before his audiences, they saw a mythical self-made man embodied in the rare Black body, a man of morality, propriety, and wisdom. It was new and thrilling, eliciting awe and admiration. And it was subversive, forcing audiences to confront their racism while never directly confronting the topic. When Lane dictated his *Narrative*, he embedded the ideal of self-making in its story of redemption and family, a progression from poor and desperate to happy and "rich," in the metaphorical sense. In time, Frederick Douglass became the embodiment of and spokesman for self-made Black manhood, but that was to come. In 1842, abolitionists, specifically White abolitionists, became enamored with Lane and his self-made manliness.[13]

It was not an easy trick for Lane to pull off. Self-making, like freedom, was a White privilege. When journalist Charles C. B. Seymour published a prosopography of self-made men in 1858, all sixty-one were White. When Harriet Beecher Stowe produced *The Lives and Deeds of Our Self-Made Men* fourteen years later, all eighteen were White. The self-made ideal suited White men who, even if they did not begin with wealth or status, benefited from the advantages afforded them by their gender and race.[14]

The ideal could not so easily be applied to or appropriated by Black men. Only a couple of Black men received recognition as self-made before the 1840s. When Thomas Paul, pastor of Boston's First Independent Baptist Church, died in 1831, William Lloyd Garrison used the term, lauding Paul's dignified manners and cultivated intellect: "As a self-made man, (and, in the present age, every colored man, if made at all, must be self-made,) he was indeed a prodigy." Self-made manhood was not intended for Black Americans, at least not before Frederick Douglass made it so in the 1850s. It was a parable of reinvention that, in a later day, became known as the American Dream but, in the mid-nineteenth century, was still a White man's ambition.[15]

From Lunsford Lane's perspective, when Black men chased it, self-made manhood became the crime of "wearing a colored skin." As an enslaved man, he could imagine acquiring a respectable manhood. His success and visibility portended citizenship and more stature than most Black men enjoyed, but his timing was horrendous. By the time he returned to North Carolina a free man in the fall of 1835, the state constitutionally had stripped free Black men of the vote and legal protections. The idea of the self-made Black man had become an abomination to White Carolinians' claim to exclusive political and economic opportunities.[16]

Once among the abolitionists, Lane assumed that his ability to purchase himself and his family fit well their basic notion that, through patience and diligence, Black men, too, could pursue happiness. The Story was a narrative told with a sense of optimism and possibility. To evidence his potential as a self-made man, Lane emphasized his hustle for the dollar, a quest that connected him as an entrepreneur to middle-class White Americans. As evidence of his self-making, Lane represented himself in *The Narrative of Lunsford Lane* as more successful than he had been, claiming that the house and lot that he owned in Raleigh was worth $500 [$17,725]. If true, then the property increased in value tenfold over four years that included the Panic of 1837. One might excuse the figure as a typographical error, the printer adding a zero to the original price of about $50, but Lunsford did not correct that error in later editions or years later when interviewed by a biographer. He wanted people to believe in his entrepreneurial success, making the case for Black self-making. Black narrators knew their stories were political. Lane chose to make his economically advantageous to himself as well.[17]

The Narrative of Lunsford Lane stretches beyond the classical hero's tale, captivity narratives, and even self-making mythology, but there was one genre in which it did not fit: slave narratives. Beginning with William Grimes's 1825 narrative, abolitionists believed such chronicles could galvanize public sentiment against the growing power of the nation's enslavers. The resulting catalog of Black autobiographies employed a common storyline, beginning with a traumatic precipitating event that led to the individual's decision to flee, then describing the escape and the challenges facing the freedom seeker in flight, and concluding with the escapee's continued fugitivity and alienation awaiting them at their destination.[18]

This is not the arc in Lunsford Lane's *Narrative*. He never truly aspired to run. There was neither an escape from enslavement nor much description of what he found in the North. Like the notion that birth into enslavement defined enslaved people, the fugitive slave narrative structure made little sense for Lunsford Lane. Most of The Story was about his experiences as a free man in which race, not enslavement, organized his life. When Lane became an actual fugitive, he was not fleeing enslavement but avoiding trial for acting a free man, part of the larger trespass of "the crime of wearing a colored skin."

Lane had a personal story to tell and, more broadly, something to say about enslavement and enslavers, statements that assured audiences that The Story was not part of the tradition of Black anger and resentment that characterized previous slave narratives. *The Narrative of Lunsford Lane* is not about the violence of enslavement. Although the darkest parts of enslavement may have touched upon the Lanes' lives, Lunsford did not include them in The Story: he is not beaten, sold, or separated from his family; his wife, mother, and daughters do not suffer sexual abuse. He does not run away and only seems to consider it once, fleetingly, when overwhelmed not with enslavement but with his frustration at Smith's mistreatment of his wife and children. Although he resents his enslavement, he does nothing to sabotage his labor or otherwise resist it. Not once in *The Narrative of Lunsford Lane* does he rage against slaveowners or condemn enslavement, dwelling "as little as possible upon the dark side—have spoken mostly of the bright."[19]

No wonder some abolitionists grew frustrated with Lane's mildness. In a moment when they sought to make White Americans uncomfortable with the atrocities of the slaveocracy, Lunsford Lane's race narrative did not condemn enslavement enough. He was too subtle, perhaps purposefully so. Maybe he sensed that racism was an accusation that White Northerners, including many abolitionists, were ill-prepared to confront. He witnessed audiences' reactions to Charles Lenox Remond's condemnations of their racism, with Remond, one of abolitionism's most powerful voices, insisting, "Complexion can in no sense be construed into crime, much less be rightfully made the criterion of rights." Remond knew otherwise, as did Lane. For years as a free man in Raleigh, during that moment as the tar oozed down his face, and for the decades that followed as he tried to negotiate the North, he witnessed how Blackness was an abomination to many White people, how complexion defined rights, and how "wearing a colored skin" could be cast as a crime. So, in his narrative and later in his first biography, Lane tempered his critiques to avoid offending the White Northerners whose empathy and donations sustained him and his family.[20]

Also distinguishing The Story from an earlier generation of narratives was the near absence of Christian influence over the narrative. Lane discarded the millennialist before-and-after storyline found in so many other slave narratives, a storyline that cast bondage as hell and freedom as hope. Given his distrust of Christianity, Lunsford credited neither godly grace nor individual faith as beacons of salvation. Instead, Lane openly questioned Christianity or at least its clergy. Months after dictating The Story, at an antislavery meeting in Essex County, Massachusetts, Lane openly agreed with Parker Pillsbury in denouncing "popular religion in this country" for sustaining slavery. He distrusted the church and its leadership, comparing God to enslavers, blaming God for destroying African lives by enslaving them on American shores, and acknowledging God as only one of many givers of good gifts, the others being his abolitionist friends. Divine intervention did not bring freedom—cash did.[21]

———

The Narrative of Lunsford Lane, Formerly of Raleigh, N.C. Embracing an Account of His Early Life, the Redemption by Purchase of Himself and Family from Slavery, and His Banishment from the Place of His Birth for the Crime of Wearing a Colored Skin arrived on July 4, 1842, printed by Joseph Gendall Torrey, once a Maine newspaper editor who, in 1834, set up a print shop on Congress Street in Boston. The volume was a pocket book, only 6″ × 3.62″ and fifty-six pages deep. Torrey used cheap, machine-cut pulp paper to reduce the printing costs. Someone in the printing office glued the pages together and then hand-stitched each of the thousand copies. Like other cheap paper-bound pamphlets, each copy sold for twenty-five cents [$9.25]. Torrey, like other printers, kept the typeset for over a month to see how the pamphlet sold. If sales were good—and they were, with the first printing selling out by mid-August—he could quickly produce a second edition. Between Lane's continued public speaking and *The Narrative of Lunsford Lane*, The Story became embedded in Northerners' imaginations and eventually in American folklore.[22]

William Lloyd Garrison advertised Lane's *Narrative* in *The Liberator,* praising it as "extremely interesting and affecting in its details" but muting its redemption-by-purchase message by warning potential buyers that his promotion of the book was not "recognition of the right of the robber to plunder, by submitting, as in the case of Lane, to his demand." In other newspapers, editors were less concerned with the politics of the book, encouraging readers to purchase *The Narrative of Lunsford Lane* to aid the family in achieving "an honest and well deserved livelihood." As one editor proclaimed, "Everybody should buy it." Thousands did, devouring the book so thoroughly that apparently only one copy of the first edition survived.[23]

Although Lane did not pen his narrative, he copyrighted it on June 28, establishing the authenticity of *The Narrative of Lunsford Lane* and claiming as much as a semiliterate person could the creative process of narrating the written story. Reviews were sparse, with one Boston newspaper simply stating that "this little book breathes a very good and well tempered spirit."[24]

Lunsford took more ownership of the book with its second edition. The differences are not vast between the first and second editions, printed one month apart, but Lunsford's voice is clearer in the second, having gone through it with a new editor. He promised in the original preface that "should another edition be called for, and should my friends advise, the work will be extended to a greater length," but his friends counseled him against it. He feared that readers would perceive his narrative as incendiary, assuring that it "does not contain a

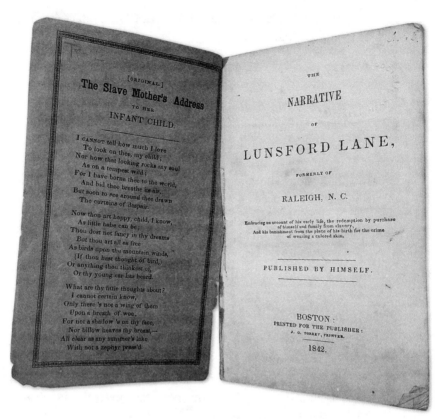

The Slave Mother's Address to her Infant Child poem and title page text shown in the photographed pamphlet.

The Narrative of Lunsford Lane, first edition, 1842. Courtesy of the American Antiquarian Society, Worcester, MA.

single period which might be twisted to convey an idea more than should be expressed." So, when Lane changed the wording for the second edition, he knew he was delivering a lesson. He was just unsure exactly what it was.[25]

Lane seemed concerned about his representations of enslavers. He had hesitated to relate the dark side of enslavement in the first edition, but he did make subtle jabs. William Boylan, Martha Lane's original enslaver, "was regarded as a very kind master to all the slaves about him; this is, to his house servants; nor did he inflict much cruelty upon his field hands, except by proxy." In the second edition, Lane deleted the final three words, absolving Boylan of the pain that his son inflicted on enslaved peoples. Why Lane made the change can only be speculated, but Martha's brother remained, crippled, on the Boylan farm in Raleigh, and they certainly feared for his safety. Lane was less generous with his characterization of Benjamin B. Smith, describing him in the first edition as "in much repute for his deep piety and devotion to religion" but upon Smith's heart, "grace (of course) had not wrought the same manner." Lane did not alter his opinion of Smith in the second edition, retaining the critique.[26]

In the end, Lane made mostly minor changes to the second edition. His ghostwriter on the original edition penned that Lane's fears of separation from his friends and family felt like "having the heart wrenched from its socket." Lane clearly did not like the action, changing it to "having the heart torn from its socket." Yes, it was minor and, yet, not insignificant—a less violent word to soften the critique.[27]

The most notable change between the editions was a poem titled "The Slave Mother's Address to Her Infant Child," which opened the first edition but slid slightly deeper into the second edition. Joshua Pollard Blanchard, a Boston bookkeeper and merchant, Quaker pacifist, and director of the American

Peace Society, authored the poem. "The Slave Mother's Address" related a woman's realization that the only way to protect her infant from a life of enslavement was to "lay thee down / To sleep beneath the sod." Blanchard imagined how the enslaved mother thought of her child's future, including a line about how, in manhood, "should some fair maiden win thy heart." The poet unthinkingly assumed feminine beauty came from being "fair," meaning, according to the American lexicographer Noah Webster, "free from spots; free from a dark hue; white; as a *fair* skin; a *fair* complexion."[28]

Still, something in the poem spoke to Lane, who kept it for the second edition. It articulated his fears during his enslavement: "Thou art a little joy to me / But soon thou may'st be sold." It addressed an unacknowledged guilt over never having been "a plantation slave, nor even a house servant under what is termed a hard and cruel master":

Thy master may be kind, and give
The every wish to thee,
Only to deny that greatest wish,
That longing to be free;
Still it will seem a comfort small
That thou hast sweeter bread,
A better hut than other slaves,
Or pillow for thy head.

It reminded him of those days at his mother's side in the kitchen behind Sherwood and Eleanor Haywood's house. Black readers who had known enslavement read the poem and the rest of *The Narrative of Lunsford Lane*, recognizing his descriptions of the lack of grace in Southern Christians and the tenderness of lost mothers and aunts who had tried to save their children. It was a particularly painful nostalgia. Like Lane, Black audiences carried their personal histories into the present. Unlike most of them, Lane intended to make money from the burden of the past.[29]

The Narrative of Lunsford Lane was Lane's meditation on himself as a Black American. A dozen years after Lunsford dictated *Narrative*, Frederick Douglass insisted that every self-made man achieved the status through the "brotherhood and inter-dependence of mankind"—that all self-made men relied on others for success. Throughout his life, Douglass consciously invested in fashioning his private self and public persona. In both, he wanted to be more than "Fredk Douglass the self educated fugitive slave," and he was ready to abandon that identity as quickly as possible. A decade earlier, Lane had already embraced the individualized identity of self-making. Maybe he convinced himself that he could, in freedom, have the liberties and privileges enjoyed by the White Americans among whom he lived, but he misunderstood his appeal to White audiences who appreciated his emphasis on family but, in the end, distrusted self-made Black Americans as different and potentially dangerous.[30]

In the *Narrative*, Lane appears upset and confused by the realization of his divergence from the White nation in which he thought he had license to participate. At one point, Lane's storytelling changes format. It is when he acknowledged the otherness of being a Black Southerner, estranging him from those who could not understand what it meant to be enslaved. At this point in *The Narrative of Lunsford Lane*, Lane no longer told The Story but interrogated it with three questions.

Describing how, at thirty-two years old as he experienced "a queer and a joyous feeling" as he finally broke free of his enslavement, he sighed, "I cannot describe my feelings to those who have never been slaves, then why should I attempt it?"—as if he did not know describing his feelings was the easiest and fastest way to raise money. Upon explaining how, when he was thirty-eight, married, and father of six, the North Carolina State Assembly refused to exempt him from the law requiring certain free Black Raleighites to leave the state, he questioned, "And why must I be banished?"—as if he had not known the penalty those many years when he flaunted the Black codes through his piddling and presence. Upon relating how, at thirty-nine years of age, he sat on the banks of a creek as a mob threatened him, he asked his reader, "How then could they suppose me to be in league with the abolitionists?"—as if he had not spent nearly a year rubbing elbows with Frederick Douglass, Anne Warren Weston, Henry Highland Garnet, William Lloyd Garrison, Wendell Philips, and so many others.[31]

The questions relate Lunsford's own thinking about how he transitioned from someone defined by enslavement to someone defined by racism, deploring those years of negotiating his otherness to satisfy White expectations of his identity and character. Contemplating what he might have done differently, Lane considered something more aligned with Charles Lenox Remond's approach to confronting racism. "I should have gone within the senate chamber," he began, but then he avoided pressing the thought further, simply stating that "no colored man has that permission," acknowledging simultaneously the White culture of power that structured his life and his own otherness that required he concede to it.[32]

The Narrative of Lunsford Lane is about what Lane imagined was behind him, in the South and in the past, but the book also hinted at something wrong with Lunsford's present, specifically his relationship with Martha. Lunsford thoughtlessly admitted in *The Narrative of Lunsford Lane* that his first love was Lucy Williams, a fact irrelevant to The Story and more suggestive that she remained on his mind if not in his heart. Although Martha could not read, she could hear. Laura Ann, learning to read in the Abiel Smith School, might have read it aloud, or possibly a well-meaning acquaintance casually asked how Martha felt discovering that Lunsford yearned for a lost love. Even though Lucy Williams was hundreds of miles away in North Carolina, Lunsford's taking on more speaking engagements added to Martha's worries. More than one Black abolitionist faced accusations of extramarital activities when away from their wives, with gossipmongers often suggesting the illicit relations involved White women. Whatever Lunsford Lane was doing on those long trips around New England, he was away from Martha and their children increasingly far too often and far too long.[33]

When *The Narrative of Lunsford Lane* appeared in the summer of 1842, the abolitionist movement stood in a transitional moment. In earlier decades, antislavery activists, many of them elite White men, had advocated a gradualist agenda of legal and legislative actions to end American slavery. The flurry of slave narratives across the late 1820s and 1830s brought direct testimony of the violence and cruelty of Southern enslavement to Northern audiences, stirring many to abandon gradualism. Enslavement was far too horrifying to wait for the slow gears of law and government to grind it down. Over the 1830s, some abolitionists adopted immediatism, including making more visible the experiences of those who intimately knew enslavement, making slave narratives popular literature.[34]

Initially, abolitionism's new literary tactic did not translate into oratorical performances, and none of the narrators of the 1830s became fixtures in American lecture halls. When Frederick Douglass spoke in Nantucket, Massachusetts, in the summer of 1841, he so impressed William Lloyd Garrison and other abolitionist leaders that his place on the lecture circuit seemed ordained. It opened a new era of Black abolitionist appearances that, like the genre of slave narratives, dramatized the cruelties of enslavement and the speakers' great escapes: William Wells Brown who, in 1834, slipped from a steamboat on which he worked when it docked in Cincinnati; Douglass who jumped aboard a northbound train near Baltimore in 1838; Milton Clarke who, along with three other enslaved men, posed as a company of musicians to perform at a ball in Cincinnati before fleeing into Ohio in 1839; Harriet Jacobs who survived seven years in a nine-by-seven-foot attic until she found a way to Philadelphia in 1842; Lewis Hayden who, with his wife and stepson, rode a carriage from Kentucky to freedom in 1844, powdering their faces with flour to appear White from a distance; Ellen Craft who posed as a White man with his manservant, her husband William Craft, mingling among the White upper crust as they rode the rails to freedom in

1846; Henry Brown who shipped himself northward in a box in 1848. Their narratives, all of which appeared after 1844, embodied the new era of narrative writing, one aligned with oratorical performance. Before audiences became familiar with these heroes and their stories, and just as they began to hear of Frederick Douglass, Lunsford Lane appeared on the scene.

Abolitionists immediately put Lane—and his family—to work. In late June 1842, after he dictated his narrative, Lunsford, Martha, and two children traveled to East Abington for the meeting of the Plymouth County Anti-Slavery Society, his first antislavery gathering as a delegate. Although not scheduled to speak, the audience entreated him to tell The Story. As "he had to do it in short hand, it was well told," praised Anne Warren Weston, yet again. Lane debated two resolutions. Did the United States Congress have "no more right to legislate for the protection of slavery, than it has for its abolition in the several States"? Lane got few words into the discussion. William Lloyd Garrison consumed more than his time, stopped only by the call for lunch. In the afternoon, Lane joined Charles Spear and others in debating "prejudice against color," praising a stage driver on the East Bridgewater and Abington line for according "colored persons equal rights and privileges."[35]

Fellow delegate Lewis Ford, who hosted the Lane family after their arrival in Massachusetts, invited Lunsford to join him weeks later in Nashua, New Hampshire. Ford contacted a Baptist church to host the event, but congregants turned him away, claiming that since the subject concerned enslavement, "it would cause hard feelings on the part of some." Next on Ford's list was the Congregationalist church, but a curt response indicated that "it was no place for lectures." Then, he wrote to the Methodists, who claimed that because they recently rejected another abolitionist's inquiry, they could not host Lane. Finally, Ford turned to the Universalists, who happily opened their meeting house. On the evening of Lane's visit, it filled to overflowing, many of the audience members from the Second Advent Society who happily delayed expectations of the imminent return of Jesus Christ to hear Lunsford tell The Story. He sold three dozen copies of *The Narrative of Lunsford Lane*.[36]

When the third annual meeting of the Massachusetts Abolition Society gathered a couple of weeks later, in late June, Lane took his family to Boston's Marlboro Chapel. It was his first break with the Old Organization. He appreciated Garrison's early interests in his cause, making Lane visible to potential donors through *The Liberator*, but Lunsford quickly lost interest in abolitionism's foremost crusader whose views on redemption-by-purchase impeded his fundraising. He found new allies among Garrison's opponents, specifically the Massachusetts Abolition Society, which arose when Congregationalist minister Charles Turner Torrey unsuccessfully challenged Garrison's leadership of the Massachusetts Anti-Slavery Society in 1839. Members of the younger society were political, evangelical, and radical, and they showed little interest in the intellectual debates with which Garrison and the Anti-Slavery Society crowd seemed enamored. Lane never met Torrey, who, beginning in 1841, busily conducted nearly four hundred freedom seekers through Washington, Baltimore, and Philadelphia. Arrested and convicted in 1844 for stealing enslaved property, Torrey died of tuberculosis in a Maryland prison two years later, becoming one of abolitionism's earliest martyrs.[37]

When Lunsford attended the Massachusetts Abolition Society meeting in the summer of 1842, Samuel Osgood, who once helped Lunsford and Laura Ann during a winter storm, was president and introduced Lane. "We had some very fair speeches, but nothing of very peculiar interest," described one attendee to the Massachusetts Abolition Society, "till the name of 'Lunsford Lane' was announced.... The *light* of the eyes and the touch of words upon the ear, the workings of the countenance are necessary to reach the heart." Lunsford masterfully told The Story, introduced his family, and passed the collection plate. "Lunsford Lane will be a John Hawkins for Abolition," declared the New-Hampshire Anti-Slavery Society, alluding to the temperance leader whom Lane had met months earlier. Just as Hawkins was an eyewitness to the sin of alcoholism, Lane experienced and survived the torments of Southern enslavement and racism. "If every freeman could *see* and *hear* Lane," declared a fan, "it would awaken them to pledge themselves in perpetual war upon slavery."[38]

On the Fourth of July, Lunsford, Maria Bell, and Laura Ann traveled to South Scituate for the festivities. Antislavery banners decorated the town meeting house where the Lanes joined a community worship service in the afternoon. Prayers, readings of scripture, singing, recitations by local children, and addresses by Lane and other guests filled the program. Most notable might have been how Maria Bell and Laura Ann "added very much to the interest of the meeting," a recognition of their own humble celebrity as the daughters of Lunsford Lane.[39]

Martha Lane, too, tested public speaking. She accompanied Mary Ida Torrey, Charles Turner Torrey's wife, to a late July meeting of the Massachusetts Female Emancipation Society, an auxiliary to the Massachusetts Abolition Society. The Emancipation Society consisted of members less wealthy and more evangelical than Anne Warren Weston and the women of the defunct Boston Female Anti-Slavery Society. It was anti-Garrisonian and integrated, the most prominent Black member of which was Nancy Beman, whose husband, Jehiel C. Beman, served as pastor of Boston's A. M. E. Zion church. In what appears to have been the only public speech Martha Lane gave, she spoke on the "afflictions of the female portion of the slave population," and the Society rejoiced in the Lane family's escape, resolving "all others God-speed in the prosecution of their efforts to escape from the prison house of the South."[40]

As Lunsford Lane participated in abolition societies and antislavery public events, he remained hesitant to wear the antislavery mantle, to become an abolitionist. Although occasionally called upon to relate The Story, it was no longer his primary purpose. Instead, he sought how to translate his rational liberty into freedom for others.

He started with someone he knew. Rumors of Lane's success in New England filtered to his friends and former Raleigh neighbors, including Isaac Hunter and Waller Freeman. Hunter, whose family flourished in New York, made a casual visit to Lane sometime during the summer of 1842. Months later, Freeman arrived with a more urgent purpose. His family had been left behind in Washington, DC, when their enslaver, George E. Badger, resigned his position as Secretary of the Navy upon President William Henry Harrison's death. Eliza and her children moved in with Waller Freeman, who promised to complete the payment of $1,800 [$66,470]. Lane arranged a fundraiser in Boston's Chardon Street Chapel where, seven months earlier, the audience had heard and cheered him. Freeman garnered $1,500 [$55,400] towards his family's freedom, but he needed $300 [$11,100] more. As news of the event spread, donations arrived at newspaper offices in Boston and New York. Attendees raised the remaining monies, eager to hear The Story and Freeman's corroborative narrative.[41]

Freeman left Boston days later with enough money to send the final payments to George E. Badger. By the end of 1842, he and Eliza set up house on M Street northeast in the nation's capital. A son, Robert, arrived in the spring of 1843, their sixth child but the first born into freedom. A couple of years later, Freeman's father, Lewis, died, leaving his son two town lots in Pittsboro, North Carolina, but Waller could not return to the state without risking his freedom. Over the next decade, three more children joined the household. The older sons took on work: William as a barber and Francis, Henry, and Robert as waiters. Eliza labored as a domestic cook, and Waller continued to rely on his carpentry. When the Civil War erupted, three sons enlisted and survived the war. Their father died in 1868, one of his last acts being a deposit of $100 [$1,900] in the Freedman's Savings and Trust Company. Eliza passed two years later. Over the previous two decades, the properties in Pittsboro had filled with squatters, and not until 1870, upon receiving their inheritance, did Freeman's heirs return to North Carolina and successfully sue for recovery of the lands.[42]

The fundraising event for Waller Freeman reignited public debates over redemption-by-purchase. Critics conceded that cases such as "that of Lunsford Lane, and Walter Freeman, make a powerful appeal to the feelings, and people will give even if it be in opposition to the dictates of their understandings." Still, they openly wondered if "it is wise or expedient to contribute money to purchase slaves of their masters," worrying that "whether in aiding an individual or a family we do not, at the same time, rivet the chains more securely on two millions and half in bondage." And they condemned any proposal to "magnanimously pay the several slave-holders a bonus or consideration for the beneficent act of emancipation."[43]

After Waller Freeman's successful visit to Boston, Lunsford and Charles Spear headed westward, first to Worcester County to attend the October 13 gathering of the Acton Anti-Slavery Society and then on to the small town of Harvard. John Gerry, a shoemaker and founder of the local Universalist society, greeted the two and invited Spear to dinner but "refused to admit Lane into his house because he was Black!" Spear declined. "His house was not large enough for me that night." The Harvard dinner invitation, the refusal of the East Abington churches to host Lane, the Springfield inn—gradually, Northern racism became part of Lunsford's story. A week later, when Lane arrived in West Boylston to dine with Joseph Warren Cross and speak at the First Congregationalist church, he related his experience from the previous December when the Springfield innkeeper turned him and Laura Ann away. Cross thought it worthwhile to broadcast the episode, writing it out to send to the newspapers. Yet, Lane had learned his lesson from the initial transcription of his narrative, insisting on hearing and approving what Cross wrote.[44]

Despite Lane's approval, when published, the letter publicly embarrassed Samuel Osgood, who had aided Lane in finding lodging that night and did not appreciate having "my good deeds trumpeted in the community." Osgood felt as if he needed to protect Springfield's reputation, insisting that "I think that the prejudice against them [Black Americans] on account of their color is fast passing away in this place, among all persons of respectability." It was a curious defense: racism should not be exposed so as not to embarrass White residents. Even well-intentioned individuals such as Osgood shifted the blame for racism from their White neighbors to Black residents, insisting that "If the character of our colored brethren can be elevated, they may soon be admitted to share in the courtesies of refined society." Osgood's reaction confirmed Lunsford's instinct that among White Northerners, even abolitionists, he needed to tiptoe around the issue of racism even as he critiqued "the crime of wearing a colored skin."[45]

After a year of hearing The Story, New England audiences began to weary of it. When, on October 18, Lunsford hosted a meeting to tell The Story and solicit donations, the audience was more interested in rumors that a Southern enslaver had tracked two freedom seekers, George and Rebecca Latimer, to Boston. On October 23, Lunsford joined five hundred friends in filling Boston's First Independent Baptist Church to denounce Latimer's arrest. William Lloyd Garrison and Charles Lenox Remond gave stirring speeches.

Committees formed—one to rouse Boston's clergy to offer antislavery sermons the following Sunday, another to visit Senator John Quincy Adams and solicit him to serve as Latimer's legal counsel. Lane volunteered for both. The following evening, Adams wrote in his journal that "just before dinner, five very respectably looking men of color, three negroes and two light mulattos, came as a delegation from a meeting of the People of colour in Boston." Although grateful to Black Bostonians for their confidence, Adams declined their request, lacking confidence in his legal skills since "for more than 30 years, I had been withdrawn from it by other occupations and except one instance about 2 years ago, when I argued before the Supreme Court of the United States the cause of the captive Africans of the Amistad, I had never resumed the practice."[46]

Six days later, when a "Great Meeting for Human Rights" convened at Boston's Faneuil Hall, Lane and the other men reported Adams's refusal, setting a tone of frustration and futility. The audience listened attentively to a White abolitionist argue for Latimer's freedom, but when the champion of antiracism, Charles Lenox Remond, took the podium, they drowned him out: "Down with the nigger! Turn the darkey over! Tip him into the pit!" Fights broke out. Frederick Douglass climbed to the stage, futilely trying to calm the ruckus as the roar of the protesters drowned his words.[47]

The violence rattled Lunsford Lane. Months earlier, in late June, after he told The Story to the antislavery meeting in East Abington, the delegates concurred with him that "mob law and anarchy are the necessary handmaids to slavery." Now he faced the corollary: Were mob rule and anarchy more acceptable when employed in the name of liberty? Lunsford seemed to think not, as did others in his circle. "Who should have thought that Boston would ever have been this desecrated?" lamented Charles Spear.[48]

Finally, a solution arose to the Latimer situation—redemption-by-purchase. In mid-November, a municipal court negotiated a price of $650 [$26,800] for James B. Gray to abandon his pursuit. For many Garrisonian abolitionists, Latimer's cause was a test case, and the proposed resolution was a grand failure. Pressured by the Massachusetts Anti-Slavery Society, the city withdrew its offer but did not abandon Latimer, surreptitiously arranging for a local Black minister to offer Gray $400 [$16,500]. The deal was made.[49]

On November 26, George Latimer accompanied Lunsford Lane to the Essex County Anti-Slavery Society meeting, where Frederick Douglass awaited them. Lane and Latimer were halfway up the aisle before "suddenly the cry was—George Latimer! Instantly there went up from the dense crowd present, a shout of greeting and joy, that made the welkin ring." There was a time when audiences had yelled "Lunsford Lane," but now their attentions went elsewhere. The three men testified about enslavement, and the meeting closed with a hymn titled "Sing On, Shout On, Ye Friends of Truth and Liberty," the audience incorporating Latimer's, Lane's, and Douglass's names into the lyrics. The audience took up a collection—for Latimer.[50]

In February 1843, Lane and Latimer attended the Plymouth County Anti-Slavery Society meeting in Hingham. On the first day, a procession of Black abolitionists, including Lane, planned to speak but were upstaged by the most recent arrival in Massachusetts, Lewis Clarke, a freedom seeker from Kentucky. Lunsford Lane, who only a year earlier was the new face of Black abolitionism, was now yesterday's news. One delegate moved that Lane recount The Story, but Charles Lenox Remond objected "to taking up the time with individual cases." Lunsford, with an axe to grind, dove into his narrative, determined to draw the audience's attention that his tarring and feathering in Raleigh resulted from "information sent by some one in Hingham, of his being present at the anti-slavery convention held here in the autumn of 1841." As the day grew long, Lane's message got lost as Remond finally took the stage. "He was argumentative or pathetic, grave or gay, tender or severe, as suited his purpose, or occasion required," described *The Liberator*. "The people stand aghast at hearing such a torrent of eloquence from a Black man, and are so enraptured with it, that they bear with the most commendable patience that which, had it come from a white man, would very likely have raised a mob at once." Remond still exceeded Lane and most others in eloquence and emotion, and as Lunsford became an elder statesman of the movement, he might never excel in speechmaking.[51]

Chapter 10

Learning Freedom

For Lunsford Lane, the climax of The Story was the family's escape from the pillory of slavery and their welcome into the cradle of liberty by his abolitionist friends. After the public adoration and celebration of the spring of 1842, the Lanes' freedom in the North meant learning the mundanity of everyday life, beginning with a home of their own.

After months of residing with Lewis and Anna Dyer Ford and other charitable abolitionists, the Lanes settled into a small rental house on Poplar Street in the southwestern end of Boston. Lunsford found work as a waiter, paying his first poll taxes and claiming his citizenship. By early 1843, the family found a house to buy in Cambridgeport, once a small village on the edge of the Charles River, which became an eastern neighborhood of Cambridge and a western suburb of Boston, connected to Beacon Hill by the West Boston Bridge. The Lanes' house was in the Lower Port, the easternmost part of the village near a canal and the wetlands that separated Cambridgeport from East Cambridge.[1]

It was a curious choice. William Lloyd Garrison lived about three blocks away at the corner of Broadway and Elm, but given Lane's distancing from the Garrisonians within the abolitionist movement, proximity to Garrison could not have been the decisive factor in his move to Cambridgeport. The village housed a small Black community, composing less than one-tenth of the population, numbering seventy in 1840, the overwhelming majority of whom had been born free in New England. Few had experienced enslavement, and maybe that contributed to the Lanes' decision—to allow their children to truly escape the shadow of the South.[2]

Or maybe John Raymond, whom Lunsford met through the abolitionist movement and accompanied when visiting John Quincy Adams, convinced the Lanes to move to Cambridgeport. In 1795, Raymond had been born free in Virginia. As in North Carolina, Virginia state law forbade free Black residents from returning after a prolonged absence. So, when Raymond traveled to New York in 1829 to speak in support of Black colonization in Canada, he knew the consequences. He found a post as pastor of Zion Baptist Church in Manhattan, returning to Virginia only briefly to collect his wife and two sons. By 1840, he led the Hamilton Street Baptist Church in Albany, New York, and was a leader in the Colored Conventions movement. Raymond also became an early supporter of the Liberty Party, attending its first annual convention in 1840. When, in February 1842, Boston's First Independent Baptist Church invited Raymond to become pastor, he accepted, and the Raymonds became Cantabrigians only months before the Lanes.[3]

Over the early 1840s, Black Cambridgeport doubled in size. Some new residents, like the Raymonds and Lanes, had experienced enslavement firsthand or observed it around them. Many others had not, having lived in New England their entire lives, relocating to Cambridgeport to find jobs as waves of Irish immigrants accepted Boston jobs for less pay, undercutting the employment of Black domestic servants and manual laborers. Boston's labor unions excluded Black workers, so many had no recourse but to abandon the city for work elsewhere. Then there was the prejudice. Black Bostonians faced daily barrages of hateful speech, as in 1844 when Frederick Douglass, attempting to view an exhibit near Boston Common, was met by the doorkeeper with "We don't allow niggers in here." Racial segregation led to unequal accommodations on trains and stages, in hotels and taverns, and in the public school system. Cambridgeport was more inviting. Dozens of Black Bostonians, particularly young couples creating families, homes, and lives, relocated across the West Boston Bridge. The Lanes' closest neighbors in the Lower Port were Black families: William H. Gray and his wife Harriet from Maryland and daughter Ann; Henry Amory of Virginia and his wife Margaret; James and Eliza Gardner's family from New York; and Benjamin and Adeline Roberts and their family from Massachusetts.[4]

One and a half miles separated Black Cantabrigians from Boston's Black neighborhood around the First Independent Baptist Church where Raymond served as minister, and the Lanes and many of their neighbors were congregants. Around 1840, the largely Black congregation wrestled with the same question that fractured the abolitionist movement: How politically active should they be? The church had served as a center for activism since its founding in 1806. The New England Anti-Slavery Society organized there in 1832. The church hosted annual Emancipation Day celebrations, marking British emancipation in its colonies as the epochal event in celebrating freedom, beginning in 1835. It sponsored the New England Freeman Association and the Boston Vigilance Committee, all-Black organizations dedicated to assisting recently arrived free and freedom-seeking Black Americans. Many members dreaded the attention brought by freedom seekers, and in 1841 when the church courted Raymond as its new pastor, about forty-six members left to form their own congregation, wary of calling such a blatantly political reformer to their pulpit. Those who remained, over 150, supported Raymond, who opened the church for "lecturers on various reforms" and participated in such events "with credit to himself and satisfaction to others."[5]

For many Black Bostonians and Cantabrigians such as John Raymond, religion and political activism were inseparable. Raymond's model of ministry drew ninety-eight new members by the end of 1842 and another 113 the following year. In early 1843, when John T. Hilton, a cofounder of the Massachusetts General Colored Association and close associate of William Lloyd Garrison and Wendell Phillips, petitioned the state legislature to investigate mistreatment of Black passengers on railroads, particularly by employees "insulting or assaulting any of their passengers on the sole ground of a difference in color," much of the protest organized at the church. Over 370 Black Bostonians signed the petition, including Lunsford, Martha, Clarissa, and the three eldest Lane children (all in the same handwriting, presumably Laura Ann's as she had been learning writing for over a year). Months later, the Lanes "signed" another petition opposing the state's prohibition on interracial marriage.[6]

In July 1843, Raymond opened the church to a meeting of Black activists, Lunsford Lane and William Nell among them. "Many important subjects will be presented, to elicit the attention of the lovers of freedom," announced *The Liberator*, "among which will be the call of a National Convention among free people of color—the introduction of two persons, just from the hot-bed of oppression, who will portray some of the delightful effects of this system upon the body and mind of our brethren. . . . Come, then, one and all, both small and great. Come, ye noble band of abolitionists, who for some 13 years have fought like Spartans for the triumph of Liberty." Lane signed the call for participants, but during the meeting, he remained largely silent, only speaking once in reaction to Nell's contention that Black Americans not act without their White allies: "It was but necessary for the colored man to imitate the example of the successful among the whites, to emulate their industry, intelligence and perseverance." It was a position that Lane understood well, having positioned himself as inheritor of White self-made manliness, but his heart was not in it. He believed Black Americans had the right to act on their own time and of their own volition, responding that the gathering should send Black delegates, Nell among them, to a national convention without any White mentors.[7]

In reporting the Boston meeting, *The Liberator* rejoiced that "the Lanes have increased among us; for they will prove a medium through which public sentiment may flow in favor of liberty of the southern bondman; demonstrating in themselves the fact that man is worthy of the boon of freedom." Not only was the Lanes' repute expanding, but the family was growing. Lunsford and Martha had their ninth child, Celia A. G. Lane, in early 1843, less an increase than a bitter trade. Lucy had made the trip northward as an infant, but late in 1842, only months before Celia's birth, Lucy died, cause unknown. The Lower Port's proximity to the Charles River marshlands created an unhealthy environment, contributing to cholera outbreaks in the 1830s and 1840s. Soon after Lucy's death, William Lloyd Garrison decided to move his family to Boston because "ever since we have resided at the port . . . we have had some one or more of the members of our family sick." Two died. "We deem our situation an unhealthy one." It was for the Lanes as well. Martha and Lunsford protected their children, particularly the youngest. But a vitamin D deficiency caused young Celia to develop rickets, her soft bones gradually becoming too weak to support her.[8]

The older children fared better. By 1843, fourteen-year-old Edward became a shoe cobbler, good enough at it to make money. Eleven-year-old Maria Bell helped her mother keep house. Seven-year-old Laura Ann and six-year-old twins, William and Lunsford Jr., attended Boston's Abiel Smith School, adjacent to the First Independent Baptist Church.

Constructed in 1835 as a successor to the earlier African School, the Smith School stood three stories high. A primary school which the twins attended was on the first floor. Laura Ann learned writing, arithmetic, and bookkeeping on the second floor. Spelling, reading, grammar, and geography awaited them on the third. Each day, when Laura Ann returned home, she taught her mother what she learned about how to write.[9]

As a public school, the Smith School proved the unequal conditions of Black education despite state laws that demanded equal instruction throughout Massachusetts. Inadequate teachers and supplies curtailed student learning, particularly in grammar. Students who excelled found little positive support from the city, which refused to recognize them at its annual Franklin Medal Scholars ceremony "to honor the graduates of the public schools, to magnify the value and importance of these institutions as the foundations and safeguards of a Republican government." As a student in the basement of the Independent Baptist Church around 1830, William Nell had been denied a Franklin Medal despite his high merit. Instead, he and the other deserving Black students received *The Life of Benjamin Franklin*. Desperate to attend the banquet for the Franklin Medal scholars at Faneuil Hall, Nell secured a position as a waiter and served the recipients. Massachusetts politician Samuel T. Armstrong, who led Nell's examination, noticed him waiting the tables and, pulling him aside, remarked, "You ought to be here with the other boys." Nell was denied because of his skin color. As the revival of the First Independent Baptist Church in Boston under Raymond's ministry bolstered the Smith School's enrollment from eighty-three in 1841 to 109 in 1842, increasingly more Black children experienced and resented their unequal treatment by the Boston school system, including Laura Ann Lane, denied her Franklin Medal in 1843.[10]

More importantly, for the Lane children and other students, the Smith School was not a safe place. Abner Forbes, the White headmaster, was abusive, resorting to corporeal punishment and violent language. He refused to allow teachers to instruct "transient and vagrant children," in other words, the children of freedom seekers. In 1844, concerned parents gathered at the First Independent Baptist Church to petition for Forbes's removal, accusing him of sexual misconduct and brutal mistreatment of the students and labeling the all-White teaching staff as racists. The Boston School Committee rejected their demands, concluding that Black students' educational weaknesses were a disability "which the Almighty has seen fit to establish, and it is founded deep in the physical, mental and moral natures of the two races. No legislation, no social customs, can efface this distinction." Just as Lunsford learned enslavement and the Haywood children learned enslaving, his children learned racial inferiority as the Boston school system taught the intellectual superiority of White children.[11]

———

After someone shot Edward Lane in the back in August 1842, he lay injured for months under Betsy John Haywood's care. News filtered northward, and Lunsford wrote Betsy John about sending his father to New England. It took Edward nearly a year to recover, and as soon as he felt up to the journey, in June 1843, he fled North Carolina, likely leaving with Betsy John's blessing, although there is no indication that she paid Edward for his services as her mother directed. She was silent about his departure in her correspondence, and neither she nor her parents' executors ever initiated the legal process for his freedom. She may have paid him enough money to make the journey, but even if Betsy John gave her blessing and a letter permitting his travel, in the eyes of the state of North Carolina, he was still legally enslaved. Like the runaways whom Lunsford had met as a child, Edward's journey northward was clandestine. He just suddenly appeared in Cambridgeport, reuniting with Clarissa, Lunsford and Martha, and the grandchildren.[12]

By mid-1843, after eighteen months of lecturing in churches and town halls, Lunsford Lane found himself in greater demand, particularly for civic events, as when the citizens of Westminster invited him as their Fourth of July speaker. The Story no longer held the novelty it once had, so before some fifteen hundred people, he transformed it from a solicitation to a lecture in which he condemned "the land of whips and yokes, and . . . the 'tender mercies' of the slave-holders and drivers." His "sorrowful calmly uttered story" dampened the "rum-soaked, powder-smoked, liberty-mocked" celebration.[13]

How could his White audience have expected otherwise? The Fourth of July never was a Black holiday, the horror of celebration-inspired White-on-Black violence shaping Lunsford's and other Black Americans' remembrances of the holiday. After the War of 1812, a new nationalism overtook the holiday that celebrated the emerging ideal of self-made manliness and the destiny of a providentially favored people, a patriotism designed for White Americans. Black Americans, then, particularly those who somehow escaped enslavement, participated in freedom celebrations with two consciousnesses—as Americans and as Black Americans. They gathered for comradery and community, rejoicing in the ideal of freedom while simultaneously sorrowing for its failed promise. Black abolitionists used Fourth of July festivities "to expose the hollow-heartedness of American liberty and Christianity, and to offset the buncombe speeches made on our national anniversary," as one planning committee noted in 1858. With little allegiance to the Fourth of July as their holiday, Black Americans embraced August 1, Emancipation Day.[14]

Weeks after Lunsford's visit to Westminster, John Murray Spear invited him to speak at the Weymouth Emancipation Day festivities. Lane took his father with him. Their journey was difficult. They tried to catch the stage from Boston, but the driver, known for his "colorphobia," refused them, insisting, "You can wait for the next stage." Racism remained commonplace in Northern transportation, a remnant of the North's own history of enslavement that expected Black travelers to journey with permission in uncomfortable segregated spaces. Stages were intimate, and White passengers often resented rubbing elbows with Black passengers. Black travelers often rode on top, alongside the driver and the baggage. The situation was so acute that antislavery societies published ratings of stage lines and drivers, as well as railroads. Transporters, such as the Worcester and Western Rail Road, drew praise for eliminating Jim Crow cars, with their porters attending "to the wants and comfort of men and women of dark features and curl locks, as to those of paler faces and land hair." The rail did not go to Weymouth, and Lunsford and Edward waited for the West Bridgewater stage with a more reputable driver known for taking on Black riders "if the passengers do not object." When the stage arrived, someone did protest because the driver regretted that he could not accommodate Lunsford and Edward.[15]

The Lanes found someone to take them because they did reach Weymouth, albeit rather late. The patient, largely Black audience enthusiastically greeted them, but Lunsford spoke only briefly, introducing his father. Edward made his first public speech, explaining how he "had always looked upon the white man as his enemy, had a shrinking and a shuddering in his presence; but now, he felt that he was in the presence of friends, it seemed to carry him up, up, up." He gave his own story, adding, without many details, his impressions of enslavement, informed by his shooting: a "slave-holder, on suspicion of insurrection or resistance, would make no more of taking his rifle and shooting down a slave, than he would of shooting a Black bear." Edward "had been brought up in such a manner, that he had sometimes thought that he was not a human being and yet he was."[16]

Although unrefined, the speech moved the audience. One observer celebrated, "There he stood, a new being in a new world, rising, as he expressed it, up, up, up. For sixty years and more, he had been looked upon as a thing—had been taught to consider himself a thing; yet the blighting curse of sixty years of slavery could not destroy the native dignity which God had given him, nor extinguish the light of a clear and penetrating intellect." Lunsford followed his father on the stage, encouraging the audience to be more active in helping freedom seekers from the South, sharing how enslaved peoples not only knew of the abolitionist movement but how it inspired their ambitions.[17]

Despite Edward Lane's successful speech at Weymouth, he showed little desire to become an orator. In July, William Nell advertised that "the father of LUNSFORD LANE is now in the city, and is desirous of employment. He has been used to *gardening*. . . . His wife is with him." No one offered work in Boston, but Edward found a position with Horace James, the recently hired co-pastor of the Original Congregational Church of Wrentham, some thirty miles southwest of Boston. James served the church for ten years, the last two as the sole clergy, and Edward Lane worked as his gardener over that decade.[18]

Wrentham was a small agricultural community, the last town through which one traveled from Boston to Rhode Island. It became Edward and Clarissa's home for the rest of their lives. Horace James paid well. Within two months, Edward saved enough money—$335 [$13,500]—to purchase about three-quarters of an acre of land along the road from Wrentham to Woonsocket, Rhode Island. Laura Ann, William, Lunsford Jr., and Alexander regularly visited their grandparents, as much to escape the unhealthy climate of Cambridgeport as to spend time with Edward and Clarissa. The Lanes' neighbors were Abner Belcher, treasurer of the Massachusetts Anti-Slavery Society, whom Lunsford met in 1842, and his wife Melansa. Belcher quickly became Edward Lane's closest friend, inviting Edward to join him as a member of the Norfolk County Anti-Slavery Society.[19]

The older children's time with Edward and Clarissa allowed Martha to nurse Celia and gave license to Lunsford to take on more lecturing opportunities. Since that first awkward meeting of the Plymouth County Anti-Slavery Society two years earlier, his speechmaking skills had matured. In late November 1843, he spoke in Keene, New Hampshire, to a standing-room-only crowd of over five hundred, "and there they stood in almost breathless silence, nearly three hours, listening to his interesting descriptions of slavery, and his solemn appeals." Isaac Colby, a local physician, praised how Lane "has made an impression on the community, that no other lecturers ever made, on the subject of slavery." Lane's oratory became his career. Audiences tipped him well, aware that "Mr Lane has a family who is dependent on his labors for a living, and he is not under pay from any society." He packed his trips with multiple lectures. Three days after Keene, Lane headed to Roxbury, Massachusetts, for a two-night performance, then Harrisville, Massachusetts, for a Sunday evening event, and finally on to Gilsum, New Hampshire.[20]

Isaac Colby was wrong, however. Although Lane earned good money for his lectures through donations, he did not rely on the collection plate. His travels through Massachusetts and New Hampshire were part of the One Hundred Conventions sponsored by the New England Anti-Slavery Society. His loyalty to the Garrisonians might have wavered over the previous two years, but the reliable salary from the One Hundred Conventions pulled him back into their sphere. The goal was to expand Garrisonian abolitionism beyond the Boston region, with speakers morally persuading their audiences to take interest in antislavery, if not commit to it. Frederick Douglass considered the One Hundred Conventions of 1843 "remarkable anti-slavery activity." Dozens of speakers participated, scattering across New Hampshire, Vermont, New York, Pennsylvania, Ohio, and Indiana. Douglass's circuit was New York and westward. Lane's was northern New England.[21]

Lane's companion on many of the trips was Lewis Clarke, the freshest face in abolitionist circles whom Lane met the previous February when Clarke upstaged him and his friend George Latimer at the Plymouth County Anti-Slavery Society meeting. Born enslaved in Kentucky in 1812, Clarke escaped in 1841 and fled to Canada. The following year, he reunited with his brother, Milton, who had flown a few years earlier. In 1843, the brothers began lecturing against enslavement, drawing Garrison's attention with their first public addresses in Centreville and Unionville, Ohio. They found their way to Massachusetts, staying with a local merchant and befriending Joseph C. Lovejoy, minister of the Second Evangelical Congregational Church. The abolitionist movement quickly began to manage their lives. Lovejoy directed them on publishing their narratives, John Murray Spear escorted them to antislavery meetings, and Garrison put them to work on the One Hundred Conventions campaign.[22]

The One Hundred Conventions campaign provoked tension and violence. In January 1843, Lewis Clarke spoke in Hollowell at the Maine Anti-Slavery Society meeting, contemplating "the subject of slavery, well spiced with wit and satire." He also watched as the meeting devolved into chaos. When a Garrisonian arose to speak, an audience member yelled for her "to sit down and behave herself modestly as a female always should," eliciting "certain women of the *bolder* sort" to come to her defense "and the shell burst with all its fury upon the grave deliberations of the meeting." The men in attendance passed a resolution to gag the women delegates. By 1843, the schisms within abolitionism were irreparable, with sides disrupting the others' efforts. When Milton Clarke spoke at the Northampton town hall eleven months later, his speech was "answered by a whig, who was replied to by a Liberty Man, and finally fists and boot toes were brought into play."[23]

Lane and Clarke journeyed across New Hampshire and Maine, employing moral suasion to encourage interest in the movement. Despite the states' proximities to Boston, the abolitionist cause manifested quite differently in northern New England. For members of the Old and New Organizations, policy differences in the abolitionist movement were overbroad, often philosophical, issues—redemption-by-purchase or women's activism. Local abolitionists in the northernmost reaches of New England expressed concern about more practical matters. They did not want to hear from White abolitionists or even Black abolitionists such as Charles Lenox Remond, who never knew enslavement. They purposefully sought out freedom seekers to illustrate the horrors of enslavement, to elicit emotions and make its physical and psychological horrors more tangible to skeptical audiences.[24]

Lunsford Lane did not delve into such cruelties in The Story. Compared to Clarke's and Douglass's narratives, Lane's story remained mild, a tale of mob violence rather than violent enslavement. Abolitionist leaders worried that it would not have the desired impact. When, in January 1844, Lewis Ford invited Lane to revisit Nashua where, two years earlier, the Baptist, Congregationalist, and Methodist churches had turned Lane away, Ford advertised The Story as "the tale of his wrongs" rather than the immorality of enslavement.[25]

Across the northern tier of New England, there were far more people indifferent to abolitionism or fully antagonistic toward it. Anticipating Lane's arrival on January 14, Ford again approached Nashua's Congregationalist North Church, and "notwithstanding all their pretensions to anti-slavery, with a slave before their eyes, longing to tell his experience, they refused to open their doors!" By evening, Lunsford found a place to speak, but Ford was unwilling to forgive the day's events. He returned to the North Church, and when the minister opened the floor to "speak or pray as they felt disposed," Ford arose and condemned the congregation for its hypocrisy. The congregants quickly cut him off, declaring that only members of the church could speak and telling him to sit down "as though I were a slave or a dog." One congregant grabbed Ford as another placed a handkerchief over his mouth to stifle him, dragging him from the church and tearing his clothes as they tossed him into the street.[26]

Although the One Hundred Conventions campaign seemed successful, the personal costs were high. Ford and other abolitionists expressed concern over the racism, violence, and other challenges faced by speakers, and for that reason, the Massachusetts Anti-Slavery Society considered defunding the project after the first year. In late January 1844, Lunsford accompanied Ford to the Society's twelfth annual meeting in Boston, hoping to convince delegates to finance the campaign for another year. Lane, Lewis Clarke, and Douglass shared their experiences. The business committee resolved that the Society should continue to support "this mission of love . . . in the cause of Righteousness and Truth, and struggling to break the chains of the oppressed." The resolution passed but with a caveat: future speaking engagements would take place "within the limits of this Commonwealth." The meetings beyond Massachusetts became too unpredictable, too contentious, too violent. The Society solicited one person from each town to arrange hospitality for the itinerant abolitionists, hoping to curb the mistreatment occasionally faced by speakers. That was good enough for Lane, who signed on for a second year. Over the next few months, he received a stipend of $32.50 [$1,310] for his travels and accepted audience donations as well.[27]

In late February, Lunsford joined Wendell Phillips in Reading, where they reported on the Massachusetts Anti-Slavery Society's efforts to engage churches in the cause. Phillips avowed that "if the meetings which follow do half as well, they will make the old Commonwealth rock to the centre, and fill the treasury of the cause to overflowing." On March 1, Lane attended a convention in Lowell, and another on March 7 when William Lloyd Garrison joined Lane and Douglass in Framingham, spending the day bashing ministers who did not support the cause. "The outcry now raised by a profligate priesthood and a corrupt church, against the faithful and uncompromising friends of the slave," resolved the convention, "is precisely the same as that which was raised against Jesus of Nazareth, eighteen hundred years ago, by the chief priests, scribes and pharisees."[28]

Abolitionists were angry at organized Christianity because many churches and clergy seemed at war with abolitionism or, if not antagonistic, at least indifferent toward addressing racism, as Lane experienced when he and Douglass visited Townsend, Massachusetts. Joining them were the Hutchinson Family Singers, a New Hampshire abolitionist family and the North's most popular entertainers by the 1840s. The Congregationalist meetinghouse, built in 1804, "bears upon it marks of the negro-hating religion it was built to promote," Douglass recalled in disgust. As they entered the hall, he and Lane saw a perch high in the wall to the right of the pulpit, twelve feet long, which an older congregant identified as the "nigger's seat." In Raleigh, Black and White congregants sat, albeit segregated, in the same spaces. In the North, segregation included physically distinct accommodations. In 1837, Congregationalist Harvey Newcomb queried, "Can anything be found in the example, precepts, or spirit of Christ's teaching, to justify the introduction of the *negro seat* into the house of God?" Four years later, the Massachusetts Anti-Slavery Society considered a motion that abolitionist ministers abolish such "negro pews" by occupying them. The resolution was tabled. The spaces persisted.[29]

Douglass was determined to occupy this one, and after a sexton aided him in finding the ladder to the balcony, Douglass made his way to the space so high that he became dizzy looking down upon the crowd. Lane did not join him. The Hutchinsons squeezed Douglass out of the loft and filled the meetinghouse with song, including lyrics from their latest standard, "Get Off the Track!" Embarrassed by the situation, minister David Stowell assured Lane and Douglass that, since the perch was no longer used, "colored people could now sit where they pleased."[30]

The trip continued. Two days later, Douglass and "friend Lane" were on their way to Acton. Snow covered the road and slowed their travel, and they did not arrive until after eight o'clock that evening, cutting their scheduled program short. The next day, they turned to New Bedford for a two-day convention. On March 10, Lane, Douglass, Parker Pillsbury, and Wendell Phillips arrived in Medford, their presence "a sufficient assurance that they [the speeches] were of the highest order." Phillips railed about ending the North's "partnership of the bloody covenant" that was the United States Constitution. "A 'Hundred' such meetings would revolutionize New England," declared Pillsbury. By April 3, when Lane attended a quarterly meeting of the Plymouth County Anti-Slavery Society in South Abington, abolitionists were in a tizzy over a local minister's denunciation of the movement as having "other objects in view paramount to the abolition of slavery." Lane and others resolved to "repudiate the charge that is assiduously circulated by pro-slavery Church and State."[31]

One another occasion, Lane, Phillips, and Douglass arrived in Groton for an antislavery gathering. Several local women invited them to dinner, along with "a very Black man, by the name of Jones." As the party sat down to the table, a rap at the door announced Abbott Lawrence, one of the most influential of New England's textile entrepreneurs and a prominent Whig, despite his reluctance to critique the enslaved labor that produced cotton for his mills. As Wendell Phillips recalled, as the host introduced Lawrence to him, the former genuflected deeply: "How do you do, sir?" Next introduced was Frederick Douglass, widely regarded as "not very Black," and Lawrence bowed a bit with a "How do you do?" Then came Lane, "about ten shades Blacker," and Lawrence nodded without greeting. Finally, Jones stepped forward, "ten degrees darker yet." Lawrence turned and left the house.[32]

When Phillips related the story to the New York Anti-Slavery Society in 1858, the punchline brought down the house, but the lesson was not meant to be funny. Lawrence and Phillips and even most antislavery society audiences took freedom for granted, never considering that racism, particularly a colorism that discriminated more against individuals with darker skins, remained powerful. Douglass, Jones, and Lane knew that achieving "freedom with their own courageous right hands" was only the first hurdle to equality, and they still faced judgment "for the crime of wearing a colored skin."[33]

Throughout 1842 and 1843, Lunsford controlled the shape and use of The Story, but some abolitionists found Lane's subtle critique of Christianity disappointing, insisting on Lane's faithfulness even when he clearly struggled with religion. Although Lunsford had not served as a spiritual leader in the Raleigh Baptist Church or in Boston's First Independent Baptist Church, the meeting president at the American Baptist Anti-Slavery Society in early August 1842 introduced Lane as a Baptist minister. There was no reason for anyone to pronounce Lane a Baptist minister except someone determined to attribute his redemption to a greater spiritual power. At events where others identified as "Reverend," Lunsford stood out, as at the 1842 Latimer meeting: "Rev. Samuel Snowden, Rev. Jeheil C. Beman, Mr. Lunsford Lane, Rev. John T. Raymond and Mr. Robert Johnson." There is only one mention of him publicly praying—at the Essex County Anti-Slavery Society in November 1842.[34]

Lunsford Lane preached only The Story, and before the American Baptist Anti-Slavery Society, he continued his secular gospel. He knew enough about the Baptist religion to petition scripture. Drawing from the Parable of the Sower in Matthew 13, he concluded, "You may take the best grain you have in your barn, and throw it out as your gravel into the field, and it never will produce a crop." A series of questions from the audience derailed him. "Did not your mistress teach you to read?" "Was your master's wife a professor?" "Did she not help you to learn to read?" "Was the mistress of your mother professedly pious?" "Did you enjoy oral instruction?" "What were your religious privileges?" "How many colored people do you suppose could read in Raleigh?" Lane respectfully answered all of them, only getting in a few requests for money, no longer for redemption-by-purchase but for the education of his children. He pontificated on how White Southerners actively deprived Black Southerners of education, and as a result, most Black Americans were "almost sure to be kept down" even in freedom. Still, in answering the Society's questions, he made no reference to God or faith, using the opportunity to reiterate his grievances with Christianity and White clergy who preached that enslaved people should "be obedient to your masters."[35]

Inevitably, The Story took on a life of its own, transforming from a personal narrative that Lane used to support himself and his family into a larger mythical narrative used by others. Already, Joseph Warren Cross had declared him an American Aeneas, and Stephen Symonds Foster had situated him as a revolutionary founder for a new American nation. When abolitionist Abby Kelley traveled to West Brookfield in the early fall of 1843, she met animosity from the First Church of Christ for her antislavery views and her activism as a woman. Her supporters situated her treatment in a mythic arc of martyr-dom, denouncing "the spirit which tarred and feathered Lunsford Lane at Ra-leigh, which scourged Amos Dresser at Nashville, which shot Lovejoy at Alton, and which hung Jesus Christ upon the cross at Calvary." Despite Lane's cynicism about the church and reluctance to identify as antislavery, he also became a Christian abolitionist martyr, albeit very much alive.[36]

Chapter 11

Yearning for Utopia

The rest of 1844 was less frenzied for Lunsford Lane—a July meeting of the Plymouth County Anti-Slavery Society in Hanson, a September convention and fair at Milford, and a Weymouth antislavery fair in November. Lunsford Lane continued speaking at abolitionist gatherings, but his interests turned to the Liberty Party and its recruiting efforts. The party appealed to many Black abolitionists who, feeling marginalized by the leadership of the American Anti-Slavery Society and disappointed with its emphasis on moral suasion, sought other outlets for their antislavery activism. "The professed object of this party is to secure the rights of *colored men* in THIS country," praised *The Colored American*, which then skeptically wondered, "In view of this state of things, what better is this third abolition *party* for us than either of the other parties?"[1]

Although still contracted in the One Hundred Conventions campaign to advocate for moral suasion, Lane began touring on behalf of the Liberty Party not only in Massachusetts but on his former circuit from Vermont to Maine. So, too, did Milton and Lewis Clarke and Henry Bibb, who, like the Clarkes, escaped enslavement from Kentucky. Bibb was eighteen years old when, in 1833, he abandoned his wife, Malinda, and children for freedom. He hoped to save them, but when he returned seven years later, they were gone, sold, and "I never expect to see her again." During their work for the Liberty Party, the four men distributed political tracts and urged churches to take strong political stances against enslavement. Months later, at its first annual meeting in Hollowell in January 1844, the Maine Liberty Association, the state party organization, praised Lunsford Lane and Lewis Clarke as the "two colored men" who "had done great service to the cause."[2]

The Clarkes' experiences with violence, Bibb's failure to save his wife, and Lane's confrontations with racism increasingly forced them, and other Black Americans, to choose between Garrisonianism's idealistic moral suasion and the Liberty Party's more straightforward offer of voting rights, protecting families, and defending against kidnapping. In particular, the Garrisonians' arguments against redemption-by-purchase discouraged Black Americans who had families and friends who could be liberated. If only Henry Bibb could have bought Malinda and his children. If only Lewis and Milton Clarke had purchased their own freedom. Redemption-by-purchase not only meant emancipation but preservation of families and freedom from a lifetime of looking over one's shoulder. There was no better example than Lunsford Lane, who enjoyed his freedom and surrounded himself with his entire family.[3]

———

Lane continued to promote redemption-by-purchase, taking advantage of a moment in August 1844 when he opened an antislavery gathering in the Milford Congregational meetinghouse. Addressing opposition to redemption-by-purchase, he asserted, "What a lie this gives to all our pretensions both to Republicanism and Christianity." He took aim at Benjamin B. Smith, condemning the man who accompanied him to New York in 1835 and protected his family in 1841 and 1842, rejecting the pretense embedded in all of Smith's actions. Smith was a devout Methodist, a church school leader, and yet an enslaver, the hypocrisy of which was as anti-Christian as Lane imagined a person could be. Lane's interrogation of religion, originated in his years listening to White preachers tell enslaved Black folk how fortunate they were, reawakened. Following his speech, the convention considered a resolution in which "the American Church and Clergy were compared with their action or inaction with regard to the giant sin of the land." Their "hypocrisy and wickedness was denounced and proved out of their own mouths."[4]

Lunsford sought something deeper, an idealism more spiritual than the shallow and insincere Christianity which he distrusted. A month after the antislavery meeting, he accepted an invitation from Adin Ballou to visit Hopedale, a Universalist utopian community near Milford, Massachusetts. Ballou was a philosophical anarchist intent on creating a socialist revolution in the United States by cultivating compassion, forgiveness, and reconciliation. He created Hopedale in 1841 as a community united in peacefully resisting governmental coercion, including its enforcement of fugitive slave laws, making the community a momentary refuge for freedom seekers, including Rosetta Hall and Frederick Douglass. Like Ballou, Lane embraced Christian ideals but had little use for the Christian church. Like Lane, Ballou appreciated redemption-by-purchase as a nonviolent form of liberation. Speaking of Lunsford's family, Ballou wondered, "but how did they obtain the boon of liberty which our mock Declaration declares is the 'inalienable' right of 'all men'? . . . He bought the right to himself, his wife and dear children with *dollars* and *cents*!"[5]

Lane's visit to Hopedale and flirtation with utopianism did not last long. In June, he attended the New England Anti-Slavery Society at Marlboro Chapel in Boston. Lunsford spoke early in the day in his typically reserved way. As the meeting proceeded, the rhetoric became fierer, sparked by the arrival of dozens of reactionary working-class men. They cheered when one speaker denounced clergy as "pirates and murderers." When Adin Ballou took the stage, the gallery, bored by his pacifistic rhetoric, shouted him down and demanded to hear Stephen Symonds Foster, who recently had published *The Brotherhood of Thieves*, in which he suggested a conspiracy among American churches to sustain enslavement. Parker Pillsbury, who often dealt with hostile crowds through nonresistance, tried to ease the tensions but eventually snarked at the audience, "Shame on your Protestantism!" The onlookers roared, "Take back what you have said," and the meeting collapsed into chaos. Pillsbury "roused a young earthquake," and the "Native American feeling burst forth with overwhelming power." Lunsford was one of only two Black abolitionists in the chapel, completely exposed to the White rage. He escaped unharmed, but the disturbing memories of yet more mob violence remained, making a permanent withdrawal to Hopedale more tempting.[6]

With a mind to leaving the lecture circuit and its increasingly inhospitable and violent audiences, in June 1845, Lane contacted Hewes & Watson, a publishing firm in Boston, to print a third edition of *The Narrative of Lunsford Lane*. As he worked on the new printing, three-year-old Celia died, her young body overcome with rickets. Lunsford and Martha, five months pregnant, buried Celia in a grave in the "public ground" of the Cambridge Cemetery, a city burial site that accommodated those who could not afford magnificent Mount Auburn Cemetery across the street or the Histon Road Cemetery, which catered to the wealthiest Cantabrigians. The city used Cambridge Cemetery as a catch-all for its poorest residents, those without kin to arrange burials, and anatomy school cadavers. Thousands of burials in Cambridge Cemetery went without headstones because the bereaved could not afford them. That Celia's grave was among them suggests just how tight money was in the Lane household. As income from public speaking and sales of the narrative dried up, Lunsford's poor financial acumen increasingly failed the family.[7]

Lunsford distracted himself from the grief with the third edition. He made only one change, dropping the poem titled "The Slave Mother's Address to Her Infant Child." The poem no longer spoke to him. Maybe Celia's loss discouraged him from thinking about childhood death so glibly. Maybe he realized the ironies: the White poet's blackface performance, assuming a Black woman's voice and emotions, imbedded in a Black man's narrative intended for a largely White readership. Maybe he just wanted to shorten the book by a couple of pages to save money. Hewes & Watson employed impositions of six pages with a final gathering of nine, allowing them to print on a single larger sheet rather than multiple sheets requiring subsequent cutting. They also bound the book more efficiently, lowering production costs and promising a better return to Lane. Like previous editions, the book arrived on the Fourth of July.[8]

Lunsford carried copies with him in August when Tremont Temple hosted an Emancipation Day celebration for a largely Black audience of some three hundred people. William Nell presided, opening with comments about how Boston still oppressed its Black residents by denying school integration. Lane was fourth to speak, and he did not open with The Story. Instead, he compared the happiness of emancipation in the West Indies to the sufferings of enslaved Black people in the United States, with a "chapter of his own experience"—The Story abridged—as an example. A youth choir followed, with a benediction and a procession to the First Independent Baptist Church for an evening of entertainments. The festivities ended with "six shouts for freedom, that made the welkin ring" again.[9]

Lunsford's address on the West Indies at the Emancipation Day celebration was a new direction for him, and it hints that he finally realized his potential as an advocate for abolition. He could be so much more than he imagined, and he needed to be if lecturing was to be his source of income. Adin Ballou noticed, "Lunsford is a man of intelligence and shrewdness," but two years of sharing the speaking circuit with the masterful Frederick Douglass and the wittily satirical Lewis Clarke took its toll. Lane occasionally apologized "for his want of ability to speak with grammatical accuracy," despite how his audiences received his words as "evidence of truthfulness and simplicity, which he can well afford to dispense with scholastic acumen." His brilliance flashed in that Emancipation Day speech, but then the doubt returned, and at the state's Liberty Party Convention at Uxbridge in mid-August, he retreated to his more familiar, well-worn script.[10]

By October 6, 1845, when Martha gave birth to Clarissa, nicknamed Clara, Lunsford was back in Cambridgeport with the family. He noted his profession in the birth records as "pedlar," although the third edition of *The Narrative of Lunsford Lane* and public performances of The Story seem to have been all that he sold. He stayed with the family for a couple of months until, in late November, the Massachusetts Anti-Slavery Society contacted him with a new project.[11]

Abner Belcher, his father's neighbor and good friend, offered to sponsor an antislavery lecture tour of "the Western Counties" of Massachusetts and Connecticut. William Lloyd Garrison planned to go himself, but when he fell ill, he called on Lunsford to go in his stead, accompanied by Erasmus D. Hudson, a physician from West Springfield who was "somewhat notorious, as a lecturer on abolition, non-resistance &c." Hudson was unconventional. In September, he helped Catherine Linda escape from a Georgia enslaver visiting Northampton. Hudson appealed to a judge to proclaim Linda free, but in court, the enslaver accused Hudson of kidnapping and "a pretended regard for her rights," as Hudson casually put it. The judge agreed, ordering

Hudson's arrest. As a non-resistor, Hudson refused to go voluntarily, forcing the sheriff to carry him first to the wagon and then into the jail, where Hudson refused to post bond, arguing that it implicitly acknowledged governmental authority. Eventually, friends bailed him out. He was still awaiting a court date when he and Lunsford began their tour.[12]

Over the next few weeks, Lane and Hudson attended twenty-five meetings in the Berkshires—East and West Granville, Rolland, Sandisfield, New Marlborough, North and South Sheffield, and Norfolk—before moving on to Hartland and Meriden, Connecticut. Meriden housed several mills reliant on Southern cotton imports and factories producing "Negro cloth," hats, boots and shoes, clocks, and other goods destined for Southern markets. The town could not escape its economic marriage to enslavement, deservedly earning the reputation along with the rest of Connecticut as "the Georgia of New England," as William Lloyd Garrison derided years later. In 1837, abolitionist Henry G. Ludlow visited Meriden, speaking in the basement of the Congregational Church to over 150 people. It was the town's oldest congregation, with a more welcoming reputation for abolitionism than the rest of Meriden. As Ludlow began, a mob banged and battered the church doors. Eventually, someone opened them from inside, and the multitude rushed the room, yelling, pushing, striking down members of the audience, and assaulting Ludlow with a barrage of eggs. He "looked like a big pumpkin pie" before friends helped him from the room.[13]

Hudson planned his and Lunsford's visit to the same Congregationalist Church. A new minister, George W. Perkins, had arrived in 1841 with an antislavery reputation, so much so that other ministers tired of him dwelling on the evils of enslavement. Still, Perkins was slow in rehabilitating the congregation, leaving segregated Sunday school classes and Jim Crow pews unchallenged. Hudson reported that Perkins "has not taught his church the first anti-slavery lesson yet" and accused the minister of conspiring with enslavers to keep congregants clueless. Perkins denied abolitionists entry to the church. "This he has done recently to Frederick Douglass, Lunsford Lane and myself for fear that we should throw an anti-slavery firebrand into his slavery and color-phobia magazine," complained Hudson, dismissing Perkins as just one of many slave-loving Christians. "The Connecticut clergy help to make up the great ecclesiastical confederation or chain," Hudson furiously penned, "that extends from Maine to Texas, which affords a stronger and more formidable power for the protection, propagation, and perpetuation of American Slavery."[14]

So, the Meriden meeting never manifested, and, relieved, Lane and Hudson headed to Wethersfield, Connecticut, to what they thought was a more welcoming Baptist Church. It was not. The threat was just less apparent.

Lane told The Story and answered questions. Hudson lectured on moral suasion. Someone did not like the messages. A month later, a letter arrived in Raleigh, the author wanting his friends in the South to know what Lunsford was up to: "The impudent scoundrel . . . is taking very well here with our hot-headed abolitionists, who have made him large contributions to aid him in inducing slaves to run away from their owners. . . . He makes high mention of a great number of your citizens," the author warned, "and urged his friends the abolitionists to take up all the money they could to send South by the first of August, when he says the white males will be about leaving for New York, and his fellows in bondage would then have a better opportunity of freeing themselves from the cursed chains of Southern slavery."[15]

Upon receiving the letter, William W. Holden, editor of the *North-Carolina Standard*, printed it, pronouncing Lunsford "more knave than fool," humbugging Northern audiences into giving money to a doomed cause. Holden had learned the printing business as a child apprentice. In 1841, he became a practicing lawyer, but his heart was in printing, and when *The Weekly Standard* became available two years later, he acquired a controlling interest. Under his editorship, the newspaper made possible the return of the Democratic Party to power in North Carolina. His hatred for Northern abolitionism drove his politics, concurring with his contact in Wethersfield that if "they think that all the gold in Boston could be so used as to seriously impair the hold which Southern masters have upon this species of property, why then let them fill this fellow's hat, and hand kerchief, and pockets and whistle for results." For those interested, "the rascal left for Boston yesterday, where he says he intends to reside."[16]

––––––––

An occasional report about Lane's New England activities kept Lunsford Lane's memory alive in Raleigh, and The Story remained popular long after he fled the South, irritating White Carolinians such as Holden. They recast him as insolent when he lived in Raleigh, resenting that he sold tobacco, worked in the State Capitol, and intermingled with the state's most powerful men. They questioned the truthfulness of his *Narrative*. Upon reading Unitarian Theodore Parker's praise of Lane's, Frederick Douglass's, and Moses Roper's narratives in 1848, Elisha Mitchell, former geologist at the University of North Carolina and a Presbyterian minister, criticized the review, finding it "a queer fact in psychology, that the man who rejects as legendary fable, I know not what part of those gospels which have commanded the reverential belief of the great and good, through so many ages, should repose implicit faith in the revelations of Moses Roper, Lunsford Lane, and the rest, some if not all of whom were under such temptations to make false or exaggerated statements."[17]

Black Carolinians responded to Lane's legacy differently, celebrating not only how Lunsford Lane raised money from Northern abolitionists but also how he had tricked White Carolinians, outwitting them to earn his freedom and that of his family. They delighted in seeing how The Story got under White Southern skins. As it began to spread by word of mouth, The Story joined flying Africans and trickster animals in the canon of folk tales that enslaved parents passed on to their own children. In honor of their hero, possibly imagining that some of Lane's qualities might be inherited by their offspring, a few parents honored their children with his name.

Lunsford remained an uncommon name, but after The Story began to circulate in 1842, some parents commemorated Lunsford Lane's trials by naming their children after him. Over the 1840s and 1850s, as his *Narrative* circulated in print and The Story spread verbally among Black Southerners, more Lunsfords appeared. An 1863 biography resurrected The Story and inspired another boost in the number of Black sons named Lunsford. The original Lunsford Lane's legacy persisted in the South through enslaved and free Black namesakes.[18]

The reasons Black parents chose to name their children after Lunsford remain hidden in history, but there are clues. When Doc and Julia Ann Lane named their son Lunsford, they commemorated a lost friendship. They knew Ned Lane and Clarissa Haywood, having worked on the Wake County farm where Ned occasionally pastured horses for John and Eliza Haywood. They were in Raleigh when Lunsford returned in 1842 to redeem his family. They experienced the terror in the aftermath of his lynching. The following year, Fabius Haywood forced them to migrate to his new Alabama cotton plantation where, two years later, they had a son—Lunsford—who would face trials of his own as "a cripple" in the cotton fields. Then, there was another enslaved man with the surname Lane, who lived in western Wake County. Most likely, he was among those scattered in the late 1790s by the dissolution of Joel Lane's estate. He knew Ned. In 1846, he had a son who received the name Lunsford who, decades later, employed the power of The Story to advance his own standing as "a colored man of the old regime, and he has a good reputation among those who know him best."[19]

Whether Lunsford Lane inspired White Americans to similarly name their sons is more difficult to trace. Although there were similar increases in the name's use in the 1840s and 1850s, most of those children arrived in Southern families already populated with Lunsfords, so their names likely represented heritage rather than admiration. Still, like the son of William and Nancy Lane, there were White Lunsfords given the name out of admiration for Lunsford Lane. In 1821, Quakers William and Nancy abandoned North Carolina for the antislavery stronghold of Orange County, Indiana. Their son,

Daniel, and his wife, Mary Collins Lane, were products of a contentious culture in which antislavery Quakers regularly clashed with bounty hunters trying to recover freedom seekers. In 1847, Daniel and Mary named their second son Lunsford, although the name was not part of the family's lineage. As a hint that this Lunsford wrestled with being named after a Black man, later in life he altered the spelling to Lansford, the name he gave his first son in 1879.[20]

As Ralph Waldo Emerson wrote in 1850, "If the companions of our childhood should turn out to be heroes, and their condition regal, it would not surprise us. All mythology opens with demigods. . . . We call our children and our lands by their names." Lunsford Lane was an American Aeneas, and like other demigods and heroes, he inspired some parents to name their children after him. The Black men—and possibly a few White men—who wore the name Lunsford because their parents admired the man who had saved his family, immeasurable as they are, embodied the reach and power of The Story.[21]

After the April 1846 meeting in Wethersfield, Connecticut, Lane returned to the small Cambridgeport rental packed to the rafters with his family. The Lanes needed a larger home. In June, Lunsford returned to the social networking that had served him previously. When he bought the house in Raleigh, he did so through his connections to and assistance from Joseph Gales and Robert W. Haywood. When purchasers and sellers knew each other, the sellers functioned as lenders. In the position to extend terms, they were people of means although the ability of someone like Lane's neighbor in Raleigh, John Campton, to extend loans to other Black Raleighites demonstrated the occasional modesty of those means.[22]

As Lane experienced in Raleigh, once mortgagee and mortgagor agreed upon the terms, the former drew up a warranty deed, a legal title that guaranteed fee simple interest in the property, meaning that there were no outstanding liens or other conditions that would burden the buyer. The warranty deed listed the sale price, and the mortgagee, Joseph Gales, remained the legal owner until mortgagor Lane met the terms of the deed. That had been Lane's experience in North Carolina in the mid-1830s when he signed the property over to Benjamin B. Smith as part of the payment for his family.[23]

In Massachusetts in the 1840s, Lane encountered a web of property laws quite different than he had known a decade earlier. Following the Panic of 1837, real estate had become less of a transaction between individuals, evolving into a business as lenders extended mortgages to greater numbers of people, many of whom they did not know and were potentially high-risk borrowers. To safeguard against loan losses, sellers demanded a remedy to slow down legal procedures that damaged so many during the Panics of 1837 and 1839. It came in the form of the mortgage deed, which secured liens on properties should mortgagors not meet the terms of the loans. It also assured the buyer an equity of redemption, meaning that they could recover the property through a court. As more individuals assumed mortgages, sometimes multiple mortgages, the number of invested parties in any given property multiplied, and the tangle of property rights bedeviled state courts. Consequently, some states prohibited mortgagees the ability to take possession, giving mortgagors greater security should they miss a payment and protecting the interests of second and third mortgagees. Some states extended equity of redemption up to twenty years even if the buyer lost the property to foreclosure. They just had to pay off the full mortgage and associated liens and taxes.[24]

The proliferation of mortgage deeds became part of a transformation of the real estate landscape, effectively acknowledging two owners—the mortgagee whom the common law recognized as holding the legal estate to protect and enforce his rights, and the mortgagor whom equity courts acknowledged as an equitable owner. The mortgage deed mimicked the warranty deed, but in reverse, with a buyer guaranteeing that, should they not meet the mortgage terms, they had not encumbered the title with liens. Mortgagees often layered mortgage deeds with all sorts of additional terms, such as requiring purchasers to pay late property taxes, assume responsibility for former liens, and acquire fire insurance, knowing that by not fulfilling all terms, mortgagors risked losing their equitable ownership of the property.[25]

Since common law granted women dower rights to one-third of the estate for their own use in case of their husbands' deaths and debts, mortgagees demanded buyers' wives sign away future claims to dower rights. (Although some states did allow wives of mortgagors, having previously relinquished claims to dower, to equity of redemption if a court so deemed.) For years, Martha made her X on each of Lunsford's mortgages, relinquishing her rights to each property. Had she not agreed, mortgagees would have refused to sell the properties and extend the loans.[26]

As Lane did in Raleigh, in Cambridgeport, he found an acquaintance, grocer Andrew Boardman, to sell him a house. Fronted by Moore Street, lot 29 was triangular, about two-fifths of an acre with a moderately-sized house. Boardman signed the warranty deed, assuring Lane that he held fee simple interest to sell the property and confirming a price of $300 [$11,820]. Lane paid $100 [$3,940] down but needed a mortgage for the remainder. Being neither wealthy nor established, he found no bank willing to extend one to him because financial institutions continued to cater to more fiscally sound purchasers. Instead, Lunsford took a loan from Boardman, agreeing in the mortgage deed to pay the balance in four annual $50 [$1,970] installments. The

Lanes moved into their Moore Street home. Lunsford paid a $1.50 [$60] property tax later that year and again in 1847, which not only covered the property but enrolled him as a voting citizen. Eighteen-year-old Edward paid a $1.50 poll tax and joined his father as an eligible voter in Cambridgeport.[27]

So, Lunsford Lane was $200 [$7,880] in debt, and he needed the new edition of *The Narrative of Lunsford Lane* to sell. His speeches drew fewer contributions, and he could no longer count on the One Hundred Conventions campaign for an income. He began advertising as a "book agent," although that entailed peddling his *Narrative* more than selling a variety of books. If Lunsford understood the maze of Massachusetts' property laws, he operated as if he lived under North Carolina property laws where White mortgagees accommodated free Black property mortgagors as much to keep their neighbors under their control as to make a profit off property sales. Gales had been flexible when Lane had missed payments. Mortgagees in the North, driven as much by capitalism as racial control, were less accommodating.[28]

The financial pressures were more than Lunsford could endure, and in late 1846, he enthusiastically considered an invitation from Gerrit Smith. In 1841, Smith had sent Lunsford $30 toward his family's redemption. Now, he invited Lane to uproot his family and settle in central New York in a community called Timbucto after the legendary center of the Mali Empire. "What people of color . . . are capable of becoming in this nation is an experiment yet to be tried," Smith contemplated years earlier. "Hitherto we have seen how far . . . they can rise under all the dead weights we attach to them." He was eager to initiate the experiment.[29]

Smith was one of the wealthiest and largest landholders in New York, owning more than one million acres in forty-eight of the state's fifty-six counties. Wealth did not bring him happiness, and in 1845, he began to reconsider his legacy. He discovered "the great delight I take in purchasing the Liberty of slaves. . . . None of my expenditures of money have brought me more gladness of heart." In 1840, he paid $450 [$15,950] to save an enslaved man. The following year, he spent $5000 [$173,770], including the $30 sent to Lane. In 1842, $6,750 [$249,260] helped nine people. When Charles Turner Torrey, organizer of the Massachusetts Abolition Society, went to the District of Columbia in 1842 to help enslaved peoples escape to freedom, Gerrit Smith underwrote much of Torrey's expenses for the next two years until Torrey's arrest. Smith continued to contribute to purchasing freedoms: another $500 [$20,140] in 1845 and $1,000 [$39,890] in 1846. At antislavery and Liberty Party meetings, Smith openly supported redemption-by-purchase, likening it to paying ransoms. So, in early 1846, he decided that "I shall have a heart to reduce myself, if not to a poor man—yet well nigh to a poor man—by purchasing the liberty of the enslaved poor." He intended to rehabilitate them in Timbucto.[30]

Although Gerrit Smith recognized that many White people needed help, he viewed his plan as more than economic reform. Poor White New Yorkers enjoyed a privilege deprived of their poor Black neighbors—they could vote, even without property ownership. The New York constitution of 1846 required Black residents, in contrast, to own property worth at least $250 [$8,850] to exercise their citizenship. "Since they must become landholders that they may be entitled to vote," Smith postulated to a friend, "they will become landholders. Vote, they will." As a leader in the Liberty Party, he believed that politics held more possibilities to end enslavement than did Garrison's fixation on moral suasion. He planned to create that political power.[31]

Smith hired Theodore S. Wright, Charles B. Ray, and James McCune Smith to recruit potential residents. Born around 1797 in Rhode Island, Wright had been free throughout his life. He became the first Black graduate of Princeton Theological Seminary. Although a founding member of the American Anti-Slavery Society, by 1853, he was estranged from the Society, becoming a proponent of Black empowerment, including violent rebellion against enslavement. Ray, born in 1807 Massachusetts, also grew up free, but he knew racism well, his enrollment at Wesleyan University disrupted by White students protesting his admission. In the 1830s, he became a Congregationalist minister and a staunch abolitionist, cofounding *The Colored American* periodical in 1838. James McCune Smith had been born enslaved in 1813 in New York City, earning his freedom in 1827 through the state's Emancipation Act. In the 1830s, denied the opportunity to study medicine in the United States, he attended the University of Glasgow in Scotland, earning a medical degree in 1837. By the mid-1840s, he had a successful medical practice in New York. Like their employer, Gerrit Smith, all three were Liberty Party men.[32]

In August 1846, the three began distributing 120,000 acres of Adirondack lands. Smith divided the lands into forty-acre parcels, planning to provide tools and work animals to three thousand future Timbucto farmers. His vision encompassed more than individual, propertied citizenship. "The owners of adjacent farms are *neighbours*," he anticipated. "There must be mutual assistance, mutual and equal dependence, mutual sympathy—and labour, the 'common destiny of the American people,' under such circumstances, yields equally to all, and makes all equal." He was intent on creating a Black community. Within two months, Wright, Ray, and Smith recruited over five hundred men.[33]

Although the recruits were to come from New York City, Gerrit Smith offered tracts to Black and White abolitionists from throughout the nation, hoping to draw their influence and leadership into his utopian community. He contacted dozens of abolitionists, including Lewis and Milton Clarke and their younger brother Cyrus, Henry Bibb, Dan C. Billings, Frederick Douglass, Lewis Hayden, and Lunsford Lane.[34]

After Lane's brief flirtation with Hopedale, Smith's offer was alluring, but early reports from the experiment were not promising. Moving to the wilds of the Adirondacks proved formidable to grantees, most wholly unprepared for the challenge. They were barbers and cooks, domestic servants and craftsmen. They did not know how to farm. Even if they had known, the land was too rocky, too hilly, and frozen too often for anyone to successfully cultivate it. And the promised wagons, tools, and horses never materialized when Smith's personal debts collided with his idealism. In the end, only about one hundred made the effort. One New Yorker skeptically questioned Smith's motivations, suggesting that since annual taxes "are fast consuming his once vast patrimony," Smith concocted Timbucto to dump his tax obligations onto unsuspecting victims.[35]

The abolitionists whom Smith recruited to help lead Timbucto were slow to arrive. In 1848, John Brown, a wool commissioner and White abolitionist from Springfield, Massachusetts, visited Timbucto, contemplating that "I can think of no place where I think I would sooner go; *all things considered* than to live with those poor despised Africans to try, and encourage them; and to show them a little so far as I am capable how to manage." Brown instead moved to Kansas territory, and another eight years passed before he arrived in Timbucto, retreating from the civil war that erupted following the territory's vote to join the United States and his murder of five proslavery settlers at Pottawatomie Creek.[36]

Brown shared his optimism about Timbucto with Willis A. Hodges, another White abolitionist, "I hope every one will be determined to not merely conduct as well as the whites, but to set them an example in all things." The Black men who dragged their families to the Adirondacks aspired to find citizenship in the dense woods and rocky fields. It was a herculean task. Although a "Nantucket Yankee who had learned to draw sustenance from the bare rocks and desert sands of his native shores, might possibly live there," observed one editorialist, "the negro unused to self-dependence never could." It was not settlers' characters that inhibited success, however, but the lack of tools and work animals, the remoteness of the lands, and the nefarious actions of White neighbors. When he went to pay his property taxes, George W. Davis discovered that someone else claimed his property by paying the bill. In 1849, Essex County officials confiscated dozens of tracts to sell at public auction. Legal fights over the county's seizures dragged on for two years. James McCune Smith circulated a letter to churches across the state informing grantees who lost lands to back taxes that they could still declare equity of redemption and recover their properties. Too many had given up the dream by then, returning to former lives in New York City.[37]

Lunsford Lane watched the disordered development of Timbucto from afar, imagining that he might join when his sons were old enough to help him scrape a life from the land. In November 1847, Smith drew up an agreement with the man "of Memorable trials at the south and now residing at Cambridge Port," selling Lunsford forty acres of land in Essex County for $1 [$37.00] on the condition that the family move immediately. Lane accepted, but apparently, Martha refused, and the family remained in Massachusetts.[38]

––––––––

In late January 1847, Lunsford Lane occupied the afternoon session at the Fifteenth Annual Meeting of the Massachusetts Anti-Slavery Society in Boston, sharing the stage with Stephen Symonds Foster, who, three years earlier, lauded Lane as a revolutionary member of abolition's founding generation. The two men commented on a series of resolutions, including one that tested the convention's support for "Dissolution of the Union, as the readiest and most effectual method of striking off the fetters of the Slave."[39]

During the meeting, visitors approached Lane about returning to work on behalf of the Liberty Party, undoubtedly with Gerrit Smith's blessing. The party had formed at the national level eight years earlier, a direct response to Garrisonian abolitionism's hesitance to engage in politics. In 1840 and again in 1844, the Liberty Party nominated Kentucky abolitionist James G. Birney as its presidential candidate, but as a third party, the ticket floundered. With abolitionist ranks divided into Old and New Organizations, party leaders struggled to shape a platform that appealed to all. Lewis Tappan, one of the founders of the American Anti-Slavery Society, doubted it possible: "The number of abolitionists is now so large here, and their views on many points of policy so various, that it will be impossible, I think, to have them united long." By 1843, Gerrit Smith emerged as the party's future. The 1844 election barely ended when he began organizing the next national Liberty Party convention and encouraged more state party conventions, all in anticipation of a greater showing in 1848.[40]

Needing the income, Lane accepted the offer to become a party spokesman. With renewed purpose, he returned to the lecture circuit. On February 7, 1847, he arrived in Worcester, scheduled to speak as "the manly and eloquent representative of three millions of human chattels." It was a Sunday, and many Worcesterites spent the day at church. Among them was Samuel M. Burnside, a man of "old New England," although not from the English stock that dominated the region's politics and history. In 1718, his maternal and paternal grandparents had come from Ireland. His father, Thomas Bumside, served in Roger's Rangers, the infamous renegade militia that wreaked havoc on French soldiers and Indigenous Americans in New York's Lake George region during the Seven Years' War. Bumside and his wife, Susannah, settled in the New Hampshire wilderness, farming and raising livestock.[41]

The Bumsides' son, M'Gregore, graduated Dartmouth College in 1805 and moved to Boston, where he began to study law. Three years later, he petitioned the Massachusetts assembly to officially change his surname from the unfortunate Bumside to the more anglicized Burnside. A year later, he petitioned the state to add the first name Samuel. He opened a law school in Worcester where he trained future lawyers such as William N. Green and Stephen Salisbury. He developed a long philanthropic record, including membership in the local antislavery society and co-leading the movement to empower democratically elected local school boards. As part of his philanthropy, he joined a group of Worcester elites to incorporate the American Antiquarian Society in 1812, with Burnside vainly inviting retired president Thomas Jefferson to join them. The Sage of Monticello did not accept.[42]

On the evening of February 12, Burnside was not feeling charitable. He spent much of the day at the Episcopal church, then visited a friend for an hour. In his diary, he recalled that as he strolled home, "it was Starlight," but he did not record what happened during his walk. As Burnside passed the crowded hall in which Lunsford Lane was speaking, he overheard the roar of the audience and angrily ripped down a broadside advertising the event, offering some choice words about a Black abolitionist holding political meetings on Sundays. A local paper sarcastically pointed out that he did so "on his way from church. A very pious and honorable act, certainly!" *The Liberator* dismissed him as "PITIFUL."[43]

Burnside's reaction represented the attitude of many White Northerners, particularly working-class Irish Americans. His was the loudest pro-Irish voice in central Massachusetts. A week earlier, he lectured to a packed house in Worcester's Lyceum, describing Ireland's Great Famine and appealing for aid. He spoke to audiences every other week on the urgency of helping their Irish neighbors, advising them to imagine unity between the White working class and Irish immigrants. He felt his appeals unheard as the abolitionist cause took center stage in the North, sucking up all the empathy in the room. "For the sufferings and outrages endured by the Irish," lectured Gerrit Smith to White audiences, "you are not responsible:—but for those endured by the slaves you are." Now, the stranger, the interloper Lunsford Lane, drew further attention from Burnside's pleas.[44]

To make matters worse, Lane had attended an 1841 meeting of the Massachusetts Anti-Slavery Society held to court Irish American support for abolitionism. Over five thousand people crowded into Boston's Faneuil Hall. William Lloyd Garrison, Wendell Phillips, Charles Lenox Remond, Frederick Douglass, Lunsford Lane, and others spoke, all seemingly oblivious to Irish Americans' desires to be accepted as White Americans rather than associated with Black Americans. Anne Warren Weston articulated the insensitivity when she described the audience to a friend, casually dismissing how "the peculiarities of the Irish peasant (& such only come among us) in connexion with his dress make him to be as easily distinguished from an American as a coloured man from a white." Irish immigrant causes and those for Black Americans clashed. Garrison touched upon the situation when, in the spring of 1842, he called out James Canning Fuller for not contributing to Lunsford's cause to redeem his family, regretting how tragic it was that Fuller saw his Irish countrymen "entrapped into the support of the horrid slave system by unprincipled leaders and crafty demagogues!" Lane's appeals in Worcester, then, distracted from Burnside's work toward Irish charity, reinforcing concerns among Irish Americans that Black Americans would shove them to the bottom of society.[45]

That Lunsford solicited for abolition and himself on a Sunday elicited Burnside's Sabbatarian ire. Over the next year, Lane and other Liberty Party speakers regularly faced criticism for holding Sunday "gatherings to carry on their electioneering, which no other party would attempt," as well as blaspheming the temples with "their calls for money" and showing "the most unblushing effrontery ever exhibited by any class of wire-pulling politicians."[46]

Lane went on from Worcester to speak across Massachusetts and Maine. At the end of his first year as a Liberty Man, Lane presented the keynote address at the Maine Liberty Association convention in Hallowell, taking one of the twins with him, either William or Lunsford Jr. He was "eloquent," producing "a deep impression," but again another speaker excelled him on the stage. Henry Bibb thrilled the meeting with a speech "unequalled except by Frederick Douglass." The next day, Lane and Bibb attended Maine's Religious Antislavery Convention, joining six other "clergy," all identified by denomination save one—Lunsford Lane, misidentified as a generic "minister." In the late 1840s, as he electioneered and fundraised on the Sabbath, Lunsford seemed even more distanced from organized religion. He spoke briefly at the Religious Antislavery Convention, again overshadowed by Bibb, who commanded the stage for over two hours, closing his oration with "a plantation song" and emotionally stirring the audience.[47]

The Liberty Party considered 1848 a pivotal election year. At the national convention in October, Gerrit Smith declared how the "men, who, under God, are to carry forward the anti-slavery cause to its triumph, are men, who identify themselves with the slaves, and are willing to be hated and despised for that identification." He counted himself among that number. He continued to hope for a political dissolution of enslavement, but he advocated any means possible: "Do my hearers . . . believe that to help a slave out of slavery by endeavors, however concealed or sly, is, not only not wrong, but perfectly and gloriously right?" Once again, Lane found himself awkwardly caught between two camps of abolitionism. Liberty Party leaders in Maine, where Lane collaborated most closely with the party, were coalitionists, hoping to create political solutions by building a Northern voting block that in time might end enslavement. They suspiciously eyed Smith's turn toward radicalism. When Smith received the presidential nomination, the coalition builders, including Nathaniel Colver, at whose church Lane had spoken years earlier, bolted the Liberty Party.[48]

Lane followed the coalitionists and found his soul. Colver was also a leader in the American Baptist Home Mission Society. Organized in 1832, the Society proposed that "heathen" Indigenous people and "infidel" White settlers living in the West eroded the nation's moral character. The American West needed evangelizing. A dozen years later, the Society added enslaved peoples in the South to their list. Southern Baptist churches, such as the one in Raleigh, once were mixed congregations, but Black members had little voice and received only verbal instruction since the law forbade them from reading. By the 1840s, many of those denominations were splintering, not only between Northern and Southern churches but between White and Black congregations. In 1843, abolitionists pushed the American Baptist Home Mission Society to consider how enslavers and their version of Baptist faith impeded conversion among enslaved peoples, and over the next six years, the Society severed all ties to Southern enslavement, rejecting donations from slaveowners, refusing to employ enslavers as missionaries, and refraining from sending missionaries into the enslaving states. Lunsford Lane finally found a Christian organization that represented what he believed—Christian principles unblemished by concessions to the slaveocracy. He became a member.[49]

Between Lunsford's speaking engagements and steady sales of the third edition of Narrative of Lunsford Lane, the Lanes' finances steadily improved. In March 1848, Lunsford purchased lot 365 in Cambridgeport, at the intersection of Medford and Clark Streets, a couple blocks northwest of the Moore Street house. At around two-thirds of an acre, the lot was slightly larger, as was the house. It was substantially more costly, sold to Lane by Walter Bryant, a Boston inventor and grate manufacturer, for $1,300 [$50,100]. Lunsford paid $100 [$3,850] down, promising in the mortgage deed an additional $300 [$11,600] within three years and the remaining $900 [$34,680] at 6 percent interest in nine annual payments. He had to provide proof of fire insurance on the house. Martha put her X on the mortgage deed, and their daughter, Laura Ann, witnessed the transaction and signed it. The house was far more than the Lanes could afford.[50]

Lunsford Lane might have taken every opportunity to reduce his debts, particularly when, within a year, he sold the Moore Street property. It was his first sale of real estate, having given away the Raleigh house when he fled. He sold it for $300 [$11,820]. The purchaser paid in full. But Lane did not embed his remaining mortgage debt into the warranty deed, retaining the load debt for a property to which he no longer had equitable or legal claim. Nor did he use the profit to pay down that debt. Since he sold the property for the price at which he bought it, Lunsford made no profit on the sale. In fact, calculating the interest that he paid on the loan, he lost money.[51]

Strapped for cash, Lane issued the fourth and final edition of *The Narrative of Lunsford Lane* in the summer of 1848, again on the Fourth of July, again printed by Hewes & Watson. Not since the first edition was it so broadly advertised, part of a larger corpus of celebrated Black biography that appeared in the late 1840s. "The few slaves who can tell the story of their wrongs, show that Slavery cannot easily be represented as worse than it is," pontificated Theodore Parker. "The lives of Moses Roper, or Lunsford Lane, or Moses Grundy, Frederic Douglas, and W. W. Brown, are before the public, and prove what could easily be learned from the advertisements of Southern newspapers, conjectured from the laws of the Southern States, or foretold outright from a knowledge of human nature itself—that the sufferings of three millions of slaves form a mass of misery which the imagination can never realize, till the eye is familiar with its terrible details." Lane revived The Story, hoping to sell books.[52]

In early May 1849, Lunsford traveled to New York City for the annual meeting of the American Baptist Home Mission Society, the symbolism of his presence as important as the message he conveyed: a Black man, formerly enslaved by White Southerners and racially restricted by the Southern Baptist church, now free and flourishing. He told The Story. The Society's membership praised him, hiring him as a colporteur to sell their literature alongside his *Narrative*. It was a welcomed offer, allowing him to define himself honestly as a book agent. After the meeting, Lane traveled upstate, arriving in Timbucto by mid-May to consult with Gerrit Smith about the forty acres.[53]

Politically, he was no longer part of Smith's Liberty Party, however. In August 1850, Lunsford arrived in Monkton, Vermont, to speak at the Free Democratic Convention. The Democratic Party had splintered as Northerners could no longer support the Southern wing of the party in its demand to protect enslavement. They became Free Democrats or, as they were termed in New York, Barnburner Democrats for their willingness to metaphorically torch the financial institutions that funded Southern enslavement and willingness to burn down the entire party as well. In 1848, they joined former members of the fading Liberty Party to form the Free Democratic Party (commonly known as the Free Soil Party), focused on one issue: opposing western expansion of enslavement, aligning with the American Home Baptist Missionary Society's concerns about the moral purity of the American West.[54]

At the Monkton meeting, Lane spoke alongside Cyrus Prindle, who seceded from the Methodist Episcopal Church in 1841 to establish the more anti-slavery Wesleyan Methodist movement, and Austin Beecher, a Baptist preacher and a cofounder of the Liberty Party who, in 1842, called out a fellow Baptist leader for suggesting "that *some* slaveholders are worthy of Christian fellowship!" In comparison to Beecher and Prindle, Lane's cautious criticisms of enslavement created an odd program for the convention, leading one critic to anticipate that "That was a strangely *matched* team!" But Lane surprised everyone, rising to the occasion, his prowess as a public speaker apparent in descriptions of his speech: "Mr. Lane is a speaker of unusual power and acuteness." So, too, were his politics as he awakened the audience to "the abhorrence of southern tyranny which should be cherished by every true freeman." Lunsford's days of dwelling as little as possible on the dark side had ended.[55]

Chapter 12

Toward Practical Abolitionism

In 1850, Lunsford and Clarissa's eldest son, Edward, became their first child to leave the house. He did not wander far. There was a small wooden cottage at the corner of the Medford Street property, out of the house but well under his parents' scrutiny. Lunsford and Martha sold Edward the cottage for $200 [$7,700] "to maintain it no longer than they permitted." Better with his finances than his father, he paid his parents in cash, needing no mortgage deed. Edward made good money from his shoe cobbling for Cambridgeport's expanding Black community. Across the 1840s, the majority of Black Cantabrigians had been from either Massachusetts or New York, but by the early 1850s, a notable number of Black Southerners had arrived, among them Milton Clarke from Kentucky. People from Delaware, Maryland, Virginia, North Carolina, Georgia, and the District of Columbia poured into the Lower Port, supposedly all of them emancipated (although if no one asked, no one told), and most of them needing shoes.[1]

Martha kept an eye on Edward from her window in the larger house nearby, but she had other children who needed attending. Maria Bell maintained the house with her mother, helping with Clara's care. Alexander joined his older siblings, Laura Ann, William, and Lunsford Jr., in school, and the three boys spent time with their grandparents in Wrentham. Lunsford took to the road more than ever, encouraging audiences to buy his *Narrative* so that he could "erect a house upon land in the State of New York, given him by Hon. Gerrit Smith, and to remove his family thereto," as he announced upon a trip to Brattleboro, Vermont. Sales stalled, however, and his dream of moving to New York faded as the family's financial circumstances deteriorated. Lunsford had agreed to too high a price on the Medford Street house and failed to pass the remaining mortgage on the Moore Street property to the next owner. In May 1850, he finally paid off the latter at the expense of a mortgage payment on the Medford Street house.[2]

The financial situation began to affect the Lanes' marriage. When the Middlesex County tax assessor visited in 1850, Martha informed him that Lunsford no longer lived with her. He had moved into an apartment at 100 Cambridge Street, Boston, behind the newly opened Taylor & Lane's Intelligence Office. The Taylor in that name was Moses M. Taylor, born enslaved in 1816, son of Frank and Allice of Fredericton, Maryland. When and how he came to live in Massachusetts is unknown, but by 1850, he was a minister in Roxbury where, the previous year, he opened an intelligence office that provided "servants of every kind supplied with good places in respectable families, and families supplied with servants, both in the city and country, at short notice, and on respectable terms."[3]

Taylor practiced practical abolitionism, a philosophy of antislavery activism whose adherents took pride in *doing* something, usually small in the grander scheme of antislavery—forming a sewing circle, holding a fair, assisting Black authors in publishing their stories, helping freedom seekers find jobs. Lunsford had surrounded himself with practical abolitionists. Moses Taylor spent his career helping freedom seekers and promoting Black American culture, including funding a reprint of Robert Benjamin Lewis's *Light and Truth*, originally published in 1836 as the first effort by a Black writer to explore the intersections of Black American and Native American histories, "the two races he so ably vindicates." "Do something and do it in earnest," Horace James, Ned and Clarissa Lane's friend, preached about practical abolitionism. Such work was "worth all the efforts to that end of all the Garrisons, Quincys, Wendells, Phillipses, and Abby Fosters in the nation." In the intelligence office, Lunsford Lane combined his older appreciation for rational liberty with the philosophy of practical abolitionism. Those with freedom had a moral obligation to spread the gospel of liberty and ensure it worked for others. "Now, if I understand the first principles of the abolition faith, it is an *active, operating faith*—a faith that will be known only by its *works*," articulated a "brother, in the cause of the oppressed."[4]

In 1850, Lunsford Lane and Moses Taylor formed Taylor & Lane as an act of practical abolitionism. The enterprise offered three services to Bostonians: providing rental properties, operating a courier service throughout the city and its environs, and serving as a job agency "whether for mechanical or laboring purposes," guaranteeing that "particular pains will be taken to furnish good, trust worthy servants in any capacity." Taylor & Lane appears to have advertised only in *The Liberator*, myopically targeting Black laborers and friendly White employers and failing to recognize the transformations within Boston's labor market. Irish laborers hesitated to walk into a Black employment office, and by the end of 1850, Boston's Black labor pool was shrinking too quickly to sustain the business. Lunsford returned to his family on Medford Street, although an emotional chasm had opened between him and Martha.[5]

Indeed, the Boston office of Taylor & Lane was less than a mile from Lane's Cambridgeport home, so why had Lunsford not stayed with his family over those months that the business operated? His and Martha's relationship was not going well. There are plenty of reasons why their marriage suffered: the unbearable grief of losing three young children over a decade, the stress of escaping the South and starting a new life, Martha's anxieties about her husband's long trips on the speaking circuits, his callous public acknowledgment of his pining for Lucy Williams, and, not least, Lunsford's entrepreneurial mediocrity and financial burdens. By March 1851, he was behind three payments on the Medford Street property and could not meet the $1,200 [$47,260] balance. Hoping to salvage the agreement, his mortgagee, Walter Bryant, offered to refinance at $1,000 [$39,380], expecting a payment of $800 [$31,500] within two years and the remaining balance a year later. But Bryant refused to be shortchanged again, and after the signing, he sold the mortgage to Cambridge merchant John P. Nichols.[6]

Lunsford was not making enough money to pay the bills, and escaping to forty acres in the Adirondacks was more tempting than ever, but the rest of the family continued to refuse. To escape his financial problems, he would have to look elsewhere. In July 1851, two letters awaited him at the Cambridgeport post office, at least one of them from Oberlin, Ohio. Lunsford had corresponded with some of his former Raleigh neighbors who, eight years earlier, had moved to Oberlin. They told him of "the mildness of the climate, and its correspondence to North Carolina,—in some respects thus reminding them of home." The possibility of starting anew energized Lunsford, particularly since he already had a support network in place. Still, he paused, opening a provisions and clothing shop in the Cambridge house, an enterprise that failed within the year.[7]

In early 1852, Lane again abandoned his family in Cambridgeport, co-renting a house at 2 Cotting Street in Boston's West End, sharing it with George H. Brown, a Black clothes cleaner from Pennsylvania. On Cotting Street, Lane returned to his roots as a tobacconist briefly. The competition was stiff with at least seventeen other established tobacconists in Boston, and months later, he abandoned the business, returning to the clothes trade briefly with little success. By the summer, he was back with his family in Cambridgeport.[8]

After the failure of Taylor & Lane, then the provisions and clothing shop, then the tobacco business, and finally the clothes sales, Lunsford's entrepreneurial reputation floundered. He learned unrepentant spending too well from the network of wealthy and powerful White Carolinians among whom he once circulated, all dying so indebted that executors sold off large parts of family inheritances just to preserve widow's dowers, and from John Chavis, who modeled that there was no reason free Black men could not carry such debt as well. Lunsford seemed unconcerned about his arrears, but it made sustaining the family from day to day more difficult. When he could not make the initial payment on the new mortgage in March 1852, Nichols foreclosed. Lunsford renegotiated with Nichols but as a renter.[9]

Lane retreated from the abolitionist world, attending only the 1852 annual meeting of the Massachusetts Anti-Slavery Society in Boston. No one asked him to tell The Story. He said little. He slowly planned to relocate, although his vision was set on neither Timbucto nor Oberlin. Over two years, as he neglected payments on the Cambridge property, he had saved enough money to make a $200 [$7,870] down payment on seven acres of "wood & sprout land" from Abner Belcher, his father's friend and neighbor. The land sat adjacent to his father's farm outside Wrentham. Belcher extended Lane a $116 [$4,570] mortgage. A month later, Lunsford bought an adjacent nine acres and a house for $450 [$17,725], taking a $400 [$15,750] loan with 6 percent interest from John A. Craig, a farmer and neighbor, and agreeing to pay it off over four years. Lunsford Lane appeared to prepare to retire to the countryside. He dropped from the roster of agents in service to the American Anti-Slavery Society, and he did not attend meetings of the American Home Baptist Missionary Society. Anticipating the family reunion, his father, Edward, had acquired a strip of land that connected his and his son's properties to the main road to Wrentham.[10]

Then, in April, Martha and Lunsford's third oldest child, Laura Ann, became ill. Tuberculosis consumed her slowly. She struggled with a dry and persistent cough, chest pains, and eventually a sore throat resulting from ulcers. In late spring 1854, she declined precipitously—the hallowing of the cheeks, the sunken eyes, and the death rattle rising from her lungs as she tried to speak. She died in mid-July, twenty years old. Her parents buried her alongside her sister, Celia, in grave 14 of range R in the Cambridge Cemetery. Local newspapers announced her death as that of a celebrity: "She was the first of the seven children who were ransomed from slavery by the untiring efforts of her estimable father, whose case excited such a sensation some years ago. While yet unborn, she was sold with her mother for $60, and at 7 years of age to her own father for $250." The part about Laura Ann being sold while in the womb was untrue, but it tugged at the sentimental heartstrings of its abolitionist readers, as intended.[11]

––––––––––

Amid marital tensions, financial struggles, the loss of a fourth child, and a general lack of purpose, Lunsford Lane drifted away from abolitionism, but abolitionism had been moving away from him for some time. Since the early 1840s, redemption-by-purchase became less a topic of conversation as abolitionists became more determined in their fights against enslavement and enslavers. Even Garrison's moral suasion lost favor as the Fugitive Slave Law of 1850 animated a revolution in abolitionist thinking. In March 1850, the South's loudest voice, Senator John C. Calhoun of South Carolina, laid responsibility for sustaining a *United* States on the North, demanding Northerners "do justice by conceding to the South an equal right in the acquired territory, and to do her duty by causing the stipulations relative to fugitive slaves to be faithfully fulfilled." The United States Senate acquiesced, passing the Fugitive Slave Law as part of the Compromise of 1850. In response, many abolitionists, particularly Black abolitionists, joined the vigilance committees to impede authorities trying to enforce the new law, by force if necessary. Lunsford Lane wanted nothing to do with the turn toward physical violence. After all, the mob that attacked him in Raleigh had been a vigilant committee as well.[12]

Although political and popular debates over the Fugitive Slave Law centered upon the contest between White property rights and Black rights to freedom, embedded in many of those arguments was a more insidious argument over the character of Black Americans. Years earlier, Calhoun contended that in the North, "the number of deaf, dumb, blind, idiots, and insane, of the negroes" was seven times higher than in the South where Black folks "improved greatly in every respect—in number, comfort, intelligence, and morals." Southern newspapers insisted that returning fugitive slaves to enslavement was "a method to keep the African race up to the point of civilization which they have already reached." With a heavy dose of sarcasm, the *Pennsylvania Freeman* replied that "the Fugitive Slave Law is, of course (next to the African slave trade which our Government should hasten to reestablish as the only hope for Africa,) the great agent for the promotion of civilization, and nothing but its full execution will save such men as Pennington, Ward, Garnet, Douglass, Crafts, Wm. W. Brown, Box Brown, Lewis Hayden, Lunsford Lane, and their fellow fugitives, from relapsing into inevitable barbarism." Of course, unlike the others, Lane had not fled enslavement, and his inclusion in the list suggests much about many White abolitionists' assumptions about the Black people around them.[13]

In Boston's First Independent Baptist Church, where the Lanes remained congregants, the Fugitive Slave Law "tore our society to pieces very much." Dozens of members fled to Canada to avoid arrest. Others transferred to the Twelfth Street Baptist Church, which had originated in 1841 when forty-six members abandoned the First Independent Baptist Church because of its overt political activism. By 1850, the Twelfth Street Baptist Church was activist, too, widely regarded as "the fugitive slave church" for its aggressive harboring of and assistance to freedom seekers. With the enactment of the Fugitive Slave Law, it experienced its own schism. Nearly sixty members took flight, as the law "struck the church like a thunderbolt, and scattered the flock." In response, remaining congregants mobilized Black Bostonians. At both churches, clergy suspended services, and renovations stalled.[14]

Freedom seekers had run in and out of Lunsford's life since his youth, hiding in Raleigh's shadows, confined in the cells of Baltimore slave pens, and arriving in New England unaware that they would quickly need strangers to help them secure their liberty. Although White Southerners often feared runaways from enslavement, it was in the North where freedom seekers challenged communal order, inspiring mob violence to protect them. In December 1850, runaway Joshua B. Smith declared at a meeting of Black Bostonians that "If liberty is not worth fighting for, it is not worth having." Six months later, Frederick Douglass wrote Gerrit Smith, "I am prepared to treat Slavery as a System of 'Lawless Violence' incapable in its nature of being legalized." There was no place for compromise or redemption-by-purchase in the polarized atmosphere created by the Fugitive Slave Act.[15]

In February 1851, United States marshals, acting on behalf of a Southern enslaver, arrested Shadrach Minkins in Boston. Minkins had flown Norfolk, Virginia, months earlier. When it appeared that a legal defense would not save Minkins, Lewis Hayden and about twenty other members of the Boston Vigilance Committee acted. Hayden and his wife, Harriet, had escaped Kentucky and enslavement in 1844, heading first to Detroit and then Canada before arriving in Boston, where they became leaders in the underground railroad movement, operating their home as a safe house for freedom seekers. Hayden and other Vigilance Committee members stormed the courtroom, grabbed Minkins, and disappeared into the crowd. Eventually, Minkins made his way to Canada, but the federal government responded with a flurry of charges against his liberators, including Hayden. Eventually, all were acquitted.[16]

About a month passed after Minkins's rescue when Boston authorities helped another Southern enslaver arrest Thomas Sims, who escaped enslavement in Georgia in February. In the scuffle to arrest Sims, he stabbed a United States marshal, Asa O. Butman, in the thigh. With the Minkins episode so fresh on their minds, authorities stationed over one hundred police around the courthouse and chained the doors as Sims went to trial, giving visual symbolism to abolitionists' complaints that the South was enslaving the entire nation. The Boston Vigilance Committee exhausted its legal efforts to help Sims, and the heavy police presence thwarted physical violence. The court ordered Sims returned to Georgia, where he was flogged and sold to a Mississippi enslaver. Abolitionists mourned their failure for years, making them more determined to succeed the next time.[17]

That moment arrived three years later, in May 1854, when Asa O. Butman, healed from his stab wound, arrested Anthony Burns and charged him with robbery. Burns had arrived in Boston months earlier from Richmond, Virginia. The Boston Vigilance Committee appealed for help throughout the

Commonwealth. "The friends here are wide awake and unanimous," wrote Samuel May to a friend in Worcester, "The country must back the city, and, if necessary, lead it." Anne Warren Weston received a letter from Anne Phillips, Wendell's wife, "Do stir up Weymouth for if this man is allowed to go back *there is no* anti-slavery in Massachusetts. We may as well disband at once if our meetings and papers are all talk and never are to do any *but* TALK." Across the Commonwealth, shopkeepers draped black cloth over doorways. City officials lowered the flag of the United States to half-mast, covering it in black as well. Effigies of the men complicit in Burns's arrest— "the Bloodhound," "the Kidnapper," "the Unjust Judge," and President Franklin Pierce, otherwise known as "Satan's Journeyman"—hung on town commons. Reverend Thomas Wentworth Higginson of Worcester's Free Church, a congregation of "comeouters" who rejected traditional denominations for refusing to denounce Southern slaveowners, accepted the invitation of Boston's Vigilance Committee to march on the Boston Courthouse. He led dozens of Worcesterites in joining the Boston mob, demanding Burns's release and condemning state officials who served the slaveocracy at the expense of Massachusetts's Liberty Act of 1843.[18]

When murder disrupted the rioting, Higginson led his army back to Worcester, even as Boston authorities charged him, Wendell Phillips, and Theodore Parker with inciting riots and impeding execution of the Fugitive Slave Law. Two nights later, hundreds of Worcesterites met at City Hall to protest Burns's arrest. Oramel Martin, president of the Worcester Freedom Club, charged the audience to "lay aside business" and march on Boston again "to meet friends of freedom and humanity from other sections of the State, and to take counsel together in the emergencies of the times." As morning broke, nearly eight hundred Worcesterites joined Martin and Higginson in Boston under the banner "Worcester Freedom Club, true to the Union and the Constitution." They burst into the already over-flowing Boston courtroom and, with hundreds of furious Bostonians and Worcesterites surrounding him, Higginson evaded arrest as they disrupted the trial and protested the slaveocracy's "authority in and over Massachusetts." Authorities were prepared, the rescue failed, and the court handed Burns over to his enslaver. Nearly twenty thousand protesters harangued the United States infantry who escorted Burns to the wharves, where he boarded a steamer to Norfolk and back to enslavement.[19]

Lunsford Lane watched these moments from afar. In 1855, the state legislature tried to temper the violence by passing a Personal Liberty Law, defining arrests of freedom seekers as kidnapping and freeing state officials from assisting enslavers and federal authorities. Jails boosted retention charges, and courts increased judicial fees, discouraging slaveowners from their pursuits.

Lane's separation from abolition was complete, however. He never joined the mobs as abolitionism turned too brutal and mobbish for him.[20]

———

By 1855, divorced from an increasingly violent abolitionist cause and struggling to make ends meet, Lunsford Lane faced a crisis of personality and purpose. He continued to fail as an entrepreneur and property owner. He rented the Medford Street property for three years, delaying payments on the lands in Wrentham where his creditors, all friends of his father, patiently pressed for their money. Edward, William, and Lunsford Jr. outgrew their parents' home, setting off in search of their futures. Maria Bell, Alexander, and Clara remained, watching their parents grow apart.

Lunsford Lane could not return to abolitionism. With his message of redemption-by-purchase faded from abolitionists' lexicon, he lost much of his celebrity and prominence, disappearing from the lecture circuit and not speaking publicly again for almost a year. He returned to soliciting donations on a smaller scale, which was the reason why, in March, Lunsford and a friend, Darby Vassall, an "Old Gentleman" of Black Boston, traveled to the Cambridge home of Harvard University professor Henry Wadsworth Longfellow.[21]

Born in 1769, Darby was the son of Catherine and Anthony, and when he was five years old, sold by Catherine's enslaver, John Vassell, to George Reed Jr. of nearby Burlington, Massachusetts. When Reed died during the Battle of Bunker Hill, Darby fled back to his parents just as George Washington took possession of the Vassall estate in July, making it his headquarters for the next ten months. Darby was seven years old, swinging on a gate, when Washington told him to go inside and be useful. He asked how much Washington would pay him, with the General refusing him anything. As Darby retold the story years later, he concluded that George Washington was "no gentleman."[22]

In the early 1790s, Darby moved to Boston with his brother, established a mutual aid association known as the African Society, and joined in establishing a school for Black children two decades before the Abiel Smith School. He became a member of Boston's Brattle Square Church, refusing to remain in "his solitary place in the negro-loft above the organ" and taking a comfortable seat near the pulpit "to the discomfort of some fastidious pewholders." Over the years, Darby Vassall became a member of the New England Anti-Slavery Society, where he met and became fast friends with William Lloyd Garrison, Wendell Phillips, and eventually Lunsford Lane. In 1855, when Lane and Vassall journeyed to Longfellow's house, Vassall was eighty-seven years old and no stranger to the poet, who had received the old Vassall estate as a wedding present from his father-in-law in 1843 and became familiar with many formerly enslaved people who visited from time to time.[23]

When Lane and Vassell approached Longfellow's door on March 21, 1855, the poet was in the middle of selling his latest poem, *The Song of Hiawatha*, to potential publisher James T. Fields. Longfellow had finished writing it the previous day, and "Of course the bells rang!" As Fields listened to Longfellow read the introduction and a chapter titled "The Peace Pipe," there was a rap at the door. "Lundy Lane and old Mr. Vassall (born a slave in this house in 1769) come to see me," Longfellow later penned in his diary, "and stay so long that Fields is driven away, and there is the end of the reading of Hiawatha."[24]

Longfellow hosted Lane and Vassall for hours, entreating Lunsford to relate The Story. When it came to discussing enslavement, Lane's attitude toward storytelling aligned with Longfellow's philosophy of poetry—"written in a kindly—not a vindictive spirit. Humanity is the chord to be touched." Lane's self-making also aligned with Longfellow's ideal of American manhood, an earnest manhood contextualized in and moderated by a sentimental dedication to family and obligation to a larger community. Delighted with their visit, the professor handed "Lundfort Lane" $10 [$354]. The two men inspired Longfellow, who, over the next month, donated hundreds of more dollars, including $6 [$212] to "Ida May, slave," $5 [$177] each to a "Fugitive Slave" and to the "African School," and $7 [$248] as a subscription to Charles Spear's newspaper, *The Prisoner's Friend*. Although Longfellow did not note it in his ledger, Lane also might have advocated for redemption-by-purchase for, soon afterward, the poet contributed $5 "to free a slave."[25]

———

Two months later, in May 1855, Lunsford attended the American and Foreign Bible Society meeting in Brooklyn, six years since his last attendance at a religion-oriented association. As delegates discussed the need to print and distribute Bibles in English, as it "was the conquering tongue of the world," Lane reminded them not to neglect sharing the Gospel with enslaved Americans. After the midday break, he continued, articulating his mild religiosity: "He had joined the Baptist church 30 years ago. . . . because his mother and grandmother were Baptists; he had been educated in the Episcopalian Church. . . . He had heard such men as Bishop [John Stark] Ravenscroft and Bishop [Lee Silliman] Ives, but he soon found out their turnings. Latterly, having examined, he liked the Baptists still; he liked them even more, but (he said) don't take too much congratulation to yourselves for that." His listeners erupted in laughter.[26]

The audience's amusement was short-lived. Lunsford explained how he recently attended a four-hour Black worship service, where the congregants "worked violently till perspiration ran down their faces; in this there was no order, no propriety; not one, when the service was over, could repeat a clear idea he had therein received." His pious listeners grew impatient with Lunsford's sleights, and the chairman bluntly asked why Lane was at the meeting. The First Independent Baptist Church in Boston had sent him to solicit $1,000 [$35,450] to complete its rebuilding, suspended years earlier as the congregation splintered in the aftermath of passage of the Fugitive Slave Act. They took a collection, falling well short of Lunsford's request. Months later, renovations began on the First Independent Baptist Church, but for the next three years, Lane continued to visit society meetings, asking for more aid.[27]

In June 1855, a state census taker rapped at the Lanes' front door. When, in 1850, a federal census taker had visited Medford Street, the house was full: Martha, Maria Bell, Laura Ann, William, Lunsford Jr., Alexander, and Clara, with Edward in the smaller adjacent building. Although Lunsford lived at the Intelligence Office in Boston, the census taker had listed him with the family. Five years later, the state official found a different household. Only Maria Bell, Alexander, and Clara remained with their parents. Laura Ann had died. Edward had moved to Oberlin, Ohio, to practice his shoemaking business. His brothers, William and Lunsford Jr., had just disappeared, possibly helping their grandparents, Edward and Clarissa, with the farm, but at eighteen years old, they could have been anywhere.[28]

With the Lanes' three oldest sons gone, Lunsford's aspiration to leave Cambridgeport deflated. He no longer had the help to operate a farm in Wrentham or carve one from the wilds of the Adirondacks, and his youngest son, Alexander, had contracted tuberculosis. Lunsford determined to stabilize the family's situation, negotiating with his landlord to repurchase the Medford Street property. In September 1855, Nichols agreed to give Lane another chance for $1,200 [$42,540]. Lunsford agreed to pay the total within one year, but Nichols had heard such promises before and took no chances, immediately selling the mortgage deed to the Cambridge Mutual Fire Insurance Company, one of many financial institutions willing to invest in riskier lending.[29]

In the fall of 1855, Lunsford owed on three properties: $316 [$11,200] on the wood and sprout land in Wrentham, $400 [$14,180] on the adjacent 9.5 acres and house, and $1,200 [$42,540] on the Medford Street property. Still dreaming of abandoning Cambridgeport, he prioritized the Wrentham house and, in early May 1856, made the final payment on the mortgage with John Craig. Yet, within a couple of months, he used the property as collateral for yet another loan. Throughout his life, Lunsford Lane's relationship to property and finances remained thorny and undisciplined. By 1857, he had defaulted on and abandoned two properties, held two mortgages totaling $1,516 [$53,780], and, with no steady work, advertised as a carpenter for which he had no training. The financial pressures became crushing. Years later, Lunsford blamed his failures on "unprincipled land speculators, who succeeded in swindling him out of nearly all the funds he had invested," but he had created his own problems.[30]

Lane desperately sought a way out from under the debts. Beginning in July 1857, he received a flurry of mail at the Boston post office, some from Edward in Oberlin. Lunsford had considered it previously, but by mid-1857, Ohio offered a real escape. Over the past nine years, Lane made not one payment from his own earnings on the Medford Street property, relying instead on new arrangements and loans on which he also did not pay. In November, Lane refinanced the Medford Street property yet again, taking another mortgage loan for $300 [$10,630] from Boston printer George P. Oakes. Amazingly, on that one property, he had held five different mortgages, been foreclosed upon, forced to rent, and allowed to repurchase. In an age before credit ratings, lenders relied on the good faith of the mortgagor, and Lunsford was effective in gaining peoples' trust. Should he fail to meet their terms, they could recover their losses by foreclosing.[31]

In December 1857, after Lane did not make the first two scheduled payments on the most recent loan, his latest mortgagee, Oakes, entered the Medford Street house "for a breach of condition" only to find it abandoned. To lay claim to the property, Oakes quickly paid the property taxes for 1857, but he would have to fight the Cambridge Mutual Fire Insurance Company in the courts over who owned the house. One thing was certain: it was not Lunsford Lane.[32]

Lunsford, Martha, Maria Bell, and Clara stealthily abandoned Cambridgeport. Alexander remained behind, too weakened by his tuberculosis to make the long journey to Ohio. Lunsford apprenticed him to William Jones, a Boston cabinetmaker who had flown enslavement in Virginia years earlier. Jones and his wife, Elisabeth, were to provide Alexander with food and a warm place to sleep. When the Lanes arrived in Oberlin in mid-December, Edward greeted his family with the painful news that, soon after the family took to the road, "of consumption, Alexander, youngest son of Lunsford and Martha Lane, aged 17 years and 5 months," died. The burials of Laura Ann and Celia years earlier showed how, even in death, the Lanes sought to keep their family together. That would not be the case with Alexander. Without their instructions, Jones buried Alexander in Woodlawn Cemetery, a rural garden cemetery in Everett, just north of Boston.[33]

Reuniting with Edward did not lessen the grief over their youngest son's death, but it was an opportunity to recreate a familiar community. In Oberlin, Edward lived with John and Mary Campton, the Lanes' former neighbors in Raleigh. Since migrating, John Campton had done well for himself as a master carpenter, acquiring two properties worth $3,000 [$104,260]. Mary and he had three more children, and in the late 1850s, they also housed four Black students from Arkansas and Kentucky who attended Oberlin College and twenty-seven-year-old Edward Lane who made shoes.[34]

Others from the 1843 migration fared just as well as the Camptons. John Lane renewed his blacksmith business and, in early 1855, married Sarah Alice Johnson from New England. He became a local leader in the Colored Conventions movement, dedicated to inspiring Black self-reliance through education, labor, and legal justice.[35]

Allen Jones, too, continued his blacksmithing. He and Polly raised their seven children, who journeyed with them from North Carolina. Jones became prominent in Ohio's Black rights movement, representing the state in the 1848 National Convention of the Colored Freemen and serving as a convention vice president. In 1856, the *Cleveland Herald* praised Jones as "one character meet for the pen of Harriet Beecher Stowe." Dedicated to education, Jones made sure his own children received their share. "Two of his six sons have graduated with college honors," continued the paper. "Two others will at next Commencement, and his other sons and daughter are examples of industry and studiousness that many of lighter skin might imitate with advantage." By the time the Lanes arrived in Oberlin, Jones was retreating from the world, mourning his wife's 1856 death and missing grown children who had migrated to Canada.[36]

John and Delilah Copeland prospered as well. John worked as a house joiner. Delilah raised eight children, only the three oldest boys remembering North Carolina. In 1854, the eldest, twenty-year-old John Anthony Copeland Jr., joined the freshman class at Oberlin College but stayed less than a year. Among the family was an adoptee. On their journey northward in 1843, somewhere in Kentucky, the Copelands had accepted Rubin Turner into their family. He had been only an infant, less than a year old, suggesting that his mother gave him to the Copelands to carry to freedom.[37]

When the Copelands arrived in Oberlin in 1843 with John Lane, Allen Jones, and the Camptons, the families represented the entire migrant population from North Carolina. By the mid-1850s, they were the forebears of an enlarging Black community in Oberlin, swelling from nineteen in 1850 to 134 a decade later. In 1853, another caravan had left North Carolina, led by the Lanes' former neighbors, Henry and Emeline Patterson and their five children, and joined by Henry's brother John and his family. In Oberlin, Henry and John set up a masonry business. Their older children enrolled in Oberlin College. The Patterson households also welcomed Oberlin students from Ohio, Texas, Bermuda, and North Carolina. A year later, Delilah Evans Copeland's brothers, Henry and Wilson Evans, led a third migration group of nineteen travelers hailing from various parts of North Carolina. By late 1857, transplanted North Carolinians composed a third of Oberlin's Black community, outnumbering migrants from Ohio and neighboring states. Oberlin, then, offered Lunsford Lane and his family not only a fresh start but a reunion with North Carolina far from its enslavement and White supremacy.[38]

———

As the Lanes began a new life in Oberlin, back in Wrentham, Lunsford's father was sick. Dozens of neighbors helped Clarissa nurse her husband, but in late February 1858, Edward Lane, born enslaved, died a free man. "So it was said, 'Mr. Lane is the only perfect gentleman in Wrentham,'" began Edward's friend, Abner Belcher, in his eulogy days later. "Though it was his lot to have all the physical comforts he could desire, yet the ruthless hand of slavery pierced his heart. He knew the liabilities to which he was exposed. Twice he was sold at auction." Drawing a sharp contrast between the pillory of slavery and the cradle of freedom, Belcher continued: "Since he resided here, he learned to read, and the progress he made in the knowledge of first principles showed a mind of the highest order. He sympathized with those he left in bonds, and with all here who make no compromise with slavery, and are laboring for its eternal overthrow." More than a man of virtuous character, Edward had been "an exalted Christian," one of such high moral principles that he could never "connect himself with the slaveholding church in his native place." Although Edward's antislavery activism was minimal, "he sympathized with those he left in bonds, and with all here who make no compromise with slavery, and are laboring for its eternal overthrow." The words contrasted sharply with another remembrance that Clarissa received in the mail a month later.[39]

In March, a letter arrived from Lucy Davis Haywood Bryan. "Miss Lucy" and her sister, "Miss Delia," had been raised by Clarissa, frequently playing with Lunsford when they were children before they learned to command him. After Edward's death, someone penned a letter on Clarissa's behalf to her sister, Matilda. Lucy intercepted the letter and assumed it licensed her to write. "I sincerely sympathize with you in the loss of your husband," Bryan wrote. "You had lived together so long and so happily that you must feel this dispensation of God as a great affliction."[40]

Lucy Bryan was more interested in comforting herself. Despite not having seen Clarissa in fifteen years, she still imagined the former cook as part of the family, an insistence that enslavers used to portray the South as a stable social and moral order that they imagined to be under threat by 1858. As one enslaving mistress decried seven years later when the end of enslavement was clear to all, "There will be no more old mammies and daddies, no more uncles and aunties. . . . The sweet ties that bound our old family servants to us will be broken and replaced with envy and ill-will." In her salutation to Clarissa, Bryan pleaded for that familial relationship, addressing the letter to "My Dear

Aunt Clarissa." She fondly recalled Clarissa being "so faithful and affectionate to our family" so that Lucy felt "great respect and affection for you" in return.[41]

Lucy Bryan's letter was her effort to momentarily escape what had transpired among the Haywoods. Her mother, Eleanor Haywood, had died in December 1855. The will scattered the enslaved Haywood community among Eleanor's heirs, according to Sherwood's original directives decades earlier. When Robert W. Haywood, Eleanor's son and executor, distributed the enslaved property, he overlooked the children of his sister, Nancy Haywood Blount, who had died thirty years earlier. William Blount and Nancy Blount Branch sued him and their other uncle, John D. Hawkins, who served as Sherwood's executor. They wanted their share of the estate, blocking the executors' efforts to sell off property and pay down the debts. The Wake County Court of Equity found in favor of Blount and Branch, ordering the executors to pay $20,000 [$723,475] plus interest. To meet the payment, in January 1857, the executors sold Eleanor's estate—two town lots and the house, the small kitchen in which Clarissa had raised her baby boy, and the Wake County farm where Lunsford had taken the horses to pasture. It was a very nasty family mess. Lucy Bryan was among the defendants in *William A. Blount and others v. John D. Hawkins and others*. Although news of Edward Lane's death elicited her sympathy, it also provided her an opportunity to reconsider the family's drama, find calm in her memories of a simpler past, and identify some humanity in the objectification of enslaved peoples as property and inheritance.[42]

Although the court forced the sale of Haywood landed properties, it did not order the executors to sell the enslaved laborers, permitting John D. Hawkins to hire out all 140 of them until the legal challenges resolved. Since it was Sherwood Haywood's will that distributed the enslaved humans among his children, Hawkins undertook to reconstruct the inventory at the time of Sherwood's death in 1828. Over the intermediate twenty-seven years until Eleanor's death, she had sold two farms in other counties and twenty-three humans. In most cases, financial pressures compelled Eleanor to make the decisions to sell, but not always. In 1834, she had sold Joe Branch, Tempe, and Needham, whose escape to New York brought public scorn upon the Haywoods, out of pure spite.[43]

Lucy Bryan's nephew and niece were greedy, challenging Hawkins's reconstructed inventory and sending the case onto the docket of the North Carolina Supreme Court. They also questioned five specific decisions that the lower court made against them on issues of unpaid interest and the profits that Eleanor made from the 1834 sales of Joe Branch, Tempe, and Needham. In mid-December 1858, the Supreme Court issued its decision, concluding that

Eleanor Haywood acted in good faith as executor of her husband's estate, freeing Robert W. Haywood to distribute the enslaved laborers according to Sherwood's instructions and auction away the sixteen enslaved peoples who remained Eleanor's domestics.[44]

Hawkins's inventorying of the Haywoods' enslaved properties sparked Lucy Bryan's recollections of Clarissa, who appeared twice on the lists: once for the $200 [$7,230] paid to purchase her; and the second time as "an old negro [who] would be 78 years old if alive—She was allowed to go with her husband to Massachusetts he being emancipated for meritorious services by Mrs John Haywood." That last part was inaccurate, of course, for Clarissa went with her son, leaving behind her still enslaved husband despite his meritorious service for which he was never emancipated.[45]

When the letter to Matilda announcing Edward Lane's death arrived in Raleigh, then, it was the first indication that Clarissa was still alive. Lucy took full advantage of the opportunity to share news. After Eleanor Haywood had died, Clarissa's sister Matilda lived with Lucy Bryan's sister, Sally Haywood Hogg, and her husband Gavin. The Hoggs granted Matilda freedom for "meritorious service." As Lucy reported to Clarissa, they "built a room for her, and Miss Sally gave her Clarissa (Matilda's own daughter) to wait on her." Matilda "looks well, and is yet a smart, active woman," and her husband, Alexander Curtis, was on the Hogg plantation with her, still enslaved. Lucy added that "Billy Noyes, (the carpenter) is still living, and Green (the teamster). Hasty (the cook) lives with me. I took her to care for her. She is quite smart and active, and cooks very well."[46]

Lucy Bryan seemed oblivious to the paradoxes in her report. The Hoggs "gave" Matilda her own daughter. Lucy took Hasty "to care for her" but made the enslaved woman do the cooking. The thoughtlessness of enslaving others flowed throughout the letter. Bryan even recalled when, years earlier, freedom tempted Clarissa to abandon Lucy during a trip to New York City. "I persuaded you to stay, . . . and when I would cry, you were so tender-hearted and kind you would promise to stay": Lucy showed no sense that Clarissa returned to North Carolina for reasons other than comforting her. Manipulation and privilege had formed the foundation of Lucy and Clarissa's relationship for decades, and Bryan was not willing to give it up, insisting that Clarissa recognize how the "abolitionists say a great deal about Southern people; but you know from your own experience, and that of your family, *that you never received any but the kindest treatment.*" It was an appeal to be remembered generously and to reimagine that, for Clarissa, enslavement had been a benevolent institution, oblivious to the ways in which enslavement left its mark on Clarissa and all the Lanes.[47]

Beyond the statement about Clarissa's sister, Lucy Bryan related other useful family news. "Sam Mac (Lunsford's uncle), as he is called,—I believe he is a brother of Uncle Ned's,—is still living," she wrote. Sixty-seven-year-old Sam remained in Raleigh, apparently in Martha Lane McKeithan Brickell's service. Upon her death in 1852, Martha had bequeathed Sam to her sister, Grizelle Lane Ryan. He outlived his sister, Cate, by thirty years and his brother, Ned, by at least a few months.[48]

Sadly, despite Lucy Bryan's familial claim to Clarissa, she said little about Clarissa's loss and grief. Neither did she include some words from Matilda. When Lucy concluded her letter, she consoled Clarissa: "I am pleased to see that you show so much Christian resignation in your trouble, and hope you will live many years to comfort your family." It was not to be. Clarissa had suffered a stroke some years earlier, and her grief over Edward's death contributed to a severe decline in her health. She died two months later, with Lunsford and his family by her side.[49]

Lunsford, Martha, Maria, and Clara were in Oberlin only a few months before news of his father's death arrived. They returned to Wrentham as stealthily as they once had abandoned Cambridgeport, arriving just in time to sit with Clarissa as she passed. Weighted with grief and lacking the funds to pay himself, Lunsford appealed to Edward and Clarissa's neighbors, John A. Craig and Silas D. Fisher, who had extended mortgages to his father over the years, to post a $100 [$3,690] bond on his behalf so that he could serve as executor. He began to inventory the farm and household to settle his parents' debts, posting a broadside notice of the estate settlement at least twice in Wrentham and advertising it three times in the *Dedham Gazette*.[50]

When an enslaved man, Lunsford Lane never had imagined the possibility of inheritance. In May 1858, he seemed eager to realize it. He mortgaged his parents' property even before he submitted paperwork to become the estate administrator, and it became clear why Craig and Fisher so willingly contributed to Lane's bond. On May 10, Lane took a loan of $500 [$18,460] from Craig, using as collateral the one acre surrounding his parents' house and five acres of the wood and sprout land that he had purchased years earlier. Three days later, Fisher bought from Lunsford a one-acre outlying parcel with a small house for $300 [$11,080], and Melansa and Abner Belcher paid $180 [$6,650] for eleven uncleared acres.[51]

For years, Lunsford had a tumultuous relationship with property ownership, and its origins can be traced to his enslavement. Denial of property ownership was a pillar of White Southern oppression of Black Southerners, and until he lost his inventory in the fire of 1832, Lane hid his meager possessions in the basement of Benjamin B. Smith's store. Then, after his emancipation, he acquired the house on Cabarrus Street and built a shack in which he stored tobacco and wood. In 1846, he bought the Moore Street house in Cambridgeport. In 1848, he obtained the Medford Street property just up the street. In 1854, Lunsford purchased the Wrentham lands. Property ownership came with freedom, but so did the ability to lose it. By 1858, he lost or sold without profit every property he had owned in the South and North. Suddenly, his parents' inheritance offered a path to some financial stability, but the promise was illusionary. On May 15, the court assigned Craig and others to appraise the estate, which they valued at only $325 [$12,000], far below the $500 mortgage Lunsford had assumed. The personal estate was worth $150.50 [$5,560], but Edward owed $132.41 [$4,890], leaving Lunsford with $18.09 [$670] and considerable debt, again.[52]

The Lanes stayed in Edward and Clarissa's house over the summer of 1858, but Lunsford planned to sell it as well. He found a new home, a rental, in Woonsocket, a textile mill village twelve miles southwest of Wrentham, just across the Rhode Island state line. The village's leading figure was Edward Harris, a maker of woolen "fancy cassimeres." By the late 1850s, eleven other textile factories operated alongside Harris's Woolen Mills, running at least fifty thousand spindles and producing cotton goods for Southern markets. Lunsford knew Harris, an abolitionist and Liberty Man, making easy the decision to settle in Woonsocket. Unlike Cambridgeport and Oberlin, the community was small, and the Black community even smaller, comprising only twenty-six people, half of whom served as domestic servants in millowners' houses. None of them worked the mills, locked out of employment by immigrant laborers. Numbering four, the Lanes became the largest Black family in 1858 and the only family from the South.[53]

As the Lanes settled into Woonsocket, Lunsford resolved the real estate situation in Wrentham. In September 1858, he paid off the $500 loan to John A. Craig, taking full ownership of the six acres, which he then sold for $500 to Mary Magee, a widowed neighbor. She put down $125 [$4,610], taking a mortgage from Lunsford for $375 [$13,850]. Lane's newfound real estate savvy was short-lived. Even as he signed the deed in Wrentham, in Cambridgeport, the Medford Street property went into court for final foreclosure.[54]

In October, the Middlesex County sheriff announced forfeiture of "all the right in equity which LUNSFORD LANE, of said Cambridge, had" and a forthcoming auction of the Medford Street property to pay off Lunsford's debt to John T. Federhen Jr., a Boston silversmith and jeweler. In the previous February, having just returned from Oberlin to Wrentham, Lane rented a house from Federhen on Briton Street Court in Boston. Whether it was for the family or yet another separation from Martha is unclear. He never paid rent and damaged the door and door frame. Federhen sued for $64.69 [$2,380], but Lane did not show up for court. The sheriff left a summons for Lane at the Medford Street house—the "last and usual place of abode"—but of course, Lane, long gone, never replied. Despite claims to the property by George Oakes and the Cambridge Mutual Fire Insurance Company, in October, the court ordered the sheriff to confiscate and sell Lane's property to meet the debts to Federhen. In December, Lunsford's "title or interest in said Estate" ended when Amory Houghton Jr. bought the property and house at public auction for twenty dollars [$740]. The sheriff did not warrant the property as free from any liens or mortgages, leaving open the possibility that there would be future legal battles.[55]

With a string of real estate disasters behind him, Lunsford made Woonsocket, not Oberlin or Wrentham or Timbucto, the new beginning. Twenty-year-old Maria Bell Lane found work as a dressmaker, twelve-year-old Clara began school, fifty-three-year-old Martha kept house, and Lunsford, the same age as his wife, remade himself. He abandoned abolitionism, lecturing, and selling books to become a doctor. He had no former training in medicine, but in his youth, he had learned herbal medicine from his mother and the art of horticulture from his father. He knew the plants that contained healing powers. While in Raleigh, he developed a reputation for his hangover recipes. Politicians had called him "Doctor," usually uttering the words in mockery. In Woonsocket, in an age when patent medicines became all the rage, Lane made and sold Dr. Lane's Vegetable Pills. Years later, a friend editorialized that although the pills "have never done much good to mankind, he promises they will do no harm." Sales were enough to sustain the family for the moment. As his labels indicated, Lunsford was now Dr. Lane.[56]

———

Twenty-nine-year-old Edward Lane stayed in Oberlin when his family returned eastward, continuing to make and peddle shoes in a shop on College Street that he shared with Hugh M. Haynes and John L. Hunter. Born enslaved in 1824, Haynes flew from North Carolina in the early 1850s, possibly as a member of Henry and Emeline Patterson's caravan, accompanied by two brothers, Isham and Edwin, and Edwin's wife Mary and son George. The third cobbler was John L. Hunter, born enslaved in 1828 in Tennessee. The shoemaking business provided a sufficient income, especially as Edward Lane continued to live with the Camptons.[57]

In August 1858, months after the rest of the Lanes returned eastward, a Kentuckian visiting Oberlin recognized a young man, John Price, who had flown enslavement two years earlier. Price hid in Oberlin, married, and began a family. The visitor enlisted a United States official in arresting Price and taking the prisoner to the Brick Hotel in Wellington, some eight miles away. Abolitionists ran throughout Oberlin, broadcasting that "they have carried off one of our men in broad daylight and are an hour on their way already." Soon, hundreds from Oberlin and Wellington surrounded the hotel, Wilson Bruce Evans, Henry Evans, Henrietta Evans, and John Anthony Copeland Jr. among them. One observer numbered the crowd as at least five hundred, with hundreds more crowding sidewalks, windows, and rooftops to watch. They refused to let the Kentuckian leave the hotel with his captive. Two groups stormed the building, one led by Copeland Jr., eventually freeing Price and escorting him back to Oberlin, where he hid for days before fleeing to Canada. In the moments following Price's escape, an activist yelled above the crowd, "We believe in State Sovereignty, and the moment a slave touches Ohio soil he is free, and all the South combined cannot carry him back, if we say No!" The crowd roared, parading back to Oberlin and celebrating through the night with chants of "Democracy" and "Liberty." The episode became known as the Oberlin-Wellington Rescue.[58]

John Copeland Jr. and his peers saved John Price out of principle, frustration, anger, and desperation. The Fugitive Slave Law of 1850, the Kansas-Nebraska Act of 1854 and its resulting violence, the caning of Senator Charles Sumner in 1856, the United States Supreme Court's *Dred Scott* decision in 1857—the arc of history seemed to bend against abolitionism. Activism against unjust law required exceptional courage, the type of bravery exhibited by thousands of Black men and women who flew enslavement and by the thousands more willing to stand up to harbor freedom seekers. As the Western Anti-Slavery Society resolved at its 1859 meeting in Canton, Ohio, the Oberlin-Wellington Rescue demonstrated that whereas "state government has either no authority or no power to protect the citizens of the State from the outrageous aggressions of the slaveholder," it was the right, indeed the duty, of the people to protect themselves, their families, and their friends.[59]

Of the thirty-seven men indicted for undermining the Fugitive Slave Law for participating in Price's rescue, one-third were Black men—three freedom seekers, six emancipated men, and three born free, including the Evans brothers. Four others were White theology students, inheritors of Oberlin College's radical origins as a home for the Lane Rebels who abandoned the more conservative Lane Seminary in 1834–1835 to find a more actively anti-slavery education. Most participants were professionals—a college professor, a bookseller, a lawyer, a shoe merchant, two cobblers, two cabinetmakers, a clerk, and a physician. Three did not even travel to Wellington but allegedly aided and abetted the crime from afar. There were a few farmers, primarily from Wellington, reputed to be conductors on an underground railroad. All of them spent time in jail, but in the end, only two of the rescuers faced trial, convicted of breaking the Fugitive Slave Law. The Evans brothers counted eighty-three days in the Cuyahoga County jail.[60]

What of those who did not join in? Edward Lane might have been among the five hundred who surrounded the hotel, but he did not participate to the point that others noticed. He may not have traveled to Wellington at all, although, by all accounts, the number of Black participants and onlookers from Oberlin was exceptionally high. His father, Lunsford, opposed mob activism and passed his reservations on to his eldest.

Edward probably felt quite lonesome in the aftermath of the Oberlin-Wellington Rescue, his family having stayed only months before returning to his grandmother's deathbed. He was not alone for long. With little money and accused of vandalizing the apartment that he rented in Boston, Lunsford abandoned Martha and their daughters in Woonsocket, returning to Oberlin, still harboring a dream to live there. In December, he paid $75 [$2,710] down on half of village lot 5 from Sidney S. Goodell, an Oberlin sashmaker (or window installer). Lane agreed to two initial annual payments of $208.83 [$7,550] and took a $464.64 [$16,800] mortgage from merchant Andrew Dutton to cover the rest of the asking price of $900 [$32,550]. He abandoned the Dr. before his name, again advertising as a book agent. Having exhausted New England's markets, he carried his stock of *The Narrative of Lunsford Lane* westward, set up an office on Main Street, and peddled, earning enough in the first year to make his first two house payments. That little taste of success inspired him to stay in Oberlin, but it did not draw Martha westward. She, Clara, and Maria Bell remained in Rhode Island.[61]

Then came Harpers Ferry. In early October 1859, John Brown—the abolitionist who wanted to join Black families in Gerrit Smith's Timbucto, settled in Kansas where he murdered five proslavery settlers in 1856 and then relocated to the Adirondacks—planned to attack the United States arsenal at Harpers Ferry, Virginia, dreaming of stirring enslaved peoples to revolt. Brown's son, John Brown Jr., recruited in Oberlin, eventually signing on only two men, both migrants from North Carolina, who acted in the Oberlin-Wellington Rescue: Lewis Sheridan Leary and John Anthony Copeland Jr. Leary left behind a wife and one-year-old daughter as he and Copeland marched off to join Brown and nineteen others, ready to start a revolution.[62]

The raid was a failure. As United States Marines surrounded the arsenal, Leary tried to escape by swimming across the Shenandoah River. He was shot in the back, suffering for nearly eight hours before dying. John Copeland Jr. remained barricaded with Brown until the Marines finally arrested them, along with three others. A week later, they went on trial. Since the *Dred Scott* decision of 1857 stripped Black Americans of citizenship rights, Copeland could not be charged with treason as were the White men. Instead, the tribunal sentenced him to death for murder and conspiracy to incite rebellion against the United States. In December 1859, awaiting execution, Copeland wrote his brother, insisting that the "blood of Black men flowed as freely as that of white men" in the Revolutionary War. "To the truth of this, history, though prejudiced, is compelled to attest." He consoled his parents to "*remember it was a holy cause*, one in which men in every way better than I am, have suffered and died." Authorities hanged John Anthony Copeland Jr. on 16 December 1859, two weeks after John Brown.[63]

Lunsford and Edward joined other mourners who gathered at the Copeland home in Oberlin to support their friends, but Delilah Copeland refused to show weakness. "If I could be the means of destroying slavery, I would willingly give up all of the menfolks," she resolved. Instead, she gave up her son's body. The Copelands enlisted an Oberlin College professor to recover their son's corpse, but before he could get to Winchester, Copeland's cadaver went to a local medical school, dissected and hidden by the students from anyone wishing to retrieve it.[64]

Weeks later, Lunsford Lane abandoned Oberlin and Edward. The Oberlin-Wellington Rescue, Harpers Ferry—he tired of the radical abolitionists and the attention they drew to the communities in which they lived. He "felt no desire to remain where there was any doubt of maintaining the freedom of himself and family." The Copelands' loss of their son possibly made him realize how he once sacrificed so much for family and seemed to have forgotten them over the past year. Maybe "unscrupulous men" swindled him, as he later claimed. Whatever the reason, he returned to Woonsocket in January 1860. Eight months later, when Goodell did not receive another mortgage payment, Ohio property laws restricted him from simply taking possession of the property. He sued Lane for the $693.17 [$25,070] balance. Wrapped up in Goodell's suit was Andrew Dutton, who had extended Lunsford the mortgage on which he still owed $424.64 [$15,360]. The Court of Common Pleas offered for Lane to pay $93.17 [$3,370] by December to redeem his original purchase, but again, Lane did not show up for court, forfeiting a second property in as many years. In December, the Court confiscated the lot, selling it in early March 1861 at auction for $650 [$23,510]. After court fees and the payoff on Dutton's loan, Goodell recuperated little owed to him. Again, Lane held others responsible for the loss of property, conceding that the Oberlin lot "had been mortgaged to other parties for far more than it was worth." He lost little compared to his mortgagee.[65]

From Cambridgeport to Oberlin to Wrentham to Woonsocket, with occasional stays in Boston, Lunsford Lane wandered through the 1850s, restless and unsure. He and Martha lost two more children, he lost both parents, and he lost a bit of himself, no longer the American Aeneas.

Chapter 13

Wartime in Worcester

As the sun rose on the first morning of August 1862, Black Worcesterites boarded omnibuses at the Zion Methodist Episcopal Church, traveling a little over three miles to the shores of beautiful Lake Quinsigamond where a "picnic excursion" awaited. Guests strolled along the lake shore and enjoyed the swings, a buffet of fish chowder, and a women's chorus that serenaded with popular religious and patriotic songs. In the evening, as dusk fell, attendees traveled home, their spirits and stomachs full.[1]

Previous Emancipation Days commemorated Britain's Slavery Abolition Act of 1833, but 1862 was different. A bit over three months earlier, in April, Abraham Lincoln signed legislation abolishing enslavement in the District of Columbia. Participants felt more patriotic. The women's chorus opened with "America": "My country! 'tis of thee / Sweet land of liberty / Of thee I sing." Guest orators praised the president and anticipated "the greater emancipation which must take place in our own country." Among them was Lunsford Lane, invited to speak by the event organizers.[2]

The good Dr. Lane's reputation preceded him. Only days earlier, he and Martha left Woonsocket with Maria Bell and Clara. William and Lunsford Jr. had not returned home and purportedly were on their way to Port Royal, South Carolina, as support personnel for a federal experiment to determine if formerly enslaved peoples could own and profit from their own farms. The dangers faced by the Lanes' twenty-five-year-old twin sons stirred empathy in Lunsford and Martha for the thousands of Northerners sending husbands, fathers, and sons off to war. It was why they were in Worcester. They spent the next year attending to young men, many about William and Lunsford Jr.'s age, either recuperating or dying in Worcester's Wellington Hospital.

––––––

Lunsford and Martha arrived in Worcester in the summer of 1862 as the town buzzed with pride over its White sons' military enlistments. Lunsford might have renewed his purpose and profit in lecturing, but it was more likely that Worcester's political atmosphere worried him. As Thomas Wentworth Higginson declared, the town was "a seething center of all of the reforms." Edward and Clarissa Lane's friend in Wrentham, Horace James, had accepted the pulpit of Worcester's Old South Church in 1852, expecting to fill

Sunday services with calls for activism. Abolition, temperance, women's rights, free people's relief, Irish charity, workingmen's rights—the town had been simmering for a long time.[3]

In Worcester, a man could go about openly as a freedom seeker, convinced that the community would protect him should the slave hunters come to town. When the Fugitive Slave Law passed in 1850, residents "white and Black, bond and free" crammed into City Hall "almost to suffocation" to denounce the Slaveocracy's invasion. Jeremiah Myers took the stage, declaring that "he had made up his mind after four escapes from slavery to go for a trial by jury. The law said otherwise, but he was determined before he went back to slavery again to have twelve Massachusetts men sit in judgment of him." Years later, Frederick Douglass remarked how "a colored man was deemed a fool who confessed himself a runaway slave, not only because of the danger to which he exposed himself of being retaken, but because it was a confession of a very *low* origin." Douglass saw it that way, but in Worcester, it was a badge of honor, at least for Myers, who reported his occupation as "{F. Slave}" in the 1850 federal census and trusted his White neighbors to safeguard his freedom.[4]

In late October 1854, alarm spread to "Look Out for Kidnappers!" as rumor circulated that the infamous Asa O. Butman had arrived in town. A mob, led by Stephen Symonds Foster, marched on Butman's hotel. Their prey emerged with gun in hand. Local police, ordered by the mayor not to cooperate with federal marshals, arrested Butman for carrying a concealed weapon, dragging him before a justice of the peace as rioters yelled and threw punches. The bedlam spilled over into the courtroom where three young Black men—barbers Alexander Hemenway and Solomon H. Dutton and wiredrawer John Angier Jr.—pummeled Butman. As authorities attempted to restore order, "the storm burst out anew," giving the three an opportunity to escape. Although the mayor pledged to his angry constituents that he would escort Butman to the train station, the crowd followed, hissing, groaning, and throwing rotten eggs and stones. Panicked upon finding the train already departed, Butman swore to never return to Worcester as he climbed aboard a hackney coach.[5]

In the aftermath of the Butman Riot, authorities charged Foster, Hemenway, Dutton, Angier, and two others with rioting and assault. In November, a Grand Jury found no cause against the three White defendants but charged the three Black men with simple assault. As they awaited trial, Foster attended the Massachusetts Anti-Slavery Society meeting in January 1855, declaring "Worcester the Canada of the United States" and taunting the slaveocracy and federal officers to come after John Jackson, a freedom seeker residing in Worcester. "If your United States officers want him, let them come and get him. . . . Worcester is in a state of insurrection to-day." The town may have been "a seething center of all of the reforms," but abolition caused the pot to boil over.[6]

Not surprisingly, then, when President Abraham Lincoln called for volunteers in June 1861, Black Worcesterites wanted to rush to war, but only White men could enlist, and they did so readily, certain that their three-year duties were sufficient. The Commonwealth set up a training facility at Camp Wool, adjacent to Worcester's fairgrounds, and when regiments marched off to war after their drills, they paraded through the town, inspiring greater war enthusiasm. By August, the Fifteenth and Twenty-First Massachusetts Infantries left for the South, the latter destined for North Carolina, first to Roanoke Island and then on to New Bern. In early 1862, the Twenty-Fifth departed, accompanied by chaplain Horace James, who resigned his pulpit at the South Church. The Thirty-Fourth Massachusetts followed in August, and the Thirty-Sixth in September.[7]

A year later, Thomas Wentworth Higginson, too, enlisted and became captain of the Fifty-First Massachusetts Infantry before rising to colonel in the South Carolina First Infantry, the first federal regiment of Black soldiers organized at Port Royal. On New Year's Day 1863, as Higginson oversaw the raising of the United States flag and a reading of the Emancipation Proclamation to a crowd of free people, one voice rose from the ranks singing "My Country 'Tis of Thee," soon joined by others. "I never saw anything so electric; it made all other words cheap; it seemed the choked voice of a race at last unloosed," Higginson recorded in his journal. "Just think of it!—the first day they had ever had a country, the first flag they had ever seen which promised anything to their people, and here, while mere spectators stood in silence, waiting for my stupid words, these simple souls burst out in their lay, as if they were by their own hearths at home!" Except, it was the *same* flag that they had seen at Fourth of July celebrations for decades, the same flag that Worcesterites draped in black when they protested slave hunters, the same flag that many abolitionists viewed as the symbol of a failed republic. They all knew that flag well and *all* that it had stood for, and they were still willing to claim the United States as their nation.[8]

Given Lunsford Lane's history, Worcester offered opportunities for acting on rational liberty, practicing practical abolitionism, and making a dime from lecturing. After the Emancipation Day celebrations, however, he showed little interest in engaging the community, restricting himself to a different call. Dr. Lane had been hired to steward Wellington's Hospital, a private military hospital.

When war erupted, Timothy W. Wellington, a local coal baron and one of Worcester's wealthier citizens, signed up for military service, but the enlistment board rejected him. Still, serving the Union was without question. In September 1861, he gave his blessing to his two eldest sons, Edward and Frank, as they marched off with the Twenty-Fifth Massachusetts Infantry. Two months later, Wellington sent one hundred mittens to his sons' company. The infantry, by then in eastern North Carolina, gratefully christened their encampment Camp Wellington, as Colonel Josiah Pickett, also of Worcester, observed, "in honor of one who, by his kindness and generosity, his acts of charity and brotherly love, his devoted patriotism, has proved himself *our true friend.*" Months later, in July 1862, Wellington "fitted up a house" in Worcester "for the use of our wounded and sick soldiers thinking it might relieve (in a measure) our crowded Hospitals," as he described to the Massachusetts adjutant general. He envisioned it as a site of healing for injured and sick soldiers, his contribution to the war effort.[9]

By August 20, Wellington enticed Dr. Lane to Worcester. The two men soon discovered that Federal military regulations did not allow battle wounded to be transferred to private hospitals. So, the patients at Wellington Hospital were men injured or taken ill at state training facilities, specifically nearby Camp Wool and Camp Meigs outside Boston. The hospital sat at 110 Mason Street, accommodating the Lane family and up to sixty patients at peak operation, with men filling twenty beds and scattered about the floors.[10]

Over the next year, Lunsford and Martha cared for about one hundred soldiers. Diarrhea was the most frequent problem, often attributed to poor food preparation. More serious diseases were rare in Massachusetts's training camps because the state aggressively vaccinated troops. Some patients arrived with broken bones and a variety of other physical ailments that warranted surgery. Oramel Martin, who once led the Worcester Freedom Club in marching on Boston before serving as regimental surgeon for the Third Massachusetts Battalion of Rifles, became head surgeon after resigning from the military in July 1862. Alongside him served Benjamin F. Heywood, a retired physician whose surname certainly reminded the Lanes of bygone days.[11]

As steward, Lunsford was to display "honest and upright character, or temperate habits, and good general intelligence." He addressed the general business of the hospital, including keeping patients' records. Given Lunsford's limited literacy, Maria Bell and Clara helped with the bookkeeping. He also disciplined, policed, purchased provisions, and tended to lighting, heating, and ventilation. He dressed wounds, applied cups and leeches, administered injections, assisted with minor surgeries, and kept the key to the dispensary. He oversaw the work of his nurses—Martha, Maria Bell, and Clara—who not only made beds, emptied chamber pots and urinals, swept the rooms, and washed patients but also prepared and served meals, laundered linens, and mended patients' clothes. Lunsford also served as the hospital's pharmacist, compounding medicines according to prescription guidelines and expanding his pharmaceutical skills.[12]

The Lanes' work at Wellington Hospital invigorated them, inspiring them to participate in Worcester's Black community. On January 1, 1863, five months after Lane's speech at Worcester's Emancipation Day festival, Lunsford and Martha joined hundreds of Worcesterites at the A.M.E. Zion Church for the Anti-Slavery and Temperance Society of Worcester's New Year's celebration. Speeches, songs, and a reading of the Emancipation Proclamation electrified the crowd.[13]

Over the next couple of months, enthusiasm for the war cooled, at least among White Massachusettsians. Fewer enlistees trained at Camps Wool and Meigs, and the number of patients at Wellington Hospital declined. Wellington's interest in the hospital waned as well. He again tried to enlist, this time successfully in the Massachusetts State Guard, charged with defending the homeland. He took trips southward, representing the state in recovering bodies. On July 6, 1863, he traveled to Gettysburg "to look after the killed and wounded belonging to our city and vicinity," reporting back that the Fifteenth Massachusetts Infantry had suffered substantial losses: nine killed, thirteen officers and twenty-nine privates wounded, three of whom had limbs amputated, and ten missing. He anticipated all would recover except for Albert H. Snow, "who was shot through the back of his head." Wellington arranged transportation back to Worcester for the body of Hans Peter Jorgensen, who died in battle.[14]

Alongside corpses, Wellington collected battlefield relics. At Gettysburg, he picked up a gray Confederate military jacket and sword, a Union cartridge box, and a handful of unidentified grapeshot. At Bull Run, he found another Confederate sword. At Cold Harbor, more grapeshot. His sons sent him souvenirs from New Bern as well: a Confederate cartridge box, a Confederate soldier's Bible presented by "the ladies of Waxhaw Creek in 1861," cannon balls from Roanoke Island, and poetry about paroled prisoners from the notorious Salisbury Prison. In time, over one hundred "rebellion relics" gathered on Wellington's shelves, acquired by the Worcester Society for Antiquity after his death in 1884. But in May 1863, it was clear that Wellington Hospital lost its benefactor's attention, although even as the beds emptied, he continued to house and pay the Lanes.[15]

On May 30, 1863, Lunsford Lane marked his sixtieth birthday with Martha, Clara, Maria Bell, and a new member of the family. Three weeks earlier, Samuel Souther, a Congregationalist missionary, officiated Maria's marriage to Henry G. Garner. Like his bride, Garner escaped enslavement as a young teen, but when he fled Fredericksburg, Virginia, he also abandoned the only family he knew—his parents, Fincastle and Hannah. In Worcester, Garner became a prominent barber and leader in the Black community, and after the war erupted, he advocated for the enlistment of Black soldiers.[16]

As the hospital work and Wellington's interests diminished, with more time on his hands, Lunsford returned to lecturing, invited to nearby Wilkinsville in June 1863 to speak on what White Americans could expect from four million free Black Americans. Two years of carnage left many Northerners weary of war, Lane acknowledged, but he hoped "to awaken a renewed interest in the colored race; hoping that advantage might be taken of this rebellion, by which great blessing might be conferred upon his unfortunate brethren in the South, who, unlike himself, were yet in bondage." He laid out a vision for an emancipated Black America that coveted rational liberty: "freedom in its truest and best sense,—not a mere license to do as we please" but "to be profitability employed, so as to benefit the State as well as ourselves." He placated the racism that underlay many White Northerners' anxieties about immediate and universal emancipation, assuring his audience that, once free, Black Southerners would stay in the South, "a clime so well suiting our constitutions." Situated on lands of their own, free men would spare wives and daughters the type of labor forced upon them in enslavement, invigorating domesticity and child-rearing. Men would turn to Massachusetts for "her hoes and ploughs and rakes and cultivators and mowing-machines," pouring money into the Northern economy. They would no longer subsist on rationed meals of bacon and corn but would expand their diets. "Healthy bread and butter and milk," he fantasized. "Tea and coffee, being unknown articles in the cabin, would then be in demand."[17]

Lunsford's message about transforming Black Americans into Americans exposed just how far he and abolitionism had diverged. Years earlier, in 1847, William Wells Brown, during a lecture to the Female Anti-Slavery Society of Salem, Massachusetts, ridiculed American identity as corrupted by the simple presence of enslavement. Liberty and enslavement were incompatible, and so "Slavery has never been represented; Slavery never can be represented." An American identity had formed without acknowledging those who experienced enslavement, concluded Brown, insisting that they were "American" nonetheless. At a Fourth of July celebration in 1852, Frederick Douglass chastised his White audience that "the existence of slavery in this country brands your republicanism as a sham, your humanity as a base pretense, and your Christianity as a lie." Still, he believed his "fellow-citizens" could redeem the nation. If "interpreted, as it *ought* to be interpreted, the Constitution is a glorious liberty document." Douglass asked, "What, to the Slave, Is the Fourth of July?" and he answered by demanding that his audience consider their complicity in the perpetuation of enslavement, his repetitive use of the second person forcing their introspection: "What have I, or those I represent, to do with *your* national independence?" "Am I, therefore called upon to bring our humble offering to the national altar, and to confess the benefits and express devout gratitude for the blessings resulting from *your* independence to us?" "*Your* high independence only reveals the immeasurable distance between us." "The rich inheritance of justice, liberty, prosperity, and independence, bequeathed by *your* fathers, is shared by *you*, not by me." "The Fourth of July is *yours*, not mine, *You* may rejoice, I must mourn."[18]

In a less eloquent manner, Lane, too, reconciled his lived experiences with the ideals at the heart of the national experiment, but he came to a different conclusion than Brown and Douglass. Rather than define how White Americans needed to revise their national identity, Lane expressed more concern with the narrative arc of Black folks themselves. His speech imagined how Black Southerners would assume an Americanness and lay claim to the Fourth of July as their holiday as well. At Wilkinsville, Lane never used the second person voice with his largely White audience. He used the collective first person over twenty times in the rather brief speech, making the case about how Black folks became fully part of the American story by remaking themselves, as he did throughout his life. "The South is *our* home; and *we* feel that there *we* can be happy, and contribute by *our* industry to the prosperity of *our* race, and leave the generation that succeeds *us* wiser and better." Black Americans could be woven into the national fabric—more farmers, more families, more citizens joining the national economy as producers and consumers.[19]

Just as White Southerners had argued about whether enslaved peoples should be economically engaged independent of their enslavers, so did White Northerners debate *how* Black Americans should participate in the nation and its economy. Lane told them. As he pled years earlier, in responding to Douglass's and William Lloyd Garrison's denouncements of redemption-by-purchase, Lane did not want to wait for "fellow-citizens." Black Americans, on their own schedules with their own ambitions, would define their freedom and their place in the United States.

———

Two of those trying to find their place were William Lane and his twin, Lunsford Jr., who had left their parents' home in 1860 when they were eighteen years old. They eventually surfaced in Troy, New York, as waiters, sharing a room in a tenement house at 115 Fifth Street with George Freeman, a cook. They were there maybe fifteen months, reappearing in Worcester sometime between July and December 1862, when they met Charlotte L. Forten. She was the same age as the twins.[20]

Charlotte knew of enslavement through her mother, Mary Virginia Wood, who once lived in Edenton, North Carolina. Wood's enslaver (and father) emancipated her, her mother, and her siblings. The family moved to Philadelphia, where the prominent Fortens, a Black family of devoted abolitionists, took interest. In 1833, Mary Wood joined the Forten women in co-founding the Philadelphia Female Anti-Slavery Society. Three years later, she married Robert Forten, and they had Charlotte the following year. When Mary died in 1840, young Charlotte fell under the care of her paternal grandmother until 1853 when Robert, hoping to educate her in an integrated public school, sent her to the home of abolitionists Amy Matilda Cassey Remond and Charles Lenox Remond in Salem, Massachusetts. In the Remonds' home, Charlotte met dozens of prominent abolitionists with whom she kept a lifelong correspondence, and she soon became a member of the Salem Female Anti-Slavery Society.[21]

In the summer of 1862, Charlotte traveled to Worcester on occasion, mingling with the town's Black and abolitionist communities, trying to gather support for her plan to go to South Carolina and share her education with the free people of Port Royal. The previous December, Federal troops had captured several of South Carolina's Sea Islands, and as Confederates fled their farms, over ten thousand Black Carolinians remained. Northern charities sent supplies, teachers, and support staff to teach not only literacy and how to farm for profit but also new patterns of living. "Whoever, under our new system, is charged with their superintendence, should see that they attend more to the cleanliness of their persons and houses," anticipated Edward L. Pierce, who previously organized free people's work in Hampton, Virginia. Sent to Port Royal in late 1861 to report on its promise, Pierce concluded that Black families, "as in families of white people, they take their meals together at a table—habits to which they will be more disposed when they are provided with another change of clothing, and when better food is furnished and a proper hour assigned for meals." In March 1862, he became superintendent over the Port Royal experiment, encouraging communities across the North to form supportive relief societies for the schools that he planned to establish.[22]

Northern organizations such as the Port Royal Relief Association of Philadelphia and New York's National Freedmen's Relief Association began recruiting educators, and Charlotte Forten volunteered. Officials warned her that "it may not be quite safe," but she insisted and by late October was on a ship tracing the Atlantic coastline through two days of turbulent weather. Accompanying her were the Lane twins, although how they came to join her is unclear. They seem to have been support staff for the National Freedmen's Relief Association. A year later, Lunsford crowed how the two "are in the federal service," stopping short of characterizing their work as military. He told a friend that his sons worked as boatmen on transports ferrying Northern teachers and missionaries, as well as military troops, from shore to shore.[23]

Over the autumn of 1862 on St. Helena, Forten and the Lane twins watched as men liberated by United States troops or who fled enslavement and found their way to Port Royal formed the First South Carolina Infantry. By November, Thomas Wentworth Higginson arrived to take charge of the regiment. The previous summer in Worcester, Forten had observed Higginson drilling the Fifty-First Massachusetts Infantry, and she applauded him for having "stood by Anthony Burns, in the old dark days, even suffering imprisonment for his sake," assurance that recruits to the infantry "might feel sure of meeting with no injustice under the leadership of such a man." William and Lunsford Jr. saw men who looked like them drill as a regiment, create comradery, and inspire a sense of purpose. The twins wrote home a letter that "breathes words of patriotism, as they witnessed the enlistment of the freedmen in our army." They heard of the newly formed Fifty-Fourth Massachusetts Infantry and promised to enlist upon their return. "Thus, the sons of escaped slaves are rendering powerful aid in the suppression of this wicked rebellion," an acquaintance of Lane cheered, "and in the emancipation of their race."[24]

Many Black Northern men looked upon the formation of the First South Carolina Infantry with envy. During the first two years of war, the Federal government refused their service, relegating them to simple gestures of support, as when Worcester barbers William H. Jankins and Gilbert Walker offered "members of the military companies to call at their hair dressing salons and get trimmed up, without charge, before leaving." White Americans assumed that it was to be a White man's war. Horace James, who climbed to the superintendency of free people in eastern North Carolina, delivered a Fourth of July address in 1862 celebrating how "the wars of 1776 and 1861 are entitled to be called the *two great Wars of America*. . . . In these two struggles the belligerents have belonged to *the same race*—Anglo-Saxons fought against Anglo-Saxons in the last century, and the same is true now."[25]

But the formation of the South Carolina First Infantry and the support work of young Black Americans like Charlotte Forten, William Lane, and Lunsford Lane Jr. belied James's assumption that only White Americans would fight for freedom's cause. Frederick Douglass publicly castigated Abraham Lincoln's hesitance to enlist Black Americans, correcting James in the process: "Colored men were good enough to fight under Washington. They are not good enough to fight under McClellan. . . . They were good enough to help win American independence, but they are not good enough to help preserve that independence against treason and rebellion."[26]

Finally, the United States Congress passed the Militia Act of 1862, authorizing Black men to enlist, and although many of them would see battle violence, the intent was that they would support White troops. The governor of Rhode Island immediately organized the Fourteenth Rhode Island Heavy Artillery, sending recruiters into neighboring states to fill its ranks. Initial reaction from White Worcester was that Black military service threatened "the harmonious and vigorous action of government in its aim to suppress the rebellion and restore the nation to its former prosperity." A month later, a "war meeting" of Black Worcesterites convinced White allies otherwise. Frustratedly, Black Worcesterites pledged that "we shall ever be found ready with patriotic and willing hearts, to promptly respond to the call of the government." A recruitment committee organized, led by Maria Bell's husband, Henry G. Garner.[27]

Not to be outdone by his Rhode Island counterpart, Massachusetts governor John A. Andrew formed the Fifty-Fourth Massachusetts Infantry. In the spring of 1863, Lewis Hayden recruited in Boston, and barber Gilbert Walker and upholsterer William Brown served as local recruiters in Worcester. Massachusetts' Black population was small, and Frederick Douglass and others recruited outside the commonwealth. But Black Massachusettsians were slow to enlist, largely because of the inequitable pay that Congress allocated. White privates received $13 [$315] per month as well as a $3.50 [$85] clothing allowance. Assuming that Black privates would not be combatants, the military capped their pay at $10 [$243] each month, with $3.00 [$73] deducted for clothing if they so elected. Black enlistees resented the prejudice and that they were ineligible for federal bounties offered to White enlistees. In March, Merrill Richardson and William Brown called a meeting at Worcester's City Hall to discuss the issue. Four wealthy White Worcesterites pledged to pay $5 [$121] to each enlistee, and Jankins convinced three of his peers to contribute one dollar [$24] per recruit. Fifteen men from Worcester immediately joined the Fifty-Fourth, including Thomas Freeman, an apprentice in William Brown's upholstery shop who signed up in April 1863, and Alexander Hemenway, itching for a fight since he beat up the federal marshal nine years earlier. As for the recruiting bonuses, "We had not our Pay yet and I never think we will," complained Freeman toward the end of the month. Even a year later, "there is men here in the regiment that have been Enlisted 13 months and have never received one cent."[28]

William Brown's other apprentice, John Johnson, also joined the Fifty-Fourth, but he was ineligible for a bonus. Bonuses only went to volunteers, theoretically at least. In August, the state drafted Johnson through the Enrollment Act of 1863. Once the military ranks opened to Black Americans, their names fell into the draft lotteries. In 1864, William Brown and William Bryant saw their names drawn. Brown claimed exemption "for bleeding at stomach." Bryant, a twenty-seven-year-old laborer, was "*not* off," although the reasons for him not joining the regiment went unexplained. He already had provided meritorious service. In the spring of 1862, Federal general Ambrose E. Burnside led an expedition in eastern North Carolina to curtail Confederate blockade running. Several Massachusetts regiments, including the Twenty-Fifth Infantry, took control of many of North Carolina's coastal towns, including New Bern and Washington. At one point during the expedition, Burnside received assistance from the then-enslaved Bryant "in the capacity of a pilot." In return, Burnside ensured that William Bryant and his wife, Mary, traveled safely to Massachusetts. They officially married as "contraband" in Worcester in 1863.[29]

Initially, some enlistees were unsure as to what they signed up for. William Brown's apprentice, Thomas Freeman, seemed particularly confused. On one occasion, he wrote that "Mrs. Bundy, Mrs. Hemenway and Sister, and a Host of Boston People Have visited our Camp. We all have a nice time and I am Happy as a King. . . . Tell Martha to Send me or Bring Me Some Home Made Gingerbread or Some Nick Nacs." On another occasion, he complained that "Slavery with all its harrows can not Equalize this for it is nothing but work from morning till night. Building Batteries Hauling Guns Cleaning Bricks cleaning up land for other Regiments to Settle on . . . and if you don't like that Some white men will Give you a crack over the Hand with his Sword."[30]

As in Worcester, war fever raged among Black Oberliners. So many of the young men who accompanied their families from North Carolina to Oberlin in the 1840s and 1850s eagerly enrolled. In April 1863, Henry and Emeline Patterson's son, Henry I. Patterson, joined the Massachusetts Fifty-Fourth Infantry, fighting alongside Thomas Freeman and Alexander Hemenway. After the Battle of Grimball's Landing outside Charleston, South Carolina, on July 16, 1863, Colonel Robert Gould Shaw promoted Henry Patterson to corporal. Two days later, the regiment spearheaded an assault on the heavily fortified Fort Wagner. Shaw fell early in the assault. Of six hundred men, 270 were killed, wounded, or captured. Henry Patterson survived, receiving the official paperwork of Shaw's promotion a month later.[31]

Wilson Evans joined the Ohio 178th Infantry in June 1863. George Freeman, who arrived from North Carolina to apprentice under Patterson, enlisted in June 1863, as did John Campton's son, Thomas, who joined the Twelfth United States Colored Artillery. In September, Rubin Turner, once adopted as an infant by the Copelands as they traveled to Oberlin, also went to war, enlisting in the Third United States Colored Artillery.[32]

Twenty-nine-year-old Edward Lane had not joined those men in the Oberlin-Wellington rescue, but he accompanied them to war, drafted in June 1863 as an undercook for Company E of the Ohio Thirty-Ninth Infantry, a White regiment. General orders assigned "two undercooks of African descent" to each regimental cook, paying $10 [$242] per month (a third of which could be in clothing) and one ration per day. On company rosters, their names sat "at the foot of the privates"—last. The infantry assigned Edward to serve under forty-year-old Mark Calomes, who began as an undercook himself before promotion to cook. The other undercook was twenty-year-old Andrew Jackson. Calomes, Lane, and Jackson served salted beef and pork, coffee, sugar, salt, dried fruits and vegetables, and, of course, the tough unleavened biscuits known as hard tack that staved off hunger. The company mustered in November, and for the first eleven months, the Thirty-Ninth camped in Memphis, but in late spring 1864, they were on the move with William Tecumseh Sherman as he slashed his way across the South, the cook and undercooks transporting the supplies, including the heavy iron kettles needed for large-scale cooking.[33]

Back in Worcester, at the end of December 1863, seven months after marrying Maria Bell, Henry G. Garner joined three friends, all barbers—Amos Webber, George Alston, and John Stevens—in enlisting for the newly formed Fifth Massachusetts Cavalry, a regiment composed of over fifteen hundred Black soldiers and White officers. The regiment mustered out in January, and Henry said goodbye to his bride. By May, the Fifth was at Camp Casey outside the nation's capital. In late June, they joined in the assault on Petersburg, Virginia, engaging Confederates in battle at Baylor Farm and along Jordan's Point Road. As the Confederates reinforced their defenses of Petersburg, the Fifth retreated to Point Lookout, Maryland.[34]

From Worcester and Oberlin to Cambridgeport and Boston, young men familiar to the Lanes, sons of friends and neighbors, joined in the effort to save the nation and destroy enslavement. So, too, did the sons of Lunsford's former peers in the abolitionist movement, taking up their parents' cause by flocking to military service. Lewis and Harriet Hayden's son, twenty-five-year-old Joseph, enlisted in the Navy in November 1861, eventually serving as a landsman on the USS Portsmouth and at Fort Gaines. Nineteen-year-old Charles Remond Douglass, Frederick and Anna's eldest son, joined the Fifty-Fourth in April 1863 and rose to lance corporal within a month. A little less than a year later, he transferred to the Fifth Calvary as a sergeant. His brother, twenty-two-year-old Lewis Henry Douglass, joined the Fifty-Fourth in March 1863, and within a month, he rose to sergeant major, the highest non-commissioned rank that Black soldiers could attain. Twenty-seven-year-old George Thompson Garrison, son of William Lloyd and Helen Eliza, enlisted in June 1863, was assigned as a second lieutenant in the Fifty-Fifth Massachusetts Infantry, and eventually rose to captain. George and Rebecca Latimer's sons enlisted in November 1864, twenty-year-old George in the Thirtieth Infantry and eighteen-year-old William H. in the Twenty-Fifth. Henry Bibb's son, twenty-year-old Napoleon, who remained enslaved with his mother Malinda in Kentucky after his father flew to freedom, enlisted in February 1864.[35]

As Lunsford Lane watched sons of friends and neighbors march off to war, he needed so desperately to believe his own sons would join in the campaign. He seemed oblivious to Edward's deployment, never mentioning it even as he celebrated his twins' desire to join the Fifty-Fourth. However, over a dozen William Lanes enlisted in the United States Colored Troops by 1864, and not one seems to have been Martha and Lunsford's son. Lunsford Jr. did not enlist either, returning to Worcester in early 1863 and finding work as a clerk for Charles A. Harrington & Co., wholesale druggists. He might have tried to register but the recruitment board did not want him: he was not well.[36]

––––––––

When Lunsford Lane delivered his address in Wilkinsville in June 1863, William G. Hawkins, minister at the Wilkinsville Episcopal Church, sat in the audience. Hawkins had met Lane twenty years earlier, in 1842, when he joined his father, John H. W. Hawkins, at a temperance meeting at the Massachusetts State House. In those days, Lane actively promoted The Story.

Born in Maryland in 1828, Hawkins grew up with an alcoholic father who drank the family into debt and often burst into the family home after a late night of drinking, "which plight his family have come to his assistance, and treated him with the utmost attention and affection, till his recovery." John Hawkins, a Baltimore hatter, tried to sober up when his wife died in 1832, leaving him with four young children, but his rehabilitation lasted barely four years as he slipped into occasional alcoholic relapses and bouts of severe depression. Young William found a more stable father figure in his step-grandfather, Methodist minister John Baxley, who enrolled William in the Episcopal High School, a boarding school outside Alexandria, Virginia. The headmaster, the Reverend Edwin A. Dalrymple, was a harsh disciplinarian, establishing a set of rules that rivaled Deuteronomy: "No student shall eat butter and molasses at once or at the same meal, nor shall any student waste in any way or leave uneaten or conceal to avoid eating"; "Every student shall be careful not to soil the table or tablecloth by spilling milk, water or anything else thereon"; "No student shall sing any negro or low song or chorus or tune in the boys' parlor or elsewhere," and so on. Transgressors met with whippings. William found his faith and discipline at the Episcopal High School and went on to become an Episcopal minister.[37]

So, William G. Hawkins escaped the darkness of his father's struggles, but he also missed his father's salvation. For decades, American temperance reformers like Lyman Beecher fought against alcoholism, but the reform movement struggled as leaders contested each other on the purpose and methods of their cause. Teetotalers advocated full abstinence. Moderationists accepted modest consumption. Other reformers pushed for laws to prohibit alcohol. Others turned to moral suasion to convince drinkers of the harm they did to their children, wives, and communities. What they all shared was the moral pedestal from which they preached down to the masses.[38]

John Hawkins became the "Great Apostle of the Washingtonian Temperance Reformation," a movement that replaced lecturers with "experience meetings," during which participants rejected King Alcohol by sharing their addiction struggles with others. Between 1840 and 1858, the movement exploded nationally, with Hawkins alone facilitating over five thousand meetings with fellow alcoholics across the country. "Poor drunkard," he often appealed to his audiences, "there is hope for you. You cannot be worse off than I was; not more degraded, or more of a slave to appetite. You can reform if you will. *Try it—Try it.*" By 1842, eight thousand members enrolled in Baltimore, sixteen thousand in New York City, twenty thousand in Philadelphia, and tens of thousands in smaller towns across the nation, including Worcester, Oberlin, and Raleigh. Illinois state legislator Abraham Lincoln, at the time, lauded members in Springfield: "And when the victory shall be complete—when there shall be neither a slave nor a drunkard on earth—how proud the title of that *Land. . . .* How nobly distinguished that People, who shall have planted, and nurtured to maturity, both the political and moral freedom of their species."[39]

When William Hawkins's father died in 1858, he wrote *The Life of John H. W. Hawkins.* He reminded himself as much as he tried to convince his readers that the drunk "*was* still a man, the immortal spark not quite quenched,—a wreck fast crumbling to decay but not quite destroyed. There are throbbings there of a noble heart, crushed and lacerated though he may be. He is still a man!" Hawkins took subscriptions for the publication and peddled it at temperance meetings and from house to house. In November 1860, he attended the Massachusetts Teachers Association meeting in Concord and went out of his way to knock on naturalist and Transcendentalist Henry David Thoreau's door. Thoreau refused to purchase a copy, telling Hawkins "that I was not much interested in the subject, as my intemperance did not lie in the direction of ardent spirits."[40]

Like Thoreau, more people refused Hawkins's overtures than not. Still, the *New-York Tribune* declared the book "interesting as a personal biography, and contains valuable materials of the history of the social reform to which the best years of his life were devoted." A Raleigh newspaper concluded that "no temperance man or woman should be without a copy." By the end of 1862, the book sold out six thousand copies. It was no *Uncle Tom's Cabin*, but it was a significant enough achievement to fill Hawkins's pockets and give him a sense of purpose.[41]

John Hawkins's rise in temperance in 1842 had coincided with Lunsford Lane's emergence as a popular storyteller, and not surprisingly, as William G. Hawkins listened to Lane speak in Wilkinsville some twenty years later, he heard echoes of his own father's activism and began to imagine in the formerly enslaved man, abolitionist, and celebrated member of Worcester's burgeoning Black community a profitable biographical subject. He anticipated awakening "a new interest in the oppressed among us" and encouraging them "to pursue a life of virtue." Hawkins approached Lane with the proposition of a biography. Lane had considered reissuing his *Narrative*, but his work at Wellington Hospital delayed the work. So, he accepted the offer, and Hawkins resigned Wilkinsville's pulpit to research Lane's life.[42]

The Civil War had entered a third year, and the emancipation of over four million enslaved people had become a paramount objective of the United States government. Hawkins insisted that his book would awaken White Americans to the "grave responsibilities resting upon them" to destroy slavery. Readers would learn from "the example of industry and patient endurance of trials, and the integrity of character unfolded in the life of Lunsford Lane." Hawkins invited his subject for an interview, reciting aloud *The Narrative of Lunsford Lane*, pausing after passages and asking for elaborations on people, places, and each important life moment.[43]

The result was slightly over three hundred machine-cut pages stuffed between a heavy 7.75″ × 5″ embossed cover, quite a contrast to the 6″ × 3.62″ fifty-four-page pocketbook that Lane produced in the 1840s. Yet, there was little new information revealed about Lunsford's life: Hawkins relied heavily on Lane's original *Narrative*, adding only one new story about Lunsford's experience in Baltimore and some minor elaborations on other stories. The rest of the book—the majority of it—comprised Hawkins's long and detailed soliloquies about enslavement, abolition, temperance, and the righteous war underway to destroy the traitorous South.[44]

With good reason, Hawkins worried that readers would question the narrative's authenticity, a constant criticism of Black narratives and biographies. Just two months after the 1838 publication of the *Narrative of James Williams, an American Slave, Who Was for Several Years a Driver on a Cotton Plantation in Alabama*, an Alabama newspaper editor claimed factual errors in the book, suggesting that John Greenleaf Whittier, the poet, abolitionist, and James Williams's ghostwriter, fabricated the story, maybe having created Williams himself from whole cloth. The American Anti-Slavery Society, the book's publisher, investigated. "While we candidly admit that it has created a doubt in our mind of the accuracy in some minute particulars," concluded the committee, "we are still disposed to give credit in the main to his narrative." Abolitionist Lydia Maria Child claimed that to those "who look on the *foundations* upon which slavery rests, it is not the slightest consequence whether James Williams told the truth or not." *The Liberator* questioned whether those who dismissed the book intended to suggest that nothing in it could have been true. "James Williams not a true story!" Garrison huffed, not assuaging anyone. "We wished it had not been true all the while we were reading it, and guess James wished so, and big Harry, and all of them. It is true that there was a James Williams who told the story, or at least that there was a John Greenleaf Whittier, who said he told it. The Whittier part we *know* is true—we have *seen* him."[45]

In 1856, Martha Griffith's *Autobiography of a Female Slave* faced similar accusations. It was not autobiographical. Griffith, a white Kentucky enslaver-turned-abolitionist, authored the book from the perspective of the women she once enslaved, making up the story and developing dialogue by exaggerating Black dialect. Critics considered it second in quality only to Stowe's *Uncle Tom's Cabin*, but in so doing, they certified its fiction. As truth, it was full of "gross representations, false theories, and most disgusting ultra anti-slavery aspirations," but as fiction, "it evinces a high order of talent and literary genius." Enslavers pointed to its fiction to question the veracity of all slave narratives. Abolitionists counted on that fiction to inspire emotions: "If a tenth part of it be true, it ought to make Abolitionists of us all."[46]

So, Hawkins took care to make his biography of Lane believable, assuring "that the narrative here given to the public is a statement of matters of fact, either received from the lips of Mr. Lane himself, or from information possessed by the compiler by a residence in the South, or drawn from well-authenticated documents." He wrote in a "plain style," but the prose was hardly dry. "Upon a pleasant afternoon in October," he began, "a slave, completing the day's labor some hours sooner than usual, his bosom swelling with emotions peculiar to a man about enjoying his first moment of freedom, when from being a chattel, he is about to experience the liberty wherewith God and nature hath made him free!" The third-person perspective distinguished Hawkins's biography from the disputed first-person voices of *Narrative of James Williams* and *Autobiography of a Female Slave*, but it also distanced Hawkins's rendition from Lane's own narrative.[47]

Aware of the potential accusations of a fictional narrative, Hawkins was surprisingly sloppy with dialogue, as in his rendering of the Haywoods' journey to Washington, North Carolina, when Lunsford met the Northern teacher, Jaquith. When Lane stepped from the shadows to interrupt Eleanor

Haywood's debate with Jaquith, he stated, "I beg your pardon, mistress, for interrupting your conversation but as we are to leave early in the morning on our journey homeward, I came to ask if you have any special order about preparations for leaving?" There is no reason to doubt the words or the properness of Lane's diction. In describing the family's return trip to Raleigh, however, when Eleanor's distant cousin showed up with his enslaved man, Hawkins created dialogue meant to distinguish the intelligent Lane from the ignorant field worker, Isaac. Confronted about loosening the ropes on his wrists, Isaac stated, "Massa, I done it myself; Lunsford nor none of the res' didn't do nuffin 'bout it." Describing how he did not get to see his family after escaping to Washington, he remarked that "the officers cotched me jus' as I git in town, and lock me in de prison." Of course, there is no reason to doubt the field worker's unpolished diction, except that Hawkins confessed that "sometimes conversations are introduced which were not in the exact language stated." He had turned to the tried-and-true practice of exaggerating Black and Southern dialects.[48]

The Baltimore story offers another example of Hawkins fictionalizing dialogue. He claimed that when Lane and Jones described the attempted kidnapping, their host, Henry Butler, reached into his jacket pocket and conveniently withdrew a newspaper clipping about Margaret Garner, who attempted to flee Kentucky enslavement with her three children. As her enslaver closed in on her hiding place, she slit her two-year-old daughter's throat and stabbed the other two children, intending to kill all three and then herself. The story was authentic; Hawkins's use of it was not. Garner's story took place in 1856, fourteen years *after* Lane and Jones visited Baltimore. Hawkins admitted, "We have antedated this event" and that although Lane's biography was a "matter of fact," he took liberties with "the class of facts introduced in the conversation at Butler's house, between Lunsford and his friends, on the evening of the day of their liberation from the hands of wicked men." Although Hawkins insisted that he was not fabricating dialogue, he demonstrated few qualms moving things around a bit.[49]

Still, Hawkins pulled heavily from Lane's own words when creating dialogue, and although he often embellished the words, he also tried to clarify them. Compare the story of Lunsford's tobacco trade. In Lunsford's words from 1842,

> I commenced the manufacture of pipes and tobacco on an enlarged
> scale. I opened a regular place of business, labelled my tobacco in a
> conspicuous manner with the names of "Edward and Lunsford Lane,"
> and of some of the persons who sold it for me,—established agencies for
> the sale in various parts of the State, one at Fayetteville, one at Salisbury,

one at Chapel Hill, and so on,—sold my articles from my place of business, and about town, also deposited them in stores on commission, and thus, after paying my mistress for my time, and rendering such support as necessary to my family, I found in the space of some six or eight years, that I had collected the sum of one thousand dollars.[50]

Recast in Hawkins's imagination,

> I now commenced business for myself, and entered upon the manufacture of pipes and tobacco upon a large scale. I opened a regular place of business,—a humble one, it is true,—and I labelled my tobacco in a conspicuous manner, attaching the names of the proprietors, "EDWARD AND LUNSFORD LANE." We (my father being in the business with me) pushed the enterprise so far as to establish agencies for the sale in various parts of the State; one at Fayetteville, one at Salisbury, and one at Chapel Hill; the latter place being the seat of the University of North Carolina and of other minor institutions made the place one of considerable importance for the slaves who were ambitious enough to supply the students and the town's people with their homely productions, and receive their pocket-money in exchange.[51]

The differences were subtle but important. Hawkins made sure his audience understood the modesty of Lunsford's enterprise—"a humble one"—despite the claim of its "large scale." He made clear that Edward Lane was more than a name on the packaging, that Lunsford's father participated in the production. Through his elaboration on Chapel Hill, Hawkins erased Lunsford's collaboration with local stores, characterizing Lunsford's sales as the type of piddling undertaken by enslaved peoples in southern towns.

Beyond the looseness with which Hawkins approached the truth of Lunsford Lane's life, there are disturbing aspects of the biography. Hawkins subtly erased the difference between Lane's original race narrative and the dozens of slave narratives with which it shared little. He transformed Lunsford into a freedom seeker. Consider the book's dedication: "To T. W. WELLINGTON, ESQ., Of whose unobtrusive benevolence and genuine sympathy of heart, The disabled Soldier in the Hospital and the wronged fugitive Slave Have received many Substantial Tokens, THIS VOLUME is respectfully inscribed." It was a noble gesture. As the biography explained, Wellington aided two groups: Massachusetts's military sons and the Lanes, indirectly situating Lunsford, Martha, and their children as *the* "fugitive Slaves" to which Hawkins alluded in the dedication. He again paralleled Lane to fugitivity when describing Lunsford's nightmare as the mob confiscated his luggage upon returning to

Raleigh: "A number seized it at once, as hungry hounds after a panting fugitive in the Southern swamps."[52]

Then, there was the title. Although planning on *The Memoir of Lunsford Lane*, Hawkins decided that Lunsford's story was just as significant as Hinton Rowan Helper's *The Impending Crisis of the South*, published in 1857, which Hawkins recently had read. Helper, a North Carolinian whom Hawkins mistakenly assumed was a professor at the state university, had dismissed religious and altruistic reasons for the abolition of enslavement, talking instead to fellow White southerners' wallets. Enslavement of Black people injured non-enslaving White people and slowed economic development in the South. As Hawkins recalled later in life, "I had just been profoundly impressed by reading 'Helpers' book, which suggested a supplementary title"—*Lunsford Lane; or, Another Helper from North Carolina*. Yet, Lunsford Lane *never* articulated enslavement as an economic problem, making Hawkins's decision to associate him with Helper just befuddling.[53]

Hawkins clearly read recently published antislavery literature, and he absorbed their messages. He tapped into a common theme of the slave narratives that emerged in the 1850s; the portrayal of White women as cruel slaveowners. "I had nothing to hope from his selfish wife," Hawkins credited Lane with saying. In his own narrative, Lane said little about Eleanor Haywood, and her decision to allow Lunsford's mother to leave North Carolina with him was hardly the action of a selfish woman. Hawkins editorialized how "Mrs. Haywood was a woman of a churlish temperament and an avaricious spirit." Amid a war against enslavement, Hawkins considered it necessary to portray Southern White women as enslavers just like their husbands, enemies of the United States. In other words, Eleanor Haywood might have been the most generous and selfless person Lunsford ever knew (she was not), but it did not suit Hawkins's purpose to portray her as such.[54]

The story of Baltimore, which did not appear in Lunsford's original narrative, may be the most telltale mark of others' impact on Hawkins. Solomon Northup's *Twelve Years a Slave*, published in 1853, described Northup's kidnapping and imprisonment in a "slave pen within the very shadow of the Capitol," and Hawkins was at least aware of Northup. The biographer wrote that "the slave-trade had not been driven from the District of Columbia; and slave-pens were in full operation there, and in the city of Baltimore." In a story about Lane, Hawkins had little reason to mention slave prisons in the nation's capital unless Northup's kidnapping was on his mind. Despite the little circumstantial evidence that suggests that Lane's Baltimore story is true, it is possible that Lunsford may never have visited Baltimore, that John Jones may not have traveled northward with him, that there may not have been a kidnapping or the possibility of Lunsford himself being sold southward. It all might have been fiction, Hawkins's nod to Northup.[55]

Finally, there were the Christian contexts that Hawkins layered onto Lane's life. Abolitionists exerted tremendous influence over the shape of slave narratives, and those who were religious translated the personal stories into conversion stories. Hawkins—clergyman and son of a reformed alcoholic—fully imbibed the ideal of the conversion narrative, reframing Lane's life from the secular biography that Lunsford told for decades into one that conflated Christian salvation with deliverance from enslavement. He cast Lane's life as a spiritual biography, interpreting Lunsford's journey from enslavement to freedom as a pilgrimage from sinfulness to grace. It was a common trope. William Craft, in his narrative three years earlier, equated freedom with grace, describing how, upon arriving in Philadelphia, "he first caught sight of the cross." In *The Narrative of Lunsford Lane*, Lane never appealed to religion as a redemptive force. Hawkins was more romantic in his religious emotionalism, tugging at his readers' hearts and sentimentality and framing Lunsford as "a man of deep religious convictions." So determined was Hawkins to transform Lane's secular narrative into a conversion narrative that he dedicated an entire chapter to "Lunsford as a Christian."[56]

Hawkins justified taking liberties with writing *Lunsford Lane* by claiming that he interviewed Lane for the project, employing signposts like "said he to the writer of this narrative." That might have been true early in the project, but there were too many errors in the published version for that to have been completely accurate. To explain how Ned Lane ended up enslaved to John Haywood, Hawkins errantly claimed that Haywood (not Henry Lane and then John Lane) served as Joel Lane's executor. He placed Lunsford's house on "Argate [Hargett] Street" rather than on Cabarrus Street. He wrote that Sherwood Haywood conceded to Lunsford's emancipation when it had been Eleanor and that Sherwood enslaved Ned and Cate when it had been his brother John. They were simple errors that Lunsford would have easily caught.[57]

Despite its flaws, *Lunsford Lane* exposed something notable: referring to Lane's own *Narrative*, Hawkins commented that it was about "what it is to be a slave, with a sensitive nature, under the most favorable circumstances." Twice more, Hawkins described Lane as "sensitive," the final time commenting that "a man less sensitive" than Lunsford could have found contentment in enslavement as a well-fed and well-dressed manservant and waiter. In that case, by "sensitive," Hawkins likely meant Lunsford's intellectual sensibilities, his perception of himself as framed by what he saw and heard around him. Hawkins employed another definition on other occasions, indicating that Lunsford had a delicate yet profound appreciation for the emotional and social complexities of enslavement. In other words, Lunsford was overly introspective, thinking deeply about enslavement and racism as they impinged upon his individual identity. Thinking back on Stephen Symonds Foster's proclamation of Black abolitionist founding fathers, in his introspection, Lane might have been a John Adams after all.[58]

In the end, the resulting biography exposed a tension between Hawkins's voice and Lane's experiences, and it was the former that filled the book. Hawkins was more preacher than biographer. As the book progressed, each chapter became less about Lunsford's story and more of a series of sermons, an interminable and at times exhausting homily about the righteousness of White Northerners. There were sermons about the desperation of enslaved peoples to reach White Northern shelter, White citizens' roles in the Oberlin-Wellington Rescue, White Massachusetts's magnanimity in forming Black military regiments during the Civil War, the treason of White Southern rebellion against the United States, the free people on the South Carolina coast and their White saviors, the glory of White New England—"The other colonies have been founded by adventurers, without family; the emigrants of New England brought with them the best elements of good order and morality." Chapter by chapter, Hawkins wove The Story into larger narratives of White United States history with the moral that Black Americans, too, could one day claim the American identity. Consequently, *Lunsford Lane* sold well among White Northerners.[59]

Strangely, though, Hawkins imagined a different audience. "It is hoped that this volume, from the plain style in which the narrative is given, may reach many of our colored fellow-citizens; and that the example of industry and of patient endurance of trials, and the integrity of character unfolded in the life of Lunsford Lane, may inspire them to the imitation of virtues, without which they can never secure the respect and sympathy of the good." His message was one of salvation for Black Americans *if* they followed Lane's model of humble enterprise. Who were "the good" for whom they were to display such character? The good were White middle-class folks enthralled with the myth of American self-making and eager to name who deserved recognition, help, and celebration. After all, Hawkins himself decided that Lane warranted respect, sympathy, and a biography, transforming the flesh-and-blood Lunsford into an antislavery exhibit that provided a virtuous model for other Black Americans—the American Aeneas, although Aeneas never displayed the integrity of character with which Hawkins adorned Lane.[60]

Hawkins commissioned a portrait to accompany the biography, and Lunsford Lane sat for J. H. Bufford's Lithography in Boston. By the late 1850s, John Henry Bufford was a major publisher of framing prints, in competition with Nathaniel Currier's shop in New York. Bufford's most famous work was *Boston Massacre, March 15th 1770*, which he produced around 1856. Taken

Lunsford Lane, 1803–79, lithograph. From William G. Hawkins, *Lunsford Lane; or, Another Helper from North Carolina* (Boston: Crosby & Nichols, 1863), frontispiece. Courtesy of the American Antiquarian Society, Worcester, MA.

from a painting by William L. Champney, *Boston Massacre* differed from previous illustrations of the event by centering the Black seaman, Crispus Attucks, certain to appeal to abolitionists and open their wallets. In early 1862, Bufford's agents were pushing his latest lithograph of *Our Generals*, a portrait of fifteen Federal generals with the Mexican War hero Winfield Scott at the center: "As a specimen of lithography this work is said to be the finest ever executed in this country." It highlighted the portraiture skills of Bufford's artists, John Perry Newell and Emile Masson.[61]

Either Bufford or one of his artists sketched Lunsford, the image signed simply "J. H. Bufford's Lith. Boston." Whether Bufford drew it or not, he trained his artists in his own techniques, so Bufford's skills are evident in the portrait. It is the only surviving likeness of Lane, making apparent the darkness of his eyes and, in his later years, the greying of his hair. Remarking on the image, the *New-York Observer* declared Lunsford "a fine-looking colored man."[62]

More so than the rest of *Lunsford Lane*, the portrait humanized the person about whom so many Americans heard and read. Too many slave narratives, as well as Lane's race narrative, offered no image, underpinning the dehumanization of enslavement despite narrators' birth claims. When, in

1854, Harriet Beecher Stowe commissioned an illustrator to bring Uncle Tom to life, many readers assumed he was a real person, and Hawkins took a lesson from Stowe, making Lunsford more visible to readers.[63]

In the portrait, the light hits Lane's face in fascinating ways, stressing the broad expanse of his forehead and one eye as it stares at the viewer, suggesting to readers that this is a man of high intelligence and insight. In the age of phrenology, the light across Lane's forehead drew attention to facilities of imitation (the ability to learn quickly), causality (power of thought and reasoning), comparison (power of analysis), suavity (politeness, a desire to do things agreeably), and mirth (merriment, full of laughter). When combined, causality and comparison indicated a "truly philosophic spirit," according to the great phrenologist Johann Gaspar Spurzheim.[64]

George C. Rand & Avery printed the book, and Crosby & Nichols marketed it. With their printing office adjacent to the Massachusetts Anti-Slavery Society, Rand & Avery had a role in the major abolitionist publications of the era, including Harriet Beecher Stowe's *Uncle Tom's Cabin* in 1858 and Harriet Wilson's *Our Nig* in 1859. Crosby & Nichols, "among the leading publishers and booksellers of this country," had bought out John P. Jewett and consequently acquired first right to Lane's biography. They marketed it extensively. It went on sale in October 1863 with simple ads relating how "it is a narrative of a slave from Raleigh, N.C., now residing in Worcester, Mass., a man of more than usual intelligence."[65]

As the Christmas season of 1863 approached, Northerners weary of war sought distractions, and in the larger cities, the publishers ramped up the advertising of "Books for the Holiday Season." *Lunsford Lane* went on sale in New York in mid-November, in Boston by the first of December, and in Philadelphia two weeks later. Advertisers assured readers that the biography was relevant to the circumstances of the day, including "the questions regarding the emancipated negroes, now pressing on the attention of all earnest patriots." Reviews were critical of Hawkins: "It shows not the darkest, but the lightest side of the institution," and "He is a little too fond of preaching, for his hero cannot sell a pipe, without his taking pains to express his disapprobation of the habit of smoking." (It was not hyperbole: upon telling the story of Lunsford's tobacco trade, Hawkins *had* interjected, "The Lanes managed to get their full share, but it is questionable whether the equivalent returned in tobacco and pipes was not greatly to the detriment of the rising generation.") Advertisements in the *New-York Times* and *The Liberator* editorialized, sarcastically presenting *Lunsford Lane* as a response to racist condemnations of Black Americans: "Ah me! What shall we do with these lazy, shiftless slaves after we have freed them?" The *Boston Traveler* announced that readers would find out "What the Colored Man can Do!"[66]

Wartime scarcity of paper ensured a pricier book than expected. In the United States, it cost one dollar [$24]; in England, five shillings [$36]. Hawkins promised the profits to Lunsford, with advertisements assuring readers that "the book is published for his benefit" and that purchasers would "while informing themselves on points of interest, aid a good man and his worthy family." The biographer was sincere, although good early sales made him reconsider. On September 3, 1863, he paid the $1 fee to register the copyright in the United States District Court in Boston, only to change his mind, having the clerk scratch through his name and give Lunsford credit for the original creation of the work and its ownership. The book sold well, demanding a second printing within a year.[67]

Among those who bought it was Samuel F. Haven, librarian at the American Antiquarian Society in Worcester, who inscribed his name into his copy of Lunsford Lane on November 6, 1863. Haven had become the librarian twenty-five years earlier after society members heard him deliver an address celebrating the bicentennial of his hometown, Dedham, and the character of early New Englanders who contributed "an honorable share of the talent, the patriotism, the domestic virtues, which created and have built up this great republic." Haven found Lunsford Lane's attention to local history and a resident celebrity interesting, but his copy of Lunsford Lane arrived in the collections of the American Antiquarian Society after his death in 1881, the cover pristine, the pages barely worn, and the spine stiff, as if never read.[68]

On January 1, 1864, John A. Green, among the founders of the American Antiquarian Society, also purchased Lunsford Lane. Green began collecting books as a young man, determined to give birth to a public library in Worcester to serve a less discriminating crowd than that found at the American Antiquarian Society. In the late 1850s and early 1860s, he donated 11,928 volumes. Upon his death in 1865, a gift of $30,000 [$559,740] and another 501 books went to the library, including his copy of Lunsford Lane. The first chapter was well-read, with pages crumpled and worn. The rest of the book was less so. Green and future library goers just did not find Hawkins's pontificating that interesting.[69]

Eleven-year-old Charles Frederick Brown printed his name inside his copy of Lunsford Lane in early 1864. By the time the book arrived in the collections at the American Antiquarian Society a century and a half later, it was well-worn, the cover faded and broken in the lower corner, the pages slightly separated as if someone had read it many times. Charles's parents, William and Martha Ann Brown, were readers, not librarians, and they taught their son to read as well. They accumulated nearly two hundred volumes in their private library and dozens of books for their son's shelves.[70]

The Browns lived on the east side of Worcester, anchoring the Liberty Street neighborhood. Decades later, locals credited the naming of Liberty Street to the fact that it was "peopled with negroes," but that was folklore. When designated in 1847, the street housed no Black residents. Like other streets in the area, its name reflected the interests of Edward Earle, a Quaker abolitionist, member of Worcester's South Division Anti-Slavery Society, and owner of much of the lands that formed the neighborhood—Edward Street, Earle Street, Wilmot Street (named for David Wilmot, the Pennsylvania congressman who attempted to ban expansion of enslavement into lands acquired through the Mexican War), and Palmer Street, apparently named for Edward Palmer, a Boston socialist and abolitionist who once wrote William Lloyd Garrison that individual liberty belonged to "all the children of God" and that "the *nominal church* and the institution of *human government* stand directly in the way of this liberty" and should be destroyed. The early residents of the Liberty Street neighborhood were the progenitors of Worcester's White middle class.[71]

William Brown's maternal uncle, John Moore Jr., had been a barber of note in Boston, and when William's father died in 1829, Moore became his legal guardian. His mother, Alice, moved the family to Worcester, and in the spring of 1849, she attended a Free Soil "Tea Party" and heard "a gentleman from Worcester and liked him very much." William found work with the dry goods firm of Chamberlain & Clark, and in 1850, he married Martha Ann Lee. Over the next decade, he became the town's leading upholsterer, making a fortune from catering to the White industrialists who were transforming the town's economic landscape. Sofas, chairs, couches, curled hair mattresses, and spring mattresses: he promised he could repick, recover, and repair them all, as well as install curtains and cut and lay carpets. He accumulated enough wealth and status to move into the middle-class Liberty Street neighborhood and become the first Black member of the Worcester County Mechanics Association, an organization that encouraged mechanical training, promoted innovation, and aided mechanics and their families distressed by illness or loss of employment. He embodied the self-made ethic that permeated New England's most industrially vibrant town, eventually acquiring patents on Brown's Patent Fruit Picker in 1867 and a New Improved Sofa Bed the following year.[72]

In 1853, William Brown contracted a carpenter to build a fine new house at 4 Palmer Street. The house boasted a parlor with Black walnut furniture and a piano, a sitting room with bookcases, a dining room table and sideboard, a chestnut and walnut master bedroom set, three upstairs bedrooms, a kitchen, and, by the 1860s, a Morning Glory coal-burning stove, the most efficient and fashionable on the market. Wallpaper adorned all the

William Brown, 1824–92.
From the Brown Family
Papers. Courtesy of the
American Antiquarian
Society, Worcester, MA.

rooms but the kitchen. Fireplaces warmed the parlor and sitting room. The house filled with furniture and people: William, Martha, and young Charlie; William's mother, Alice Moore Bush; his brother, Frederick A. Brown; John Henry Johnson, an apprentice upholsterer; and William M. Davis, who was "reading law." Many boarders who preceded them had apprenticed under William Brown: Henry Stockbridge, Henry Bowman, and Martha's brother, Thomas Freeman. Above a fireplace hung a portrait—almost unheard of in Black American homes—of William Brown's uncle and legal guardian, John Moore Jr. William Brown knew and celebrated his genealogy.[73]

Young Charlie Brown's library was that of a schoolboy: William Ward's *A View of All Religions* (1824), J. T. Headley's *Imperial Guard of Napoleon* (1851), *Putnam's Home Cyclopedia: Handbook of Literature and the Fine Arts* (1852), Eliza Robbins's *The Guide to Knowledge, Adapted for Young Persons* (1853), *Europe and the Allies of the Past and of Today* (1855), R. M. Zornlin's *Physical Geography, for Families and Schools* (1855), *The Child's*

Anti-Slavery Book (1859), M. J. Michelet's *Woman (La Femme)* (1860), an 1864 edition of the Koran, and William H. Thayer's *The Pioneer Boy and How He Became President* (1864). In 1864, the Browns added Hawkins's *Lunsford Lane* to their son's collection.[74]

Most of Charlie's books had been written for White children, offering racial lessons disguised as moral ones. In *The Pioneer Boy and How He Became President*, the author fabricated a conversation between Abraham Lincoln's father and a neighbor that included Thomas Lincoln deciding to leave Kentucky because poor White settlers could not excel poor Black settlers, "and I am sick of it." *A View of All Religions* described how "that unhappy portion of our population" enslaved in the South experienced "the rudiments of education and the leading principles of the gospel." *Physical Geography for Families and Schools* explained how the "most refined and civilized as well as the most powerful nations of the earth have belonged to the Caucasian race." Michelet's *Woman* taught that, of all women, Black women were "most loving, the most generating . . . from the richness of her heart" and that "the river thirsts for the clouds, the desert for the river, the Black woman for the white man." What must Charlie have thought about his Black neighbors, particularly those displaced by war, embodying the unhappy and uneducated cotton pickers portrayed in his books? Lessons of Blackness, written by White authors, presented them as unrefined and uncivilized, limited in their education and religiosity, at the lowest rung of economy and society, and lusting for Whiteness both carnally and as inspiration toward civilization, faith, and refinement.[75]

The school books that lined Charlie Brown's shelves might have distorted his view of his neighbors, but he owned another, *The Child's Anti-Slavery Book*, which spoke to Black children. Its three stories centered upon enslaved peoples' greatest anxiety: separation from family. The accompanying illustrations—*A Slave Father Sold Away from His Family* and *Little Lewis Sold*—horrified young readers who saw their own families in the images. A brief epilogue told of a West Indian man taught to read by a missionary, differentiating the literate child who owned *The Child's Anti-Slavery Book* from the illiterate enslaved man and reinforcing the importance of Black children's ownership of books.[76]

Around the same time that Charlie added *Lunsford Lane* to his library, Wellington Hospital closed, and Lunsford and Martha Lane moved into a rental just around the corner from the Brown family. Naturally, one of Worcester's leading Black families made acquaintance with the new celebrity in the neighborhood. Yet, the families did not become fast friends. The Lanes' economic struggles might have played a role. Lunsford's lecture at Wilkinsville did not translate into a sustained speaking tour. The biography did not yield enough cash. Banking on his reputation as a hospital steward, he returned to making medicines for a living, but the sales never met his

No. 660.

LITTLE LEWIS SOLD.

Little Lewis Sold. From *The Child's Anti-Slavery Book* (Boston: American Tract Society, 1859), 18–19. Courtesy of the American Antiquarian Society, Worcester, MA.

needs. Money was tight, and the Lanes lived humbly compared to the Browns, who, by 1865, held a landed wealth of $2,480 [$46,270] and moved in different social circles.[77]

During the war, the Liberty Street neighborhood filled with migrants. In 1863, Black residents occupied only five households: William and Martha Ann Brown; Charles W. and Sarah Bulah from New Jersey and Pennsylvania, respectively; Maryland freedom seekers Isaac and Anne Mason; Gilbert Walker and his Massachusetts-born wife, Sarah; and William H. H. Geary, who came to Worcester to learn the barber trade from "the well known Professor Walker." Within two years, the number quadrupled, the Lanes arriving alongside new neighbors from North Carolina, Missouri, and Maryland, as well as several New England states.[78]

The Lanes struggled to fit in with the rest of Black Worcester. Lunsford no longer enjoyed the reputation of representing redemption-by-purchase or even antislavery, and after President Abraham Lincoln issued the Emancipation Proclamation, and it became apparent to all that the war was about ending slavery, those topics did not matter anymore. On January 1, 1864, the Anti-Slavery and Temperance Society of Worcester sponsored an anniversary celebration of the Emancipation Proclamation. Dr. Lane was one of four featured speakers, alongside two ministers and longtime activist Allen Walker. His colleagues' speeches moved the audience to donate toward recently freed people in eastern North Carolina, but Lunsford was unimpressive. In a review of the event, a reporter praised Walker, Reverends Brown and Richardson, "and others."[79]

In the latter months of the war, as a steady stream of refugees and freedom seekers arrived in Worcester seeking support and protection, many Black Worcesterites opened their homes and expanded their families. In the Liberty Street neighborhood, Gilbert and Sarah Walker took in Thomas and Eliza Barber from North Carolina, Addie Parker of Pennsylvania, Robert Brown from Virginia, and Augustus Toney, who had grown up in Worcester. Isaac and Anne Mason took in Stephen Taylor, once enslaved in Missouri, and his wife Mary Taylor from Pennsylvania, as well as William and Rachel Bostic of Pennsylvania. Allen and Sarah Walker took in William Gurry from Virginia. Charles and Sarah Bulah took in John Clark, a Massachusetts-born painter. Henry and Lydia Boscom housed Eliza Chaplin, a cook from Connecticut, and Rosa Hazard from Rhode Island. The Lanes do not appear to have opened their home to anyone.[80]

The war ended in April 1865. Although Timothy Wellington's eldest son arrived home safely, it was with heavy heart that, on July 1, 1865, he hosted an elegant community feast to celebrate Worcesterites' wartime sacrifices. So many of Worcester's soldiers already had returned home. Speeches and music enlivened the day, concluding with a parade that included Wellington coal wagons, each filled with "Black diamonds" and drawn by horses covered with red, white, and blue blankets. For Wellington, the words painted on the side of each wagon became painful to read: T. W. Wellington & Sons. His second youngest, George, fought for only five months when, in April 1864, Confederates captured him at Plymouth, North Carolina, confining him at Andersonville Prison in Georgia. For four months, he suffered from scurvy and bleeding gums, surviving on cob meal and molasses as he gradually wasted away and became delirious. George died on August 10, 1864. A hostess presented Wellington with a bouquet of remembrance.[81]

Although absent from the July 1865 celebration, war-wearied Black men had returned to Worcester months earlier. Henry Garner's three friends all returned: George Alston in June 1864, disabled and no longer able to fight; Amos Webber, quartermaster sergeant of the Fifth Cavalry, in October 1864; and John Stevens a year later. Alexander Hemenway rose to First Sergeant in the Massachusetts Fifty-Fourth and walked into his parents' home in late April 1865. William Brown's apprentice, Thomas Freeman, wounded at the

Battle of Honey Hill in November 1864, arrived home in Worcester and strug-gled with typhoid until he died in early 1866. Brown's other apprentice never returned. A night sentinel accidentally shot John Johnson on June 11, 1864, on Morris Island, South Carolina.[82]

Among the Lanes' friends in Oberlin, Rubin Turner returned to the Copeland home in early summer 1865 from Fort Pickering in Memphis, discharged as disabled. "Consumption of both lungs and chronic Diarrhea contracted in the line of duty," diagnosed the company surgeon. "This Sol-dier has done very liteel duty since joining the regiment. . . . He will never be fit for Military duty. He is not fit for the Veteran Reserve Corps." Rubin lan-guished for a month in Oberlin, dying in late August. He was twenty-one years old. Henry Patterson, now a sergeant, returned to Oberlin late in the summer of 1865, as did Wilson Evans. Thomas Campton, stationed in Louisville, Kentucky, expected to muster out in July 1865 but instead transferred to another company of the Twelfth United States Colored Heavy Artillery. By August, he was absent without leave, returning only upon threat of court-martial. He finally mustered out and arrived in Oberlin in February 1866.[83]

As the Lanes watched young men return from war and received reports from their friends in Oberlin, they heard nothing from their own soldiers. After the siege of Atlanta, Edward Lane and the Thirty-Ninth Ohio Infantry marched on with William Tecumseh Sherman to Savannah and into the Carolinas, eventu-ally engaging Joseph E. Johnston at the Battle of Bentonville. In April 1865, twenty-three years after he fled Raleigh as a young teenager, Edward returned as an occupier. Three months later, he mustered out in Louisville, Kentucky.[84]

His sister, Maria Bell Lane Garner, also sought word about her husband, Henry. When the state census taker visited in the spring of 1865, she expectantly listed him as a member of their household, but she would not see Henry again. Maria shared only six months with him. They had just begun to know each other when he marched off to war. After the Battle of Petersburg, the Fifth Calvary transferred to Texas. At the end of October, his regiment mustered out at Clarksville. Ten days later, Henry died from chronic diarrhea in the Hospital Corps d'Afrique in New Orleans, buried the same day in section 65, plot 15 of the Chalmette Cemetery, his grave marked by a small wooden cross. A decade later, the cross was gone, replaced by a regulation military headstone.[85]

In January 1866, Maria Bell Lane Garner signed the paperwork for her widow's pension with the help of Henry's friend and fellow cavalryman, Amos Webber. The United States had passed the Widow's Pension Act in July 1862, providing an $8 [$150] monthly pension for "total disability." Applicants found the process a bureaucratic nightmare. The clerk questioned Maria's "alleged marriage" to Henry, forcing her to apply for a copy of her marriage certifi-cate. In March, the adjutant general's office rejected her application because

"Henry G Garner does not appear on any Muster Roll." After a little research, they conceded his service, but in April, the office again wrote, warning that there "is no evidence of his Death on file in this office." In 1865 and 1866, the Commissioner on Pensions received thousands of applications, and slight delays were to be expected, but Maria heard nothing more for another year. She gathered testimonials from Webber and other soldiers who fought alongside her husband, including Andrew F. Chapman of Boston, who, in December 1866, testified that Henry rose to sergeant in Company D just before he died. Maria wrote to the commissioner, pleading that he accept Chapman's affidavit because she did not know the hospital surgeon who could verify Henry's death and did not know how to find him since "he resides somewhere in the South," signing "Mrs. Maria B garner." Six months later, she found Frederick G. Parker of Maine, the company surgeon, who confirmed Henry's death. Not until August 24, 1867, did F. E. Pequette, the surgeon at Hospital Corps d'Afrique, certify that Henry had died nearly two years earlier. Still, it was another two months until Maria received her first pension payment: $8 a month beginning in September 1867, with back payments to November 1865. Another year passed before Henry's effects arrived from the Hospital Corps d'Afrique: two dollars [$38] found in his pocket.[86]

By then, Maria had met Gustavus Rose. He had fled Virginia and enslavement in the late 1840s with his sister, Martha Patterson, leaving behind their parents, John and Hannah. The siblings settled in Manhattan, where Martha met a man and eventually had two sons, William and John. By 1855, the boys' father was out of the picture, and Martha's youngest died. A census taker found Gustavus moved in with his sister and young Willie, sharing a tenement apartment with John Thomas and his two young sons, who had escaped enslavement in Maryland.[87]

John Thomas was a waiter, and he likely helped Gustavus Rose secure a job because the thirty-five-year-old showed up a second time on the federal census that year, listed among the staff in the private four-story brick home of millionaire Amos Richards Eno, one of the city's great capitalists. Eno recently built the Fifth Avenue Hotel at Madison Square, the city's first "uptown" luxury hotel. The five-story hotel was ahead of its age. Anticipating that 23rd Avenue would become a commercial center, Eno built his hotel on the northern reaches of the city, facing Madison Square Park. Rumors that the site had been a potter's field that once served victims of the 1797 yellow fever epidemic and later as Bellevue Hospital's cemetery did not slow Fifth Avenue Hotel from becoming the most opulent guesthouse in Manhattan, a building of imported marble with public spaces often compared to European palaces and the city's second passenger elevator, a steam-powered "vertical screw railway" designed by Otis Tufts.[88]

Commonwealth of Massachusetts.

City Clerk's Office,

Worcester, *January 30th 1866.*

I, *Samuel Smith* hereby certify that I hold the Office of City Clerk, and have the custody of the Records of this City relating to Births, Marriages, and Deaths; and I further certify that it appears by the Registry of *Marriages,* that *Henry G. Garner and Maria Bell Lane* were Married in *this city* on the *third* day of *May A.D. 1863.* By *Samuel Souther a clergyman of Worcester.*

Witness my hand and Seal of the City. *Samuel Smith City Clerk.*

Marriage certificate for Maria Bell Lane and Henry G. Garner, 1866. From Case Files of Approved Pension Applications of Widows and Other Veterans of the Army and Navy Who Served Mainly in the Civil War and the War with Spain, Compiled 1861–1934, Record Group 15, Records of the Veterans Administration. Courtesy of the National Archives, Washington, DC.

In New York and other Northern cities, waiting was increasingly a Black occupation. Hotel and restaurant owners and private employers like Eno assumed that Black waiters, many of whom with experience not only in private Southern homes but at public dinners and civic festivities, would act "naturally" deferential towards White customers. It was a tall order for Black waiters who felt attacked on two fronts—wealthy White customers, many of them Southern who refused to acknowledge the humanity of waiting staff, and thousands of Irish immigrants who, willing to work for lesser wages, became sudden threats to job security. Black waiters countered the threat of losing jobs to Irish immigrants by forming unions. As an organizer described in March 1853, the job demanded "an active, intelligent man, of good moral character and honesty," and Irish waiters were "in a manner, ashamed of being so, and are consequently indifferent." As Lunsford Lane had learned decades earlier, serving the Marquis de Lafayette, "If you now be true to yourselves, you will dignify your calling and character." Leaders of the Waiters' Protective Union Society planned a strike to pressure employers to raise salaries to $18 [$710] a month. When approached by a White waiters' union to collaborate on the strike, the Waiters' Protective Union Society gladly accepted, but another group—the First United Association of Colored Waiters—rejected interracial activism, recognizing the threat of White waiters willing to work for the same rates.[89]

Over the next decade, racial tensions among New York waiters smoldered until, in July 1863, hundreds of working-class New Yorkers, many of them Irish immigrants and Irish Americans, rioted over the Enrollment Act, a draft instituted by the United States Congress to raise more troops. Irish and German immigrants who recently received citizenship resented their recruitment, particularly since wealthier White men could buy substitutes. The rioters took their anger out on Black New Yorkers, killing over 119 people and pillaging and ransacking lower Manhattan, including the Colored Orphan Asylum (terrorizing the 237 orphans as they fled), the Colored Sailors' Home, James McCune Smith's pharmacy, and several hotels, among them Crook's Hotel which consequently lost all its Black waiters as they bolted for Philadelphia. They were among the thousands of Black New Yorkers who abandoned the city. The riots spread beyond Manhattan. In Troy, New York, protestors assaulted the Troy House, planning "to make a demonstration on the colored waiters." They were dissuaded by a guest, the famed bare-knuckle boxer John Morrissey, who owned gaming houses in nearby Saratoga Springs and appreciated Black waiters' professionalism.[90]

In the atmosphere of racialized terror and Black professional aspirations, Gustavus Rose was the only Black staff member—the waiter—in the Eno home, working alongside five Irish coachmen and domestics. When the Enrollment Act passed in June 1863, Rose registered for the draft, but he never served and remained in the Eno household for two more years. When the end of war brought thousands of White men back to New York City, displacing Black laborers, Rose abandoned the city, taking on work in Worcester and living with several other waiters in a boarding house. If he met Maria Bell Lane Garner then, she was still married and waiting for Henry to return home.[91]

At war's end, thousands of arrivals from Ireland, Germany, the former Confederacy, and across the North sought work in Worcester's machine shops, wire factories, textile mills, and other industrial works, transforming the town into the center of New England manufacturing and transportation. With industrialization came wealth, a lot of it, drawing investors and inventors and energizing a hospitality industry. Hoping to take advantage of the demand for good hospitality, in early August 1864, John S. Thomas took over the Bay State House, the town's largest hotel, renovating the interior and advertising for new employees. Gustavus Rose joined the staff, thirty-four strong—cooks, bell boys, laundresses, porters, housekeepers, bar keepers, chamber girls, billiards keepers, domestics, scrub girls, stable keepers, and waiters. He and Charles E. Bailey, both formerly enslaved men, were the waiters, the only two Black employees on the hotel staff, boarding together in a Worcester tenement house from which Rose courted a young widow.[92]

Chapter 14

Return to Carolina

Just as the Civil War brought industrial and demographic change to Worcester, so too did it transform Raleigh. In the early years of the war, hundreds of White women and children, fleeing Federal troops in the eastern part of the state, crowded as war refugees into the town's boarding houses, hotels, and private homes. Initially, there were plenty of White men in Raleigh, exempted from Confederate conscription laws because of their status as state officials, to provide a sense of security. Still, rumors of insurrection spread among a desperately paranoid population. In 1863, the state legislature futilely established a Home Guard to defend the homeland, but the regiment of older men could do little to salvage the town's economy and community. By summer of 1863, rents tripled their 1861 rates, food was scarce, and "everyone is melancholy and dejected, not at the ill success of our arms, but at the certain disaster."[1]

By late 1864, White men were becoming so scarce in Raleigh that fifteen Black men joined Raleigh's Home Guard, causing one newspaper to question rumors that the Confederacy planned "to raise negro troops to fight under the Confederate flag! Has it come to that? . . . It is so ridiculous, so ruinous even at the first blush, and so full of madness that we shall not discuss it." In spring 1865, White Raleighites anticipated "the final struggle of the war will soon occur in the old North State." Federal troops, including Edward Lane's Thirty-Ninth Infantry, spread across eastern North Carolina, occupying the capital town in April with hundreds of Black refugees in tow seeking protection and opportunity. With war's end, John M. Schofield, the commanding Union general in North Carolina, promised Black Carolinians their freedom, asking them to remain on the farms where they worked and encouraging their former enslavers to "employ them as hired servants at reasonable wages." Some free people stayed where they were, unsure of where else to go or what to do should they leave. Others abandoned the sites and memories of enslavement as fast as they could.[2]

With Emancipation, the fears that framed White Carolinians' relations with their Black neighbors over two centuries evolved into disdain. The primary target became the Freedmen's Bureau, which provided food, clothing, shelter, schools, medical care, and employment advice to needy Black and White Carolinians. White women from the North whom the Bureau brought into North Carolina to teach Black Southerners became subject to rumors that they, "not of the masculine gender, the more effectually to accomplish their dark and nefarious designs, eschew the society of the whites, and have taken up their bed and board with the Blacks." Violence against Black Southerners exploded. One bureau agent suspected that White residents' first inclination in dealing with their Black neighbors "was to take a gun and put a bullet into him or a charge of shot." In May 1865, near New Bern, a former enslaver shot Jack three times for trying to visit a relative on the farm. In Wilmington in late June, a White man shot and killed a Black woman who was trying to "get away from the presence of a drunken and brutal paramour." One newspaper justified the murder. The woman assumed "privileges beyond those enjoyed by any other class of community."[3]

Amid the chaos, the racial anxieties, and the violence of the summer of 1865, Benjamin Wisner Pond, a superintendent for the New York National Freedmen's Relief Association, arrived in Raleigh. Pond had been born and raised in Bangor, Maine, the son of Julia Ann and Enoch Pond, a Congregationalist minister and theology professor at the Bangor Theological Seminary. Benjamin followed his father into the ministry, leaving it between 1864 and 1867 to work with newly free Black Southerners. He became principal of the free people's high school in the District of Columbia where over fifty students learned English and algebra from nine teachers, including Sojourner Truth. In June 1865, the Association sent Pond southward to inspect free people's schools. Accompanying him was Lane's biographer, William G. Hawkins, now the Association's secretary and editor of *The National Freedman*, the Association's monthly journal. Hawkins headed to Virginia and Pond to North Carolina.[4]

Raleigh offered no school for free people, despite the numbers of refugees who congregated in the town. Pond suspected a "few schools may be put in operation there (there is not field for many) with promise of excellent results," and on July 5, on behalf of the Association, Pond christened the new Johnson School, named for Raleigh-born President Andrew Johnson. White Raleighites, displeased with Emancipation, threatened "that no man, woman, or child in their employ shall attend school and remain in their employ." For Black residents, it was a difficult choice between education and employment. Pond hoped to inspire them toward education.[5]

So, a week later during a packed meeting of Black Raleighites, Pond announced that Lunsford Lane was coming. Lane accompanied Hawkins and Pond on the journey southward, continuing with Pond into North Carolina. The announcement electrified the crowd. Pond noted how "strong men and women shook with intense feeling, and that day brought great rejoicing to many." He tried to explain the reaction to the White Northern readership of *The National Freedman*: "Raleigh was the scene of the history of the slave-man, Lunsford Lane. The narrative of his difficulties in escaping from bondage, even after he purchased himself and his family, was published and widely read in New England two years ago. The history was enacted here in Raleigh some thirty years ago, and enlisted the sympathies of the entire Black population here, so that they whisper the name and memory of Lunsford Lane as the name of a banished favorite; and that not alone because he was a martyr, but because he had been a sort of leader and prince among them."[6]

Prince Lunsford was not in Raleigh yet. He was in New Bern, accompanied by his sons Edward, William, and Lunsford Jr. They had not traveled southward together. Although unclear as to which son, either Edward or William had found work as a steward on a New Bern-bound steamer from New York. During the journey, that son, the ship's captain, and the first mate brawled, the latter two pummeling Lunsford's son with marlinspikes. The provost marshal arrested all three. Lunsford turned to William G. Hawkins to help. That the assault had been racially motivated gradually became apparent. Hawkins warned Brigadier General Charles Jackson Paine, district commander in New Bern, that "outrages are committed upon these unoffending people: do not be surprised if they at some time take the law in their own hands, and use their muskets." Paine released Lunsford's son, promising to make an example of the sailors.[7]

———

The Fourth of July celebration in 1865 was the first in Raleigh's nineteenth-century history during which speakers did not endorse enslavement as a corollary to White liberty. Few White Carolinians attended—"no ladies, no flags, orations met with silence, maybe three hundred." Instead, five thousand Black Carolinians filled the streets, embracing the United States for the first time as *their* nation with a parade, music, and banners. Rumor was that they sang "My Country 'Tis of Thee."[8]

Then, two weeks later, Lunsford Lane arrived to much fanfare, heralded by those who knew him as a long-lost friend who once saved his family and survived being tarred and feathered. It had been twenty-three years since he last saw Raleigh, and the town's population was mostly unfamiliar. Former neighbors and friends had moved to Oberlin. Benjamin B. Smith had died in 1855, as had Eleanor Haywood and former governor Edward Dudley. The last of the original Haywood brothers, Henry, died in 1857. Lunsford's former employer, C. C. Battle, passed in 1859. William Boylan followed in July 1861. Of the 122 people enslaved by Eleanor Haywood when Lunsford and Clarissa stepped off the Raleigh estate for the last time, Eleanor had sold nineteen, forty-three had died by the outbreak of the Civil War, and the rest scattered with Emancipation. It is unknown whether Lunsford's aunt Matilda, uncle Sam Mac, and cousins Montford and Davy remained in Raleigh or even were alive. The White Haywood children were grown with families of their own. Raleigh was full of strangers: thousands of Black and White war refugees and a new generation of Black Raleighites who knew enslavement only as a childhood nightmare.[9]

Yet, Lunsford Lane returned to Raleigh a hero. The Story had preserved his memory among Black Raleighites and introduced him to younger generations. Among the people who crowded Lane as he arrived in town were new admirers, people such as Anna Julia Haywood and her brothers and Charles Norfleet Hunter and Osborne Hunter Jr.—all too young to have known Lunsford or even his children before the Lanes abandoned Raleigh. Instead, they heard The Story and wanted to see the genuine hero for themselves.[10]

Anna Julia Haywood's mother was Hannah. Their enslaver, Washington Haywood, had been born a year before Lunsford Lane and had been a childhood playmate. He went on to a distinguished legal career and became a star in North Carolina's Whig Party. Washington often repaired his siblings' mistakes. After Eliza Haywood's death in 1832, her youngest son, Alfred, was not attending college, not interested in courting, and languishing on a farm in the St. Mary's district where he managed the enslaved laborers he inherited from his father. In 1833, without conferring with his siblings, he used his and their shares of Eliza's estate—the house and the enslaved peoples—as security for a $1,026 [$37,110] loan. Horrified at his younger brother's carelessness, Washington and his brothers John and Fabius bailed Alfred out to save the house and most of the enslaved peoples. In return, Alfred used his enslaved laborers as collateral should he default on their loan. When he failed to pay, Hannah, who once worked alongside Ned Lane in the Haywood home, was among ten enslaved people divided among Alfred's patrons.[11]

Hannah and her two-month-old son, Rufus, went into Washington Haywood's household. The details of Hannah's private life are hidden, but Washington's sister, Rebecca Haywood Hall, rumored that Robert White had fathered Rufus. Andrew Jackson, born eleven years later, and Anna Julia, born another eleven years later, appeared as "mulatto" in official records, and it seems they were the children of Hannah and Washington Haywood. Anna had little use for her Haywood lineage. "My mother was a slave and the finest woman I have ever known," she recalled decades later. If it was true that Washington Haywood was her father, "I owe him not a sou & she was always too modest & shamefaced ever to mention him."[12]

Hannah's father seems to have been Jacob Stanley, an enslaved carpenter in the household of Fabius Haywood, Washington's brother. Years later, Anna Julia celebrated her grandfather in a poem, describing him as "a broad chested upstanding black man" and noting how "family tradition" took pride in his having helped construct the State Capitol in the 1830s. Anna Julia Haywood was seven years old when Federal troops occupied Raleigh, bringing emancipation as well as hope that the war was near its end.[13]

Anna Julia Haywood knew the Hunter brothers, enslaved children on the estate of William Dallas Haywood, son of Stephen and Delia Haywood. Their father, Osborne Hunter, was a skilled carpenter who hired out his time and lived independently of his enslaver. He, in turn, hired an enslaved woman, Mary, to work in his shop, and in 1848, they had their first child, Harriet. Two years later, Osborne arrived, followed by Charles the next year, and another sister, her name lost, a couple of years later. By 1856, both parents had died, and the boys and their sisters went to Dallas Haywood's estate where their father's kin cared for them. On an inventory that numbered over one hundred enslaved peoples, Charles and Osborne enjoyed a privileged position, moderating Charles's opinions about enslavement later in life. An "injury done to a Haywood Negro was injury done to a Haywood white and vice versa," he reminisced about his youth. Of course, an injury done to an enslaved Haywood was damage to property and loss of monetary value, a point that he did not seem to grasp or conveniently overlooked. When Federal troops marched into Raleigh in 1865, Charles was twelve years old.[14]

In July 1865, Charles Hunter and Anna Julia Haywood were feeling their emancipations as children, experiencing Raleigh's racial convulsions as the system of enslavement collapsed and Federal troops instilled a new order. As members of the extended Black Haywood families, they, too, knew the tales of Lunsford Lane. They joined in the revelry when he returned to Raleigh.[15]

Who knows how an event like the return of a local hero affected young, free Black Raleighites? Soon after Lane's visit, Anna Julia began attending Raleigh's newly formed St. Augustine's Normal School and Collegiate Institute, an outreach project of the Freedmen's Commission of the Protestant Episcopal Church. Nine years later, she married George Cooper, a St. Augustine's theology teacher. When he died in 1879, Anna Cooper remained in Raleigh briefly as a teacher before leaving for Oberlin College where she earned her bachelor's and master's degrees. She went on to teach high school in Washington, DC. In 1892, she was a central figure in forming the Colored Women's League, devoted to improving the lives of Black women and children, particularly in cities. Cooper became outspoken about empowering Black women through education and social opportunities. As their status climbed, so too did that of the Black community. She articulated these views in *A Voice from the South*, published in 1892, and the following year in her presentation on "The Intellectual Progress of the Colored Women of the United States since the Emancipation Proclamation" at the World's Congress of Representative Women in Chicago. In 1925, she earned a doctoral degree from the Université de Paris-Sorbonne with a dissertation titled "The Attitude of France on the Question of Slavery between 1789 and 1848."[16]

Throughout her work and her writings, Cooper returned time and again to memory, folklore, and family traditions. She made no reference to that day in 1866 when, as an eight-year-old, she heard rumor that Lunsford Lane was coming and witnessed his return to Raleigh, but the enthusiasm of the crowds, the rumors of his heroism, and The Story itself must have struck a chord. It was the first public celebration of her life that centered Black history. The Story became part of the corpus of local folklore from which Black Americans contested White narratives of the past. Later in life, Anna Julia Cooper became a central figure in the Hampton Folklore Society, which, by the 1890s, began collecting and preserving Black heritage. She saw the society's project as a validation of the distinctiveness and redemptive potential of Black American culture.[17]

Charles and Osborne Hunter also went on to do important things. They attended a free people's school in Raleigh. Osborne became active in the Republican Party, coediting the partisan *Raleigh Daily Constitution* beginning in 1875. He contributed to national conversations about Black Americans' futures, testifying in investigations about the exodus of thousands of Black Carolinians to Indiana in the late 1870s and culminating in an 1884 essay titled "What's Next?" in which he argued that, distracted by their "political welfare," Black Americans had neglected "wealth and education—the two great highways that lead to prosperity and success."[18]

Months after Lane's visit, fourteen-year-old Charles Hunter snuck into the state's first freedmen's convention. Delegates gathered in Raleigh, passing resolutions praising the tenet that all men are created equal, proclaiming their freedom, appealing to state leaders for security as Federal troops began to depart Raleigh, and arguing for the centrality of education for Black success. He took it to heart, beginning a teaching career in 1875 that consumed the rest of his life, over the years serving as a teacher and school superintendent in several rural North Carolina counties as well as in Durham, Goldsboro, and Raleigh. He became Raleigh's first Black postmaster in 1881, and he took on the associate editor position at *The Banner* newspaper that year as well.[19]

Hunter believed that an education in history was foundational to successful citizenship. His first effort to bring history to Black Carolinians was a Fourth of July celebration that he organized in 1869, followed the next year by the state's first Emancipation Day gathering, which he also planned. Although less than twenty years old, Hunter already served as the state's repository of Black memory. Speeches, songs, and parades highlighted the events. Over the next fifty years, Hunter keynoted many of them, often drawing on the theme that "The past has its lessons: let us study time." In 1879, with his brother Osborne, Charles founded the North Carolina Industrial Association in 1879, a Black civic organization "to encourage and promote the development of the industrial and educational resources of the colored people of North Carolina." They initiated the North Carolina Colored Industrial Fair, a celebration of Black handicrafts, agriculture, industry, and art to inspire racial pride. In 1906, he developed the state's exhibit for the Jamestown Exposition, a national celebration of the tricentennial of the founding of Jamestown. He traveled the state collecting documents related to Black history to fill the exhibit, situated in the exposition's Negro Building. Hunter viewed all these efforts as meeting the most important duty of Black Carolinians—educating their children.[20]

In 1907, Charles N. Hunter, who met Lane as a child and played a central role in creating North Carolina's Negro State Fair, visited Raleigh's Shaw University. His lecture at Shaw began with questions: "Who knew anything, or had heard anything of John Chavis, the noted Negro scholar, teacher, and preacher"? Not a hand went up. "George M. Horton, The Slave Poet of North Carolina"? No hand. "Lunsford Lane, of Raleigh, who distinguished himself in Massachusetts during the days of the Abolition conflict"? Again, no one. Hunter's spirits fell. After the lecture, students crowded him, imploring him to publish sketches of Chavis, Horton, and Lane to "render them available for study."[21]

Hunter believed that Black Americans had "no adequate appreciation of the essential place which history must hold in determining racial values." To know themselves, they needed to know their forbears. To understand White people who sought to oppress them, Black folks needed to know those forbears as well. So, Hunter began work on the biographies, quickly sketching out Chavis's and Horton's lives and acquiring a typescript of the fourth edition of Lane's *Narrative*. Thirteen years later, he was still investigating, traveling to the Boston Public Library in 1920 to research "remarkable Negro characters which were developed during the days of slavery," specifically Lane and Horton. Hunter did not have skills as historian or biographer, however, and he struggled to complete the work, leaving "Negro Life in North Carolina Illustrated" unrealized. Still, in his draft of the Horton biography, Hunter concluded with what he considered the cause of the era: "Give us history. Give us history."[22]

When Lunsford Lane returned to Raleigh in the summer of 1865, Black Raleighites' celebration of The Story not only inspired but reminded of the racial violence of the old regime. A generation later, historian and sociologist W. E. B. Du Bois fulminated how, despite Emancipation, three million Black folk in the mid-1860s remained in the shadow of slavery, represented by two figures: the White enslaver, "a blighted, ruined form," and the Black mother who once "quailed at that white master's command, had bent in love over the cradles of his sons and daughters, and closed in death the sunken eyes of his wife," and still saw "her dark boy's limbs scattered to the winds by midnight marauders riding after 'damned Niggers.'" The increasing violence of post-war North Carolina evidenced that little had changed from the days when the "slave mother" lamented, "Thou art a little slave, my child / And much I grieve and mourn / That to so dark a destiny / A lovely babe I've borne." The Story embodied a racialized terrorism that continued through Emancipation, haunting Anna Julia Haywood, Charles Hunter, and other youth who went out to see the folk hero as he shared new tales of life in the North. Deciding that he would not allow it to haunt his own children, Lunsford Lane sent Edward, William, and Lunsford Jr. northward soon after the Raleigh reunion.[23]

––––––––

The arrest of Lunsford's son, the celebratory return to Raleigh—distractions drew Lane from his purpose for traveling to North Carolina: to establish a school "to fit these people for republican government," as Horace James articulated. Private societies like the Worcester Freedmen's Aid Society loosely coordinated with the American Missionary Association, the National Freedmen's Relief Association, and the Freedmen's Bureau to send supplies and teachers southward. Horace James, Superintendent of the Eastern District in North Carolina, insisted on the need for more schools to teach mechanic arts, specifically soliciting coopering tools to set up barrel productions for local turpentine industries. When Lane left Massachusetts for North Carolina, he had already communicated with James about setting up a school, one like the superintendent's lauded efforts on Roanoke Island. Lane also conversed with his biographer, Hawkins, who, as a leader on the National Freedmen's Relief Association's Committee on Teachers and Publications, was a critical partner in establishing schools in New Bern, Wilmington, Oxford, Washington, and Roanoke Island. Hawkins, as editor of the association's national newspaper, *The Freedman's Advocate*, during its run from 1864 to 1865 and the monthly journal, *The National Freedman*, from 1865 to 1866, also controlled the news about those schools.[24]

Success depended on the good graces of local residents. Upon arriving outside New Bern, Lane found someone to support his mission—Edward H. Hill, a successful farmer born enslaved in 1835. He was an extremely religious man, quickly becoming an elder and deacon in the New Bern A.M.E. Zion Church when it organized in 1864. It was the first A.M.E. Zion congregation to form in the disintegrating Confederacy, and in May, Hill represented the congregation—indeed the entire Black South—when he attended the denomination's General Conference in Philadelphia. The following year, he organized the Clinton Chapel A.M.E. Zion Church in Charlotte. Lunsford Lane arrived in New Bern as Edward Hill returned home from Charlotte, and they planned the manual labor school together. Within a month, they recruited thirty "hands" to work the farm—men, women, children, and families. They also approached Richard M. C. Tucker, Moses P. Kennedy, and John R. Good to serve as an advisory council.[25]

Tucker, born enslaved around 1818, apprenticed as a carpenter and coffin-maker in his youth. In the 1830s, he married Emeline, enslaved on a nearby farm, in a ceremony officiated by a Black clergyman, although such weddings were neither legal nor recognized by White authorities. Over the years, they had fifteen children. "I have eight head living and seven head dead," Emeline shared with Horace James in 1865. Emeline's enslaver, Raymond Castix, sold seven of the children, forcing Richard Tucker to beg his enslaver, John Flanner, to purchase Emeline and the last child for their own security. Tucker paid Flanner fifteen dollars [$280] a month in return. Once the Federal Army controlled New Bern, Richard and Emeline approached James about officially marrying them. "They took each the other by the hand, as their lawful and wedded mate," recalled James, "and tears of grateful joy streamed down their serious faces." Upon emancipation in 1865, Tucker's training situated him well. He became a prominent undertaker, burying "nearly all, both white and colored," and managing New Bern's Black cemetery. He also became political, attending the 1866 Freedmen Convention in Raleigh and the 1868 North Carolina Constitutional Convention. He and Emeline eventually tracked down four of their stolen children. Like Hill, Tucker became a leader in the A.M.E. Zion church. Impressed by Tucker "as a leading and influential colored man in Newbern," Horace James connected Lane to him.[26]

Moses Kennedy had been born into enslavement in 1783, the son of Peggy. He lived the next seventy-seven years enslaved to John Wright Stanly Jr. As a nineteen-year-old, Moses witnessed Stanly, a Federalist, kill a political opponent and former governor, Richard Dobbs Spaight, in the state's most notorious duel. In his early thirties, Kennedy served as a drummer in the War of 1812. When Stanly died, his son, Edward, inherited Moses and emancipated him, partially because Moses once "plunged without suggestion or command into the angry stream then swarming with alligators and swam to the opposite shore" to get a boat to safely transport his enslaver to the farm. Freedom brought a surname—Kennedy—and a career as a barber, but it also brought heartache. His wife, Siddy, who gained her freedom by 1861, took advantage of her independence to leave "my bed and board without any cause," as Moses advertised, warning readers to not let her charge anything to his accounts. Three years later, his son, Dow, ran to the Federal troops as they marched through eastern North Carolina and became an incidental casualty during battle.[27]

In 1815, John R. Good was also born enslaved. Thirty-nine years later, the State Assembly granted him his emancipation. Good became a barber. He joined Edward Hill in 1864 in a delegation to meet Abraham Lincoln, the first group of Black southerners to do so, petitioning the President "to finish the noble work you have begun, and grant unto your petitioners that greatest of privileges when the State is reconstructed, to exercise the right of suffrage." The men then went on to New York, attending a public reception at the city's A.M.E. Zion Church. Hill spoke first, praising John Brown as "the only man who had the skill and power to break" through the entrenched influence of the slaveocracy, making "a passage way so large that Abraham Lincoln and all his hosts had ample room to pass through." Good, emotionally overwhelmed by the moment, addressed and shocked his audience with tales of living "amid the horrors of slavery so long."[28]

For Good, Kennedy, Tucker, Hill, and other Black Carolinians, founding a school promised to build new communities as enslavement collapsed. For Lunsford Lane, it was an enterprise, one that reflected his commitment to rational liberty and practical abolitionism, and one that might make money. For months, Horace James bragged through Northern newspapers of his profitable work on Roanoke Island, particularly the evening schools where soldiers taught free people. He appealed to fellow abolitionists back in Worcester to send missionary teachers and funds to support schools for free people, receiving such a good response that one soldier wrote home, "New Bern abounds with Worcester faces."[29]

In mid-1865, James stepped down as Superintendent of the Eastern District, taking a minor bureaucratic role as Assistant Superintendent of Pitt County, where he invested in two farms—Avon and Yankee Hall—which sat on opposing banks of the Tar River. He recruited residents, paying boys $6 [$110] a month and men $15 [$280], and providing rations for the families. Each family had a cabin and a private garden and kept hogs and hens. Each farm had a school run by a White Northern volunteer: Hattie Billings at Yankee Hall and Katie Means at Avon. The schools, the good pay, the provisions—all were meant to inspire refugees to abandon the overcrowded camps near the Federal troops where disease and food shortages threatened. By helping themselves, free people also helped James, providing labor for his enterprises.[30]

Horace James, 1818–75. From J. Waldo Denny, *Wearing the Blue in the Twenty-Fifth Mass. Volunteer Infantry, with Burnside's Coastal Division, 18th Army Corps, and Army of the James* (Worcester, MA: Putnam & Davis, 1879), opposite page 20, North Carolina Collection. Courtesy of Wilson Special Collections Library, University of North Carolina at Chapel Hill.

Lunsford's school similarly arose on a former farm near a small stop along the Atlantic & North Carolina Rail Road known as Rouse Depot. Federal troops damaged sections of the railroad during the war, and although Rouse Depot sat only some twenty-five miles west of New Bern, it was cut off from the world. Unlike James, Lane did not have federal connections, forcing him to rely on often inconsistent donations from the Freedmen's Aid Society, a Black community-based charity that organized throughout Northern towns to support the American Missionary Association's aspirations to educate Black Southerners. Funds and supplies trickled slowly to New Bern and, given the condition of the railroad, even more slowly to Rouse Depot, compelling Lane to negotiate with the landowner to rent the property because he could not commit to the $6,000 [$111,950] purchase price. One-quarter of the annual yield from the fields went to the landowner. Eventually, thirty residents moved into the old cabins, worked the fields daily as their children learned reading and writing, and attended classes themselves in the evenings. Lane purchased a mule and wagon, but the mule died within months, leaving residents without a work animal to plow the ground. In the first year, they raised only

375 bushels of corn and one hundred bushels of sweet potatoes, far less than Lane hoped.[31]

William G. Hawkins, having visited the National Freedmen's Relief Association's Roanoke Island industrial school, caught up to Lunsford Lane in Raleigh. He obsessively spent much of the next few weeks seeking out witnesses to Lane's previous life, confirming the facts outlined in his biography of Lane.[32]

By the end of July, Lane and Hawkins were back in New Bern, and a month later, on August 28, Lane attended a meeting of Black New Bernians who gathered to select representatives to the freedmen's convention in Raleigh into which young Charles Hunter would sneak. Chairing the meeting was Abram H. Galloway, who escaped enslavement in North Carolina in 1857 by hiding among barrels of pine tar and turpentine aboard a schooner to Philadelphia. After years in Canada, he returned to New Bern in 1864, leading the delegation that met with President Lincoln and included John R. Good and Edward Hill. He was, by far, among the most radical of Southern Black orators, denouncing the term "freedmen" which suggested that Black Americans did not earn their liberty but received it as a gift, and demanding the use of "freemen" and all that came with the status—voting rights, testifying in court, learning to read and write. He condemned White privileges and refused to concede his place in line to White customers or to step aside to let White pedestrians pass on the street. He openly ridiculed White Carolinians' efforts to demean Black Carolinians. In arguing for voting rights, he laughed about overhearing two White men worrying that "if they are allowed to vote they have the majority here in New Bern, and the first thing they will do, will be to elect that scoundrel, Galloway, Mayor." He assured his audience, "I don't wish to be elected Mayor; I wouldn't begin so low as that," and he did not. In 1868, he became one of three Black senators in the North Carolina General Assembly, voting to ratify both the Fourteenth and Fifteenth Amendments.[33]

In the 1865 community meeting, Galloway mustered enthusiasm for a statewide freemen's convention. "The white people of this State and of the other Southern States are about to hold conventions for the purpose of reconstruction," he declared, "and it is necessary that the colored people should take such steps as may influence these conventions and promote good." Black New Bernians supported the cause but disagreed over where to hold the meeting. For symbolic purposes, Galloway wanted Raleigh "where legislation has been made upon the subject of slavery, and where the slave code and all its horrors, thumbscrews, etc., . . . have been enacted." Raleigh was also where politicians planned to convene the new constitutional convention, and Galloway intended the two meetings to occur simultaneously. Opposition to

Raleigh came from the newcomer, Lunsford Lane, who, "in a long and forcible speech" informed by years of well-organized and well-funded abolitionist meetings, worried that the "colored people of Raleigh were very poor and unable to attend to the wants of the inner man that would necessarily come up, where there was such a large gathering." The "colored people of Raleigh had large-hearts, but the members of the Convention could not subsist on large hearts," he protested. His objection was unconvincing, and the vote for the capital town was nearly unanimous.[34]

Lane had run headlong into a collective grassroots activism that Galloway and others constructed to provide community needs and pursue political rights among free people. His school would become part of New Bern's communal networks, but Lunsford was not part of that organic community. Unlike Raleigh, where the crowd greeted Lunsford Lane as the conquering hero, he was just another Northerner in New Bern, an outsider, a carpetbagger who seemed as interested in reconciliation with White Carolinians as uplifting Black Carolinians. Lane was proud that, during his return southward, he "made a point to mingle with that class termed secesh, and whether from principle or policy, as a general thing, they readily acquiesced in that radical change—the emancipation of the slave—and a great number told me they thought that the colored man ought to have equal rights under the law." In the manner with which he always approached race relations, Lane was generous in his assumptions about White folk, concluding that they, having "begun farms" and hired "colored laborers," were "far more liberal then I thought they would have been." In the immediate aftermath of an overwhelming war, faced with a devastated economy and an occupying Federal army, most White Carolinians saw few options but to hire anyone willing to do the work.[35]

When Federal generals visited North Carolina months later to investigate the proliferation of unauthorized schools for free people, they did not find the secesh crowd so acquiescent. There was widespread resentment toward the Freedmen's Bureau and "working plantations, running saw-mills, manufacturing turpentine and tar, etc.," all operations run by Northern-born investors that distracted emancipated people from taking jobs with local White enterprises. Lane's friend, Horace James, warned that White Southerners' "minds are not changed," and they "do their best to create a state of wretchedness, and want . . . and then point to it and say: 'Behold the legitimate fruit of your policy of emancipation.'"[36]

Local animus toward James and other plantation school administrators "armed with the official positions" became so strong that, in February 1866, a rumor spread quickly and easily within and beyond North Carolina that an angry mob, determined "to set things right," tracked James down. He "was assailed by rowdies and most shamefully beaten." On his travels to Washington, North Carolina, James tried to curb the rumors, announcing that the report was "wholly without foundation," but news in the North circulated that James "had been brutally murdered by rebels in North Carolina."[37]

Lunsford Lane did not experience violence or rumor of it. He surrounded himself with locally important men, partners in Galloway's communal activism, who validated his presence and were happy to let Lane run the day-to-day operations of the Rouse Depot farm while they pursued grander ambitions. John R. Good attended the 1865 Freedmen's Convention in Raleigh, organizing a campaign to petition the constitutional convention for greater equal rights. Edward Hill chased politics, rising to a leadership role in the state Republican Party by the spring of 1866. As his collaborators spent less time in New Bern, Lane found himself without immediate support, and he traveled back to Worcester to appeal for assistance, taking samples of sweet potatoes and corn as evidence of the farming success of his plantation school.[38]

Upon arriving in Massachusetts, Lane found the old abolitionists scattered and unfocused. As Northerners, particularly Black Northerners, imagined the end of enslavement, they shifted their visions from antislavery to aid and relief for the millions of anticipated free people. James Miller McKim, a Pennsylvania abolitionist and advocate for Black military participation, expressed a loss of purpose: "We have passed through the *pulling down* stage of our movement; the building-up—the constructive part—remains to be accomplished."[39]

Lunsford sought out his neighbor, Martha Ann Brown, the only Black member of Worcester's Ladies Benevolent Society and Ladies' Relief Society. With their contributions of clothing, food, school supplies, and teachers, grassroots relief societies such as the Ladies' Relief Society sought to fuel emancipated peoples' transitions to freedom. Martha Ann Brown also led the local Freedmen's Aid Society, coordinating contributions to free peoples' schools and organizing a meeting of Worcesterites to discuss free peoples' "claims on the consideration and charities of public," which "have never been more pressing than now." She promised Lunsford more supplies and money.[40]

Lane did not remain in Worcester long, spending little time with his wife Martha. When he returned to New Bern a couple of months later, Tucker and Good were preparing to attend a second freedmen's convention in the fall and planning to form the State Equal Rights League and a Freedmen's Educational Association charged with establishing nonsectarian schools for Black and White Carolinians, "especially among the freedmen." Over the spring and summer of 1866, Lane again found himself bearing the responsibility of running the farm and school, waiting for needed supplies from Massachusetts.[41]

Martha Ann Lee Brown, ca. 1821–89. From the Brown Family Papers. Courtesy of the American Antiquarian Society, Worcester, MA.

While Lane was in New England, free people in eastern North Carolina began to raise concerns with the Freedmen's Bureau about the schools, among them Horace James's Pitt County school, a private partnership with Eliphalet Whittlesey, assistant commissioner of the Freedmen's Bureau in North Carolina, and Maine abolitionist Winthrop Tappan. James aspired to reconstruct all Southerners in his small corner of the old Confederacy, loaning "public animals" to White and Black farmers who could not afford their own beasts of burden and offering financial loans to local White Southerners willing to employ free Black laborers. The Freedmen's Bureau sent a committee in May 1866 to investigate the James School as well as ones set up in Pitt County by Isaac Rosenkranz, United States Commissary of Subsistence, and in Wayne County by Frederick A. Seely, Superintendent of the Bureau of the Eastern District of North Carolina. Plantation schools became large-scale industries profiting former and active Federal officers. Beyond those of James,

Whittlesey, Rosenkranz, and Seely, at least five other such profit-oriented farms arose in Kinston, Goldsborough, and Wilmington.[42]

At all the schools, corporeal punishment was widespread. A former chaplain testified that he witnessed two occasions when a free man was hung by his wrists for four to six hours, another occasion when a man was imprisoned for three months for fighting with his wife publicly, and the imprisonment of six children for ten days for playing on the Sabbath. Most horrific was that, upon arriving in New Bern, the military commissioners heard rumor of "the alleged killing of a freedman by a white employee of Colonel WHITTLESEY . . . and REV. HORACE JAMES" two months earlier.[43]

In March, Alsbury Reel, accused of stealing from Whittlesey's commissary at the Yankee Hall farm, traveled across the river to Avon farm, where Horace James sentenced him to dig ditches under the supervision of John Izzy, a Black overseer. On a Saturday evening, as several men cast nets into the river to catch fish, the overseer heard Reel's "shoes cracking." Reel decided to fly, "pursued by Izzy and James's clerk, David Boyden, who arrived at the bank of a river while the free man was attempting to cross in a canoe. Boyden ordered him to return, "telling him if he did not he would shoot, and the freedman, disregarding this order, Boyden fired." Reel disappeared into the water, but Boyden did not report the incident until the next day. When Whittlesey, as superintendent of the local Bureau, investigated, he insisted that since "the affairs seems to have occurred at night and as the body of the negro has not yet been discovered, it does not appear certain that the shot took effect." The case was closed. But when Alsbury Reel's body floated ashore on March 25, Black New Bernians became outraged at how quickly authorities dismissed the killing of one of their own.[44]

The federal investigators convened a military commission in Raleigh on September 14. They reprimanded Whittlesey for not looking into Reel's death, as well as for covering up his and other federal officers' involvement in profiting from free labor. The commission saved its wrath for Horace James, accusing him of misconduct in office. He allegedly partnered with Whittlesey and Tappan in employing 140 free people on Pitt County farms, pursued a free man who attempted to leave the farm, and, without provocation, authorized his clerk to shoot the man. James pled "not guilty."[45]

James defended himself. Yes, he cultivated farms and employed free people, but he did so as a private citizen. Although titled as an agent for the Bureau of Refugees, Freedmen, and Abandoned Lands in Pitt County, James no longer worked for the Freedmen's Bureau, choosing instead to undertake "large agricultural matters, in which I shall have a personal interest." In late 1865, he made clear in a request for demotion that he wanted "to engage in the culture of a plantation, as other citizen agents were permitted to do." On that farm, he served the nation by employing free people who refused to work for White Southerners, and he paid them "generously and promptly." How dare the commissioners condemn him for his efforts: "I should receive their approbation, and even their praise, for having performed a service at once delicate and important to the State and the Nation."[46]

White Southerners delighted in "the long Black list of perversion of official position for the subserviency of private ends." They accused Federal officers of selling donations for private gain, abusing the free people by forcing them to work in chain gangs, and, at least with Horace James, covering up a murder. White Southerners laid the ultimate responsibility for Alsbury Reel's death with Reel himself, not because he stole some goods and deserved punishment, but because he supposed himself free and "being in the hands of men who paid nothing for him, and with whom discipline is of more value than negroes, the poor fellow had made a slight mistake in his reckoning." Reel never stood a chance against the good Reverend James, "a smooth, oily, slick, slippery villain, in no official capacity, but simply as 'master of a plantation.'"[47]

Northern Democrats took the opportunity to disparage what James and others were doing in the name of the Freedmen's Bureau. Isaac Van Auden, editor of the *Brooklyn Daily Eagle*, echoed White Southerners' complaint that "the singular feature of the whole is that the worst cases of malfeasance are found at the doors of New England philanthropists." Some, such as James, "have secured positions as agents of the Bureau, have been making a handsome thing out of their positions," continued Van Auden. "The negro, it will be seen, has not profited by a change of masters," he continued. "He finds the New Englander a harder taskmaster, with a more cold-blooded indifference to his fate than ever the Southern slaveholder exhibited."[48]

In the end, the commission absolved James of all charges, giving him what he demanded: a complete vindication of his manly reputation and Christian service to the free people. Still, James was done with plantation schools, the Freedmen's Bureau, and North Carolina. His father, Galen James, planned to retire the editorship of *The Congregationalist and Recorder* newspaper in Lowell, Massachusetts, and Horace returned to New England in late September 1866 to accept the pulpit of Lowell's First Congregational Church and continue his father's work with "the oldest religious newspaper in the world."[49]

Lane's dream of aiding Black Southerners dissipated in Carolina's late summer heat. By August 1866, even before James's trial was underway, Northern public support for the plantation schools dried up. With James and others under investigation, the future of the plantation school movement seemed fated. Lane did not wait to hear the verdicts for either James's or the schools' futures, setting out for Worcester by the end of the month.

In the following years, the men who partnered with Lunsford Lane—Tucker, Hill, and Good—continued to reconstruct North Carolina and to create Black community. In 1870, Hill was among several men who incorporated the A.M.E. Singing School of Newbern, served as treasurer of the A.M.E. Zion Church Educational Society, and, with Good and Tucker, organized the Mechanics and Laborers' Mutual Aid Society of North Carolina, which, upon members' deaths, covered the cost of burials and ensured proper funerary displays—white gloves, white flowers, and white headstones. That year, voters sent Tucker to the state House of Representatives, where he pushed to create an Assistant Superintendent of Public Instruction. Two years later, Good and Tucker co-organized the Newbern Educational Association, and Good followed Tucker to the House of Representatives. In 1874, citizens reelected Good and sent Hill to the House of Representatives with him, as Tucker moved on to the state Senate.[50]

By the 1870s, however, Black legislators saw their influence decline. Many of their Northerner supporters, such as James, had returned to the North, and many Southern White Republicans had switched parties out of racial loyalties. Good and Hill joined the other Black representatives in protesting the Amnesty and Pardon Bill, passed in March 1872, which exempted members of the "the Heroes of America, Loyal Union League, Red Strings, Constitutional Union Guard, White Brotherhood, Invisible, Empire, Ku-Klux Klan, North Carolina State Troops, North Carolina Militia, Jay Hawkers, or any other organization, association or assembly, secret or otherwise" from prosecution for all crimes other than rape, murder, arson, and burglary committed before September 1871. They argued that the law encouraged "the tendency of bad men to commit crime by organizing secret societies."[51]

The election of all three men to state office threatened conservative White Carolinians, who became loud in their resentment of Reconstruction and Black politicians. "The chief argument for supporting the Conservative cause, is to whip out the negro party," declared *The Charlotte Observer*, pointing to the Craven County ticket as a prime example: "For Senator, Richard Tucker, a negro; for Representatives, John R. Good and Edward H. Hill, negroes; . . . The only offices, it will be perceived, that are given to Southern white men are the Register of Deeds, the Surveyor—both comparatively unimportant—and three of the County Commissioners, all of whom are miserable scallawags." The Ku Klux Klan made its presence known in February 1870, assassinating Wyatt Outlaw, a former member of the US Colored Cavalry and attendee at the 1866 Freedmen's Convention. A month later, John W. Stephens, a state senator and Freedmen's Bureau agent, died at the Klan's hands as well. By 1874, the editor of *The Observer* hoped to rally more violence: "White men of North

Carolina, will you basely bend your necks to the yoke of Negro Rule?" Even the local New Bern paper questioned the newly elected representatives. "How unfortunate it is that old Craven has no one to represent her good people except three 'civil rights' negroes. John Good, that impersonification of pomposity, walks about the streets as if he was nothing short of an Emperor; and Dick Tucker is the hardest looking member of the General Assembly, white or Black." In less than a decade, the secesh crowd whom Lunsford Lane found contrite and potentially conciliatory turned dangerously violent.[52]

White resentment took another form in the myth of the Lost Cause. Of the four men who once aided Lunsford Lane in the plantation school, Moses Kennedy proved the least politically active, so it should not be surprising that, as the Lost Cause took shape in North Carolina, anti-Black voices adopted the tale of Kennedy fending off alligators for his enslaver's comfort as a staple of the "loyal slave" mythology. After Moses died in 1878, White storytellers appropriated his voice and image, quite literally. In 1896, John D. Whitford, once president of the Atlantic & North Carolina Rail Road and, by the 1890s, a self-proclaimed historian, showed off his tintype of Moses and wrote reminiscences in which Moses figured prominently. A former Confederate, Whitford situated Kennedy as a witness to the honorable manhood of the Old South: the Stanly-Spaight duel of 1802; an 1812 duel in which speaker of the House of Commons Louis D. Henry killed Stanly's brother, Thomas J. Stanly, over a woman that they met at a party; and the 1844 death of the great North Carolina jurist William Gaston. Whether Moses Kennedy witnessed these events did not matter. As Lunsford Lane could attest, when others took control of one's narrative to create myth—in this case the myth of the "faithful slave"—accuracy was seldom a concern.[53]

Chapter 15

Loss and Loneliness

With the Rouse Depot school behind him, Lunsford Lane returned to Worcester's Liberty Street, finding dozens of unfamiliar faces but not his family. Martha and his daughters lived in a different house, blocks away at 26 Wilmot Street, in an overwhelmingly White neighborhood. The property measured about two-thirds of an acre with a house and smaller buildings as well as a walkway to a well. Martha, Maria Bell, and Clara bought it from Lewis Thayer, a local wool manufacturer and real estate dealer, and his wife Eliza. They accepted the $1,400 [$26,680] asking price, assumed a $300 [$5,720] loan already attached to the property by the State Mutual Life Assurance Company, and agreed to carry insurance "against the hazard of fire."[1]

Throughout their marriage, Martha always depended upon Lunsford to secure her accommodations. American common law dictated that a husband owned his wife's property because marriage joined them as one legal identity—his. Even had Martha been free in Raleigh in the late 1830s, she would not have been allowed, or even expected, to sign off on her husband's property sale. Had she any dower property of her own, she would have needed his signature to sell it. As Martha experienced in Cambridgeport and Oberlin, women suffered from their husbands' poor economic decisions, and the nation's exploding market economy introduced new threats to their security.[2]

Starting with Mississippi in 1839, state legislatures passed married women's property acts to protect women from such losses, empowering them to purchase and control property independent of their husbands. In 1845, Massachusetts followed, granting women full authority over property that they brought into marriages and rights to acquire or bequeath property during marriages "free from the interference or control of her husband." A decade later, concerned over men's continued attempts to pocket women's earnings, legislatures sharpened their laws. In Massachusetts, lawmakers assured that the wife could "bargain, sell and convey her real and personal property, and enter into any contract . . . as if she were sole," and that her property "shall remain her sole and separate property, notwithstanding her marriage, and not be subject to the disposal of her husband, or liable for his debts."[3]

Homestead exemption laws also began to appear, the first passed in the Republic of Texas in 1839. They designated the house as part of the one-third of the estate owned by wives, ensuring that, should their husbands lose a fortune or pass away, women would still have roofs over their heads. The Haywood widows of Raleigh—Delia, Eliza, and Eleanor—would have benefited from such homestead exemptions, relieving them from the fear of losing their houses so that they could better have protected their families and inheritances, but homestead exemptions and married women's property rights did not arrive in North Carolina until Reconstruction.[4]

In the North, in contrast, by the late 1840s, homestead exemption and other protections for women became central tenets of abolitionism. To broaden the Liberty Party's appeal in 1848, Gerrit Smith had endorsed homestead exemptions as part of the party platform. Why fight so hard for Black men's economic rights if their wives could so easily lose everything? The 1849 National Convention of Colored Citizens celebrated homestead exemption alongside "Free Soil, Free Speech, Free Labor, and Free Men." The following year, arguing in favor of homestead exemption laws, Indiana Whig Schuyler Colfax reasoned that "Mercantile debts, business liabilities, endorsements, I would recognize them all, but above them—higher, holier, than any of them—is the debt to the family." Dozens of Northern states passed homestead exemption laws in the early 1850s, among them Massachusetts. The law restricted men from paying off debts by mortgaging or selling their homes without the consent of their wives. Upon a husband's or father's death, a creditor could not evict a family even if he held superior title to the property.[5]

So, when Martha, Maria Bell, and Clara bought 26 Wilmot, they protected themselves from Lunsford's financial whims and failures. The warranty deed explicitly gave "sole and separate use free from the control or interference of any present or future husband." Still, they needed a mortgage loan, and in 1855, the Commonwealth had revised its married women's property law, adding an interesting caveat: that although women had rights to purchase and own without men's permission, they could not sell or convey property without "the assent, in writing, of her husband" (or by successfully petitioning a state justice). The law protected the husband from *her* indebtedness: should a wife die, her husband would not have been burdened with any mortgage debts that she owed.[6]

Traditionally, wealthy individuals such as the Thayers offered real estate mortgages by collaborating with others to share the risk. In Worcester, wealthy residents monopolized the mortgage market by the 1860s, extending loans to purchasers who could barely make monthly payments and leading critics to worry that, should too many mortgagors default, the resulting redistribution of landed property into the hands of the wealthy few would expose "the whole real estate to be knocked off under the hammer of the auctioneer." With the promise of potentially retaking the property should his mortgagors default, Lewis Thayer offered a $700 [$13,340] mortgage to the Lanes. In contrast to the warranty deed, the primary signatory on the mortgage deed was Lunsford Lane, granting his consent to his wife and daughters' investment. So, Thayer and Lunsford wrote up a four-year payment plan. Maria Bell and Clara signed off on the mortgage, and Martha made her X. Thayer then sold the Lanes' mortgage to Frederick E. Abbott, an insurance claims agent.[7]

Although now indebted to Abbott, the Lanes also owed the $300 State Mutual Life Assurance Company's loan that came with the house. Corporate mortgage lenders emerged in the wake of the Panic of 1837, but they did not proliferate until the 1870s, when westward agricultural expansion, urbanization, and increased emphasis on single-family homeownership transformed the mortgage markets. In the 1860s, institutions such as the State Mutual Life Assurance Company, chartered in 1844, saw an opportunity to diversify their investments and began to extend minor mortgages to individuals. The aversion of three former owners of 26 Wilmot to pay off that $300 loan suggests the respect still granted the traditional private individual mortgagee over institutional mortgagees.[8]

———

Next door, at 24 Wilmot, lived the street's only other Black family, William and Mary Bryant. In August 1865, they renewed their lease on the house for $75 [$1,400] a month from Ebenezer E. Abbott, agreeing to paint and shingle the house and dig a cistern in the cellar. William was a bit of a Jack-of-all-trades, advertising his services as "Windows Washed, Carpet Cleaned, and General Housework Done in the Best Manner."[9]

The Lanes and Bryants did not get along, although the reasons are vague. As Lunsford Lane's former glory faded, William Bryant enjoyed a rising celebrity in Worcester as the man who had helped Ambrose Burnside's Federal troops invade eastern North Carolina. The local newspaper celebrated the "intelligent and fine looking 'contraband,' who . . . deserved immediate employment here . . . understands garden and farm work and the care of animals." The Bryants became known among Black Worcesterites for their charity to free people, such as an 1867 mortgage that William extended to Lacy and Ruth Lyle, recently arrived from Virginia. Lunsford, in contrast, became a has-been, his celebrity behind him, his plantation school enterprise failed, his book sales dried up, and his wife and daughters' real estate ventures reminding him that he was not even necessary in the household.[10]

Then, there were Clara Lane's continued property acquisitions. Her signature on the deed to 26 Wilmot whetted her appetite for more real estate ventures. Massachusetts's women's property laws granted her the right, as a single woman, to buy and sell without her father's or any man's approval. In August 1868, she purchased the lot next door, lot 24, which the Bryants leased. She paid $100 [$2,130] down on the $1,000 [$21,350] price, taking a $900 [$19,220] mortgage from Ebenezer Abbott as well as agreeing to keep fire insurance on the house. Although Clara conceded that the Bryants could lease the property through the end of their contract in April 1871, the relationship of the new landlady to her lessees became tense.[11]

Regardless of the reasons, the tension between the Lanes and Bryants manifested in debate over the use of a well. In purchasing 26 Wilmot, the Lanes took control of the accessway, and the Bryants complained. Years later, when Clara decided to sell part of 24 Wilmot, they insisted that she make clear that use of the well was "subject to any rights of William Bryant as Lessee," with Clara snippily adding "if he has any."[12]

As Lunsford's wife and daughters dabbled in real estate, he occupied himself with the election of 1868. In late August, he attended a Republican Party meeting at Mechanics Hall. The crowd was overwhelmingly working-class, coming together to celebrate the party's selection of Ulysses S. Grant and Schuyler Colfax as its presidential ticket. They elected Lane as one of a dozen vice presidents for the meeting, reminding him that he was not forgotten, at least not in Worcester.[13]

In that position, Lunsford became a member of the newly formed Grant and Colfax Club, led by his old employer, Timothy W. Wellington. Grant and Colfax Clubs began popping up earlier in the year—in Indianapolis in March, Chicago and Madison in April, Brooklyn and Sacramento in May. Over the summer, hundreds more organized, their collective mission to support the Republican Party's presidential ticket. "Let our Republicans, young and old, call and sign and prepare for earnest work," declared the chapter in Yonkers, New York. Across the former Confederacy, Black folk formed chapters with their carpetbagger allies. Black women took the lead in Houston. Texas. In Washington, North Carolina, Charles H. Moore, a descendent of people once enslaved by a Haywood at Chocowinity, served as president of the local chapter. In Raleigh, George O. Spooner, an agent for the Freeman's Bureau from Boston, and Joseph W. Holden, a co-editor of the pro-Reconstruction *Weekly Standard*, organized a chapter. "There has never been such a popular uprising and outpouring of the people since the days of Clay," concluded a Raleigh newspaper. "Every hamlet has its Grant and Colfax club."[14]

Confederate resentment boiled beneath the surface. Some sniped at the gall of Northern carpetbaggers and Southern scalawags as they empowered Black republicanism. One newspaper snarked that the uniform of the local Grant and Colfax Club was "a linen duster, to be worn in travelling, and carpet-bag, to be carried in the hand." When only thirty-six people turned out for a midsummer 1868 meeting in Chambersburg, Pennsylvania, local Democrats prophesized that "conservative men" finally realized "the precipice over which they are invited to plunge. Negro-equality and military power have no charms for them." They were wrong. Participation declined because the Grant and Colfax Clubs had run their course: Grant won the election.[15]

The political club was the extent of Lunsford's renewed activism. Personal issues encroached on his time and energy. The family lived thinly, with Lunsford bringing in a meager income from sales of his vegetable pills. Clara developed a sore throat and a dry and persistent cough, symptoms the Lanes knew all too well from when Laura Ann and Alexander had become ill. Tensions with the next-door neighbors worsened, devolving into occasional verbal altercations between Lunsford and William Bryant.

Shortly after midnight on April 17, 1869, Lunsford, Martha, Maria Bell, and Clara awakened to smoke filling the house. Some neighbors rushed to help the Lanes extinguish the flames, but the fire singed most of the exterior before they quelched it. "INCENDIARISM" concluded the local newspaper, noting that it was, after all, the respected Dr. Lane, "a colored physician on Laurel Hill," whom the arsonist had targeted. "It was a hellish attempt," exclaimed an observer, "and but for the providential awakening of Mr. Lane, he with his wife and two daughters would have been burned to death with their dwelling."[16]

Initial reports suggested that someone tossed kerosene on the side of the house and laid kerosene-saturated straw on a porch. The fuel, introduced in the United States only sixteen years earlier, provided an "illuminating power . . . twice as brilliant as ordinary coal gas," and "without the spirits of Turpentine or alcohol, is warranted to be not explosive." Beginning in the early 1860s, kerosene fires belied the marketing. In 1861, there were kerosene explosions in Washington, DC; Waltham and Williamsburg in Massachusetts; Scranton, Pennsylvania; and Newark, New Jersey. Massachusetts's state assayer concluded that "light and very volatile oils, which are very explosive," such as "kesoline," often resulted during kerosene production, making kerosene dangerous if used improperly. The arsonist at Lunsford Lane's house counted on that volatility, creating a devious weapon by filling a butter firkin with kerosene to function as a bomb once the oil-drenched walls fully flamed.[17]

Lunsford immediately accused neighbor William Bryant. The *Worcester Evening Gazette* declared, even before an arrest and trial, that Byant was "the culprit who threw kerosene upon the house of L. Lane on Reservoir Hill on the evening of the 17, and then touched a match to the building." A little over a week later, constables arrested Bryant. A justice set bond at $3,000 [$66,470], well beyond Bryant's means, and so he sat in the Worcester jail overnight. When the Municipal Court convened on April 27, the judge dismissed the case for want of evidence, but the damage to Bryant's reputation was irreparable.

The Bryants remained at 24 Wilmot for a couple more months, abandoning Worcester by July 1869.[18]

The Lanes began to restore their house and their lives. Their mortgagee had required them to carry fire insurance, so they soon restored 26 Wilmot. The family was shrinking. When Maria Bell Lane Garner's beau, Gustavus Rose, took a waiting position in New York City, he asked her to marry him. On October 9, they wed and left Worcester, abandoning sickly Clara to care for Lunsford and Martha. Working as a dressmaker and dabbling in real estate with her mother, Clara tried to hold the family together. She picked up Lunsford's careless over-mortgaging habits, however, taking another mortgage on 26 Wilmot for $2,000 [$44,310] in July 1869, using part of the loan four days later to pay off the $700 mortgage that the family secured three years earlier. By April 1870, the Lanes—at least the women—decided that they no longer wished to stay in Worcester. Clara orchestrated a flurry of real estate activity, culminating in early April when she sold part of lot 24 for $600 [$13,290], and she and her mother sold 26 Wilmot for another $600. Sarah R. Knight, wife to one of the town's more successful boot and shoemakers, purchased both properties. From Eliza D. Thayer to Martha Lane and her daughters to Sarah R. Knight, the chain of real estate dealings associated with lots 24 and 26 in the late 1860s attested to the success of married women's property acts in opening opportunities to women, White and Black.[19]

In July 1871, Clara sold the rest of lot 24 to James S. Rogers, a local coal dealer, for $450 [$11,230]. She, Martha, and Maria Bell still owed $900 [$22,470] on a mortgage to Ebenezer Abbott, which he sold for $672 [$16,775] to Edward Earle, who once had owned all of Laurel Hill. When the Lanes left Worcester, Earle could not expect the $900.[20]

———

During the war, Lunsford and Martha's son, William Curtis Lane, took a waiting position in Philadelphia, but by late 1866, he moved to Manhattan where he met Rebecca Ann Mitchell. Her father, James, had flown South Carolina's enslavement by 1845, making a home in New York where he learned the barber trade and married Mary Ann Lewis. The Mitchells were members of Manhattan's burgeoning Black middle class—tailors, craftsmen, barbers, and waiters. They had two children, Rebecca and her younger brother, James, but Mary Ann might have died in childbirth or soon thereafter because the children had no mother by 1850. When Rebecca turned twenty-three years old, she married William Lane, and the young couple started their life together—William as a waiter and Rebecca as a dressmaker—but in a new town. They found a small one-story rental at 1 Webster Street, Cambridgeport. It sat off the street, a former outbuilding for the larger houses nearby and maybe too secluded for

Rebecca to peddle her dresses. They stayed there less than a year, finding a larger and more prominent rental at 105 Harvard Street.[21]

In late 1870, Lunsford, Martha, and Clara also returned to Cambridgeport, moving into the west side of a small frame duplex—42 Washington Street— blocks south of William and Rebecca. It was one of a handful of duplex rentals situated among multiple tenement houses, and the Lanes did not remain long, moving the next year to a two-story frame duplex a block westward in a more single-family neighborhood. Months later, they migrated a little farther westward. Lunsford returned to peddling his medicines, at least for the next two years.[22]

Lunsford and Martha found few familiar faces, although Milton Clarke continued to live in Cambridgeport, having been there since 1851. In the aftermath of Emancipation, the town's Black population exploded, and like William and Rebecca Lane, hundreds of new Cantabrigians took advantage of its flourishing economy, packing into the duplexes and tenements along Washington and Harvard Streets. In 1870, their votes helped Clarke win election to the town's Common Council, the first Black Cantabrigian to serve in public office.[23]

Although the Black community consisted of young families, some older luminaries relocated to Cambridgeport in the 1860s, including William Wells Brown and Harriet Jacobs, both of whom had begrudgingly accepted their freedom through redemption-by-purchase. Lunsford Lane knew Brown from the abolitionist circuits and conventions of an earlier era. Brown, his wife Anne Elizabeth Gray, and daughter Annie lived in one of his in-laws' Cambridgeport properties. Harriet Jacobs was a new face to the Lanes. Although she published her *Incidents in the Life of a Slave Girl* in 1861 under a pseudonym, by 1870, Jacobs's name was well known. She translated her fame into support for Black war veterans and educational opportunities for Black Americans. She and her daughter Louisa rented a house on the western edge of Cambridgeport near Harvard College, where she served as a house mother of sorts for four Harvard students, a professor of law, a "scientific professor," and four domestic servants—two women immigrants and two formerly enslaved women.[24]

Lunsford and Martha settled into Cambridgeport, then, with a more coherent Black community around them than they had known twenty years earlier. Clara lived with them, taking care of her aging parents, and for two years, all seemed well, although her parents recognized in horror the graveyard cough, the gradual wasting away, and finally, the death rattle. In spring 1872, like Laura Ann and Alexander, twenty-eight-year-old Clara Lane died of tuberculosis. The local paper noted her as "daughter of Lunsford Lane" but little more. There was no memorial service. The Lanes managed to pay about

$75 [$1,870] for a burial plot adjacent to her sisters Laura Ann and Celia in Cambridge Cemetery. Like her sisters' grave, Clara's went without a headstone. Still, she had a private plot. A dozen years later, when William Wells Brown died and was buried about eight hundred feet from Clara, Laura Ann, and Celia Lane, it was in a shared "city" plot where his mother-in-law also lay. Brown, too, had no headstone, and over the decades, the city buried other bodies with no familial relationship beside and on top of him. At least the Lane girls rested in peace.[25]

Like most twenty-eight-year-olds, Clara did not have a last will and testament. When she died, she still owned part of lot 26 in Worcester. Months later, in October, Martha traveled to Worcester to meet Edward Earle. She could not pay the mortgage that Clara, Maria Bell, and she took two years earlier, so Martha signed over the deed to lot 26, putting her X on the line.[26]

That Martha made that journey alone signaled the end of her relationship with Lunsford. For decades, the quiet tensions of their marriage brought her to this point. Having left Raleigh's Black community and her brother, Martha never found a new network of support to replace them. In 1842, when she connected with the community of the Massachusetts Female Emancipation Society, Lunsford soon thereafter moved the family from their temporary housing in Boston to the new home in Cambridgeport, separating her from the opportunity. He had traveled widely, speaking and advocating for change, leaving her for long periods. So often, she was alone among unfamiliar neighbors, expected to raise the children on Lunsford's meager income, even birthing children in Lunsford's absence on occasions.

When Martha returned from Worcester after settling her daughter's estate, then, she remained in Cambridgeport for a short time. Her son William had found work as a railroad porter in Jersey City, New Jersey, and as he and Rebecca prepared to move, Martha decided to leave Lunsford. She accompanied William to a Jersey City duplex. The young couple occupied half of the house, and Martha resided in the other half.[27]

Suddenly alone, Lunsford abandoned Cambridgeport, finding a job in John H. Cranston's printing press manufactory in Norwich, Connecticut. On the factory wall hung two mottos: "First learn to do things well, then learn to do them quickly" and "Produce the best possible work for the purposes intended." Six years later, Cranston patented his own press—The Cranston—which became famous for its inking apparatus and durability. In 1872, the manufactory employed only two people: Lunsford, who assembled presses on contract, and Ellen Leahey, an Irish domestic. The following year, Cranston added a clerk to his factory and hired a new assemblyman: Lunsford Lane Jr. At sixty-nine years of age, the elder Lunsford's body struggled to manage the industrial work, so, just as Ned had once taught

Lunsford the horticultural trade, Lunsford trained Lunsford Jr. to replace him on the factory floor. He returned to Cambridgeport briefly in 1873, hauling wood and coal for a local business, but it was a lonely town without family, and before the year was out, Lunsford went back to Norwich to take care of Cranston's horses, deliver orders, and spend time with Lunsford Jr.[28]

Time with grown children became precious: Martha lived with William, and Lunsford worked with Lunsford Jr. Maria Bell was with Gustavus not too far away in Brooklyn, having moved there in 1871 and renting an apartment on Vanderbilt Avenue for months before investing in a home at 119 High Street in Brooklyn Heights, a racially and ethnically diverse neighborhood near the ferry to Manhattan. Over a quarter of a million people commuted daily between the two boroughs. Just the previous year, the New York and Brooklyn Bridge Company planted the caissons for a new bridge into the riverbed. The Roses and their neighbors did not realize how the finished bridge would physically displace their neighborhood. By mid-1873, the Brooklyn-side tower arose, and the future of High Street was inevitable. The Roses moved three blocks eastward to 241 Pearl Street.[29]

On July 15, 1874, Maria Bell Lane Garner Rose was in her Pearl Street home while, 180 miles away, residents of Worcester honored her former husband, Henry G. Garner, at the dedication of the Soldiers' Monument. The granite and bronze monument stood sixty-five feet high at a cost of $50,000 [$1,343,000]. On each corner of the foundation stood a bronze figure representing the Navy, Infantry, Artillery, and Cavalry. On the pillar were white granite bas-reliefs of Abraham Lincoln, a dying soldier, Governor John A. Andrew, and an inscription "ERECTED BY THE PEOPLE OF WORCESTER, TO THE MEMORY OF HER SONS WHO DIED *For the Unity of the Republic*, A. D. 1861–1865." At its pinnacle arose the Goddess of Victory, raising her sword in military conquest. As the drapery that concealed the monument fell to the ground, thousands of spectators cheered, Horace James among them, and a band burst into "Keller's American Hymn": "Speed our Republic, O Father on high / Lead us in pathways of justice and right." A light artillery fired a salute.[30]

The dedication speaker, former governor Alexander H. Bullock, delivered a long, rambling address that considered the whole of American military history and how Worcester's sons, 398 of them, died for "the unity of the republic." Preserving the republic had been important, but for Henry G. Garner and other Black Worcesterites who had marched off to war—fifteen in the Massachusetts Fifty-Fourth Infantry, five in the Fifty-Fifth Infantry, and twenty-two in the Fifth Cavalry—destroying enslavement was *the* reason for war and enlistment. Garner had fought alongside Joshua Dunbar, whose son,

Soldiers' Monument, Worcester, MA. From *Dedication of the Soldier's Monument at Worcester* (Worcester: Monument Committee, 1875), frontispiece. Courtesy of the American Antiquarian Society, Worcester, MA.

Paul Laurence Dunbar, one day encapsulated his father's purpose in the poem "The Colored Soldiers."

> Yes, the Blacks enjoy their freedom,
>   And they won it dearly, too;
> For the life blood of their thousands
>   Did the southern fields bedew.
> In the darkness of their bondage,
>   In the depths of slavery's night,
> Their muskets flashed the dawning,
>   And they fought their way to light.

Among those honored on the Soldiers' Monument, Henry Garner and John Cheesman of the Fifth Cavalry and John H. Johnson of the Fifty-Fourth Infantry had died to win freedom for millions of Black Americans.[31]

In testimony to the comradery of military service, engravers listed names on the monument's plaques, but the monument's sculptor and the guest speakers on dedication day seemed to misunderstand that some of the celebrated dead were Black men, that their cause was not White Worcester's cause, and that their enthusiasm for war ascended from a deeper place in their souls. The Soldiers' Monument celebrated White sacrifice, its four military statues adorned with White faces and the insignia of White units, and its White granite subliminally declaring the memorial as one to Whiteness.

Maria Bell Lane Garner Rose left no records, no evidence of how she grieved Henry G. Garner, about life with Gustavus, or how she felt when her father showed up at her door in 1874, expecting to live out his old age with her. Brooklyn was a new place for him to peddle his book, his medicines, and The Story. He became Dr. Lane again, returning to his vegetable pills. In December, he gave his last public speech, traveling to Belfast, Maine, as part of a speaker series, delivering a history lesson on "slavery and its influences at the North." He lived with Maria Bell and Gustavus only about eighteen months before finding his own place on Cranston Street, near the southern coast of Brooklyn along Jamaica Bay.[32]

Certainly, Lunsford's children made sure he heard of Martha on occasion. On May 8, 1875, he received word that she had died. She was seventy-two years old. She had negotiated enslavement, escaped the South with her family, suffered the loss of five children, dealt in real estate, and spent over forty years with her husband. In Martha's loss, the children came together and not just to say "goodbye." Lunsford Jr. traveled from Norwich, where he had replaced his father as hosteler for the Cranston factory. He would not return to Connecticut, moving into William's home and finding work as a farrier. By the end of the year, Maria Bell Lane Garner Rose also moved into William's home, Gustavus having disappeared—no record of death or abandonment, just gone.[33]

———

Late in 1876, soon after Maria Bell Lane Garner Rose went to live with William Lane's family, Lunsford Lane moved again to 15 Cornelia Street in Greenwich Village, once the most pastoral part of Manhattan. The nineteenth century brought change. The ferry from Weehawken, New Jersey, originally intended to deliver farm produce to New York's markethouses, began carrying passengers, The ferry docked at Christopher Street, ushering new residents directly into the village, driving real estate values down and prompting property owners to sell their farms and move uptown. Catering to thousands of Irish and German immigrants in the 1840s and 1850s, new investors converted elegant estates into boarding houses. In 1853, a four-story brick Italianate tenement replaced the farmhouse. By 1870, six million people ferried into Greenwich Village annually.[34]

And yet, even as Greenwich Village filled with immigrant residents, a quarter of Black New Yorkers lived in and around Greenwich. In 1863, the White working-class violence waged against conscription and Black New Yorkers boiled over into the village where, on July 13, rioters destroyed Black homes, targeted restaurants that hired Black waiters, looted Black stores, and beat and mutilated Black men. Over the next two years, as thousands fled the city, its Black population plummeted to its lowest numbers since 1820.[35]

After the war, a wave of Black migrants from the South arrived, escaping to the opportunity and anonymity of Manhattan. Many avoided moving into the city proper, settling on its peripheries—Jersey City, Brooklyn, Weeksville, Carrsville, and Greenwich. Among them was twenty-nine-year-old Jacob Dyett, who fled enslavement in Maryland and joined the United States Navy in 1861, serving as a cook on the USS Alabama. After his service ended in 1862, he met and married Mary, but the Conscription Act of 1863 inspired him to reenlist. Also among the refugees was James J. Hopewell, who served on the USS Wyandank in 1865. After the war, he met Anna, recently emancipated from Virginia.[36]

Both the Dyetts and Hopewells resided at 15 Cornelia Street at least for the next fifteen years, the only two families to live there for so long. The rest of the tenants, numbering around fifty, came and went. Although the census taker in 1880 lazily identified all the residents as "mulatto," they represented the kaleidoscope of Black America, harkening from North and South, pursuing a variety of jobs—cooks and waiters, washwomen and chambermaids, longshoremen, dressmakers, coalers, railroad porters, clerks, and hostelers—and competing for opportunity with thousands of other New Yorkers. In 1867, "A respectable colored woman wishes gentlemen's washing at her house, 15 Cornelia st., first floor." In 1875, "A situation wanted—by a young colored man, as porter in a store or to drive; can come well recommended. Apply at 15 Cornelia st., third floor, back room." In 1876, "To Travel—a colored young man to travel with a gentleman as nurse. Call on J. S. W., No. 15 Cornelia st."[37]

So, Lunsford Lane joined the porters, nurses, and washing women of 15 Cornelia. The life and activities of a seventy-six-year-old elderly man estranged from his family are difficult to recover. He probably continued to peddle medicines and *The Narrative of Lunsford Lane*, although he did not promote himself in city directories. He likely visited Mother A.M.E. Zion Church nearby, at the corner of West 10th and Bleecker Streets, where Frederick Douglass, Sojourner Truth, and Harriet Tubman occasionally attended. He might have sought out Isaac H. Hunter Jr., a hotel keeper and son of the man targeted alongside Lunsford by Raleigh's magistrates in late 1840. Lunsford probably told The Story any chance given him, reminiscing about what had once been good about life so long ago before it had all gone bad.[38]

Whatever Lunsford Lane did during the days, in the evenings, he returned to his apartment at 15 Cornelia and the loneliness that he had cultivated. Maria Bell and the twins, William and Lunsford Jr., were in Jersey City, just across the Hudson River, but the ties that bind had severed. Upon returning from North Carolina, Edward disappeared into the chaos of Reconstruction-Era America. Lunsford's other children were also gone: Lucy, Celia, and an infant lost early; Laura Ann, Alexander, and Clara consumed by tuberculosis. Martha was no longer there to comfort him through the losses and the grief. She had not been for years.[39]

Nineteenth-century Americans conceptualized chronic disease in two ways: as either the emaciation associated with consumption, from which Laura Ann, Alexander, and Clara had suffered, or as bloated and distorted bodies so often associated with dropsy. Lunsford suffered fatigue, his limbs engorged, his kidneys releasing too much protein and leaving him susceptible to stroke or heart attack. Only months after arriving at 15 Cornelia, in June 1879, he collapsed and died. The physician attributed it to dropsy, noting Lane's edema—swelling of the legs and arms.[40]

Maybe it was destiny that Lunsford Lane died in Manhattan, only a few blocks away from an overstuffed tenement on 34th Street where, a dozen years earlier, Horatio Alger, a graduate of Harvard College and former Unitarian minister, wrote *Ragged Dick; or, Street Life in New York*. Alger had transformed the self-made ideal into a rags-to-riches legend that inspired the optimism of the exploding Gilded Age. In Alger's tales, character begets hard work and opportunity which in turn results sometimes in wealth but always in worthiness. Anyone—a White American without the benefit of heritage or education, an immigrant with no family and who could not speak English, and a Black American newly empowered with freedom and little more—could aspire to rise from their meager backgrounds to find success. It was a moral that Lunsford Lane had embraced in his public speaking and his private ambitions, even though he often fell short of it. His legend—The Story—had inspired Americans decades before Alger described the American Dream.[41]

———

New York Bay Cemetery was a rural cemetery that sat on the outskirts of Jersey City, its manicured landscapes inspiring "feelings of solemnity, reverence and tender respect for the memory of the dead," inviting the living to commune with their ancestors and reminding visitors of "our own mortality and that of our friends." It occupied about one hundred acres on a hillside that gently slopped eastward, down to the bay. From its southeastern corner, where the tree line was low, one could see the tip of Manhattan and Bedloe's Island where, in 1884, citizens would lay a cornerstone for a statue of liberty.[42]

Although originally designed to allure middle-class residents, over the decades, New York Bay Cemetery housed hundreds of working-class immigrants, with a monument to the martyrs of the 1848 revolutions in Hungary and the Italian states. The cemetery offered group rates to the New-York Fire Department and the Independent Order of Odd Fellows, a fraternal organization of the city's mechanics and laborers. In January 1850, Tradesman's Lodge 314 of the Odd Fellows, representing mostly German laborers, accepted a similar deal. The British and North American Royal Mail Steam Packet Company purchased plots for its sailors and laborers who worked the docks on the Jersey City waterfront. When, in 1851, New York City banned interments inside the city, residents looked beyond the city for burial plots. New York Bay Cemetery set aside "a beautiful spot" with "access by land or water" with prices so low "that the Poor, to a large extent, may possess suitable burial grounds." Among the cemetery's interments in the 1850s and 1860s were Jewish New Yorkers, most immigrants and members of the Sol Benjamin Society and the United Order of the Sons of David. The cemetery filled with magnificent granite and marble markers engraved with names, dates of birth and death, references to the Rhineland, Bavaria, and Alsace that declared their occupants' Germanness, and Stars of David that celebrated their Jewishness.[43]

In the shadows of the beautiful monuments to working-class and immigrant New Yorkers, William, Maria Bell, and Lunsford Jr. buried their parents four years apart in section P North of New York Bay Cemetery, reserved for those who could afford plots but no gravestones. Its emptiness was inescapable but deceptive, for there were hundreds lying beneath the topsoil of

P North, among them, Martha Lane in row N, grave 10. In the summer of 1879, Lunsford joined her in row N. His grave was number 7. The space that came between husband and wife in life followed them into death. Two empty plots separated them as if waiting for others.[44]

As William Lane arranged his father's burial, thousands of Black Southerners were on the move, abandoning the restoration of White rule in Southern states and the poverty of Southern tenant farming for the hope of land ownership west of the Mississippi River. The Kansas Exodus proved one of the greatest migrations in American history, championed by former abolitionists. In Worcester, William Wells Brown organized a fundraiser to aid Black migrants. In Ohio, John Brown Jr., son of the man whose soul went marching on, pledged his service and money to the Sandusky Emigrant Aid Society to fulfill "his cherished plan of personally attending to settling the colored refuges in Kansas." Wendell Phillips declared that "the negro whose freedom and citizenship are the plume in the cap of the old and trued Republican party is flying by thousands, and wishing and planning to fly hundreds of thousands from the lawlessness and intolerable oppression" of the South. At a meeting of the John Brown Association in 1870, he moved that rental fees from John Brown's former farmstead in the old Timbucto tract benefit Exodusters.[45]

One former abolitionist was less supportive. During a late summer 1879 speech at Saratoga Springs, New York, Frederick Douglass insisted that "in anything like a normal condition of things the South is the best place for the Negro. Nowhere else is there for him a promise of a happier future. Let him stay there if he can, and save both the South and himself to civilization." For Douglass, it was not just a problem of where his fellow Black Americans lived but a validation of the abolitionist revolution. The migration was, he insisted, an "untimely concession to the idea that white people and colored people cannot live together in peace and prosperity unless the whites are a majority and control the legislation and hold the offices of the State."[46]

Another former revolutionary, Lewis Clarke, who in 1843 had joined Lunsford Lane on the One Hundred Conventions campaign, read a newspaper account of Douglass's comments. He thought Douglass hypocritical, complaining to fellow abolitionists Lewis and Harriet Hayden in early January 1880 that, "if it is not best for those that are leaving now then you and I and Lane and Brown and Doughless Should not of left but should of staid thare and fight it out and if I was to tell them that they should stay and fight it out I should think it my duty to go and help to fight it out then it would look like I ment what I said." Clarke contended that Douglass, indeed any of those who had fled enslavement, would have rejected as madness the idea that they should have stayed enslaved to "save both the South and himself to civilization." Douglass was wrong, insisted Clarke. Those who fled enslavement before the war and tenant farming after the war did not betray the revolution: they *were* the revolution. Anyone who thought they should have stayed, "eaven if it had been Garrison or Garrod Smith or eather of the Tappens or aney one," was the true traitor.[47]

Clarke, the Haydens, William Wells Brown, Frederick Douglass, Lunsford Lane—"there are a few of the oald vetons still alive hare and thare," Clarke lamented, "thoe they are getting verrey scurs and fiew and fair between but as a genurel thing they stand firm and studdy on the oald principle of Human rits." He was mistaken. Seven months earlier, Lane was gone, the first of Clarke's roster of abolitionist revolutionaries to die.[48]

Did anyone beyond Lunsford's immediate family know that he died in 1879? Hayden did not know. No letters suggest that news traveled southward to what remained of the Haywood families. Frederick Douglass did not note it, nor did Wendell Phillips or Anne Warren Weston or Henry Highland Garnett. There was no obituary in the newspapers. Ironically, given Lunsford's financial struggles in life, he apparently left no debt in death, but no inheritance either. His children could not afford a gravestone in New York Bay Cemetery, neither for Martha nor for him—nothing for descendants to revere and historians to scrutinize.[49]

A lifetime earlier, in describing his fears of being sold to the cotton planters of Alabama, Lunsford Lane had mourned those he knew who were "at times transported to a climate where, in a few years they die, and then borne without ceremony, and with few mourners, to their last resting-place beneath the sod." Such was the fate of Black Americans on the pillory of slavery. So, too, could it become their fate in the cradle of liberty. Over the decades, Lunsford lost five children, each buried without ceremony and grave markers. Although he and Martha lived long lives, they too were borne without ceremony to their resting places beneath the New Jersey grass, the absent tombstones declaring that they had become forgotten and maybe even erased, forever in the shadows of others' monuments, the all-to-common conclusion to nineteenth-century Black American lives in South and North.[50]

———

In Roman mythology, Venus had named her son "Aeneas," presumably because of the αἰνόν ἄχος—the "terrible grief"—that she knew awaited her upon her mortal son's death. When Aeneas fell in battle with the Rutuli not far from Rome, Venus, with Jupiter's consent, commanded the river god Numicus to wash away her son's mortality: "His mother anointed his body *thus* purified with divine odours, and touched his face with ambrosia, mingled with sweet nectar, and made him a God. Him the people of Quirinus called Indiges, and endowed with a temple and with altars." "Aeneas" also evokes αἰνός, meaning "praise" and "story." Praise for his story manifested in the temple and at the altars. The story, a worthy one, lived on through Greek, Roman, and Anglo-Saxon mythologies.[51]

Lunsford Lane, too, had a story, one of a reluctant warrior who fought the battle. Maybe, his hesitance or his refusal to dedicate a lifetime to the cause is the reason why, by his death, Lane had become forgotten. In 1852, Black nationalist Martin Robinson Delany omitted Lane from *The Condition, Elevation, Emigration, and Destiny of the Colored People of the United States*. William Nell did not list Lane alongside other Black Carolinians such as David Walker, Jonathan Overton, Delph Williamson, and George M. Horton in 1855's *The Colored Patriots of the American Revolution*. William Wells Brown did not recall Lane in *The Black Man* in 1863. Delany, Nell, and Brown were active abolitionists who had known Lane, so his exclusion from their works seems to suggest that they considered Lunsford historically irrelevant.[52]

Then, in autumn 1894, fifteen years after Lane's death, Stephen B. Weeks wandered the aisles of a Connecticut bookstore and came across "a book containing the life of a North Carolina negro." Its scent tickled the historian's nose as he turned the volume back and forth in his hands, leafing the well-worn pages, skimming the lengthy table of contents, noting the author and publication date—William G. Hawkins, 1863. He bought it, and when Weeks arrived home in the nation's capital, he placed *Lunsford Lane* in his library, excitedly sending word southward that he found "perhaps the only biography of a North Carolina negro ever written." His announcement resurrected Lane, elevating him in the consciousness of Black and White America as the great entrepreneur who purchased his and his family's freedom, and transforming his story into American mythology.[53]

Epilogue

Children of the American Aeneas

After a parent dies, even if their children are at their deathbed, they think of the things they should have asked over the years. What was their childhood like? How did they meet their spouse? What did they dream for themselves and their children? They recall the stories their parents told—the tall tales, the half-truths, and the authenticities. Over their lifetimes, Edward, Maria Bell, William, and Lunsford Jr. heard their father tell The Story many times, experiencing much of it with him, from enslavement in Raleigh to fleeing the terror of a White mob, riding the rails northward, their introduction to the American Anti-Slavery Society in cavernous Broadway Tabernacle, and the seas of White audiences who gazed at them and then dropped money in their baskets. Like the answers to their unasked questions, the opportunity to hear The Story one last time evaporated as they buried their father in New York Bay Cemetery. Of the three known children who remained in 1879, their own histories evidence no remembrances of the man who saved himself and his family from freedom. They had their own stories to write, on pages dimly watermarked by their father's legacy, taking it up to create a new birthright of family, community, and Black self-empowerment.

———

Not long after burying his father, Lunsford Jr. packed up and left his brother William's home, moving to Philadelphia. William rented out Lunsford's former half of the duplex to Isaac Walker, enslaved as a child in South Carolina before heading northward after Emancipation. In 1879, Walker was twenty years old, a barber, and married to Virginia, whom he had met in New York. By the time they moved into the duplex alongside William and Rebecca Lane, they had their only child, Edith. The two families became close friends. Living with the Lanes in the other half of the duplex were Maria Bell Lane Garner Rose and two borders: Lewis Thomas and Abner Thompson.[1]

Thomas and Thompson worked with William Lane as sleeping car porters, often laboring as much as one hundred hours per week for minimal pay and little prospect of promotion. They went to the Jersey City rail station early in the mornings to set up the cars, make the beds, and lay out combs and brushes. As passengers arrived, they carried luggage and shined shoes. On the long rail trips, they stayed awake well into the night to serve travelers, probably reminding William of that journey so many years earlier, when he was five years old, aboard the trains as they phizzz-zzz-zzzed from Raleigh to Jersey City. Like the hotel owners and private individuals who hired Gustavus Rose and other waiters in the 1860s, railroad companies counted on Black porters acting "naturally" deferential towards wealthy White passengers. Formerly enslaved men such as Lewis Thomas, who came from North Carolina after Emancipation, and William Lane, who fled with his family decades earlier, could feign that deference. Such subservience often resulted in large tips but often at an exacting price to porters' self-esteem. "The sleeping car porters are subjected to more indignities from both the railroad managers and the traveling public than any set of men on earth," expounded the railroad porters' union years later.[2]

In 1881, William and Rebecca Lane began a family. Their first child, Catherine, survived only months. In June, they buried her in the empty space between Lunsford and Martha Lane in New York Bay Cemetery. A little over a year later, in late December 1882, triplets Maria, Mabel Curtis, and Maud Hasard entered the world. Five months later, when the Lanes had their daughters baptized at Saint Matthew's Protestant Episcopal Church in Jersey City, Maria was no longer with her sisters, having joined her grandparents as well. The Lanes' neighbor, Virginia Walker, became godparent to Mabel, and a family friend, Grace Hasard, served as Maud's godmother. Sadly, the baptism was a rushed ritual because Mabel had contracted pneumonia. She died soon thereafter, and her parents again returned to New York Bay Cemetery, the third time in two years.[3]

Every pregnancy stirred months of anticipation and joy. Each death crushed the dreams that the Lanes imagined for their children. William and Rebecca threw themselves into distractions. He became involved in the railroad porters' union, an organization that lobbied on behalf of its members, raising money "to take care of a hard-working class of the community." He rose in the union ranks, serving as vice president of the New York chapter by 1883. Rebecca found solace in doting on Maud and attending social functions. "Mrs. Wm. C. Lane and her daughter Maud, of Jersey City, arrived home Sep 1, after spending the month of August at Little Neck, L.I., the guests of Mrs. Dempsey," announced the *New York Globe* in 1884. Every spring, the porters' union hosted an annual ball in Manhattan where Rebecca and William mingled with Manhattan's Black society and occasionally the city's White society, as in 1888 when organizers invited officers of railroad corporations to join the festivities. From a distance, the White businessmen watched as the porters danced.[4]

Meanwhile, when Lunsford Lane Jr. moved to Philadelphia in 1879, he secured employment as a waiter and found accommodations in a house kept by Priscilla Waters, a widow formerly enslaved in Delaware. Within months, Lunsford was out, by choice or by force. Times were hard, and he could not keep a woman or a job. He moved to 405 Blight Street with Francis Gurley, a floor supervisor in a local manufactory where Lunsford Jr. had found new employment.[5]

Lunsford Lane Jr. had not been well for years. The circumstances surrounding his 1882 admission to the State Hospital for the Insane in Norristown are unknown, but he was among its earliest patients. The hospital opened in 1880, fifteen miles northeast of Philadelphia. Shedding the old model of a monstrous, prison-like institution, the new asylum promised more progressive facilities and therapies. It accommodated 750 residents, divided into cottages of up to one hundred residents, segregated by gender, with access to "more out-door freedom than has hitherto been afforded them," as one regional newspaper described. Robert H. Chase, a notable doctor from Washington, DC, accepted the position as the hospital's resident physician. By 1884, over one thousand inmates overcrowded the hospital, overwhelming Chase and his staff, which may explain the brevity with which the doctor filled out Lunsford Jr.'s death certificate on October 22, attributing his passing to general paresis, a severe neuropsychiatric disorder that manifests in late-stage syphilis.[6]

After an autopsy, Lunsford Jr.'s body traveled to the Philadelphia School of Anatomy, joining a parade of late-nineteenth-century Black bodies involuntarily supplied to medical school dissecting tables. His brain remained at the State Hospital, sitting in storage until 1906, when the facility opened a museum, not for the public but for medical students and physicians. Two years later, a pathologist examined and indexed each of the 1180 brains on display. Lane had suffered a long time with paralytic dementia, losing memories and eventually dying from a brain aneurysm.[7]

The early to mid-1880s were difficult for William Lane. Babies died, his twin lost his mind and died, and, apparently, Maria Bell Lane Garner Rose died as well. Soon after Maud Lane's birth in 1882, fifty-year-old Maria Bell vanished from her brother's household, and, like her husband Gustavus, left no traces as to what happened. William's co-workers, Lewis Thomas and Abner Thompson, also left the duplex, starting their own families nearby. The Lanes—William, Rebecca, and Maud—became a nuclear middle-class family, one that continued to experience tragedy. When she was four years old, Maud Lane greeted a new sister, Vanessa Preston, but months after her birth, Vanessa, too, was buried alongside Catherine, Maria, and Mabel between their grandparents.[8]

The few bright spots in the Lanes' lives were Maud's childhood and William's climb through the porter union's ranks, which opened social opportunities for Rebecca. In late 1891, he became president of the reorganized Railroad Porters Mutual Protective Union. With Edward's whereabout unknown, William was possibly the only surviving child of Lunsford and Martha Lane. He lived two more years, dying at fifty-seven years old in 1894. Without her husband's connections, Rebecca Mitchell Lane lost status in Manhattan's social circles, but she soon married Samuel S. Jackson, a Jersey City coal merchant nineteen years her elder, a relationship that situated her and young Maud financially in ways that Lane's porter's earnings never had. Maud graduated from old No. 1 School in 1897, one of two Black students in a class of twenty-one. In 1903, Rebecca cofounded the Afro-American Woman's Industrial Club, a Jersey City organization dedicated to the "help and uplift of the women and girls of our race along many lines of usefulness." The following year, the clubwomen voted to join the Northeastern Federation of Afro-American Women's Clubs, which organized regional conferences such as one in 1909 on how to be politically active against lynching. Rebecca Ann Mitchell Lane Jackson rose to vice president of the federation in 1907 and became president of the local chapter by 1910. She hosted the chapter's tenth-anniversary meeting in her home, where twenty-seven-year-old Maud, trained in voice and piano, performed. When, in 1909, W. E. B. Du Bois decided to update *Some*

Efforts of American Negroes for Their Own Social Betterment, a study originally written eleven years earlier that documented activism in Black churches, fraternities and sororities, benevolent organizations, and insurance societies, he contacted Rebecca Jackson to write the history of the Afro-American Woman's Industrial Club. She bragged that the chapter purchased a six-bedroom house to accommodate Black women needing assistance and protection. The rooms filled, and the club could not meet the community's needs.[9]

———

Lunsford and Martha Lane's bloodline remained with their granddaughter, Maud. Strangely, the census taker of 1900 wrote Maud Lane's name into the Jackson household and then scratched through, replacing it with the name of her stepbrother, eleven-year-old Charles Jackson. Only weeks prior to the census taker's visit, seventeen-year-old Maud married Samuel T. Cole and moved to his home at 23 Jewett Street in Jersey City. Cole's parents, William T. and Rachel A. Jackson Cole, may have known enslavement, but Samuel told census takers different things about their origins: in 1900, only his mother, from Maryland, had been enslaved, and his father had been born free in Pennsylvania; in 1910, both were from Maryland; in 1920, his mother from Maryland and his father's origins unknown; in 1930, they came from South Carolina. Regardless of their origins, in the 1870s, they migrated to New Jersey, where Samuel was born in 1878. By 1900, he worked as a waiter on a dining car for the Lehigh Valley Rail Road, the termini for which were Jersey City and Niagara Falls.[10]

Having learned the importance of social activism and visibility from her mother, Maud Cole became the matriarch of a prominent Jersey City family, regularly appearing in the *New York Age*, a regional Black newspaper that wielded a great deal of social influence. Although the paper missed the 1905 baptism announcement for the Coles' first child, Jeannette Lane, it did not overlook their other children—Eleanor Quinn in 1907 and William Thomas in 1909. *The New York Age* particularly noted how, on each occasion, Maud's mother and stepfather attended the ceremonies. In 1911, when the Lehigh Valley Rail Road promoted Samuel Cole to conductor, his wife and mother-in-law took advantage of his new position, traveling to Niagara Falls the following summer to stay with a friend in Buffalo. The *New York Age* noticed, as it did a month later when the Coles visited Samuel's mother in Germantown, Pennsylvania, and again in late April 1915 when over one hundred guests attended the Coles' fifteenth-anniversary reception in their home, "beautifully decorated with smilax and pink and white carnations." Guests enjoyed a buffet dinner, and a "profuse and beautiful array of cut glass presents was shown upstairs in the pink room."[11]

Maud Cole enjoyed a leisurely life. She and her mother continued to summer with other society women, no longer running away to Long Island or Niagara Falls but to the briny air of the Jersey shore, where they stayed with other Black socialites at hotels such as Marguerite Cottage in Long Branch, Whitehead House in Asbury Park, and Laster Cottage in Spring Lake Beach for weeks of "bathing, crabbing, and sightseeing." At Spring Lake Beach in 1922, they dined with Nina Gomer Du Bois, wife of W. E. B., again announced by *The New York Age*. Not since the early 1840s, when Lunsford Lane traveled and intermingled with New England's Black abolitionist elite, had a Lane become so integrated into Black America's social circles. When Rebecca Ann Mitchell Lane Jackson moved in with the Coles upon her second husband's death in 1917, they found more opportunities to socialize, leaving the children with their grandmother. She lived with them another nine years, dying in 1926 and buried in Bayview Cemetery, adjacent to New York Bay Cemetery and near the four infant daughters she lost in life.[12]

Just as Maud Cole's mother had the Afro-American Woman's Industrial Club, Maud adopted causes of her own. She cofounded the Church of the Incarnation, Jersey City's Black Episcopal congregation. She joined the Friendly Big Sisters, an organization that aided in "racial adjustment" by attending juvenile courts and schools to intercede on behalf of the "needy" and make sure that "whatever cases brought them has been given attention." She became a leader in Jersey City's Helping Hand Society, a women's voluntary organization that grew out of the Women's Christian Temperance Union to aid disadvantaged women and families dealing with men's alcoholism. She joined the Daughters of Wesley, a sorority that often met as Sunday School classes and quilting bees, and the Court of Calanthe, a Black women's insurance society which, in an age when most burial associations in Black America were controlled by male undertakers, invested and shared monies among women to cover the costs of burials.[13]

When Maud's children were young, she taught them the necessary social graces, including years of piano lessons. She involved them in her charity work. Still, despite the refinement that their mother tried to teach them, Jeannette, Eleanor, and William were children, difficult and mischievous at times. They frequently antagonized a local launderer, a Chinese immigrant whom they enjoyed startling by sticking their heads through the laundry window and jabbering imitations of Mandarin before running away, shrieking with laughter.[14]

The mid-1910s were a challenging time for the Coles. Young William died in 1916, devastating the family. Months later, Samuel registered for the World War I draft. Although the Army did not call him into service, Maud thought it important to support the war effort. She became heavily involved in the

Circle of Negro War Relief, which made comfort kits, issued educational pamphlets about Black soldiering, and supplied military families with Christmas trees, Victrolas, and records. With their son's death, both Maud and Samuel Cole seemed to cling more tightly to their daughters. Jeannette began to accompany Samuel to the Wicoma Tennis Club where she learned the sport, becoming a tournament-winning player by her late teens. The girls accompanied Maud to meetings of the Young Women's Christian Association for which she served as chair of the membership committee and a representative to the 1920 national convention in Cleveland. A decade later, Maud Lane Cole became one of two Black women who integrated the Jersey City YWCA, arranging a conference for girls, including her daughters, to live as "guests in homes of the opposite race."[15]

Maud and Samuel Cole emphasized education for their daughters, both of whom started school by 1915. Eleanor graduated from Dickinson High School nine years later and then attended the Pratt Institute in Brooklyn, earning a diploma in Household Sciences and Arts. She advertised as a dressmaker. Jeannette, after her graduation in 1922, pursued a bachelor's and a master's degree in English at New York University. In 1928, she took a teaching position at Saint Paul's Normal and Industrial School in Lawrenceville, Virginia. To assure themselves of Jeannette's happiness and safety, Maud, Samuel, and Eleanor traveled southward in the summer of 1930 to visit her, and Maud reassured herself again in July 1931. The culture shock was dramatic for Jeannette Lane Cole. Each summer, even those when her family visited her, she traveled to Jersey City to escape the South and enjoy a little tennis.[16]

After Jeannette's departure, Maud and Eleanor Cole remained active in Jersey City society, attending teas, leading study groups at the House of Friendliness YWCA, arranging Red Cross benefits, and participating in the Daughters of Wesley. In late December 1931, Maud suffered an unidentified illness noteworthy enough to alarm the social reporters at the *New York Age*. Four months later, she vacationed in Asbury Park to recuperate, and in May, she attended the national YWCA conference in Minneapolis. She seemed to have recovered from whatever afflicted her, but in late September, she was "stricken with paralysis and never spoke again." She died days later. "No woman was more active in the life of the community than the deceased," opined her obituary. Samuel Cole buried her in Bayview Cemetery, near her mother, grandparents, and sisters. He joined her there eight years later.[17]

The Lane lineage pulsed through Eleanor and Jeannette Cole, and in time, it died with them. Eleanor retreated from the social scene and eventually set up house with her cousin, Marguerite Cole, who tried to continue in Manhattan's

Black society, attending a ladies' gathering in 1938 at Hazel Green Royalle's home where rumor circulated that "Marguerite and Barnie are still at it." Marguerite and Barnie did not stay at it long. She and Eleanor grew older together, Marguerite taking on work as a hotel chambermaid as Eleanor continued to make dresses. In 1943, Eleanor met and married Edward Johnson, but their life together did not last. She died three years later, laid beside her mother in Bayview Cemetery.[18]

Eleanor's sister, Jeannette Cole, never married. After her mother's death, she stayed in Virginia throughout the summers. Lawrenceville was a small town some seventy miles southwest of Richmond, bound to the rest of the nation by rail lines. In 1888, John Solomon Russell selected the community for Saint Paul's Normal and Industrial School. Born enslaved in 1857 in Mecklenburg County, Virginia, Russell attended Hampton Normal and Agricultural Institute beginning in 1874, and then the Bishop Payne Divinity School in Petersburg in 1878, where he became an Episcopal minister. He studied Booker T. Washington's theories of industrial education but was unconvinced that Black Americans should just settle for hard work, discipline, and self-help. Russell aspired for more for his graduates, believing they could pursue intellectualism. His theological studies led him to imagine education as about preparing students to use their minds as much as their hands. So, he established a school to train Black school teachers to work in southeastern Virginia. Jeannette's commitment to that vision of education was strong. She stayed at Saint Paul's for fifty years.[19]

Soon after Jeannette Lane Cole arrived at the school in 1928, the national economy collapsed. Lawrenceville's four banks failed, and hundreds of residents lost their jobs. Poverty became so great that the town benefited significantly from New Deal programs. The Works Progress Administration installed curbs and gutters along the streets and constructed a community swimming pool, bath house, and baseball stadium—Black Virginians banned from each. As in any small Southern town in the 1930s and 1940s, Jim Crow segregation was powerful, and racial tensions were high. Years later, Jeannette remembered the "White" and "Colored" signs around Lawrenceville. She never went to the movies, refusing to sit on the balcony. She resented that when she took the train, she sat on uncomfortable benches in a segregated, open-air car. Saint Paul's, which in 1941 became Saint Paul's Polytechnic Institute, worked to ease those tensions. The school provided agricultural and domestic extension services, healthcare, youth programs, and continuing education to all citizens of Lawrenceville, regardless of race.[20]

In the 1930s, Saint Paul's faculty lived in collective housing, and Jeannette Cole shared a house with ten other single Black women from Virginia, North Carolina, Pennsylvania, Ohio, and Alabama—five teachers, three secretaries, and one librarian. An adjacent building housed seven men, all from North Carolina and Virginia, who served as teachers, a dean, an agriculturalist, a steward, and an accountant. As the college faced financial strains during the Great Depression, faculty took on multiple roles, a tradition that continued into better times because, as a small Black college, Saint Paul's was never flush with money. Cole taught English, but her years of piano lessons positioned her in 1934 to become the college's organist and musical director. Over the decades, she also served as chair of the English Department, and, when the school restructured in 1957 as Saint Paul's College, she became head of the Humanities Department.[21]

As with every professor who enjoys a long tenure at one institution, "Miss Cole," as she became known on campus, became somewhat of a folk hero, her personality wrapped up in college lore. She was quirky. Students remembered fondly how she so often began a sentence with "Now maybe I'm a little old fashioned, but in my day . . ." She was sentimental, attending the local Episcopal Church but refusing to move her membership from the Church of the Incarnation in Jersey City.[22]

And she emulated the long legacy of women in the Lane family. From Martha Lane's introduction to the American Anti-Slavery Society in 1842 to Clarissa Lane's real estate investments, to Maria Bell Lane Garner Rose's and Rebecca Mitchell Lane Jackson's engagements with New York City's emerging Black middle class, to Maud Hasard Lane Cole and her daughters' immersion in Jersey City's social clubs, the Lane women epitomized the arc of self-actualization that Black America experienced across the late nineteenth and early twentieth centuries. It was a legacy of women's empowerment that Lunsford Lane clearly never imagined when he once declared to a Massachusetts audience that Emancipation returned Black women "to the duties of home in the rearing of our neglected offspring, giving far more attention to their cleanliness and comfort."[23]

The Lane women and many other Black women pursued a politics of respectability intended to counter White America's stereotypes. Thinking of themselves as members of the "Talented Tenth," they conceded to the ideal of the "respectable Negro" that ironically worked against many Black Americans. As journalist and activist Ida B. Wells-Barnett complained, "It was not the servant or working class of Negroes, who know their places, with whom the white people objected to riding, but the educated, property-owning Negro who thought himself the white man's equal." Jeannette Lane Cole knew well the White insistence on staying in her place and the male insistence also. Although her female ancestors often relied on husbands' and fathers' activities to create their own opportunities, she required no man to soar.[24]

Still, it was difficult for Jeannette Cole, as a Northern Black woman in rural Virginia, to emulate her mother. Lawrenceville was no Jersey City, and opportunities for service and social comradery were scarce. She found a friend in Nellie Pratt, who arrived as faculty at Saint Paul's in 1913 and soon married J. Alvin Russell, son of the school's founder.

During Pratt's sophomore year at Howard University in 1909, she had been a member of the first initiated class of a newly formed sorority, Alpha Kappa Alpha. Four years later, the sorority splintered. Although often described as a disagreement over official colors, symbols, and name, the schism also involved differences over visions of activism. In the original sorority, women such as Pratt, whose degrees were primarily in Liberal Arts, insisted on social activism to uplift Black Americans. The breakaway group, most of them pursuing degrees in Education, wanted to act more politically. (How reminiscent of the moral suasion versus political activism schism that fissured the abolitionist movement of the late 1830s and 1840s.) Months later, the breakaway group formed a new sorority, Delta Sigma Theta, which participated in the Women's Suffrage March of 1913, weathering jibes and insults from the White crowd and the White suffragettes. By 1922, as Southern senators blocked consideration of antilynching legislation, sisters of Alpha Kappa Alpha came to realize that their vision of social activism was not enough. Using Christmas cards, campaign buttons, and newsletters, they began to engage politically, drawing attention to the continued need for antilynching legislation well into the 1940s.[25]

Nearly forty years after Nellie Pratt joined Alpha Kappa Alpha, she established Lawrenceville's alumnae chapter of the sorority and Saint Paul's undergraduate chapter. She convinced Jeannette Cole to join in the first initiated class, and Jeannette's great-grandparents' world crashed into her own. White Americans during Lunsford Lane's lifetime, and more than a few Black Americans, assumed that darker-skinned Black folk were better field laborers and lighter-skinned Black folk were more capable of mastering domestic work and artisan skills. As a man whom White people viewed as moderate in complexion, Lunsford Lane enjoyed privileges denied to darker-skinned enslaved peoples among whom he lived. He had received at least a recognition when, upon joining Frederick Douglass and Mr. Jones in Groton, a state politician judged each on his skin tone before turning on his heels and fleeing when faced with the darkest skin. When, in 1842, *The Liberator* described the "bright looking children" who walked into Broadway Tabernacle with Lunsford and Martha Lane, and when, in 1886, a Pennsylvania newspaper described Frederick Douglass as "a bright example of the capability of the colored race," their use of the euphemism "bright" related how the politics of complexion remained powerful. A caste system of assumptions about intelligence and skin tones emerged among Black Americans on southern farms and in southern towns, and it remained after Emancipation, through Jim Crow, and into the Civil Rights era. By the mid-twentieth century, some Black organizations, particularly sororities like Alpha Kappa Alpha, acquired reputations for perpetuating the caste of colorism. A "brown paper bag" test arose as an allegorical measure of Black women's beauty and character.[26]

Dark-skinned Jeannette Cole "had probably never been beautiful," recalled one of her colleagues, "always short, stocky, pug-nosed." Despite her upbringing, she struggled to physically display refinement. She walked with difficulty, her knees painful from years of tennis, the trophies for which she displayed in her campus office. In contrast to Nellie Pratt Russell, who worked about fifteen hours a week as an English instructor, Cole averaged forty-five hours a week teaching and rehearsing with the college choir. So, Cole did not find community in Alpha Kappa Alpha, attending few meetings and leaving sponsorship of the local chapter to Russell.[27]

Throughout her career at Saint Paul's, Cole dealt with structural prejudice. The greater challenges were, as Anna Julia Cooper once acknowledged for all Black women, "a woman question and a race question." Colorism bubbled up in the sorority system and among Saint Paul's all-Black faculty, staff, and students. Cole learned to negotiate or avoid the Jim Crow racism that was endemic in Lawrenceville. Sexism, and a bit of intellectual elitism, were the challenges that she faced most often. Over four decades, the school's yearbooks filled with photographs of professors labeled by their doctoral titles, contrasting with occasional nods to "Miss Jeannette L. Cole." As a professor at Saint Paul's who never pursued doctoral work, she became frustrated as more degreed scholars, most of them men, took positions at the college. Then, one day in 1973, Jeannette Cole decided to change her title. She was not so presumptuous, as her great-grandfather had been, to declare herself "Dr.," but she did insist that authorities discard the "Miss." Future yearbooks identified her as simply "Jeannette L. Cole," even as other non-degreed women continued to be identified as "Miss." As a colleague suspected, "early on she must have learned to use her energy and her supple mind to achieve the notice beauty would not bring her." She countered the intellectual elitism by directing her energies as a lifelong member of Alpha Kappa Mu National Honor Society, founding Saint Paul's chapter in 1953, sponsoring the chapter throughout her later career, and serving as national president between 1975 and 1978.[28]

A simple change in title was just her first foray into fighting sexism. When, in 1974, Richard Conway arrived on campus to interview for an English teaching position, he realized two things: "Mine was the only white skin as far as the eye could see," and that one of his interviewers, Jeannette Cole, faced incessant interruptions by the college president and the dean, both of whom impressed Conway as "men more interested in form than substance." Cole held her own. "Age gave her the added dimension of self-knowledge. It seemed that her composure could not now be ruffled by senators or disturbed by lovers. Should either most surprisingly present themselves, she would be what the rest of us labor fruitlessly all our lives to become. Just herself."[29]

Saint Paul's offered Conway the position, and over the next few months, Cole befriended him. Having lived in the western United States, Conway could not adjust to the South's racialized culture and lasted only the one year, convinced that he "did not want my children . . . to grow up in that tangled web of race relations, caught between the oppressors and the oppressed, learning both exploitation and hostility." Jeannette Lane Cole had tolerated that culture for forty-six years.[30]

Cole, growing notably deaf, retired four years later in May 1978. She finally received a doctorate as an honorary degree from St. Augustine's College in Raleigh in recognition of her fifty-year career at a historically Black college. She remained in Virginia until her death in August 1997. Although her obituary mentioned her parents, it said nothing of her descent from Lunsford Lane or her sister Eleanor, with whom she arranged to be buried in Jersey City's Bayview Cemetery. Cole left an endowment of $100,000 [$191,200] to Saint Paul's as a scholarship fund for members of Alpha Kappa Mu. To become a Cole Scholar, students had to submit an essay on the challenges in promoting James Solomon Russell's original vision for the school, an ideal toward which she had dedicated her career. Jeannette Lane Cole's former colleague, Richard Conway, honored her with a homage and poem. He was "tempted to say that she represented the indomitable spirit of African-American womanhood. One thinks of brave examples from American life and literature: the mighty Sojourner Truth, say, or Sue, the intrepid heroine of Richard Wright's 'Bright [and] Morning Star.'"[31]

Beyond those heroes, though, Jeannette Lane Cole might have just glanced backward through her family history: to a mother who advocated for justice for criminally accused Black juveniles and assisted Black women who were victims of their husbands' alcoholism and a father who was willing to fight for a nation unwilling to grant him equality; to a grandmother who worked to empower abandoned and disadvantaged women and a grandfather who organized Black railroad porters. Had any of them ever read *The Narrative of Lunsford Lane* or even William Hawkins's *Lunsford Lane*? Had they shared The Story from generation to generation, or had they, like the American public, forgotten Jeannette Lane Cole's great-grandmother, who survived enslavement and raised a family, and great-grandfather who might have faltered in his own self-making but persisted, and through The Story—incomplete and flawed as it might have been—inspired others to pursue their own stories.

Acknowledgments

This book represents over a decade of journeying with Lunsford Lane, taking me to over three dozen repositories where I patiently and relentlessly sought him and his family in others' papers and memories. Because Lane did not leave behind copious documentation and was not completely forthcoming in the materials he did create, his is not an easy life to reconstruct, which is why I am so appreciative of the many people who supported and helped me.

I am grateful beyond measure for my friendships with Lorri Glover and Ami Pflugard-Jackisch, fellow members of the Southern Biography Circle and to whom I am heavily indebted. They read chapters and then the entire manuscript. I burdened them with more stories about Lunsford Lane than they deserved. They rewarded me with honest and useful criticism. For their invaluable feedback and moral support, I also thank the readers for UNC Press—Douglas R. Egerton, Antwain K. Hunter, and Richard S. Newman. Their suggestions made this a deeper and more complex story. I am truly fortunate to count such incredible and inspiring people as fellow travelers through historical research and writing.

The generosity of the scholarly community always buoys me. For the small and large ways in which they contributed to my work, I thank L. Diane Barnes, Andrew Diemer, Edward J. Balleisen, Charlene Boyer Lewis, Patrick Breen, Karen Bullock, Chloe Chapin, Megan L. Cherry, Justene Hill Edwards, Annette Gordon-Reed, Sean Griffin, Carmen Harris, Donald Holmes, Reeve Huston, Karen A. Johnson, Ebony Jones, Mark Kelley, Gary Kornblith, Carol Lasser, Alex Leslie, Caleb McDaniel, Kevin McGruder, Don James McLoughlin, Katherine Mellen Charron, Christina Michelon, Rachel Miller, David Mills, Florence Mitchell, Sharon Ann Murphy, Margaret Newell, Holly A. Pinheiro Jr., Claire Priest, Cassandra Pybus, Stacey Robertson, Julia Rudolph, Karen Sanchez-Eppler, Whitney Stewart, Matthew Suazo, Megan Walsh, Trudy Williams, Peter H. Wood, my colleagues in the NCSU History Department, and the Triangle Early American History Seminar. For sharing traces of Lunsford's story that they ran across in their own scholarship, I thank Julia Wallace Bernier, Sande Bishop, Thomas Doughton, Natalie Joy, Kathleen King, Belle Long, Shirley Moody-Turner, Jonathan Wells, and Garrett Wright. For their generosity in hosting me in their homes during research trips, I am indebted to Douglas Egerton and Leigh Fought, Liz Covart and Tim Wilde, Carol Lasser and Gary Kornblith, and Mike Cormier and Steve Carlin. I owe much to Phillip M. Bass and Brian Hollingsworth for counseling during particularly challenging times.

An American Antiquarian Society-National Endowment for the Humanities fellowship and a scholarly fellowship from the Gilder Lehrman Institute of American History aided my research. The support was invaluable. My choices on how to present Lane are my own and do not represent the National Endowment for the Humanities, the American Antiquarian Society, or the Gilder Lehrman Institute of American History.

I am particularly grateful to individuals who gave of their time to assist me with research: Lannie Hubbard and Meaghan Nappo at the Joel Lane Museum House; Joshua Hager, Alison Thurman, and the other archivists at the State Archives of North Carolina; Jason Tomberlin, Taylor de Klerk Butler, and Sarah Carrier at the Southern Historical Collection at the University of North Carolina at Chapel Hill; Elizabeth Pope, Ashley Cataldo, Laura Wasowicz, Nan Wolverton, Kimberly Toney, Dan Boudreau, and the curators and staff at the American Antiquarian Society. Additionally, I thank Anna LeBlanc-Mulder at the Amistad Research Center at Tulane University; Diane S. Smyczynski and Lisa Jackson at Bayview-New York Bay Cemetery; Neeley Bersch at the Brunswick Public Library; Maureen Morris at the Cambridge Cemetery; Kathleen L. Rawlins at the Cambridge Historical Commission; Maggie Hoffman at the Cambridge Historical Society; Alyssa Pacy at the Cambridge Public Library; Kristy Wallisch at Chalmette National Cemetery; Claudia Schumacher at the Fiske Public Library; Sarah Horowitz at Haverford Special Collections; Kate Hanson Plass at the Longfellow House-Washington's Headquarters Historic National Site; Keith Vezeau and Catherine Gaggioli at the Massachusetts State Archives; Jennifer McLamb and Doug Porter at the Mordecai House; Stephen Pinkerton at Mount Auburn Cemetery; Marcia Kirk and Joe Van Nostrand of the New York Department of Records and Information Services; Maren McKee at the Oberlin Heritage Center; Rebecca E. Lesny at the Pennsylvania State Archives; Wendy Essery at the Worcester Historical Museum; Joy Hennig of the Worcester Public Library. I am also grateful to Betsy Haywood, whom I befriended late in the project. She has been generous in sharing her time, knowledge, and paintings of her ancestors.

Over the years, I have benefited from the mentorship and friendship of Theda Perdue. She is among the most genuine and generous people whom I have known. From the moment that she encouraged me, an eighth-grade social studies teacher, to pursue a career in academia, she has been a constant encouragement and inspiration. Thank you so much for everything.

I am forever indebted to Debbie Gershenowitz for her belief in this project, her guidance in its development, and her editorial eye. She piloted me in finding my purpose, helped me tackle the challenge of shortening a lengthy manuscript (yes, it was longer), advised on the flow of the narrative, and answered the phone when I called. Once a conference acquaintance, Debbie has become someone I highly respect as an editor and cherish as a friend.

I dedicate this book to Roderick Glenn Turner. When we met in 1994, I thought he was the most loving, genuine, and beautiful person I had ever met. When we married in 2015, I felt the same. In my heart, nothing has changed over our thirty years together: I soar with his laughter, I melt with his tears, and I treasure every moment. That he chose me is the most important honor of my life.

Notes

Abbreviations

AAN	African American Newspapers Collection, Accessible Archives, https://www -accessible-archives.com/collections/african-american-newspapers/
AAS	American Antiquarian Society, Worcester, MA
AccArch	Accessible Archives, https://www-accessible-archives.com
AncC	Ancestry.com, https://www.ancestry.com/
BPL	Boston Public Library, Boston, MA
CPL	Archives and Special Collections, Cambridge Public Library, Cambridge, MA
CRNC	William L. Saunders, ed., *The Colonial Records of North Carolina*, 10 vols. (Raleigh: State of North Carolina, 1886–90), *Documenting the American South*, https://docsouth.unc.edu/csr/
EHC	Ernest Haywood Collection of Haywood Family Papers, 1752–1967, Southern Historical Collection, Wilson Library, University of North Carolina, Chapel Hill
GSP	Gerrit Smith Papers, Special Collections Research Center, Syracuse University Libraries, Syracuse, NY
HSP	Historical Society of Pennsylvania, Philadelphia
HT	HathiTrust Digital Library, https://www.hathitrust.org/
IntArch	Internet Archive, https://archive.org/
JAH	*Journal of American History*
JER	*Journal of the Early Republic*
LOC	Library of Congress, Washington, DC
MHS	Massachusetts Historical Society, Boston
NARA	National Archives and Records Administration, Washington, DC
NASN	North American Slave Narratives, *Documenting the American South*, University Library, University of North Carolina at Chapel Hill, https://docsouth.unc.edu /neh
NCC	North Carolina Collection, Wilson Library, University of North Carolina, Chapel Hill
NCHR	*North Carolina Historical Review*
NCRD	Norfolk County Registry of Deeds, Dedham, MA, https://www.norfolkdeeds.org/
NewsC	Newspapers.com, https://www.newspapers.com/
NJSA	New Jersey State Archives, Trenton
NYHS	New-York Historical Society, New York City
Ohio5	Five Colleges of Ohio, https://dcollections.oberlin.edu/digital/
PAW	Case Files of Approved Pension Applications of Widows and Other Veterans of the Army and Navy Who Served Mainly in the Civil War and the War with

Spain, Compiled 1861–1934, Records of the Veterans Administration, RG 15, NARA, *Fold3*, https://www.fold3.com/

RLDU   Rubenstein Library, Duke University, Durham, NC

SANC   State Archives of North Carolina, Raleigh

SHC   Southern Historical Collection, Wilson Library, University of North Carolina, Chapel Hill

SLNC   State Library of North Carolina, Raleigh

SMRRL   South Middlesex Recorded/Registered Land, Registry of Deeds, Cambridge, MA, hwww.masslandrecords.com/MiddlesexSouth/

SRNC   Walter Clark, ed., *The State Records of North Carolina*, vols. 11–26 (Raleigh: State of North Carolina, 1895–1906), *Documenting the American South*, https://docsouth.unc.edu/csr/

WCRD   Wake County Register of Deeds, Consolidated Real Property Index, Raleigh, NC, www.wakegov.com/rod

WDRRL   Worcester District Recorded/Registered Land, Registry of Deeds, Worcester, MA, www.masslandrecords.com/Worcester/

WPL   Worcester Public Library, Worcester, MA

Introduction

1. Henry Louis Gates Jr. and Maria Tatar, *The Annotated African American Folktales* (New York: W. W. Norton, 2018), 65–72, 133–42.

2. Joel Chandler Harris, *Uncle Remus, His Songs and His Sayings: The Folk-Lore of the Old Plantation* (New York: D. Appleton, 1880), 24; interview with Priscilla McCullough, in Georgia Writers' Project of the WPA, *Drums and Shadows: Survival Studies among the Georgia Coastal Negroes* (Athens: University of Georgia Press, 1940), 154; interview with Mose Brown, in Georgia Writers' Project of the WPA, *Drums and Shadows*, 18; Virginia Hamilton, *The People Could Fly: American Black Folktales* (New York: Knopf, 1993), x. From Joel Chandler Harris to Works Projects Administration recorders, White story collectors of the late nineteenth and early twentieth centuries transformed Black English vernacular dialect into minstrel-like dialogue; see Catherine A. Stewart, *Long Past Slavery: Representing Race in the Federal Writers' Project* (Chapel Hill: University of North Carolina Press, 2016), 5–7. Folklorists are divided on whether verbatim representations of such informal speech perpetuate negative stereotypes; see Shane White and Graham White, *The Sounds of Slavery: Discovering African American History through Songs, Sermons, and Speech* (Boston: Beacon Press, 2005), 80–83; John A. Burrison, ed., *Storytellers: Folktales and Legends from the South* (Athens: University of Georgia Press, 1989), 17–18. I have elected to retain features of relaxed speech but to clarify and celebrate the stories' creativity by reducing dialectic distortions. Lawrence W. Levine would certainly disapprove; see *Black Culture and Black Consciousness: Afro-American Folk Though from Slavery to Freedom* (New York: Oxford University Press, 1977), xv–xvi.

3. Lunsford Lane, *The Narrative of Lunsford Lane, Formerly of Raleigh, N.C. Embracing an Account of His Early Life, the Redemption by Purchase of Himself and Family from Slavery, and His Banishment from the Place of His Birth for the Crime of Wearing a Colored Skin. Published by Himself*, 2nd ed. (Boston: J. G. Torrey, 1842), 6–29, AAS. Of no significance at all, May 30 is also my birthday.

4. Lane, *Narrative of Lunsford Lane*, 2nd ed., 51–52.

5. Anne Warren Weston to Deborah Weston, 25 January 1842, Anti-Slavery Collection, BPL.

6. *The Liberator* (Boston, MA), 3 June 1842, NewsC.

7. Entry for 9–10 May 1842, Charles Spear Journal, microfilm, BPL; *The Liberator*, 13 May 1842, 3 June 1842; *National Anti-Slavery Standard* (New York, NY), 9 June 1842, AccArch.

8. W. Sherman Savage, "The Influence of John Chavis and Lunsford Lane on the History of North Carolina," *Journal of Negro History* 26 (January 1940): 24.

9. "Self-made woman" conceptually arrived in the 1860s, primarily associated with actresses such as Mollie Williams and Adelaide Ristori; see *Buffalo (NY) Evening Post*, 13 June 1863, NewsC; *Brooklyn (NY) Daily Eagle*, 8 February 1867, NewsC. An articulation of the attributes of the self-made woman — "the energetic woman" — first appeared in 1869; see *Brooklyn (NY) Union*, 24 February 1869, NewsC.

10. Lane, *Narrative of Lunsford Lane*, 2nd ed., iv; W. E. B. Du Bois, *The Souls of Black Folk: Essays and Sketches* (Chicago: A. C. McClung & Co., 1903), 8, 53.

11. Ibram X. Kendi, *Stamped from the Beginning: The Definitive History of Racist Ideas in America* (New York: Nation Books, 2016), 55–56; Nell Irvin Painter, *The History of White People* (New York: W. W. Norton, 2010), 34–58.

12. Painter, *History of White People*, 104–5.

13. Yue Gu, "Narrative, Life Writing, and Healing: The Therapeutic Functions of Storytelling," *Neohelicon* 45 (2018): 479–89; Hans Render, "Biography in Academia and the Critical Frontier in Life Writing: Where Biography Shifts into Life Writing," in *Theoretical Discussions of Biography*, ed. Hans Renders and Binne de Haan (Boston: Brill, 2014), 169–78; Annette Gordon-Reed, "Writing Early American Lives as Biography," *William and Mary Quarterly* 71 (October 2014): 491–516; Jill Lepore, "Historians Who Love Too Much: Reflections on Microhistory and Biography," *JAH* 88 (June 2001): 129–44.

14. Edward G. Parker, *The Golden Age of American Oratory* (Boston; Whittemore, Niles, and Hill, 1857), 1, 12; Carolyn Eastman, *A Nation of Speechifiers: Making an American Public after the Revolution* (Chicago: University of Chicago Press, 2009); Carolyn Eastman, *The Strange Genius of Mr. O: The World of the United States' First Forgotten Celebrity* (Chapel Hill: University of North Carolina Press, 2021), 6.

15. Parker, *Golden Age of American Oratory*, 12.

16. *The Emancipator and Free American* (New York, NY), 3 November 1842, NYHS; Homer, *The Iliad*; Virgil, *The Aeneid*; Titus Livius, *The History of Rome: Sir Gawain & the Green Knight*, ed. J. R. R. Tolkien and E. V. Gordon (Oxford: Claredon Press, 1925), 1.1.5; Charles Anthon, *The Æneïd of Virgil, with English Notes, Critical and Explanatory, a Metrical Clavis, and an Historical, Geographical, and Mythological Index* (New York: Harper & Bros., 1843), xii-xiii, 892; Carolyn Sale, "Black Aeneas: Race, English Literary History, and the 'Barbarous' Poetics of *Titus Andronicus*," *Shakespeare Quarterly* 62 (Spring 2011): 27–28.

17. *The Liberator*, 3 June 1842.

18. William Shakespeare, *Titus Andronicus*, ed. Barbara A Mowat and Paul Werstine (Washington, DC: Folger Library, n.d.), https:www.folger.edu/explore/shakespeares-works/titus-andronicus/read/, 63, 65, 67; Sale, "Black Aeneas," 28–29.

19. Shakespeare, *Titus Andronicus*, 139; Sale, "Black Aeneas," 29–30.

20. W. E. B. Du Bois, "The Talented Tenth," in *The Negro Problem: A Series of Articles by Representative Negroes of To-Day* (New York: James Pott & Co, 1903), 33; Janice Gassam Asare, "Our Obsession with Black Excellence is Harming Black People," *Forbes*, 1 August 2021, https://www.forbes.com/sites/janicegassam/2021/08/01/our-obsession-with-black-excellence-is-harming-black-people/?sh=32312afb2fd9.

21. W. Sherman Rogers, *The African American Entrepreneur: Then and Now* (Santa Barbara, CA: Praeger, 2010), 1, 31–33; Pat McCrory, "Proclamation, Troop 3432 African American History Month Patch, March 2015," Governors' Papers: Pat McCrory, *North Carolina Digital Collections*, http://digital.ncdcr.gov/cdm/ref/collection/p16062coll5/id/21831.

22. Badia Ahad, "The Burden of Demanding Black Excellence," 16 February 2021, *DAME*, https://www.damemagazine.com/2021/02/16/the-burden-of-demanding-black-excellence/. On my familiarity with Lunsford Lane as a historical person, see Craig Thompson Friend, "Lunsford Lane and Me: Life-Writings and Public Histories of an Enslaved Other," *JER* 39 (Spring 2019): 1–26.

23. Values are estimated as 2023 rates based on considerations found at Alan Eliasen, "Historical Currency Conversions," https://futureboy.us/fsp/dollar.fsp; "$10,000 in 1778 → 2018/Inflation Calculator," US Official Inflation Data, https://www.officialdata.org/1778-dollars-in-2018?amount=10000; Robert Sahr, "Inflation Conversion Factors for years 1774 to estimated 2028," https://liberalarts.oregonstate.edu/spp/polisci/research/inflation-conversion-factors.

24. Elizabeth Stordeur Pryor, *Colored Travelers: Mobility and the Fight for Citizenship before the Civil War* (Chapel Hill: University of North Carolina Press, 2016), 5–6, 10–43; Elizabeth Stordeur Pryor, "The Etymology of Nigger: Resistance, Language and the Politics of Freedom in the Antebellum North," *JER* 36 (Summer 2016): 207.

25. Nancy Coleman, "Why We're Capitalizing Black," *New York Times*, 5 July 2020, https://www.nytimes.com/2020/07/05/insider/capitalized-black.html; American Psychological Association, quoted in Kwame Anthony Appiah, "The Case for Capitalizing the *B* in Black," *The Atlantic*, 18 June 2020, https://www.theatlantic.com/ideas/archive/2020/06/time-to-capitalize-blackand-white/613159; Nell Irvin Painter, "Why 'White' Should Be Capitalized, Too," *Washington Post*, 22 July 2020, https://www.washingtonpost.com/opinions/2020/07/22/why-white-should-be-capitalized/. For an alternative perspective, see Whitney Nell Stewart, "White/white and/or the Absence of the Modifier," *JER* 43 (Spring 2003): 101–8.

Chapter 1

1. William G. Hawkins, *Lunsford Lane; or, Another Helper from North Carolina* (Boston: Crosby & Nichols, 1863), 64, NCC; Frederick Douglass, *My Bondage and My Freedom*, Part 1, *Life as a Slave* (New York: Miller, Orton & Mulligan, 1855), 34, NASN; François Weil, *Family Trees: A History of Genealogy in America* (Cambridge, MA: Harvard University Press, 2013), 29–30, 50.

2. Hawkins, *Lunsford Lane*, 16; Joseph Lane to Joel Lane, 20 October 1763, Halifax County Record of Deeds, 9: 851, SANC; William Pullum to Joel Lane, 5 May 1765, Halifax County Record of Deeds, 9: 548; Florence Mitchell, "Joel Lane and the Enslaved People Who Lived on His Plantation," unpublished manuscript, 2010, Research Collection, Joel Lane Museum House, Raleigh, NC.

3. Marvin L. Michael Kay and Lorin Lee Cary, *Slavery in North Carolina, 1748–1775* (Chapel Hill: University of North Carolina Press, 1995), 26–27, 230–31: Table 1–5, 234–35: Table 1–8; Thomas A. Foster, *Rethinking Rufus: Sexual Violations of Enslaved Men* (Athens: University of Georgia Press, 2019), 63–67.

4. Rodham Atkins to John Haywood, 30 December 1801, EHC; Hawkins, *Lunsford Lane*, 16.

5. Michel-Rolph Trouillot, *Silencing the Past: Power and the Production of History* (Boston: Beacon Press, 1995), 48–49.

6. Weil, *Family Trees*, 30–32, 47–48; John Bennett Boddie, *Southside Virginia Families*, 2 vols. (1955; reprint, Baltimore: Genealogy Publishing Co., 1966), 2: 290–93, 294, SLNC; "Minutes of the Lower House of the North Carolina General Assembly," 7 May 1760, *CRNC*, 6: 383–84; "Minutes of the Lower House of the North Carolina General Assembly," 18 November 1760, *CRNC*, 6: 481–82; "Minutes of the Lower House of the North Carolina General Assembly," 5 December 1769, *CRNC*, 8: 106; Marshall DeLancey Haywood, *Joel Lane, Pioneer and Patriot: A Biographical Sketch* (Raleigh: Alford, Bynum, & Christophers, 1900), 5, NCC.

7. "Minutes of the Lower House of the North Carolina General Assembly," 17 December 1770, *CRNC*, 8: 324; "An Act for erecting part of Johnston, Cumberland, and Orange Counties, into a separate and Distinct County, by the Name of Wake County and St. Margaret's Parish," in "Acts of the General Assembly, 1770–1771," *SRNC*, 23: 819–23; Haywood, *Joel Lane*, 6–7; Elizabeth Reid Murray, *Wake: Capital County of North Carolina*, Vol. 1, *Prehistory through Centennial* (Raleigh: Capital County Publishing Co., 1983), 41–49; will of Joseph Lane, 29 November 1773, Halifax County Record of Wills, 1758–1824, SANC, 2: 43; Boddie, *Southside Virginia Families*, 2: 295; Florence Mitchell, *Joel Lane and His Slaves*, 1:07:43, C-SPAN, 3 February 2011, http://www.c-span.org/video/?297837-1/joel-lane-slaves; will of Joel Lane, 22 October 1794, June term 1795, Minutes Docket 1777–1868, Wake County Court of Pleas and Quarter Sessions, 3: 69–70, SANC; inventory of the Estate of Mary Lane, dec'd, 19 December 1799, Wake County: Records of Wills, Inventories, Settlements of Estates, 1794–1802, 4: 38, SANC; Hawkins, *Lunsford Lane*, 16. Joel Lane held thirty-two slaves in 1794, but paid taxes on only seventeen of them, indicating that the rest were either under twelve years of age or over fifty years of age, although the latter appears unlikely; see Tax List for 1794, Wake County Tax Lists: 1781–1860, SANC.

8. *State v. Samuel*, 19 N.C. 177 (N.C. 1836), in *Reports of Cases at Law Argued and Determined in the Supreme Court of North Carolina, from December Term, 1836, to December Term, 1837, Both Inclusive*, ed. Thomas P. Devereux and William H. Battle, 2 vols. (Raleigh: Turner & Hughes, 1838), 2: 183, IntArch.

9. "An Act Concerning Servants & Slaves," in "Acts of the North Carolina General Assembly, 1715–1716," *SRNC*, 23: 62–66. On the evolution of the Black code in North Carolina, see Rosser Howard Taylor, "Humanizing the Slave Code of North Carolina," *NCHR* 2 (July 1925): 328–29; Ernest James Clark Jr., "Aspects of the North Carolina Slave Code, 1715–1860," *NCHR* 39 (Spring 1962): 148–64. Traditionally, historians have used "slave codes" for laws passed in colonial America and the Southern United States before 1865, and "Black codes" for laws passed in Northern states before 1865 and Southern states following Reconstruction. Although a term used at the time, "slave code" is problematic, not only because many of the laws addressed and applied to all Black folks whether enslaved or not, but also because it was a term purposely devised to "other" free Black people as noncitizens.

10. "Minutes of the Upper House of the North Carolina General Assembly," 16 August 1740, *CRNC*, 4: 542; "An Act Concerning Servants and Slaves," in "Acts of the North Carolina General Assembly, 1741," *SRNC*, 23: 191–204, quote from 201; "An Act directing the trial of Slaves, committing capital crimes; and for the more effectual punishing conspiracies and insurrections of them; and for the better government of Negros, Mulattos, and Indians, bond or free," May 1723, in William Waller Hening, ed., *The Statutes at Large; Being a Collection of all the Laws of Virginia*, 12 vols. (Richmond: privately printed, 1820), 4: 132, Rare Books Room, Law Library, University of North Carolina at Chapel Hill.

11. "An Act Concerning Servants and Slaves," 23: 191–204.

12. "An additional Act to an Act concerning servants and slaves," in "Acts of the North Carolina General Assembly, 1753," *SRNC*, 23: 388–90; "An Additional Act to an Act, intitled, An Act concerning Servants and Slaves," in "Acts of the General Assembly, 1758," *SRNC*, 23: 488–89; Alan D. Watson, "North Carolina Slave Courts, 1715–1785," *NCHR* 60 (January 1983): 24–36; Sally E. Hadden, *Slave Patrols: Law and Violence in Virginia and the Carolinas* (Cambridge, MA: Harvard University Press, 2001), 34–38.

13. Halifax County Deed Book 8: 38, 103, 163, Register of Deeds, Halifax County Courthouse, Halifax, NC; Boddie, *Southside Virginia Families*, 2: 294–95; "Minutes of the North Carolina Governor's Council," 11 October 1749, *CRNC*, 4: 966; "An additional Act to an Act concerning servants and slaves," 23: 388–90; "Report by the Committee of both Houses of the North Carolina General Assembly concerning public claims," 19 December 1758, *CRNC*, 5: 982; will of Joseph Lane, 6 December 1757, North Carolina Original Wills, 1663–1790, Secretary of State Papers, SANC; W. C. Allen, *History of Halifax County* (Boston: Cornhill Co., 1918), 11, 12, NCC.

14. Accounts of the United States with North Carolina, Revolutionary War Accounts, Treasurer and Comptroller Records, Military Papers, Secretary of State Papers, SANC, H: 46; Joel Lane, December 1780, April 1781, April 1782, and June 1782, Revolutionary Vouchers, Military Papers; Wake County Warrants, Plats, etc., file nos. 111, 112, 113, 114, 356, 425, 426 (1778), also 116, 132, 133, 525, 614 (1779), and 468 (1780), Land Grant Section, Secretary of State Papers; "Minutes of the North Carolina Senate," 14 July 1781, *SRNC*, 17: 876 and 18 April 1783, *SRNC*, 20: 130; "Minutes of the North Carolina House of Commons," 14 July 1781, *SRNC*, 17: 973; Jerry L. Cross, "Chameleon on the Crabtree: The Story of Joel Lane," 13, 14–15, 19, 24, manuscript, NCC. The £15,000 reimbursements are indicative of the inflation that struck the states late in the war; see Haywood, *Joel Lane*, 14–15.

15. "Minutes of the North Carolina Senate," 22 December 1777, *SRNC*, 12: 242, 243; "Minutes of the North Carolina Senate," 26 November 1787, *SRNC*, 20: 328; "Minutes of the North Carolina Senate," 17 November 1788, *SRNC*, 20: 514.

16. "Minutes of the North Carolina Constitutional Convention at Hillsborough," 21 July–4 August 1788, *SRNC*, 22: 28–29; "An Act to confirm the proceedings of the Commissioners appointed under an act of the last General Assembly," in *The Acts of the General Assembly of the State of North-Carolina Passed during the Sessions held in the Years 1791, 1972, 1793, and 1794* (New Bern: Francois X. Martin, 1795), 48, NCC; "Report of the commission to locate the capital," 2 and 5 April 1792, 6 June 1792, Miscellaneous Papers, Secretary of State Papers, SANC; Murray, *Wake*, 78–84; US Census, 1790: North Carolina.

17. Will of Joel Lane, 22 October 1794; inventory of the Estate of Joel Lane, June 1795, Wake County: Records of Wills, Inventories, Settlements of Estates, 1794–1802, 4: 195–97; Frances Holloway Wynne, *Abstract of Record of Wills, Inventories, Settlements of Estates,*

1771–1802: Wake County, North Carolina (Fairfax, VA: privately published, 1985), 118, 150–51, SLNC.

18. Will of Joel Lane, 22 October 1794.

19. Will of Joel Lane, 22 October 1794; *North-Carolina Journal* (Halifax), 15 August 1796, NewsC.

20. "An Act for the Better Care of Orphans, and Security and Management of their Estates," 1762, *SRNC*, 23: 577–83; will of Joel Lane, 22 October 1794; Haywood, *Joel Lane*, 19–20. Between the writing of the 1794 will and the 1795 inventory, Jack, the last of Joel Lane's original enslaved laborers, disappeared: hence, the discrepancy in numbers; see will of Joel Lane, 22 October 1794; inventory of the Estate of Joel Lane.

21. List of debts collected by Henry Lane, n.d., Joel and Mary Lane folder, Wake County Estate Records, 1771–1952, SANC; John Lane v. John Hinton, June 1800, Joel and Mary Lane folder; *John Lane v. John Hinton*, December term 1800–1801, Minutes Docket 1777–1868.

22. Guardianship agreement, Wake County Court, 20 September 1797, copy, Research Collection, Joel Lane Museum House; *North-Carolina Journal*, 22 October 1798; Nathaniel Jones to Martin Lane, 7 March 1800, bk. R: 60, WCRD.

23. Estate of Col. Joel Lane dec'd, 1798, Wake County: Records of Wills, Inventories, Settlements of Estates, 1794–1802, 4: 54–57; bond for Jimboy, 8 January 1799, Joel and Mary Lane folder; bond for Jimboy, 8 January 1800, Joel and Mary Lane folder; bond for Jeffrey, 8 January 1804, Joel and Mary Lane folder; bond for Jeffrey, 8 January 1805, Joel and Mary Lane folder; *State Gazette of North-Carolina* (New Bern), 29 November 1787, NewsC; *Hall's Wilmington (NC) Gazette*, 15 November 1798, North Carolina Newspapers, DigitalNC, https://www.digitalnc.org/collections/newspapers/; Linda Baumgarten, *What Clothes Reveal: The Language of Clothing in Colonial and Federal America* (Williamsburg, VA: Colonial Williamsburg Foundation, 2002), 134–35, 247 n74.

24. "A Bill to establish Raleigh as the capital of the state, to set forth and name the public squares, and to provide for the construction of a building to house the General Assembly and the state officers on Union Square," 31 December 1792, House Bills/Senate Bills: November 20–December 14, General Assembly Session Records, November 1792–January 1793, SANC; James Williamson to John Haywood, 22 June 1797, bk. Q: 366–67, WCRD.

25. *Heads of Families at the First Census of the United States Taken in the Year 1790: North Carolina* (Washington, DC: Government Printing Office, 1908), 193; Christine L. Ingram Hockaday and William G. Koch, eds., *The Slave Deeds of New Hanover County, North Carolina*, Series 1: *1734–1820* (Wilmington, NC: Cape Fear Community College, 2014), 44; Alfred Moore Waddell, *A History of New Hanover County and the Lower Cape Fear Region*, Vol 1, *1723–1800* (Wilmington, NC: n. p., 1909), 55.

26. Williamson to Haywood, 22 June 1797; John Haywood to James Ingles, 18 June 1800, bk. Q: 367, WCRD; US Census, 1800: Wake County, NC; Murray, *Wake*, 117; John Haywood to Eliza Haywood, 26 June 1798, EHC; John Haywood to Eliza Haywood, 12 July 1798, EHC; Jane Williams to Eliza Haywood, 16 August 1798, EHC.

27. Jane Williams to Eliza Haywood, 28 October 1798, EHC; Jane Williams to Eliza Haywood, 5 November 1798, EHC.

28. *Weekly Raleigh (NC) Register*, 2 February 1802, NewsC; John Haywood to Eliza Haywood, 22 February 1799, EHC; bond for Jimboy, 8 January 1799.

29. William R. Davie to John Haywood, 25 April 1799, EHC; John Haywood to Eliza Haywood, 19 March 1799, EHC; James H. Craig, *The Arts and Crafts in North Carolina,*

1699–1840 (Winston-Salem, NC: Museum of Early Southern Decorative Arts, 1965), 293, 304, 307.

30. Haywood to Haywood, 22 February 1799; Richard L. Bushman, *The Refinement of America: Persons, Houses, Cities* (New York: Alfred A. Knopf, 1992), 127–31.

31. John Haywood to Eliza Haywood, 10 April 1799, EHC. On the sexual commodification of enslaved women, see Edward E. Baptist, "'Cuffy,' 'Fancy Maids,' and 'One-Eyed Men': Rape, Commodification, and the Domestic Slave Trade in the United States," *American Historical Review* 106 (December 2001): 1619–50; Daina Ramey Berry, *The Price for Their Pound of Flesh: The Value of the Enslaved, from Womb to Grave, in the Building of a Nation* (Boston: Beacon Press, 2017), 78–83.

32. John Haywood to Eliza Haywood, 6 February 1799, EHC.

33. Haywood to Haywood, 10 April 1799; Richard Dobbs Speight to John Haywood, 27 May 1798, EHC; Lawrence E. Abbott Jr., John D. Davis, and Paul A. Russo, *N.C. Museum of History Project: Text Excavations in an Urban Setting*, March 1989, 6, North Carolina Office of State Archaeology, Raleigh.

34. Haywood to Haywood, 10 April 1799; John Haywood to Eliza Haywood, 23 April 1799, EHC; Jane Williams to Eliza Haywood, 28 May 1799, EHC.

35. Lane, *Narrative of Lunsford Lane*, 2nd ed., 4–5.

36. Benjamin B. Smith to Lunsford Lane, bill of sale, 25 April 1842, reprinted in Lane, *Narrative of Lunsford Lane*, 2nd ed., 53–54.

37. Will of William Haywood, 25 November 1779; Lane, *Narrative of Lunsford Lane*, 2nd ed., 5; Haywood to Haywood, 6 February 1799; James Glasgow to John Haywood, 16 August 1799, bk. Q: 471–72, WCRD; John Haywood to Sherwood Haywood, 8 February 1800, bk. 5: 659–60, WCRD; Smith to Lane, 25 April 1842, 53–54. Lunsford confirmed that his maternal grandmother lived on the Haywood estate with Clarissa and him and that she attended the Baptist church; *Christian Watchman* (Boston, MA), 17 May 1852, AAS.

38. Michael Olmert, *Kitchens, Smokehouses, and Privies: Outbuildings and the Architecture of Daily Life in the Eighteenth-Century Mid-Atlantic* (Ithaca: Cornell University Press, 2009), 23–73; Alexandra A. Chan, *Slavery in the Age of Reason: Archaeology at a New England Farm* (Knoxville: University of Tennessee Press, 2007), 197–226.

39. Hugh Jones, *The Present State of Virginia: A Particular and Short Account of the Indian, English, and Negro Inhabitants of that Colony* (1724; reprint, New York: Joseph Sabin, 1865), 23; John Michael Vlach, *Back of the Great House: The Architecture of Plantation Slavery* (Chapel Hill: University of North Carolina Press, 1993), 43–44; Olmert, *Kitchens, Smokehouses, and Privies*, 23–73.

40. US Census, 1800: Wake County, NC; US Census, 1830: Wake County, NC; will of Philomen Hawkins, 22 July 1801, Hawkins Family Papers, 1738–1895, SHC; Manly Wade Wellman, *The County of Warren, North Carolina, 1586–1917* (Chapel Hill: University of North Carolina Press, 1959), 57, 75; Hawkins, *Lunsford Lane*, 281.

41. William Haywood to John Haywood, 18 December 1799, EHC; inventory of the Estate of Mary Lane, dec'd, 19 December 1799; Mary Lane Estate Sale, 21 April 1800, Wake County Record Book 5: 216, SANC; "Account of Sales of the Estate of Mary Lane dec'd," 27 February 1800, Wake County: Wills, 1771–1966, 4: 38, 216, SANC.

42. "Account of Sales of the Estate of Mary Lane dec'd," 4: 216.

43. *Raleigh Minerva*, 5 January 1802; bond of payment to Martin Lane, 8 January 1799, Joel and Mary Lane folder; Martin Lane to William Hill, 20 October 1807, bk. U: 285,

WCRD; Thomas Lane to William Shaw, 20 June 1807, bk. U: 147, WCRD; Thomas Lane to John Jackson, 14 February 1807, bk. U: 10, WCRD; Thomas Lane to Allen Gilchrist, 13 December 1808, bk. V: 49–51, WCRD; Thomas Lane power of attorney to Allen Gilchrist, 22 November 1807, bk. U: 232, WCRD; *Weekly Raleigh Register*, 15 December 1801.

44. Nathaniel Lane to John Haywood, 22 November 1800, bk. Q: 520, WCRD; Jane Williams to Eliza Haywood, 2 May 1812, EHC. Nathaniel Lane accepted a monetary loss in selling Cate, Davy, and Montford. He was in some financial difficulties which precipitated the sale; see Isaac Hutchins to Theophilus Hunter/State of North Carolina, 12 January 1801, bk. Q: 487, WCRD; Isaac Hutchins to Edmond Lane, 19 February 1801, bk. Q: 489, WCRD; Nathaniel Lane and Benjamin Pulliam to Theophilus Hunter, 23 June 1801, bk. Q: 491–93, WCRD.

45. Joseph Tagert to John Haywood, 26 May 1796, EHC; Robert Donnell to John Haywood, 3 November 1797, EHC.

46. John Davis to John Haywood, 21 January 1800, EHC; Theophilus Hunter to John Haywood, bill for March–April 1799 and February–March 1800, 21 July 1800, EHC; *Raleigh Minerva*, 3 June 1800; John Haywood to Nathaniel Jones, Isaac Hunter, and Isham Symms, 16 June 1800, EHC; John Haywood to John Ingles, 20 June 1800, bk. O: 367–68, WCRD; Linda Mackie Griggs, "Haywood Hall," unpublished manuscript, 3 vols., November 1984, 1: 182, SANC.

47. John Haywood to Mr. Young, November 1801, EHC; James Mairs to John Haywood, bill for January 1799–October 1801, EHC; Andrew McDonough to John Haywood, bill for October 1801, EHC; Griggs, "Haywood Hall," 1: 10–12.

48. John Haywood to Eliza Haywood, 4 November 1801, EHC.

49. "Stable, Haywood Hall, 211 New Bern Ave., Raleigh, Wake County, NC," Survey HABS NC-229 RAL 8, sheet 20, Historic American Buildings Survey, LOC; "Kitchen, Haywood Hall, 211 New Bern Ave., Raleigh, Wake County, NC," HABS NC-229 RAL 8, sheet 19, Historic American Buildings Survey.

50. "Schedule of Slaves in being at S. Haywood's death & in his actual possession," *William A. Blount and Others v. John D. Hawkins and Others*, 57 N.C. 162 (December 1858), Supreme Court Original Cases, 1800–1809, SANC; "Schedule of Slaves of the estate of S Haywood," *William A. Blount and Others v. John D. Hawkins and Others*, 57 N.C. 162; listings of shoe purchases for slaves, 1839, 1843, 1845, Account Books, vols. 16 and 18, EHC; Frances Holloway Wynne, "Slaves Named in the Inventory of the Estates of Sherwood Haywood: Wake County, North Carolina," *Journal of the Afro-American Historical and Genealogical Society* 6 (1985): 34–35.

51. Herbert G. Gutman, *The Black Family in Slavery and Freedom, 1750–1925* (New York: Vintage Books, 1976), 241–44; John C. Inscoe, "Carolina Slave Names: An Index to Acculturation," *Journal of Southern History* 49 (November 1983): 527.

52. Jane Williams to Eliza Haywood, 18 August 1801, EHC; John Haywood to Eliza Haywood, 22 November 1801, EHC: James Read to John Haywood, 6 April 1801, EHC.

53. John Haywood to unknown, n.d., EHC.

54. Lucy D. Bryan to Clarissa Lane, 23 February 1858, reprinted in Hawkins, *Lunsford Lane*, 281–83; Williams to Haywood, 2 May 1812; Williams to Haywood, 18 August 1801; Jane Williams to Eliza Haywood, 11 June 1801, EHC; Sally McMillen, *Motherhood in the Old South: Pregnancy, Childbirth, and Infant Rearing* (Baton Rouge: Louisiana State University Press, 1990), 5–6.

55. Eliza Haywood to Jane Williams, 18 March 1802, EHC.

56. John Haywood personal notes, 31 December 1791, EHC; Tax List for 1799, Wake County Tax Lists: 1781–1860; John Haywood to Jezekiah Spain, 18 November 1817, EHC; US Census, 1800: Wake County, NC; Thomas Brown to John Haywood, 22 September 1801, EHC; Cullen Darman to John Haywood, 24 November 1801, EHC; Atkins to Haywood, 30 December 1801; Tax List for 1802, Wake County Tax Lists: 1781–1860; Eliza Haywood to Jane Williams, 20 December 1803, EHC.

57. Tax List for 1802; Haywood to Haywood, 8 February 1800; John Harvey to Stephen Haywood, 10 October 1801, bk. R: 177, WCRD; *Weekly Raleigh Register*, 10 December 1799; US Census, 1800: Wake County, NC; Zella Armstrong, comp., *Notable Southern Families*, 2 vols. (Chattanooga, TN: Lookout Publishing, 1933), 2: 152–56, SLNC; Williams to Haywood, 28 October 1798; John Harvey to Stephen N. Haywood, 14 December 1801, bk. R: 177, WCRD; Stephen Haywood to Rodham Atkins, 8 August 1799, bk. Q: 214, WCRD; Rodham Atkins to Hogg & Adams, 19 June 1800, bk. Q: 214–15, WCRD.

58. "Plan of the City of Raleigh, First Published in the Year 1834" (Raleigh: Walter, Hughes and Co., 1834), NCC; Williams to Haywood, 28 October 1798; *Weekly Raleigh Register*, 10 December 1799; Lane, *Narrative of Lunsford Lane*, 2nd ed., 5–6; Murray, *Wake*, 274.

Chapter 2

1. *Weekly Raleigh (NC) Register*, 9 May 1803, NewsC; Jane Williams to Eliza Haywood, 27–28 May 1803, EHC; Rebecca Christine Williams to Ferebee Hall, 26 October 1803, EHC; Marshall DeLancey Haywood, "John Haywood," in *Biographical History of North Carolina from Colonial Times to the Present*, ed. Samuel A'Court Ashe, Stephen B. Weeks, and Charles L. Van Noppen, 8 vols. (Greensboro, NC: Charles L. Van Noppen, 1906), 6: 287–88; Vance E. Swift, "Haywood Pioneered Using Chloroform," *The State* 47 (November 1979): 21.

2. William G. Hawkins, *Lunsford Lane; or, Another Helper from North Carolina* (Boston: Crosby & Nichols, 1863), 281, NCC.

3. Lunsford Lane, *The Narrative of Lunsford Lane, Formerly of Raleigh, N.C. Embracing an Account of His Early Life, the Redemption by Purchase of Himself and Family from Slavery, and His Banishment from the Place of His Birth for the Crime of Wearing a Colored Skin. Published by Himself*, 2nd ed. (Boston: J. G. Torrey, 1842), 5, AAS.

4. Lane, *Narrative of Lunsford Lane*, 2nd ed., 6.

5. US Census, 1800; US Census, 1820; US Census, 1830; US Census, 1840; US Census, 1850; Patrick Hanks, *Dictionary of American Family Names: G-N* (New York: Oxford University Press, 2013), 474; "Minutes of the North Carolina Constitutional Convention at Fayetteville," 16–22 November 1789, SRNC, 22: 37, 48; *North-Carolina Journal* (Halifax), 6 August 1794, 29 May 1797, NewsC; US Census, 1790: Edgecombe County, NC; will of Nicholas Long, 13 June 1787, in Charles Hughes Hamlin, comp., *They Went Thataway*, 3 vols. (1965; reprint, Baltimore: Genealogical Publishing Co., 1985), 2: 7–8; John Bennett Boddie, *Southside Virginia Families*, 2 vols. (1955; reprint, Baltimore: Genealogy Publishing Co., 1966), 1: 81; Cadwallader Jones, *A Genealogical History* (Columbia, SC: Ye Bryan Printing Co., 1900), 11, 18–19, SLNC; Mary Polk Branch, *Memoirs of a Southern Woman "Within the Lines"* (Chicago: Joseph G. Branch Publishing Co., 1912), 58, SLNC.

6. "Minutes of the North Carolina House of Commons," 2 December 1790, SRNC, 21: 1068; *Weekly Raleigh (NC) Register*, 12 November 1807, NewsC; Hawkins, *Lunsford Lane*, 16–17.

7. *Rebecca and Mary Long v. Lunsford Long's Ex'r,* July 1811, in A. D. Murphy, *Reports of Cases Argued and Adjudged in the Supreme Court of North-Carolina from the Year 1811 to the Year 1813, Inclusive, and at July Term, 1818,* 2 vols. (Raleigh: J. Gales & Son, 1826), 2: 19–21, IntArch.

8. "Stable, Haywood Hall, 211 New Bern Ave., Raleigh, Wake County, NC," Survey HABS NC-229 RAL 8, sheet 20, Historic American Buildings Survey, LOC; "Kitchen, Haywood Hall, 211 New Bern Ave., Raleigh, Wake County, NC," HABS NC-229 RAL 8, sheet 19, Historic American Buildings Survey.

9. Entry for 27 April 1828, Minutes 1812–1832, First Baptist Church, Vol. 1, 1828, 5, microfilm, Special Collections & Archives Reading Room, Z. Smith Reynolds Library, Wake Forest University, Winston-Salem, NC; W. Glenn Jonas Jr., *Nurturing the Vision: First Baptist Church, Raleigh, 1812–2012* (Macon: Mercer University Press, 2012), 87.

10. Lane, *Narrative of Lunsford Lane,* 2nd ed., 7–8.

11. *North-Carolina Journal,* 12 February 1798.

12. "An Act Concerning Slaves and Free Persons of Color: Revised Code—No. 105" (Raleigh: General Assembly, 1831), # 38, NCC; *North-Carolina Journal,* 7 May 1798; Kemp P. Battle, "The Trial of James Glasgow and the Supreme Court of North Carolina," *North Carolina Booklet* 3 (May 1903): 5–11, SLNC.

13. Public Notice, 29 January 1798, Governor's Papers: Ashe, SANC; Basil Gaither and Samuel Purviance to William R. Davie, 28 June 1799, "Glasgow Land Frauds, Vol I, 1798–1800," Secretary of State Papers, SANC; Governor Samuel Ashe to General Assembly, 18 December 1797, Governor's Messages, General Assembly Session Records, November–December 1797, SANC; *Weekly Raleigh Register,* 31 December 1799; Elizabeth Reid Murray, *Wake: Capital County of North Carolina,* Vol. 1, *Prehistory through Centennial* (Raleigh: Capital County Publishing Co., 1983), 404.

14. "Petition of John Peter Bird of Raleigh," 11 December 1798, Select Committee Reports, General Assembly Session Records, November–December 1798, SANC.

15. US Census, 1800: Wake County, NC. Bird moved to Chatham County, where he died in February 1820; see Inventory of the Estate of Peter Bird, 1 December 1820, Orange County District and Probate Courts, SANC.

16. Lane, *Narrative of Lunsford Lane,* 2nd ed., 7–8; John Hope Franklin, *The Free Negro in North Carolina, 1790–1860* (Chapel Hill: University of North Carolina Press, 1943), 54–55.

17. James H. Broussard, *The Southern Federalists, 1800–1816* (Baton Rouge: Louisiana State University, 1978), 287–90; Mary L. Thornton, "Public Printing in North Carolina, 1749–1815," *NCHR* 21 (July 1944): 181–202; Robert N. Elliott Jr., *The Raleigh Register, 1799–1863* (Chapel Hill: University of North Carolina Press, 1955), 16–18.

18. *Raleigh (NC) Minerva,* 19 October 1802, NewsC. "Cousin German" references a first cousin.

19. Thomas Jefferson, *Notes on the State of Virginia* (Philadelphia: Prichard & Hall, 1788), 148, Rare Book Collection, Wilson Library, University of North Carolina, Chapel Hill; Winifred Gales and Joseph Gales, "Reminiscences," 139, Gales Family Papers, SHC; Scott King-Owen, "To 'Write Down the Republican Administration': William Boylan and the Federalist Party in North Carolina, 1800–1805" *NCHR* 89 (April 2012): 155–83. Jefferson probably derived the notion from John Locke who once wrote that "if History lie not," African "women have conceived by drills"; see *Locke's Essay Concerning Human Understanding,* annotated by Alexander Campbell Fraser, 2 vols. (New York: Dover Publications, 1959), 2: 75.

20. Hawkins, *Lunsford Lane*, 19.

21. Lane, *Narrative of Lunsford Lane*, 2nd ed., 52; *Weekly Raleigh Register*, 2 March 1802, 16 March 1802, 8 August 1803, 17 May 1810; *Raleigh Minerva*, 17 August 1802, 11 April 1803; Sergio A. Lussana, *My Brother Slaves: Friendship, Masculinity, and Resistance in the Antebellum South* (Lexington: University Press of Kentucky, 2016), 114–24.

22. Thomas Blount to John Gray Blount, 28 June 1802, in *The John Gray Blount Papers*, ed. Alice Barnwell Keith and William H. Masterson, 3 vols. (Raleigh: State Department of Archives and History, 1965), 3: 516–17; *The Evening Post* (New York, NY), 21 June 1802, NewsC; *The Times* (Philadelphia, PA), 9 August 1802, HSP; "An Act Concerning Slaves and Free Persons of Color: Revised Code—No. 105," # 36–40; Freddie L. Parker, *Running for Freedom: Slave Runaways in North Carolina, 1775–1840* (New York: Routledge, 1993); Guion Griffis Johnson, *Ante-Bellum North Carolina* (Chapel Hill: University of North Carolina Press, 1937), 510–13; R. H. Taylor, "Slave Conspiracies in North Carolina," *NCHR* 5 (January 1928): 31–32; Douglas R. Egerton, *Gabriel's Rebellion: The Virginia Slave Conspiracies of 1800 & 1802* (Chapel Hill: University of North Carolina Press, 1993), 129–31.

23. S. Collure to John Haywood, 14 July 1805, EHC.

24. Hawkins, *Lunsford Lane*, 19. On runaways who harbored in Southern towns, see Viola Franziska Muller, *Escape to the City: Fugitive Slaves in the Antebellum Urban South* (Chapel Hill: University of North Carolina Press, 2022).

25. Figures come from surveying the *Weekly Raleigh Register*, *Raleigh Minerva*, and *North-Carolina Star* (Raleigh), NewsC.

26. Tax List for 1800, Wake County Tax Lists: 1781–1860, SANC; US Census, 1800: Wake County, NC; Lisa C. Tolbert, *Constructing Townscapes: Space and Society in Antebellum Tennessee* (Chapel Hill: University of North Carolina Press, 1999), 195–96. The State did not require taxes on enslaved children under twelve, so tax lists do not necessarily align with census records. For example, in 1800, John Haywood listed twenty-nine enslaved people with the census taker but only twenty-four with the tax collector, meaning that there were five younger enslaved people, all on his Wake County farm. Sherwood Haywood enrolled twenty-four enslaved with the census, with the same number on his tax rosters, which means that Lunsford, born three years later, was among the first children born into enslavement on his Raleigh estate.

27. George M. Stroud, *Sketch of the Laws Relating to Slavery in the Several States of the United States of America*, 2nd ed. (Philadelphia: Kimber and Sharpless, 1827), 97, IntArch.

28. Lane, *Narrative of Lunsford Lane*, 2nd ed., 6; Bertis D. English, *Civil Wars, Civil Beings, and Civil Rights in Alabama's Black Belt: A History of Perry County* (Tuscaloosa: University of Alabama Press, 2020), 86–90.

29. Lane, *Narrative of Lunsford Lane*, 2nd ed., 13; Hawkins, *Lunsford Lane*, 18.

30. Jane Williams to Eliza Haywood, 4 January 1816, EHC; M. M. Goflenny to Betsy John Haywood, undated, EHC; Ann E. Gales to Eliza Haywood, undated, EHC; Abigail Jacobsen and J. Dustin Williams, "Back Shelf: Tales from the Archives—Prince Family Nurseries," *Bulletin of the Hunt Institute for Botanical Documentation* 21 (Spring 2009): 4–7; William Prince Jr., *A Short Treatise on Horticulture* (New York: T&J Swords, 1828), IntArch; Betsy John Haywood to George W. Haywood, 4 January 1839, EHC; Linda Mackie Griggs, "Haywood Hall," unpublished manuscript, 3 vols., November 1984, 3: Appendix N: "Plants and Seeds Acquired or Ordered for the Garden, 1806–1832," SANC.

31. Thomas Haywood to William Prince, November 1827, EHC.

32. James Read to John Haywood, 6 November 1800, EHC; Haywood to Williams, 18 March 1802; Jane Williams to Rebecca Moore, 11 December 1804, EHC; Ferebee Hall to Jane Williams, 11 February 1806, EHC.

33. Jane Williams to Eliza Haywood, 5 January 1810, EHC; Jane Williams to Eliza Haywood, 29 May 1812, EHC; Williams to Haywood, 4 January 1816. Also, see Jane Williams to Eliza Haywood, 20 December 1812, EHC.

34. John Haywood to George Washington Haywood, 7 August 1818, EHC; John Haywood to Fabius Haywood, 1 July 1826, EHC.

35. John Haywood to Eliza Haywood, 28 June 1824, EHC; will of John Haywood, November 1827, Wills and Estate Papers, Wake County, 1663–1978, SANC.

36. Entries for 12 March 1819, 11 September 1819, 1 October 1819, and 30 November 1819, E. Haywood Account Book, Vol. 2, EHC; A. Moore to Jane Williams, 15 January 1818, EHC; John Hill to John Haywood, 26 November 1820.

37. Lane, *Narrative of Lunsford Lane*, 2nd ed., 6; Lucy D. Bryan to Clarissa Lane, 23 February 1858, reprinted in Hawkins, *Lunsford Lane*, 281–83.

38. *Christian Reflector* (Worcester, MA), 3 August 1842, AAS; Stephanie Jones-Rogers, *They Were Her Property: White Women as Slave Owners in the American South* (New Haven, CT: Yale University Press, 2019), 16–17; Wilma King, *Stolen Childhood: Slave Youth in Nineteenth-Century America* (Bloomington: University of Indiana Press, 1995), 107–49; Katherine Fishburn, *The Problem of Embodiment in Early African American Narrative* (Westport, CT: Greenwood Press, 1997), 100.

39. Lane, *Narrative of Lunsford Lane*, 2nd ed., 7–8.

40. *North-Carolina Star*, 26 April 1816; "The Goodman Family," *The Pathfinder* 6 (2001): 7–8; *Weekly Raleigh Register*, 27 June 1817; Murray, *Wake*, 244 n46; J. Collin contract with John Haywood, 5 July 1820, EHC; William Sneed to John Haywood, 26 October 1824, EHC; Nancy Venture Smith to John Haywood, 5 February 1825, EHC; Catherine W. Bishir, "Black Builders in North Carolina," in *Southern Built: American Architecture, Regional Practice* (Charlottesville: University of Virginia Press, 2009), 72, 79.

41. "Funds for Candidates for the Ministry," *Catalogue of Princeton University: One Hundred and Sixty-Fourth Year, 1910–1911* (Princeton, NJ: The University, 1910), 370, HT; Helen Chavis Othow, *John Chavis: African American Patriot, Preacher, Teacher, and Mentor (1763–1838)* (Jefferson, NC: McFarland & Co., 2001), 52–58; *Weekly Raleigh Register*, 14 July 1806, 25 August 1808; Stephen B. Weeks, "John Chavis: Antebellum Negro Preacher and Teacher," *The Southern Workman* 63 (February 1914): 102, NCC; Franklin, *The Free Negro in North Carolina*, 170–73.

42. William E. Roberts to John Chavis, 28 June 1815, bk. 3: 336–37, WCRD; John Chavis to John Haywood, 17 May 1822, John Haywood Papers, 1790–1903, SHC; John Chavis to John Haywood, October 1817, John Haywood Papers; John Chavis to John Haywood, 3 July 1822, in *The Papers of Willie Person Mangum*, ed. Henry Thomas Shanks, 5 vols. (Winston-Salem: Winston Printing Co., 1950), 1: 41–42; John Chavis to John Haywood, 1 April 1823, EHC; John Haywood to Willie P. Mangum, 15 October 1824, in Shanks, ed., *Papers of Willie Person Mangum*, 1: 155–56; John Chavis to Willie P. Mangum, 28 January 1825, in Shanks, ed., *Papers of Willie Person Mangum*, 1: 184–85; Othow, *John Chavis*, 72–73.

43. Chavis to Mangum, 3 September 1831, 1: 412; John Chavis to Willie P. Mangum, 10 March 1832, in Shanks, ed., *Papers of Willie Person Mangum*, 1: 507; Shanks, ed., *Papers of Willie Person Mangum*, 1: 41n45.

Chapter 3

1. Entry for 7 March 1812, Minutes 1812–1832, First Baptist Church, Vol. 1, 1828, 5, micro-film, Special Collections & Archives Reading Room, Z. Smith Reynolds Library, Wake Forest University, Winston-Salem, NC; *First Baptist Church, Wilmington and Morgan Streets, Raleigh, NC, 1812–1962* (Raleigh: Irving-Swain Press, 1962); W. Glenn Jonas Jr., *Nurturing the Vision: First Baptist Church, Raleigh, 1812–2012* (Macon: Mercer University Press, 2012), 24; Moses N. Amis, *Historical Raleigh, with Sketches of Wake County (from 1771) and Its Important Towns*, rev. ed. (Raleigh: Commercial Printing Co., 1913), 102, SLNC.

2. William G. Hawkins, *Lunsford Lane; or, Another Helper from North Carolina* (Boston: Crosby & Nichols, 1863), 18, NCC; *Christian Watchman and Reflector* (Boston, MA), 17 May 1857, AAS; *Sketches of Church Histories in North Carolina: Addresses and Papers by Clergymen and Laymen of the Dioceses of North and East Carolina* (Wilmington, NC: Wm. L. De Rosset Jr., 1892), 276–77, IntArch; N. Brooks Graebner, "The Episcopal Church and Race in Nineteenth-Century North Carolina," *Anglican and Episcopal History* 78 (March 2009): 86–87.

3. Lunsford Lane, *The Narrative of Lunsford Lane, Formerly of Raleigh, N.C. Embracing an Account of His Early Life, the Redemption by Purchase of Himself and Family from Slavery, and His Banishment from the Place of His Birth for the Crime of Wearing a Colored Skin. Published by Himself*, 2nd ed. (Boston: J. G. Torrey, 1842), 20–21, AAS; Hawkins, *Lunsford Lane*, 65; Ephesians 6:5, King James Version; Luke 12:47, King James Version.

4. *Raleigh (NC) Minerva*, 9 January 1820, NewsC; *The National Gazette* (Philadelphia, PA), 11 September 1822, HSP. As for Crudup's own enslavement of humans, the records for 1820 are unrevealing, but he owned thirty-nine laborers by 1830; see US Census, 1830: Wake County, NC.

5. *Weekly Raleigh (NC) Register*, 29 October 1824, NewsC.

6. Hawkins, *Lunsford Lane*, 64.

7. "Comptroller's Reports on the Treasurer's Accounts," 1 July 1790, SRNC, 21: 869–70; "Minutes of the North Carolina House of Commons," 4 January 1787, SRNC, 18: 444.

8. Archibald DeBow Murphey to William Polk, 22 January 1822, Polk-Yeatman Papers, SHC; *Hillsborough (NC) Recorder*, 29 November 1820, NewsC; William K. Boyd, *History of North Carolina*, Vol. 2, *The Federal Period, 1783–1860* (New York: Lewis Publishing Company, 1919), 109–13.

9. John Haywood to John Gray Blount, 8 August 1794, in *The John Gray Blount Papers*, ed. Alice Barnwell Keith and William H. Masterson, 3 vols. (Raleigh: State Department of Archives and History, 1965), 2: 424–25.

10. "Minutes of the North Carolina Governor's Council," 12 April 1753, CRNC, 5: 33; "Minutes of the Lower House of the North Carolina General Assembly," 22 December 1758, CRNC, 5: 1089–93; Thornton W. Mitchell, "The Granville District and Its Records," NCHR 70 (April 1993): 114; Joseph Kelly Turner and John L. Bridgers Jr., *History of Edgecombe County* (Raleigh: Edwards and Broughton, 1920), 95, SLNC.

11. "Minutes of the Lower House of the North Carolina General Assembly," 15 May 1759, CRNC, 6: 106; Wayne E. Lee, *Crowds and Soldiers in Revolutionary North Carolina: The Culture of Violence in Riot and War* (Gainesville: University Press of Florida, 2001), 23–28.

12. John Haywood to the Honourable the Speaker and Members of the House of Commons, 16 December 1819, John Haywood Letters, 1800–1865, RLDU; *Weekly Raleigh (NC) Register*, 24 November 1820, NewsC.

13. *Report of the Committee Appointed to Investigate the State of the Treasury, and to Enquire into the Official Conduct of John Haywood, Esq., Public Treasurer of North-Carolina* (Raleigh: T. Henderson Jr., 1820), 3, NCC.

14. William H. Haywood Jr to Elizabeth E. Haywood, 22 February 1831, EHC.

15. *Raleigh Minerva*, 30 June 1806.

16. *Weekly Raleigh Register*, 11 March 1805, 15 August 1817, 21 August 1818; *Newbern (NC) Sentinel*, 28 August 1819, NewsC; *Raleigh Minerva*, 9 June 1820; W. H. Howerton, comp., *The Legislative Manual and Political Register of the State of North Carolina, for the Year 1874* (Raleigh: Josiah Turner, 1874), 354, NCC; Marshall DeLancey Haywood, *Joel Lane, Pioneer and Patriot: A Biographical Sketch* (Raleigh: Alford, Bynum, & Christophers, 1900), 19–20, NCC.

17. *Raleigh (NC) Register*, 14 September 1824, 17 September 1824, NewsC.

18. Haywood to Haywood, 22 February 1831; *Weekly Raleigh Register*, 3 December 1824, 28 October 1825; Tax Lists for 1825 and 1827–28, Wake County Tax Lists: 1781–1860, SANC.

19. *Weekly Raleigh Register*, 22 October 1824, 10 June 1825, 28 October 1825, 4 November 1825, 24 September 1829; will of Stephen Haywood, 15 April 1823, Wills and Estate Papers, Wake County, 1663–1978, SANC; William Nichols to the Newbern Bank, 1 June 1826, bk. 7: 142–43, WCRD; *North-Carolina Star* (Raleigh), 8 November 1827, 6 November 1828, NewsC; Stephanie Jones-Rogers, *They Were Her Property: White Women as Slave Owners in the American South* (New Haven, CT: Yale University Press, 2019), 97.

20. *North-Carolina Star*, 15 April 1830; *Raleigh Register*, 28 December 1827; estate of Stephen Haywood to Delia Haywood, 5 January 1826, bk. 7: 64, WCRD; codicil to Stephen Haywood's will, 1 April 1823, bk. 19: 387, WCRD; receipt to Stephen Haywood for hire of Carpenters for Old West, May 26, 1823, University of North Carolina Papers, University Archives, University of North Carolina at Chapel Hill; *Raleigh Register*, 2 December 1828.

21. Hawkins, *Lunsford Lane*, 19.

22. *Weekly Raleigh Register*, 11 March 1825; Auguste Levasseur, *Lafayette in America in 1824 and 1825; or, Journal of a Voyage to the United States*, 2 vols. (Philadelphia: Carey and Lea, 1829), 1: 33, IntArch; Marshall De Lancey Haywood, "The Visit of General Lafayette to North Carolina in 1825," *American Historical Register* 1 (May 1897): 185n*.

23. Catherine W. Bishir, *North Carolina Architecture* (Chapel Hill: University of North Carolina Press, 2005), 124; Kemp P. Battle, *The Early History of Raleigh, The Capital City of North Carolina* (Raleigh: Edwards & Broughton, 1893), 124–25, SLNC; Haywood, "Visit of General Lafayette," 185. There is no historical evidence to support the lore of Lafayette's interactions with the Haywoods; see Elizabeth Reid Murray, *Wake: Capital County of North Carolina*, Vol. 1, *Prehistory through Centennial* (Raleigh: Capital County Publishing Co., 1983), 226 n145.

24. *Weekly Raleigh Register*, 11 March 1825; Levasseur, *Lafayette in America*, 1: 33.

25. Thomas Clarkson to Gerrit Smith, 20 February 1844, GSP; Thomas Clarkson to Mrs. H. G. Chapman, 3 October 1845, in *The Liberty Bell* (Boston: Massachusetts Anti-Slavery Fair, 1846), 63–64, RLDU; Lafayette to his Daughters and Grand-daughters, 15 April 1825, Manuscripts, Arthur H. and Mary Marden Dean Lafayette Collection, 1520–1973, Division of Rare and Manuscript Collection, Cornell University Library, Ithaca, NY.

26. *Memphis (TN) Daily Appeal*, 2 November 1867, NewsC; Daniel Walker Howe, *Making the American Self: Jonathan Edwards to Abraham Lincoln* (New York: Oxford University Press, 1997), 48–57.

27. Edmund Burke, "Reflections on the Revolution in France," in *Burke: Select Works*, ed. E. J. Payne, 3 vols. (Oxford, UK: Clarendon Press, 1877), 2: 102; Max Skjönsberg, *The Persistence of Party: Ideas of Harmonious Discord in Eighteenth-Century Britain* (New York: Cambridge University Press, 2021), 309–25.

28. Albert Gallatin to the Marquis de La Fayette, 21 April 1814, in *The Writings of Albert Gallatin*, ed. Henry Adams, 2 vols. (Philadelphia: J. B. Lippincott & Co., 1879), 605.

29. *Hartford (CT) Courant*, 11 January 1825, NewsC; *Charleston (SC) Mercury*, 12 January 1825, NewsC.

30. Hawkins, *Lunsford Lane*, 289–90.

31. "Remarks at Raleigh," 11 November 1825, in *Papers of John C. Calhoun*, Vol. 10, *1825–1829*, ed. Clyde N. Wilson and W. Edwin Hemphill (Columbia: University of South Carolina Press, 1977), 53; *North-Carolina Star*, 18 November 1825; John C. Calhoun to Christopher Van Deventer, 22 September 1825, in *Annual Report of the American Historical Association for the Year 1899*, Vol 2: *Calhoun's Correspondence*, ed. J. Franklin Jameson (Washington, DC: Government Printing Office, 1900), 232–33.

32. *Christian Watchman* (Boston, MA), 17 May 1852, AAS; Hawkins, *Lunsford Lane*, 288; Murray, *Wake*, 221.

33. Hawkins, *Lunsford Lane*, 21, 290–91; John Ernest, *Liberation Historiography: African American Writers and the Challenge of History, 1794–1861* (Chapel Hill: University of North Carolina Press, 2004), 225, 237.

34. Hawkins, *Lunsford Lane*, 171–73.

35. Zella Armstrong, comp., *Notable Southern Families*, 2 vols. (Chattanooga, TN: Lookout Publishing, 1933), 2: 154; Hawkins, *Lunsford Lane*, 33–45.

36. Thomas Marshall, first son of US Supreme Court Chief Justice John Marshall, delivered a fiery speech favoring the gradual abolition of slavery in the Virginia House of Delegates in January 1832; see Beverly Bland Munford, *Virginia's Attitude toward Slavery and Secession* (Richmond: L. H. Jenkins, 1909), 92, IntArch.

Chapter 4

1. *North-Carolina Star* (Raleigh), 24 December 1829, 7 January 1830, NewsC; *Weekly Raleigh (NC) Register*, 9 December 1830, NewsC; Elizabeth Reid Murray, *Wake: Capital County of North Carolina*, Vol. 1, *Prehistory through Centennial* (Raleigh: Capital County Publishing Co., 1983), 158–59; Fabius J. Haywood to Duncan Cameron, 5 February 1828, Cameron Family Papers, 1757–1978, SHC; Robert S. Richard, "Panic and Power: North Carolina's first Great Depression, 1819–1833" (PhD diss., University of North Carolina, 2020), 199–200.

2. Haywood to Cameron, 5 February 1828; "List of Bonds due the Executors of John Haywood, died 21 August 1828," John Haywood Letters, 1800–1865, RLDU; *North-Carolina Star*, 13 December 1827; will of John Haywood, November 1827, Wills and Estate Papers, Wake County, 1663–1978, SANC; *Message of His Excellency Montford Stokes of the General Assembly of North Carolina* (Raleigh: Lawrence & Lemay, 1831), 4, SHC.

3. "Statement of Sales of John Haywood's Land & Negros by Commissioners," Miscellaneous Group: John Haywood, 1828–1837, Treasurer's and Comptroller's Papers, SANC;

Eliza E. A. Haywood to State: Account of Sales and Agreement with Commissioners, 21 February 1828, Miscellaneous Group: John Haywood, 1828–1837; William H. Haywood Jr to Elizabeth E. Haywood, 22 February 1831, EHC; Sharon Ann Murphy, *Banking on Slavery: Financing Southern Expansion in the Antebellum United States* (Chicago: University of Chicago Press, 2023), 97–100. The process of seizure and sale of debtors' properties little changed from the colonial era, see Claire Priest, "Creating an American Property Law: Alienability and Its Limits in American History," *Harvard Law Review* 120 (December 2006): 401–2, 405n63.

4. Haywood to Cameron, 5 February 1828; will of John Haywood, November 1827.

5. William S. Robards to Mayor Cook of Newbern, 7 August 1828, Miscellaneous Group: John Haywood, 1828–1837; *North-Carolina Star*, 12 June 1828, 1 January 1829; *Weekly Raleigh Register*, 5 December 1828, 9 January 1829, 13 January 1829, NewsC.

6. William R. Hinton, Sheriff, to State of North Carolina, 1 September 1830, bk. 9: 489–90, WCRD; *Weekly Raleigh Register*, 10 February 1831, 2 December 1831; *Message of His Excellency Montford Stokes*, 4, 17, 23; *Report of the Public Treasurer on the State of the Finances of North Carolina* (Raleigh: Charles R. Ramsey, 1833), 4, SHC; *North-Carolina Star*, 22 November 1833; Alfred Moore to Betsy John Haywood, 1832, EHC.

7. *Raleigh (NC) Register*, 16 September 1828, 19 May 1829, 27 September 1830, NewsC; David L. Swain to Eleanor Swain, 13 November 1829, David Lowry Swain Papers, NCC.

8. Handbill advertisement, August 1831, EHC; James L. Belden Garden Seeds order form, 1831, EHC; Lois M. Wieder, *The Wethersfield Story* (Guilford, CT: Globe Pequot, 1966), 39.

9. Lunsford Lane, *The Narrative of Lunsford Lane, Formerly of Raleigh, N.C. Embracing an Account of His Early Life, the Redemption by Purchase of Himself and Family from Slavery, and His Banishment from the Place of His Birth for the Crime of Wearing a Colored Skin. Published by Himself*, 2nd ed. (Boston: J. G. Torrey, 1842), 20, AAS; entry for 1823, Minutes 1812–1832, First Baptist Church, Vol. 1, 1828, 9, microfilm, Special Collections & Archives Reading Room, Z. Smith Reynolds Library, Wake Forest University, Winston-Salem, NC; roster of Black members for 1826, First Baptist Church, Vol. 1, 1828; Jordan Womble, "The History of the First Raleigh Baptist Church from 1812," Minutes 1812–1832, First Baptist Church, Vol. 1, 1828; *Journals of the Senate and House of Commons of the General Assembly of the State of North-Carolina at Its Session in 1822* (Raleigh: Bell & Lawrence, 1823), 52, 179, SANC; W. Glenn Jonas Jr., *Nurturing the Vision: First Baptist Church, Raleigh, 1812–2012* (Macon: Mercer University Press, 2012), 32–34.

10. Entry for 27 April 1828, Minutes 1812–1832, First Baptist Church, Vol. 1, 1828; "Religious Intelligence," in *The General Assembly's Missionary Magazine; or Evangelical Intelligencer for 1805*, ed. William P. Farrand, 2 vols. (Philadelphia: William P. Farrand & Co., 1806), 1: 449, IntArch; William G. Hawkins, *Lunsford Lane; or, Another Helper from North Carolina* (Boston: Crosby & Nichols, 1863), 64–65, NCC.

11. Lane, *Narrative of Lunsford Lane*, 2nd ed., 21; George Washington Freeman, *The Rights and Duties of Slaveholders: Two Discourses Delivered on Sunday, November 27, 1836, in Christ Church, Raleigh, North Carolina* (Raleigh: J. Gales & Son, 1837), RLDU.

12. Auguste Levasseur, *Lafayette in America in 1824 and 1825; or, Journal of a Voyage to the United States*, 2 vols. (Philadelphia: Carey and Lea, 1829), 2: 242, IntArch; Anne C. Loveland, *Emblem of Liberty: The Image of Lafayette in the American Mind* (Baton Rouge: Louisiana State University, 1971), 30.

13. Lane, *Narrative of Lunsford Lane*, 2nd ed., 20; Marie-Joseph-Paul-Yves-Roch-Gilbert du Motier, *Memoirs of General Lafayette, With an Account of His Visit to America, and of His Reception by the People of the United States; from His Arrival, August 15th, to the Celebration at Yorktown, October 19th, 1824* (Boston: E. G. House, 1824), 96, 180, IntArch.

14. Hawkins, *Lunsford Lane*, 65; Lane, *Narrative of Lunsford Lane*, 2nd ed., iv, 20.

15. Lane, *Narrative of Lunsford Lane*, 2nd ed., 6, 8–9; Hawkins, *Lunsford Lane*, vi; "Several Answers of John D. Hawkins, surviving executor of Sherwood Haywood," 1858, *William A. Blount and others v. John D. Hawkins and others*, 57 N.C. 162 (December 1858), Supreme Court Original Cases, 1800–1809, SANC; "Answer of Mr. [Will R.] Poole," 1858, *William A. Blount and others v. John D. Hawkins and others*, 57 N.C. 162.

16. Hawkins, *Lunsford Lane*, 23–24; Lane, *Narrative of Lunsford Lane*, 2nd ed., 8–9; receipt to Mrs. John Haywood from B. B. Smith & Co., 31 May 1826, John Haywood Papers, 1790–1903, SHC; "Sherwood Haywood's account with Joseph and William Peace," 1828–1829, *William A. Blount and others v. John D. Hawkins and others*, 57 NC 162.

17. Lane, *Narrative of Lunsford Lane*, 2nd ed., 9; Hawkins, *Lunsford Lane*, 25–26, 48.

18. Pat McCrory, "Proclamation, Troop 3432 African American History Month Patch, March 2015," Governors' Papers: Pat McCrory, *North Carolina Digital Collections*, http://digital.ncdcr.gov/cdm/ref/collection/p16062coll5/id/21831.

19. David Dodge, "The Free Negroes of North Carolina," *Atlantic Monthly* 57 (January 1886): 20, https://www.theatlantic.com/magazine/toc/1886/01/.

20. Jean-Baptiste Say, *Catéchisme d'Économie Politique*, 3rd ed. (1826; reprint, Paris: O. Zeller, 1966), 20, IntArch.

21. *Charleston (SC) Daily Courier*, 14 September 1822, NewsC; Say, *Catéchisme d'Économie Politique*, 20.

22. On early nineteenth-century banks and their catering of loans to local elites, see Naomi Lamoreaux, *Insider Lending: Banks, Personal Connections, and Economic Development in Industrial New England* (New York: Cambridge University Press, 1994), 11–30.

23. Noah Webster, *An American Dictionary of the English Language*, 2 vols. (New York: S. Converse, 1828), 1: 640, IntArch; *An American Dictionary of the English Language*, rev. ed. (Springfield, MA: George & Charles Merriam, 1848), 507, IntArch; Noah Webster, *An American Dictionary of the English Language* (Springfield, MA: George and Charles Merriam, 1860), 1: 886. Examples of the traditional usage of "entrepreneur" include *New-York (NY) American*, 23 November 1822, 27 January 1829, NYHS; *Weekly Herald* (New York, NY), 21 September 1844, IntArch.

24. Edward E. Baptist, *The Half Has Never Been Told: Slavery and the Making of American Capitalism* (New York: Basic Books, 2014), 86–90; Harry L. Watson, "'The Common Rights of Mankind': Subsistence, Shad, and Commerce in the Early Republican South," *Journal of American History* 83 (June 1996): 13–43; Craig Thompson Friend, "Merchants and Markethouses: Reflections on Moral Economy in Early Kentucky," *JER* 17 (Winter 1997): 553–74.

25. Dylan C. Penningroth, *The Claims of Kinfolk: African American Property and Community in the Nineteenth-Century South* (Chapel Hill: University of North Carolina Press, 2003), 46–68; John Hope Franklin, *The Free Negro in North Carolina, 1790–1860* (Chapel Hill: University of North Carolina Press, 1943), 121–50; Juliet E. K. Walker, *The History of Black Business in America: Capitalism, Race, Entrepreneurship*, Vol. 1, *To 1865* (New York: Macmillan Press, 1998), 68, 345; John Sibley Butler, *Entrepreneurship and Self-Help among*

Black Americans: A Reconsideration of Race and Economics, rev. ed. (Albany: SUNY Press, 2005), 45, 53; Ira Berlin and Philip D. Morgan, "Introduction," in *The Slaves' Economy: Independent Production by Slaves in the Americas*, ed. Ira Berlin and Philip D. Morgan (London: Frank Cass, 1991), 19.

26. "An Act to Prohibit the Trading with Slaves, Except in the Manner Therein Prescribed" (1826), in *Acts Passed by the General Assembly of the State of North Carolina at Its Session, Commencing on the 25th of December, 1826* (Raleigh: Lawrence & Lemay, 1827), 7–8, SANC.

27. "An Act to Prohibit," 7–8.

28. *Waddill v. Martin*, 38 NC 562 (June 1845), 445; Charles Lewis Neir III, "The Shadow of Credit: The Historical Origins of Racial Predatory Lending and Its Impact upon African American Wealth Accumulation," *University of Pennsylvania Journal of Law and Social Change* 11 (2008): 139–40. On the legal privileges that granted enslaved persons property ownership, see Dylan C. Penningroth, *Before the Movement: The Hidden History of Black Civil Rights* (New York; Liveright, 2023), 13–14. In *Waddill v. Martin* (1845), the North Carolina Supreme Court concluded that enslaved people's ownership of meager property was acceptable throughout North Carolina, comparing their petty assets to "the savings of a wife in housekeeping, by sales of milk, butter, cheese, vegetables, and so forth, are declared to be, by the husband's consent, the property of the wife," see *Waddill v. Martin*, 38 NC 562, 444.

29. Butler, *Entrepreneurship and Self-Help*, 244; Walker, *History of Black Business*, 157–62; William L. Andrews, *Slavery and Class in the American South: A Generation of Slave Narrative Testimony, 1840–1865* (New York: Oxford University Press, 2019), 192. On the role that such networks played in self-purchase, see Julia W. Bernier, "'Never be free without trustin' some person': Networking and Buying Freedom in the Nineteenth-Century United States," *Slavery & Abolition* 40 (April 2019): 341–60.

30. Hawkins, *Lunsford Lane*, 289; *Weekly Raleigh Register*, 23 July 1816, 9 July 1824; *First Presbyterian Church, Raleigh, North Carolina, 1816–1941* (n. p.: n. p., 1941), 1–2, SLNC.

31. *Weekly Raleigh Register*, 7 November 1817, 2 July 1819, 18 June 1819, 8 July 1825; "Memorial of the Raleigh Auxiliary Society for Colonizing the Free People of Colour of the United States," undated, General Assembly Session Records, November–December 1819, SANC; *The Annual Reports of the American Society for Colonizing the Free People of Colour of the United States*, 10 vols. (New York: Negro Universities Press, 1969), 3: 139, 5: 118; Kemp P. Battle, *The Early History of Raleigh, The Capital City of North Carolina* (Raleigh: Edwards & Broughton, 1893), 52, 57, SLNC.

32. *Third Annual Report of the American Society for Colonizing the Free People of Color of the United States* (Washington, DC: Davis and Force, 1820), 139, IntArch; *Weekly Raleigh Register*, 22 April 1825; Robert G. Harper to Elias B. Caldwell, 20 August 1817, in *First Annual Report of the American Society for Colonizing the Free People of Colour of the United States* (Washington, DC: D. Rapine, 1818), 32, IntArch; *First Presbyterian Church, Raleigh, North Carolina, 1816–1941*, 12. In Hawkins's biography of Lunsford Lane, he repeatedly misidentified Thomas Hunt as "Heath" and William McPheeters as "McPhetus," a suggestion of how poorly he listened to Lane; see *Lunsford Lane*, 69–79, 289.

33. Hawkins, *Lunsford Lane*, 69–70; T. P. Hunt, *Life and Thoughts of Rev. Thomas P. Hunt: An Autobiography* (Wilkes-Barre, PA: Robt. Baur & Son, 1901), 10, 52–78, NCC; "Rev. Thomas B. Hunt," in *The National Temperance Offering: And Sons and Daughters*

of Temperance Gift, ed. S. F. Cary (New York: R. Vandien, 1850), 225–27, IntArch; *The Temperance Text-Book: A Collection of Facts and Interesting Anecdotes, Illustrating the Evils of Intoxicating Drinks*, 3rd ed. (Philadelphia: E L. Carey and A. Hart, 1837) 3, 154, IntArch.

34. Hawkins, *Lunsford Lane*, 73–74.

35. Hawkins, *Lunsford Lane*, 78.

36. Marshall DeLancey Haywood, "William Boylan," in *Biographical History of North Carolina from Colonial Times to the Present*, ed. Samuel A'Court Ashe, Stephen B. Weeks, and Charles L. Van Noppen, 8 vols. (Greensboro, NC: Charles L. Van Noppen, 1906), 4: 89–93; will of William Boylan, 18 June 1858, Wills and Estate Papers, Johnston County, 1663–1978, SANC; Scott King-Owen, "To 'Write Down the Republican Administration': William Boylan and the Federalist Party in North Carolina, 1800–1805," *NCHR* 89 (April 2012): 155–83; Hope Summerell Chamberlain, *History of Wake County, North Carolina, with Sketches of Those Who Have Most Influenced Its Development* (Raleigh: Edwards & Broughton, 1922), 144, SLNC.

37. Christopher Curtis, 22 February 1797, no. 1209, North Carolina Land Grants, microfilm, SANC; Christopher Curtis to Rhody McGuffie, 11 June 1814, bk. Y: 76, WCRD; *Raleigh (NC) Minerva*, 21 June 1816, NewsC; *North-Carolina Star*, 20 January 1815, 16 July 1815, 1 December 1815, 21 June 1816, 5 July 1816; Murray, *Wake*, 145; Anderson Curtis to Sherwood Haywood, 12 May 1817, bk. 2: 96, WCRD.

38. Peter Brown to William Boylan, 25 May 1818, bk. 3: 255, WCRD; "Schedule of Slaves in being at S. Haywood's death & in his actual possession," *William A. Blount and others v. John D. Hawkins and others*, 57 N.C. 162 (December 1858), Supreme Court Original Cases, 1800–1809, SANC; "Schedule of Slaves of the estate of S Haywood," *William A. Blount and others v. John D. Hawkins and others*, 57 N.C. 162; US Census, 1830: Wake County, NC; Wynne, "Slaves Named in the Inventory of the Estates of Sherwood Haywood: Wake County, North Carolina," *Journal of the Afro-American Historical and Genealogical Society* 6 (1985): 34–35. Although her brother's name went unrecorded, given the naming patterns for Martha's sons, it is probable that Martha's brother was William Curtis. The evidence on Martha's mother is simply one line in Lunsford Lane's *Narrative* that Martha's mother became wet nurse to Boylan's children; see *Narrative of Lunsford Lane*, 2nd ed., 11.

39. Lane, *Narrative of Lunsford Lane*, 2nd ed., 11–12; interview with Elias Thomas, in Federal Writers' Project, *Slave Narratives: A Folk History of Slavery in the United States from Interviews with Former Slaves*, Vol. 2, *North Carolina Narratives*, Part 2, *Jackson-Yellerday* (Washington, DC: Works Progress Administration, 1941), 343; US Census, 1860: Chatham County, NC; US Census, 1870: Chatham County, NC; will of William Boylan; will of John H. Boylan, 20 March 1869, Record Books of Wills, Inventories, Settlement of Estates (1771–1902), SANC; Hawkins, *Lunsford Lane*, 27, 171.

40. Franklin Bowditch Dexter, *Biographical Sketches of the Graduates of Yale College*, Vol. 4, *September 1805–September 1815* (New Haven, CT: Yale University Press, 1912), 548–49, IntArch; US Census, 1830: Wake County; Hawkins, *Lunsford Lane*, 26; Lane, *Narrative of Lunsford Lane*, 2nd ed., 10.

41. Lane, *Narrative of Lunsford Lane*, 2nd ed., 11; Patrick W. O'Neil, "Bosses and Broomsticks: Ritual and Authority in Antebellum Slave Weddings," *Journal of Southern History* 75 (February 2009): 35; Albert J. Raboteau, *Slave Religion: The Invisible Institution* (1978; reprint, New York: Oxford University Press, 2004), 228; *State v. Samuel*, 19 N.C. 177 (N.C. 1836), in *Reports of Cases at Law Argued and Determined in the Supreme Court of*

North Carolina, from December Term, 1836, to December Term, 1837, Both Inclusive, ed. Thomas P. Devereux and William H. Battle, 2 vols. (Raleigh: Turner & Hughes, 1838), 2: 183, IntArch.

42. Lane, *Narrative of Lunsford Lane*, 2nd ed., 11; Hawkins, *Lunsford Lane*, 27.

43. Lane, *Narrative of Lunsford Lane*, 2nd ed., 11; *Raleigh Minerva*, 19 December 1817; A. W. Mangum, "The Introduction and History of Methodism in Raleigh, North Carolina," in *Centennial of Methodism in North-Carolina*, ed. L. S. Burkhead (Raleigh: J. Nichols, 1875), 93, 96, 109, SLNC. The dating of 1833 to 1834 is determined by Smith's taxes: he began paying for a second enslaved adult beginning in 1834; Tax Lists for 1824–25 and 1826–36, Wake County Tax Lists: 1781–1860, SANC.

44. Hunt, *Life and Thoughts*, 52–78, quote on 61; "Rev. Thomas B. Hunt," 225–27.

45. Hawkins, *Lunsford Lane*, 284–85; marriage bond of Benjamin B. Smith and Laura Worthington, 3 February 1819, Wake County, NC, North Carolina County Registers of Deeds, RG 48, microfilm, SANC.

46. Marriage bond of Benjamin B. Smith and Laura Worthington, 3 February 1819; Lane, *Narrative of Lunsford Lane*, 2nd ed., 11–14; Hawkins, *Lunsford Lane*, 30. For Smith's use of "Patsy," see Smith to Lane, 25 April 1842, 53–54.

47. Laura F. Edwards, *The People and Their Peace: Legal Culture and the Transformation of Inequality in the Post-Revolutionary South* (Chapel Hill: University of North Carolina Press, 2009), 142–43.

48. Lane, *Narrative of Lunsford Lane*, 2nd ed., 7.

49. Hawkins, *Lunsford Lane*, 19.

50. "An Act transferring the duties of commissioner of loans to the Bank of the United States, and abolishing the office of commissioner of loans," 14th Cong., 2nd Sess., 3 March 1817, in *The Public Statutes at Large of the United States of America*, 8 vols. (Boston: Charles C. Little & James Brown, 1850), 3: 360–61, IntArch; *North-Carolina Star*, 21 June 1816; will of Sherwood Haywood, 26 September 1829, *William A. Blount and others v. John D. Hawkins and others*, 57 NC 162.

51. "Several Answers of John D. Hawkins," 1858.

52. *Raleigh Register*, 25 February 1830; *Edenton (NC) Gazette*, 6 March 1830, NewsC; Lucy D. Bryan to Clarissa Lane, 23 February 1858, reprinted in Hawkins, *Lunsford Lane*, 281–83.

53. Lane, *Narrative of Lunsford Lane*, 2nd ed., 19.

54. "Hiring Out list," *William A. Blount and others v. John D. Hawkins and others*, 57 NC 162; "John D. Hawkins's Answers to Bill of Complaint," *William A. Blount and others v. John D. Hawkins and others*, 57 NC 162; "Account showing receipts by the executor other than the profits of the farm and other," 1858, *William A. Blount and others v. John D. Hawkins and others*, 57 NC 162; receipts from Bank of Newbern, 26 March 1830 and 22 June 1831, EHC; US Census, 1830: Wake County, NC; *North-Carolina Star*, 27 May 1830.

55. Thomas P. Devereux to Eleanor Haywood, 25 April 1840, bk. 14: 129, WCRD; William Boylan to Thomas P. Devereux, 11 March 1819, bk. 3: 196–97, WCRD; Thomas P. Devereux & William H. Haywood Senior to William H. Haywood Junior, 25 February 1831, bk. 20: 121–24, WCRD; Thomas P. Devereux to Eleanor Haywood, 25 April 1840, bk. 14: 129, WCRD.

56. *Weekly Raleigh Register*, 7 July 1831; Lane, *Narrative of Lunsford Lane*, 2nd ed., 14–15; "1794 c406 s1: Slaves not to hire their time Penalty and Proceedings," in *Laws of the State of*

North Carolina Revised, Under the Authority of the General Assembly, ed. Henry Potter, 2 vols. (Raleigh: J. Gales, 1821), 1: 740–41, IntArch.

57. Lane, *Narrative of Lunsford Lane*, 2nd ed., 14–15; Hawkins, *Lunsford Lane*, 48. Historians such as Juliet E. K. Walker have claimed that Lane's tobacco product spread statewide, but there is no evidence to support that claim; see *History of Black Business*, 75–81. There is a mention of "Lane's Smoking Tobacco" in an advertisement for John E. Patterson's store in Fayetteville, but the ad is titled "Just received by Steam Boat, Henrietta," which suggests that the product came from abroad and not sixty-five miles up the road; *Fayetteville (NC) Weekly Observer*, 27 June 1838, 13 July 1838, NewsC. Even if "Lane's Smoking Tobacco" *was* Lunsford Lane's product, it is mentioned only by that singular store only on two occasions.

58. John Sugg to Sherwood Haywood, 28 March 1826, bk. 11: 263–64, WCRD; "Eleanor Haywood's Claim," 1834, *William A. Blount and others v. John D. Hawkins and others*, 57 N.C. 162; "Several Answers of John D. Hawkins," 1858; *Roanoke Advocate* (Halifax, NC), 2 February 1832, NewsC; *Weekly Raleigh Register*, 15 May 1829, 4 May 1832; Stephanie Jones-Rogers, *They Were Her Property: White Women as Slave Owners in the American South* (New Haven, CT: Yale University Press, 2019), 38–41.

59. *Roanoke Advocate*, 2 February 1832; *Richmond (VA) Enquirer*, 26 January 1832, NewsC; indenture of Rufus Haywood, March 1834, EHC.

Chapter 5

1. Will of John Craven, 20 May 1807, Wills and Estate Papers, Wake County, 1663–1978, SANC; James Turner to John Hall, 25 December 1808, privately held, *Warren Co, North Carolina*, https://www.ncgenweb.us/ncwarren/misc/hall_j-ltr.htm; *Haywood v. Craven's Executors*, July 1816, in *North Carolina Reports*, Vol. 4, *Embracing Carolina Law Repository, Vols. 1 and 2, January Term 1811 to July Term 1816, and North Carolina Term Reports, July Term 1816 to January Term 1818, Inclusive* (Raleigh: Mitchell Printing Co., 1921), 280–82, SANC; Executors of John Craven to Stephen & Dallas Haywood, 13 July 1817, bk. 1: 306–8, WCRD; A. E. Keir Nash, "Reason of Slavery: Understanding the Judicial Role in the Peculiar Institution," *Vanderbilt Law Review* 32 (1979): 111n345. Justices cited *Haywood v. Craven's Executors* in fifteen future cases and revised how testators might emancipate by last will; see "An Act to Regulate the Emancipation of Slaves in this State," in *Acts Passed by the General Assembly of the State of North Carolina at the Session of 1830-31* (Raleigh: Lawrence & Lemay, 1831), 12–14, SANC.

2. *Raleigh (NC) Register*, 22 February 1830, NewsC; *State v. Mann*, Superior Court, fall term 1829, Chowan County Slave Records, n2, SANC; *State v. Mann*, 13 N.C. 263 (December 1829), 263–69, quote on 266; Mark V. Tushnet, *Slave Law in the American South: State v. Mann in History and Literature* (Lawrence: University Press of Kansas, 2003), 264–67; Sally Greene, "*State v. Mann* Exhumed," *North Carolina Law Review* 87 (2009): 702–55.

3. *State v. Mann*, 13 N.C. 263, 268; Greene, "*State v. Mann* Exhumed," 748; Laura F. Edwards, *The People and Their Peace: Legal Culture and the Transformation of Inequality in the Post-Revolutionary South* (Chapel Hill: University of North Carolina Press, 2009), 9.

4. *North-Carolina Star* (Raleigh), 14 October 1830, NewsC.

5. David Walker, *Walker's Appeal, in Four Articles*, 3rd ed. (Boston: David Walker, 1830), 3, 18, 44, 76–77, IntArch; Thomas Jefferson, *Notes on the State of Virginia* (Philadelphia: Prichard & Hall, 1788), 152, Rare Book Collection, Wilson Library, University of North

Carolina, Chapel Hill; *Weekly Raleigh (NC) Register*, 22 September 1831, NewsC; Peter P. Hinks, *To Awaken My Afflicted Brethren: David Walker and the Problem of Antebellum Slave Resistance* (University Park: Pennsylvania State University Press, 1997), 200–212; Gene Andrew Jarrett, *Representing the Race: A New Political History of African American Literature* (New York: New York University Press, 2020), 40–42.

6. *North-Carolina Star*, 14 October 1830; T. P. Hunt, *Life and Thoughts of Rev. Thomas P. Hunt: An Autobiography* (Wilkes-Barre, PA: Robt. Baur & Son, 1901), 138.

7. "An Act Concerning Slaves and Free Persons of Color: Revised Code—No. 105" (Raleigh: General Assembly, 1831), # 29, 31, 34, 36, 78, 79, 81, 82, 87, NCC; "An Act to prevent all persons from teaching slaves to read or write, the use of figures excepted," in *Acts Passed by the General Assembly of the State of North Carolina at the Session of 1830–31*, 11; *North Carolina Spectator and Western Advertiser* (Rutherfordton, NC), 24 December 1830, NewsC.

8. "An Act to regulate the emancipation of slaves in this State," in *Acts Passed by the General Assembly of the State of North Carolina at the Session of 1830–31*, 12–14; John Hope Franklin, *The Free Negro in North Carolina, 1790–1860* (Chapel Hill: University of North Carolina Press, 1943), 27, 70–73.

9. "An Act Concerning Slaves and Free Persons of Color: Revised Code—No. 105," #59, 60, 61, 62, 63; *Journals of the Senate and House of Commons of the General Assembly of North-Carolina at It Session of 1830/31* (Raleigh: Lawrence & Lemay, 1831), 169, 209, 265, 266, SANC.

10. "An act pointing out the mode whereby the militia of this State shall hereafter be called into service in cases of insurrection or invasion, and outlawed and runaway slaves," in *Acts Passed by the General Assembly of the State of North Carolina at the Session of 1831–32* (Raleigh: Lawrence & LeMay, 1832), 28–29, SANC; R. H. Taylor, "Slave Conspiracies in North Carolina," *NCHR* 5 (January 1928): 28–29; William G. Hawkins, *Lunsford Lane; or, Another Helper from North Carolina* (Boston: Crosby & Nichols, 1863), 41, NCC.

11. *North-Carolina Free Press* (Halifax, NC), 17 January 1832, NewsC; *Newbern (NC) Sentinel*, 21 September 1831, NewsC; *Weekly Raleigh Register*, 15 September 1831, 22 September 1831; "An Act to Amend the First Section of an Act, Passed in the Year One Thousand Eight Hundred and Thirty, Which Authorizes Free Persons of Colour to Hawk and Peddle Out of the Limits of the County in Which They Reside," in *Acts Passed by the General Assembly of the State of North Carolina at the Session of 1831–32*, 24; Walter Eugene Milteer Jr., *North Carolina's Free People of Color, 1715–1885* (Baton Rouge: Louisiana State University Press, 2020), 37–39; Charles Edward Morris, "Panic and Reprisal: Reaction in North Carolina to the Nat Turner Insurrection, 1831," *NCHR* 62 (January 1985): 29–52.

12. *Weekly Raleigh Register*, 13 January 1831; "An Act to preserve the public buildings in the city of Raleigh," in *Acts Passed by the General Assembly of the State of North Carolina at the Session of 1830–31*, 9; *North-Carolina Star*, 27 January 1831; *Weekly Raleigh Register*, 23 June 1831; *North-Carolina Free Press*, 28 June 1831; Catherine W. Bishir, "Black Builders in Antebellum North Carolina," *NCHR* 61 (October 1984): 423–61.

13. *Weekly Raleigh Register*, 14 June 1816, 23 June 1831, 30 June 1831; *Fayetteville (NC) Weekly Observer*, 11 January 1832, NewsC; *North-Carolina Star*, 10 February 1832.

14. *Raleigh Register* extra, 7 January 1832, reprinted in *Roanoke Advocate* (Halifax, NC), 12 January 1832, NewsC.

15. Thomas B. Haywood, "Obituary," July 1832, EHC; will of Elizabeth E. A. Haywood, 12 July 1832, Wills and Estate Papers, Wake County; Elizabeth Reid Murray, *Wake: Capital*

County of North Carolina, Vol. 1, *Prehistory through Centennial* (Raleigh: Capital County Publishing Co., 1983), 163.

16. *Executors of Charles James v. William B. Masters*, in A. D. Murphey, *North Carolina Reports*, Vol. 7, *Reports of Cases Argued and Adjudged in the Supreme Court of North Carolina during the Year 1819* (Raleigh: Nach Brothers, 1910), 87–90, SANC; *Pride, Executor of Jones, v. Pulliam*, in Francis L. Hawks, *North Carolina Reports*, Vol. 11, *Cases Argued and Determined in the Supreme Court of North Carolina, December Term 1825 and June Term 1826* (Raleigh: Commercial Printing Co., 1917), 22–24, SANC; *Rebecca and Mary Long v. Lunsford Long's Executor*, July 1811, 20–21. Three emancipation petitions were rejected by the legislature between 1826 and 1829: *Journals of the Senate and House of Commons of the General Assembly of North-Carolina at It Session of 1826/1827* (Raleigh: Lawrence & Lemay, 1827), 186, SANC; *Journals of the Senate and House of Commons of the General Assembly of North-Carolina at It Session of 1827/1828* (Raleigh: Lawrence & Lemay, 1828), 57, 75, 151, 204, SANC.

17. "A South-Carolinian," *A Refutation of the Calumnies Circulated against the Southern & Western States Respecting the Institution and Existence of Slavery among Them* (Charleston, SC: A. E. Miller, 1822), 83, IntArch; *Raleigh Register*, 23 January 1827; "An Act to prevent free persons of colour from migrating into this State, for the good government of such persons resident in the State, and for other purposes," in *Acts Passed by the General Assembly of the State of North Carolina, at its Session, Commencing on the 25th of December 1826* (Raleigh: Lawrence & Lemay, 1827), 13–16, SANC; Franklin, *Free Negro*, 43.

18. "An Act to emancipate Isaac, a slave," in *Laws of the State of North Carolina, passed by the General Assembly at the Session of 1836–37* (Raleigh: Thos. J. Lemay, 1837), 328, SANC; "An Act to emancipate Caroline Cook and her four children, viz: Pamelia, Archibald T., James Ellis, and Martha Jane," in *Acts Passed by the General Assembly of the State of North Carolina at the Session of 1835* (Raleigh: J. Gales & Son, 1839), 157, SANC; *Journals of the Senate and House of Commons of the General Assembly of North-Carolina at It Session of 1832/1833* (Raleigh: Lawrence & Lemay, 1833), 47, 68, 71, 95, 107–108, 160, 173, 178, 184, 188–89, 211, 212, 243, SANC; *Journals of the Senate and House of Commons of the General Assembly of North-Carolina at It Session of 1833/1834* (Raleigh: Lawrence & Lemay, 1834), 22, 23, 28, 40, 48, 144, 147, 148, 153, 154, 164, 166, 168, 169, 176, SANC; *Journals of the Senate and House of Commons of the General Assembly of North-Carolina at It Session of 1834–35* (Raleigh: Lawrence & Lemay, 1835), 13, 24, 37, 108, 142, 149, 154, 157, 159, 160, 162, 164, 169, 170, 191, 196, 206, 214, 215, 232, SANC.

19. *First Annual Report of the American Anti-Slavery Society* (New York: Dorr & Butterfield, 1834), 55–56, IntArch; *The Emancipator* (New York, NY), 1 April 1834, AAS; *Fayetteville Weekly Observer*, 29 July 1834; "Eleanor Haywood's Claim," 1834, *William A. Blount and others v. John D. Hawkins and others*, 57 N.C. 162 (December 1858), Supreme Court Original Cases, 1800–1809, SANC; Account showing receipts by the executor other than the profits of the farm and other," 1858, *William A. Blount and others v. John D. Hawkins and others*, 57 NC 162; William M. Wiecek, *The Sources of Antislavery Constitutionalism in America, 1760–1848* (Ithaca, NY: Cornell University Press, 1977), 159.

20. *Jack, a negro man, v. Mary Martin*, 12 Wend. 311 (July 1834): 311–29; Thomas D. Morris, *Free Men All: The Personal Liberty Laws of the North, 1780–1861* (Union, NJ: Lawbook Exchange, 2001), 64–68; Christopher James Bonner, *Remaking the Republic: Black Politics and the Creation of American Citizenship* (Philadelphia: University of

Pennsylvania Press, 2020), 103–106; Paul Finkelman, "Chief Justice Hornblower of New Jersey and the Fugitive Slave Law of 1793," in *Slavery & the Law*, ed. Paul Finkelman (Madison, WI: Madison House, 1997), 126.

21. *Jack, a negro man, v. Mary Martin*, 14 Wend. 507, 507–39, quote on 538; *Fayetteville Weekly Observer*, 29 July 1834; inventory of slaves, 1858, *William A. Blount and others v. John D. Hawkins and others*, 57 N.C. 162.

22. *Fayetteville Weekly Observer*, 29 July 1834; *The Emancipator*, 1 April 1834, 17 June 1834; *The National Gazette and Literary Register* (Philadelphia, PA), 24 July 1834, HSP.

23. *First Annual Report*, 48–49, 56; Lunsford Lane, *The Narrative of Lunsford Lane, Formerly of Raleigh, N.C. Embracing an Account of His Early Life, the Redemption by Purchase of Himself and Family from Slavery, and His Banishment from the Place of His Birth for the Crime of Wearing a Colored Skin. Published by Himself*, 2nd ed. (Boston: J. G. Torrey, 1842), 6–7, AAS. At least one other Haywood man sexually used enslaved women. In her 1860 will, Betsy John Haywood bequeathed Montfort and his wife, Julia, to Montfort's half-brother Burke Haywood, son of Montfort's "said father, my brother E. Burke Haywood." Montfort and Julia's daughter, Jane, went to her grandfather; see will of Eliza E. Haywood, 10 March 1860, Wills and Estate Papers, Wake County.

24. *Weekly Raleigh Register*, 18 January 1833, 25 January 1833, 16 April 1833, 9 July 1833; *North-Carolina Constitutionalist and Peoples' Advocate* (Raleigh), 9 July 1933, NewsC; Henry Seawall, in *Debate in the Legislature of North-Carolina on a Proposed Appropriation for Re-building the Capitol, and on the Convention Question in the Months of December and January, 1831–1832* (Raleigh: Joseph Gales & Son, 1832), 5, SLNC; Thomas E. Jeffrey, *State Parties and National Politics: North Carolina, 1815–1861* (Athens: University of Georgia Press, 1989), 56–57.

25. *Proceedings of the Friends of Convention: at a meeting held in Raleigh, December 1822* (Raleigh: Thomas Henderson, 1822), 3, NCC; William Henry Haywood III, in *Debate in the Legislature of North-Carolina on a Proposed Appropriation for Re-building the Capitol*, 27; Jeffrey, *State Parties and National Politics*, 30, 40, 57–58.

26. Harry L. Watson, *Jacksonian Politics and Community Conflict: The Emergence of the Second American Party System in Cumberland County, North Carolina* (Baton Rouge: Louisiana State University Press, 1981), 199–201; "Amendments to the Constitution, as Ratified by the People," art. 1, sec. 3, in *Proceedings and Debates of the Convention of North-Carolina, Called to Amend the Constitution of the State, Which Assembled at Raleigh, June 4, 1835 to Which are Subjoined the Convention Act and the Amendments to the Constitution, Together with the Votes of the People* (Raleigh: Joseph Gales & Son, 1836), 421, NCC.

27. *The Weekly Standard* (Raleigh, NC), 19 June 1835, NewsC; *Newbern (NC) Spectator*, 20 November 1835; *Proceedings and Debates of the Convention of North-Carolina*, 61, 65, 67; Franklin, *Free Negro*, 71–, 74, 109–15, 351–52; Lacy K. Ford, *Deliver Us from Evil: The Slavery Question in the Old South* (New York: Oxford University Press, 2009), 418–47; Warren Eugene Milteer Jr., *Beyond Slavery's Shadow: Free People of Color in the South* (Chapel Hill: University of North Carolina Press, 2021), 156–58.

28. *Weekly Raleigh Register*, 25 June 1838; John Chavis, "Letter upon the Doctrine of the Extent of the Atonement of Christ" (1833), in Helen Chavis Othow, *John Chavis: African American Patriot, Preacher, Teacher, and Mentor (1763–1838)* (Jefferson, NC: McFarland & Co., 2001), 32–44, also 94–95; *Weekly Raleigh Register*, 25 June 1838; Timothy B. Tyson, *Blood Done Sign My Name: A True Story* (New York: Three Rivers Press, 2004), 132–33.

29. "Declaration of Sentiments of the American Anti-Slavery Convention," in *Selections from the Writings and Speeches of William Lloyd Garrison* (Boston: R. F. Wallcut, 1852), 68, AAS; *The Liberator* (Boston, MA), 20 July 1831, NewsC; Larry E. Tise, *Proslavery: A History of the Defense of Slavery in America, 1701–1840* (Athens: University of Georgia Press, 1987), 308, 323–46.

30. *Weekly Raleigh Register*, 12 July 1836; *Report of Commissioners appointed to Superintend the Re-Building of the State Capitol, December 4th, 1834* (Raleigh: Phil White, 1834), 7–8, SHC; Friday Jones, *Days of Bondage: Autobiography of Friday Jones, Being a Brief Narrative of His Trials and Tribulations in Slavery* (Washington, DC: Commercial Pub. Co., 1883), 7, J. Y. Joyner Library, East Carolina Library, Greenville, NC.

31. Don Holmes, "'a clever fellow': The Subversive Trickster in *The Narrative of Lunsford Lane*," unpublished manuscript, 2019, in possession of author.

32. Lane, *Narrative of Lunsford Lane*, 2nd ed., 15, 16, 26.

33. Hawkins, *Lunsford Lane*, 31–32; US Census, 1840: Wake County, NC; Sidnoie Smith, *Where I'm Bound: Patterns of Slavery and Freedom in Black American Autobiography* (Westport, CT: Greenwood Press, 1974), 14–16.

34. Henry Louis Gates Jr., *The Signifying Monkey: A Theory of African-American Literary Criticism* (New York: Oxford University Press, 1988), 25–27; Robert D. Pelton, *The Trickster in West Africa: A Study of Mythic Irony and Sacred Delight* (Berkley: University of California Press, 1980), 113–63; Lawrence W. Levine, *Black Culture and Black Consciousness: Afro-American Folk Though from Slavery to Freedom* (New York: Oxford University Press, 1977), 121–32.

35. Hawkins, *Lunsford Lane*, 32.

36. Lane, *Narrative of Lunsford Lane*, 2nd ed., 15.

37. Lane, *Narrative of Lunsford Lane*, 2nd ed., 9, 15.

38. Lane, *Narrative of Lunsford Lane*, 2nd ed., 14–15; Hawkins, *Lunsford Lane*, 51.

39. *Weekly Raleigh Register*, 28 April 1835; Dylan C. Penningroth, *The Claims of Kinfolk: African American Property and Community in the Nineteenth-Century South* (Chapel Hill: University of North Carolina Press, 2003), 55; Sumner Eliot Morrison, "Manumission by Purchase," *Journal of Negro History* 33 (April 1948): 155; Stephanie Jones-Rogers, *They Were Her Property: White Women as Slave Owners in the American South* (New Haven, CT: Yale University Press, 2019), 98.

40. It is noteworthy that William and Lunsford Jr. were twins, as were their uncles Montford and Davy. In 1882, William and his wife, Rebecca Ann Mitchell Lane, would have triplets: Maria, Mabel, and Maud. Although a "twin gene" can run in families, it does so only with fraternal twins, which happens when two eggs are simultaneously fertilized. Since men have no influence over the number of eggs that a woman releases and since the births in the Lane family were related through men, there was seemingly no "twin gene" coursing through Lunsford Lane's genetic heritage; Anaha O'Connor, "The Claim: Twins Always Skip a Generation," *New York (NY) Times*, 2 October 2007, https://www.nytimes.com/2007/10/02/health/02real.html.

41. Lane, *Narrative of Lunsford Lane*, 2nd ed., 17–18.

42. "An Act for the gradual abolition of slavery," 29 March 1799," in *Laws of the State of New York Passed at the Sessions of the Legislature Held in the Years 1787, 1798, 1799, and 1800, inclusive, Being the Twentieth, Twenty-First, Twenty-Second, and Twenty-Third Session* (Albany: Weed, Parsons and Co., 1887), 388–89, IntArch; "An Act relative to slaves

and servants," 21 March 1817, in *Laws of the State of New-York, Passed at the Thirty-Ninth, Fortieth and Forty-First Sessions of the Legislature, Commencing January 1816 and Ending April 1818* (Albany: Websters and Skinners, 1818), 136–44, IntArch; Leslie M. Harris, *In the Shadow of Slavery: African Americans in New York City, 1626–1863* (Chicago: University of Chicago Press, 2003), 70–71, 94; *Abstract of the Returns of the Fifth Census* (Washington, DC: Duff Green, 1832), 6; *Compendium of the Enumeration of the Inhabitants and Statistics of the United States* (Washington: Thomas Allen, 1841), 22.

43. "Act relative to slaves," 136–44; Lane, *Narrative of Lunsford Lane*, 2nd ed., 9, 15.

44. *Raleigh Register*, 1 April 1825, 8 July 1828; *North-Carolina Star*, 5 April 1827.

45. *Weekly Raleigh Register*, 29 September 1835; *The Weekly Standard*, 27 August 1835, 10 September 1835; *North-Carolina Star*, 1 October 1835.

46. Frederick Douglass, "The Horrors of Slavery and England's Duty to Free the Bondsman: An Address Delivered in Taunton, England, on September 1, 1846," in *The Frederick Douglass Papers: Series One—Speeches, Debates, and Interviews*, Vol. 1, *1841–1846*, ed. John Blassingame et al. (New Haven, CT: Yale University Press, 1979), 371; *Raleigh Register*, 20 October 1835; *North-Carolina Standard* (Raleigh), 6 October 1836, 13 October 1836, 20 October 1836, NewsC; *Weekly Raleigh Register*, 9 July 1838, 16 July 1838; "An act to prohibit free persons of colour from peddling and hawking out of the limits of the county in which they respectively reside," in *Acts Passed by the General Assembly of the State of North Carolina at the Session of 1830–31*, 11–12.

47. *The Weekly Standard*, 6 October 1836; *Weekly Raleigh Register*, 20 October 1835, 16 October 1837, 9 July 1838; Lane, *Narrative of Lunsford Lane*, 2nd ed., 10; *Wilmington (NC) Chronicle*, 20 April 1842, 20 August 1843, NewsC; *Fayetteville Weekly Observer*, 5 November 1835; *Newbern Spectator*, 9 June 1837; *The People's Press and Wilmington (NC) Advertiser*, 17 December 1834, 22 November 1839, NewsC; *Newbern Sentinel*, 1 February 1833.

48. *Fayetteville Observer*, quoted in *Weekly Raleigh Register*, 26 January 1836; Jeffrey, *State Parties and National Politics*, 72; *The Weekly Standard*, 7 January 1836; *North-Carolina Star*, 14 April 1836, 1 September 1836; *Charlotte (NC) Journal*, 6 May 1836, NewsC; *Newbern Spectator*, 12 August 1836.

49. *The Carolina Watchman* (Salisbury, NC), 20 August 1836, NewsC; *Weekly Raleigh Register*, 3 January 1837; *The Weekly Standard*, 29 November 1837; Burton Alva Konkle, *John Motley Morehead and the Development of North Carolina, 1796–1866* (Philadelphia: William J. Campbell, 1922), 175; Benjamin L. Huggins, *Willie Mangum and the North Carolina Whigs* (Jefferson, NC: McFarland Press, 2016), 104–5.

50. *North-Carolina Star*, 28 June 1837; *Weekly Raleigh Register*, 10 July 1837.

51. H. B. Battle, Lois Yelverton, and W. J. Battle, *The Battle Book: A Genealogy of the Battle Family in America* (Montgomery, AL: Paragon Press, 1930), 194–95, Olivia Raney Local History Library, Raleigh, NC; *North-Carolina Standard*, 29 November 1837, 22 January 1840, 27 January 1841, 8 December 1841; *The Weekly Standard*, 29 November 1837, 27 January 1841, 1 February 1841; Hawkins, *Lunsford Lane*, 90; US Census, 1840: Wake County, NC.

52. *Report of the Comptroller's Department of North-Carolina to the Legislature of the State showing the Receipts and Disbursements of the Treasury Department for the Fiscal Year, ending November 1, 1838* (Raleigh: J. Gales and Son, 1838), 39–40, SANC; *Christian Reflector* (Worcester, MA), 3 August 1842, AAS.

Chapter 6

1. John Haywood to Betsy John Haywood, 21 March 1822, EHC; David L. Swain to George Swain 18 May 1822 and 28 June 1822, David L. Swain Papers, SHC; Betsy John Haywood to John Haywood, 29 May, 2 June 1824, EHC.

2. Will of Elizabeth E. A. Haywood, 12 July 1832, Wills and Estate Papers, Wake County, 1663–1978, SANC; *The Weekly Standard* (Raleigh, NC), 26 December 1838, NewsC; Betsy Charles Manly to Betsy John Haywood, January 1839, bk. 13: 40, WCRD; Betsy John Haywood to George W. Haywood, 4 January 1839, EHC.

3. C. H. Dudley to Albert Hall, 4 March 1835, EHC; Alfred Moore Haywood to George Washington Haywood, 8 November 1838, EHC; Betsy John Haywood to George Washington Haywood, 6 December 1838, EHC; Eliza E. Haywood and George W. Haywood to Charles Manly, December 1838, bk. 13: 383, WCRD.

4. Mr. and Mrs. H. Waddell to Betsy John Haywood, 7 March 1841, EHC; Certificate of Guardianship, 22 February 1839, Guardians' Records, 1772–1948, Wake County Clerk of Superior Court Records, SANC; William Davie Haywood to George W. Haywood, 6 November 1836, EHC; William Davie Haywood to George W. Haywood, 3 July 1837, EHC; William H. Haywood Jr. to Eliza Haywood, undated, EHC; Thomas Burgess Haywood to Betsy John Haywood, 29 December 1826, EHC; Kemp P. Battle, *The History of the University of North Carolina from Its Beginning to the Death of President Swain, 1789–1868* (Raleigh: Edwards & Broughton, 1907), 315, NCC.

5. Haywood to Haywood, 6 December 1838; John Steele Haywood to George W. Haywood, 17 March 1839, EHC; *Weekly Raleigh (NC) Register*, 20 July 1839, NewsC. On the patterns of forced migration from North Carolina to Alabama, see Whitney Nell Stewart, *This Is Our Home: Slavery and Struggle on Southern Plantations* (Chapel Hill: University of North Carolina Press, 2023), 75–78.

6. Petition of Henry Patterson, 26 November 1838, General Assembly Session Records, November 1838–January 1839, SANC; *Journals of the Senate and House of Commons of the General Assembly of the State of North Carolina, at Its Session in 1838–39* (Raleigh: Thos. J. Lemay, 1859), 315, 341, 382, SANC.

7. Lunsford Lane, *The Narrative of Lunsford Lane, Formerly of Raleigh, N.C. Embracing an Account of His Early Life, the Redemption by Purchase of Himself and Family from Slavery, and His Banishment from the Place of His Birth for the Crime of Wearing a Colored Skin. Published by Himself*, 2nd ed. (Boston: J. G. Torrey, 1842), 22–23, AAS; Carla Kaplan, *The Erotics of Talk: Women's Writings and Feminist Paradigms* (New York: Oxford University Press, 1996), 47–68.

8. Invitation to tea, 28 December 1836, EHC.

9. *The Weekly Standard*, 15 March 1837; *Tarboro' (NC) Press*, 26 October 1839, NewsC; US Census, 1830: Wake County, NC; US Census, 1840: Wake County, NC.

10. Weston R. Gales to Lunsford Lane, 2 October 1838, bk. 14: 404, WCRD; Christopher K. Odinet, "Modernizing Mortgage Law," *North Carolina Law Review* 100 (December 2021): 91; Sharon Ann Murphy, *Banking on Slavery: Financing Southern Expansion in the Antebellum United States* (Chicago: University of Chicago Press, 2023), 62.

11. Gales to Lane, 2 October 1838; *The Weekly Standard*, 15 April 1840; *Tarboro' Press*, 26 September 1840; Leonard A. Jones, *A Treatise on the Law of Mortgages of Real Property*, 2 vols. (Boston: Houghton, Osgood, and Co., 1878), 1: 45, IntArch; H. W. Chaplin, "The

Story of Mortgage Law," *Harvard Law Review* 4 (April 1890): 12; K-Sue Park, "Money, Mortgages, and the Conquest of America," *Law & Social Inquiry* 41 (Fall 2015): 1006–35.

12. William G. Hawkins, *Lunsford Lane; or, Another Helper from North Carolina* (Boston: Crosby & Nichols, 1863), 169–70, NCC.

13. Tax Lists for 1838–1840 and 1835–1840, Wake County Tax Lists: 1781–1860, SANC.

14. US Census, 1840: Wake County, NC; "1831 c 4 s 3 Free negros not to inter marry with slaves," in "An Act Concerning Slaves and Free Persons of Color: Revised Code—No. 105" (Raleigh: General Assembly, 1831), # 79, NCC; Hawkins, *Lunsford Lane*, 16; Tax Lists for 1838–1840, 1835–1840; Laura F. Edwards, *Only the Clothes on Her Back: Clothing & the Hidden History of Power in the 19th-Century United States* (New York: Oxford University Press, 2022), 112–13.

15. *State v. Lunsford Lane & Isaac Hunter*, November term 1839, Minutes Docket 1837–1842, 227, Wake County Court of Pleas and Quarter Sessions, SANC.

16. Tax Lists for 1838–1840, 1835–1840.

17. Tax Lists for 1838–1840, 1835–1840; US Census, 1840: Wake County, NC.

18. *North-Carolina Star* (Raleigh), 15 July 1840, NewsC.

19. John Campton to Mary Porch, 4 February 1837, bk. 23: 341–42, WCRD; Weston R. Gales to John Campton, 14 October 1839, bk. 13: 570, WCRD; Weston R. Gales to John Campton, 8 August 1840, bk. 14: 208 WCRD; William F. Clark and John H. Christopher to John Campton, 29 March 1840, bk. 15: 151, WCRD; John Campton to John H. Kirkham, 23 March 1841, bk. 14: 539, WCRD; Ephriam Holmes to Waller Freeman, 17 August 1840, bk. 14: 367–68, WCRD; Sam Jones to Henry J. Patterson & others, 3 September 1842, bk. 15: 182–83, WCRD.

20. Holmes to Freeman, 17 August 1840; *Journals of the Senate and House of Commons of the General Assembly of the State of North Carolina at Its Session in 1840–41* (Raleigh: Thomas J. Lemay, 1841), 393, 404, 465, SANC. On the variety of marriage practices and family formations that enslaved and free Black Americans created, see Tera W. Hunter, *Bound in Wedlock: Slave and Free Black Marriage in the Nineteenth Century* (Cambridge, MA: Belknap Press, 2017).

21. US Census, 1820: Chatham County, NC; US Census, 1830: Chatham County, NC; George E. Badger to Lewis Freeman, 6 October 1832, bk. 11: 120, WCRD; *Journals of the Senate and House of Commons of the General Assembly of the State of North Carolina, at the Session of 1834–35* (Raleigh: Philo White, 1835), 85, 108, 171, 191, SANC; probate of Waller Freeman, 14 July 1870, Wills and Estate Papers, Chatham County, SANC; Holmes to Freeman, 17 August 1840; US Census, 1840: Wake County, NC.

22. Hawkins, *Lunsford Lane*, 50; *Weekly Raleigh (NC) Register*, 2 October 1812, NewsC; "Report of Committee on Propositions & Grievances," undated, House Resolutions: November 19–December 9, General Assembly Session Records, November 1840–January 1841, SANC; US Census, 1840: Wake County, NC; John Hope Franklin, *The Free Negro in North Carolina, 1790–1860* (Chapel Hill: University of North Carolina Press, 1943), 29, 142, 145.

23. *New York (NY) Evangelist*, 15 December 1842, NewsC; "Report of Committee"; William Boylan to Isaac Hunter, 28 June 1839, bk. 13: 401, WCRD.

24. *National Anti-Slavery Standard* (New York, NY), 11 October 1856, AccArch; Thomas P. Devereux to Allen Jones, 1 March 1829, bk. 9: 153, WCRD; Charles Parish to Allen Jones, 25 September 1829, bk. 9: 139–40, WCRD; Sarah Mitchell to Allen Jones, 21 January 1836, bk. 12: 392, WCRD; Thomas P. Devereux to Allen Jones, 18 October 1838,

bk. 14: 333–34, WCRD; Sally Mitchell to Allen Jones, 28 April 1841, bk. 14: 369–70, WCRD; Allen Jones to William H. Hollowman, 9 February 1843, bk. 15: 386–87, WCRD; Henry Patterson & others to Rachel Campton & others, 15 January 1838, bk. 19: 394–95, WCRD; Jones to Patterson & others, 3 September 1842, bk. 15: 181–83, WCRD.

25. Thomas Devereux to Henry Wise, 10 November 1856, Wise Family Papers, 1836–1928, LOC; US Census, 1840: Wake County, NC; US Census, 1850: Wake County, NC.

26. US Census, 1840: Wake County, NC; US Census, 1850: Wake County, NC; Joseph Gales to Margaret Eastwood, 13 June 1834, bk. 13: 354, WCRD; *The Weekly Standard*, 7 July 1841, 14 July 1841; Campton to Kirkham, 23 March 1841; "Report: Commissioners Appointed to Superintend the Re-building of the State Capitol, December 4th, 1834" (Raleigh: Philo White, 1834), 8, SLNC; Emily West, *Family or Freedom: People of Color in the Antebellum South* (Lexington: University Press of Kentucky, 2012), 56–65.

27. Lane, *Narrative of Lunsford Lane*, 2nd ed., 18–19; *North-Carolina Standard* (Raleigh), 4 January 1837, NewsC.

28. "An Act for the Regulation of the Patrol," in *Acts Passed by the General Assembly of the State of North Carolina at the Session of 1830–31* (Raleigh: Lawrence & Lemay, 1831), 17–18; "General Regulation #8," in *Laws for the Government of the City of Raleigh, containing all Legislative Enactments relative thereto, and the Ordinances of the Board of Commissioners, Now in Force; from the First Act of Incorporation to 1838* (Raleigh: Raleigh Register, 1838), 48, 57, NCC; Sally E. Hadden, *Slave Patrols: Law and Violence in Virginia and the Carolinas* (Cambridge, MA: Harvard University Press, 2001), 48; Laura F. Edwards, *The People and Their Peace: Legal Culture and the Transformation of Inequality in the Post-Revolutionary South* (Chapel Hill: University of North Carolina Press, 2009), 4.

29. *The Weekly Standard*, 11 July 1838, 1 August 1838; *Newbern (NC) Spectator*, 16 November 1838, 14 January 1839, NewsC; *Western Carolinian* (Salisbury, NC), 21 December 1836, NewsC; *Weekly Raleigh Register*, 23 May 1837, 26 March 1838, 31 December 1838; *Tarboro' Press*, 27 May 1837; Thomas E. Jeffrey, *State Parties and National Politics: North Carolina, 1815–1861* (Athens: University of Georgia Press, 1989), 81.

30. *North-Carolina Standard*, 29 November 1837, 22 January 1840; *Weekly Raleigh Register*, 4 December 1837, 28 December 1839; *Report of the Comptroller's Department of North-Carolina to the Legislature of the State showing the Receipts and Disbursements of the Treasury Department for the Fiscal Year, ending November 1, 1838* (Raleigh: J. Gales and Son, 1838), 39, 40, SANC; *Report of the Comptroller's Department of North Carolina to the Governor of the State, showing the Receipts and Disbursements at the Treasury Department for the Fiscal Year, ending November 1, 1839* (Raleigh: Thos. J. Lemay, 1840), 35, 46, SANC; *Report from the Comptroller's Department of North Carolina to the Governor of the State, showing the Receipts and Disbursements at the Treasury Department for the Fiscal Year, ending November 1, 1840* (Raleigh: Thos. J. Lemay, 1841), 34, SANC; Robert S. Jones to Lunsford Lane, 2 October 1838, bk. 14: 406, WCRD; Hawkins, *Lunsford Lane*, 82.

31. Jordan Womble, "The History of the First Raleigh Baptist Church from 1812," Minutes 1812–1832, First Baptist Church, Vol. 1, 1828, 10a, microfilm, Special Collections & Archives Reading Room, Z. Smith Reynolds Library, Wake Forest University, Winston-Salem, NC; *North-Carolina Constitutionalist and People's Advocate* (Raleigh), 23 June 1833; *North-Carolina Star*, 15 September 1831; *Weekly Raleigh Register*, 28 January 1839, 6 January 1846; *The Weekly Standard*, 20 October 1839; *State v. Lunsford Lane &*

Isaac Hunter; W. Glenn Jonas Jr., *Nurturing the Vision: First Baptist Church, Raleigh, 1812–2012* (Macon: Mercer University Press, 2012), 47–54, 76 n67; Edwards, *People and Their Peace*, 71.

32. James Graham to William A. Graham, 19 March 1840, in *The Papers of William Alexander Graham*, ed. J. G. de Roulhac Hamilton and Max R. Williams, 5 vols. (Raleigh: Division of Archives and History, 1957–73), 2: 77; *The Weekly Standard*, 18 March 1840; *American Farmer* (Baltimore, MD), 9 January 1828, HT.

33. *The Weekly Standard*, 22 January 1840; *Raleigh Register*, 19 January 1841, 21 January 1842; *Weekly Raleigh Register*, 21 September 1839, 25 September 1839.

34. *Raleigh Register*, 28 April 1840.

35. *The Weekly Standard*, 6 May 1840, 10 June 1840; *Weekly Raleigh Register*, 9 October 1840; *North-Carolina Star*, 1 April 1840, 22 June 1840; Burton Alva Konkle, *John Motley Morehead and the Development of North Carolina, 1796–1866* (Philadelphia: William J. Campbell, 1922), 194–95; Harry L. Watson, *Jacksonian Politics and Community Conflict: The Emergence of the Second American Party System in Cumberland County, North Carolina* (Baton Rouge: Louisiana State University Press, 1981), 275–76.

36. *State v. Lunsford alias Lunsford Lane & Benjamin B. Smith*, and *State v. Isaac alias Isaac Hunter & Benj. B. Smith*, February term 1840, Minutes Docket 1837–1842, 254; *State v. Lunsford Lane*, May term 1840, Minutes Docket 1837–1842, 286.

37. *Weekly Raleigh Register*, 24 April 1840, 19 June 1840; *Raleigh Register*, 16 June 1840; *The Rasp* (Raleigh, NC), 4 February 1842, NewsC.

38. *Raleigh (NC) Microcosm*, 20 March 1839, NewsC; Konkle, *John Motley Morehead and the Development of North Carolina*, 221.

39. *Raleigh Register*, 21 August 1840; Lane, *Narrative of Lunsford Lane*, 2nd ed., 24.

40. US Census, 1850: Wake County, NC; Lane, *Narrative of Lunsford Lane*, 2nd ed., 24–25.

41. Lane, *Narrative of Lunsford Lane*, 2nd ed., 27.

42. Lane, *Narrative of Lunsford Lane*, 2nd ed., 29–31; "Petition of Lunsford Lane," in Hawkins, *Lunsford Lane*, 93.

43. *State v. Lunsford Lane & Robert W. Haywood, State v. Isaac Hunter & B. B. Smith*, and *State v. Waller Freeman, Charles Manly, & A. B. Stith*, November term 1840, Minutes Docket 1837–1842, 341; Juliet E. K. Walker, *The History of Black Business in America: Capitalism, Race, Entrepreneurship*, Vol. 1, *To 1865* (New York: Macmillan Press, 1998), 157–62.

44. *Raleigh Register*, 3 November 1840, 17 November 1840, 20 November 1840, 24 November 1840, 27 November 1840, 9 December 1840, 11 December 1840; "Report of Committee,"; Petition of Isaac Hunter, undated, Senate Bills: November 20–January 11, General Assembly Session Records, November 1840–January 1841; "Petition of Lunsford Lane," 93; *Journals of the Senate and House of Commons of the General Assembly of the State of North Carolina, at the Session of 1840–41* (Raleigh: Thomas J. Lemay, 1841), 414, 451–53, SANC.

45. *Weekly Raleigh Register*, 7 November 1840, 10 November 1840, 13 November 1840, 17 November 1840, 20 November 1840, 24 November 1840, 27 November 1840, 11 December 1840; *The Weekly Standard*, 13 January 1841.

46. "Message from House of Commons," 11 December 1840, House Messages: December–January, General Assembly Session Records, November 1840–January 1841; *Journals of the Senate and House of Commons of the General Assembly of the State of North Carolina, at*

the Session of 1840–41, 115, 160, 165, 196, 441; "Resolution in Favor of Isaac Hunter," in *Laws of the General Assembly at the Session of 1840–41* (Raleigh: W. R. Gales, 1841), 207, 536, SANC; *Raleigh Register*, 10 November 1840, 13 November 1840, 17 November 1840, 27 November 1840.

47. *Journals of the Senate and House of Commons of the General Assembly of the State of North Carolina, at the Session of 1840–41*, 441, 551; "Memorial to General Assembly of the State of North Carolina," undated, House Resolutions: November 19–December 9, General Assembly Session Records, November 1840–January 1841.

48. *Journals of the Senate and House of Commons of the General Assembly of the State of North Carolina, at the Session of 1840–41*, 564, 567, 696, 705; *Weekly Raleigh Register*, 29 December 1840; Lane's petition, reprinted in *The Liberator* (Boston, MA), 17 September 1841, NewsC.

49. "Resolution in favor of Lunsford Lane," 9 January 1841, House Resolutions: December 10–31, General Assembly Session Records, November 1840–January 1841; *Journals of the Senate and House of Commons of the General Assembly of the State of North Carolina, at the Session of 1840–41*, 291–92, 298; *The Weekly Standard*, 2 December 1840.

50. "Resolution in favor of Lunsford Lane," 9 January 1841.

51. Edwards, *People and Their Peace*, 60, 199.

52. "A Bill to amend the Revised Statute entitled 'An act concerning Slaves and Free persons of Color," 21 December 1840, House Bills: December 14–21, General Assembly Session Records, November 1840–January 1841; *Journals of the Senate and House of Commons of the General Assembly of the State of North Carolina, at the Session of 1840–41*, 715; Benjamin L. Huggins, *Willie Mangum and the North Carolina Whigs* (Jefferson, NC: McFarland Press, 2016), 124–25.

53. "Petition of Isaac Hunter, a Man of Color," undated, House Resolutions: November 19–December 9, General Assembly Session Records, November 1840–January 1841; William Boylan to Isaac Hunter, 14 February 1842, bk. 14: 583, WCRD; *Brooklyn (NY) Evening Star*, 29 November 1842, 22 May 1852, 31 May 1852, NewsC; US Census, 1850: Kings County, NY; *Brooklyn (NY) Union*, 15 August 1876, NewsC.

54. *The Liberator*, 9 September 1842.

55. *Journals of the Senate and House of Commons of the General Assembly of the State of North Carolina, at the Session of 1840–41*, 291; "Report on the Committee on Finance, Doc. No. 26, Legislature of North Carolina, 21 Dec. 1840," in *Documents Printed by Order of the General Assembly of North Carolina at Its Session of 1849* (Raleigh: Weston R. Gales, 1849), 3–4, SANC; *Public Acts of the State of North Carolina, Passed by the General Assembly, at the Session of 1840–41* (Raleigh: W. R. Gales, 1841), 204, SANC; *The Weekly Standard*, 27 January 1841; *North-Carolina Standard*, 27 January 1841, 8 December 1841.

56. "Resolution in favor of Lunsford Lane," 23 December 1840, House Resolutions: December 10–31, General Assembly Session Records, November 1840–January 1841; *Comptroller's Report ending November 1, 1841* (Raleigh: Weston Gailes, 1842), 41, SANC; *North-Carolina Standard*, 8 December 1841.

57. *State v. Waller Freeman, Charles Manly & A. B. Stith, State v. Isaac Hunter & B. B. Smith*, and *State v. Lunsford Lane, B. B. Smith, & Robert W. Haywood*, February term 1841, Minutes Docket 1837–1842, 376. Lunsford did not attend the February court, but in his 1863 biography, he blamed the delay in his trial on "my prosecutors were not ready for trial, and the case was laid over three months, to the next term"; see Hawkins, *Lunsford Lane*, 92.

Chapter 7

1. William G. Hawkins, *Lunsford Lane; or, Another Helper from North Carolina* (Boston: Crosby & Nichols, 1863), 102, NCC; US Census, 1850: Bristol County, MA; recommendation letter of Henry D. Turner, reprinted in *The Liberator* (Boston, MA), 17 September 1841, NewsC.

2. Hawkins, *Lunsford Lane*, 105–6.

3. *The Liberator*, 15 July 1831, 28 July 1832; Richard Bell, *Stolen: Five Free Boys Kidnapped into Slavery and Their Astonishing Odyssey Home* (New York: Simon & Schuster, 2019).

4. Adam Malka, *The Men of Mobtown: Policing Baltimore in the Age of Slavery and Emancipation* (Chapel Hill: University of North Carolina Press, 2018), 3–4, 25, 163; Carol Wilson, *Freedom at Risk: The Kidnapping of Free Blacks in America, 1780–1865* (Lexington: University Press of Kentucky, 1994), 40–41, 43–44.

5. *Craig's Business Directory and Baltimore Almanac for 1842* (Baltimore: Daniel H. Craig, 1842), 124, IntArch; *The Fugitive Slave Bill: Its History and Unconstitutionality* (New York: William Harned, 1850), 5; *The Friend: A Religious and Literary Journal* 20 (26 June 1847): 316; *Baltimore (MD) Sun*, 9 July 1838, NewsC; Jennie K. Williams, "Trouble the Water: The Baltimore to New Orleans Coastwise Slave Trade, 1820–1860," *Slavery & Abolition* 41 (Spring 2020): 275–76; Joseph Sturge, *A Visit to the United States in 1841* (London: Hamilton, Adams & Co., 1842), 32–35, IntArch; Christopher Phillips, *Freedom's Port: The African American Community in Baltimore, 1790–1860* (Urbana: University of Illinois Press, 1997), 230–31.

6. *Matchett's Baltimore Directory Corrected Up to June 1837* (Baltimore: Directory Office, 1837), 80, Maryland State Archives, Annapolis.

7. *Matchett's Baltimore Directory Corrected Up to June 1837*, 282, 287, 288, 318; *Matchett's Baltimore Directory or Register of Householders Corrected Up to June 1843* (Baltimore: Directory Office, 1843), 386, Maryland State Archives, Annapolis; *The Pilot and Transcript* (Baltimore, MD), 28 April 1840, NewsC; Henry E. Shepherd, *History of Baltimore, Maryland from its Founding as a Town to the Current Year, 1729–1898* (Baltimore: S. B. Nelson, 1898), 264–67, Maryland Historical Society, Baltimore; Conway W. Sams and Elihu S. Riley, *The Bench and Bar of Maryland: A History, 1634 to 1901*, 2 vols. (Chicago: Lewis Publishing Co., 1901), 2: 419.

8. Hawkins, *Lunsford Lane*, 110–11.

9. Hawkins, *Lunsford Lane*, 111–12. On Northup's experience with kidnapping and imprisonment, see Solomon Northup, *Twelve Years a Slave: Narrative of Solomon Northup, a Citizen of New-York, Kidnapped in Washington City in 1841 and Rescued in 1853, from a Cotton Plantation Near the Red River in Louisiana* (Auburn, NY: Derby and Miller, 1853), 37–53, AAS.

10. Hawkins, *Lunsford Lane*, 138; *New-York Tribune* (New York, NY), 7 May 1841, NewsC.

11. Testimonial of William Hill et al., reprinted in *The Liberator*, 17 September 1841; certification of Madison B. Royster, reprinted in *The Liberator*, 17 September 1841; Lunsford Lane, *The Narrative of Lunsford Lane, Formerly of Raleigh, N.C. Embracing an Account of His Early Life, the Redemption by Purchase of Himself and Family from Slavery, and His Banishment from the Place of His Birth for the Crime of Wearing a Colored Skin. Published by Himself*, 2nd ed. (Boston: J. G. Torrey, 1842), 39, AAS.

12. *State v. Lunsford Lane & R. W. Haywood*, and *State v. Isaac Hunter & B. B. Smith*, May term 1841, Minutes Docket 1837–1842, 413, Wake County Court of Pleas and Quarter Sessions, SANC; Hawkins, *Lunsford Lane*, 139–40; Benjamin B. Smith to Lunsford Lane, 17 May 1841, reprinted in Lane, *Narrative of Lunsford Lane*, 2nd ed., 53.

13. Recommendation letter of Henry D. Turner.

14. Lane, *Narrative of Lunsford Lane*, 2nd ed., 34; Hawkins, *Lunsford Lane*, 141; *Commercial Advertiser and Journal* (Buffalo, NY), 15 May 1841, NewsC; *The Madisonian* (Washington, DC), 14 May 1841, NewsC. On the splintering of the anti-slavery movement, see Manisha Sinha, *The Slave's Cause: A History of Abolition* (New Haven, CT: Yale University Press, 2016), 262–65.

15. *The Liberator*, 16 June 1832; *The North Star* (Danville, VT), 27 January 1834, NewsC; Margaret M. R. Kellow, "Conflicting Imperatives: Black and White American Abolitionists Debate Slave Redemption," in *Buying Freedom: The Ethics and Economics of Slave Redemption*, ed. Kwame Anthony Appiah and Martin Bunzl (Princeton, NJ: Princeton University Press, 2007), 202–3.

16. *The Liberator*, 15 January 1847.

17. *The Liberator*, 17 September 1841, 1 October 1841, 14 January 1842.

18. *Vermont Telegraph* (Brandon, VT), 2 June 1841, NewsC; *The Liberator*, 21 May 1841, 1 October 1841.

19. *Hingham (MA) Patriot*, 2 October 1841, AAS.

20. *Hingham Patriot*, 2 October 1841; *The Liberator*, 8 October 1841.

21. Entries for 1 November and 2 November 1841, Charles Spear Journal, microfilm, BPL.

22. *Hingham Patriot*, 30 October 1841; *The Monthly Offering* (November 1841): 164, AAS.

23. *The Liberator*, 15 October 1841; Leigh Fought, *Women in the World of Frederick Douglass* (New York: Oxford University Press, 2017), 52–58; Gregory P. Lampe, *Frederick Douglass: Freedom's Voice, 1818–1845* (East Lansing: Michigan State University Press, 1998), 49–50, 58–73; *Boston (MA) Journal*, 13 September 1886, MHS.

24. "Recollections of the Anti-Slavery Conflict: An Address Delivered in Louisville, Kentucky," 21 April 1873, in *The Frederick Douglass Papers: Series One—Speeches, Debates, and Interviews*, Vol. 4, *1864–1880*, ed. John Blassingame and John R. McKivigan (New Haven, CT: Yale University Press, 1991), 368; Frederick Douglass, *My Bondage and My Freedom*, Part 1, *Life as a Slave* (New York: Miller, Orton & Mulligan, 1855), 356, NASN; William Lloyd Garrison, "Preface," in Frederick Douglass, *Narrative of the Life of Frederick Douglass, an American Slave. Written by Himself* (Boston: Anti-Slavery Office, 1845), iv, NASN; *Hingham Patriot*, 30 October 1841.

25. *Hingham Patriot*, 6 November 1841, 13 November 1841.

26. *The Liberator*, 12 November 1841.

27. *Hingham Patriot*, 13 November 1841; *The North Star* (VT), 27 January 1834; *National Anti-Slavery Standard* (New York, NY), 18 November 1841, AccArch; *The Liberator*, 26 November 1841.

28. *Hingham Patriot*, 13 November 1841; *The Liberator*, 26 November 1841; Lampe, *Frederick Douglass*, 73–75.

29. *The Liberator*, 26 November 1841.

30. *National Anti-Slavery Standard*, 18 November 1841; *Hingham Patriot*, 20 November 1841.

31. *Hingham Patriot*, 22 November 1841.

32. *The Weekly Standard* (Raleigh, NC), 24 November 1841, NewsC.

33. Lane, *Narrative of Lunsford Lane*, 2nd ed., 48; *Boston (MA) Daily Atlas*, 15 December 1841, MHS.

34. *The Emancipator and Free American* (New York, NY), 3 November 1842, NYHS.

35. *The Emancipator and Free American*, 3 November 1842.

36. *The Liberator*, 7 January 1842; *Boston (MA) Courier*, 10 January 1842, AAS; *Boston (MA) Evening Transcript*, 12 January 1842, NewsC.

37. Charles Spear, *Essays on Imprisonment for Debt* (Hartford, CT: B. Sperry, 1833), 5, 7, 17–18, 20, IntArch; entries for 10, 24, and 25 January 1842, Charles Spear Journal; Louis P. Masur, *Rites of Execution: Capital Punishment and the Transformation of American Culture, 1776–1865* (New York: Oxford University Press, 1989), 127–28.

38. Anne Warren Weston to Deborah Weston, 25 January 1842, Anti-Slavery Collection, BPL.

39. Weston to Weston, 25 January 1842.

40. *The Liberator*, 18 February 1842.

41. *The Liberator*, 18 February 1842, 22 February 1842; entry for 26 January 1842, Charles Spear Journal; *Tenth Annual Report of the Board of Managers of the Massachusetts Anti-Slavery Society, presented January 26, 1842* (Boston: Dow & Jackson's Press, 1842), appendix: 6, IntArch.

42. *The Liberator*, 18 February 1842, 11 March 1842; Edward G. Parker, *The Golden Age of American Oratory* (Boston; Whittemore, Niles, and Hill, 1857), 411.

43. Stephen S. Foster, *The Brotherhood of Thieves; or, a True Picture of the American Church and Clergy* (Boston: Anti-Slavery Office, 1844), 20, AAS.

44. Entries for 28 January 1842, 2 February 1842, 4 February 1842, Charles Spear Journal; *The Liberator*, 4 February 1842; *Tenth Annual Report of the Board of Managers of the Massachusetts Anti-Slavery Society*, appendix: 6.

45. *The Emancipator and Free American*, 4 March 1842; Benjamin Quarles, *Black Abolitionists* (New York: Oxford University Press, 1969), 184.

46. *The Liberator*, 25 March 1842, 3 June 1842.

47. *The Weekly Standard*, 19 January 1842; *Raleigh Register*, 21 January 1842.

48. *North-Carolina Star* (Raleigh, NC), 6 April 1842; *The Weekly Standard*, 6 April 1842; Benjamin L. Huggins, *Willie Mangum and the North Carolina Whigs* (Jefferson, NC: McFarland Press, 2016), 148–52.

49. *Journals of the Senate and House of Commons of the General Assembly of the State of North-Carolina, at Its Session in 1836–37* (Raleigh: J. Gales & Son, 1837), 402–404, SANC; Lane, *Narrative of Lunsford Lane*, 2nd ed., 38.

50. Lane, *Narrative of Lunsford Lane*, 2nd ed., 43.

51. Entry for 29 February 1842, Diary of Sidney Bumpas, Bumpas Family Papers, 1838–1972, SHC; *Minutes of the Annual Conferences of the Methodist Episcopal Church for the years 1839–1845*, 4 vols. (New York: T. Mason and G. Lane, 1848), 3: 207, 310, IntArch; David W. Stone to Thomas Ruffin, 3 May 1842, in *The Papers of Thomas Ruffin*, ed. J. G. De Roulhac Hamilton, 4 vols. (Raleigh: Edwards & Broughton, 1918), 2: 205–206; US Census, 1840: Wake County, NC; Lane, *Narrative of Lunsford Lane*, 2nd ed., 43, 46; *Raleigh Register*, 23 October 1840; *The Weekly Standard*, 16 August 1848; Hawkins, *Lunsford Lane*, 160;

"Memorial to General Assembly of the State of North Carolina," undated, House Resolutions: November 19–December 9, General Assembly Session Records, November 1840–January 1841, SANC.

52. Lane, *Narrative of Lunsford Lane*, 2nd ed., 44–45.

53. *The Liberator*, 22 September 1837; Benjamin H. Irvin, "Tar, Feathers, and the Enemies of American Liberties, 1768–1776," *New England Quarterly* 76 (June 2003): 200–204; Alfred F. Young, "English Plebian Culture and Eighteenth-Century American Radicalism," in *The Origins of Anglo-American Radicalism*, ed. Margaret Jacob and James Jacob (London: Allen & Unwin, 1984), 185–212.

54. Lane, *Narrative of Lunsford Lane*, 2nd ed., 46.

55. Lane, *Narrative of Lunsford Lane*, 2nd ed., 47.

56. *The Liberator*, 3 June 1842; Hawkins, *Lunsford Lane*, 156; Amy Kate Bailey and Steward E. Tolnay, *Lynched: The Victims of Southern Mob Violence* (Chapel Hill: University of North Carolina Press, 2015), 208–10; Laura F. Edwards, *The People and Their Peace: Legal Culture and the Transformation of Inequality in the Post-Revolutionary South* (Chapel Hill: University of North Carolina Press, 2009), 111–21; Irvin, "Tar, Feathers, and the Enemies," 205–6.

57. *The Rasp* (Raleigh, NC), 17 July 1841, NewsC; Benjamin Franklin, *Autobiography of Benjamin Franklin*, ed. Frank Woodworth Pine (New York: Henry Holt & Co., 1916), 146; Lewis Henry Boutell, *The Life of Roger Sherman* (Chicago: A. C. McClurg and Company, 1896), 165.

58. *Raleigh Register*, 10 August 1824, 29 October 1824, 7 October 1828; *The National Gazette* (Philadelphia, PA), 11 March 1830, HSP; *Sentinel and Democrat* (Burlington, VT), 12 March 1830, NewsC; *Brattleboro' (VT) Messenger*, 14 May 1831, NewsC; *Arkansas Gazette* (Arkansas Post, AR), 6 July 1831, NewsC; *The Liberator*, 24 September 1831; *Boston (MA) Post*, 17 August 1832, NewsC; *Vermont Gazette* (Bennington, VT), 12 February 1833, NewsC; *Illinois State Register* (Springfield, IL), 8 December 1837, NewsC; *The Madisonian*, 25 December 1838; *Southern Citizen* (Asheboro, NC), 21 June 1839, NewsC; Nehemiah Cleaveland and Alpheus Spring Packard, *History of Bowdoin College with Biographical Sketches of Its Graduates from 1806 to 1870, Inclusive* (Boston: James Ripley Osgood & Co., 1882), 158, IntArch; Henry Clay, "The American System," 2, 3, and 6 February 1832, in *The Senate, 1789–1989: Classic Speeches, 1830–1993*, comp. Robert C. Byrd, ed. Wendy Wolff, 4 vols. (Washington, DC: US Government Printing Office, 1994), 3: 100; Charles C. B. Seymour, *Self-Made Men* (New York: Harper & Brothers, 1858), IntArch; Harriet Beecher Stowe, *The Lives of Self-Made Men* (Hartford, CT: Worthington, Dustin & Co., 1872), IntArch. On the power of self-making ideology in the early Republic, see Daniel Walker Howe, *Making the American Self: Jonathan Edwards to Abraham Lincoln* (New York: Oxford University Press, 1997), 136–56. *The United States Gazette* (Philadelphia, PA), 2 August 1825, NewsC; *Genius of Universal Emancipation* 1 (September 1830): 86–87, AAS; *The Liberator*, 14 July 1832.

59. Hawkins, *Lunsford Lane*, 82.

60. Lane, *Narrative of Lunsford Lane*, 2nd ed., 48.

61. Lane, *Narrative of Lunsford Lane*, 2nd ed., 48–49.

62. Lane, *Narrative of Lunsford Lane*, 2nd ed., 50; *The Liberator*, 3 June 1842; Rebecca Hall to John S. Haywood, 1 August 1836, EHC. Lunsford's cousin, Davy, disappeared from the Haywood rosters in the 1830s. It is possible that John Steele Haywood had taken him to the Alabama farm.

63. Benjamin B. Smith to Lunsford Lane, 2 December 1842, reprinted in Hawkins, *Lunsford Lane*, 163.

64. Entry for 29 February 1842, Diary of Sidney Bumpas; Stone to Ruffin, 3 May 1842; *The Rasp*, 30 April 1842, 11 June 1842.

65. *The Rasp*, 11 June 1842.

66. *The Rasp*, 26 June 1841, 12 March 1842, 30 April 1842; US Census, 1850: Wake County, NC.

67. "Memorial on Subject of Slaves and Free Negroes," 29 November 1842, November Petitions, General Assembly Session Records, November 1842–January 1843, SANC.

68. *Raleigh Register*, 7 March 1843; *Raleigh (NC) Microcosm*, 22 October 1842, NewsC; *National Anti-Slavery Standard*, 11 October 1856; Walter Eugene Milteer Jr., *North Carolina's Free People of Color, 1715–1885* (Baton Rouge: Louisiana State University Press, 2020), 52–53. One reporter confused Jones's lynching with that of Lunsford Lane, and the resulting article should be used cautiously; see *Fayetteville (NC) Weekly Observer*, 26 October 1842, NewsC.

69. *Oberlin (OH) Weekly News*, 19 August 1881, Ohio5; *Raleigh Register*, 10 March 1843; *The Rasp*, 9 April 1842; John Campton to John Primrose, 2 March 1843, bk. 53: 15–16, WCRD; Steven Lubet, *The "Colored Hero" of Harper's Ferry: John Anthony Copeland and the War against Slavery* (New York: Cambridge University Press, 2015), 32–37; Gary J. Kornblith and Carol Lasser, *Elusive Utopia: The Struggle for Racial Equality in Oberlin, Ohio* (Baton Rouge: Louisiana State University Press, 2018), 40–43. Interestingly, newspaper accounts from four decades later did not include John Campton in the scenarios. Possibly, the Camptons did not travel with the original group. Maybe the storyteller was unaware of them or just neglected them.

70. Priscilla Shaw to Henry J. Patterson, 20 April 1837, bk. 14: 292–93, WCRD; Henry J. Patterson to Charles Manly, 21 September 1842, bk. 15: 198, WCRD; Henry J. Patterson to Weston R. Gales, 28 July 1843, bk. 16: 55, WCRD; Henry J. Patterson to Weston R. Gales, 26 November 1844, bk. 16: 448, WCRD; Weston R. Gales to Henry J. Patterson, 21 August 1845, bk. 17: 216, WCRD; Henry J. Patterson to Charles Manly, 1 March 1847, bk. 17: 246, WCRD; US Census, 1840: Wake County, NC.

71. *The Rasp*, 30 April 1842.

Chapter 8

1. *Raleigh (NC) Register*, 24 March 1840, 20 June 1845, NewsC; *Wilmington (NC) Chronicle*, 27 January 1841, NewsC; *New York (NY) Daily Herald*, 2 May 1843, NewsC; Burton Alva Konkle, *John Motley Morehead and the Development of North Carolina, 1796–1866* (Philadelphia: William J. Campbell, 1922), 183–84.

2. Lunsford Lane, *The Narrative of Lunsford Lane, Formerly of Raleigh, N.C. Embracing an Account of His Early Life, the Redemption by Purchase of Himself and Family from Slavery, and His Banishment from the Place of His Birth for the Crime of Wearing a Colored Skin. Published by Himself*, 2nd ed. (Boston: J. G. Torrey, 1842), 50, AAS; Walter Clark, *History of the Raleigh & Gaston Railroad Company* (Raleigh: Raleigh News Steam Job Print, 1877), 141; US Census, 1850: Wake County, NC.

3. *The Liberator* (Boston, MA) 3 June 1842, NewsC. As with his siblings, Alexander appears to have been named after a relative: Clarissa's brother-in-law Alexander Curtis.

4. *The Liberator*, 3 June 1842.

5. *Proceedings of the Session of Broadway Tabernacle against Lewis Tappan, with the action of the Third Presbytery of New-York and General Assembly* (New York: S. W. Benedict, 1839), 10–11, AAS; William Lloyd Garrison, *An Address Delivered to the Broadway Tabernacle, N.Y., August 1, 1838* (Boston: Isaac Knapp, 1838), AAS; Kevin Pierce Thornton, "Andrew Harris, Vermont's Forgotten Abolitionist," *Vermont History* 83 (Summer/Fall 2015): 119-56; Susan Hayes Ward, *The History of the Broadway Tabernacle Church, from Its Organization in 1840 to the Close of 1900, Including Factors Influencing Its Formation* (New York: Trow Print, 1901), xii, 28–29, 41, 79, IntArch; Marcus Rediker, *The Amistad Rebellion: An Atlantic Odyssey of Slavery and Freedom* (New York: Penguin, 2013), 196, 197, 202, 284–85n27.

6. *The Liberator*, 3 June 1842.

7. *The Liberator*, 13 May 1842, 20 May 1842, 27 May 1842, 3 June 1842, 17 June 1842; *Lamoille Standard* (Johnson, VT), 21 May 1842, NewsC.

8. *The Liberator*, 3 June 1842; *National Anti-Slavery Standard* (New York, NY), 19 May 1842, AccArch; *The Oberlin (OH) Evangelist*, 22 June 1842, Ohio5; Donald M. Scott, "The Popular Lecture and the Creation of a Public in Mid-Nineteenth-Century America," *Journal of American History* 66 (March 1980): 792-94, 801.

9. *The Liberator*, 3 June 1842.

10. *The Liberator*, 3 June 1842; entry for 9–10 May 1842, Charles Spear Journal, microfilm, BPL; *National Anti-Slavery Standard*, 11 July 1844. On some White abolitionists' concession to Black speakers as the best authorities on topics related to enslavement, see Dickson D. Bruce Jr., *The Origins of African American Literature, 1680–1865* (Charlottesville: University Press of Virginia, 2001), 220–27.

11. *The Liberator*, 21 January 1842, 3 June 1842, 24 February 1844; *The Herald of Freedom* (Concord, NH), 27 May 1842, NewsC; Frederick Douglass, *My Bondage and My Freedom*, Part 1, *Life as a Slave* (New York: Miller, Orton & Mulligan, 1855), 360, NASN; John Ernest, *Liberation Historiography: African American Writers and the Challenge of History, 1794–1861* (Chapel Hill: University of North Carolina Press, 2004), 225.

12. William G. Hawkins, *Lunsford Lane; or, Another Helper from North Carolina* (Boston: Crosby & Nichols, 1863), 288, NCC.

13. Terry Baxter, *Frederick Douglass's Curious Audiences: Ethos in the Age of the Consumable Subject* (New York: Routledge, 2004), 33–37. On Douglass's introduction to oratory, see Frederick Douglass, "Boyhood in Baltimore: An Address Delivered in Baltimore, Maryland, on 6 September 1891," in *The Frederick Douglass Papers: Series One—Speeches, Debates, and Interviews*, Vol. 5, *1881–1895*, ed. John Blassingame et al. (New Haven, CT: Yale University Press, 1992), 25–33.

14. Charles Lenox Remond, "The Rights of Colored Citizens in Traveling," 1842, in *Lift Every Voice: African American Oratory, 1787–1900*, ed. Philip S. Foner and Robert James Branham (Tuscaloosa: University of Alabama Press, 1990), 190; Charles Lenox Remond, "For the Dissolution of the Union," 1844, in Foner and Branham, eds., *Lift Every Voice*, 208; Charles Lenox Remond, "Slavery as It Concerns the British," 1841, in Carter G. Woodson, *Negro Orators and Their Orations* (Washington, DC: Associated Publishers, 1925), 128; David Walker, *Walker's Appeal, in Four Articles*, 3rd ed. (Boston: David Walker, 1830), 3; Hosea Easton, "A Treatise on the Intellectual Character, and Civil and Political Condition of the Colored People of the U. States; and the Prejudice Exercised

towards Them: with a Sermon on the Duty of the Church to Them," in *To Heal the Scrouge of Prejudice: The Life and Writings of Hosea Easton*, ed. George R. Price and James Brewer Stewart (Amherst: University of Massachusetts Press, 1999), 119; IntArch; Sarah N. Roth, *Gender and Race in Antebellum Popular Culture* (New York: Cambridge University Press, 2014), 38–49.

15. *The Liberator*, 12 March 1831, 25 February 1832; Peter P. Hinks, *To Awaken My Afflicted Brethren: David Walker and the Problem of Antebellum Slave Resistance* (University Park: Pennsylvania State University Press, 1997), 269–70: Appendix E; Manisha Sinha, *The Slave's Cause: A History of Abolition* (New Haven, CT: Yale University Press, 2016), 196–214.

16. Frederick Douglass, "Love of God, Love of Man, Love of Country," 24 September 1847, in *The Frederick Douglass Papers: Series One—Speeches, Debates, and Interviews*, Vol. 2, *1847–54*, ed. John Blassingame et al. (New Haven, CT: Yale University Press, 1982), 102; Frederick Douglass, *Narrative of the Life of Frederick Douglass, an American Slave. Written by Himself* (Boston: Anti-Slavery Office, 1845), 65–66, 71, NASN; *The Liberator*, 4 February 1842; Sarah N. Roth, "'How a Slave was Made a Man': Negotiating Black Violence and Masculinity in Antebellum Slave Narratives," *Slavery & Abolition* 28 (August 2007): 255–75.

17. *National Anti-Slavery Standard*, 9 June 1842; *The Liberator*, 4 February 1842; David N. Johnson, *Sketches of Lynn: The Changes of Fifty Years* (Lynn, MA: Thos. P. Nichols, 1880), 230–31, IntArch; Baxter, *Frederick Douglass's Curious Audiences*, 4.

18. Anne Warren Weston to Deborah Weston, 25 January 1842, Anti-Slavery Collection, BPL; entry for 9–10 May 1842, Charles Spear Journal; *Boston Courier*, 10 January 1842.

19. *The Oberlin Evangelist*, 22 June 1842.

20. *The Liberator*, 3 June 1842; *National Anti-Slavery Standard*, 18 November 1841; Baxter, *Frederick Douglass's Curious Audiences*, 74–75.

21. Entry for 9–10 May 1842, Charles Spear Journal.

22. Lewis Ford, *The Variety Book, Containing Life Sketches and Reminiscences* (Boston: Geo. E. Crosby & Co., 1892), 25–26, IntArch.

23. Entries for 15 May and 23–26 May 1842, Charles Spear Journal; *Christian Reflector* (Worcester, MA), 25 May 1842, AAS; "Charge Mrs. Haywood for Negroes sold of estate," 1858, *William A. Blount and others v. John D. Hawkins and others*, 57 N.C. 162 (December 1858), Supreme Court Original Cases, 1800–1809, SANC.

24. *New York (NY) Evangelist*, 26 May 1842, NewsC; *Boston (MA) Post*, 28 May 1842, NewsC; *The Liberator*, 3 June 1842; *The Emancipator and Free American* (New York, NY), 2 June 1842, NYHS; *Vermont Baptist Journal* (Middlebury, VT), 3 June 1842, NewsC; William George Hawkins, *Life of John H. W. Hawkins* (Boston: J. P. Jewett & Co., 1859), 222–27, AAS.

25. *The Herald of Freedom*, 3 June 1842; *The Liberator*, 3 June 1842.

26. Mary Weston to Deborah Weston, 3 July 1842, Anti-Slavery Collection, BPL; *The Liberator*, 15 June 1842.

27. *The Rasp* (Raleigh, NC), 5 March 1842, 21 May 1842, 16 July 1842, NewsC.

28. Hawkins, *Lunsford Lane*, 170–71.

29. Thomas Jefferson, *Notes on the State of Virginia* (Philadelphia: Prichard & Hall, 1788), 149, Rare Book Collection, Wilson Library, University of North Carolina, Chapel Hill.

30. George Bancroft, *History of the Colonization of the United States*, 3 vols., 3rd ed. (Boston: Charles C. Little and James Brown, 1838), 2: 466–67, AAS; Samuel Ringgold Ward, *Autobiography of a Fugitive Negro: His Anti-Slavery Labours in the United States, Canada & England* (London: John Snow, 1855), 185–86, IntArch; Michael D. Hattem, *Past*

and Prologue: Politics and Memory in the American Revolution (New Haven, CT: Yale University Press, 2020), 236, 247–48.

31. *The Liberator*, 13 July 1860.

32. "Minutes of the Fourth Annual Convention of the Free People of Colour in the United States" (New York: the Convention, 1834), 27, *Colored Conventions Project Digital Records*, https://omeka.coloredconventions.org/items/show/276; James W. C. Pennington, *A Text Book of the Origin and History, &c. &c. of the Colored People* (Hartford, CT: L. Skinner, 1841), 51–52, IntArch; Ernest, *Liberation Historiography*, 39–94; Benjamin Quarles, "Black History's Antebellum Origins," *Proceedings of the American Antiquarian Society* 89 (1979): 91.

33. *The Liberator*, 2 March 1833; Henry Highland Garnet, *A Memorial Discourse* (Philadelphia: Joseph M. Wilson, 1865), 50, IntArch; *The Colored American* (New York, NY), 30 May 1840, AAN.

34. Henry Highland Garnet, "Address to the Slaves of the United States of America," 16 August 1843, in *The Black Abolitionist Papers*, ed. C. Peter Ripley et al., 5 vols. (Chapel Hill: University of North Carolina Press, 1985–92), 4: 409; Patrick Rael, *Black Identity & Black Protest in the Antebellum North* (Chapel Hill: University of North Carolina Press, 2002), 224–25, 273–74.

35. J. W. Loguen, *The Rev. J. W. Loguen, as a Slave and as a Freeman. A Narrative of Real Life* (Syracuse: J. G. K. Truair & Co., 1859), viii, IntArch; James McCune Smith, "The German Invasion," *Anglo-African Magazine* 1 (February 1859): 48, AAS.

36. Weston to Weston, 3 July 1842.

37. *Carolina Federal Republican* (New Bern, NC), 21 March 1818, NewsC; *The Emancipator and Free American*, 3 November 1842; William Richard Cutter, *Genealogical and Personal Memoirs Relating to the Families of Boston and Eastern Massachusetts*, 4 vols. (New York: Historical Publishing Co., 1908), 3: 1264, AAS; John C. Shields, *The American Aeneas: Classical Origins of the American Self* (Knoxville: University of Tennessee Press, 2001), xxviii-xxxiii, 165–204, 297–333; Carl J. Richard, *The Golden Age of the Classics in America: Greece, Rome, and the Antebellum United States* (Cambridge, MA: Harvard University Press, 2009), 4–5, 17–19, 23; Carl J. Richard, "Vergil and the Early American Republic," in *A Companion to Vergil's* Aeneid *and Its Tradition*, ed. Joseph Farrell and Michael C. J. Putnam (Malden, MA: John Wiley & Sons, 2010), 355–65.

38. Stephen S. Foster, *The Brotherhood of Thieves; or, a True Picture of the American Church and Clergy* (Boston: Anti-Slavery Office, 1844), 20, AAS.

39. Thomas Jefferson to Samuel Adams Wells, 12 May 1819, in *The Papers of Thomas Jefferson: Retirement Series*, ed. J. Jefferson Looney, 15 vols. (Princeton, NJ: Princeton University Press, 2011), 14: 293; Pauline Maier, *The Old Revolutionaries: Political Lives in the Age of Samuel Adams* (New York: Alfred A. Knopf, 1980), 3–50; *The Liberator*, 15 March 1844.

40. William C. Nell, *The Colored Patriots of the American Revolution, with Sketches of Several Distinguished Colored Persons* (Boston: Robert F. Wallcut, 1855), 380, AAS; William Wells Brown, *The Negro in the American Rebellion: His Heroism and His Fidelity* (Boston: Lee & Shepard, 1867), AAS; Sinha, *Slave's Cause*, 205–6; Erica L. Ball, *To Live an Antislavery Life: Personal Politics and the Antebellum Black Middle Class* (Athens: University of Georgia Press, 2012), 113.

41. John Adams, *Discourses on Davila; a Series of Papers on Political History, by an American Citizen*, in *The Works of John Adams, Second President of the United States; with*

a Life of the Author, Notes and Illustrations, ed. Charles Francis Adams, 10 vols. (Boston: Charles C. Little and James Brown, 1851), 6: 280, AAS; Margaret M. R. Kellow, "Conflicting Imperatives: Black and White American Abolitionists Debate Slave Redemption," in *Buying Freedom: The Ethics and Economics of Slave Redemption*, ed. Kwame Anthony Appiah and Martin Bunzl (Princeton, NJ: Princeton University Press, 2007), 204.

42. Sumner Eliot Morrison, "Manumission by Purchase," *Journal of Negro History* 33 (April 1948): 155; Dylan C. Penningroth, *Before the Movement: The Hidden History of Black Civil Rights* (New York; Liveright, 2023), 15.

43. *The United States Gazette* (Philadelphia, PA), 2 August 1825, NewsC; *Genius of Universal Emancipation* 1 (September 1830): 86–87; *The Liberator*, 14 July 1832. A simple word search in *Newspapers.com* and *Accessible Archives* resulted in zero matches for "redemption by purchase" and "redemption-by-purchase." So, Lane's use of the term was rather unique. Julia Wallace Bernier noted that, during the nineteenth century, Americans more commonly used the term "compensated manumission" to indicate buying someone else's freedom; see "A Papered Freedom: Self-Purchase and Compensated Manumission in the Antebellum United States" (PhD diss., University of Massachusetts Amherst, 2017), 2.

44. *Genius of Universal Emancipation* 2 (January 1832): 121–22, 2 (May 1832): 191; *The Liberator*, 3 March 1832; Bernier, "A Papered Freedom," chaps. 2–3.

45. *Genius of Universal Emancipation* 2 (August 1832): 208; *The Liberator*, 15 September 1832.

46. *The Liberator*, 16 June 1832, 31 August 1833, 7 September 1833, 9 August 1834; *The North Star* (Rochester, NY), 27 January 1834, AAN.

47. *The Liberator*, 27 September 1834; *Southern Christian Herald*, reprinted in *The Liberator*, 14 March 1835.

48. *The Liberator*, 17 September 1841; Kellow, "Conflicting Imperatives," 200–212.

49. "Declaration of Sentiments of the American Anti-Slavery Convention," in *Selections from the Writings and Speeches of William Lloyd Garrison* (Boston: R. F. Wallcut, 1852), 69, AAS; *The North Star* (NY), 27 January 1834.

50. *The Liberator*, 17 September 1841, 8 July 1842.

51. *National Anti-Slavery Standard*, 19 May 1842.

52. *The Liberator*, 15 January 1847, 22 January 1847, 29 January 1847, 19 February 1847, 5 March 1847; William Lloyd Garrison to Elizabeth Pease, 1 April 1847, in *The Letters of William Lloyd Garrison*, Vol. 3, *No Union with Slave-Holders 1841–1846*, ed. Walter Merrill (Cambridge, MA: The Belknap Press, 1973), 474; Kellow, "Conflicting Imperatives," 204–6; Sinha, *Slave's Cause*, 426–27; Aileen S. Kraditor, *Means and Ends in American Abolitionism: Garrison and His Critics on Strategy and Tactics, 1834–1850* (New York: Pantheon Books, 1967), 220–22.

53. Lane, *Narrative of Lunsford Lane*, 2nd ed., 17; Edie L. Wong, *Neither Fugitive nor Free: Atlantic Slavery, Freedom Suits, and the Legal Culture of Travel* (New York: New York University Press, 2016), 165.

Chapter 9

1. *Stimpson's Boston Directory* (Boston: Charles Stimpson, 1842), 32–35.

2. *Boston (MA) Post*, 14 June 1842, NewsC; Lunsford Lane, *The Narrative of Lunsford Lane, Formerly of Raleigh, N.C. Embracing an Account of His Early Life, the Redemption by*

Purchase of Himself and Family from Slavery, and His Banishment from the Place of His Birth for the Crime of Wearing a Colored Skin. Published by Himself, 2nd ed. (Boston: J. G. Torrey, 1842), iii–iv, AAS.

3. Lane, *Narrative of Lunsford Lane*, 2nd ed., iii–iv; Frederick Douglass, *My Bondage and My Freedom*, Part 1, *Life as a Slave* (New York: Miller, Orton & Mulligan, 1855), 361, NASN. On the pressure placed on narrators to tailor stories to their sponsors' agendas, see Valerie Smith, *Self-Discovery and Authority in Afro-American Narrative* (Cambridge, MA: Harvard University Press, 1987), 9–10. On White editors' revision of narratives for political purposes, see Ann Fabian, *Unvarnished Truth: Personal Narratives in Nineteenth-Century America* (Berkeley: University of California Press, 2000), 79–116.

4. James Olney, "'I Was Born': Slave Narratives, Their Status as Autobiography and as Literature," *Callaloo* 20 (Winter 1984): 50–52, 68n6.

5. Olney, "'I Was Born,'" 52; Frederick Douglass, *Narrative of the Life of Frederick Douglass, an American Slave. Written by Himself.* (Boston: Anti-Slavery Office, 1845), 1, NASN; Douglass, *My Bondage and My Freedom*, 34; Frederick Douglass, *The Heroic Slave*, in *Autographs for Freedom* (Boston: John P. Jewett & Co., 1853), 177, BPL; B. Eugene McCarthy and Thomas L. Doughton, "General Introduction," in *From Bondage to Belonging: The Worcester Slave Narratives*, ed. B. Eugene McCarthy and Thomas L. Doughton (Amherst: University of Massachusetts Press, 2007), xlix. In his later years, Douglass moved the birth claim back to the first paragraph of *Life and Times of Frederick Douglass: His Early Life as a Slave, His Escape from Bondage, and His Complete History to the Present Time* (Hartford, CT: Park Publishing Co., 1881), 13, NASN.

6. Lane, *Narrative of Lunsford Lane*, 2nd ed., 7; Sterling Lecater Bland Jr., *Voices of the Fugitives: Runaway Slave Stories and Their Fictions of Self-Creation* (Westport, CT: Praeger, 2000), 67–68; Joseph Campbell, *The Hero with a Thousand Faces: Commemorative Edition* (Princeton, NJ: Princeton University Press, 2004), 28–36; Evans Lansing Smith, *The Hero Journey in Literature: Parables of Poesis* (Lanham, MD: University Press of America, 1997), 232–38.

7. Jo Burr Margadant, "Introduction: Constructing Selves in Historical Perspective," in *The New Biography: Performing Femininity in Nineteenth-Century France*, ed. Jo Burr Margadant (Berkeley: University of California Press, 2000), 2, 7; Daniel Walker Howe, *Making the American Self: Jonathan Edwards to Abraham Lincoln* (New York: Oxford University Press, 1997), 107–114; William L. Andrews, *To Tell a Free Story: The First Century of Afro-American Autobiography, 1760–1865* (Urbana: University of Illinois Press, 1986), 112–18.

8. Don Holmes, "'a clever fellow': The Subversive Trickster in *The Narrative of Lunsford Lane*," unpublished manuscript, 2019, in possession of author; Francis Smith Foster, *Witnessing Slavery: The Development of Anti-Bellum Slave Narratives* (Madison: University of Wisconsin Press, 1979), 5–6; Lane, *Narrative of Lunsford Lane*, 2nd ed., 50; Andrews, *To Tell a Free Story*, 206.

9. Richard Slotkin, *Regeneration through Violence: The Mythology of the American Frontier, 1600–1860* (Norman: University of Oklahoma Pres, 1973), 440–44; David Wall, "'A Chaos of Sin and Folly': Art, Culture, and Carnival in Antebellum America," *Journal of American Studies* 42 (December 2008): 515–35.

10. Ralph Waldo Emerson, *The Works of Ralph Waldo Emerson, in 12 vols.*, Fireside ed. (Boston: n. p., 1909), 5: 288; Nell Irvin Painter, *The History of White People* (New York:

W. W. Norton, 2010), 174–77; Kirk Savage, *Standing Soldiers, Kneeling Slaves: Race, War, and Monument in Nineteenth-Century America* (Princeton, NJ: Princeton University Press, 1997), 30.

11. Michel Sobel, "The Revolution in Selves: Black and White Inner Aliens," in *Through a Glass Darkly: Reflections on Personal Identity in Early America*, ed. Ronald Hoffman, Mechal Sobel, and Fredrika J. Teute (Chapel Hill: University of North Carolina Press, 1997), 171–2. On expectations of subservience within White abolitionists' imagining of Blackness, see Toni Morrison, *The Origins of Others* (Cambridge, MA: Harvard University Press, 2017), 9–14.

12. Allyson Hobbs, *A Chosen Exile: A History of Racial Passing in American Life* (Cambridge, MA: Harvard University Press, 2014), chap. 1; P. Gabrielle Foreman and Cherene Sherrard-Johnson, "Racial Recovery, Racial Death: An Introduction in Four Parts," *Legacy* 24 (2007): 160–61; Laura Doyle, "Atlantic Modernism at the Crossing: The Migrant Labours of Hurston, McKay, and the Diasporic Text," in *Modernism and Race*, ed. Len Platt (New York: Cambridge University Press, 2011), 116; Stephen Butterfield, *Black Autobiography in America* (Amherst: University of Massachusetts Press, 1974), chap. 3; Gary S. Selby, "The Limits of Accommodation: Frederick Douglass and the Garrisonian Abolitionists," *Southern Communication Journal* 66 (2000): 52–66; McCarthy and Doughton, "General Introduction," xxiv.

13. Howe, *Making the American Self*, 136–56; Margadant, "Introduction," 1–10. On Lane's narrative as part of a larger literary movement in the 1840s that minimized violence in slave narratives to emphasize the protagonists' admirable manliness, see Sarah N. Roth, "'How a Slave was Made a Man': Negotiating Black Violence and Masculinity in Antebellum Slave Narratives," *Slavery & Abolition* 28 (August 2007): 255–75.

14. Charles C. B. Seymour, *Self-Made Men* (New York: Harper & Brothers, 1858), IntArch; Harriet Beecher Stowe, *The Lives of Self-Made Men* (Hartford, CT: Worthington, Dustin & Co., 1872), IntArch; Howe, *Making the American Self*, 136–56.

15. *The United States Gazette* (Philadelphia, PA), 2 August 1825, NewsC; *Genius of Universal Emancipation* 1 (September 1830): 86–87; *The Liberator* (Boston, MA), 14 July 1832, NewsC; Howe, *Making the American Self*, 136–37.

16. *The Liberator*, 16 April 1831, 7 December 1838; Erica L. Ball, *To Live an Antislavery Life: Personal Politics and the Antebellum Black Middle Class* (Athens: University of Georgia Press, 2012), 37–61; Willard B. Gatewood Jr., "'To Be Truly Free': Louis Sheridan and the Colonization of Liberia," *Civil War History* 29 (December 1983): 332–48.

17. Butterfield, *Black Autobiography in America*, 29–30; John Ernest, *Liberation Historiography: African American Writers and the Challenge of History, 1794–1861* (Chapel Hill: University of North Carolina Press, 2004), 17; Margaret M. R. Kellow, "Conflicting Imperatives: Black and White American Abolitionists Debate Slave Redemption," in *Buying Freedom: The Ethics and Economics of Slave Redemption*, ed. Kwame Anthony Appiah and Martin Bunzl (Princeton, NJ: Princeton University Press, 2007), 209. Although the parcel of lot 53 was too small to warrant a property tax when Lane owned it, when Benjamin B. Smith took control of it, combined with his other properties, it showed up in the Wake County tax lists, but only for one year. The meager increase in Smith's property taxes indicates it was certainly not worth $500; see Tax List for 1842, Wake County Tax Lists: 1781–1860, SANC; Lane, *Narrative of Lunsford Lane*, 2nd ed., 84; William G. Hawkins, *Lunsford Lane; or, Another Helper from North Carolina* (Boston: Crosby & Nichols, 1863), 147, NCC.

18. William Grimes, *Life of William Grimes, the Runaway Slave* (New York: n. p., 1825), 50–52, NASN; Andrews, *To Tell a Free Story*, 62–66.

19. Lane, *Narrative of Lunsford Lane*, 2nd ed., iv; Cynthia A. Current, "Lunsford Lane: 1803-?" in *The North Carolina Roots of African American Literature: An Anthology*, ed. William L. Andrews (Chapel Hill: University of North Carolina Press, 2006), 139–43.

20. Lane, *Narrative of Lunsford Lane*, 2nd ed., iv; Charles Lenox Remond, "The Rights of Colored Citizens in Traveling," 1842, in *Lift Every Voice: African American Oratory, 1787–1900*, ed. Philip S. Foner and Robert James Branham (Tuscaloosa: University of Alabama Press, 1990), 190; Charles Lenox Remond, "Slavery as It Concerns the British," 1841, in Carter G. Woodson, *Negro Orators and Their Orations* (Washington, DC: Associated Publishers, 1925), 128; William L. Andrews, *Slavery and Class in the American South: A Generation of Slave Narrative Testimony, 1840–1865* (New York: Oxford University Press, 2019), 47.

21. Lane, *Narrative of Lunsford Lane*, 2nd ed., 11, 20, 52; *The Liberator*, 9 December 1842; John Stauffer, "Foreword," in McCarthy and Doughton, eds., *From Bondage to Belonging*, xvi; Ernest, *Liberation Historiography*, 162; Sidonie Smith, *Where I'm Bound: Patterns of Slavery and Freedom in Black American Autobiography* (Westport, CT: Greenwood Press, 1974), 13; Bland, *Voices of the Fugitives*, 65.

22. *The Emancipator and Free American* (New York, NY), 21 July 1842, NYHS; *The Weekly Standard* (Raleigh, NC), 13 May 1846, NewsC; *Stimpson's Boston Directory* (Boston: Charles Stimpson Jr., 1840), 404, BPL; US Census, 1840: Roxbury, MA; Charles H. Nichols, "Who Read the Slave Narratives?" *Phylon Quarterly* 20 (1959): 149–50; Michael Winship, "Manufacturing and Book Production," in *A History of the Book in America*, Vol. 3, *The Industrial Book, 1840–1880*, ed. Scott E. Casper et al. (Chapel Hill: University of North Carolina Press, 2008), 46, 51, 61–62; Joseph Griffin, ed., *History of the Press of Maine* (Brunswick: Joseph Griffin, 1872), 166, IntArch. Historian John W. Blassingame suggested that Lane's ghostwriter was William George Hawkins who, in 1863, penned Lane's biography; see *Slave Testimony: Two Centuries of Letters, Speeches, Interviews, and Autobiographies* (Baton Rouge: Louisiana State University Press, 1977), xix. Although plausible, it is unlikely. Hawkins was eighteen years old in 1842 and had lived in Massachusetts for only two months. Also, Hawkins claimed in 1863 that he only recently had met Lane; see *Lunsford Lane*, v; William George Hawkins, *Life of John H. W. Hawkins* (Boston: J. P. Jewett & Co., 1859), 222, AAS.

23. *The Liberator*, 8 July 1842; *The Emancipator and Republican* (Boston, MA), 21 July 1842, AAS; *The Emancipator and Free American*, 21 July 1842; Andrews, *To Tell a Free Story*, 108.

24. Copyright Ledger: District of Massachusetts, 1842, Vol. 59: 177, Early Copyright Records Collection, Rare Book and Special Collections Division, LOC; *Boston (MA) Musical Visitor*, 6 October 1842, AAS; Sadie Van Vranken, "Lunsford Lane," *Black Self-Publishing*, https://www.americanantiquarian.org/Blackpublishing/lunsford-lane.

25. Lunsford Lane, *The Narrative of Lunsford Lane, Formerly of Raleigh, N.C. Embracing an Account of His Early Life, the Redemption by Purchase of Himself and Family from Slavery, and His Banishment from the Place of His Birth for the Crime of Wearing a Colored Skin. Published by Himself*, 1st ed. (Boston: J. G. Torrey, 1842), iii, AAS. This is the only extant original edition that I have located, and as I held it in the reading room of the American Antiquarian Society, I realized that, sometime in 1842, Lunsford Lane had handled it, momentarily, as he passed it to a purchaser. His fingerprints are all over this book,

but a forensic analyst would be hard-pressed to distinguish them from the fingerprints of many others—the purchaser, the collector, the librarians, the researchers—who have turned its pages since 1842.

26. Lane, *Narrative of Lunsford Lane*, 1st ed., 11; Lane, *Narrative of Lunsford Lane*, 2nd ed., 11; Gay Wilentz, "Authenticating Experience: North Carolina Slave Narratives and the Politics of Place," *North Carolina Literary Review* 1 (Summer 1992): 122.

27. Lane, *Narrative of Lunsford Lane*, 1st ed., 8; Lane, *Narrative of Lunsford Lane*, 2nd ed., 8.

28. "The Slave Mother's Address to Her Infant Child," 1842, in Lane, *Narrative of Lunsford Lane*, 1st ed., inside front and back cover; Lane, *Narrative of Lunsford Lane*, 2nd ed., iii; Noah Webster, *An American Dictionary of the English Language*, 2 vols. (New York: S. Converse, 1828), 1: 713, IntArch. On the term "fair" as a synonym for "White," see "The United States and the Slave Trade," *The United Service Magazine and Naval and Military Journal, 1842: Part II* (June 1842): 171–78, IntArch, in which the author denounced the United States as "a land where dark and fair skins are not even allowed equal privileges of approaching their common Creator" (175).

29. "The Slave Mother's Address to Her Infant Child"; Russ Castronovo, *Necro Citizenship: Death, Eroticism, and the Public Sphere in the Nineteenth-Century United States* (Durham: Duke University Press, 2001), 37; McCarthy and Doughton, "General Introduction," l; Melvin Dixon, "The Black Writer's Use of Memory," in *History and Memory in African-American Culture*, ed. Genevieve Fabre and Robert O'Meally (New York: Oxford University Press, 1994), 18–27. John Stauffer suggested that we assume Black narrators "wrote, at least in part, for northern free Blacks"; see "Foreword," xiii. We know that was true for Lunsford Lane, who was writing for anyone willing to pay.

30. Frederick Douglass, "Self-Made Men: An Address Delivered in Carlisle, Pennsylvania in March 1893," in *The Frederick Douglass Papers: Series One—Speeches, Debates, and Interviews*, Vol. 5, *1881–1895*, ed. John Blassingame et al. (New Haven, CT: Yale University Press, 1992), 545–75, quotes on 549–50; Frederick Douglass to James Redpath, 29 July 1871, Alfred Williams Anthony Collection, New York Public Library, New York; Booker T. Washington, *The Story of the Negro*, Vol. 1, *The Rise of the Race from Slavery* (London: T. Fisher Unwin, 1909), 296–309; Howe, *Making the American Self*, 149–56; Robert Steven Levine, *Martin Delaney, Frederick Douglass, and the Politics of Representative Identity* (Chapel Hill: University of North Carolina Press, 1997), 4; Sarah N. Roth, *Gender and Race in Antebellum Popular Culture* (New York: Cambridge University Press, 2014), 84.

31. Lane, *Narrative of Lunsford Lane*, 2nd ed., 6–7, 17–18, 31, 45.

32. Lane, *Narrative of Lunsford Lane*, 2nd ed., 30.

33. Over the 1840s and 1850s, several Black abolitionists became subject to rumors of marital infidelity, including William Wells Brown and Frederick Douglass; see Ezra Greenspan, *William Wells Brown: An African American Life* (New York: W. W. Norton, 2014), 256–66; Leigh Fought, *Women in the World of Frederick Douglass* (New York: Oxford University Press, 2017), 85–87, 95–96, 109–11; David W. Blight, *Frederick Douglass: Prophet of Freedom* (New York: Simon & Schuster, 2018), 221.

34. Richard Newman, *The Transformation of American Abolitionism: Fighting Slavery in the Early Republic* (Chapel Hill: University of North Carolina Press, 2002), 4–8; Andrews, *To Tell a Free Story*, 61–66.

35. Mary Weston to Deborah Weston, 3 July 1842, Anti-Slavery Collection, BPL; *The Liberator*, 15 July 1842.

36. Lewis Ford, *The Variety Book, Containing Life Sketches and Reminiscences* (Boston: Geo. E. Crosby & Co., 1892), 19–20, IntArch.

37. *The Liberator*, 28 June 1839, 26 July 1844; E. Fuller Torrey, *The Martyrdom of Abolitionist Charles Torrey* (Baton Rouge: Louisiana State University Press, 2013); Corey M. Brooks, *Liberty Power: Antislavery Third Parties and the Transformation of American Politics* (Chicago: University of Chicago Press, 2016), 32–33; Frederick D. Torrey, *The Torrey Families and Their Children in America*, 2 vols. (Lakehurst, NJ: privately published, 1924–1929), 1: 81, 191, 275, 277, 2: 35, 71.

38. *The Herald of Freedom* (Concord, NH), 1 July 1842, NewsC; Charles J. G. Griffin, "The 'Washingtonian Revival': Narrative and the Moral Transformation of Temperance Reform in Antebellum America," *Southern Communication Journal* 66 (Fall 2000): 67–78; Milton A. Maxwell, "The Washington Movement," *Quarterly Journal of Studies on Alcohol* 11 (September 1950): 422–23.

39. *The Liberator*, 12 August 1842.

40. *The Emancipator and Free American*, 21 July 1842, 25 August 1842; Julie Roy Jeffrey, "The Liberty Women of Boston: Evangelicalism and Antislavery Politics," *New England Quarterly* 85 (March 2012): 38–77.

41. *The Weekly Standard*, 10 November 1841, 19 January 1842; *Raleigh (NC) Register*, 16 November 1841; *The Liberator*, 9 September 1842; Hawkins, *Lunsford Lane*, 50. Hunter apparently did not rely on a trip to New England to raise money, listing only Philadelphia, New York, and Washington as the sites of fundraisers; *Brooklyn (NY) Evening Star*, 29 November 1842, NewsC.

42. US Census, 1850: Washington, DC; US Census, 1860: Washington, DC; *Journals of the Senate and House of Commons of the General Assembly of the State of North Carolina, at the Session of 1840–41* (Raleigh: Thomas J. Lemay, 1841), 536, 564, SANC; Estate of Waller Freeman, 19 July 1870, Wills and Estate Papers, Chatham County, SANC; *National Republican* (Washington, DC), 2 April 1879, NewsC; Thomas Hutchinson, comp., *Boyd's Washington and Georgetown Directory* (Washington, DC: Thomas Hutchinson, 1862), 85; *Hutchinson's Washington and Georgetown Directory* (Washington, DC: Hutchinson and Brother, 1863), 93, IntArch; Andre Boyd, comp., *Boyd's Washington and Georgetown Directory* (Washington, DC: Hudson Taylor, 1865), 200, IntArch; Civil War Union Draft Records, District of Columbia, Consolidated Enrollment Lists, 1863–1865, 5 vols., 1: 314, Records of the Provost Marshal General's Bureau, RG 110, War Department, National Archives, Washington, DC, Fold3, https://www.fold3.com/; record for Waller F. Freeman, #1447, *Registers of Signatures of Depositors in Branches of the Freedman's Savings and Trust Company, 1865–1874*, July 11, 1865–December 30, 1871, Records of the Office of the Comptroller of the Currency, RG 101, NARA.

43. *The American and Foreign Anti-Slavery Reporter* (New York, NY), 1 September 1842, AAS; *The Abolitionist* (Cazenovia, NY), 11 October 1842, AAS.

44. Entry for 13–14 October 1842, Charles Spear Journal, microfilm, BPL; Henry Stedman Nouse, *History of the Town of Harvard, Massachusetts: 1732–1893* (Harvard, MA: Warren Hapgood, 1894), 249–50, AAS; US Census, 1850: Worcester County, MA; *The Emancipator and Free American*, 3 November 1842.

45. *The Emancipator and Free American*, 17 November 1842, 24 November 1842.

46. *The Liberator*, 28 October 1842, 11 November 1842; entry for 24 October 1842, Diary 43: 1 January 1842–8 July 1843, *The Diaries of John Quincy Adams*, MHS, https://www.masshist.org/jqadiaries/php.

47. *Boston Post*, 1 November 1842; *Boston (MA) Daily Atlas*, 11 November 1842, MHS; *The Emancipator and Free American*, 3 November 1842; *Bangor (ME) Daily Whig and Courier*, 2 November 1842, NewsC; *Wisconsin Democrat* (Green Bay, WI), 29 November 1842, NewsC; Manisha Sinha, *The Slave's Cause: A History of Abolition* (New Haven, CT: Yale University Press, 2016), 391; Stanley Harrold, *Border War: Fighting over Slavery before the Civil War* (Chapel Hill: University of North Carolina Press, 2010), 100–101, 107.

48. *National Anti-Slavery Standard* (New York, NY), 28 July 1842, AccArch; entries for 18 October 1842 and 19 November 1842, Charles Spear Journal.

49. *The Liberator*, 25 November 1842.

50. *The Herald of Freedom*, 16 December 1842; *The Liberator*, 9 December 1842.

51. *The Liberator*, 27 January 1843; *National Anti-Slavery Standard*, 9 February 1843.

Chapter 10

1. Tax book, 1843: Ward 5, 53, Real Estate, Personal Estate and Poll Tax Records, City of Boston Archives, West Roxbury, MA; Transfer book, 1843: Ward 5, 56, Real Estate, Personal Estate and Poll Tax Records; Valuation book, 1843: Ward 5, 46, Real Estate, Personal Estate and Poll Tax Records.

2. Cambridge Assessor's Records, Ward 2—Annotated, 1842, CPL; William Lloyd Garrison to George William Brown, 20 September 1839, Anti-Slavery Collection, BPL; US Census, 1840: Middlesex County, MA. Lunsford Lane does not appear in the assessor's records for 1843, 1844, or 1845, although the Lanes lived in the house on Medford Street.

3. *The Life of Arthur Tappan* (New York: Hurd and Houghton, 1870), 180, AAS; *Minutes of the State Convention of Colored Citizens, Held at Albany, on the 18th, 19th, and 20th of August, 1840, for the Purpose of Considering Their Political Condition* (New York: Piercy & Reed, 1840), 6, 7, 9, 25, AAS; *The Liberator* (Boston, MA), 11 February 1842, 1 July 1842, 19 August 1842, 11 November 1842, NewsC; *National Anti-Slavery Standard* (New York, NY), 10 October 1850, AccArch; William C. Nell, *The Colored Patriots of the American Revolution, with Sketches of Several Distinguished Colored Persons* (Boston: Robert F. Wallcut, 1855), 356, AAS; David E. Swift, *Black Prophets of Justice: Activist Clergy before the Civil War* (Baton Rouge: Louisiana State University Press, 1989), 166; James Oliver Horton and Lois E. Horton, *In Hope of Liberty: Culture, Community and Protest among Northern Free Blacks, 1700–1860* (New York: Oxford University Press, 1997), 242; George H. Hansell, *Reminiscences of Baptist Churches and Baptist Leaders in New York City and Vicinity, from 1835–1898* (Philadelphia: American Baptist Publication Society, 1899), 7, 26, HT. On the Colored Citizens Conventions, see *The Colored Conventions Movement: Black Organizing in the Nineteenth Century*, ed. P. Gabrielle Foreman, Jim Casey, and Sarah Lynn Patterson (Chapel Hill: University of North Carolina Press, 2021).

4. *Boston Courier*, reprinted in *The Emancipator and Free American* (New York, NY), 28 July 1842, NYHS; *The Liberator*, 30 January 1846; *Report to the Primary School Committee, June 15, 1846, on the Petition of Sundry Colored Persons, for the Abolition of the Schools for Colored Citizens* (Boston, MA: Primary School Committee, 1846), Boston School Committee Papers, BPL; *Sarah C. Roberts v. The City of Boston*, 59 Mass. 198, 5 Cush. 198 (November 1849), in *Encyclopedia of African American History, 1619–1895: From the Colonial Period to the Age of Frederick Douglass*, ed. Paul Finkelman (New York: Oxford University Press, 2009), 198–210; George A. Levesque, *Black Boston: African American Life and*

Culture in Urban America, 1750–1860 (New York: Garland Publishing, 1994), 116–28; James Oliver Horton and Lois E. Horton, *Black Bostonians: Family Life and Community Struggle in the Antebellum North* (New York: Holmes & Meier, 1979), 78–79; Roderick T. Baltimore and Robert F. Williams, "The State Constitutional Roots of the 'Separate but Equal' Doctrine: *Roberts v. City of Boston*," *Rutgers Law Journal* 17 (1986): 537–52; Cambridge Assessor's Records, Ward 2—Annotated, 1842, 15, 47.

5. Nell, *Colored Patriots*, 364; Roy E. Finkenbine, "Boston's Black Churches: Institutional Centers of the Antislavery Movement," in *Courage and Conscience: Black & White Abolitionists in Boston*, ed. Donald M. Jacobs (Bloomington: Indiana University Press, 1993), 171, 175–80; Mitch Kachun, *Festivals of Freedom: Memory and Meaning in African American Emancipation Celebrations, 1808–1915* (Amherst: University of Massachusetts Press, 2003), 56; Horton and Horton, *Black Bostonians*, 41–43; Stephen and Paul Kendrick, *Sarah's Long Walk: The Free Blacks of Boston and How Their Struggle for Equality Changed America* (Boston: Beacon Press, 2004), 75–76; Robert C. Hayden, *The African Meeting House in Boston: A Celebration of History* (Boston: Museum of Afro-American History, 1987), 19.

6. *Christian Reflector* (Worcester, MA), 3 August 1842, AAS; "Petition of John T. Hilton + 375 other colored Citizens of Boston praying for equal rights in travelling on railroads," House Unpassed Legislation 1843, docket 1230A, series 230, seq. 60–70, Digital Archive of Massachusetts Anti-Slavery and Anti-Segregation Petitions, Harvard College Library, Harvard University, Cambridge, MA, https://id.lib.harvard.edu/ead/wid00004/catalog; "Petition of John T. Hilton," House Unpassed Legislation 1843, docket 1286, series 230, seq. 11–21, Digital Archive of Massachusetts Anti-Slavery and Anti-Segregation Petitions; Adelaide M. Cromwell, *The Other Brahmins: Boston's Black Upper Class, 1750–1950* (Fayetteville: University of Arkansas Press, 1994), 39, 44, 225. Presumably, someone other than the Lanes wrote their names on the petitions because, on the first petition, the signatory wrote "Emeline Lane" instead of "Maria Bell Lane," correcting the error slightly on the second petition with "M Lane."

7. *The Liberator*, 28 July 1843, 4 August 1843; Finkenbine, "Boston's Black Churches," 173.

8. *The Liberator*, 4 August 1843; *Vital Records of Cambridge, Massachusetts, to the Year 1850*, comp. Thomas W. Baldwin, 2 vols. (Boston: Wright & Potter, 1915), 632, LOC; William Lloyd Garrison to George William Benson, 1 April 1843, Anti-Slavery Collection; William G. Hawkins, *Lunsford Lane; or, Another Helper from North Carolina* (Boston: Crosby & Nichols, 1863), vi, NCC.

9. "School Committee Semi-Annual Report, 1843," Boston School Committee Papers.

10. *Triumph of Equal School Rights in Boston: Proceedings of the Presentation Meeting Held in Boston, December 17, 1855* (Boston: R. F. Wallent, 1856), 5, AAS; Martin Moore, *Boston Revival, 1842: A Brief History of the Evangelical Churches of Boston, Together with a More Particular Account of the Revival of 1842* (Boston: John Putnam, 1842), 95, AAS; City of Boston School Committee Minutes, Vol. 3, 1838, 122–23, Boston School Committee Papers, 317–59; Kendrick and Kendrick, *Sarah's Long Walk*, 85; Dorothy Parker Wesley, "Integration versus Separation: William Cooper Nell's Role in the Struggle for Equality," in Jacobs, ed., *Courage and Conscience*, 208–9.

11. "School Committee Semi-Annual Report, 1843," Boston School Committee Papers; "Resolutions by a Meeting of Boston Blacks Convened at the First Independent Baptist Church of People of Color in Boston, Boston, Massachusetts, 18 June 1844," in Ripley et al., eds., *The Black Abolitionist Papers*, 3: 446–49; Primary School committee report, quoted

in Charles Sumner, *Orations and Speeches*, 2 vols. (Boston: Ticknor, Reed, and Fields, 1850), 2: 352; Horton and Horton, *Black Bostonians*, 71, 74; Crystal Lynn Webster, *Beyond the Boundaries of Childhood: African American Children in the Antebellum North* (Chapel Hill: University of North Carolina Press, 2021), 107–110; Kendrick and Kendrick, *Sarah's Long Walk*, 76.

12. Hawkins, *Lunsford Lane*, 196–97.

13. *The Emancipator and Free American* 10 August 1843; *The Liberator*, 21 July 1843, 4 August 1843; *The Practical Christian* (Hopedale, MA), 9 July 1843, AAS; Kachun, *Festivals of Freedom*, 26–27, 56.

14. "Report of the West Indian Emancipation Committee, October 13, 1858," American Negro Historical Society Papers, Leon Gardiner Collection, HSP; William B. Gravely, "The Dialectic of Double-Consciousness in Black American Freedom Celebrations, 1808–1863," *Journal of Negro History* 67 (Winter 1982): 304–306; W. E. B. Du Bois, "Strivings of the Negro People," *Atlantic Monthly* 80 (August 1897): 194–95; Kachun, *Festivals of Freedom*, 56, 70, 77; Steven Watts, *The Republic Reborn: War and the Making of Liberal America, 1790–1820* (Baltimore: Johns Hopkins University Press, 1987), 298; David Waldstreicher, *In the Midst of Perpetual Fetes: The Making of American Nationalism, 1776–1820* (Chapel Hill: University of North Carolina Press, 1997), 335–42; Kachun, *Festivals of Freedom*, 26–27.

15. *The Liberator*, 25 August 1843; *The Free American* (Boston, MA), 11 November 1841, AAS; Elizabeth Stordeur Pryor, *Colored Travelers: Mobility and the Fight for Citizenship before the Civil War* (Chapel Hill: University of North Carolina Press, 2016), 46, 62–65.

16. *The Liberator*, 11 August 1843.

17. *Christian Reflector*, 23 August 1843; *The Liberator*, 11 August 1843.

18. *The Liberator*, 7 July 1843; Frederick Newman Rutan, "Historical Sermon on the Reverend Horace James: Delivered September First, Nineteen Hundred and Seven, in the Congregational Church, Wrentham" (n. p.: n. p., 1907), 6, AAS.

19. "Eighth Annual Report of the Board of Managers of the Mass. Anti-Slavery Society, Presented January 22, 1840," in *Annual Report Presented to the Massachusetts Anti-Slavery Society by Its Board of Managers, 1st–21st: Jan. 1833–Jan. 1853* (Westport, CT: Negro Universities Press, 1970), lix, liv, HT; *Tenth Annual Report of the Board of Managers of the Massachusetts Anti-Slavery Society, presented January 26, 1842* (Boston: Dow & Jackson's Press, 1842), appendix: 6, IntArch; *Eleventh Annual Report Presented to the Massachusetts Anti-Slavery Society by Its Board of Managers, January 25, 1843* (Boston: Oliver Johnson, 1843), 51, 85, IntArch; *Twelfth Annual Report Presented to the Massachusetts Anti-Slavery Society by Its Board of Managers, January 24, 1844* (Boston: Oliver Johnson, 1844), 69, 88, IntArch; Rebecca Fisher to Edward Lane, 21 September 1843, bk. 142: 580, NCRD; *The Liberator*, 1 November 1844; Massachusetts Census, 1845: Norfolk County, AncC; Jordan D. Fiore, *Wrentham, 1673–1973: A History* (Wrentham: Town of Wrentham, 1973), 88.

20. Isaac Colby to Milan Harris, 21 November 1843, Quaker Special Collections, Haverford College Libraries, Haverford, PA; "Physicians of Concord," *The New Hampshire Repository* 2 (October 1849): 141, IntArch; Silvanus Hayward, *History of the Town of Gilsum, New Hampshire, from 1752 to 1879* (Manchester, NH: John R. Clark, 1881), 89, AAS.

21. "Register of the One Hundred Conventions Held by Vote of the New England Anti-Slavery Society Convention," 159–64, Anti-Slavery Collection; Frederick Douglass, "One Hundred Conventions," in *The Frederick Douglass Papers: Series Two—Autobiographical*

Writings, ed. John R. McKivigan et al., 3 vols. (New Haven, CT: Yale University Press, 2012), 3: 175–80; Thomas D. Hamm, *God's Government Begun: The Society for Universal Inquiry and Reform, 1842–1846* (Bloomington: Indiana University Press, 1995), 89; Reinhard O. Johnson, *The Liberty Party, 1840–1848: Antislavery Third-Party Politics in the United States* (Baton Rouge: Louisiana State University Press, 2009), 103.

22. *Narrative of the Sufferings of Lewis Clarke, During a Captivity of More than Twenty-Five Years, among the Algerines of Kentucky, One of the So-Called Christian States of North America. Dictated by Himself* (Boston: David H. Ela, 1845), Treasure Room Special Collections, James E. Shepard Memorial Library, North Carolina Central University, Durham; *National Anti-Slavery Standard*, 9 February 1843; *Vermont Union Whig* (Rutland, VT), 30 November 1843, NewsC.

23. *The Liberator*, 10 February 1843; *Bangor (ME) Daily Whig and Courier*, 24 April 1843, NewsC; *New York (NY) Daily Herald*, 30 December 1843, NewsC.

24. Austin Willey, *The History of the Antislavery Cause in State and Nation* (Portland, ME: Brown Thurston and Hoyt, Fogg & Donham, 1886), 241–42, AAS; Edward Schriver, "Black Politics without Blacks: Maine 1841–1848," *Phylon* 21 (1970): 194–201.

25. Lewis Ford to Brother Rogers, 21 January 1844, in Lewis Ford, *The Variety Book, Containing Life Sketches and Reminiscences* (Boston: Geo. E. Crosby & Co., 1892), 26–28, IntArch.

26. Lewis Ford to Brother Rogers, 21 January 1844; *The Liberator*, 9 February 1844.

27. *Twelfth Annual Report Presented to the Massachusetts Anti-Slavery Society, by Its Board of Managers, January 24, 1844*, 80; *Thirteenth Annual Report, Presented to the Massachusetts Anti-Slavery Society, by Its Board of Managers, January 22, 1845* (Boston: Massachusetts Anti-Slavery Society, 1845), 67, IntArch; *The Liberator*, 2 February 1844, 31 January 1845.

28. *The Liberator*, 1 March 1844, 15 March 1844.

29. Frederick Douglass to William Lloyd Garrison, 6 March 1844, in *The Frederick Douglass Papers, Series Three—Correspondence*, ed. John R. McKivigan et al., 3 vols. (New Haven, CT: Yale University Press, 2009), 1: 20–21; Harvey Newcomb, *The "Negro Pew": Being an Inquiry Concerning the Propriety of Distinctions in the House of God, on Account of Color* (Boston: Isaac Knopf, 1837), 79, Special Collections, Harvard Divinity School Library, Harvard University, Cambridge, MA; *The Liberator*, 27 August 1841.

30. Douglass to Garrison, 6 March 1844.

31. Douglass to Garrison, 6 March 1844; *The Liberator*, 1 March 1844, 22 March 1844, 19 April 1844.

32. *The Liberator*, 28 May 1858; *National Anti-Slavery Standard*, 29 May 1858. Although presented as factual, quite possibly, this was an apocryphal story that Wendell used to draw attention to colorism.

33. *National Anti-Slavery Standard*, 29 May 1858.

34. *Morning Star* (Limerick, ME), 24 August 1842, LOC; *The Emancipator and Free American*, 3 November 1842, NYHS; *The Liberator*, 9 December 1842. The myth of Lane as a preacher seems to have begun with Trinity College history professor John Spencer Bassett in "Religious Conditions of Slavery in North Carolina," *The Farmer and Mechanic* (Raleigh, NC), 19 December 1899.

35. *Christian Reflector* (Worcester, MA), 3 August 1842, AAS.

36. *An Exposition of Difficulties in West Brookfield, connected with Anti-Slavery Operations* (West Brookfield, MA: Anti-Slavery Society, 1844), 11–12, AAS.

Chapter 11

1. *The Colored American* (New York, NY), 10 October 1840, AAN; Manisha Sinha, *The Slave's Cause: A History of Abolition* (New Haven, CT: Yale University Press, 2016), 467–68.

2. *National Anti-Slavery Standard* (New York, NY), 11 July 1844, 26 September 1844, AccArch; *The Liberator* (Boston, MA), 4 October 1844, 29 November 1844, NewsC; *Narrative of the Life and Adventures of Henry Bibb, An American Slave, Written by Himself* (New York: the author, 1849), 147–48, J. Y. Joyner Library, East Carolina Library, Greenville, NC; "Register of the One Hundred Conventions Held by Vote of the New England Anti-Slavery Society Convention," 159–64, Anti-Slavery Collection, BPL; Edward O. Shriver, *Go Free: The Antislavery Impulse in Maine, 1833–1855* (Orono: University of Maine Press, 1970), 104 n19; James L. Huston, "The Experiential Basis of the Northern Antislavery Impulse," *Journal of Southern History* 56 (November 1990): 620–40.

3. Reinhard O. Johnson, *The Liberty Party, 1840–1848: Antislavery Third-Party Politics in the United States* (Baton Rouge: Louisiana State University Press, 2009), 245, 250, 252–53; James Oliver Horton and Lois E. Horton, "The Affirmation of Manhood: Black Garrisonians in Antebellum Boston," in *Courage and Conscience: Black & White Abolitionists in Boston*, ed. Donald M. Jacobs (Bloomington: Indiana University Press, 1993), 127–53; Thomas Hudson McKee, *The National Conventions and Platforms of All Political Parties, 1789–1900* (Baltimore: Friedenwald Co., 1900), 52, IntArch; Peter Wirzbicki, *Fighting for the Higher Law: Black and White Transcendentalists against Slavery* (Philadelphia: University of Pennsylvania Press, 2021), 194–95.

4. *The Practical Christian* (Hopedale, MA), 28 August 1844, 12 October 1844, AAS; Daryl Cumber Dance, "Wit and Humor in the Slave Narratives," *Journal of Afro-American Issues* 5 (Spring 1977): 125–34.

5. *The Practical Christian*, 26 October 1844; Wirzbicki, *Fighting for the Higher Law*, 124–25.

6. *The Liberator*, 6 June 1845.

7. *Vital Records of Cambridge, Massachusetts, to the Year 1850*, comp. Thomas W. Baldwin, 2 vols. (Boston: Wright & Potter, 1915), 2: 632, LOC; Laura Ann Lane and Celia A. G. Lane, range R, grave 14, Cambridge Cemetery Records, Cambridge Cemetery, Cambridge, MA; "Map of the Cambridge Cemetery, Massachusetts, 1855," Harvard Map Collection, Harvard College Library, Harvard University, Cambridge, MA; Elizabeth T. Hurren, "A Pauper Dead-House: The Expansion of the Cambridge Anatomical Teaching School under the Late-Victorian Poor Law, 1870–1914," *Medical History* 48 (January 2004): 69–94.

8. Lunsford Lane, *The Narrative of Lunsford Lane, Formerly of Raleigh, N.C. Embracing an Account of His Early Life, the Redemption by Purchase of Himself and Family from Slavery, and His Banishment from the Place of His Birth for the Crime of Wearing a Colored Skin. Published by Himself*, 3rd ed. (Boston: Hewes & Watson, 1845), AAS; S. N. Dickinson, *The Boston Almanac for 1848* (Boston: B. B. Mussey & Co., 1848), 102, BPL; Sadie Van

Vranken, "Lunsford Lane," *Black Self-Publishing*, https://www.americanantiquarian.org /Blackpublishing/lunsford-lane.

9. *The Emancipator and Weekly Chronicle* (Boston, MA), 6 August 1845, AAS; *The Liberator*, 8 August 1845.

10. *The Practical Christian*, 28 August 1844, 26 October 1844; *The Emancipator and Weekly Chronicle*, 13 August 1845; *The Liberator*, 27 June 1845.

11. Baldwin, comp., *Vital Records of Cambridge, Massachusetts to the Year 1850*, 1: 423; "Return of Number of Births in City of Cambridge, during the Year next preceding May 1, 1846," 7, Massachusetts Vital Records, 1840–1911, New England Historic Genealogical Society, Boston, MA.

12. *Fourteenth Annual Report Presented to the Massachusetts Anti-Slavery Society by Its Board of Managers, January 28, 1846* (Boston: Scarlett & Laing, 1846), 51, IntArch; *Vermont Phoenix* (Brattleboro, VT), 18 September 1845, NewsC; *The Liberator*, 3 October 1845; *Fifteenth Annual Report Presented to the Massachusetts Anti-Slavery Society by Its Board of Managers, January 27, 1847* (Boston: Andrews & Prentiss, 1847), appendix: 60, IntArch.

13. *The Liberator*, 20 February 1846, 23 March 1846, 9 April 1846; *Hartford (CT) Courant*, 5 February 1839, NewsC; *Vermont Standard* (Woodstock, VT), 6 July 1855, NewsC; Edward Hungerford, *Centennial Sermons on the History of the Center Congregational Church of Meriden, Conn.* (Hartford: Case, Lockwood & Brainard Co., 1877), 54–55, AAS; *Contributions to the Ecclesiastical History of Connecticut* (New Haven, CT: J. H. Benham, 1861), 420–21, IntArch; C. Bancroft Gillespie, *An Historic Record and Pictorial Description of the Town of Meriden, Connecticut and the Men Who Have Made It* (Meriden, CT: Journal Publishing Co., 1906), 359–60, AAS.

14. *The Liberator*, 3 April 1846; Hungerford, *Centennial Sermons on the History of the Center Congregational Church of Meriden*, 56–57.

15. *The Weekly Standard* (Raleigh, NC), 13 May 1846, NewsC; *North-Carolina Standard* (Raleigh), 4 February 1846, NewsC.

16. *The Weekly Standard*, 13 May 1846; *North-Carolina Standard*, 4 February 1846; Edgar Estes Folk, "W. W. Holden and the North Carolina Standard, 1843–1848: A Study in Political Journalism," *NCHR* 19 (January 1942): 22–47.

17. *The Liberator*, 15 January 1847; Elisha Mitchell, "Reaction to Theodore Parker's appreciation for Lane, Roper, et al.," in *The Other Leaf of the Book of Nature and the Word of God* (n. p.: n. p., 1848), 65, IntArch.

18. US Census, 1840; US Census, 1850; US Census, 1860; US Census, 1870. In 1840, there were approximately thirty Black Southern men named Lunsford, only two of whom were free: Lunsford Lane and another Wake County resident, Lunsford Worrell. Many, like Lane, carried a name given or inspired by a local White benefactor or friend, and there were plenty of White Southerners named Lunsford to inspire the name. Between 1842, when Lunsford started telling The Story, and 1858, a decade following the publication of the fourth and final edition of *The Narrative of Lunsford Lane*, six free Black children and about thirty enslaved children received the name. In the 1860s, following publication of the biography, eleven more Lunsfords arrived, all emancipated.

19. *Raleigh (NC) Register*, 23 November 1827, 6 January 1829, NewsC; Fabius Haywood to Alfred Williams, 20 February 1836, EHC; "List of Laborers Employed on the Plantation of Williams & Haywood for the present year, 13 June 1865," EHC; US Census, 1870: Wake County, NC; US Census, 1880: Wake County, NC; John Spencer Bassett, *Anti-Slavery*

Leaders of North Carolina (Baltimore: Johns Hopkins Press, 1898), 74; *Durham Sun*, 17 January 1899.

20. Coy D. Robbins, *Forgotten Hoosiers: African Heritage in Orange County, Indiana* (Bowie, MD: Heritage Cooks, 1994), 110, 112, 168, 177, 178, 183, 185, 215; US Census, 1840: Orange County, IN; US Census, 1850: Orange County, IN; US Census, 1860: Orange County, IN; US Census, 1870: Orange County, IN; US Census, 1880: Vigo County, IN; US Census, 1900: Vigo County, IN; *The Orleans (NE) Progress*, 12 May 1892, NewsC; Death Certificates 1903, microfilm, Indiana State Board of Health, Indiana Archives and Records Administration, Indianapolis. Three Lunsfords appeared in northern White families in the 1840s and 1850s, and they might have been named Lunsford by antislavery parents, but that is speculative as best. The spelling of *this* Lane's name is inconsistent in transactional records, evolving from Lunsford to Lanceford, Laneford, and finally Lansford on his grave marker in Mount Pleasant Cemetery in Terre Haute. His son's name is consistently spelled as Lansford; see US Census, 1910: Stark County, ND; US Census, 1920: Hettinger County, ND.

21. 1850 US Census: Osage County, MO; Ralph Waldo Emerson, *Representative Men: Seven Lectures* (Boston: Phillips, Sampson & Co., 1850), 9, AAS.

22. Steven J. Kochevar, "The Rise of Institutional Mortgage Lending in Early Nineteenth-Century New Haven," *Yale Law Journal* 124 (October 2014): 164–65.

23. Leonard A. Jones, *A Treatise on the Law of Mortgages of Real Property*, 2 vols. (Boston: Houghton, Osgood, and Co., 1878), 1: 32, IntArch.

24. H. W. Chaplin, "The Story of Mortgage Law," *Harvard Law Review* 4 (April 1890): 2–3; Kochevar, "The Rise of Institutional Mortgage Lending in Early Nineteenth-Century New Haven," 166–67; Edmund Trowbridge, "Of Mortgages," 8 Mass. 550 (1811–12), 550–60; William E. Nelson, *Americanization of the Common Law: The Impact of Legal Change on Massachusetts Society, 1760–1830* (Cambridge, MA: Harvard University Press, 1975), 6; *Runyan v. Mersereau*, 11 Johns (NY) 524 (1814); *Rockwell v. Bradley*, 2 Conn. 1 (1816); "Proceedings to compel the determination of claims to real property, in certain cases" (1828), in *The Revised Statutes of New-York*, 3 vols. (Albany: Packard and Van Benthuysen, 1829), 2: 312–15, IntArch; Jones, *A Treatise on the Law of Mortgages of Real Property*, 1: 15.

25. Chaplin, "The Story of Mortgage Law," 12–13; Nelson, *Americanization of the Common Law*, 42, 253 n1000.

26. Chaplin, "The Story of Mortgage Law," 12–13; Jones, *A Treatise on the Law of Mortgages of Real Property*, 1: 15.

27. Andrew Boardman to Lunsford Lane, 3 June 1846, bk. 485: 373–74, SMRRL; Lunsford Lane to Andrew Boardman, 3 June 1846, bk. 520: 489–90, SMRRL; Cambridge Assessors' Records for 1846: Ward 2—annotated, 39, CPL; Valuation List for 1846, 62, CPL; Cambridge Assessors' Records for 1847: Ward 2—annotated, 43, CPL; Valuation List for 1847, 62, CPL; Charles M. Sullivan to Natalie Friendly, 23 September 1982, Lunsford Lane folder, Cambridge Historical Commission, Cambridge, MA.

28. US Census, 1850: Middlesex County, MA.

29. Gerrit Smith to John H. Cooke, 11 December 1840, GSP.

30. Gerrit Smith to Ezekial Birdseye, 8 July 1845, GSP; Gerrit Smith to L. Chaplin, & January 1846, GSP; Norman K. Dunn, *Practical Dreamer: Gerrit Smith and the Crusade for Social Reform* (Hamilton, NY: Log Cabin Books, 2009), 459–61; Stanley Harrold, "On the Borders of Slavery and Race: Charles T. Torrey and the Underground Railroad,"

JER 20 (Summer 2000): 273–92; John Stauffer, *The Black Hearts of Men: Radical Aboli-tionists and the Transformation of Race* (Cambridge, MA: Harvard University Press, 2002), 141–44.

31. Art. III, Sec. 1, Third Constitution of New York, 1846, Digital Collection, New York State Archives, Albany, https://dicitalcollections.archives.nysed.gov/index.php/Detail /objects/57721; *Vermont Freeman* (Norwich, VT), 16 September 1843, NewsC; Gerrit Smith to Theodore S. Wright, Charles B. Ray, and James McCune Smith, 14 November 1846, GSP; Gerrit Smith, *Address to the Three Thousand Colored Citizens of New-York Who Are the Owners of One Hundred and Twenty Thousand Acres of Land in the State of New-York, Given to Them by Gerrit Smith, Esq. of Petersboro* (New York: 1846), 5, AAS; Ralph Volney Harlow, *Gerrit Smith: Philanthropist and Reformer* (New York: Henry Holt & Co., 1939), 174–75, 242–53.

32. Bella Gross, "Life and Times of Theodore S. Wright, 1797–1847," *Negro History Bul-letin* 3 (June 1940): 133–38; M. N. Work, "The Life of Charles B. Ray," *Journal of Negro His-tory* 4 (October 1919): 361–71; John Stauffer, "Introduction," in *The Works of James McCune Smith: Black Intellectual and Abolitionist,* ed. John Stauffer (New York: Oxford University Press, 2006), xiii–xl.

33. Smith, *Address to the Three Thousand Colored Citizens of New-York,* 10; Gerrit Smith to Messrs. Wright, Ray, Smith, 3 October 1846, GSP; Stauffer, *Black Hearts of Men,* 127–31; Sinha, *Slave's Cause,* 357.

34. "Account of My Distribution of Land among Colored Men," Register, Vol. 88: 37, GSP.

35. *Sandusky (OH) Clarion,* 6 October 1846, NewsC; Carol M. Hunter, *To Set the Captives Free: Reverend Jeremiah Wesley Loguen and the Struggle for Freedom in Central New York, 1835–1872* (New York: Garland, 1993), 179–80; Harlow, *Gerrit Smith,* 246.

36. John Brown to Owen Brown, 10 January 1849, in *A John Brown Reader: John Brown, Frederick Douglass, W. E. B. Du Bois, and Others* (New York: Dover Pub., 2021), 40.

37. John Brown to Willis Hodges, 22 January 1849, in *The Evening Post* (New York, NY), 20 December 1859, NewsC; *Sandusky Clarion,* 6 October 1846, NewsC; Charles B. Ray and James McCune Smith to Gerrit Smith, 4 December 1847, GSP; James McCune Smith to Gerrit Smith, 7 July 1848, GSP; G. W. Grimbly to Gerrit Smith, 31 August 1849, GSP; "To Gerrit Smith Grantees! Redeem Your Lands!!" 4 October 1854, GSP; Stauffer, *Black Hearts of Men,* 222–24; Harlow, *Gerrit Smith,* 252.

38. Index Essex County (NY) Deeds—Grantees, 1800–1852, Book L: 261 Essex County Clerk's Office County Records, *CountyOffice.org,* https://www.countyoffice.org/ny-essex -county-land-records/; Deeds, 1850, Vol. HH: 264–65, Essex County Clerk's Office County Records.

39. *Fifteenth Annual Report Presented,* appendix: 90.

40. Harlow, *Gerrit Smith,* 136–62; Lewis Tappan to John Scoble, 10 December 1839, in *A Side-Light on Anglo-American Relations, 1839–1858, Furnished by the Correspondence of Lewis Tappan and Others with the British and Foreign Anti- Slavery Committee,* ed. Annie Heloise Abel and Frank J. Klingberg (Washington, DC: Association for the Study of Negro Life and History, Inc., 1927), 62; Sinha, *Slave's Cause,* 467–68.

41. Charles Knowles Bolton, *Scotch Irish Pioneers in Ulster and America* (Boston: Bacon and Brown, 1910), 94, 106, 119, 146, 155, 239–66; Georgia Drew Merrill, *History of Coos County, New Hampshire* (Syracuse: W. A. Ferguson, 1888), 539–49, IntArch; Caleb Stark,

Memoir and Official Correspondence of Gen. John Stark (Concord, NH: G. Parker Lyon, 1860), 487–88, AAS.

42. "An Act to change the name of Samuel M. Burnside, of Charlestown, in the County of Middlesex, and to render valid the doings of said Samuel, under the name of Samuel M. Burnside," 17 November 1808, in *Private and Special Statutes of the Commonwealth of Massachusetts from February 1806 to February 1814*, 7 vols. (Boston: Wells and Lilly, 1823), 4: 196, AAS; "An Act to Alter the Names of Certain Persons Therein Mentioned," 4 March 1809, in *Private and Special Statutes of the Commonwealth of Massachusetts from February 1806 to February 1814*, 4: 226–27; "An Act to Incorporate the American Antiquarian Society," 24 October 1812, in *Private and Special Statutes of the Commonwealth of Massachusetts from February 1806 to February 1814*, 4: 461; entry for 24 February 1847, Samuel M. Burnside diary, Octavo 19: January 1, 1847–December 31, 1848, Samuel M'Gregore Burnside Papers, 1808–1848, AAS; *The National Aegis* (Worcester, MA), 29 October 1845, BPL; *The Pittsfield (MA) Sun*, 9 June 1880, NewsC; Samuel M. Burnside to Thomas Jefferson, 23 January 1815, in *The Papers of Thomas Jefferson: Retirement Series*, ed. J. Jefferson Looney, 15 vols. (Princeton, NJ: Princeton University Press, 2011), 8: 207–8; William Lincoln, *History of Worcester, Massachusetts: From Its Earliest Settlement to September 1836* (Worcester, MA: Charles Hersey, 1862), 201–202, 211, 229, WPL; Franklin P. Rice, *The Worcester Book: Diary of Noteworthy Events in Worcester from 1657 to 1883* (Worcester, MA: Putnam, Davis & Co., 1884), 80, 94, 122, WPL; John Nelson, *Worcester County: A Narrative History*, 3 vols. (New York: American Historical Society, 1934), 2: 690–91, WPL.

43. Burnside diary, 7 February 1847; *The Liberator*, 12 February 1847.

44. *Worcester (MA) Daily Spy*, 18 February 1842, AAS; Anne Warren Weston to Elizabeth Pease Nichol, 30 January 1842, Anti-Slavery Collection.

45. Burnside diary, 21 January 1847, 16 February 1847; "To the People of the County of Madison," 16 March 1847, GSP; *The Liberator*, 11 March 1842, 25 March 1842; *Boston (MA) Post*, 28 February 1834, NewsC; Gilbert Osofsky, "Abolitionists, Irish Immigrants, and the Dilemmas of Romantic Nationalism," *American Historical Review* 80 (October 1975): 898–90; J. M. Opal, *Beyond the Farm: National Ambitions in Rural New England* (Philadelphia: University of Pennsylvania Press, 2008), 91; Sinha, *Slave's Cause*, 359–63; David R. Roediger, *The Wages of Whiteness: Race and the Making of the American Working Class* (London: Verso, 1991), 134–50. On Irish Americans' antagonism toward Black Americans and abolition, see Nell Irvin Painter, *The History of White People* (New York: W. W. Norton, 2010), 143–44. On Black Americans' juxtaposition of their native-born status to the foreignness of the Irish, see Christopher James Bonner, *Remaking the Republic: Black Politics and the Creation of American Citizenship* (Philadelphia: University of Pennsylvania Press, 2020), 87–91.

46. *Portland (ME) Advertiser*, 15 February 1848, AAS.

47. Joseph Williamson, *History of the City of Belfast in the State of Maine, from Its First Settlement in 1770 to 1875* (Portland: Loring, Short, and Harmon, 1877), 324, IntArch; Austin Willey, *The History of the Antislavery Cause in State and Nation* (Portland, ME: Brown Thurston and Hoyt, Fogg & Donham, 1886), 330–33, AAS.

48. *Proceedings of the National Liberty Convention, Held at Buffalo, NY, June 14th & 15th, 1848* (Utica, NY: S. W. Green, 1848), 49, 51, IntArch; Douglas M. Strong, *Perfectionist Politics: Abolitionism and the Religious Tensions of Democracy* (Syracuse, NY: Syracuse University Press, 1999), 146–53.

49. Henry L. Morehouse, "Historical Sketch of the ABHMS for Fifty Years," in *Baptist Home Missions in North America; Including a Full Report of the Proceedings and Address of the Jubilee Meeting, and a Historical Sketch of the ABHMS, Historical Tables, Etc., 1832–1882* (New York: American Baptist Home Mission Society, 1883), 386–95, IntArch.

50. Walter Bryant and Leopold Herman to Lunsford Lane, 9 March 1848, bk. 520: 491–92, SMRRL; Lane to Boardman, 3 June 1846; Cambridge Assessors' Records for 1848: Ward 2—annotated, 36, CPL; Valuation List for 1848, 34, CPL; John Ford, *Cambridge Directory* (Cambridge, MA: Chronicle Office, 1848), 73, CPL. Bryant's business partner, Leopold Herman, joined him as seller on the deed, but when their business relationship collapsed in 1849, apparently Herman withdrew from the arrangement with the Lanes; see *Boston (MA) Evening Transcript*, 7 September 1849, NewsC.

51. Lunsford Lane to Daniel McClure, 31 May 1849, bk 540: 552–53, SMRRL.

52. Van Vranken, "Lunsford Lane"; Dickinson, *The Boston Almanac for 1848*, 102; Theodore Parker, *A Letter to the People of the United States Touching the Matter of Slavery* (Boston: J. Munroe & Co., 1848), 34, AAS; *The National Era* (Washington, DC), 13 January 1848, AAN; *The Pennsylvania Freeman* (Philadelphia, PA), 13 January 1848, HSP; *Congregational Journal* (Concord, NH), 3 February 1848, AAS; *The North Star* (Rochester, NY), 4 February 1848, AAN. Torrey employed an imposition of eight pages throughout the text.

53. *New York (NY) Daily Herald*, 15 May 1849, NewsC; William G. Hawkins, *Lunsford Lane; or, Another Helper from North Carolina* (Boston: Crosby & Nichols, 1863), 177, NCC; Derek Chang, *Citizens of a Christian Nation: Evangelical Missions and the Problem of Race in the Nineteenth Century* (Philadelphia: University of Pennsylvania Press, 2010), 20–21. In his typically sloppy manner, Hawkins misidentified the association and the year it met in New York City.

54. *Burlington (VT) Courier*, 22 August 1850, NewsC; *Vermont Patriot and State Gazette* (Montpelier, VT), 7 February 1850, NewsC; *St. Albans (VT) Weekly Messenger*, 29 August 1850, NewsC; Eric Foner, *Free Soil, Free Labor, Free Men: The Ideology of the Republican Party before the Civil War*, rpt. ed. (New York: Oxford University Press, 1995), 124–26; Sinha, *Slave's Cause*, 484.

55. *Argus and Patriot* (Montpelier, VT), 18 April 1872, NewsC; *Vermont Telegraph* (Brandon, VT), 7 September 1842, NewsC; *Burlington (VT) Courier*, 22 August 1850, NewsC.

Chapter 12

1. John Ford, *Cambridge Directory and Almanac for 1850* (Cambridge, MA: Chronicle Office, 1850), 40, CPL; Lunsford and Martha Lane to Edward Lane, 21 May 1850, bk. 570: 121–22, SMRRL; William G. Hawkins, *Lunsford Lane; or, Another Helper from North Carolina* (Boston: Crosby & Nichols, 1863), 178, NCC; US Census, 1840: Suffolk County, MA; US Census, 1850: Suffolk County, MA; US Census, 1850: Middlesex County, MA; Adelaide M. Cromwell, "The Black Presence in the West End of Boston, 1800–1864: A Demographic Map," in *Courage and Conscience: Black & White Abolitionists in Boston*, ed. Donald M. Jacobs (Bloomington: Indiana University Press, 1993), 157.

2. Cambridge Assessors' Records for 1850: Ward 2—annotated, 13, 42, CPL; Walter Bryant to Lunsford Lane, 22 December 1851, bk. 610: 18–20, SMRRL; US Census, 1850:

Middlesex County, MA; annotation for 2 May 1850, on Lunsford Lane to Andrew Board-man, 3 June 1846, bk. 520: 489–90, SMRRL; *Semi-Weekly Eagle* (Brattleboro, VT), 28 October 1850, NewsC; US Census, 1850: Norfolk County, MA.

3. Penciled annotation, Valuation List for 1850, 61, CPL; *Directory of the City of Boston* (Boston: George Adams, 1850), 305, 364, IntArch; George Adams, *The Roxbury Directory* (Roxbury, MA: James T. Bicknell, 1850), 109, IntArch; *The Liberator* (Boston, MA), 19 January 1849, NewsC.

4. *The Anti-Slavery Bugle* (New Lisbon, OH), 3 December 1847, NewsC; *Baltimore (MD) Sun*, 20 April 1848, NewsC; Robert Benjamin Lewis, *Light and Truth; Collected from the Bible and Ancient & Modern History, Containing the Universal History of the Colored and the Indian Race, From the Creation of the World to the Present Time*, 2nd ed. (Boston: Moses M. Taylor, 1851), iii, AAS; Roxbury, Norfolk County 1860 census, Non-Population Census Schedule for Massachusetts, 1850–1880, 4, NARA; *The Liberator*, 9 June 1837; *Vermont Telegraph* (Brandon, VT), 13 July 1837, NewsC; Norman K. Dunn, *Practical Dreamer: Gerrit Smith and the Crusade for Social Reform* (Hamilton, NY: Log Cabin Books, 2009), 38. On the philosophy of radical practical abolitionism, see Jesse Olsavsky, *The Most Absolute Abolition: Runaways, Vigilance Committees, and the Rise of Revolutionary Abolitionism, 1835–1861* (Baton Rouge: Louisiana State University Press, 2022), 54–57; Richard Bell, "Counterfeit Kin: Kidnappers of Color, the Reverse Underground Railroad, and the Origins of Practical Abolition," *JER* 38 (Summer 2018): 199–230.

5. *The Liberator*, 22 February 1850, 5 April 1850; Cambridge Assessors' Records for 1851: Ward 2—annotated, n. p., CPL; Valuation List for 1851, 82, CPL; John Ford, *The Cambridge Directory and Almanac for 1851* (Cambridge, MA: Chronicle Office, 1851), 106, IntArch.

6. Bryant to Lane, 22 December 1851, bk. 610: 18–20, SMRRL; Lunsford Lane to Walter Bryant, 22 December 1851, bk. 610: 20–21, SMRRL; annotation for 17 July 1852, Lane to Bryant, 22 December 1851, bk. 610: 20. Not surprisingly, Bryant led an effort to have the Massachusetts legislature modify mortgage, usury, and lien laws just a few years later; *Boston (MA) Evening Transcript*, 22 February 1854, NewsC.

7. *Cambridge (MA) Chronicle*, 19 July 1851, CPL; Hawkins, *Lunsford Lane*, 178; US Census, 1850: Middlesex County, MA.

8. John Ford, *The Cambridge Directory and Almanac for 1852* (Cambridge, MA: Chronicle Office, 1852), 118, IntArch; *Boston Directory for the Year 1852* (Boston: George Adams, 1852), 37, 152, 310, BPL; US Census, 1850: Suffolk County, MA; Assessor's List: J-P 1852, 113, Real Estate, Personal Estate and Poll Tax Records, City of Boston Archives, West Roxbury, MA; Tax Books: 1852, Ward 5, 69, Real Estate, Personal Estate and Poll Tax Records; Valuation Books: 1852, Ward 5, 2, Real Estate, Personal Estate and Poll Tax Records; Transfer book, 1852: Ward 5, Real Estate, Personal Estate and Poll Tax Records; Tax book, 1852: Ward 5, 69, Real Estate, Personal Estate and Poll Tax Records; US Census, 1850: Middlesex County, MA; Cambridge Assessors' Records for 1853: Ward 2—annotated, n. p., CPL.

9. Cambridge Assessors' Records for 1852: Ward 2—annotated, n. p., CPL; Valuation list for 1852, 79, CPL; Charles M. Sullivan to Natalie Friendly, 23 September 1982, Lunsford Lane folder, Cambridge Historical Commission, Cambridge, MA.; K-Sue Park, "Race, Innovation, and Financial Growth: The Example of Foreclosure," in *Histories of Racial Capitalism*, ed. Destin Jenkins and Justin Leroy (New York: Columbia University Press, 2021), 32.

10. *National Anti-Slavery Standard* (New York, NY), 12 February 1852, AccArch; *The Liberator*, 6 February 1852; Abner Belcher to Lunsford Lane, 15 March 1854, bk. 224: 566–67,

NCRD; Lunsford Lane to Abner Belcher, 16 March 1854, bk. 224: 567–68, NCRD; Robert Holmes to Lunsford Lane, 5 April 1854, bk. 229: 59–60, NCRD; Lunsford Lane and Martha Lane to John A. Craig, 20 March 1854, bk. 229: 380–81, NCRD; Abner Belcher to Edward Lane, 6 May 1850, bk. 224: 566, NCRD; Massachusetts Census, 1855: Norfolk County, AncC; *Proceedings of the Massachusetts Anti-Slavery Society at the Annual Meetings Held in 1854, 1855 & 1856* (Boston: Massachusetts Anti-Slavery Society, 1856), 24, 49, IntArch; Valuation List for 1854, 41, CPL; Cambridge Assessors' Records for 1854: Ward 2—annotated, n. p., CPL.

11. Sheila M. Rothman, *Living in the Shadow of Death: Tuberculosis and the Social Experience of Illness in American History* (Baltimore: Johns Hopkins University Press, 1994), 16–17; "Deaths Registered in the City of Cambridge for the Year 1854," Massachusetts Vital Records, 1840–1911, New England Historic Genealogical Society, Boston, MA; Laura Ann Lane and Celia A. G. Lane, range R, grave 14, Cambridge Cemetery Records, Cambridge Cemetery, Cambridge, MA; *The Liberator*, 21 July 1854; *National Anti-Slavery Standard*, 29 July 1854.

12. John C. Calhoun, "Speech on the Slavery Question," 4 March 1850, in *The Works of John C. Calhoun*, 6 vols. (New York: D. Appleton & Co., 1857), 4: 572; Kellie Carter Jackson, *Force and Freedom: Black Abolitionists and the Politics of Violence* (Philadelphia: University of Pennsylvania Press, 2019), 40; Olsavsky, *Most Absolute Abolition*, 88–94.

13. *Signal of Liberty* (Ann Arbor, MI), 3 June 1844, *Ann Arbor District Library*, https://aadl.org/files/documents/pdf/signal/SL_18440603.pdf; *Richmond Dispatch*, quoted in *The Pennsylvania Freeman* (Philadelphia, PA), 20 March 1851, HSP.

14. "An Appeal," First Independent Baptist Church (Africans), Arlington Street Church (Boston, Mass.) Records, 1730–1979, Special Collections, Harvard Divinity School Library, Harvard University, Cambridge, MA; "Circular," First Independent Baptist Church (Africans), Arlington Street Church (Boston, Mass.) Records; *The Pennsylvania Freeman*, 25 August 1853; George W. Williams, *History of the Twelfth Street Baptist Church, Boston, Mass., from 1840 to 1874* (Boston: James H. Earle, 1874), 20; Roy E. Finkenbine, "Boston's Black Churches: Institutional Centers of the Antislavery Movement," in Jacobs, ed., *Courage and Conscience*, 173, 181–82.

15. *The Liberator*, 11 October 1850; Frederick Douglass to Gerrit Smith, 1 May 1851, GSP.

16. James Oliver Horton and Lois E. Horton, *Black Bostonians: Family Life and Community Struggle in the Antebellum North* (New York: Holmes & Meier, 1979), 112–18; Gary Lee Collison, *Shadrach Minkins: From Fugitive Slave to Citizen* (Cambridge, MA: Harvard University Press, 1998).

17. Leonard W. Levy, "Sims' Case: The Fugitive Slave Law in Boston in 1851," *Journal of Negro History* 35 (January 1950): 39–74; Stanley W. Campbell, *The Slave Catchers: Enforcement of the Fugitive Slave Law, 1850–1860* (Chapel Hill: University of North Carolina Press, 1970), 117–21.

18. Campbell, *Slave Catchers*, 126–32; Samuel J. May to Thomas Wentworth Higginson, 25 May 1854, in "Trial of Anthony Burns, 1854," *Proceedings of the Massachusetts Historical Society* 44 (1910–11): 323; Anne G. Phillips to Anne and Deborah Weston, 25 May 1854, in "Trial of Anthony Burns, 1854," 322; Jackson, *Force and Freedom*, 71–75; *Massachusetts Spy* (Worcester, MA), 31 May 1854, AAS; Harold Schwartz, "Fugitive Slave Days in Boston," *New England Quarterly* 27 (June 1954): 191–212; "An Act to Protect the Rights and Liberties of the People of the Commonwealth of Massachusetts," *Acts and Resolves Passed by the*

General Court of Massachusetts, in the Year 1854 (Boston: William White, 1855), 924–29, IntArch; Thomas D. Morris, *Free Men All: The Personal Liberty Laws of the North, 1780–1861* (Union, NJ: Lawbook Exchange, 2001), 166–86.

19. *Massachusetts Spy*, 31 May 1854, 13 December 1854; *History of Worcester, Massachusetts* (Philadelphia: J. W. Lewis & Co., 1889), 1449–1450, AAS; Worcester Freedom Club, 20 September 1852, broadside, AAS; *Daily Evening Telegraph* (Boston, MA), 15 September 1854, AAS; *Albany (NY) Journal*, 30 May 1854, NewsC; Albert J. Von Frank, *The Trial of Anthony Burns: Freedom and Slavery in Emerson's Boston* (Cambridge, MA: Harvard University Press, 1998), 122–39.

20. Campbell, *Slave Catchers*, 170–86.

21. Cromwell, "The Black Presence in the West End of Boston," 159.

22. *The Liberator*, 22 November 1861; Samuel Francis Batchelder, *Notes on Colonel Henry Vassall (1721–1769), His Wife Penelope Royall, His House at Cambridge, and His Slaves Tony and Darby* (Cambridge, MA: n. p., 1917), 46–49, 68, 71; *A Bloody Butchery, by the British Troops: or, The Runaway Fight of the Regulars, To which is annexed A funeral elegy to the imortal memory of those worthies, who were slain in the battle of Concord, 1775* (Salem, MA: E. Russell, 1775), Rare Book and Special Collections Division, LOC; Batchelder, *Notes on Colonel Henry Vassall*, 61–78; "A Home of the Olden Time," *New England Historical and Genealogical Register* 25 (January 1871): 44–45.

23. *The Liberator*, 14 June 1844, 22 November 1861; Andrew P. Peabody, ed., "Memoir of the Rev. Samuel K. Lothrop, D. D.," in *Proceedings of the Massachusetts Historical Society*, Vol. 3, *Second Series, 1886–1887* (Boston: The Society, 1888), 169; Charles C. Calhoun, *Longfellow: A Rediscovered Life* (Boston: Beacon Press, 2004), 167.

24. Henry Wadsworth Longfellow to James Thomas Fields, 21 March 1855, in *The Letters of Henry Wadsworth Longfellow*, ed. Andrew Hilen, 4 vols. (Cambridge: Belknap Press, 1972), 3: 470; entry for 22 March 1855, in *Life of Henry Wadsworth Longfellow: With Extracts from His Journals and Correspondence*, ed. Samuel Longfellow, 2 vols. (Boston: Ticknor and Company, 1886), 2: 255, AAS; Angela Sorby, *Schoolhouse Poets: Childhood, Performance, and the Place of American Poetry, 1865-1917* (Durham: University of New Hampshire Press, 2005), 4–12; Christoph Irmscher, *Public Poet, Private Man: Henry Wadsworth Longfellow at 200* (Amherst: University of Massachusetts Press, 2009), 109. The familiar "Lundy Lane" suggests that Lane and Longfellow may have met previously, but Longfellow did not mention him elsewhere in his voluminous journals. More likely, Lundy is how Vassall introduced his friend to Longfellow.

25. Henry Wadsworth Longfellow to John Forster, 15 December 1842, in Hilen, ed., *The Letters of Henry Wadsworth Longfellow*, 2: 481; entries for 24 and 30 March 1855, 24 and 29 April 1855, 22 March 1856, 13 June 1856, Personal Account Book 1840–1882, 78–79, Henry Wadsworth Longfellow Papers 1819–1928, Houghton Library, Harvard University, Cambridge, MA.

26. *Anti-Slavery Bugle*, 19 May 1855.

27. *Anti-Slavery Bugle*, 19 May 1855; *Christian Watchman* (Boston, MA), 17 May 1852, AAS; *Richmond (VA) Dispatch*, 11 May 1855; *Boston (MA) Herald*, 4 January 1855, BPL; Hawkins, *Lunsford Lane*, 198.

28. US Census, 1850: Middlesex County, MA; Massachusetts Census, 1855: Middlesex County, AncC; Massachusetts Census, 1855: Norfolk County; US Census, 1860: Lorain County, OH.

29. John P. Nichols to Lunsford Lane, 1 September 1855, bk. 720: 259–60, SMRRL; Lunsford Lane to John P. Nichols, 1 September 1855, bk. 720: 260–62, SMRRL; John P. Nichols to Cambridge Mutual Fire Insurance Co., 5 September 1855, bk. 720: 260, SMRRL; Cambridge Assessors' Records for 1855: Ward 2—annotated, n. p., CPL; Steven J. Kochevar, "The Rise of Institutional Mortgage Lending in Early Nineteenth-Century New Haven," *Yale Law Journal* 124 (October 2014):161; Lamoreaux, *Insider Lending*, 52–83.

30. Annotation for 3 May 1856, Lane and Lane to Craig, 20 March 1854; Lunsford Lane and Martha Lane to Robert Holmes, 20 May 1856, bk. 246: 94–95, NCRD; John Ford, *The Cambridge Directory and Almanac for 1856* (Cambridge, MA: Chronicle Office, 1856), 129, IntArch; Cambridge Assessors' Records for 1856: Ward 2—annotated, 83, CPL; Valuation List for 1856, 48, CPL; Hawkins, *Lunsford Lane*, 178–79.

31. Lunsford Lane to George P. Oakes, 20 November 1857, bk. 790: 564–65, SMRRL.

32. Cambridge Assessors' Records for 1857: Ward 2—annotated, CPL; William E. Nelson, *Americanization of the Common Law: The Impact of Legal Change on Massachusetts Society, 1760–1830* (Cambridge: Harvard University Press, 1975), 251n62.

33. US Census, 1860: Suffolk County, MA: *Boston Directory for the Year 1857* (Boston: George Adams, 1857), 195, IntArch; *Boston Evening Transcript*, 26 October 1850; *Boston Herald*, 15 July 1857, 28 October 1857, 9 December 1857; Lane to Oakes, 20 November 1857; *Zion's Herald & Wesleyan Journal* (Boston, MA), 23 December 1857, AAS; "Deaths in Boston during the Month of December 1857," Massachusetts Vital Records, 1840–1911.

34. US Census, 1860: Lorain County, OH; Gary J. Kornblith and Carol Lasser, *Elusive Utopia: The Struggle for Racial Equality in Oberlin, Ohio* (Baton Rouge: Louisiana State University Press, 2018), 40; William E. Bigglestone, *They Stopped in Oberlin: Black Residents and Visitors in the Nineteenth Century* (Oberlin, OH: Oberlin College, 2002), 31–32.

35. "Minutes and Address of the State Convention of the Colored Citizens of Ohio, Convened at Columbus, January 10th, 11th, 12th, & 13th, 1849," in *Proceedings of the Black State Conventions, 1840–1865*, ed. Philip S. Foner and George E. Walker, 2 vols. (Philadelphia: Temple University Press, 1979), 1: 220.

36. *The Liberator*, 20 October 1848; *Cleveland Herald*, 28 August 1856, reprinted in *National Anti-Slavery Standard*, 11 October 1856; *Oberlin (OH) Weekly News*, 4 November 1881, Ohio5; Kornblith and Lasser, *Elusive Utopia*, 74–75; Bigglestone, *They Stopped in Oberlin*, 125.

37. *General Catalogue of Oberlin College, 1833–1908: Including an Account of the Principal Events in the History of the College, with Illustrations of the College Buildings* (Oberlin, OH: Oberlin College, 1909), 220, IntArch; Bigglestone, *They Stopped in Oberlin*, 50–52.

38. US Census, 1850, Lorain County, OH; US Census, 1860: Lorain County, OH; Kornblith and Lasser, *Elusive Utopia*, 53; Bigglestone, *The Stopped in Oberlin*, 31–32; *Tarborough (NC) Southerner*, 26 November 1859, NewsC; US Census, 1850: Cumberland County, NC; Oswald Garrison Villard, *John Brown, 1800–1859: A Biography Fifty Years After* (New York: Houghton Mifflin Co., 1910), 645–86.

39. *The Liberator*, 1 November 1844, 26 February 1858.

40. Lucy D. Bryan to Clarissa Lane, 23 February 1858, reprinted in Hawkins, *Lunsford Lane*, 281–83.

41. Bryan to Lane, 23 February 1858; Eliza Frances Andrews, *War-Time Journal of a Georgia Girl, 1864–1865* (New York: D. Appleton & Co., 1908), 347, IntArch; Eugene Genovese, "'Our Family, Black and White': Family and Household in the Southern Slaveholders;

World View," in *In Joy and Sorrow: Women, Family, and Marriage in the Victorian South, 1830–1900*, ed. Carol Bleser (New York: Oxford University Press, 1991), 69–87.

42. *Fayetteville (NC) Weekly Observer*, 31 December 1855, NewsC; *The Weekly Standard* (Raleigh, NC), 11 February 1857, NewsC; *Weekly Raleigh (NC) Register*, 12 March 1856, 2 December 1857, NewsC; "List of slaves," *William A. Blount and others v. John D. Hawkins and others*, 57 N.C. 162 (December 1858), Supreme Court Original Cases, 1800–1809, SANC; "Several Answers of John D. Hawkins, surviving executor of Sherwood Haywood," *William A. Blount and others v. John D. Hawkins and others*, 57 N.C. 162; *The Semi-Weekly Standard* (Raleigh, NC), 30 January 1856, 31 January 1857, NewsC.

43. *The Weekly Standard*, 20 January 1856; "Several Answers of John D. Hawkins."

44. *William A. Blount and others v. John D. Hawkins and others*, in Hamilton C. Jones, *North Carolina Reports*, Vol. 57, *Cases in Equity Argued and Determined in the Supreme Court of North Carolina, from June Term, 1858, to August Term, 1859, Inclusive* (Raleigh: E. M. Uzzell & Co., 1904), 160–63.

45. "Notes by R. B. & R. W. Haywood," *William A. Blount and others v. John D. Hawkins and others*, 57 N.C. 162; Bryan to Lane, 23 February 1858; Hawkins, *Lunsford Lane*, 198. The lawyers mistakenly recorded the payment that Lunsford made on his mother's behalf as $250 rather than $200.

46. Bryan to Lane, 23 February 1858; Zella Armstrong, comp., *Notable Southern Families*, 2 vols. (Chattanooga, TN: Lookout Publishing, 1933), 2: 153. Matilda Haywood and Alexander Curtis's son (Lunsford's cousin), Alexander Haywood Curtis, was taken to Alabama in 1839 by Rufus Haywood to work one of the Haywood farms. He purchased himself in 1859 and, like Lunsford, went to Manhattan to secure his freedom. He returned to Alabama where, after the Civil War, he enjoyed a distinguished political career in the state House of Representatives; see Bertis D. English, *Civil Wars, Civil Beings, and Civil Rights in Alabama's Black Belt: A History of Perry County* (Tuscaloosa: University of Alabama Press, 2020), 86–90.

47. Bryan to Lane, 23 February 1858.

48. 1850 Census, Slave Schedule: Wake County, NC; will of Martha Brickell, undated, Wake County, NC, SANC; Bryan to Lane, 20 February 1858.

49. Bryan to Lane, 23 February 1858; Hawkins, *Lunsford Lane*, 198.

50. Administration, Probate Records for 1858, Vol. 99: 275, Norfolk County Registry of Probate, Dedham, MA, MHS; *Probate Index: Norfolk County, Massachusetts, 1793–1900*, Vol. 2, *L-Z* (Dedham: Transcript Press, 1910), 636, IntArch.

51. Lunsford Lane to John A. Craig, 10 May 1858, bk. 265: 524–25, NCRD: Lunsford Lane to Silas P. Fisher, 13 May 1858, bk. 269: 399–400, NCRD; Lunsford and Martha Lane to Melansa Belcher, 13 May 1858, bk. 317: 556–57, NCRD; No. 11.309, Probate Docket Book 10.903–12.723, Dedham, Norfolk, Massachusetts, 113, MHS; Accounts of Administrator, Probate Records for 1858, Vol. 102: 374, Norfolk County Registry of Probate; Affidavits, Probate Records for 1858, Vol. 102: 479, Norfolk County Registry of Probate; Accounts of Administrator, Probate Records for 1858, Vol. 102: 275, Norfolk County Registry of Probate.

52. Inventory Assignments, Probate Records for 1858, Vol. 102: 662, Norfolk County Registry of Probate. Historians have produced little on Black property ownership in the nineteenth-century North, in contrast to studies on Black property ownership in the nineteenth-century South; see Dylan C. Penningroth, *The Claims of Kinfolk: African American Property and Community in the Nineteenth-Century South* (Chapel Hill:

University of North Carolina Press, 2003); Roy W. Copeland, "In the Beginning: Origins of African American Real Property Ownership in the United States," *Journal of Black Studies* 44 (September 2013): 646–64; Loren Schweninger, *Black Property Owners in the South, 1790–1915* (Urbana: University of Illinois Press, 1990).

53. Richard Mather Bayles, *History of Providence County, Rhode Island*, 2 vols. (New York: W. W. Preston & Co., 1891), 2: 301, 311–13, Rhode Island Historical Society, Providence, RI.

54. John A. Craig and Sophia J. Craig to Lunsford Lane, 6 September 1858, bk. 283: 14, NCRD; Lunsford Lane and Martha Lane to Mary Magee, 9 September 1858, bk. 283: 14–15, NCRD; annotation for 9 November 1860, Mary Magee to Lunsford Lane, 9 September 1858, bk. 283: 15–16, NCRD.

55. Massachusetts Census, 1855: Suffolk County, AncC; summary of *Federhen v. Lane*, 7 October 1858, *John Federhen Jr. v. Lunsford Lane*, Suffolk County Superior Court Records, Massachusetts Supreme Judicial Court Archives and Records Preservation, Boston; order of execution, 24 June 1858, *John Federhen Jr. v. Lunsford Lane*; plaintiff's declaration, 29 September 1858, *John Federhen Jr. v. Lunsford Lane*; court order, 7 October 1858, *John Federhen Jr. v. Lunsford Lane*; *Cambridge Chronicle*, 16 November 1858; annotation for 27 September 1858, Lane to Oakes, 20 November 1857; Lane's Estate to Amory Houghton Jr., 11 December 1858, bk. 830: 250–52, SMRRL; Lunsford Lane to William Heath, 19 May 1860, bk. 870: 387, SMRRL; Edward J. Balleisen, *Navigating Failure: Bankruptcy and Commercial Society in Antebellum America* (Chapel Hill: University of North Carolina Press, 2001), 80–81.

56. US Census, 1860: Providence County, RI; Hawkins, *Lunsford Lane*, 195; Sharla M. Fett, *Working Cures: Healing, Health, and Power on Southern Slave Plantations* (Chapel Hill: University of North Carolina Press, 2002), 68–78; Paul Starr, *The Social Transformation of American Medicine* (New York: Basic Books, 1982), 47–48; James Harvey Young, "Patent Medicines and the Self-Help Syndrome," in *Sickness and Health in America: Readings in the History of Medicine and Public Health*, ed. Judith Walzer Leavitt and Ronald L. Numbers, 2nd ed. (Madison: University of Wisconsin Press, 1985), 71–78; Edmund A. Schofield, "Thoreau, the Reverend 'Book-Hawker Hawkins,' Horace James, and Dr. Lunsford Lane," *Thoreau Society Bulletin* 266 (Spring 2009): 8.

57. *C. S. Williams' Medina, Elyria & Oberlin City Directory, City Guide, and Business Mirror* (Cincinnati.: C. S. Williams, 1859), 98–99, IntArch; US Census, 1870: Hamilton County, OH.

58. *New-York Daily Tribune* (New York, NY), 18 September 1858, LOC; *The Evening Star* (Washington, DC), 14 August 1908, NewsC; Joseph R. Shipherd, comp., *History of the Oberlin-Wellington Rescue* (Boston: John P. Jewett & Co., 1859), 1–4, 11–13, 131, MHS; Nat Brandt, *The Town that Started the Civil War* (New York: Laurel, 1990), 88–111; Manisha Sinha, *The Slave's Cause: A History of Abolition* (New Haven, CT: Yale University Press, 2016), 523–24.

59. *Anti-Slavery Bugle*, 10 September 1859.

60. Brant, *Town that Started*, 116–17, 125; Bert Klandermans and Jacqueilien van Stekelenburg, "Why People Don't Participate in Collective Action," *Journal of Civil Society* 10 (October 2014): 341–52.

61. Transfer book, 1858: Ward 5, 77, Real Estate, Personal Estate and Poll Tax Records, City of Boston Archives; Valuation book, 1858: Ward 5, 71, Real Estate, Personal Estate and Poll Tax

Records, City of Boston Archives; US Census, 1860: Huron County, OH; US Census, 1860: Lorain County, OH; General Index for Deeds, Lorain Co.—Grantees, 225, Lorain County Recorder's Office, Elyria, OH, https://www.loraincountyrecorder.us/; Sidney S. Goodell to Lunsford Lane, 23 December 1858, bk. 12: 540–41, Lorain County Recorder's Office.

62. J. Brent Morris, *Oberlin, Hotbed of Abolitionism: College, Community, and the Fight for Freedom and Equality in Antebellum America* (Chapel Hill: University of North Carolina Press, 2014), 224–31; Brandt, *Town That Started*, 241–44.

63. *The Oberlin (OH) Evangelist*, 21 December 1859, Ohio5; *Cleveland (OH) Daily Leader*, 12 December 1859; *The Liberator*, 13 January 1860; *Harper's Weekly* 3 (29 October 1859): 694–95, 3 (24 December 1859): 823, IntArch.

64. *Independent Democrat* (Elyria, OH), 2 November 1859, LOC; James Monroe, *Oberlin Thursday Lectures, Addresses and Essays* (Oberlin: Edward J. Goodrich, 1897), 170–73, IntArch; Steven Lubet, *The "Colored Hero" of Harper's Ferry: John Anthony Copeland and the War against Slavery* (New York: Cambridge University Press, 2015), 206–7.

65. *Lorain County News* (Oberlin and Wellington, OH), 2 May 1860, 4 May 1860, 16 May 1860, 30 May 1860, 6 June 1860, Ohio5; Hawkins, *Lunsford Lane*, 179; General Index to Deeds, Lorain Co.—Grantors, 245, Lorain County Recorder's Office; Sheriff to Edward J. Goodrich, 4 April 1861, bk. 15: 262–63, Lorain County Recorder's Office; "The Mortgage; Its Origins and History—Principles Presiding over Its Application to Real and Personal Property—Remedies," *American Law Register* (June 1856): 458, IntArch; Joshua Williams, *Principles of the Law of Real Property, Intended as a First Book for the Use of Students in Conveyancing* (London: S. Sweet, 1845), 334–36, IntArch; *Harkraker v. Leiby*, 4 Ohio St. 602 (1855).

Chapter 13

1. *Massachusetts Spy* (Worcester, MA), 6 August 1862, AAS; *Worcester (MA) Daily Spy*, 31 July 1862, AAS.

2. *The Rasp* (Raleigh, NC), 20 August 1842, NewsC; *Worcester Daily Spy*, 31 July 1862, 4 August 1862; *The Liberator* (Boston, MA), 5 December 1845, NewsC; Nick Salvatore, *We All Got History: The Memory Books of Amos Webber* (New York: Times Books, 1996), 113–24.

3. Thomas Wentworth Higginson, *Cheerful Yesterdays* (Boston: Houghton, Mifflin & Co., 1890), 131, AAS; D. Butler to Horace James, 5 January 1853, Horace James Correspondence, 1852–1870, AAS; Warren Burton to Horace James, 15 May 1856, Horace James Correspondence.

4. Frederick Douglass, *My Bondage and My Freedom*, Part 1, *Life as a Slave* (New York: Miller, Orton & Mulligan, 1855), 361, NASN; *Worcester Daily Spy*, 5 October 1850; US Census, 1850: Worcester County, MA; Ethan J. Kytle, *Romantic Reformers and the Antislavery Struggle in the Civil War Era* (New York: Cambridge University Press, 2014), 206–52.

5. *Massachusetts Spy*, 1 November 1854; *Daily Evening Journal* (Worcester, MA), 30 October 1854, AAS; "The Butman Riot: Oct. 30, 1854," *Proceedings of the Worcester Society of Antiquity, for the Year 1878* (Worcester: by the Society, 1879): 85–93; Janette Thomas Greenwood, *First Fruits of Freedom: The Migration of Former Slaves and Their Search for Equality in Worcester, Massachusetts, 1862–1900* (Chapel Hill: University of North Carolina Press, 2009), 17–19; Albert J. Von Frank, *The Trial of Anthony Burns: Freedom and Slavery in Emerson's Boston* (Cambridge, MA: Harvard University Press, 1998), 305–6.

6. *Tri-Weekly Commercial* (Wilmington, NC), 5 December 1854, NewsC; *The Weekly Union* (Manchester, NH), 15 November 1854, NewsC; *Boston (MA) Investigator*, 6 December 1854, AAS; *Worcester Daily Spy*, 23 January 1855, 24 January 1855.

7. Charles Nutt, *History of Worcester and Its People*, 4 vols. (New York: Lewis Historical Publishing Co., 1919), 2: 581–606; Pamela J. Cummings, "Worcester County Soldiers in the Civil War," *Historical Journal of Massachusetts* 20 (Winter 1992): 32–52; John L. Brooke, *The Heart of the Commonwealth: Society and Political Culture in Worcester County, Massachusetts, 1713–1861* (New York: Cambridge University Press, 1989), 389–97; "Annual Report for 1865 and History," in National Freedmen's Relief Association, *The Abolition of Slavery in America* (London: W. H. Collingridge, 1862), 3, NYHS.

8. *Massachusetts Soldiers, Sailors, and Marines in the Civil War*, 8 vols. (Norwood, MA: Norwood Press, 1932), 4: 546–47, 555, AAS; Thomas W. Higginson, *Army Life in a Black Regiment* (Boston: Fields, Osgood, & Co., 1870), 41, AAS.

9. T. W. Wellington to William J. Dale, 31 July 1862, quoted in Sande P. Bishop, "Dale Hospital—A Civil War Hospital with Community Support," *Civil War Rx*, 28 November 1999, http://civilwarrx.blogspot.com/2016/07/dale-hospital-civil-war-hospital-with.html; Sande P. Bishop, "Lunsford Lane: A Fascinating Story in Worcester's Medical History," *Worcester Medicine* 60 (Fall 1996): 22–24, Worcester District Medical Society, Worcester, MA; Abijah P. Marvin, *Worcester in the War of the Rebellion* (Worcester: the author, 1880), 133, 417; *Massachusetts Soldiers, Sailors, and Marines*, 3: 48; J. Waldo Denny, *Wearing the Blue in the Twenty-Fifth Mass. Volunteer Infantry, with Burnside's Division, 18th Army Corps, and the Army of the James* (Worcester: Putnam & Davis, 1879), 34, 244, IntArch.

10. Wellington to Dale, 31 July 1862; *Massachusetts Spy*, 23 July 1862, 18 September 1862; William G. Hawkins, *Lunsford Lane; or, Another Helper from North Carolina* (Boston: Crosby & Nichols, 1863), 208, NCC; Henry J. Howland, *The Worcester Almanac, Directory, and Business Advertiser for 1863* (Worcester: Henry J. Howland, 1863), 104, IntArch; 80; Samuel B. Woodward, "Early Charitable Organizations in Worcester," *Worcester Historical Society Publications* 1 (April 1934): 400.

11. *Report of the Surgeon-General of Massachusetts to His Excellency the Commander-in-Chief, December 1st, 1862*, in *Annual Report of the Adjutant-General of the Commonwealth of Massachusetts with Reports from the Quartermaster-General, Surgeon-General, and Master of Ordinance, for the Year Ending December 31, 1862* (Boston: Wright & Potter, 1863), 24–25, AAS; D. Hamilton Hurd et al., *History of Worcester County, Massachusetts, with Biographical Sketches of Many of Its Pioneers and Prominent Men*, 2 vols. (Philadelphia: J. W. Lewis & Co., 1889), 2: 1573, AAS; Howland, *The Worcester Almanac, Directory, and Business Advertiser for 1863*, 80; Hawkins, *Lunsford Lane*, 207–209; *Massachusetts Soldiers, Sailors, and Marines*, 5: 304, 6: 768.

12. J. J. Woodward, *The Hospital Steward's Manual: For the Instruction of Hospital Stewards, Ward Master, and Attendants in Their Several Duties* (Philadelphia: Lippincott & Co., 1862), 20, 38–39, 41–44, 54–55, 129, 285–94, IntArch. It was commonly understood that Lane was not an actual doctor, with a historian less than twenty-five years later placing the title in quotation marks: "'Dr.' Lunsford Lane, once a slave, was in charge and was assisted by his wife and daughter"; see Hurd et al., *History of Worcester County, Massachusetts*, 2: 1573.

13. *Worcester Daily Spy*, 2 January 1863; Hurd et al., *History of Worcester County, Massachusetts*, 2: 1560–61, 1573, 1586; George Warren Nason, *History and Complete Roster of the*

Massachusetts Regiments: Minute Men of '61 (Boston: Smith & McCance, 1910), 277, AAS; Hawkins, *Lunsford Lane*, 207–9.

14. *Worcester Daily Spy*, 6 July 1863, 8 July 1863, 15 July 1863, 22 July 1863; Marvin, *Worcester in the War*, 431–33; *Massachusetts Soldiers, Sailors, and Marines*, 2: 138; Drew Gilpin Faust, *This Republic of Suffering: Death and the American Civil War* (New York: Alfred A. Knopf, 2008), 85–93.

15. Albert S. Roe, "Military History: The Wellington Collection of Rebellion Relics," *Proceedings of the Worcester Society of Antiquity for the Year 1883* (Worcester: Worcester Society of Antiquity, 1884), 231–38.

16. Hawkins, *Lunsford Lane*, 207–209; Marriage Register, Massachusetts Vital Records, 1840–1911, New England Historic Genealogical Society, Boston, MA; Henry J. Howland, *The Worcester Almanac, Directory, and Business Advertiser for 1862* (Worcester: Henry J. Howland, 1862), 92, IntArch; Howland, *The Worcester Almanac, Directory, and Business Advertiser for 1863*, 70; Marriages Registered in the City of Worcester, County of Worcester, 1863, in Jay Mack Holbrook, *Massachusetts Vital Records to 1850: Worcester 1719–1890* (Oxford, MA: Holbrook Research Institute, 1984), 113–14, AAS.

17. Hawkins, *Lunsford Lane*, 204–6.

18. William Wells Brown, *A Lecture Delivered before the Female Anti-Slavery Society of Salem, at Lyceum Hall. Nov. 14, 1847* (Boston: Massachusetts Anti-Slavery Society, 1847), 4, AAS; Frederick Douglass, "What, to the Slave, Is the Fourth of July?" in *Lift Every Voice: African American Oratory, 1787–1900*, ed. Philip S. Foner and Robert James Branham (Tuscaloosa: University of Alabama Press, 1990), 39–40, 81, 265–66; David W. Blight, *Frederick Douglass' Civil War: Keeping Faith in Jubilee* (Baton Rouge: Louisiana State University Press, 1989), 74–75.

19. Hawkins, *Lunsford Lane*, 206; Mitch Kachun, *Festivals of Freedom: Memory and Meaning in African American Emancipation Celebrations, 1808–1915* (Amherst: University of Massachusetts Press, 2003), 70.

20. US Census, 1860: Rensselaer County, NY. The Lane sons are not listed in Troy's city directory for 1860, but the other residents in their tenement house are, suggesting that Lunsford Jr. and William arrived late in 1860; see *The Troy Directory of the Year 1860* (Troy: William H. Young, 1860), 109, 135, 153, 180, IntArch; also, *The Troy Directory of the Year 1861* (Troy: Young & Benson, 1861), 112, 123, 189, IntArch.

21. Mary Maillard, "'Faithfully Draw from Real Life': Autobiographical Elements in Frank J. Webb's *The Garies and Their Friends*," *Pennsylvania Magazine of History and Biography* 137 (July 2013): 265–67; Julie Winch, *A Gentleman of Color: The Life of James Forten* (New York: Oxford University Press, 2004), 279–80, 321. 343, 347–50; Brenda Stevenson, ed., *The Journals of Charlotte Forten Grimké* (New York: Oxford University Press, 1988), 9, 17–18.

22. Abijah P. Marvin, *History of Worcester in the War of the Rebellion* (Worcester, MA: the author, 1870), 417, AAS; *The Negroes at Port Royal: Report of E. L. Pierce, Government Agent, to the Hon. Salmon P. Chase, Secretary of the Treasury* (Boston: R. F. Wallcut, 1862), 8, AAS; John Greenleaf Whittier, *Anti-Slavery Poems: Songs of Labor and Reform*, 7 vols. (Boston: Houghton, Mifflin & Co., 1892), 3: 230–33, IntArch; Willie Lee Rose, *Rehearsal for Reconstruction: The Port Royal Experiment* (Indianapolis: Bobbs-Merrill Co., 1964).

23. *Boston (MA) Traveller*, 4 November 1863, AAS; Hawkins, *Lunsford Lane*, 218; Ray Allen Billington, ed., *The Journal of Charlotte L. Forten* (New York: Dryden Press, 1953),

115, 121, 122–26. Contrary to Hawkins's framing, William and Lunsford Jr. were not transporting the troops that invaded Port Royal in December 1861. The three hundred oarsmen and coxswains who launched the transports were "soldier oarsmen" who joined their platoons after landing; see T. W. Sherman, General Orders No. 19, 23 October 1861, in *The War of the Rebellion: A Compilation of the Official Records of the Union and Confederate Armies*—Series. 1: Vol. 6. (Washington, DC: Government Printing Office, 1882), 182.

24. Billington, ed., *Journal of Charlotte L. Forten*, 137; Higginson, *Army Life*, 8–14.

25. Horace James, "An Oration delivered in Newbern, North Carolina, before the Twenty-Fifth Regiment Massachusetts Volunteers, July 4, 1862" (Boston: W. F. Brown & Co., 1862), 9, NYHS. On James's career as Superintendent of Negro Affairs for the Department of North Carolina during the war, see Judkin Browning, *Shifting Loyalties: The Union Occupation of Eastern North Carolina* (Chapel Hill: University of North Carolina Press, 2011), 81–104.

26. *New-York Daily Tribune* (New York, NY), 13 February 1862, LOC.

27. *Worcester Daily Spy*, 19 April 1861, 6 August 1862, 11 August 1862, 12 September 1862, 17 September 1862.

28. *Worcester Daily Spy*, 12 March 1863; *Massachusetts Spy*, 18 March 1863; *Massachusetts Soldiers, Sailors, and Marines*, 4: 696, 697; Thomas Freeman to William Brown, 16 May 1864, Brown Family Papers, AAS; Thomas D. Freeman to Martha Brown, 25 April 1864, Brown Family Papers; T. D. Brown to William Brown, 26 March 1864, Brown Family Papers; Douglas R. Egerton, *Thunder at the Gates: The Black Civil War Regiments that Redeemed America* (New York: Basic Books, 2016), 63–77; Steven M. LaBarre, *The Fifth Massachusetts Colored Cavalry in the Civil War* (Jefferson, NC: Macfarland & Co., 2016), 14–15; Marvin, *History of Worcester*, 573, 547.

29. Enlistment Lists, 1864, Worcester, Massachusetts Collection, 1686–1941, AAS; Vital Records: Marriages, 1841–1915, 240, Massachusetts State Archives, Boston; *Worcester Daily Spy*, 28 June 1862.

30. Kachun, *Festivals of Freedom*, 70; Thomas D. Freeman to William Brown, 8 May 1864, Brown Family Papers; Freeman to Brown, 26 March 1864.

31. "Henry J. Patterson," card 18, Carded Records Showing Military Service of Soldiers Who Fought in Volunteer Organizations During the American Civil War, compiled 1890–1912, documenting the period 1861–1866, Records of the Adjutant General's Office, 1762–1984, RG 94, War Department, National Archives, Washington, DC, *Fold3*, https://www.fold3.com/; Egerton, *Thunder at the Gates*, 69–93, 123–33.

32. Civil War Union Draft Records, Ohio: 14th Congressional District, 3 vols., 1: 70, 145, 2: 432, 3: 75, Records of the Provost Marshal General's Bureau, RG 110, War Department, National Archives, Washington, DC, *Fold3*, https://www.fold3.com/; "Rubin Turner," Certificate of Disability for Discharge, 20 July 1865, Carded Records Showing Military Service of Soldiers Who Fought in Volunteer Organizations During the American Civil War; William E. Bigglestone, *They Stopped in Oberlin: Black Residents and Visitors in the Nineteenth Century* (Oberlin, OH: Oberlin College, 2002), 202.

33. Civil War Union Draft Records, Ohio: 14th Congressional District, 2: 277; "Edward Lane," Indexes to the Carded Records of Soldiers who Served in Volunteer Organizations during the Civil War, Records of the Adjutant General's Office, 1762–1984, RG 94; General Orders, No. 323, in *General Orders of the War Department, Embracing the Years 1861, 1862*

& 1863 Adapted Specially for the Use of the Army and Navy of the United States, 2 vols. (New York: Derby & Miller, 1864), 2: 542, IntArch.

34. *Worcester Daily Spy*, 14 August 1896; *Massachusetts Soldiers, Sailors, and Marines*, 6: 506, 509, 510; Marvin, *History of Worcester*, 546–47; Christopher Cox, *History of Massachusetts Civil War Regiments: Artillery, Cavalry, and Infantry* (Raleigh: Lulu Publishing, 2013), 41–42; Egerton, *Thunder at the Gates*, 251–99; P. C. Headley, *Massachusetts in the Rebellion: A Record of the Historical Position of the Commonwealth and the Services of the Leading Statesmen, the Military, the Colleges, and the People in the Civil War of 1861–1865* (Boston: Walker, Fuller, and Co., 1866), 497–98.

35. US Census, 1850: Suffolk County, MA; Massachusetts Census, 1865: Suffolk County, AncC; *Massachusetts Soldiers, Sailors, and Marines*, 4: 686, 758, 6: 528, 8: 151; Egerton, *Thunder at the Gates*, 77–78, 254; Register of Enlistments in the US Army, 1798–1914, 172, War Department, Records of the Adjutant General's Office, 1762–1984, RG 94; US Census, 1880: Logan County, KY; Civil War Union Draft Records, Kentucky, 3 vols., 1: 21, Records of the Provost Marshal General's Bureau, RG 110.

36. Hawkins, *Lunsford Lane*, 218; Howland, *The Worcester Almanac, Directory, and Business Advertiser for 1863*, 73; Henry J. Howland, *Worcester City Directory Advertiser for 1865* (Worcester: Henry J. Howland, 1865), 80.

37. "A Teetotaler," in *The New Impulse; or Hawkins and Reform: A Brief History of the Origin, Progress, and Effects of the Present Astonishing Temperance Movement: and of the Life and Reformation of John H. W. Hawkins, the Distinguished Leader* (Boston: Samuel N. Dickinson, 1841), 12, AAS; William George Hawkins, *Life of John H. W. Hawkins* (Boston: J. P. Jewett & Co., 1859), 11, 49–60, AAS; US Census, 1850: Fairfax County, VA.

38. *Baltimore (MA) Sun*, 31 August 1858, NewsC; *Vermont Chronicle* (Bellows Falls, VT), 28 September 1858, NewsC; *The Liberator*, 25 March 1859; Rossiter Johnson, "Hawkins, William George," *Biographical Dictionary of America*, 10 vols. (Boston: American Biographical Society, 1906), 5: 169; *Journal of the Proceedings of the Bishops, Clergy, and Laity of the Protestant Episcopal Church in the United States of America* (Philadelphia: King & Baird, 1854), 386; *Journal of the Sixty-First Annual Convention of the Protestant Episcopal Church in Maryland* (Baltimore: Joseph Robinson, 1849), vii.

39. Hawkins, *Life of John H. W. Hawkins*, 26; *The Liberator*, 1 October 1841; "A Teetotaler," 12; Frank Colgrove, "Some Worcester Contacts with the Washington Temperance Movement," *Worcester Historical Society Publications* 1 (April 1930): 107; Abraham Lincoln, "An Address Delivered before the Springfield Washington Temperance Society," 22 February 1842, in *Collected Works of Abraham Lincoln*, ed. Roy P. Basler, 8 vols. (New Brunswick, NJ: Rutgers University Press, 1953), 1: 279; Charles J. G. Griffin, "The 'Washingtonian Revival': Narrative and the Moral Transformation of Temperance Reform in Antebellum America," *Southern Communication Journal* 66 (Fall 2000): 67–78; Milton A. Maxwell, "The Washington Movement," *Quarterly Journal of Studies on Alcohol* 11 (September 1950): 422–23.

40. Hawkins, *Life of John H. W. Hawkins*, 425; Henry David Thoreau, quoted in Thomas Blanding and Edmund A. Schofield, "E. Harlow Russell's Reminiscences of Thoreau," *The Concord Saunterer* 17 (August 1984): 11; Edmund A. Schofield, "Thoreau, the Reverend 'Book-Hawker Hawkins,' Horace James, and Dr. Lunsford Lane," *Thoreau Society Bulletin* 266 (Spring 2009): 5; George Faber Clark, *History of the Temperance Reform in Massachusetts, 1813–1883* (Boston: Clarke & Carruth, 1888), 50, 236, 244, 248, 250.

41. *New-York Daily Tribune*, 26 March 1859; *The Spirit of the Age* (Raleigh, NC), 16 February 1859, NewsC.

42. *The Herald of Freedom* (Concord, NH), 1 July 1842, NewsC; *Worcester Daily Spy*, 18 February 1863; Hawkins, *Lunsford Lane*, 204–6.

43. Hawkins, *Lunsford Lane*, v–vii.

44. Hawkins, *Lunsford Lane*; *Christian Advocate and Journal* (New York, NY), 24 December 1863, LOC.

45. James Williams, *Narrative of James Williams, an American Slave, Who Was for Several Years a Driver on a Cotton Plantation in Alabama* (Boston: Isaac Knapp, 1838), NASN; Lydia Maria Child to Theodore Weld, 29 December 1838, in *Letters of Theodore Weld, Angelina Grimké Weld, and Sarah Grimké, 1822–1844*, 2 vols. (New York: D. Appleton-Century Co., 1934), 2: 735, also 730–32; *The Liberator*, 21 September 1838.

46. Martha Griffith Browne, *Autobiography of a Female Slave* (New York: Redfield, 1857), NASN; *Ohio Farmer* (Cleveland, OH), 27 December 1856, AAS; *Richmond (VA) Whig & Public Advertiser*, 2 January 1857, AAS; *The Liberator*, 9 January 1857.

47. Hawkins, *Lunsford Lane*, vii, viii, 16, 137; Kimberly R. Smith, *The Dominion of Voice: Riot, Reason, and Romance in Antebellum Politics* (Lawrence: University Press of Kansas, 1999), 182.

48. Hawkins, *Lunsford Lane*, 84.

49. Hawkins, *Lunsford Lane*, 119, 137.

50. Lunsford Lane, *The Narrative of Lunsford Lane, Formerly of Raleigh, N.C. Embracing an Account of His Early Life, the Redemption by Purchase of Himself and Family from Slavery, and His Banishment from the Place of His Birth for the Crime of Wearing a Colored Skin. Published by Himself*, 2nd ed. (Boston: J. G. Torrey, 1842), 15–16, AAS.

51. Hawkins, *Lunsford Lane*, 48.

52. Hawkins, *Lunsford Lane*, vi.

53. *Worcester Daily Spy*, 17 September 1863; Hawkins, *Lunsford Lane*, 66; William George Hawkins to John S. Bassett, 23 October 1899, John Spencer Bassett Papers, 1770–1978, Manuscripts Division, LOC; Hinton Rowan Helper, *The Impending Crisis of the South: How to Meet It* (New-York: Burdick Brothers, 1857), NCC.

54. Hawkins, *Lunsford Lane*, 14, 19; Sarah N. Roth, *Gender and Race in Antebellum Popular Culture* (New York: Cambridge University Press, 2014), 78.

55. Solomon Northup, *Twelve Years a Slave: Narrative of Solomon Northup, a Citizen of New-York, Kidnapped in Washington City in 1841 and Rescued in 1853, from a Cotton Plantation Near the Red River in Louisiana* (Auburn, NY: Derby and Miller, 1853), 40–49, quote on 43, AAS; Hawkins, *Lunsford Lane*, 103, 137.

56. Manisha Sinha, *The Slave's Cause: A History of Abolition* (New Haven, CT: Yale University Press, 2016), 248; William Craft, *Running a Thousand Miles for Freedom; or, the Escape of William and Ellen Craft from Slavery* (London: William Tweedie, 1860), 313, NASN; Hawkins, *Lunsford Lane*, 15, 63–80, 175; William L. Andrews, *To Tell a Free Story: The First Century of Afro-American Autobiography, 1760–1865* (Urbana: University of Illinois Press, 1986), 62.

57. Hawkins, *Lunsford Lane*, 19, 40, 43, 83–84, 137–38.

58. Hawkins, *Lunsford Lane*, vi, 18, 31.

59. Hawkins, *Lunsford Lane*, 76; Eugene McCarthy and Thomas L. Doughton, "General Introduction," in *From Bondage to Belonging: The Worcester Slave Narratives*, ed. B. Eugene

McCarthy and Thomas L. Doughton (Amherst: University of Massachusetts Press, 2007), xxiv.

60. Hawkins, *Lunsford Lane*, vii, 195–98; Terry Baxter, *Frederick Douglass's Curious Audiences: Ethos in the Age of the Consumable Subject* (New York: Routledge, 2004), 92, 104–7; Roy E. Finkenbine, "Boston's Black Churches: Institutional Centers of the Antislavery Movement," in *Courage and Conscience: Black & White Abolitionists in Boston*, ed. Donald M. Jacobs (Bloomington: Indiana University Press, 1993), 178; McCarthy and Doughton, "General Introduction," xlix; Andrews, *To Tell a Free Story*, 99–100.

61. David Tatham, "John Henry Bufford: American Lithographer," *Proceedings of the American Antiquarian Society* 86 (April 1976): 47–73; *Hartford (CT) Courant*, 4 January 1862, NewsC; J. H. Bufford, "Boston Massacre, March 5, 1770," chromolithograph (Boston: Henry Q. Smith, 1856), MHS.

62. *New-York (NY) Observer*, 26 November 1863, NewsC.

63. Lynn A. Camier-Paz, "Slave Narratives and the Rhetoric of Author Portraiture," *New Literary History* 34 (Winter 2003): 93, 102, 105.

64. G. Spurzheim, *Outlines of Phrenology* (Boston: Marsh, Capen and Lyon, 1832), 49–51, 69–71; O. S. Fowler, *Fowler's Practical Phrenology* (New York: Fowlers and Wells, 1850), 64–65; Susan Branson, "Phrenology and the Science of Race in Antebellum America," *Early American Studies* 15 (Winter 2017): 164–93.

65. *Buffalo (NY) Morning Express*, 10 October 1863, AAS; *The Publishers' Weekly* 72 (July–December 1907), 667, HT; *American Literary Gazette and Publishers Circular* 2 (2 November 1863): 31, IntArch; Hawkins, *Lunsford Lane*, 48; Susan S. Williams, "Authors and Literary Authorship," in *A History of the Book in America*, Vol. 3, *The Industrial Book, 1840–1880*, ed. Scott E. Casper et al. (Chapel Hill: University of North Carolina Press, 2008), 96; Marcy J. Dinius, *The Camera and the Press: American Visual and Print Culture in the Age of Daguerreotype* (Philadelphia: University of Pennsylvania Press, 2021), 131–36; John Tebbell, *A History of Book Publishing in the United States*, Vol. 1: *The Creation of an Industry, 1630-1865* (New York: R. R. Bowder, 1972), 429.

66. *New York (NY) Times*, 23 November 1863, NewsC; *The Liberator*, 4 December 1863; *Boston (MA) Evening Transcript*, 4 November 1863, NewsC; *Boston Traveller*, 4 November 1863, 23 November 1863; *Bangor (ME) Daily Whig and Courier*, 11 February 1864, NewsC.

67. *Boston Evening Transcript*, 5 November 1863; *Publishers' Circular and General Records of British and Foreign Literature* 26 (8 December 1863): 630, IntArch; *Boston Traveller*, 4 November 1863; entry for 3 September 1863, Copy Right Entries and Fees, 1860–1864, US District Court for the District of Massachusetts, 1789–, Records of District Courts of the United States, 1685–2009, National Archives at Boston, Waltham, MA. On the wartime scarcity of paper in Massachusetts, see "Report of the Librarian," April 1863, *Proceedings of the American Antiquarian Society Annual Meeting, in Boston* (Boston: John Wilson and Son, 1863), 19.

68. Inscription inside front cover, Haven copy of William G. Hawkins, *Lunsford Lane; or, Another Helper from North Carolina* (Boston: Crosby & Nichols, 1863), AAS; "Proceedings: Annual Meeting of the Society, October 16, 1907, at the Hall of the Society in Worcester," *Proceedings of the American Antiquarian Society, New Series*, Vol. 18, *October 24, 1906-October 16, 1906* (Worcester: American Antiquarian Society, 1907), 280, AAS; Samuel F. Haven, *An Historical Address Delivered before the Citizens of the Town of Dedham, on the Twenty-First of September, 1836, Being the Second Centennial Anniversary of the*

Incorporation of the Town (Dedham: Herman Mann, 1837), 48, AAS; Philip F. Gura, *The American Antiquarian Society, 1812–2012: A Bicentennial History* (Worcester: American Antiquarian Society, 2012), 86, 115–16, 128; Charles Deane, *Memoir of Samuel F. Haven, LL.D.* (Cambridge, MA: John Wilson and Son, 1885), 9, AAS.

69. *Worcester (MA) Palladium*, 9 January 1861, 13 June 1866, AAS; *The National Aegis* (Worcester, MA), 24 October 1863, 21 October 1865, 25 October 1865, 28 October 1865, AAS; *Massachusetts Spy*, 27 October 1865; Samuel Sweet Green, *The Public Library Movement in the United States, 1853–1893* (Boston: Boston Book Co., 1913), 8; Gura, *American Antiquarian Society*, 22, 137; Samuel S. Greene, *A Genealogical Sketch of the Descendants of Thomas Green[e] of Malden, Mass.* (Boston: Henry W. Dutton & Son, 1858), 62, AAS; bookplate inside front cover, Green copy of William G. Hawkins, *Lunsford Lane; or, Another Helper from North Carolina* (Boston: Crosby & Nichols, 1863), Dr. Green Collection, WPL.

70. Inscription inside front cover, Brown copy of William G. Hawkins, *Lunsford Lane; or, Another Helper from North Carolina* (Boston: Crosby & Nichols, 1863), AAS; inventory of Brown Family Library, AAS; transcription inside front cover, William H. Thayer, *The Pioneer Boy and How He Became President* (Boston: Walker, Wise, & Co., 1864), AAS.

71. *The Daily Enterprise* (Marlborough, MA), 5 June 1901, BPL; *The Liberator*, 31 January 1840; Nutt, *History of Worcester*, 1: 492, 2: 604, 4: 603–604; *Dictionary of Worcester and Its Vicinity* (Worcester: F. S. Blanchard & Co., 1889), 88–90, IntArch; Henry J. Howland, *The Worcester Almanac, Directory, and Business Advertiser for 1864* (Worcester: Henry J. Howland, 1864), 74, IntArch; Theodore Parker to Edward Earle, 16 October 1847, Edward Earle Papers, AAS; Ivan Sandrof, *Your Worcester Street* (Worcester: Franklin Publishing Co., 1948), 94; Warren Lazell, *Map of the City of Worcester, Worcester County, Massachusetts, from Original Surveys by H. F. Walling* (Worcester: n. p., 1851), AAS; Edward Palmer to William Lloyd Garrison, 9 August 1837, Anti-Slavery Collection, BPL.

72. Salvatore, *We All Got History*, 98, 108; *Fiske's Pocket Business Manual of the City of Worcester for the Year 1863* (Worcester: Edward R. Fiske, 1863), 41, WPL; Howland, *The Worcester Almanac, Directory, and Business Advertiser for 1863*, 104; Patent No. 61709, 5 February 1867, Brown Family Papers; Patent No. 81065, 18 August 1868, Brown Family Papers; J. Cotton Eastman to William Brown, 30 May 1867, Brown Family Papers; Greenwood, *First Fruits of Freedom*, 52; Alice Bush to "dear sons," n.d., Brown Family Papers (the letter is situated between one dated January 28 and one dated March 25).

73. William R. Hooper to William Brown, 20 July 1853, bk. 513: 203–204, WDRRL; contract between Anson Bangs and William Brown, 1 April 1853, Brown Family Papers; S. H. Bowman to William Brown, 11 March 1853, Brown Family Papers; agreement between Joseph F. Clarke and Wm. Brown, 5 March 1868, Brown Family Papers; *Stimpson's Boston Directory* (Boston: Stimpson and Clapp, 1832), 347, IntArch; US Census, 1850: Worcester County, MA; Massachusetts Census, 1855: Worcester County; US Census, 1860: Worcester County, MA. D. G. Littlefield, *The Morning Glory: Origin of the Base-Burning Stove* (Albany: n. p., 1869), AAS; William P. Codman, *John Moore Jr.*, 1826, oil on canvas, AAS; Lauren B. Hewes, *Portraits of the Collection of the American Antiquarian Society* (Worcester: American Antiquarian Society, 2004), 245–47; Florence T. Allen, comp., *Worcester House Directory Arranged by Streets* (n. p.: n. p., 1954), AAS; François Weil, *Family Trees: A History of Genealogy in America* (Cambridge, MA: Harvard University Press, 2013), 149–50. Thomas Freeman referenced this sibling relationship in Thomas D. Freeman to Martha Ann Brown, 23 April 1865, Brown Family Papers.

74. William Ward, *A View of All Religions* (Hartford, CT: William D. Cooke, 1824), AAS; J. T. Headley, *Imperial Guard of Napoleon: From Marengo to Waterloo* (New York: Scribner, 1851), AAS; George Ripley and Bayard Taylor, eds., *Putnam's Home Cyclopedia: Handbook of Literature and the Fine Arts* (New York: George P. Putnam, 1852), AAS; Eliza Robbins, *The Guide to Knowledge, Adapted for Young Persons* (New York: Appleton, 1853), AAS; *Europe and the Allies of the Past and of Today* (New York: Edward Livermore, 1855), AAS; R. M. Zornlin, *Physical Geography, for Families and Schools* (Boston: J. Munroe & Co., 1855), AAS; Harriot K. Hunt, *Professional Life* (Boston: John P. Jewett and Co., 1856), AAS; *The Child's Anti-Slavery Book: Containing a Few Words about American Slave Children, and Stories of Slave Life* (Boston: American Tract Society, 1859), AAS; M. J. Michelet, *Woman (La Femme)* (New York: Rudde and Carleto, 1860) AAS; the Koran *(Boston: T. O. H. P. Burnham, 1864), AAS.*

75. Thayer, *Pioneer Boy*, 43; Ward, *A View of All Religions*, 242–43; Zornlin, *Physical Geography*, 136; Michelet, *Woman*, 132; Laurie F. Maffly-Kipp, *Setting Down the Sacred Past: African-American Race Histories* (Cambridge, MA: Belknap Press, 2010), 48–49.

76. *Child's Anti-Slavery Book*, 158.

77. *Fiske's Pocket Business Manual*, 74; Howland, *The Worcester City Directory Advertiser for 1865*, 80; Henry J. Howland, *The Worcester Directory Advertiser for 1866* (Worcester: Asa B. Adams, 1866), 140, WPL; *Worcester Daily Spy*, 13 July 1865.

78. Massachusetts Census, 1865: Worcester County, AncC; Howland, *The Worcester Directory Advertiser for 1866*, 56, 58, 63, 67, 70, 91, 115, 132, 140, 150, 181, 183, 186, 207, 211.

79. *Worcester Daily Spy*, 1 January 1864, 2 January 1864, 5 November 1864.

80. Massachusetts Census, 1865: Worcester County, AncC; Nancy Kathryn Burns and Janette Thomas Greenwood, *Rediscovering an American Community of Color: The Photography of William Bullard, 1897–1917* (Worcester: Worcester Art Museum, 2017), 21, 106–7. The Massachusetts census of 1865 listed Charles L. Lane, age sixteen, in the Lane household. Efforts to identity Charles L. Lane were fruitless, leading to the conclusion that this is a misidentification of Clara Lane, who was sixteen at the time and is found nowhere else in the census; see Massachusetts Census, 1865: Worcester County.

81. *Worcester Daily Spy*, 6 July 1865; Greenwood, *First Fruits of Freedom*, 92; *Massachusetts Soldiers, Sailors, and Marines*, 5: 725; Marvin, *History of Worcester*, 417, 448.

82. R. Robinson to William Brown, 12 June 1864, Brown Family Papers; *Massachusetts Soldiers, Sailors, and Marines*, 4: 686, 696, 697, 6: 506, 508, 509, 510.

83. "Rubin Turner," Certificate of Disability for Discharge, 20 July 1865; Bigglestone, *They Stopped at Oberlin*, 202; *Massachusetts Soldiers, Sailors, and Marines*, 4: 688, 9: 584.

84. *Official Roster of the Soldiers of the State of Ohio in the War of the Rebellions, 1861–1866*, Vol 4, *37th–53rd Regiments—Infantry* (Akron, OH: Werner Printing and Manufacturing Co., 1867), 81, 107, IntArch.

85. *Worcester Daily Spy*, 8 November 1864; Marvin, *History of Worcester*, 310; *Massachusetts Soldiers, Sailors, and Marines*, 6: 492, 508; Massachusetts Census, 1865: Worcester County; *Massachusetts Spy*, 21 July 1865; James L. Bowen, *Massachusetts in the War, 1861–1865* (Springfield, MA: C. W. Bryan & Co., 1889), 781–83, AAS; Civil War Record Books, 1861–1865, Worcester, Massachusetts Collection; National Park Service, Chalmette National Cemetery—Headstones, 19 August 2006, 95, Chalmette National Cemetery, New Orleans, LA.

86. Widow's Certificate File 100230, PAW; Chapter 166: "An Act to Grant Pensions," 14 July 1862, *Acts and Resolutions of the Second Session of the Thirty-Seventh Congress, Begun*

on Monday, December 2, 1861, and Ended on Thursday, July 17, 1862 (Washington, DC: Government Printing Office, 1862), 566–69, IntArch; Adjutant General's Office to Henry C. Rice, 14 March 1866, PAW; Adjutant General's Office to Henry C. Rice, 3 April 1866, PAW; Chapman affidavit, 10 December 1866, PAW; Parker affidavit, 30 July 1867, PAW; Surgeon General's Office to Henry C. Rice, 24 August 1867; Claim for Widow's Pension, 19 September 1867, PAW; Megan J. McClintock, "Civil War Pensions and the Reconstruction of Union Families," *Journal of American History* 83 (September 1996): 456–80.

87. New York State Census, 1855: New York City, Ward 9, AncC; US Census, 1860: New York City, Ward 9; Leslie M. Harris, *In the Shadow of Slavery: African Americans in New York City, 1626–1863* (Chicago: University of Chicago Press, 2003), 181.

88. US Census, 1860: New York City, Ward 18; "Fifth Avenue Hotel," *The Granite Monthly* 10 (January 1887): 317–25, AAS; W. Sloane Kennedy, "The Vertical Railway," *Harper's New Monthly Magazine* 65 (November 1882): 891; Edwin G. Burrows and Mike Wallace, *Gotham: A History of New York City to 1898* (New York: Oxford University Press, 1999), 672.

89. *New York (NY) Daily Herald*, 31 March 1853, 5 April 1853, 13 April 1853, 16 April 1853, NewsC.

90. *The Liberator*, 24 July 1863; *New York Times*, 14 July 1863; Harris, *In the Shadow of Slavery*, 245, 279–88; James C. Nicholson, *The Notorious John Morrissey: How a Bare-Knuckle Brawler Became a Congressman and Founded Saratoga Race Course* (Lexington: University Press of Kentucky, 2016), 61–84.

91. Enrollment Lists and Corrections to Enrollment Lists, 1863–65, New York: 13th Congressional District, 3 vols., 3: 211, Records of the Provost Marshal General's Bureau, RG 110; Massachusetts Census, 1865: Worcester County.

92. Massachusetts Census, 1865: Worcester County; *Massachusetts Soldiers, Sailors, and Marines*, 4: 664, 6: 33; *Fall River (MA) Daily Evening News*, 22 July 1864, 1 August 1865, 4 August 1865, NewsC; Howland, *Worcester City Directory Advertiser for 1865*, 81.

Chapter 14

1. "An Act to exempt certain persons from enrollment for service in the armies of the Confederate States," 21 April 1862, in *Public Laws of the Confederate States of America, Passed at the First Session of the First Congress* (Richmond: R. M. Smith, 1862), 51–52, HT.

2. "A Bill to Amend an Act in Relation to the Militia and a Guard for Home Defence" (Raleigh: W. W. Holden, 1863), 1–2, NCC; "An Act to Amend an Act Entitled an Act to Increase the Efficiency of the Home Guard Organization," 7 February 1865, in *Public Laws of the State of North-Carolina Passed by the General Assembly at Its Adjourned Session of 1865* (Raleigh: Cannon & Holden, 1865), 12–13, IntArch; *The Weekly Standard* (Raleigh, NC), 19 October 1864, NewsC; *Worcester (MA) Daily Spy*, 9 March 1865, AAS; *Daily Progress* (Raleigh, NC), 29 April 1865, NewsC; Elizabeth Reid Murray, *Wake: Capital County of North Carolina*, Vol. 1, *Prehistory through Centennial* (Raleigh: Capital County Publishing Co., 1983), 489–91.

3. *Daily Progress*, 26 May 1865, 19 July 1865; *Wilmington (NC) Herald*, 24 June 1865, NewsC.

4. "Extract from Annual Report of Rev. H. James, Sup't Negro Affairs in N. C.," *National Freedman* 1 (1 May 1865): 123–24, NYHS; "Obituary Record, 1919–1920," *Bowdoin College Bulletin* 109 (February 1921): 46, IntArch.

5. B. W. Pond to William G. Hawkins, 19 July 1865, reprinted in *National Freedman* 1 (15 August 1865): 220–22.

6. "Lunsford Lane," *National Freedman* 1 (15 August 1865): 221.

7. "Report of Secretary of Teachers' Committee," *National Freedman* 1 (15 September 1865): 276–77.

8. *National Anti-Slavery Standard* (New York, NY), 29 July 1865, AccArch.

9. "Lunsford Lane," *National Freedman*, 221; *The Weekly Standard*, 31 January 1855, 7 November 1855, 17 July 1861; *Weekly Raleigh (NC) Register*, 12 March 1856, NewsC; *The Semi-Weekly Standard* (Raleigh, NC), 13 October 1852, 10 June 1857, 1 June 1859, NewsC; Dorothy A. Gay, "Crisis of Identity: The Negro Community in Raleigh, 1890–1900," *NCHR* 50 (April 1973): 121.

10. *Worcester Daily Spy*, 29 March 1866; "Lunsford Lane," *National Freedman*, 221; "List of slaves," *William A. Blount and others v. John D. Hawkins and others*, 57 N.C. 162 (December 1858), Supreme Court Original Cases, 1800–1809, SANC.

11. Alfred M. Haywood to Geo. W. Haywood & others, 9 March 1833, bk. 11: 66–68, WCRD; Alfred M. Haywood to Cyrus Whitaker & Others, 8 March 1833, bk. 11: 128–29, WCRD.

12. US Slave Schedule, 1850: Wake County, NC; US Census, 1870: Wake County, NC; US Census, 1880: Wake County, NC; Rebecca Hall to John S. Haywood, 1 August 1836, EHC; Anna Julia Cooper, handwritten autobiographical note, AC-MS8, Anna Julia Cooper Papers, 1881–1958, Moorland-Spingarn Research Center, Howard University, Washington, DC. Literary scholar Mary Helen Washington speculated that George Washington Haywood was Cooper's father; see "Introduction," in Anna Julia Cooper, *A Voice from the South* (New York: Oxford University Press, 1988), xxxi, lii n8–9. Others have suggested Anna's father was another brother, Fabius Julius Haywood; see Vivian M. May, *Anna Julia Cooper, Visionary Black Feminist: A Critical Introduction* (Taylor & Francis, 2007), 88, 190 n4; Louise Daniel Hutchinson, *Anna J. Cooper, a Voice from the South* (Washington, DC: Smithsonian Institution Press, 1981), 3–6.

13. Karen Johnson, *Uplifting the Women and the Race: The Educational Philosophies and Social Activism of Anna Julia Cooper and Nannie Helen Burroughs* (New York: Garland Pub., 2000), 33–37; Anna J. Cooper, "Grapes from Thorns: The First Step 3 Poems," 1958, Personal Papers, Anna Julia Cooper Papers; Hutchinson, *Anna J. Cooper*, 3–17.

14. US Census, 1870: Wake County, NC; US Census, 1880: Wake County, NC; *Haywood School Register*, October 1922, clipping, Scrapbook 1891–1928, 48, Scrapbook Series, 1866–1932 and undated, Charles N. Hunter Papers, 1850s–1932 and undated, RLDU; John H. Haley, *Charles N. Hunter and Race Relations in North Carolina* (Chapel Hill: University of North Carolina Press, 1987), 1–2.

15. Haley, *Charles N. Hunter*, 5–12.

16. US Census, 1880: Wake County, NC; Washington, "Introduction," xxvii–liv.

17. Shirley Moody-Turner, *Black Folklore and the Politics of Representation* (Jackson: University Press of Mississippi, 2014), 88–94; Alice Mabel Bacon, "Work and Methods of the Hampton Folklore Society," *The Black Perspective on Music* 4 (July 1976): 151–55.

18. *The Tarborough (NC) Southerner*, 13 August 1875, NewsC; *The Raleigh (NC) News*, 29 January 1880, NewsC; *Wilmington (NC) Morning Star*, 14 December 1884, NewsC.

19. *National Anti-Slavery Standard*, 14 October 1865, 21 October 1865; Haley, *Charles N. Hunter*, 9–10; *The Weekly Star* (Wilmington, NC), 15 April 1881, NewsC; *Wilmington (NC)*

Post, 25 December 1881, NewsC; *Official Register of the United States, Containing a List of the Officers and Employees in the Civil, Military, and Naval Service on the First of July 1887*, Vol. 1, *Legislative, Executive, Judicial* (Washington, DC: Government Printing Office, 1887), 527.

20. "Address Delivered on the Occasion of the Celebration of Emancipation Day, Raleigh N. C., January 1, 1912," Celebration of Emancipation Day Speeches, 1895, 1899, 1912, 1923 and undated, Charles N. Hunter Papers; *News and Observer* (Raleigh, NC), 20 October 1907; Haley, *Charles N. Hunter*, 23–24, 46–48; "An Act to Incorporate the North Carolina Industrial Association," in *Laws and Resolutions of the State of North Carolina, passed by the General Assembly at its session of 1879* (Raleigh: The Observer, 1879), 799–800.

21. Charles N. Hunter, *Review of Negro Life in North Carolina with My Recollections* (Raleigh: Charles N. Hunter, 1925), 6, RLDU.

22. Charles N. Hunter, "George M. Horton: Historical Sketches No. 1," typescript, undated, 24, Charles N. Hunter Papers; Charles N. Hunter, "The Story of John Chavis," handwritten, undated, Charles N. Hunter Papers; Charles N. Hunter, "History of John Chavis: The Negro Scholar, Preacher and Teacher," typescript, undated, Charles N. Hunter Papers; Lunsford Lane, "The Narrative of Lunsford Lane," 4th ed., typescript copy, undated, Charles N. Hunter Papers; *New York (NY) Age*, 26 June 1920, NewsC; Haley, *Charles N. Hunter*, 162–63.

23. W. E. B. Du Bois, *The Souls of Black Folk: Essays and Sketches* (Chicago: A. C. McClung & Co., 1903), 29–30; Gregory Laski, *Untimely Democracy: The Politics of Progress after Slavery* (New York: Oxford University Press, 2018), 52–53; Lunsford Lane, *The Narrative of Lunsford Lane, Formerly of Raleigh, N.C. Embracing an Account of His Early Life, the Redemption by Purchase of Himself and Family from Slavery, and His Banishment from the Place of His Birth for the Crime of Wearing a Colored Skin. Published by Himself*, 2nd ed. (Boston: J. G. Torrey, 1842), 4, AAS; William G. Hawkins, *Lunsford Lane; or, Another Helper from North Carolina* (Boston: Crosby & Nichols, 1863), 61, NCC.

24. "Report of Rev. Horace James," *National Freedman* 1 (1 June 1865): 153; William George Hawkins to John S. Bassett, 23 October 1899, John Spencer Bassett Papers, 1770–1978, Manuscripts Division, LOC; US Census, 1870: Craven County, NC; Joe M. Richardson, *Christian Reconstruction: The American Missionary Association and Southern Blacks, 1861–1890* (Athens: University of Georgia Press, 1986), 71–84; *The Republican-Register* (Aurora, NE), 27 April 1882.

25. US Census, 1870: Craven County, NC; J. W. Hood, *Sketch of the Early History of the African Methodist Episcopal Zion Church with Jubilee Souvenir and an Appendix* (Charlotte: A. M. E. Zion Publishing House, 1914), 33, 84–85, 91, Treasure Room Special Collections, James E. Shepard Memorial Library, North Carolina Central University, Durham; J. W. Hood, *One Hundred Years of the African Methodist Episcopal Zion Church; or, the Centennial of African Methodism* (New York: A. M. E. Zion Book Concern, 1895), 87–88, 297, IntArch; Sandy Dwayne Martin, *For God and Race: The Religious and Political Leadership of AMEZ Bishop James Walker Hood* (Columbia: University of South Carolina Press, 1999), 58.

26. Horace James, "A Freedman's Wedding," in *Household Reading: Selections from The Congregationalist, 1849–1867* (Boston: W. L. Greene & Co., 1868), 285–86, IntArch; *Worcester (MA) Daily Spy*, 29 March 1866, AAS; US Census, 1850: Carteret County, NC; US Census, 1860: Craven County, NC; US Census, 1870: Craven County, NC; *The New*

Berne (NC) Times, 7 March 1865, 21 October 1869, 9 July 1873, NewsC; Catherine W. Bishir, *Crafting Lives: African American Artisans in New Bern, North Carolina, 1770–1900* (Chapel Hill: University of North Carolina Press, 2013), 288–89.

27. *Daily Review* (Wilmington, NC), 22 June 1878; *The Observer* (Raleigh, NC), 9 December 1877; *Newbern (NC) Daily Progress*, 4 June 1861, NewsC; *The Raleigh (NC) Sentinel*, 2 September 1871; *Daily Journal* (New Bern, NC), 17 September 1882, NewsC; *New Bern (NC) Weekly Journal*, 27 December 1904.

28. *The New Berne Times*, 21 May 1864; Bishir, *Crafting Lives*, 168–69; David W. Cecelski, *The Fire of Freedom: Abraham Galloway & the Slaves' Civil War* (Chapel Hill: University of North Carolina Press, 2012), 115–17.

29. *Worcester Daily Spy*, 10 December 1862; Patricia C. Clark, *Time Full of Trial: The Roanoke Island Freedmen's Colony, 1862–1867* (Chapel Hill: University of North Carolina Press, 2001), 191–95.

30. Frederick Newman Rutan, "Historical Sermon on the Reverend Horace James: Delivered September First, Nineteen Hundred and Seven, in the Congregational Church, Wrentham" (n. p.: n. p., 1907), 10, AAS.; "Trial of Rev. Horace James, before a special military commission, convened by direction of Andrew Johnson, president of the United States, in September 1866" (Raleigh: n. p., 1866), 6, 12, 18, 20–21, AAS.

31. *Worcester Daily Spy*, 29 March 1866; *The Twenty-Second Annual Report of the American Missionary Association, and the Proceedings at the Annual Meeting Held in Springfield, Mass., October 28th and 29th, 1868* (New York: American Missionary Association, 1868), 20, AAS.

32. Hawkins to Bassett, 23 October 1899; Clark, *Time Full of Trial*, 146.

33. William Still, *The Underground Railroad. A Record of Facts, Authentic Narratives, Letters, &c. Narrating the Hardships Hair-breadth Escapes and Death Struggles of the Slaves in Their Efforts for Freedom* (Philadelphia: Porter & Coates, 1872), 150–52, IntArch; *The New Berne Times*, 30 August 1865; Cecelski, *Fire of Freedom*, 179–88; Jonathan White, *A House Built by Slaves: African American Visitors to the Lincoln White House* (New York: Random House, 2022), 93–96.

34. *Newbern Daily Progress*, 1 September 1865; Cecelski, *Fire of Freedom*, 179–82.

35. *The Congregationalist* (Boston, MA), 6 April 1866, BPL; Thulani Davis, *The Emancipation Circuit: Black Activism Forging a Culture of Freedom* (Durham: Duke University Press, 2022), 2–5, 115–20.

36. *Army and Navy Journal* 3 (19 May 1866): 616, HT; *The Nineteenth Annual Report of the American Missionary Association, and the Proceedings at the Annual Meeting Held in Brooklyn, N. Y., October 25th and 26th, 1865* (New York: American Missionary Association, 1865), appendix, AAS.

37. *Wilmington (NC) Daily Dispatch*, 1 February 1866, NewsC; *The New Berne Times*, 13 February 1866; *Chicago (IL) Tribune*, 19 February 1866, NewsC.

38. *National Anti-Slavery Standard*, 14 October 1865; *Daily Standard* (Raleigh, NC), 23 August 1866, NewsC.

39. *The Liberator* (Boston, MA), 30 May 1862, NewsC.

40. *Worcester Daily Spy*, 15 November 1865, 1 January 1866, 29 March 1866; *National Anti-Slavery Standard*, 3 May 1862; Janette Thomas Greenwood, *First Fruits of Freedom: The Migration of Former Slaves and Their Search for Equality in Worcester, Massachusetts, 1862–1900* (Chapel Hill: University of North Carolina Press, 2009), 71–72; Thavolia Glymph,

The Women's Fight: The Civil War's Battles for Home, Freedom, and Nation (Chapel Hill: University of North Carolina Press, 2020), 138–51.

41. US Census, 1860: Craven County, NC; *Journals of the Senate and House of Commons of the General Assembly of the State of North-Carolina at Its Session of 1854-'55* (Raleigh: Holden & Wilson, 1855), 60, 75, 90, 108, 154, 169, 203, 242, SANC; *Journal of Freedom* (Raleigh, NC), 6 October 1865, NewsC; *Daily Progress*, 3 October 1865; *Minutes of the Freedmen's Convention Held in the City of Raleigh* (Raleigh: Standard Book and Job Office, 1866), 27–30, NCC; *Daily Standard*, 4 October 1866, 11 October 1866, 20 June 1867; *The New Berne Times*, 23 May 1872, 13 June 1872.

42. Rutan, "Historical Sermon," 10–12; *Army and Navy Journal* 3 (19 May 1866): 617; *The New Berne Times*, 25 December 1865.

43. *Army and Navy Journal* 3 (19 May 1866): 617; "Trial of Rev. Horace James," 270.

44. Testimony of A. Coats, in Executive Document No. 123: Letter from the President of the United States Transmitting a Communication from the Secretary of War in Reference to the Operations of the Bureau of Refugees, Freedmen, and Abandoned Lands, 31 May 1866, in *Executive Documents Printed by the Order of the House of Representatives during the First Session of the Thirty-Ninth Congress, 1865-'66*, 16 vols. (Washington, DC: Government Printing Office, 1866), 12: 14–15; *Army and Navy Journal* 3 (19 May 1866): 617; "Trial of Rev. Horace James," 9–10.

45. "Trial of Rev. Horace James," 1–4; *The New Berne Times*, 27 June 1866.

46. "Trial of Rev. Horace James," 25–26; Horace James to Michael Strieby, 5 December 1865, North Carolina: 1852 June-1866 January 25, American Missionary Association archives, Amistad Research Center at Tulane University, New Orleans, LA.

47. *Wilmington Daily Dispatch*, 10 May 1866; *The New Berne Times*, 11 May 1866; *Daily Standard*, 12 May 1866; *Weekly Sentinel* (Raleigh, NC), 15 May 1866, NewsC.

48. *Wilmington Daily Dispatch*, 10 May 1866; *Brooklyn (NY) Daily Eagle*, 8 May 1866, NewsC.

49. *Worcester Daily Spy*, 25 August 1866; *New York (NY) Daily Herald*, 1 February 1867, NewsC; Rutan, "Historical Sermon," 12; *The New Bern (NC) Republican*, 4 June 1867, NewsC; *Brooklyn (NY) Union*, 28 May 1867, NewsC; "The Congregationalist and Boston Recorder," in *Household Reading*, 513–15.

50. *Minutes of the North Carolina Annual Conference of the African Methodist Episcopal Zion Church in America, 1865* (Hartford, CT: Case, Lockwood & Co., 1865), 1, microfilm, Duke Divinity School Library, Durham, NC; *Journal of the House of Representatives of the General Assembly of the State of North Carolina, at Its Session of 1870-'71* (Raleigh: James H. Moore, 1871), 623; *Private Laws of the State of North Carolina, Passed by the General Assembly at Its Session 1870-'71* (Raleigh: James H. Moore, 1871), 41, IntArch; "An Act to Incorporate the Mechanics' and Laborers' Mutual Aid Society of North Carolina," *Public Laws and Resolutions Together with the Private Laws of the State of North Carolina Passed by the General Assembly at Its Sessions 1872-'73* (Raleigh: Stone & Uzell, 1873), 472–74, IntArch; Karla F C Holloway, *Passed On: African American Mourning Stories* (Durham, NC: Duke University Press, 2003), 33–36; "An Act to Incorporate the Newbern Educational Association," *Private Laws of the State of North Carolina Passed in 1871-72* (Raleigh: Holden & Wilson, 1872), 90–91; Registers of Signatures of Depositors in Branches of the Freedman's Savings and Trust Company, 1865–1874, New Bern, NC, November 2, 1869-July 25, 1874, Records of the Office of the Comptroller of the Currency; *The New Berne*

Times, 6 September 1872, 11 June 1874, 26 June 1874, 25 August 1874; *Turner's North Carolina Almanac for the Year of Our Lord 1875* (Raleigh: Edwards, Broughton & Co., 1875), 36, Int-Arch; Benjamin R. Justesen, *George Henry White: An Even Chance in the Race of Life* (Baton Rouge: Louisiana State University Press, 2001), 66n6, 69.

51. *Journal of the House of Representatives of the General Assembly of the State of North Carolina at Its Session of 1874–'75* (Raleigh: Josiah Turner, 1875), 4, 113–14; "An Act for Amnesty and Pardon," March 1873, in *Public Laws and Resolutions, Together with the Private Laws of the State of North Carolina, Passed by the General Assembly at Its Session 1872–'73* (Stone & Uzzell, 1873), 298–300.

52. *Weekly Era* (Raleigh, NC), 11 February 1875, NewsC; Carole Watterson Troxler, "'To Look More Closely at the Man': Wyatt Outlaw, a Nexus of National, Local, and Personal History," *NCHR* 77 (October 2000): 413–14; *Charlotte (NC) Observer,* 15 July 1874, NewsC; *The Newbernian* (New Bern, NC), 10 December 1874, NewsC.

53. *The Observer,* 9 December 1877, 26 June 1878; *Daily Review,* 22 June 1878; *Daily Journal,* 25 December 1891, 4 September 1896; "The Code in North Carolina: Contributions to the History of the Duello," *Magazine of American History* 26 (December 1891): 450; David W. Blight, *Race and Reunion: The Civil War in American Memory* (Cambridge, MA: Belknap Press, 2001), 287.

Chapter 15

1. Lewis Thayer to Martha Lane &c., 18 August 1866, bk. 730: 294–95, WDRRL; Henry J. Howland, *The Worcester Directory for 1866* (Worcester: Henry J. Howland, 1866), 69, 110, 227, WPL; D. Hamilton Hurd et al., *History of Worcester County, Massachusetts, with Biographical Sketches of Many of Its Pioneers and Prominent Men,* 2 vols. (Philadelphia: J. W. Lewis & Co., 1889), 2: 1607. The $300 mortgage had passed with the property through several owners; see George Peckham to William Hatch, 23 May 1862, bk. 652: 573–75, WDRRL; William Hatch to Joseph Beauregard Jr, 1 April 1863, bk. 667: 85–87, WDRRL; Joseph Beauregard Jr. to Frederick Abbott, 26 March 1866, bk 721: 189–91, WDRRL; Frederick Abbott to Lewis Thayer, 18 August 1866, 730: 301–2, WDRRL.

2. Jessica M. Lepler, *The Many Panics of 1837: People, Politics, and the Creation of a Transatlantic Financial Crisis* (New York: Cambridge University Press, 2013), 145.

3. "An Act in Addition to the Several Acts Concerning Husband and Wife," in *Acts and Resolves Passed by the General Court of Massachusetts in the Years 1843, 1844, 1845: Together with the Rolls and Messages* (Boston: Dutton and Wentworth, 1843–1845), 531–33, IntArch; "An Act to Protect the Property of Married Women," 1855, in *Acts and Resolves Passed by the General Court of Massachusetts in the Year 1855: Together with the Messages* (Boston: William White, 1855), 710–11, IntArch; Sharon Ann Murphy, *Banking on Slavery: Financing Southern Expansion in the Antebellum United States* (Chicago: University of Chicago Press, 2023), 207; Bernie D. Jones, "Revisiting the Married Women's Property Acts: Recapturing Protection in the Face of Equality," *Journal of Gender, Social Policy & the Law* 22 (2013): 98–99; Kathleen M. O'Connor, "Marital Property Reform in Massachusetts: A Choice for the New Millennium," *New England Law Review* 34 (1999): 289–92; Richard H. Chused, "Married Women's Property Law: 1800–1850," *Georgetown Law Journal* 71 (1983): 1398–1412; Carole Shammas, "Re-Assessing the Married Women's Property Acts," *Journal of Women's History* 6 (Spring 1994): 9–30. On why married women's property laws

originated in the South, see Woody Holton, "Equality as Unintended Consequence: The Contracts Clause and the Married Women's Property Acts," *Journal of Southern History* 81 (May 2015): 313–40.

4. "An Act to Exempt from Levy on Execution of the Homestead of a Householder Having a Family," ch. 340, sec. 2, 24 May 1851, in *Acts and Resolves Passed by the General Court of Massachusetts, in the Years 1849, 1850, 1851: Together with the Messages* (Boston: Button and Wentworth, 1851), 844–45, IntArch; William B. Aycock, "Homestead Exemption in North Carolina," *North Carolina Law Review* 29 (1951): 143; Lee Harrington, "Time for Change: Bringing Massachusetts Homestead and Personal Property Exemptions into the Twenty-First Century," *University of Massachusetts Law Review* 4 (January 2009): 6; Edward J. Balleisen, *Navigating Failure: Bankruptcy and Commercial Society in Antebellum America* (Chapel Hill: University of North Carolina Press, 2001), 96.

5. Paul Goodman, "Emergence of Homestead Exemption in the United States: Accommodation and Resistance to the Market Revolution, 1840–1880," *Journal of American History* 80 (September 1993): 483–88; H. Fowler, *Report of the Debates and Proceedings of the Convention for the Revision of the Constitution of the State of Indiana, 1850*, 2 vols. (Indianapolis: A. H. Brown, 1850), 2: 748, IntArch; *The Liberator* (Boston, MA), 27 July 1849, NewsC; Alison D. Morantz, "There's No Place Like Home: Homestead Exemption and Judicial Constructions of Family in Nineteenth-Century America," *Law and History Review* 24 (Summer 2006): 246, 258–66.

6. "Act to Protect the Property," 711; Thayer to Lane &c., 18 August 1866.

7. *New England Farmer* (Boston, MA), 8 June 1831, NewsC; Henry J. Howland, *The Worcester Directory for 1867* (Worcester: Wm. H. Sanford & Son, 1867), 209, WPL; Henry J. Howland, *Worcester Directory for 1870* (Worcester: Luther H. Bigelow, 1870), 57, WPL; Jeanne Ellen Whitney, "'An art that requires capital': Agriculture and Mortgages in Worcester County, Massachusetts, 1790–1850" (PhD diss., University of Delaware, 1991), 83–89, 181–83; Lunsford Lane &c. to Lewis Thayer, 18 August 1866, bk. 730: 295–98, WDRRL.

8. William H. Cunningham, *Protecting Three Generations: Commemorating Ninety Years of Life Insurance Service by the State Mutual Life Assurance Co. of Worcester, Massachusetts* (Worcester: privately printed, 1935),14; Sheldon Ames, *A Systematic View of the Science of Jurisprudence* (London: Longmans, Green, & Co., 1872), 269–70; Kenneth A Snowden, *Mortgage Banking in the United States, 1870–1940* (Washington, DC: Research Institute for Housing America, 2013), 3; Tamara Plakins Thornton, "'A Great Machine' or a 'Beast of Prey': A Boston Corporation and Its Rural Debtors in an Age of Capitalist Transformation," *JER* 27 (Winter 2007): 567–97.

9. E. E. Abbott to William Bryant, 26 August 1865, bk. 709: 22–23, WDRRL; *Worcester (MA) Daily Spy*, 28 October 1869, AAS; Janette Thomas Greenwood, *First Fruits of Freedom: The Migration of Former Slaves and Their Search for Equality in Worcester, Massachusetts, 1862–1900* (Chapel Hill: University of North Carolina Press, 2009), 93–95.

10. *Massachusetts Spy* (Worcester, MA), 28 June 1862, AAS; Martha Goulding to Ruth Liel, 6 December 1866, bk. 746: 443, WDRRL; Ruth Liel to William Bryant, 12 June 1867, bk. 746: 444–45, WDRRL.

11. Ebenezer E. Abbott to Clara A. Lane, 4 August 1868, bk. 776: 90–91, WDRRL; Clara A. Lane to Ebenezer E. Abbott, 24 August 1868, bk. 774: 239–42, WDRRL.

12. Clara A. Lane to Sarah R. Knight, 1 April 1870, bk. 812: 382–83, WDRRL.

13. *Worcester (MA) Palladium*, 26 August 1868, AAS.

14. *Weekly Republican* (Plymouth, IN), 26 March 1868, NewsC; *New-York Tribune* (New York, NY), 22 May 1868, NewsC; *Chicago (IL) Tribune*, 2 May 1868, NewsC; *Brooklyn (NY) Union*, 25 May 1868, NewsC; *Daily Evening Express* (Lancaster, PA), 26 May 1868, NewsC; *The Folsom (CA) Telegraph*, 30 May 1868, NewsC; *The Yonkers (NY) Statesman*, 4 June 1868, AAS; US Census, 1870: Beaufort County, NC; *Wilmington (NC) Post*, 23 August 1868, NewsC; *Daily Standard* (Raleigh, NC), 21 July 1868, 30 September 1868, NewsC; US Census, 1870: Wake County, NC; *The Weekly Standard* (Raleigh, NC), 1 July 1868, NewsC; Ruthe Winegarten, *Black Texas Women: 150 Years of Trial and Triumph* (Austin: University of Texas Press, 1995), 66.

15. *The Tarborough (NC) Southerner*, 20 August 1868, NewsC; *Valley Spirit* (Chambersburg, PA), 17 June 1868, NewsC.

16. *Worcester (MA) Evening Gazette*, 19 April 1869, AAS; *Worcester Daily Spy*, 20 April 1869.

17. *North-Carolina Star* (Raleigh), 12 October 1853, NewsC; *New-York Tribune* (New York, NY), 2 February 1856, NewsC; *Fall River (MA) Daily Evening News*, 30 March 1861, NewsC; *Brooklyn (NY) Evening Star*, 19 April 1861, NewsC; *The Philadelphia (PA) Inquirer*, 5 July 1861, NewsC; *Gazette and Courier* (Greenfield, MA), 19 August 1861, AAS; *Hartford (CT) Courant*, 12 December 1861, NewsC; *Daily Missouri Republican* (St. Louis), 13 April 1861, NewsC; *Worcester Daily Spy*, 20 April 1869.

18. *Worcester Evening Gazette*, 27 April 1869; *Worcester Daily Spy*, 27 and 29 April 1869; *Massachusetts Spy*, 30 April 1869; Greenwood, *First Fruits of Freedom*, 95; Lane to Knight, 1 April 1870; Clara Ann Lane to James S. Rogers, 5 July 1870, bk. 850: 110–11, WDRRL.

19. Marriages Registered in the City of Worcester, County of Worcester, 1869, in Jay Mack Holbrook, *Massachusetts Vital Records to 1850: Worcester 1719–1890* (Oxford, MA: Holbrook Research Institute, 1984), 136–37, AAS; Martha Lane &c. to Franklin Whipple &c., 13 July 1869, bk. 798: 15–17, WDRRL; Franklin Whipple &c. to Martha Lane &c., 13 July 1869, bk. 798: 17–18, WDRRL; Lane to Knight, 1 April 1870; Sarah R. Knight to Martha Lane &c., 1 April 1870, bk. 812: 378–80, WDRRL; annotation for 17 July 1869, Lane &c. to Thayer, 18 August 1866; *Berkshire County Eagle* (Pittsfield, MA), 22 March 1860, AAS; US Census, 1860: Worcester County, MA; Massachusetts Census, 1865: Worcester County, AncC; US Census, 1870: Worcester County, MA.

20. Lane to Rogers, 5 July 1870; Ebenezer E. Abbott to Edward Earle, 6 July 1871, bk. 850: 110, WDRRL.

21. US Census, 1850: New York City, Ward 5; Clarence Taylor, *The Black Churches of Brooklyn* (New York: Columbia University Press, 1994), 14–20; Marriage Certificate 3425, Index to New York City Marriages, 1866–1937, Division of Vital Statistics, Department of Health, New York City Municipal Archives, NY; Dudley & Greenough, *The Cambridge Directory for 1869* (Cambridge, MA: Sever, Francis & Co., 1869), 186; Dean Dudley & Co., *The Cambridge Directory for 1870* (Cambridge, MA: Sever, Francis & Co., 1870), 196; *Sanborn First Insurance Map from Cambridge, Middlesex County, Massachusetts*, Sanborn Map Company, Vol. 1, 1900: plate 19, Manuscript Division, LOC, https://www.loc.gov/item/sanborn03701_002/; *Atlas of the City of Cambridge, Middlesex Co., Massachusetts* (Philadelphia: G. M. Hopkins, 1873), plates J and L.

22. Dean Dudley, *The Cambridge Directory for 1871* (Cambridge, MA: Sever, Francis & Co., 1871), 220; Dean Dudley, *The Cambridge Directory for 1872* (Cambridge, MA: Charles W. Sever, 1872), 195; Greenough, Jones & Co., *Cambridge Directory for 1873* (Cambridge,

MA: B. H. Richardson, 1873), 225; *Sanborn First Insurance Map from Cambridge*, Vol. 1, 1900: plates 51 and 53; *Atlas of the City of Cambridge*, plate O.

23. *The Soldiers' Monument in Cambridge, MA: Proceedings in Relation to the Building and Dedication of the Monument Erected in the Years 1869–70 by the City Government of Cambridge, Mass.* (Cambridge, MA: John Wilson and Son, 1870), 68; Massachusetts Census, 1855: Middlesex County, AncC.

24. *The Pennsylvania Freeman* (Philadelphia, PA), 20 April 1854, HSP; *National Anti-Slavery Standard* (New York, NY), 11 September 1854, AccArch; *The Liberator*, 13 October 1854; Ezra Greenspan, *William Wells Brown: An African American Life* (New York: W. W. Norton, 2014), Greenspan, *William Wells Brown*, 359; *The Cambridge Directory for 1863–64* (Cambridgeport: George Fisher, 1863), 18; US Census, 1870: Middlesex County, MA.

25. *Cambridge (MA) Chronicle*, 27 April 1872, CPL; Massachusetts Vital Records, 1840–1911; card 58, Cambridge Cemetery Records, Cambridge Cemetery, Cambridge, MA; *Boston (MA) Globe*, 8 November 1884, 10 November 1884, NewsC; Greenspan, *William Wells Brown*, 505; Sheila M. Rothman, *Living in the Shadow of Death: Tuberculosis and the Social Experience of Illness in American History* (Baltimore: Johns Hopkins University Press, 1994), 16–17. Three cases of tuberculosis in one family over two decades suggest a genetic susceptibility among the Lanes and not just random environmental causes; see Laurent Abel et al., "Human Genetics of Tuberculosis: A Long and Winding Road," *Philosophical Transactions of the Royal Society of London, Series B: Biological Sciences* 369 (19 June 2014), National Institute of Health, *National Library of Medicine*, https://www.ncbi.nlm.nih.gov/pmc/issues/237833/.

26. Annotation for 7 October 1872, Lane to Abbott, 24 August 1868.

27. Isaac Costa, comp., *Gopsill's Jersey City and Hoboken Directory for the Year Ending April 30th 1874* (Jersey City: John H. Lyon, 1874), 382–83, HT; Isaac Costa, comp., *Gopsill's Jersey City and Hoboken Directory for the Year Ending April 30th 1876* (Jersey City: Jersey City Directory Co., 1876), 113, 139, 276, 372, HT.

28. *The Inland Printer: A Technical Journal* 7 (August 1890): 999–1000; *Annual Report of the Commissioner of Patents for the Year 1879* (Washington, DC: Government Printing Office, 1880), 43; John W. Stedman, *Stedman's Directory of the City and Town of Norwich* (Norwich: Norwich Printing Co., 1872), 155, 154; John W. Stedman, *Stedman's Directory of the City and Town of Norwich* (Norwich: Norwich Printing Co., 1873), 175; Greenough, Jones & Co., *Cambridge Directory for 1873*, 225; Dudley, *The Cambridge Directory of 1872*, 195.

29. George T. Lain, *The Brooklyn City and Business Directory for the Year Ending May 1st 1871* (Brooklyn: Lain & Co., 1871), 617; George T. Lain, *The Brooklyn City and Business Directory for the Year Ending May 1st 1872* (Brooklyn: Lain & Co., 1872), 639; Carla L. Peterson, *Black Gotham: A Family History of African Americans in Nineteenth-Century New York City* (New Haven, CT: Yale University Press, 2013), 311–12; Taylor, *Black Churches of Brooklyn*, 7–8; William C. Conant, "The Brooklyn Bridge," *Harper's New Monthly Magazine* 6 (May 1885): 938–39.

30. *Boston Globe*, 15 July 1874; *Massachusetts Spy*, 17 July 1874; *The National Aegis* (Worcester, MA), 18 July 1874, AAS; *Dedication of the Soldiers' Monument at Worcester, Massachusetts, July 15, A. D. 1874* (Worcester: Monument Committee, 1875), 10–11.

31. *Dedication of the Soldiers' Monument*, 27; Abijah P. Marvin, *History of Worcester in the War of the Rebellion* (Worcester, MA: the author, 1870), 398, AAS; Paul Laurence

Dunbar, "The Colored Soldiers," in *The Complete Poems of Paul Laurence Dunbar* (New York: Dodd, Mead & Co., 1922), 50–52; Greenwood, *First Fruits of Freedom*, 131–32.

32. George T. Lain, *The Brooklyn City Directory and Business Directory, 1987–71* (Brooklyn: Lain & Co., 1875), 725; *New York State 1874 Business Directory* (New York: Charles Van Beutheysen & Sons, 1874), 978; *The Republican Journal* (Belfast, ME), 17 December 1874, NewsC; George T. Lain, *Brooklyn City and Business Directory for the Year ending May 1st, 1875* (New York: Wynkoop & Hallenbeck, 1875), 472, 725.

33. New Jersey Deaths, 1670–1988, Division of Archives and Records Management, New Jersey Department of State, Trenton; John W. Stedman, *Stedman's Directory of the City and Town of Norwich* (Norwich: Norwich Printing Co., 1874), 155; John W. Stedman, *Stedman's Directory of the City and Town of Norwich* (Norwich: Norwich Printing Co., 1875), 110; George T. Lain, *Brooklyn City and Business Directory for the Year ending May 1st, 1876* (New York: Wynkoop & Hallenbeck 1876), 768; US Census, 1880: Hudson County, NJ.

34. Alfred Pommer and Eleanor Winters, *Explore the Original West Village* (Charleston, SC: The History Press, 2011), 15–17; Olivia Klose, "Greenwich Village Historic District Extension II: Designation Report," 22 June 2010, Landmarks Preservation Commission, New York City, NY, 5–6, 142, https://media.villagepreservation.org/wp-content/uploads/2020/03/15123045/Greenwich-Village-Historic-District-Extension-II-Designation-Report.pdf.

35. Edwin G. Burrows and Mike Wallace, *Gotham: A History of New York City to 1898* (New York: Oxford University Press, 1999), 888–95; Leslie M. Harris, *In the Shadow of Slavery: African Americans in New York City, 1626–1863* (Chicago: University of Chicago Press, 2003), 280–87; Graham Russell Hodges, *Root & Branch: African Americans in New York & East Jersey* (Chapel Hill: University of North Carolina Press, 1999), 262–63.

36. Naval Enlistment Rendezvous, 1855–1891, 110 vols., Records of the Bureau of Naval Personnel, RG 24, NARA, 16: 72; Interment Control Forms, 1928–1962, Interment Control Forms, Records of the Office of the Quartermaster General, 1774–1985, RG 92, National Archives at College Park, College Park, MD, *Fold3*, https://www.fold3.com/; Burrows and Wallace, *Gotham*, 897.

37. *New York Daily Herald*, 6 April, 1848, 15 February 1867, 23 July 1875; *New York Times* (New York, NY), 24 September 1876, NewsC; US Census, 1880: New York City, NY; *Trow's New York City Directory*, Vol. 42, *for the year ending May 1, 1879* (New York: Trow City Directory Co., 1878), 64, 203, 410, 663, 722, 868; *Trow's New York City Directory*, Vol. 43, *for the year ending May 1, 1880* (New York: Trow City Directory Co., 1879), 18, 175, 208, 259, 421, 641, 714, 1025, 1115, 1181, 1498, 1579.

38. "Persons who Died during the Year ending May 31, 1880, enumerated in New York City, in the County of N.Y., State of N.Y.," 55, US Census Mortality Schedules: New York, 1850–1880, microfilm, New York State Education Department, Albany; David W. Dunlap, *From Abyssinian to Zion: A Guide to Manhattan's Houses of Worship* (New York: Columbia University Press, 204), 148–49; US Census, 1880: New York City, NY.

39. Despite years of searching, I could not trace Edward Lane's life after the Civil War. There are no matching Edward Lanes in the 1870 or 1880 United States censuses or in hundreds of governmental and transactional records that were consulted. He does not show up in Oscar Sheppard, *Fuller's Ohio Brigade, 27th, 39th, 43d, and 63d Regiments, Ohio Volunteer Infantry: List of Survivors, with Post-Office Addresses So Far as Known to the Secretary, January 1, 1891* (Dayton, OH: United Brethren Publishing House, 1891).

40. Steven J. Peitzman, "From Dropsy to Bright's Disease to End-Stage Renal Disease," *Milbank Quarterly* 67 Supplement 1 (1989): 17–19; "Persons who DIED during the Year ending May 31, 1880," 55; Burrows and Wallace, *Gotham*, 978.

41. US Census, 1870: New York, Ward 21; John William Tebbel, *From Rags to Riches: Horatio Alger, Jr., and the American Dream* (New York: MacMillan Pub. Co., 1963), 10–14; Carol Nackenoff, *The Fictional Republic: Horatio Alger and American Political Discourse* (New York: Oxford University Press, 1994), 3, 11.

42. Robert Feldra, comp., *History of Hudson County: Genealogies of Prominent Families* (Union, NJ: Michel & Rank, 1917), 19; Alexander McLean, *History of Jersey City, N.J.: A Record of Its Early Settlement and Corporate Progress* (Jersey City: Jersey City Printing Co., 1895), 87; "Reports of Committees: Burial Place Committee," *The Underhill Society of America: Fourteenth Annual Report, May Twelfth, 1906* (Brooklyn: The Society, 1906), 33; "The Planting of Rural Cemeteries," *The Country Gentleman* (5 November 1857), 306, AAS.

43. *Baltimore (MA) Sun*, 19 September 1849, NewsC; Howard R. Marraro, "Italians in New York during the First Half of the Nineteenth Century," *New York History* 26 (July 1945): 292; *The Evening Post* (New York, NY), 8 October 1849, NewsC; *New York Daily Tribune* (New York, NY), 16 August 1849, 13 December 1849, 14 January 1850, 24 February 1851, 7 March 1860, LOC.

44. Interment File for Graves #6–10, Row #N-7, P North Section, Bayview-New York Bay Cemetery, Jersey City, NJ.

45. *Memphis (TN) Daily Appeal*, 13 July 1879, NewsC; *Pottawatomie County Herald* (Louisville, KS), 2 July 1879, NewsC; *Lawrence (KS) Tribune*, 28 August 1879, NewsC; *Dubuque (IA) Sunday Herald*, 28 February 1892, LOC; Nell Irvin Painter, *Exodusters: Black Migration to Kansas after Reconstruction* (New York: Alfred A. Knopf, 1977), 246–47.

46. Unidentified newspaper clipping, Brown Family Papers, AAS; Frederick Douglass, "The Negro Exodus from the Gulf States," *Journal of Social Sciences* 11 (May 1880): 19; *National Republican* (Washington, DC), 5 May 1879, NewsC; Lewis B. Clarke to Lewis and Harriet Hayden, 3 January 1880, Charles Chapman Papers, 1791–1901, Moorland-Spingarn Research Center; David W. Blight, *Frederick Douglass' Civil War: Keeping Faith in Jubilee* (Baton Rouge: Louisiana State University Press, 1989), 603–604; Painter, *Exodusters*, 247–50; Milton Sernatt, *Bound for the Promised Land: African American Religion and the Great Migration* (Durham, NC: Duke University Press, 1997), 12–14.

47. Clarke to the Haydens, 3 January 1880.

48. Clarke to the Haydens, 3 January 1880.

49. Interment File for Graves #6–10, Row #N-7, P North Section. The third of P North section that has no markers is not a publicly owned potter's field. Families paid for the burial plots but could not afford headstones.

50. William G. Hawkins, *Lunsford Lane; or, Another Helper from North Carolina* (Boston: Crosby & Nichols, 1863), 53, NCC.

51. Ovid, *The Metamorphoses*, trans. Henry T. Riley (London: Georege Bell & Sons, 1889), 506; Avi Kepech, "Aeneas," *Mythopedia*, https://mythopedia.com/topics/aeneas; Titus Livius, *The History of Rome: Sir Gawain & the Green Knight*, ed. J. R. R. Tolkien and E. V. Gordon (Oxford: Claredon Press, 1925), 1.1.5; *The Brut, or The Chronicles of England*, ed. Friedrich W. D. Brie, 2 parts (London: Kegan Paul, Trench, Trübner & Co., 1906), 1: 5.

52. Martin Robinson Delany, *The Condition, Elevation, Emigration, and Destiny of the Colored People of the United States, Politically Considered* (Philadelphia: by author, 1852),

92–109, IntArch; William C. Nell, *The Colored Patriots of the American Revolution, with Sketches of Several Distinguished Colored Persons* (Boston: Robert F. Wallcut, 1855), 231–35, AAS; William Wells Brown, *The Black Man: His Antecedents, His Genius, and His Achievements* (New York: Thomas Hamilton, 1863), AAS.

53. *The Semi-Weekly Messenger* (Wilmington, NC), 25 October 1894, NewsC; *News and Observer* (Raleigh, NC), 19 October 1824, NewsC; Weeks's copy of William G. Hawkins, *Lunsford Lane; or, Another Helper from North Carolina* (Boston: Crosby & Nichols, 1863), NCC.

Epilogue

1. US Census, 1880: Hudson County, NJ; US Census, 1920: Hudson County, NJ; *Gopsill's Jersey City and Hoboken Directory for the Year Ending April 30th 1879* (Jersey City: Jersey City Directory Co., 1879), 773, HT.

2. Eric Arnesen, *Brotherhood of Color: Black Railroad Workers and the Struggle for Equality* (Cambridge, MA: Harvard University Press, 2011), 16–18, 21; Christopher R. Reed, "Pullman Porters in the Late 19th and Early 20th Centuries before the Formation of the Brotherhood of Sleeping Car Porters (1925)," in *An Anthology of Respect: The Pullman Porters National Historic Registry of African-American Railroad Employees*, ed. Lyn Hughes (Chicago: Hughes Peterson Publishing Co., 2009), 14–15.

3. Certificate of death, 7 June 1881, Death Records, June 1878–December 1900, NJSA; Birth Records, May 1, 1848–December 31, 1920, NJSA; Records of the Parish of Saint Matthew, October 1874 to May 1899, Episcopal Diocese of Newark, Newark, NJ, AncC; certificate of death, 9 May 1883, Death Records, June 1878–December 1900, NJSA.

4. *New York (NY) Globe*, 17 November 1883, 8 March 1884, 6 September 1884, Center for Research Libraries, https://crl.edu; *New York (NY) Freeman*, 2 October 1886, Center for Research Libraries; *New York (NY) Tribune*, 10 March 1887, LOC; *The Evening World* (New York, NY), 6 April 1888, LOC.

5. *Gopsill's Philadelphia City Directory for 1879* (Philadelphia: Canton Press, 1879), 925, 1156, 1678, 1711, HT; US Census, 1870: Philadelphia, PA; *Gopsill's Philadelphia City Directory for 1880*, comp. Isaac Costa (Philadelphia: James Gopsill, 1880), 705, 974, HT; *Gopsill's Philadelphia City Directory for 1881*, comp. Isaac Costa (Philadelphia: James Gopsill, 1881), 678, 942, HT.

6. *Reading (PA) Times*, 24 May 1880, NewsC; *Harrisburg (PA) Telegraph*, 7 August 1883, NewsC; *The Inquirer* (Lancaster, PA), 15 March 1884, NewsC; D. Hack Tuke, *The Insane in the United States and Canada* (London H. K. Lewis, 1885), 154–57, IntArch; Registration of Deaths, Aug. 1884–Dec. 1884, 176–77, Death Certificates, Department of Records, Philadelphia City Archives, Philadelphia, PA; Certificate of Death for Lunsford Lane Jr., 22 October 1884, Death Returns, Board of Health, microfilm, roll 1152, Department of Records, Philadelphia, PA, PhillyHistory.org.

7. *Sixth Annual Report of the State Hospital for the Insane for the S. E. District of Pennsylvania at Norristown, Pa. for the Year Ending September 30, 1885* (Norristown: Hospital Printing Office, 1885), 62, Records of the Department of Human Services, Office of Mental Health, Norristown State Hospital, Pennsylvania State Archives, Harrisburg; back of Certificate of Death for Lunsford Lane Jr., 22 October 1884; William W. Keen, *The History of the Philadelphia School of Anatomy and Its Relations to Medical Teaching* (Philadelphia:

J. B. Lippincott & Co., 1875), 22, 24, 31, IntArch; Michael Soppal, *A Traffic in Dead Bodies: Anatomy and Embodied Social Identity in Nineteenth-Century America* (Princeton, NJ: Princeton University Press, 2018), 256–59; *Fourth Annual Report of the State Board of Health and Vital Statistics of the Commonwealth of Pennsylvania* (Harrisburg: Edwin K. Meyers, 1889) 332; H. J. Sommer, *Index of 1180 Post-Mortems on the Insane: State Hospital for the Insane, Norristown, Pa.* (Norristown: Hospital Printing Office, 1908), i–ii, 1, Records of the Department of Human Services. No patients were listed by name in the *Annual Report* or the *Index*, but there is only one listing under 1884 for a forty-seven-year-old man, and the medical descriptions correlate with Lane's condition.

8. William H. Boyd, comp., *Gopsill's Jersey City and Hoboken Directory for the Year Ending April 30, 1881* (Washington, DC: John W. Harrison, 1881), 349, HT; William H. Boyd, comp., *Gopsill's Jersey City and Hoboken Directory for the Year Ending April 30, 1882* (Washington, DC: John W. Harrison, 1882), 336, HT; William H. Boyd, comp., *Gopsill's Jersey City and Hoboken Directory for the Year Ending April 30, 1883* (Washington, DC: John W. Harrison, 1883), 449, HT; certificate of death, 11 July 1886, New York City Deaths, 1795–1949, New York, New York Death Index, 1862–1948, New York City Department of Records, Manhattan; US Census, 1880: Hudson County, NJ.

9. *New York (NY) Age*, 14 November 1891, 19 December 1891, 9 September 1909, 1 June 1911, 4 July 1912, NewsC; New Jersey State Census, 1895: Jersey City, AncC; certificate of death, 30 January 1894, New York City Deaths, 1795–1949; *Jersey City (NJ) News*, 26 June 1897, NewsC; *Brooklyn (NY) Daily Eagle*, 6 August 1907, NewsC; W. E. B. Du Bois, ed., *Efforts for Social Betterment among Negro Americans,* Atlanta University Publications No. 14 (Atlanta: Atlanta University Press, 1909), 59–60, IntArch; *Corporations of New Jersey: List of Certificates Filed in the Department of State during the Year 1908* (Trenton: John L. Murphy, 1909), 7, New Jersey State Library, Trenton.

10. US Census, 1900: Hudson County, NJ; US Census, 1910: Hudson County, NJ; Index to Deaths, Geographical, 1916–1929: Jersey City, 1916–19, NJSA.

11. *New York Age*, 29 August 1907, 16 May 1907, 18 November 1909, 6 July 1911, 20 July 1911, 24 August 1911, 6 May 1915; W. Andrew Boyd, comp., *Boyd's Jersey City and Hoboken Directory, 1910–11* (Jersey City: Howell & Co., 1910), 135, New Jersey State Library.

12. *New York Age*, 29 August 1907, 18 January 1917, 8 July 1922, 15 July 1922; Carla L. Peterson, *Black Gotham: A Family History of African Americans in Nineteenth-Century New York City* (New Haven, CT: Yale University Press, 2013), 314–16; interment file for Grave #1, Lot #53S, West Edgewood Section, Bayview-New York Bay Cemetery, Jersey City, NJ.

13. *New York Age*, 4 November 1915, 3 August 1918, 29 March 1930, 5 April 1930, 18 October 1930, 2 May 1931 (quote), 21 November 1931, 23 January 1932; Rebecca Sharpless, "'Us Has Ever Lived De Useful Life': African American Women in Texas, 1874–1900," in *Black Women in Texas History*, ed. Bruce A. Glasrud and Meline Pitre (College Station: Texas A&M University, 2008), 91–92; Karla FC Holloway, *Passed On: African American Mourning Stories* (Durham, NC: Duke University Press, 2003), 33–35; Graham Russell Gao Hodges, *Black New Jersey: 1664 to the Present Day* (New Brunswick: Rutgers University Press, 2018), 106, 118, 131.

14. *New York Age*, 15 June 1916; Richard Conway, "Homage to Miss Cole," *Weber: The Contemporary West* 19 (Winter 2002), https://www.weber.edu/weberjournal/Journal _Archives/Archive_C2/Vol_19_2/RConwayEss.html.

15. *New York Age*, 23 September 1915, 7 October 1915, 14 October 1915, 25 January 1917, 27 September 1917, 9 March 1918, 26 October 1918, 20 August 1919, 1 May 1920, 12 March 1921,

24 March 1923, 11 August 1923, 31 January 1931, 21 March 1931, 28 March 1831, 4 April 1931, 25 April 1931, 30 May 1931, 6 June 1931; Hudson County NJ, draft board 6, World War I Selective Service System Draft Registration Cards, 1917–1918, NARA; *R. L. Polk & Co.'s 1918 Jersey City, Hoboken and Bayonne Directories* (Jersey City: R. L. Polk & Co., 1918), 408, New Jersey State Library; US Census, 1920: Hudson County, NJ; Emmet J. Scott, *Scott's Official History of the American Negro in the World War* (Chicago: Homewood Press, 1919), 387–90, HT.

16. *New York Age*, 15 November 1930, 17 January 1931, 13 July 1931, 18 July 1931, 14 November 1931, 26 December 1931, 6 February 1932, 16 April 1932, 14 May 1832; US Census, 1930: Hudson County, NJ; *The Standard Union* (Brooklyn, NY), 19 June 1925, NewsC; *Brooklyn Daily Eagle*, 19 June 1925; *The Gnome* yearbook, William L. Dickinson High School, 1924, New Jersey Room, Jersey City Free Public Library, Jersey City, NJ; James D. Brown, *Black Education in the South, 1860–1935* (Chapel Hill: University of North Carolina Press, 1988), 244–45.

17. *New York Age*, 12 March 1921, 13 July 1929, 15 November 1930, 17 January 1931, 24 January 1931, 7 March 1931, 14 November 1931, 26 December 1931, 16 January 1932, 6 February 1932, 19 March 1932, 16 April 1932, 14 May 1832, 24 September 1932; Peterson, *Black Gotham*, 137–38; Alessandra Lorini, *Rituals of Race: American Public Culture and the Search for Racial Democracy* (Charlottesville: University Press of Virginia, 1999), 24; US Census, 1930: Brunswick County, VA; interment file for Grave #2, Lot #53S, West Edgewood Section, Bayview-New York Bay Cemetery.

18. US Census, 1940: Hudson County, NJ; *New York Age*, 19 November 1938; Marriage Index: Brides: 1943, NJSA; interment file for Grave #1, Lot #53S, West Edgewood Section, Bayview-New York Bay Cemetery.

19. Worth Earlwood Norman Jr., *James Solomon Russell: Former Slave, Pioneering Educator and Episcopal Evangelist* (Jefferson, NC: McFarland & Co., 2012), 121–56; Frances Ashton Thurman, "The History of Saint Paul's College, Lawrenceville, Virginia, 1888–1959" (PhD diss., Howard University, 1978), 15–126.

20. *Richmond (VA) Times Dispatch*, 8 May 1941, NewsC; US Census, 1940: Brunswick County, VA; "Lawrenceville Historic Resource Survey Report," 12 May 2000, 6–8, Special Collections, Department of Historic Resources, Richmond, VA; Conway, "Homage to Miss Cole."

21. Thurman, "The History of Saint Paul's College, Lawrenceville, Virginia, 1888–1959," 163–66, 190–222; *The Living Church* (Milwaukee, WI), 15 April 1945, TLC Archive of Back Issues of *The Living Church*, https://livingchurch.org/tlc-archive-back-issues/; *Pittsburgh (PA) Courier*, 28 April 1945, 20 November 1965, NewsC; "English and Modern Language Department Chairmen, 1965–66," *PMLA* 80, pt. 2: Supplement (September 1965): 205; Carolyn R. Smith and Geneva C. Davis, *Education Directory, Colleges & Universities, 1980–81* (Washington, DC: National Center for Education Studies, 1981), 437; US Census, 1930: Brunswick County, VA; *Carolina Times* (Durham, NC), 29 March 1975, NewsC.

22. *South Hill (VA) Enterprise*, 13 August 1997, Dr. William McCaddin Pritchett Local History Room, Brunswick County Library, Lawrenceville, VA; *The Tiger* (Lawrenceville, VA: 1949), 76, Dr. William McCaddin Pritchett Local History Room.

23. Speech in Wilkinsville, Massachusetts, June 1863, reprinted in William G. Hawkins, *Lunsford Lane; or, Another Helper from North Carolina* (Boston: Crosby & Nichols, 1863), 204, NCC.

24. Ida B. Wells-Barnett, "Booker T. Washington and His Critics," in *The World To-Day* 6 (April 1904): 520, HT; Evelyn Brooks Higginbotham, *Righteous Discontent: The Women's Movement in the Black Baptist Church, 1880–1920* (Cambridge, MA: Harvard University Press, 1993); Stephanie Shaw, *What a Woman Ought to Be and To Do: Black Professional Women Workers during the Jim Crow Era* (Chicago: University of Chicago Press, 1996).

25. Deborah Elizabeth Whaley, *Disciplining Women: Alpha Kappa Alpha, Black Counterpublics, and the Cultural Politics of Black Sororities* (Albany: SUNY Press, 2010), 36–39; Michael H. Washington and Marjorie H. Parker, *Alpha Kappa Alpha through the Years, 1908–1988* (Chicago: Mobium Press, 1990), 35, 298, 319; Cheryl L. Nuñez, "Education, Racial Uplift, and the Rise of the Greek-Letter Tradition: The African American Quest for Status in the Early Twentieth Century," in *African American Fraternities and Sororities: The Legacy and the Vision,* ed. Tamara L. Brown, Gregory S. Parks, and Clarenda M. Phillips (Lexington: University Press of Kentucky, 2009), 169–70; Jacqueline M. Moore, *Leading the Race: The Transformation of the Black Elite in the Nation's Capital, 1880–1920* (Charlottesville: University Press of Virginia, 1999), 117; *The Crisis* 23 (March 1922): 218, IntArch.

26. Anna Julia Cooper, *A Voice from the South* (Xenia, OH: Aldine Printing, 1892), 134; Walter Johnson, *Soul by Soul: Life Inside the Antebellum Slave Market* (Cambridge, MA: Harvard University Press, 1999), 137–40; Audrey Elisa Kerr, "The Paper Bag Principle: Of the Myth and the Motion of Colorism," *Journal of American Folklore* 118 (Summer 2005): 271–89; *The Liberator* (Boston, MA), 3 June 1842, NewsC; *Oxford (PA) Press*, 2 January 1886, HSP; Blain Roberts, *Pageants, Parlors, and Pretty Women: Race and Beauty in the Twentieth-Century South* (Chapel Hill: University of North Carolina Press, 2014), 74–86; Ibram X. Kendi, *Stamped from the Beginning: The Definitive History of Racist Ideas in America* (New York: Nation Books, 2016), 243–44; JeffriAnne Wilder, *Color Stories: Black Woman and Colorism in the 21st Century* (Santa Barbara: ABC-CLIO, 2015), 71; Deborah Elizabeth Whaley, "The Empty Space of African American Sorority Representation: Spike Lee's *School Daze,*" in Brown, Parks, and Phillips, eds., *African American Fraternities and Sororities*, 418–33; US Census, 1950: Brunswick County, VA.

27. Conway, "Homage to Miss Cole"; Paula Giddings, *In Search of Sisterhood: Delta Sigma Theta and the Challenge of the Black Sorority Movement* (New York: HarperCollins, 1988), 53.

28. *The Tiger* (Lawrenceville, VA: 1973), 18, Dr. William McCaddin Pritchett Local History Room; assembly program, 21st Annual Convention, 20 March 1959, Alpha Kappa Mu Honor Society, April 1953–March 20, 1959, Horace Mann Bond Papers, Special Collections and University Archives, University of Massachusetts at Amherst; *Alpha Kappa Mu Newsletter* 32 (December 2012): 2, 5, Alpha Kappa Mu Honor Society publications, https://www.alphakappamu.org/publications.html; *The Daily Press* (Newport News, VA), 31 March 1980.

29. Conway, "Homage to Miss Cole."

30. Conway, "Homage to Miss Cole."

31. *News and Observer* (Raleigh, NC), 12 October 1978, NewsC; certificate of death, 9 August 1997, Death Records, 1912–2014, Virginia Department of Health, Richmond; Interment File for Grave #1, Lot #53S, West Edgewood Section, Bayview-New York Bay Cemetery; Saint Paul's College Bulletin 88 (2008–2011), 18, James Solomon Russell/Saint Paul's College Museum & Archives, Lawrenceville, VA; Conway, "Homage to Miss Cole."

Index

Italic page numbers refer to illustrations.

234; on genealogy, 15, 153; infidelity of, 361n33; and Kansas Exodus, 299–300; and lecture circuit, 188, 190; and Lunsford Lane, 127, 130–31, 131, 151, 155, 159, 160, 179, 190–92, 197, 198, 204, 207, 208; as narrator, 163, 358n5; and racism, 182, 190–91, 198; and redemption-by-purchase, 126–27, 159; as revolutionary, 155; and recruitment of Black soldiers, 241–42; and self-making, 166, 172; speaking skills of, 3, 6, 7, 125–26, 130–31, 147–49, 151, 162, 197, 208, 238–39. *See also* "What, to the Slave, Is the Fourth of July?" (Douglass)

dower rights, 36, 202, 214, 285

Draft Riots, 265

Dresser, Amos, 139–40, 193

dropsy, 297

Du Bois, Nina Gomer, 308

Du Bois, W. E. B., 8, 272–73, 306–7

Dudley, Edward B., 97–99, 109, 112, 113, 117, 268

Dunbar, Paul Laurence, 294–95

Dutton, Andrew, 231, 232

Earle, Edward, 257, 290, 292

Easton, Hosea, 147–48

Eastwood, Peggy, 108

elections: of 1800, 41–42; of 1819 and 1820, 54–55; of 1836, 97; of 1838 and 1839, 109–10; of 1841, 133; of 1844, 206; of 1848, 208–9; of 1868, 288–89; of 1870 and 1872, 283, 291; of 1872, 283; constitutional procedure for, 90

emancipation: by will, 338n1; Emancipation of 1865, 266, 267, 269, 272–73, 291, 311; immediate, 159; laws in New York, 95–96, 204; laws of 1741 (North Carolina), 18; laws of 1830–31 (North Carolina), 84, 85, 92; petitions for, 340n16; procedures of, 2, 86–88, 115; Slavery Abolition Act of 1833 (Great Britain), 158, 233. *See also* redemption-by-purchase; self-purchase

Emancipation Day, 182, 186, 197, 233, 237, 271

Emancipation Proclamation, 235, 237, 260–61, 270

Emerson, Ralph Waldo, 8, 165, 201

Eno, Amos Richards, 263, 264

Enrollment Act of 1863, 242, 265

enslaved property: abolition as theft of, 176; as collateral, 78; and debt, 55, 63; display of, 146–47; humans as, 157–58, 161, 270; and inheritance, 225–26; Lunsford Lane and, 124, 146, 156, 158; recovery of, 81; taxation of, 321n7, 328n26. *See also* property

enslavement: childhood in, 42, 45, 270, 328n26; domestic, 28, 34–35, 39, 43–44; enforcement of, 18–19, 20, 70–71, 87; family identities in, 15–16, 18, 32, 95, 336n38; and fieldwork, 59, 75, 238; flight from, 42–43, 73, 144; marriage within, 75–76; in New York, 95–96; property rights in, 335n28; racism and, 41–42; religious hypocrisy and, 66–67; resistance to, 18, 43–44, 83–85, 87, 93–94, 139; violence in, 42–43; and Whiteness, 82–83, 91–92. *See also* emancipation

entrepreneurialism: among Black Americans, 9, 70–71; definitions of, 69, 70; Lunsford Lane and, 68–69, 70–71, 96–97, 164, 167, 214, 219, 301; mythology of, 9, 68–69, 249–50; piddling within, 69–70. *See also* self-making

Essex County Anti-Slavery Society, 179, 192

Èṣù, 93, 132

Europe and the Allies of the Past and of Today (anonymous), 258

Evans, Henry, 223, 230–31

Evans, Wilson Bruce, 223, 230–31, 243, 262

"exceptional Negro," 8, 9. *See also* "respectable Negro"

Exodusters. *See* Kansas Exodus

fatherhood: among Black Americans, 6, 46, 68, 105–6, 147, 149, 177, 231, 250, 303; among White Americans, 89, 100, 245, 259, 269

Federalist Party, 41, 74, 274

Federhen, John T., Jr., 228–29

Fields, James T., 220

Finney, Charles G., 144

First Independent Baptist Church of People of Color, 83, 182, 184–85, 192, 197, 216, 221

First United Association of Colored Waiters, 264

Fisher, Silas D., 227

Flora (enslaved), 15–16, 17

flying Africans, 42, 73, 144, 200, 414

folklore, 93, 163, 169, 257, 271, 318n2

Forbes, Abner, 185–85

Ford, Anna Dyer, 150, 181

Ford, Lewis, 150, 175, 181, 189

Forten, Charlotte L., 240–41

Forten, Mary Virginia Wood, 240

Forten, Robert, 240

Foster, Abby Kelley, 3, 123, 131, 156, 193, 213

Foster, Stephen Symonds: as abolitionist, 3, 125, 156, 193; and Butman riot, 234; mythmaking by, 155; as orator, 196, 206

Fourth of July: and Black Americans, 185–86, 238–39; celebrations, 72, 90, 92, 136, 176, 235, 241; as publication date of *Narrative of Lunsford Lane* (Lane), 196, 210

Franklin, Benjamin, 57, 136, 154, 166

Franklin Medal Scholars, 184

Frederick (enslaved), 32, 34

free Blacks: cohabitation with enslaved people, 84, 104; emigration of, 139, 140; in Maryland, 120, 121; in North Carolina, 9, 19, 41, 48–50, 66, 69, 71, 72, 73, 84, 87, 90–91, 96, 97, 104, 107, 108–9, 110, 111, 115, 116, 136, 167, 173, 203

Free Democratic Party, 210–11

Freedmen Convention, 274, 277

Freedmen's Bureau, 266, 273, 278, 280, 281, 282, 283

freedom seekers: assistance for, 88–89, 176, 187, 195, 213, 216, 220, 260–61; Frederick Douglass as, 160, 172; embracing identity of, 124; Ned Lane as, 138; Lane family portrayed as, 143, 250; as narrators, 7, 189; and rescue attempts, 178–79, 217, 218, 230; Whites' fears of, 42–44, 73, 135, 182, 185

Freeman, Eliza (enslaved), 108, 117, 177

Freeman, George (apprentice), 243

Freeman, George (cook), 239

Freeman, George Washington, 66

Freeman, Thomas, 242, 243, 258, 261–62, 386n73

Freeman, Waller: emancipation of, 104, 106, 108; land owned by, 105; legal accusations against, 112–13, 114, 118, 122, 139; petition for freedom by, 115, 116, 117, 134; solicitation of money by, 177–78

Free Soil Party. *See* Free Democratic Party

French Revolution, 57–58

Fugitive Slave Law of 1793, 88, 119

Fugitive Slave Law of 1850, 215–16, 217, 218, 221, 230–31, 234

fugitive slaves. *See* freedom seekers

Fuller, James Canning, 131, 132, 208

Gales, Joseph, 41–42, 72–73, 103, 105, 201, 203

Gales, Weston, 119, 123, 140

Gales and Seaton, 119

Gallatin, Albert, 58

Galloway, Abram H., 277, 278, 279

gardening: William Bryant and, 287; Eliza Haywood and, 45–46; at Haywood home, 26, 44, 45, 65, 100; Ned Lane and, 26, 30, 45–46, 100, 187

Garner, Henry G.: death of, 262; enlistment of, 242; marriage of, 238, 264; as military recruiter, 238; military service of, 242, 263; in popular memory, 293–94

Garner, Margaret, 249

Garnet, Henry Highland, 3, 132, 153, 154, 156, 173, 216

Garrison, Helen Eliza, 244

Garrison, William Lloyd: in Cambridge-port, 184; and Lewis and Milton Clarke, 188; and Frederick Douglass, 126, 146, 148, 160, 174; as editor, 91, 123–24, 131, 132, 138, 162, 248; and Lunsford Lane, 123, 160, 169, 173, 175–76, 181; and moral suasion, 122–23, 204, 215; and redemption-by-purchase, 157–60, 161, 239; as public speaker, 6, 125, 127, 131, 144, 175, 178, 190, 197, 198, 207, 208; and self-made manhood, 166; Darby Vassall, 219

Garrisonians. *See* Old Organization

Gaston, William, 59, 91

Lane, Clarissa "Clara" (enslaved; daughter of Lunsford and Martha Lane): birth of, 197; as daughter, 4, 219, 221, 222, 227, 229, 231, 233, 237, 289; death of, 291–92, 297; illness of, 289; land ownership by, 285, 286, 287–88, 290; misidentification of in census, 387n80; at Wellington Hospital, 236–37

Lane, Daniel (of Indiana), 200–201

Lane, Edward (enslaved; son of Lunsford and Martha Lane): on abolitionist stages, 145, 159; as citizen, 203; departure from home, 219; disappearance of, 297, 306, 397n39; as enslaved, 17, 76, 104; land ownership by, 212; military service of, 244, 245, 262, 266; naming of, 76, 95; in Ohio, 221, 222–23, 229, 231, 232; return to North Carolina, 268, 273; as shoemaker, 184, 221

Lane, Edward "Ned" (enslaved; father of Lunsford Lane): birth of, 15, 16; death of, 4, 224–27; as enslaved, 20, 21, 22, 26, 29, 30, 33, 34, 44, 46–47, 63, 64, 128–29, 200, 252; as father of Lunsford Lane, 2, 36, 38, 39, 40–41, 66, 292–93; as gardener, 26, 45–46, 65, 187; as grandparent, 187, 221; and Eliza Haywood, 46–47; as head of family, 137–38; hiring out of, 23, 25; home of, 31, 37; and Horace James, 213; land ownership by, 187, 215, 227–28; marriage of, 35, 79, 144, 185, 187; naming of, 11, 32, 33, 97; and opportunity for freedom, 86–88, 100, 101, 185; public speaking by, 186–87; and racism, 186; shooting of, 152, 185; as storyteller, 1, 41; as tobacconist, 68, 97, 109, 249–50

Lane, Henry, 15, 21, 22, 252

Lane, James, 15, 21, 22

Lane, Joel (1739–95): death of, 21; as enslaver, 15–16, 17, 18, 19–21, 30, 36, 86, 134, 321n7; genealogy of, 16; home of, 17; land ownership by, 20

Lane, Joel H. (1790–1832), 22

Lane, John (free Black man), 139, 223

Lane, John (son of Joel Lane), 22, 23, 29–30, 252

Lane, Joseph, 19

Lane, Laura Ann (enslaved; daughter of Lunsford and Martha): on abolitionist stages, 176; birth of, 95; burial of, 222, 292; death of, 215, 221, 297; education of, 130, 132, 145, 146, 173–74, 184, 212; as enslaved, 104; and grandparents, 187; literacy of, 183, 209; in Massachusetts, 129, 130, 132; naming of, 95; in New York, 122; purchase of, 122, 123, 132, 160; and racism, 129, 178

Lane, Lucy (enslaved), 4, 137, 145, 159, 183–84, 297

Lane, Lunsford (1803–79): as abolitionist, 2, 3, 4, 133–35, 143, 149, 151, 300; arrest of, 104; birth of, 35; and Blackness, 5, 8; biography of, 245–53; as bookseller, 175, 203, 210, 229, 231, 287, 295; burial of, 298–99; and Cate (sister), 15–17, 30, 227; childhood of, 35–36, 39, 43, 44–45, 47–48; and Christianity, 66–67, 77, 168–69, 192–93, 195, 252; as clothier, 214; and clothing, 76, 77, 104; death of, 297–98; as doctor, 229, 235–37, 259, 261, 289, 291, 295, 380n12; as enslaved, 35–96; and enslaved property, 124, 146, 156, 158; entrepreneurialism of, 68–69, 70–71, 96–97, 164, 167, 214, 219, 301; as free, 96–297; and Free Democratic Party, 210; genealogy of, 200–201, 324n37; hiring out of, 80, 94; identity as Black American, 6, 167, 172–73, 178, 193, 253; as inspiration for naming of children, 200–201, 368n18, 369n20; intelligence of, 61, 155, 197, 236, 255; inventory of, 71, 86, 109, 128, 228; and Lafayette, 58–59, 264; and land ownership, 9, 103, 167, 202–3, 210, 212–14, 215, 219, 221–22, 227–29, 232, 276, 359n17, 363n2; and Liberty Party, 132, 194, 197, 206, 208, 209, 210–11; literacy of, 48, 66, 67, 94, 112, 192; lynching of, 3, 134–35; marriage of, 4, 75–77, 95, 104, 137, 173–74, 202, 206, 212, 213–14, 229, 231, 279, 285, 289, 290, 291, 292, 293; mythologization of, 7–10, 154–55, 163–69, 192–93, 199–201, 248–52, 269, 297–98; naming of, 36, 39,

Monroe, James, 56
Montfort (enslaved), 341n23
Montford (enslaved; son of Cate), 22, 38, 45, 64, 269, 325n44, 342n40
Moore, John, Jr., 257, 258
moral suasion: Garrisonian tactic of, 145, 189, 194, 199, 215, 312; Liberty Party's rejection of, 204; in temperance, 246; as theme of One Hundred Conventions, 194
Morehead, John Motley, 110, 111, 112, 132–33
Morrissey, John, 265
mortgage deed, 202, 209, 212, 221, 286–87, 373n6, 393n1
Moses (enslaved), 34, 63, 64, 86
Mount Pleasant Cemetery, 369n20
Murray, Daniel, 133
My Bondage and My Freedom (Douglass), 163
Myers, Jeremiah, 234

naming: as commemorative, 200–201, 267, 295, 300–301, 368n18, 369n20; among enslaved people, 31, 36, 97; as exerting ownership, 97, 249–50, 256–57; among Lane's children, 76, 95, 144, 336n38, 353n3; origin of Lunsford as name, 11, 36; surnames, 11, 31–32, 39, 74–75, 125, 144, 274
Narrative of Colonel Ethan Allen's Captivity, A (Allen), 164
Narrative of James Williams (Whittier), 247–48
Narrative of Lunsford Lane, The (Lane): copyright for, *171*; first edition of, 168–69, *170*, 360–61n25; fourth edition of, 210; as life-writing, 172–74; mildness of, 170–71; reviews of, 169; second edition of, 170–71; storytelling in, 3, 163–67; third edition of, 196, 197, 203, 209; vs. *Lunsford Lane* (Hawkins), 252
Narrative of the Adventures and Escape of Moses Roper (Roper), 17, 210
Narrative of the Life of Frederick Douglass (Douglass), 17, 210
Narrative of the Life of Mrs. Mary Jemison (Seaver), 164
National Convention of Colored Peoples, 153

National Freedmen's Relief Association, 240–41, 267, 273, 277
Negro cloth, 23, 198
"Negro Life in North Carolina Illustrated" (Hunter), 272
Negro pew, 190–91, 198, 219
Nell, William C., 153, 156, 183, 184, 187, 197, 301
New England Anti-Slavery Society, 150, 151, 182, 188, 195, 219
New England Freeman Association, 182
New-Hampshire Anti-Slavery Society, 176
New York Age (newspaper), 307, 308, 309
New York Anti-Slavery Society, 96, 191
New York Bay Cemetery, 298, 300, 303, 304, 308, 398n49
New York Supreme Court of Judicature, 88–89
Nichols, John P., 214, 221
Norfolk County Anti-Slavery Society, 187
Northampton rebellion, 43
North Carolina Colored Industrial Fair, 272
North Carolina Constitutional Convention of 1835, 90–91, 99
North Carolina Constitutional Convention of 1868, 274, 277–78, 279
North Carolina General Assembly: and Black codes, 18–19, 71, 80, 83–85, 140; Black members of, 277, 284; and William Boylan, 74, 140, 277; constitutional reorganization of, 90; election of 1838, 109; election of 1840, 98–99; and Glasgow land fraud, 40; and Delia Haywood, 55; and Eliza Haywood, 33; and John Haywood, 52, 54, 63; and Joel Lane, 17, 20–21; and meritorious service, 40, 86–87; and petitions, 102, 105, 106, 114, 115, 116, 117, 134, 139, 275; and reconstruction of capitol, 86
North Carolina House of Commons: and emancipation, 116; and Waller Freeman, 115; and Isaac Hunter, 114–15; individual members of, 23, 52, 54–55, 111, 113, 283, 284; investigation of John Haywood, 52–54; and Lunsford Lane, 114–15; petitions to, 114, 115

North Carolina Provincial Congress, 20

North Carolina Senate: election of Black members to, 283; and Stephen Haywood, 54–55; Isaac Hunter and, 114–15; and Lunsford Lane, 115–16, 117, 173; vote for constitutional convention by, 90; voting rights for, 110; Whig victory for, 112

Northup, Solomon, 121, 251–52

Nye, Susan D., 72, 73

Oakes, George P., 222, 229

Oberlin-Wellington rescue, 229–30, 231, 232, 240, 253

Ohio Thirty-Ninth Infantry, 244, 262, 266

Old Colony Anti-Slavery Society, 125, 126, 128

Old Ned (enslaved), 15, 16, 17, 22, 29, 32, 34

Old Organization, 123, 175

One Hundred Conventions, 188–89, 194, 203, 299

oratory, 6–7, 52, 59, 125–26, 131, 147–49, 188

Osgood, Samuel, 129, 176, 178

Our Generals (Bufford), 254

Our Nig (Wilson), 255

Paine, Charles Jackson, 268

Panics: of 1819, 47; of 1837, 101, 102, 167, 201, 287; of 1839, 110

Parker, Edward Griffin, 6–7

Parker, Theodore, 199, 210, 218

Patterson, Emeline, 102, 140, 223, 229

Patterson, Henry I. (1804–86), 102, 105, 107, 140, 223, 229, 243

Patterson, Henry I., Jr. (1844–99), 140, 243, 262

Patterson, John E., 223, 338n57

Peace, Joseph, 68, 113

Peace, William, 68, 72, 113

Peace Party, 74

Pennington, James W. C., 153, 216

Pequette, F. E., 263

personal liberty laws, 218–19

Philadelphia Female Anti-Slavery Society, 240

Philadelphia School of Anatomy, 305

Phillimon (enslaved), 40, 53

Phillips, Anne, 218

Phillips, Wendell: as abolitionist, 131, 219; at antislavery meeting, 190, 191–92, 207; and Burns riot, 218; as orator, 3, 6, 299, 300, 366n32

phrenology, 255

Physical Geography for Families and Schools (Zornlin), 258

Pierce, Edward L., 240

Pierce, Franklin, 218

Pillsbury, Parker, 168, 191, 196

Pioneer Boy and How He Became President, The (Thayer), 259

plantation schools: Avon School, 275, 281; Johnson School, 267; Rouse Depot School, 276, 279; Yankee Hall School, 275, 281

Plymouth County Anti-Slavery Society, 151, 154, 175, 180, 188, 191, 194

Polk, William, 56, 57, 72, 73–74

Pond, Benjamin Wisner, 267

Port Royal Relief Association of Philadelphia, 240

Powers, Hiram, 165

practical abolitionism, 213, 235, 275

Presbyterian Church (Raleigh), 51, 71, 94, 109

Prindle, Cyrus, 211

property: as constitutional right, 124, 156; in Massachusetts, 201–202, 203, 285, 286, 373n6; in New York, 88; in North Carolina, 103, 199, 201, 203, 286; in Ohio, 232. *See also* enslaved property; landed property; mortgage deed; warranty deed

proslavery thought, 52, 85, 92, 158

Punch, John, 5

Putnam's Home Cyclopedia (anonymous), 258

Quincy, Edmund, 125, 213

racism: against Black Americans, 194; and John Chavis, 50; and Jeannette Lane Cole, 310, 313; and Isaac Hunter, 117; and Lunsford Lane, 164, 166, 168, 173, 178–79, 238, 253; within politics, 42; Charles Lenox Remond, 147–48, 173, 179; on